ALSO BY JULIE GREENE

Pure and Simple Politics:
The American Federation of Labor and Political Activism, 1881–1917

Labor Histories:
Class, Politics, and the Working-Class Experience
(Coeditor, with Eric Arnesen and Bruce Laurie)

THE CANAL BUILDERS

THE CANAL BUILDERS

MAKING AMERICA'S EMPIRE
AT THE PANAMA CANAL

JULIE GREENE

THE PENGUIN PRESS

NEW YORK

2009

THE PENGUIN PRESS
Published by the Penguin Group
Penguin Group (USA) Inc., 375 Hudson Street, New York, New York 10014, U.S.A. • Penguin Group (Canada),
90 Eglinton Avenue East, Suite 700, Toronto, Ontario, Canada M4P 2Y3 (a division of Pearson Penguin Canada
Inc.) • Penguin Books Ltd, 80 Strand, London WC2R 0RL, England • Penguin Ireland, 25 St. Stephen's
Green, Dublin 2, Ireland (a division of Penguin Books Ltd) • Penguin Books Australia Ltd, 250 Camberwell
Road, Camberwell, Victoria 3124, Australia (a division of Pearson Australia Group Pty Ltd) • Penguin Books
India Pvt Ltd, 11 Community Centre, Panchsheel Park, New Delhi–110 017, India • Penguin Group (NZ),
67 Apollo Drive, Rosedale, North Shore 0632, New Zealand (a division of Pearson New Zealand Ltd) • Penguin
Books (South Africa) (Pty) Ltd, 24 Sturdee Avenue, Rosebank, Johannesburg 2196, South Africa

Penguin Books Ltd, Registered Offices:
80 Strand, London WC2R 0RL, England

First published in 2009 by The Penguin Press,
a member of Penguin Group (USA) Inc.

1 3 5 7 9 10 8 6 4 2

Frontispiece photo © Hulton Archive/Getty Images

"A Worker Reads History" from *Selected Poems* by Bertolt Brecht, translated by H. R. Hays. Copyright 1947 by
Bertolt Brecht and H. R. Hays and renewed 1975 by Stefan S. Brecht and H. R. Hays. Reprinted by permission of
Houghton Mifflin Harcourt Publishing Company and Ann Elmo Agency, Inc.

"The 13th Labor of Hercules" poster by Perham Nahl courtesy of the Larson Collection, Special Collections
Research Center, California State University, Fresno.

Library of Congress Cataloging-in-Publication Data

Greene, Julie, 1956–
The canal builders : making America's empire at the Panama Canal / Julie Greene.
p.   cm.—(The Penguin history of American life)
Includes bibliographical references and index.
ISBN 978-1-59420-201-8
1. Panama Canal (Panama)—History.   2. Canals—Panama—Design and construction—History.
3. Canal Zone—History.   I. Title.
F1569.C2G66   2009
972.87'5051—dc22   2008028650

Printed in the United States of America

DESIGNED BY MARYSARAH QUINN
MAPS BY JEFFREY L. WARD

FOR JIM AND SOPHIE
my beloved

CONTENTS

A WORKER READS HISTORY

Who built the seven gates of Thebes?
The books are filled with names of kings.
Was it the kings who hauled the craggy blocks of stone?
And Babylon, so many times destroyed.
Who built the city up each time? In which of Lima's houses,
That city glittering with gold, lived those who built it?
In the evening when the Chinese wall was finished
Where did the masons go? Imperial Rome
Is full of arcs of triumph. Who reared them up? Over whom
Did the Caesars triumph? Byzantium lives in song.
Were all her dwellings palaces? And even in Atlantis of the legend
The night the sea rushed in,
The drowning men still bellowed for their slaves.

Young Alexander conquered India.
He alone?
Caesar beat the Gauls.
Was there not even a cook in his army?
Philip of Spain wept as his fleet
Was sunk and destroyed. Were there no other tears?
Frederick the Great triumphed in the Seven Years War. Who
Triumphed with him?

Each page a victory.
At whose expense the victory ball?
Every ten years a great man,
Who pays the piper?

So many particulars.
So many questions.

—BERTOLT BRECHT

UNITED STATES

TEXAS

LOUISIANA

MISSISSIPPI

ALABAMA

GEORGIA

Atlanta

Mobile

Houston

New Orleans

FLORIDA

Miami

Gulf of Mexico

Havana

CUBA

CAYMAN ISLANDS

Mexico City

MEXICO

BELIZE

GUATEMALA

HONDURAS

EL SALVADOR

NICARAGUA

Pacific

Ocean

COSTA
RICA

Bocas del Toro

Colón

Panama City

PANAMA

0 Miles   200   400

0 Kilometers   400

© 2009 Jeffrey L. Ward

THE CARIBBEAN BASIN

BAHAMAS

Atlantic

Ocean

TURKS AND CAICOS

DOMINICAN
REPUBLIC

Santiago de Cuba

HAITI

PUERTO
RICO

BRITISH
VIRGIN ISLANDS

Kingston

VIRGIN
ISLANDS

ANTIGUA AND
BARBUDA

JAMAICA

ST. KITTS AND NEVIS

MONTSERRAT

GUADELOUPE

Caribbean Sea

DOMINICA

MARTINIQUE

ST. LUCIA

BARBADOS

NETHERLANDS
ANTILLES

ST. VINCENT AND
THE GRENADINES

Bridgetown

ARUBA

GRENADA

TRINIDAD
AND TOBAGO

VENEZUELA

COLOMBIA

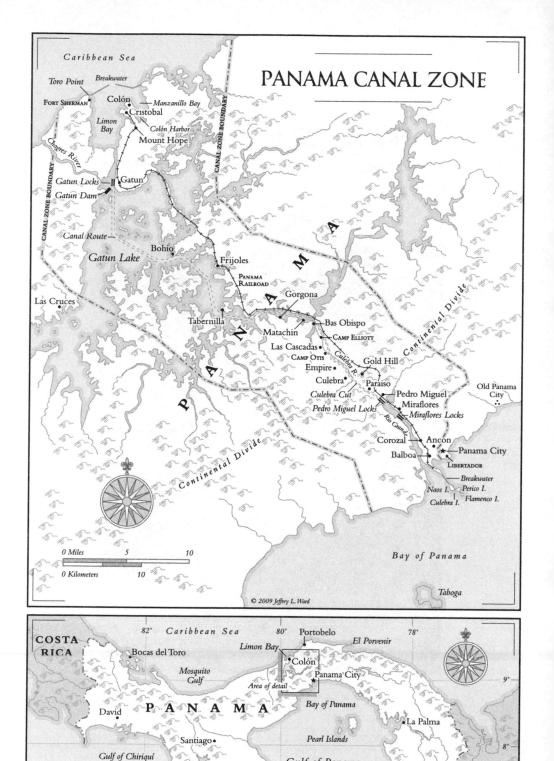

PANAMA CANAL ZONE

Caribbean Sea

Toro Point Breakwater
Fort Sherman Colón Manzanillo Bay
Cristobal
Limon Bay Colón Harbor
Mount Hope

CANAL ZONE BOUNDARY

Chagres River

CANAL ZONE BOUNDARY

Gatun Locks Gatun
Gatun Dam

Canal Route

Gatun Lake

Bohio

Las Cruces

Frijoles

PANAMA RAILROAD

Tabernilla

Gorgona

Bas Obispo
Matachin CAMP ELLIOTT
Las Cascadas
CAMP OTIS Gold Hill
Empire Culebra R.
Culebra Paraiso
Culebra Cut
Pedro Miguel Locks Pedro Miguel
Miraflores
Miraflores Locks

Río Grande

Continental Divide

Old Panama City

Corozal Ancon
Balboa Panama City
LIBERTADOR
Breakwater
Naos I. Perico I.
Culebra I. Flamenco I.

P A N A M A

Continental Divide

Bay of Panama

© 2009 Jeffrey L. Ward

0 Miles   5   10
0 Kilometers   10

Taboga

COSTA RICA

82° Caribbean Sea 80° Portobelo El Porvenir 78°
Bocas del Toro Limon Bay
Mosquito Gulf Colón
Area of detail Panama City

David

P A N A M A

Bay of Panama

9°

Santiago

Gulf of Chiriquí

Las Tablas

Coiba I.
Cebaco I.

Pearl Islands

Gulf of Panama

La Palma

8°

Pacific Ocean

0 Miles   50   100
0 Kilometers   100

COLOMBIA

The Thirteenth Labor of Hercules

Perham W. Nahl (1869-1935)

INTRODUCTION

I N 1915, as Americans planned a grand world's fair to celebrate the completion of the Panama Canal, California artist Perham Nahl created a lithograph he called *The Thirteenth Labor of Hercules*. In Greek mythology Hercules, the brave and strong son of Zeus, had to complete twelve arduous labors, including such unimaginable tasks as diverting rivers and carrying the earth on his shoulders. With the construction of the canal, Nahl suggested, Hercules—symbolizing the United States—had finally and triumphantly completed his thirteenth labor.

Nahl depicted Hercules thrusting apart a mountain range, his back pushing against one side while his arm forces away the far side. His mighty labor allows a gentle stream of water to pass by at his feet. A small boat traverses the distance toward a mythic city on a hill. Hercules shows no sweat; his muscles are poised but not straining. He is turned away from us, his head lowered as if in benediction. We do not see his face. What we see is his masculine body conquering Mother Earth and making possible a great wonder of the world. By connecting the canal construction to Greek mythology, Nahl's image brilliantly invoked the spirit of the canal while honoring the nation that built it and linking it to the greatest ideals of Western civilization. America now stood as a Hercules, achieving a godlike task through a bloodless conquest over nature.

The lithograph of Hercules helped draw people in 1915 to the Panama-Pacific International Exposition in San Francisco, where more than eighteen million visitors marveled at the wonders of American industrialism—including many of the technologies that helped make the Panama Canal possible. The fair emphasized the links between industrialism and America's emergence as a leading world power. Nothing exemplified those links more clearly than the recently completed canal, hailed by observers around the world as a miracle of engineering and industrial technology. The fair, like Nahl's lithograph, celebrated the canal while diminishing the role of the tens of thousands of men and women required to build it.[1]

These are the aspects most of us remember about the canal—it's a tale enshrined in popular memory and innumerable histories and novels. Most narratives begin by pointing out that the dream of a canal was centuries old, but only the Americans achieved it. In 1880 the French, under the leadership of Ferdinand de Lesseps (who had previously constructed the Suez Canal to great acclaim), began trying to build a canal across the Isthmus of Panama. France's effort ended in failure in 1889 due to mismanagement, devastating disease, financial problems, and engineering mistakes. In 1904 the United States took over the job, with the ingenious President Theodore Roosevelt leading the way. Breakthroughs in medicine, technology, and science and wise engineering decisions, according to traditional accounts of the project, allowed the United States to succeed where France had failed. Engineers who had helped build the transcontinental railroad and diverted rivers in the United States applied their experience and determination amid the chaos (and debilitating humidity and rain showers) of the Isthmus of Panama. The engineers brilliantly figured out how to dig through the Continental Divide, how to dispose of all that dirt, and how to handle the mudslides. Most important of all, they decided they must rely on locks to raise and lower the ships, rather than attempting to build the canal at sea level. It was built ahead of schedule and under budget, costing only $352 million. The Panama Canal opened to tremendous celebration in August 1914, and it marked the emergence of the United States as a world leader at the very moment when World War I broke out and split the nations of Europe apart.

It was a difficult, challenging task—in a word, Herculean—but thanks to a few individuals of genius, it worked. And through it all the will and spirit of Americans never wavered. Indeed, central to this common narrative is the notion that the canal project demonstrated the superior character of the American people. In 2005 the historian David McCullough, author of *The Path Between the Seas* (1977), a bestselling account of the canal's history, took a cruise through the canal. Afterward he noted, "I think often about why the French failed at Panama and why we succeeded. One of the reasons we succeeded is that we were gifted, we were attuned to adaptation, to doing what works, whereas they were trained to do everything in a certain way. We have a gift for improvisation." In this speech as in his book, McCullough, like so many Americans, was particularly fascinated by the work of the engineers who built the canal. He described the landslides and floods the engineers confronted and the way they succeeded against all the odds. He gave as an example the engineers' ability to make concrete stronger and more durable than anyone expected: "That ingenious contrivance by the American engineers is a perfect expression of what engineering ought to be at its best—man's creations working with nature." The canal, he concluded, is "an extraordinary work of civilization."[2]

The industrial prowess that enabled the canal also earned a place for it in popular memory as an affirmation of American national identity. McCullough's comments provide just one indication of the force these ideas still hold today. Yet this emphasis on the canal as above all a feat of engineering has obscured some of the most significant and dramatic elements of the construction project. This book tells a different story. It takes as its starting point the perspective of the chief engineer George Washington Goethals, who oversaw construction of the canal from 1907 until its completion in 1914. Years later Goethals reflected on the success of the American project. Despite prevalent ideas about the canal, he argued, its construction required no innovations from the standpoint either of engineering or of medicine. The engineering challenges were solved by applying "known principles and methods." Eradicating yellow fever and malaria likewise required tactics and rules previously developed in Cuba, India, and Egypt. It was the human rather than the technological or scientific dimensions of the project that struck Goethals as most challenging. The size of the workforce and the fact that workingmen and -women came so far from home both required efficient forms of government: "a novel problem in government was presented by the necessity of ruling and preserving order within the Canal Zone." Goethals would have agreed that the canal was a major engineering achievement, but he took even more pride in his ability to govern the vast and unwieldy population of employees and family members. We have long perceived the canal as involving conquest over nature, and there's some truth in that. But it also involved conquest over the tens of thousands of men and women in the Canal Zone and in the Republic of Panama.[3]

Working people journeyed to the Canal Zone from all over the globe: from the United States and Canada, the Caribbean, northern and southern Europe, and India. Each group brought different strategies for responding to conditions and policies on the isthmus. Workingmen who repaired steam shovels, ran lathes, dug dirt, or drilled dynamite had their own dreams and visions, as did workingwomen who washed laundry and cleaned houses. Their ideas often complicated officials' plans. In the Republic of Panama, which provided critical support for the construction effort, everyone from politicians to sewer diggers, servants, prostitutes, bartenders, and chauffeurs experienced the transformation of their cities as a result of the American occupation and found diverse ways of responding. U.S. government officials—charged with building towns across the isthmus to supply employees and families with food, housing, medical care, and entertainment—found the chore of constructing the canal large but relatively straightforward. More challenging was the task, endlessly discussed and debated by bureaucrats, of determining how best to motivate, manage, and discipline the people of the isthmus. This book explores the ways working people interacted with one another and with a U.S. government determined to build the canal quickly and efficiently. With a debt to Bertolt Brecht and his questions about the seven gates of Thebes, it asks: Who built the Panama Canal and how? And how does looking at the construction project from their perspective change our understanding of this moment in history?[4]

In 1912 an American named John Hall published a book of poems that tried to capture both the idealism of the canal project and the challenge it involved as an exercise of power. Hall had been living in the Canal Zone for five years and had watched men digging, dynamiting, and commanding steam shovels. In his poem "The Canal Builders," he tried to capture the diversity of the workforce building the canal: "They have come from every nation, / Every breed in all creation." The workers differed, he said, in many ways, in their language and social station, but all were helping to build America's new empire. He declared: "For Empire they toil, / In an alien soil." In their focus on workers and in designating their labor as contributing to the making of America's empire, Hall's simple rhymes captured a key element of the canal project. Another of Hall's poems, titled "The Price of Empire," noted that many men died while working on the canal, but they did not die in vain:

> *A mighty Nation, by their deeds,*
> *Stands girthed from sea to sea,*
> *And high o'er their graves proudly waves*
> *The Emblem of the Free.*

Like much of American political culture at the time, this lyric mixed idealistic notions of America's gifts to world civilization with pride in its rising stature as a first-class imperial power.[5]

These dual notions about American power were reflected at the turn of the twentieth century in numerous events. When the United States went to war against Spain in 1898 and won a victory within a few months, suddenly acquiring formal and informal colonies stretching from Cuba and Puerto Rico in the Caribbean to Guam, Hawaii, and the Philippines in the Pacific, it seemed to have embarked on a new and more promising role as a world power. The defeat of Spain caused much pride and celebration across the United States. Yet the war's aftermath generated unforeseen conflicts. Exercising power in the Philippines, Puerto Rico, Cuba, and Hawaii proved daunting. Most sobering of all were the actions taken by the people of the Philippines, who immediately went to war against the United States to win their independence. Filipinos had not expected that America's victory against Spain would simply substitute one colonialist power for another, and the United States became mired in a seemingly endless war. Where America's fight against Spain had been justified as a noble crusade against a corrupt imperial power that trampled on basic human rights, now America found itself in the position of colonialist, fighting to suppress indigenous peoples' rights. As the war dragged on, tales of cruelty by U.S. soldiers against Filipino soldiers and civilians made their way into American newspapers. By the time the war ended in uneasy victory for the United States and subjugation of the Filipino people in this country's first formal colony, many Americans had grown disillusioned with empire building. They worried that it violated American ideals, that it was corrupting their nation's democracy, and that it was unjust to the world's citizens.[6]

The early twentieth century, therefore, might not have seemed an auspicious time for a colossal canal-building project. And at first America's project in Panama was beset by controversy. Americans had wanted to build a canal across Nicaragua or Panama since the mid-nineteenth century, and as soon as Theodore Roosevelt became president in 1901, he began negotiations with Colombia for the right to build a canal across the Isthmus of Panama, then under Colombian control. When discussions broke down, Roosevelt opportunistically formed an alliance with a group of Panamanians seeking independence from Colombia. In November 1903 he sent warships to the isthmus to support the Panamanians' clandestine independence movement. When Panama achieved independence, Roosevelt immediately negotiated a treaty with the new republic that created the Panama Canal Zone and gave the United States complete and perpetual control over it as well as extensive rights in the Republic of Panama. The gentleman representing Panama in the negotiations was himself not even Panamanian, but a representative of the French company that still owned the rights to the canal—and that stood to make a huge profit by selling those rights to the United States.[7]

Writing sixty years later, William Appleman Williams declared Roosevelt's seizing of the isthmus "as brazen a bit of imperial land-grabbing as is recorded in modern history," and his sentiment was shared by many at the time. The editors of the *New York Times,* writing just days after the U.S.-backed coup brought independence to Panama, declared the situation a "national disgrace" and added that if Roosevelt now followed by building a canal across the isthmus, the United States would "incur the censure of just men and civilized Governments . . . [and] put a stain upon the country's good name by such a policy of dishonorable intrigue and aggression."[8] Of course, Roosevelt followed by doing precisely that.

At the project's outset, the gigantic challenge of building a canal across the isthmus became a symbol of governmental inefficiency, corruption, graft, and immorality. Exposés charged the U.S. government with everything from creating a quicksand of bureaucratic red tape in the Canal Zone to importing prostitutes for the comfort of canal employees. Congressmen kept busy during these years investigating various scandals and accusations and seeking ways to improve the U.S. government's performance on the isthmus. At first, then, the canal project seemed to fit within a larger, troubling pattern of America's weak and ineffective role in world affairs. It might easily have become an example of the U.S. government's fecklessness and ineptitude. Instead, it became an icon of what a strong, progressive federal government could accomplish in world affairs.

How did this happen? The canal construction project married values, ideals, and strategies that many Americans admired in their nation to the new challenges involved in managing life and labor in the international setting of the Panama Canal Zone. It was not always an easy or comfortable marriage, and much of the story in these pages concerns the tensions between the two. Those tensions suggest the need for a double focus, one that looks closely at events in the Panama Canal Zone while rethinking the relationship between U.S. domestic and international history. We need to disrupt the boundaries between domestic and "off-site" history in order to focus on the connections between them.

Looking about their country at the dawn of the twentieth century, many Americans observed problems, certainly, but overall they felt optimistic. They possessed a deep faith in progress, and it seemed warranted. Their nation was now the top-ranking industrial power in the world, its technological and scientific expertise widely envied. While city dwellers saw skyscrapers rapidly rising around them and streetcars and subways stretching out to the suburbs, and as millions of immigrants arrived yearly to labor in the nation's factories, new conflicts became apparent. The unchecked power of corporations worried some, though others looked to business leaders to solve the pervasive working-class discontent. Labor unions, socialists, single-tax advocates, progressives, and African American and immigrant leaders all voiced critiques of the status quo.

Those Americans actively working to eradicate social problems during the early twentieth century tended to coalesce around the progressive movement. Progressives combined an optimistic belief in progress and scientific achievement with a fervor for greater government intervention to achieve changes in the nation's political economy. Their movement became a terrific force throughout the land as progressive reformers created voluntary organizations (such as settlement houses), new strategies of labor management, and corporate welfare policies and fought for new levels of state intervention. Bureaucracies emerged to tackle a wide array of perceived problems at the municipal, state, and federal levels. Reformers experimented with new approaches to urban planning, municipal government, direct democracy, and laws to regulate working and living conditions.

As numerous historians have pointed out, there was another aspect of the progressive movement that emphasized social order and discipline. This strain of progressivism focused on racial segregation, disenfranchisement of African Americans and immigrants, new forms of judicial and prison discipline, vagrancy laws, and moral sanitation efforts such as the temperance movement. Historians have deemed these dual aspects the social justice and social control wings of the progressive movement. Although they might seem contradictory, both influences remained prevalent throughout the era, and each strain contributed to give the early-twentieth-century United States its particular shape.[9]

Each powerfully influenced life and work in the Panama Canal Zone as well. Canal engineers would employ not only the latest in technology, like Bucyrus steam shovels, but also new ideas about state intervention, labor management, urban planning, judicial and prison discipline, and the modern utility of segregation systems based on race, ethnicity, and nationality. Welfare policies borrowed from a triumphant corporate capitalism proved important, as did ideas about women's indispensable role in taming a wilderness. These strategies combined with prevailing ideas regarding civilization and citizenship to make the canal construction project a spectacular success. And its success, in turn, reinforced these virtues for American and world audiences. To many, the genius of the Panama Canal lay precisely in the fact that it seemed unconnected to imperialism; instead, it was seen as a display of America's *domestic* strengths in a world setting. In its triumph, the Panama Canal articulated American expansionism as a positive, humane, and beneficial activity, one equally valuable to world civilization and to American national identity. Emerging as the apparent antithesis of empire, the Panama Canal ironically helped make American empire possible. Yet as officials in the Canal Zone confronted the diverse cultures of a global workforce as well as disease, a tropical climate, and a rough mountainous terrain, they found themselves struggling to revise and adapt their initial ideas and strategies. Officials felt caught between faith that benevolent state intervention could create a more pleasant and just civilization and the belief that they must master, discipline, and control the population around them. These turned out to be the key approaches in the U.S. program to rule over the men and women of the isthmus.

THUS THE canal project became a signal moment in the building of America's new empire, and it also became a moment wrapped up inextricably with idealism and notions of selfless gifts to civilization. This book originated in my desire to uncover the history of America's empire and its ties with U.S. domestic politics and culture. In 1993 the literary scholar Amy Kaplan published an essay on Americans' peculiar and historic reluctance to perceive their nation as an empire, and it initiated an exciting intellectual ferment that gave rise to the "new imperial" school of historical and literary research. As Kaplan noted, she was not the first scholar to make this observation. William Appleman Williams had argued in 1955 that "one of the central themes of American historiography is that there is no American empire." American national identity, according to this view, has historically accepted that the United States is a world power while denying that it operates with imperial intentions or consequences. Even as Kaplan's essay returned scholars to Williams's original argument, historians grew increasingly interested in the historical relationship between the United States and the world. Numerous studies have appeared in recent years that explore U.S. empire from different perspectives—for example, in the Philippines, Hawaii, Puerto Rico, Cuba, and Mexico. The new scholarship on empire, however, has failed to explore how the construction of the Panama Canal shaped this crucial period. *The Canal Builders* addresses this absence as a way to contribute to a broader rethinking of America's "new empire" in the aftermath of 1898.[10]

In the early twentieth century the canal construction project resonated not with notions of empire but with civilization, progress, humanity, and the proper role of government. Much of the canal's significance—and perhaps a key explanation for why the recent scholarship on empire has neglected it—derived from this. This book explores how the canal became a positive symbol of American power, how it helped shape Americans' perception of their role in the world as something bigger and better than empire, and how in this way it helped to justify and make possible America's empire in the decades to come. While some, like the poet John Hall, saw the canal as empire building, for many others, whether Theodore Roosevelt or maids and diggers from Barbados or Jamaica, the canal's potential legacy went beyond empire. At its heart the canal project involved the construction of a global infrastructure; the early roots of globalization; the easier and faster flow of commerce, labor, and military vessels; and state intervention on an international level.

More than forty years ago, Walter LaFeber published *The New Empire*, in which he sought to link the rise of American empire to U.S. industrialization: "It was not accidental that Americans built their new empire at the same time their industrial complex matured."[11] *The New Empire* focuses on agricultural and industrial leaders' demands for more markets in the late nineteenth century. Since LaFeber's book appeared, a vast scholarship has enriched our understanding of U.S. industrialization and the political, social, and cultural history that accompanied it. Transnational methodologies that focus attention on the flow of people, ideas, and capital—and that transcend the boundaries of the nation-state—have more recently given us a fruitful vantage point from which to explore the canal, its construction, and its significance for U.S. history. As the scholar Isabel Hofmeyr observed, "The claim of transnational methods is not simply that historical processes are made in different places but that they are constructed in the movement between places, sites, and regions."[12] Hofmeyr's perspective suggests that we consider how the canal project shaped the United States economically, militarily, politically, and culturally and how it influenced even debates considered purely "domestic" affairs. By acquiring territory around the globe, the United States itself had grown larger and more complex. American experiences in territories quite distant from Washington, D.C., would now influence the nation-state's history. *The Canal Builders* thus integrates fields of scholarship that have traditionally remained separate, bringing the domestic history of industrialization, the working class, and state building into dialogue with the history of empire building and transnational methodologies.[13]

Scholars have shown that many Americans, despite reluctance to describe their nation as an empire, fervently believed in expansionism since the founding of the Republic. Thomas Jefferson, for example, perceived expansion of the nation as essential for the continuation and blossoming of freedom. Such ideas inspired territorial acquisitions and wars of conquest against indigenous peoples and foreign nations throughout the nineteenth century. By the 1890s the popularity of social Darwinism, the belief in a racial hierarchy of the world's cultures, and the presumed superiority of Western civilization had made expansionism seem more desirable than ever. The so-called new empire that blossomed in the 1890s was hardly new, but rather a matter of pushing expansionism, which had heretofore been focused on the North American continent, into the overseas arena. Once the conquest of the American West was complete, Americans could begin to apply Manifest Destiny to foreign shores. By defeating Spain in the War of 1898 and engaging in other opportunistic moves around the same time, the United States acquired territories that stretched halfway around the globe and included control over Puerto Rico, Cuba, Guam, Hawaii, and the Philippines. These were heady days for politicians like Theodore Roosevelt and Albert Beveridge, who had advocated a strenuous expansionism for years, as they watched their nation rapidly attain a new status as a world power.[14]

Yet the new empire generated a lengthy and heated debate. Would expansionism contradict the ideals of the Republic? And what form should it take? Even before news and scandals from the Philippine-American War began fully to shape the debate, many Americans argued against formal imperialism from a pragmatic and pro-business perspective. In 1899 and 1900, Secretary of State John Hay issued famous declarations in response to his perception that the European powers were being given unequal access to Chinese ports and markets. Hay's writings, known as the Open Door Notes, articulated an alternative to formal imperialism, one that would ultimately come to dominate twentieth-century American foreign policy. Hay argued for free and equal access to Chinese markets and announced the desire of the United States to safeguard China's territorial integrity while upholding the rights guaranteed to all nations by international law. In this way the United States sketched out a different approach to world power, one based on its spectacular industrialization. The American strategy would eschew formal territorial control, annexation, or colonialism in favor of economic and commercial relationships and, when necessary, military intervention. This approach paved the way for the Panama Canal project, which would in turn transform Americans' notions of the nation's proper role in world affairs.[15]

So this is a book about empire, and yet, following the canal's own strange career, it is also about a project that does not fit easily into our notions of imperialism. It is about the ways diverse visions, expectations, hopes, dreams, and realities clashed against one another. It is about how a scandalous moment in the history of the United States became transformed into one widely seen as profound, idealistic, and triumphant. It is about how the world became larger and smaller at the same time. It is about the movement of tens of thousands of people, who left jobs in Mississippi or New Jersey, who departed plantations in Barbados or Antigua or rocky fields in Galicia, Spain, to work on the Americans' canal. It is about the creation of a global infrastructure that enhanced the flow of commerce and military personnel in order to assert U.S. economic, military, and diplomatic power. It is about struggles over the meaning and significance of the construction project, how it was received and how it transformed American history at home and in the world. It is, ultimately, a story about fortune and misfortune, about the making of America's empire in all its idealism, enthusiasm, and tragedy.

PRESIDENT ROOSEVELT'S STEAM SHOVEL

I N THE AUTUMN of 1906, President Theodore Roosevelt and his wife boarded the battleship USS *Louisiana* for a trip to the Panama Canal Zone. The president wanted to inspect the construction sites of the canal, a project he would forever consider his greatest achievement. Never before had a president of the United States left the country while in office. During the six days they spent on the ship, Roosevelt, rather bored, read Milton, tagged along as officers inspected the ship, or, as he wrote in letters to his children, sat and envisioned the history of the region he was passing through—and his place in that history. As the battleship and its accompanying warships passed by Cuba and Haiti, "two great, beautiful, venomous islands," as Roosevelt described them, his thoughts turned to Columbus, Spanish explorers, buccaneers and pirates, the rise of the slave trade, and "the turning of Hayti into a land of savage negroes, who have reverted to voodooism and cannibalism." Roosevelt believed by contrast that Cuba and Puerto Rico, thanks to the wise leadership of the United States, were making steady steps toward progress. He found it fascinating to compare his current journey with the trip he took eight years earlier to Santiago, Cuba, amid a fleet of warships, to fight in the Spanish-American War: "It seems a strange thing to think of my now being President, going to visit the work of the Panama Canal, which I have made possible."[1]

How much had changed in eight years, and how impressed the president felt at all he and his nation had achieved: "It is a beautiful sight, these three great warships standing southward in close column, and almost as beautiful at night when we see not only the lights but the loom through the darkness of the ships astern." He proudly described the Navy officers and crew: "The men are such splendid-looking fellows, Americans of the best type, young, active, vigorous, with lots of intelligence." The names given to the guns of the battleship also charmed Roosevelt: among them, Invincible, Peacemaker, Tedd, and The Big Stick.[2]

His wife, Edith, "pretty and dainty in white summer clothes," enjoyed the days at sea. Roosevelt himself could barely wait to hit the shores of Panama. He paced impatiently, and to pass the time, he retreated into more dreams of history. He saw centuries of "wild and bloody romance" as Vasco Núñez de Balboa crossed the isthmus, Spaniards conquered the indigenous peoples, and lonely tradespeople carried gold and silver across the isthmus to waiting ships. He imagined the wars of rebellion against Spanish domination and then the heroic Panamanians, aided by their friends in the United States, winning their independence from Colombia. In his mind's eye Roosevelt saw the building of the Panama Railroad with its "appalling loss of life," and finally the efforts of the French canal company, doomed to failure because of inefficiency and greed.[3]

At long last Roosevelt saw on the horizon the shore. He shook himself out of his reverie and waited eagerly as the mountains and jungles of Panama inched closer. When the ship docked, the president wanted to begin his explorations right away, though a ferocious storm hit during his first two days in the Zone and the Chagres River swelled higher than it had in years. Nonetheless, Roosevelt was elated. He toured the newly built villages of the Canal Zone, now knee-deep in water; observed the rivers flooding through the jungle; examined the machine shops, cafeterias, and dormitories; and spent a day in the awesome waste of Culebra Cut, where thousands of workers struggled to dig through the Continental Divide.

Nothing seems to have impressed Roosevelt more than the ninety-five-ton Bucyrus steam shovels. He watched as the gigantic machines dug into the mountainside, shaking as they pulled out to dump tremendous piles of rock and dirt into waiting train cars: "With intense energy men and machines do their task, the white men supervising matters and handling the machines, while the tens of thousands of black men do the rough manual labor where it is not worth while to have machines do it. It is an epic feat, and one of immense significance."[4]

Roosevelt could not resist the temptation to master one of the monstrous machines. He hoisted himself into the cab and posed for all the world to see, in triumph, as a steam-shovel driver and engineer. In that famous photograph, the president appears completely in control, efficiently and single-handedly directing the work himself. The machine and the president dominate the picture, working together to destroy a mountain. Absent from the picture are the thousands of workingmen who actually dug the canal.[5]

The photograph represented to the world the values U.S. officials sought to associate with the canal project: American efficiency, technological superiority, conquest over nature, and leadership. Roosevelt's journey to the isthmus, and his fleeting moment aboard the steam shovel, would prove a milestone in the history of the canal—and a turning point in the effort to construct a triumphalist narrative of America's role in the world. It could not have come at a better moment, for the canal project had become associated with scandal, corruption, and ineptitude in most Americans' minds. Perhaps only Roosevelt could have turned the situation around, for he brilliantly combined the great themes of the early twentieth century: progressivism, optimism, masculinity, and a vivacious belief that America was destined to play a leadership role in world affairs.

To Roosevelt, expansionism was a virtuous and necessary course for any great nation. National virtue and duty demanded that the United States play a vigorous role in the world. Roosevelt grew up in a wealthy New York family, a young man who adored his father but who was aware of the great disappointment of his father's life—that he had not fought in the Civil War. Roosevelt's struggle against physical frailty, especially asthma, and his campaign to transform himself into a robust and physically active young man have been noted by many historians. A Victorian code of manliness was part of the culture in which Roosevelt grew up, and a projection of masculinity was essential to his success as a man and as a politician.[6]

As a college student, young Theodore had already demonstrated an intense interest in sea power and the fate of the nation. He majored in history and wrote his senior thesis on the naval war of 1812. In the next decade and a half, as he entered politics, he began advocating an aggressive policy of expansionism. By the 1890s, when Roosevelt secured a series of government positions, a persuasive group of men had joined him in arguing that the United States must build up its military and acquire new territory in order to become a great and influential nation in the twentieth century. These included Alfred T. Mahan, whose *Influence of Sea Power upon History* reinforced Roosevelt's arguments that a strong navy was essential for any nation aspiring to greatness, and Henry Cabot Lodge, Roosevelt's mentor and friend.[7]

When making his case for an expansionist policy in these years, Roosevelt relied on a vocabulary quite different from that used by the anti-imperialists—the men and women who opposed empire on constitutional, economic, moral, and racial grounds.[8] Roosevelt eschewed the term "empire" in describing the United States. Instead, he talked about national greatness and the virtues and responsibilities of the Anglo-Saxon race. Speaking before the Naval War College in 1897, just weeks after having won appointment as assistant secretary of the Navy, Roosevelt argued that preparing for war would be the best way to ensure peace. America had never manifested a warlike spirit, so no one should worry that a strong military would lead to war. To the contrary, he claimed, "an unmanly desire to avoid a quarrel is often the surest way to precipitate one; and utter unreadiness to fight is even surer."[9] Expansionists like Roosevelt observed the drive toward empire being made by European powers and vowed that the United States must stand up, demonstrate its greatness, and keep the Old World out of the Western Hemisphere. Roosevelt fervently believed that the United States should not let Europeans dominate and carve up the Americas as they had Africa.

Even as Roosevelt addressed these naval students, the nation was watching events in Cuba with greater urgency. While William Randolph

Hearst and Joseph Pulitzer galvanized Americans' humanitarian concern for the plight of Cuban citizens with sensational tales of Spanish concentration camps on the island, the true expansionists, people like Roosevelt and Lodge, focused more on the opportunity Cuba's war afforded for realizing their expansionist dreams. Although President William McKinley shared their desire to see his nation play a more assertive role in the world, he initially hesitated to fight Spain. When the USS *Maine* exploded in Havana harbor in February 1898, he at last obliged them. Roosevelt's famous Rough Riders volunteer regiment—made up of cowboys, Indian fighters, and Ivy League athletes—his mythic charge up San Juan Hill, and his own remarkable skills at self-promotion made him a media darling and paved his way to political stardom. His vigorous posturing and military record helped him win the coveted vice presidential nomination in 1900. Then, in the autumn of 1901, President McKinley's assassination at the hands of an anarchist catapulted Roosevelt to the presidency.

At the young age of forty-three Roosevelt had achieved a major goal—even he may have been impressed by his precociousness. Meanwhile, the United States had easily bested the Spanish Empire in the War of 1898, thereby acquiring Puerto Rico, Guam, and the Philippines, as well as decisive control over Cuba. For years American plantation owners in Hawaii had been demanding that their nation annex the islands, and in 1898 McKinley finally agreed and added Hawaii to the list of new U.S. possessions. Now it remained to build up and manage this empire, consolidate American citizens' support for expansionism, and turn the United States at last into a great world power.

R OOSEVELT FREQUENTLY demonstrated his concern for such matters in his speeches in these years. His believed the United States *must* take its place among the world's great powers. It was the only possible course for a strong and virile race. "If we refrain from doing our part of the world's work, it will not alter the fact that work has got to be done, only it will have to be done by some stronger race, because we will have shown ourselves weaklings. I do not speak merely from the standpoint of American interests, but from the standpoint of civilization and humanity."[10] No one, he stressed, would advocate that the nation enter rashly into international relationships or acquire a colonial empire. Yet neither could Americans neglect their international duties, even if those duties required strenuous effort. America must act to make the world a better place.

This broad context helped revive for Roosevelt and like-minded expansionists the old dream of an Isthmian canal. A canal would demonstrate to Americans and to the world the beneficent potential of American power. A canal would shift attention away from America's suppression of Filipino hopes for independence and focus it instead on a seemingly more innocent conquest over nature. A canal would allow Roosevelt to enhance the nation's new identity as a world power while consolidating U.S. might throughout the Caribbean and Central America. A canal would tie images of a triumphant nation-state to notions of engineering prowess and industrial and economic superiority.

And what could be better than a construction project that would slice the continents in two, creating a spectacular waterway that would make military and commercial movements alike cheaper and more efficient? Sea power was integral to Roosevelt's visions of America's future. The War of 1898 won for the United States an empire that stretched halfway around the world, but it simultaneously demonstrated the weakness of the U.S. Navy and the need for a canal. All eyes were on the USS *Oregon* as it made the nearly fifteen-thousand-mile journey from Seattle to Florida, forced to go around Cape Horn in order to join the forces in Cuba. It took the battleship more than two months to arrive, a perilously slow transit during a time of war. An Isthmian canal would cut the distance a ship needed to traverse by more than eight thousand miles and consequently place the United States in a bigger league in terms of sea power as well as commercial might.

Roosevelt decided the canal should be built across the Isthmus of Panama rather than in Nicaragua. The United States had already been involved in building the railroad across Panama in the 1850s, and in the 1880s the French effort to construct a canal there had made some headway before failing altogether. The United States could benefit from France's work if it chose Panama as the construction site. U.S. diplomats urged Colombia to accept a treaty that would effectively eliminate its sovereignty over the isthmus, granting to the United States complete control over the Canal Zone. Roosevelt's administration offered what seemed to the Colombian government only a paltry sum of money in return. When Colombia expressed dismay over the deal, the U.S. secretary of state, John Hay, resorted to threats, warning that if the Colombian senate rejected the treaty, "action might be taken by the Congress next winter which every friend of Colombia would regret." Perhaps unable to grasp the determination of U.S. officials to have their canal—and assert their hegemony over the region—at any cost, the Colombian senate rejected the offer.[11]

Outraged, Roosevelt argued Colombia must not be allowed to "bar one of the future highways of civilization." He and his advisers seriously considered taking the isthmus by military force. But they knew Colombia would resist and the war that ensued would doubtlessly be attacked at home as imperialistic. With a political election coming up, Roosevelt did not want a major war on his hands. Thus he sought another way to acquire rights to build the canal. This led him to engage with the independence movement that had existed in Panama for some years.[12]

Roosevelt had little motivation to take the independence movement seriously until Colombia rejected the deal he offered. Then the insurgents suddenly appeared as a surrogate way to acquire control over the isthmus. When leading representatives of the New Panama Canal Company became involved as well, especially the Frenchman Philippe Bunau-Varilla, Roosevelt began to trust that the movement for independence could succeed. Without declaring any explicit intentions, he signaled to Bunau-Varilla that the United States would support a coup attempt and ordered four battleships to Panama. The coup took place in the evening of November 3, 1903. Colombians fled Panama City on November 4, and on November 6 the United States gave its recognition to the new Republic of Panama. That morning, a member of the U.S. Army raised the flag of Panama over the city of Colón.[13]

All that was left to do was to negotiate terms with the new Republic of Panama. Its government appointed Bunau-Varilla as diplomat in charge of negotiations with Secretary of State Hay. The Hay–Bunau-Varilla Treaty of 1903 gave astonishing rights to the United States while it virtually eliminated any sovereignty the Republic of Panama might have possessed. Bunau-Varilla's New Panama Canal Company made $40 million from the sale of the rights and equipment to the United States. Nervous after the horse had left the stable about what Bunau-Varilla was negotiating, Panamanian Manuel Amador Guerrero (who, months later, would become Panama's first president) rushed to Washington, D.C., but the treaty had already been signed when he arrived. His horror over the rights Bunau-Varilla had given away was plainly visible.[14] The U.S. Senate fiercely debated the Hay–Bunau-Varilla Treaty, with opponents arguing that it was the child of conspiratorial machinations by Roosevelt and Bunau-Varilla and that it violated Colombian sovereignty. In the end, however, the Senate ratified the treaty by a strong majority.[15]

The United States had won not only a monopoly over construction of the canal but also complete and perpetual control (as "if it were sovereign") over the Canal Zone, a ten-mile-wide territory that stretched across the isthmus, effectively splitting the Republic of Panama in two, and the right to purchase or otherwise control any land or buildings in the cities of Panama and Colón deemed necessary for constructing the canal or for sanitation work; and in the notorious Article 7 of the treaty, the United States gained the right to intervene in the cities of Panama and adjacent territory to maintain or restore public order "in case the Republic of Panama should not be, in the judgment of the United States, able to maintain such order." In return the United States agreed to guarantee the independence of the Republic of Panama and to pay the republic $10 million plus an annual sum of $250,000.[16] Roosevelt finally had control over the isthmus he coveted and could build a waterway to provide quick transit between the oceans, give the United States ready access to its new empire in Hawaii and the Philippines, and provide the rationale for a strenuous policing effort and military intervention by the United States throughout the Caribbean.

But what of the Republic of Panama? Its citizens were not a wealthy people, and they were ruled by a small oligarchy of merchants, land-owners, bankers, and businessmen. Even as these groups took their young nation into a Faustian bargain with the United States, they hoped their independence and their friendship with the United States would provide a ticket to wealth, power, and respect in the eyes of the world. But the U.S. occupation of the Canal Zone and the construction project instead generated tremendous strains on all Panamanians economically and culturally, regardless of their ethnicity, race, or class status. Living in a small and scarcely populated province of Colombia, the people of the isthmus had historically felt ignored and disrespected by Colombian leaders. The merchants and businessmen who dominated the region feared and disliked the working masses around them and sought to iso-late themselves from any demands urban workers might make. Caught between the disdain of Colombian leaders and the working-class people they themselves disdained, Panama's leaders had for nearly a century sought the protection of a strong foreign power. Over the course of the nineteenth century they looked to Great Britain, France, and the United States for support.[17]

These men also felt anxious to make use of whatever advantages they could to propel forward the economic fortunes of the isthmus— as well as their own political and economic fates, naturally seeing the two as virtually indistinguishable. Throughout the nineteenth century and into the twentieth, this required exploiting their remarkable geography. Pan-ama had little coffee or sugar to sell, but, poised on a narrow strip of land between two great oceans, it had served as a crossing point for explorers and conquerors for hundreds of years. In the mid–nineteenth century, Panamanian elites negotiated construction of a railroad with American contractors, and later they hoped to benefit from the French project to construct a canal. Each of these projects generated destabiliz-ing social and economic change, leading Panama's merchants and busi-nessmen to worry about their security and future. Nonetheless, they remained convinced that alliance with a powerful foreign nation would provide the best route to prosperity and political might. More than that, the historian Peter Szok has demonstrated, this small group of elites shared, like so many across Latin America, a deep belief in liberalism: the idea that progress and civilization must be brought to the isthmus. They hoped to achieve this through a relationship with a power like France or the United States—a nation that could help them profit from their unrivaled location—and by luring foreign investment and creating a Western-style government in the region. This would not only bring civilization to the isthmus but also help insulate elites from the demands and protests of lower-class Panamanians, most of them people of African or mestizo descent. Economically vulnerable but demographically dominant, the lower classes of Panama had long seemed a threat to the Panamanian upper class, with its European background, and so the latter had developed notions of liberalism and nationalism that carefully excluded all other social groups.[18]

And yet there was always a sharp edge to the alliance between the merchants of Panama and the Americans. The Frenchman Bunau-Varilla, representing Panama in the negotiations with the United States, reportedly threatened the young nation's leaders that if he did not play the central role, the United States might refuse to support independence. Although their alliance guaranteed Panama's independence, the relationship was fundamentally unequal. As time went on, the canal construction project and U.S. policies together generated a major social transformation of Panama, heightening divisions within the country, and the rift in the friendship grew ever larger.

The early days of Panamanian independence proved difficult. A constitution was passed that included a clause granting the United States the right to intervene anywhere in the republic to restore public peace, and established an interim revolutionary government to rule until February 1904, when the National Assembly elected the elderly conservative Manuel Amador Guerrero as the nation's first president. Amador hung a photograph of President Theodore Roosevelt on the wall behind his desk and got to work. Many controversies arising out of Panama's revolution required handling: Colombia remained problematic; relations with the United States generated difficult issues; and, perhaps most important, Amador needed to isolate those within his country who might cause problems, including liberals and nationalists who criticized the Hay–Bunau-Varilla Treaty as granting too much to the United States, and the lower and middle classes who were angry over their exclusion from so much of Panama's public and political life.[19]

B ACK IN the United States, Roosevelt received criticism for the way he had acquired the Canal Zone. The *New York Times* referred to the Zone as "stolen property" and declared that Roosevelt's partners in the crime were "a group of canal promoters and speculators and lobbyists who came into their money through the rebellion we encouraged, made safe, and effectuated." The anti-imperialist Moorfield Storey declared Roosevelt's seizing of the canal to be morally and legally objectionable: "It teaches the weaker republics of this hemisphere to distrust and fear us. . . . It sets an unhappy example of lawlessness to our citizens [and] . . . it lowers the moral standard of our whole people."[20] Stung by the criticism, Roosevelt released documents and developed arguments to defend his actions. His main justification will sound familiar today, in an age of acknowledged globalization: the interests of world trade transcended international law. The needs of civilization itself were at stake, and this trumped any mere sovereignty of Colombia. "If ever a Government could be said to have received a mandate from civilization to effect an object the accomplishment of which was demanded in the interest of mankind, the United States holds that position with regard to the interoceanic canal," Roosevelt declared.[21]

Yet despite condemnation from the press and from some anti-imperialists, Roosevelt's taking of the Canal Zone generated few widespread protests. The Anti-Imperialist League tried but failed to generate a campaign opposed to the canal. At the annual convention of the American Federation of Labor, the longtime activist Andrew Furuseth introduced a measure criticizing the government for violating Colombia's sovereignty. The AFL instead passed a resolution hailing the construction of an Isthmian canal as "the most important public work ever assumed by this or any other nation." Roosevelt's shift away from formal colonialism had made it easier for AFL leaders to support his actions, and the canal's importance as a public works project made it seem necessary to them.[22] Traditional opponents of empire among both the working class and the middle class seemed to be losing their fire. Disturbed by the lack of opposition to the U.S. role in Panama, the philosopher and anti-imperialist William James noted in a letter to a friend: "The organization of slick success in our age is only equalled by the organization of political acquiescence. Between them we shall live in a new form of society."[23]

As expansionists like Roosevelt hungrily looked to begin the construction project, serious questions awaited them. There was a great deal of contemplation across the United States in the early twentieth century about what it meant to be an imperial power, what it should look like, and how to tackle the challenges involved in empire building generally and in constructing the canal more specifically. The United States had to succeed, and succeed marvelously, if it was to exploit the construction effort for maximum effect. The French effort to build a canal across the isthmus from 1880 to 1889 had failed spectacularly due to persistent disease, inadequate technology, insufficient funds, high labor turnover, and, most damaging of all, unfortunate engineering decisions. It cost the lives of at least twenty thousand people. In the aftermath, Ferdinand de Lesseps, the hero of France who had supervised the building of the Suez Canal and who had been expected to triumph in Panama as well, was tried and convicted of fraud and breach of trust.[24] Having dishonored France, de Lesseps was surely on American officials' minds as they plotted their own success. They understood that the French failure gave them an opportunity to showcase the promise and talents of young America. The project would be a gigantic one, requiring the labor and energy of tens of thousands. It would necessitate creating an entire society in the Canal Zone, housing the workers, keeping them healthy, protecting them, disciplining them, and managing their work. How might all this be done?

A rush of books and articles appeared in these years, introducing readers to America's new possessions, questioning their potential impact on the Republic, and analyzing some of the challenges and quandaries they presented. Authors devoted endless pages simply to describing the new U.S. territories, from Puerto Rico to Panama, from Guam to Hawaii. For some, clarifying the relationship between the United States and Panama proved a preoccupation. In the anthology *America Across the Seas: Our Colonial Empire,* John Wallace wrote that "while it would hardly be proper to style the Republic of Panama one of the colonial possessions of the United States," the United States does have complete control over the strip of land known as the Canal Zone. Another book referred to the Panama Canal Zone as "our most important colony." Some writers celebrated the canal project in ways that must have pleased Roosevelt. William Boyce proclaimed in his book *United States Colonies and Dependencies: The Travels and Investigations of a Chicago Publisher,* "The Panama Canal is the greatest industrial undertaking ever attempted and successfully carried to completion by any nation of the world, and we should all feel proud of our country, and that we are citizens of the United States of North America."[25]

Yet many others voiced concerns. The English writer Benjamin Kidd had forcefully raised the problems inherent in tropical conquest in his 1898 book *The Control of the Tropics,* which declared that the white man could never adapt to tropical climates or to the peoples who lived there. Kidd wrote that "in the midst of races in a different and lower stage of development; divorced from the influences which have produced him, from the moral and political environment from which he sprang, the white man does not in the end . . . tend so much to raise the level of the races amongst whom he has made his unnatural home, as he tends himself to sink slowly to the level around him." In an article in the *Atlantic Monthly* that closely followed upon publication of his book, Kidd specifically addressed these questions with regard to the United States. He anticipated that it was the destiny of the United States to be the "leading world-power of the next century" and noted that this could not be accomplished without a major commitment to world trade. Kidd took the expansionism of the United States as a given, but he repeated that the white man "can never be acclimatized in the tropics." Rather, the "*natural* inhabitants" must continue to people those regions, and the United States must be sure to govern them "as a trust for civilization." As Kidd's comments suggest, the "tropics" loomed as a great source of anxiety to many in the early twentieth century. Tropical climates were particularly associated with the absence of civilization—and hence with the same threat of degeneration people had observed in the Philippines.[26]

James Morton Callahan, author of *An Introduction to American Expansion Policy,* likewise commented on the fears that colonization of the tropics would bring trouble, especially race problems, and that the people of the tropics could not possibly be governed by democratic means. People worry, he noted, that "some system of forced or indentured labor will be necessary to develop large industries" and that this will threaten the American Republic. Yet Callahan sided with those more optimistic observers who "are telling us that the trade of the tropics will be the largest factor in the era upon which we are entering; that the trend of modern history seems to be toward colonization and protectorates for less civilized peoples; and that it will be futile for any first class power to fold its hands and stand aloof from regions which, although they cannot perhaps be colonized by whites, must be governed by a base in the temperate zones—by the United States and other nations whose duty it is to undertake the work in the interest of all as a trust for civilization." Expansionists, he noted, merely laugh at the anti-imperialists, and he described the latter as "shrieking at the self-conjured ghost of imperialism, as if empire could grow on freedom's soil." To the contrary, he urged, civilization must "reach out in helpfulness to lift the less enlightened to liberty's plane, to search for fresh resources, to transform seas into paths for ships, and yoke nature to serve man."[27] Thus did Callahan state the expansionists' cheerful vision of American imperialism.

Through such books and articles Americans who never laid foot on the Isthmus of Panama would become acquainted with its geography. Bounded on the Atlantic (Caribbean) side by the city of Colón and on the Pacific shore by Panama City, the Republic of Panama possessed a climate shaped powerfully by the proximity of the ocean. Three and a half million years earlier the oceans had met there and sharks had swum freely through the water. The oceans' impact could still be felt in tremendous downpours of rain, particularly in the wet season, which lasted from

May to December and, when combined with high temperatures and humidity, made life across the isthmus a challenge. During one of the downpours that came daily during the wet months, an inch or two of rain could fall within minutes, flooding streets, complicating the construction process, and making almost unbearable the workers' time on the job. James Anthony Froude had described Panama in 1885 as "a hideous dung heap of physical and moral abomination . . . a damp, tropical jungle, intensely hot, swarming with mosquitoes, snakes, alligators, scorpions, and centipedes; the home, even as Nature made it, of yellow fever, typhus, and dysentery and now made immeasurably more deadly by the multitudes of people who crowd thither."[28]

The memoirs of those who traveled to the isthmus during the French and early American eras repeat such horrifying images over and over again. Marie Gorgas, the wife of the sanitation director, William Gorgas, and one of the first to arrive in Panama, recalled, "Nature herself seemed to have set aside the Isthmus as the headquarters of the worst manifestations of the human spirit. The whole forty-mile stretch was one sweltering miasma of death and disease." She saw on the isthmus "an apparently hopeless tangle of tropical vegetation, swamps whose bottoms the engineers had not discovered, black muddy soil, quicksands, intercepted now and then by a tall volcanic mountain or crossed by rivers that, at flood tide, sometimes rose twenty feet and more in a single night." The floods regularly "obliterated the landscape." Altogether it impressed her as a land of "dank terror."[29] As Americans prepared to head for the isthmus, conquer the tropics, and build a new civilization, they knew the task would be formidable.

MEANWHILE, MEN and women around the world heard of the Yankees' project and began to think of making their own trip. Their journeys and experiences in the Canal Zone were different—but no less important, and no less rich in meaning—from those of Theodore Roosevelt. U.S. government officials had established offices in the Caribbean and in Europe to begin recruiting labor for the construction project, and their labor agents fanned out around the globe looking for able-bodied men. The islands of the Caribbean emerged as their main target, with Barbados feeling the impact most intensively. Sugarcane plantations of a few hundred acres each dominated Barbados and were worked by a rural proletariat of African descent. The typical plantation manager had moved to Barbados from Britain and knew his workers by name—these were not the distant corporate owners that dominated many Caribbean islands. The Barbadians who harvested and processed the cane, or who worked as blacksmiths or wheelwrights, were for the most part impoverished. Many owned no shoes. Estate workers who sought better-paying work elsewhere often faced prosecution for deserting the job. Some managed to acquire small plots for growing a few vegetables, which helped them survive. When hunger grew desperate, particularly among the children, a rough form of justice known as the potato raid might be carried out, where hundreds of estate workers would loot a potato crop, beating off anyone who tried to stop them.[30]

Considering their circumstances back home, it is perhaps not surprising that over the course of a decade, twenty thousand Barbadians signed contracts with the U.S. government and traveled to Panama. Probably at least that many more went to work in Panama without a contract, many of them wives or children of contract laborers. As migrants headed for Bridgetown to catch a steamer, their excitement must have been as palpable as the planters' horror. One estate worker remembered a song that spread through the estates after Panama migration began:

> We want more wages, we want it now,
> And if we don't get it, we going to Panama.
> Yankees say they want we down there,
> We want more wages, we want it now.[31]

Those who left for Panama were eager for adventure, the chance to make more money, and freedom from the toil of plantation work, but they were also nervous about leaving loved ones behind for the unknown world of the Yankees. One Barbadian woman remembered the night before the boats left: there was such a big party that some didn't make it to the boat the next day.[32] The preparations for departure could be extensive: saving up money and purchasing shoes and a suit coat, perhaps a nice hat, and a canvas folding chair for the journey. Old kerosene tins often served as suitcases. Across the island one would see men saying good-bye to their families before joining others to hike to meet the ship in Bridgetown. It became a common sight, these men marching across the island, dressed in suit coats and heading for Panama.

Beresford Skinner was one such man, an estate worker in the parish of St. Lucy, at the northern tip of the island. Skinner left his home with a few other men and headed for the village of Speightstown, where they could catch a cheap schooner to Bridgetown. They stopped to pick up a friend along the way, but the man's wife was hanging on to his shoulders, crying and pleading with him not to go away. The friend told Skinner to go on without him, but Skinner responded, "My wife's home crying too, and I left her, come with us." Yet the man stayed behind, and finally Skinner turned away and headed for Panama.[33] Skinner and his friends surely passed by plantation workers as they traveled and exhorted them to join their parade. And when one group of migrants heading for Panama passed by estate workers in a field, a member of the party shouted out, "Why you don't hit de manager in de head, and come along wid we!"[34]

Such scenes played out on islands across the Caribbean as workers packed their bags for Panama. The majority of those who signed contracts with the Isthmian Canal Commission were Barbadian men, due to the difficulties U.S. government officials faced when negotiating with other Caribbean governments. Yet with or without a contract, workingmen on islands like Grenada, Martinique, St. Lucia, and Jamaica made the journey as well. Most migrants were male, but over time more women began making the journey, often to join husbands or lovers. Years later Bea Waldron remembered traveling with her mother to join her father in Panama. Once there her mother would add to the family income by selling fruits and coal and washing clothes. Her mother instructed Bea, "Be sweet when you get to Panama. Forget Barbadian." By this, she meant dialect—she wanted her daughter to sound properly Panamanian.[35]

The trip Bea made shared little with Theodore Roosevelt's pampered journey. Her ship took six days to go from Barbados to Panama, with no stops. No sleeping accommodations were provided for people like Bea and her mother; hence immigrants carried their own deck chairs. No food was provided, though on some ships immigrants received coffee each morning. An awning might be spread to protect them from the sun. Winifred James, an Englishwoman who traveled to Panama to meet her husband, described the West Indians she observed: "On the journey they lie about inert, listless and unwashed. But on the day of arrival there is a great awakening. The parcels are undone, clean dresses and marvellous hats appear out of the brown-paper parcels. . . . I have seen them make their toilet in the full blaze of morning light, with no more thought than as if they were in the screened privacy of a jealously guarded bedchamber."[36]

For West Indians such as these, the Panama Canal project had already begun to act as a global magnet, drawing families away from their homeland and setting in motion wide-ranging changes involving migration, labor supply, and the distribution of economic wealth and social status. The project would bring a measure of economic prosperity to the nations of the Caribbean and turn many estate workers into globe-trotters familiar with a larger landscape, one ranging from Panama to Costa Rica and Colombia and, for a great many, onward to the United States. And though the canal project mostly drew migrants from the Caribbean, thousands of others came from northern and southern Europe and from as far away as India and China. Peruvians, Colombians, Costa Ricans, and Mexicans all packed suitcases for the Canal Zone. No official recruitment of these groups took place, but foremen might hire them if they showed up. Chinese came to the Canal Zone from south China or from Panama City and Colón, the latter two residences for many Chinese who had first arrived during the French construction effort. Now they moved into the new towns of the Zone to open small shops, selling tobacco and household items, pots and pans, and clothing and handkerchiefs to the new residents of towns like Empire and Gorgona. Many Indians similarly had first migrated as indentured servants to Caribbean islands like Trinidad, but some made the six-month-long journey from their homes in India.[37]

In much larger numbers men and women migrated to the Canal Zone from the United States. Many were similar to Ted Sherrard, a young man from Kansas, fresh out of college with a major in engineering, eager for adventure and opportunity. While working in Pittsburgh as an apprentice at Westinghouse, Ted learned the federal government was recruiting men for jobs in the Panama Canal Zone. He applied for a position and within a few weeks received a telegram offering work as an assistant switchboard operator. His foreman urged him to take the job, saying it would be "the best thing in the world to do." If he did well, the foreman added, the government would find him another job after that one ended. Ted soon made up his mind. Surely, he must have thought, a job in the Panama Canal Zone would bring adventure, good pay, and good experience. He wrote to his mother, "I will be on one of the healthiest chunks of soil that Uncle Sam owns. . . . I have talked with fellows who have been down there and they say the conditions there are first rate." He packed his bags and headed to New York City, where he caught a ship to Panama. Assigned on the ship to a tiny room right over the propeller, Ted described a noise that sounded like "an empty lumber wagon on a rocky road." But he enjoyed meeting workingmen who were on their way back to Panama after a vacation in the States, and he managed the trip with only a few bouts of seasickness.[38]

Henry Williams of Houston, Texas, also found the recruiter's terms attractive. An African American born in 1870, Henry was a stout man of 210 pounds. At the age of ten he had begun working at farm labor in Texas, then moved into such jobs as longshoreman, railroad track worker, and freight loader. Gradually, he moved his way up into the job of blacksmith helper for the Southern Pacific Railroad. In 1907 a government labor agent hired Henry to work on the canal as a blacksmith helper at forty-four cents gold per hour. This must have seemed to him a great stroke of luck—working at a prestigious job for the federal government. Perhaps he also hoped that leaving Texas for the Canal Zone would bring him respite from the harshness of Jim Crow segregation, economic discrimination, and racial violence. And so Henry said good-bye to his mother and his daughter, Henrietta, and traveled to Panama for a job in the town of Empire, working in the vast mechanical shops there that repaired and maintained tools and steam shovels throughout the Canal Zone.[39]

As conditions on the isthmus improved, after 1906, American women gradually began packing bags for Panama so they might work as secretaries or nurses (many of the latter traveling from Manila or Havana), or, more commonly, to join husbands already there and provide a home for them. In 1907, Elizabeth Kittredge joyfully received a note from her fiancé, Charlie, who worked in the Department of Labor, Quarters, and Subsistence in the Canal Zone. At last, he said, he felt the Zone had become safe enough, with the yellow fever now eradicated, for her to join him. Young Elizabeth traveled to Colón with a chaperone, watching the blue Caribbean sea flow by during the six-day trip.[40] Arriving in Colón, she observed, with some trepidation, "the blackest man I'd ever seen" hoist her trunk onto his head and carry it up the hill to a small wooden house poised high on stilts. The house belonged to Charlie's boss, and it would serve as the couple's wedding chapel. She entered the house and noted the bare wooden walls. More worrisome yet was the boss's wife, "a lanky woman with faded hair and colorless cheeks. . . . I wondered, subconsciously, how soon the tropics would fade my shining hair and take the color from my red cheeks." Elizabeth cleaned herself up, changed clothes, and headed into the living room to be married by a missionary. Afterward everyone sat down to a wedding luncheon served on the house's screened-in porch. On the table were nice white china and fancy silver, pâté de fois gras, champagne, and roast turkey, but "all served awkwardly by a little Jamaican maid in a gingham dress." That evening a gang of West Indians carried the couple's belongings to a new bungalow that awaited them with two rooms, two enclosed porches, a bathroom, and a kitchen. "In the soft glow of the kerosene lamps, we unpacked our wedding gifts, hung our clothes in the crude wardrobe—and the little house became our home."[41]

The one other group that journeyed to Panama in large numbers, comparable to those of the Americans, was Europeans. Frenchmen, Germans, English, and Swedes were almost uniformly destined for supervisory or skilled jobs, while the thousands of Spaniards, Italians, and Greeks who came found themselves working unskilled jobs as tracklayers, freight loaders, or diggers. Labor recruiters were especially keen on importing

Spaniards, believing they would work better than West Indians. When they discovered the Spaniards worked only marginally better but caused a great deal more trouble (in the form of food riots, strikes, and other protests), they nonetheless continued to recruit a few of them to goad the Caribbeans to work harder. One Spaniard who traveled to the isthmus was Antonio Sanchez, a thirty-year-old who would spend more than four years laying track in Culebra Cut. The Spaniards with whom he traveled, he later recalled, arrived in Panama with one belief: "Everything here was gold and all things were as sweet as honey. However, they were to find out the gold was silver and the fruits were sour."[42]

THUS THE Panama Canal project beckoned to working people from around the world, as well as to expansionists like Theodore Roosevelt. As many Americans saw it, the War of 1898 had ended in victory and made their country a power in the world. John Foster Carr wrote in the *Outlook* that U.S. expansionism had "made the Pacific almost an American ocean." The United States needed to use the power it had won in 1898 to consolidate its empire; exercise power in significant, productive, and impressive ways; win its citizenry over to a new identity as an imperial power; and impress the people and nation-states of the world. If the United States could accomplish this, it would emerge as one of the world's great nations.[43]

Industrialization at home and the broad range of social, economic, and cultural changes associated with it had the majority of Americans focused on their immediate lives, on their jobs and families. They were saving money, perhaps for a beachside trip or new shoes for their children. In ways they likely did not grasp, however, their lives at home had become connected, inextricably, to events and movements occurring all over the globe. Within the United States one could see this most obviously in the millions of immigrants trudging down the ships to enter American ports, crowding into cities, and rushing to sign up for jobs in the booming factories. In neighborhoods like the Lower East Side in New York, you could barely find room to cross the streets, so crowded were they with people, dogs, horses, and carriages. Immigrants, especially those from southern and eastern Europe, seemed to bring a new world to America's doorstep, bringing with them also new ways of dressing and speaking and relating to the world. To some, everything about the new immigrants seemed to threaten traditional cultures and manners in the United States.

But the Isthmus of Panama was also now, in effect, on America's doorstep, and thousands of immigrants from the Caribbean, Europe, Asia, Latin America, and the United States would build a different world there in the years to come, one that would shape and be shaped by conditions, cultures, and circumstances back home. As the United States dug more deeply into the Isthmus of Panama, officials struggled to build a comfortable and nurturing society for white Americans—one they might proudly call a civilization—in the Canal Zone. Simultaneously, they sought ways of managing, disciplining, and maintaining order among the men and women they employed. Officials needed to succeed in this venture, as a great deal was riding on it—the reputation of America in the world, the status of Roosevelt and his government at home. How they attempted this grand adventure and how the people of the Isthmus of Panama forced reckonings of many kinds is the story of the pages that follow.

CHAPTER ONE

A MODERN STATE
IN THE TROPICS

I N 1906 the journalist John Foster Carr traveled from New York City to Panama in order to observe the construction project. In a series of articles for the *Outlook,* he stressed the "splendid human story" being written in the Panama Canal Zone. What he found most fascinating was the challenge to develop an effective form of government there: "You begin to understand that our Republic is doing something more on the Isthmus than the mere building of a canal. It is creating a State with all the machinery and equipment of our home civilization adapted to strange needs." Carr, like most other observers, stressed that the canal was made possible by the great democratic ideals of the American Republic.

Ironically, he also noted that government in the Zone was evolving in a way very different from its counterpart in the United States. The water supply, the fire department, the postal service, and more, he argued, were "such as might be provided by a progressive and strongly centralized European government." However much Americans hoped to transplant the culture and politics of their "home civilization," something happened along the way. Challenged on all sides by a difficult climate, a colossal construction project, rampant disease, and tens of thousands of workers and their families who emigrated from all over the world, officials struggled to govern and manage the isthmus. They needed to create a civilized and efficient society in the Canal Zone while establishing a firm boundary between the Zone and the Republic of Panama. At times, particularly in the early days, it seemed they would not succeed. Before the project was more than a few years old, Roosevelt had been forced to find a second and then a third chief engineer to supervise the construction after their predecessors had resigned, unable or unwilling to tolerate the poor conditions and difficult challenges.[1]

The Zone was a territory ten miles wide (five miles on either side of the projected canal), covering dense jungle, mountains, and swampy lowlands across the nearly fifty-mile-long isthmus. The construction of the canal officially lasted ten years, from May 1904 to August 1914, and was characterized by experimentation and strategic reorganizations of the Canal Zone's government, a process that overlapped to a large extent with the tenure of the three chief engineers. John Wallace, the first one, lasted only one year and oversaw an anxious and poorly organized period. His successor, the railroad engineer John Stevens, remained on the job less than two years (June 1905 to April 1907), but his tenure was vastly more effective, and he played a key role by convincing Congress to build a lock rather than a sea-level canal. The third and final chief engineer, George Washington Goethals, oversaw most of the actual construction and continued with the job through its completion. Goethals's era witnessed the construction of the spectacular lock gates, the completion of Gatun Dam, the flooding of Gatun Lake, and the first ship's successful traversing of the canal in 1914. The latter occurred just as World War I erupted in Europe, somewhat overshadowing the U.S. success with the canal. Nonetheless, the next year the United States emphatically celebrated its triumph at the Panama-Pacific International Exposition in San Francisco.

The three chief engineers each faced the challenge of how to govern the Zone's growing population and how to overcome the engineering and medical difficulties the region posed. The construction project formally began in 1904 as a small group of men—surveyors, geographers, engineers, doctors—and a handful of female nurses boarded ships for the isthmus. The French failure was fresh on Americans' minds as they arrived to find ghostly mementos of the earlier construction effort lurking in every swamp hole—old, rusting machinery, locomotives, dilapidated houses. Philippe Bunau-Varilla had written about his time working on the French project, "Death was constantly gathering its harvest about me." Convincing workers to go to Panama—and keeping them alive once they arrived—would prove daunting tasks indeed.[2]

THE GREAT PROBLEM OF LABOR

As the U.S. occupation of the Canal Zone began, Roosevelt chose the Army doctor William Gorgas to head the U.S. sanitation effort. Born in 1854, Gorgas grew up in a household profoundly affected by the Civil War. His father, a Pennsylvanian trained at West Point, moved to Richmond during the war and joined the Confederate cause. Jefferson Davis appointed him chief of ordnance, and William grew up in a social world that included the top leaders of the Confederacy. He later remembered fleeing with his family as the war came to an end: "I first came to Baltimore a ragged, barefoot little rebel, with empty pockets and an empty stomach. My father had gone south with the army. At the fall and destruction of Richmond my mother's house, with all that she had, was burned, leaving her stranded with six small children. She came to Baltimore, and was cared for by friends." After the war the family was impoverished until, after some years, William's father won a job as head of the University of the South.[3]

William dreamed of a military career but failed to win admission to West Point. He decided to become an Army doctor in spite of his father, who objected that it was not an honorable career. After attending medical school, William Gorgas spent twenty years as an Army doctor in North Dakota, Texas, and Florida. When the War of 1898 began, the Army sent Gorgas to Havana to fight the spread of yellow fever among soldiers there, and after the war he was appointed chief sanitary officer of Cuba. In these years the U.S. government realized that yellow fever threatened its effort to control and clean up cities like Havana. Under the leadership of the Army physician and research scientist Walter Reed, and following the earlier ideas of the Cuban Carlos Finlay, doctors demonstrated that yellow fever was spread by mosquitoes. Gorgas then helped implement sanitation measures to rid Cuba of the disease.

Gorgas and his wife, Marie, would be among the first Americans to venture into Panama. Their ship arrived at Colón, and as they wandered the city, they found the streets "unspeakably dirty and mud-filled, swarmed with naked children; the ugly frame houses rested on piles, under which greenish slimy water formed lagoons. Such dilapidation and desolation!" They gamely enjoyed the train ride across the isthmus to Panama City, finding their mood lifted by the beautiful mountains and jungle, and then descended again into mud and a slow carriage ride up to Ancon Hospital, where living quarters had been arranged for them. After dinner they sat with friends in their living quarters, which happened to be a reconversion of the old officers' ward. This ward, Marie Gorgas noted, had been the site of more yellow fever deaths than any other spot on the isthmus during the French period. It was a grim reminder of the difficulties awaiting them.[4]

Could they possibly bring order, health, sanitation, indeed civilization itself, to this rude corner of the world? Tropical nature was seen as threatening the health and civilization of white men who ventured to Panama. Although an earlier discourse had associated the tropics with the Garden of Eden, by the early twentieth century it had come to be seen as sinister. The climate, the heavy rainfall, the prevalence of disease, and the perceived indolence of those native to the tropics all loomed as highly problematic.[5]

Gorgas believed that succeeding in the tropics depended first and foremost upon eradicating or containing disease. Toward this end he employed the same strategies relied on earlier in Cuba. Years later, in an essay that sounded a triumphant response to Benjamin Kidd's earlier warnings, titled "The Conquest of the Tropics for the White Race," Gorgas explained his procedures. He and his staff worked to destroy all possible breeding places of the mosquitoes carrying malaria or yellow fever. Throughout the Zone they drained or filled in ditches, sprayed oil or petroleum over water that could not be drained, used chemicals to kill algae in streams, and cut brush where mosquitoes dwelled. As extra precautions, windows in houses (at least those houses intended for whites) built by the Isthmian Canal Commission, or ICC, received screens, and officials made quinine available to all employees.[6]

The U.S. government also worked to rebuild the urban environments of Panama City and Colón, which were seen as crucial bases for the canal project, to enhance sanitation and eradicate disease. The streets of each city were suddenly filled with American sanitary officials in white coats and West Indian laborers under their direction. West Indians worked at street sweeping, fumigation, mosquito destruction, draining or oiling of water, building and paving roads and sidewalks, constructing sewers and water lines, and poisoning hundreds of stray dogs and thousands of rats. Officials went door-to-door throughout the cities, again and again, inspecting every home. When inspectors found mosquito larvae in someone's home, they reported the residents to the mayor of Panama City, who imposed a fine. When they found illness or mosquitoes, they fumigated. ICC officials estimated the total cost of improvements to the cities of Panama to be nearly $2 million.[7]

These early days were dark ones for officials like Gorgas and the chief engineer John Wallace. Named by Roosevelt to head the construction effort, Wallace came to the Zone with experience as engineer and general manager of the Illinois Central Railroad. He suffered through the most difficult and experimental period of the U.S. occupation and possessed less authority than later chief engineers, because the U.S. government's strategy initially centered power on the ICC—the members of which resided in the United States. Wallace saw his administration hindered by bureaucracy and lengthy delays as he requested provisions and equipment from Washington, D.C. His requests were often questioned or denied by the commissioners, who were concerned about limiting expenditures. Wallace nonetheless accomplished a significant amount: under his supervision, workers repaired hundreds of old French houses and built a few dozen new ones, extended the railroad, conducted extensive surveys, and added to the excavation already done by the French.

Wallace complained vociferously about the inefficient bureaucracy hindering his work. In the spring of 1905, President Roosevelt undertook the first of several reorganizations, replacing every member of the ICC with a new commissioner and centralizing its operations. Yet Wallace seemed, almost from the beginning, defeated by the job and by the climate and terrain. He saw the unhappiness of workers, their constant flight back to the United States, and accurately evaluated the problem: not only were the men worried about yellow fever, but they felt that housing was inadequate, amusements and diversions were nonexistent, and food prices were much too high. And they were homesick. He knew better quarters would gradually become available, yet he despaired of fixing other problems: "It could hardly be expected that the United States should maintain theatres, dance-halls, bowling alleys . . . and vaudevilles for the delectation of its employees." He noted also that a few men had brought their wives with them, but this had added to their misery rather than curing it, because conditions were unpleasant. Wallace concluded, "I have personally done all I could to discourage the coming hither of families until a man could see that he was in a position to take care of his dependents when they arrived."[8]

The biggest problem was yellow fever. Like French officials before him, Wallace had arrived in Panama with a coffin to carry him home in case he became victim to an epidemic. During the first year of the occupation disease was by far the greatest threat, and hence Gorgas's role became the most important. As men and women headed to the Canal Zone to prepare the way for digging, yellow fever began to break out. By the end of 1904, cases were appearing every week. Next bubonic plague appeared, and then malaria and pneumonia. Terror struck the isthmus, and old-timers compared these days to the worst of the French period. They found little solace in the many French cemeteries dotting the isthmus. The majority of Americans packed suitcases and headed home to the United States. That summer Wallace did the same. He resigned, as John Foster Carr put it, "like a general deserting on the field of battle."[9] Those who remained in the Canal Zone seemed paralyzed by fear or given to outbursts. A man known for his calmness exploded one night during dinner, swearing "by the living God" he would henceforth eat alone if his dinner companions mentioned yellow fever one more time.[10]

Fortunately, the measures taken earlier by Gorgas and his staff soon contained the yellow fever. By the autumn of 1905 the epidemic had subsided, and government officials had stopped bringing metal caskets with them to the isthmus. In the long run, doctors would find the struggle to eliminate malaria and pneumonia much more difficult. (Indeed, they would never fully succeed.) As late as December 1905 the new chief engineer, John Stevens, still complained bitterly that the exodus from the isthmus continued, causing severe labor shortages. Men hoping to escape to their various Caribbean islands often could not find room on the ships. "The Jamaicans are returning [home] almost universally," Stevens observed.[11] Yet Stevens's presence and his energetic action to prepare the way for construction seemed to signal that the crisis was ending and that death would not spread into every household on the isthmus.[12]

In his months on the job, from mid-1905 through April 1, 1907, the autocratic Stevens profoundly shaped the character of the construction project. Stevens was a fifty-two-year-old railroad man. He had cut his teeth helping build James J. Hill's Great Northern Railroad, which stretched seventeen hundred miles from St. Paul to Seattle. Stevens brought many engineers who had worked under him on the Great Northern to the Canal Zone, and he approached the job as a railroad man, conceiving the railroad as the Canal Zone's central artery. It would distribute laborers, engineers, foremen, equipment, supplies, and food, as well as family members, politicians, and even tourists. It would also carry away the excavated dirt and rocks. Accordingly, once at work in the Canal Zone, Stevens transformed the existing railroad, replacing the narrow rails with five-foot-gauge ones for almost the entire forty-seven miles of the isthmus and adding double tracks so locomotives could go both directions at once. Thus carloads of dirt would head out for the coasts while empty cars shuttled back for more. The mightiest locomotives available—a world apart from the light equipment the French had used—were sent to the Canal Zone, and the new wide-gauge rails could handle them. Getting rid of the excavated dirt efficiently was one of Stevens's great contributions. The French had not moved their excavated spoil far away, and the piles of dirt and rock so near the construction had generated more landslides. Stevens, on the other hand, used the spoil to reclaim land from the Pacific Ocean in order to build the American town of Balboa and the Fort Amador military base, both near Panama

City; he also used it to construct Gatun Dam, Miraflores Locks, and an enormous breakwater stretching out from Panama City to four different islands.[13]

As a result of Stevens's work, the Zone became thoroughly dominated by the railroads and the men who worked them. There was little transportation within or across the Canal Zone except by railroad. If trains proved inconvenient, people typically walked, most often using the vacant tracks as their footpath and jumping off when a train approached. Once the excavation work was going at full steam, as many as eight hundred trains filled with dirt and rocks would pass by the towns of the Zone each day. The rumble of trains and the dynamite explosions set off at 11:30 and 5:30 each day made the digging site a "noisy, smoky, canal," as the Zone policeman and census taker Harry Franck put it. The sounds and smells of machinery were ever present. An Englishwoman visiting the heart of the construction site remembered, "The whole earth seems to tremble with the bellow of dynamite, the roar of machinery, and the dull vibration of the loaded trains. All along our route of some ten miles we were never out of sight of dense masses of workmen, nor clear of the black smoke of straining engines, which clanked, groaned, shrieked and whistled through miles of construction track." Even out at sea one could feel the trembling of the dynamite explosions.[14]

The noisiest and most dangerous part of the canal was Culebra Cut, the long, devastating stretch that sliced through the Continental Divide. Tourists looking down from observation decks thought of it as a great gorge, a canyon, an unimaginable ditch. The engineers and their army of laborers were, as the American writer Arthur Bullard commented, "gouging out a canyon 10 miles long, 300 feet wide, and in some places over 250 feet deep. Think about that for a minute and then be proud that you are an American." Culebra Cut was many construction projects going on simultaneously. There were numerous levels to it, and each, set ten or fifteen feet above another, had its own set of train tracks and its own steam shovels, uploaders, and track shifters. Several of the machines, including spreaders (to distribute the excavated spoil after unloading it) and track shifters, were invented in the Canal Zone to answer the demands of construction. The steam shovels, most of them ninety-five-ton monsters, were the "backbone and sinew" of the construction project. More than a hundred of them ate away at the mountains, each one worked by two skilled white Americans, who in turn were assisted by a team of West Indian laborers.[15]

Although tourists most often remarked on the great machines of Culebra Cut, closer observers were often fascinated by the complex world of laborers in the Zone. Harry Franck observed, "Everywhere are gangs of men, sometimes two or three gangs working together at the same task. Shovel gangs, track gangs, surfacing gangs, dynamite gangs, gangs doing everything imaginable with shovel and pick and crowbar, gangs down on the floor of the canal, gangs far up the steep walls of cut rock, gangs stretching away in either direction till those far off look like upright bands of the leaf-cutting ants of Panamanian jungles; gangs nearly all, whatever their nationality, in the blue shirts and khaki trousers of the Zone commissary, giving a peculiar color scheme to all the scene." Culebra Cut was the most feared by the laborers: regular landslides, premature dynamite explosions, flooding from the daily rains during the wet season, and the constant railroad traffic and other machines made it an extremely dangerous place to work. Even when one's life was not at risk, the scorching sun, high temperatures, humidity, and rain showers made daily work extremely difficult. Laborers worked amid water and mud that sometimes reached up to their waists, shoveling, breaking rocks, drilling holes, or performing a multitude of other tasks, the constant rains making the cut a wet and slippery place.[16]

Even moving away from the cut and into the jungle, an observer would see gangs of laborers scattered about. Harry Franck described traveling through the jungle on a train car not pulled by an engine—it was instead, he explained, a "six-negro-powered-car." Franck would order the car stopped every few minutes as he came upon another gang of thirty or so men: "Antiguans shoveling gravel, Martiniques snarling and quarreling as they wallowed thigh-deep in swamps and pools, a company of Greeks unloading train-loads of ties, Spaniards leisurely but steadily grading and surfacing, track bands of 'Spigoties' chopping away the aggressive jungle with their machetes—the one task at which the native Panamanian . . . is worth his brass-check. Every here and there we caught labor's odds and ends, diminutive 'water-boys,' likewise of varying nationality." Interviewing every worker and resident he could find, Franck came to know the Canal Zone like few other people did.[17]

Managing the men deployed across the construction site was itself an awesome task. The workday began early. The white American machinists, pattern makers, blacksmiths, and carpenters as well as their West Indian helpers often lived near enough to their workplace, in towns such as Empire and Gorgona, to walk to work. Thousands of others would catch the labor train with its segregated cars. Skilled white American workers traveled in passenger cars, while West Indian workers rode in open-air boxcars fully stuffed with men sitting, standing, and hanging off the sides. Trains would transport the men to their site, carry them back to towns for their midday lunch break, and back and forth again for an afternoon of work. This made transportation a dominant source of employment; railroad workers—the conductors, brakemen, engineers, and firemen—were among the most common employees in the Zone.[18]

When Stevens came to the isthmus in 1905, the U.S. government had still not decided on its plan for building the canal. The question loomed, most importantly, of whether the canal should be built as a sea-level or lock canal. The French had attempted to build a sea-level canal, which required not only cutting a pathway through the mountains but lowering that route to the level of the sea. A lock canal, by contrast, would use lock chambers to raise ships gradually eighty-five feet up to the level of a huge lake, itself created by damming the powerful Chagres River. Ships would traverse the lake to another set of locks that would then lower them back down to sea level. Some engineers and politicians worried about the safety and efficiency of a dam. An international board appointed by Roosevelt recommended that the canal be built at sea level, just as the Suez Canal had been. Stevens at first supported a sea-level canal, but over time the torrential rains and flooding of the Chagres River convinced him that only locks would succeed. He declared a lock canal would take only eight years to build, whereas a sea-level canal would take twenty-four years. Once the senators became confident that the huge dam could be constructed in a way that ensured safety, they voted, by a narrow margin, to authorize construction of a lock canal.[19]

Even before excavation began, Stevens took steps to provide for the massive working population that would be needed to build the canal. "Civilized" life in the Zone would require a complete infrastructure: a fire department, post offices, a police force, sanitation services, hospitals, bachelor and family housing, separate cafeterias for different nationalities (white U.S. workers, Caribbean workers, and European workers all ate at different cafeterias), hotels, schools, churches, a judicial system, jails, and a penitentiary. The government laid out towns; built roads, bridges, sidewalks, and sewage disposal plants; installed streetlamps; planted trees; and drained ditches to bring the mosquito population under control. Stevens estimated that he had overseen the construction of more than five thousand buildings, including more than forty hotels and restaurants, plus piers, docks, and warehouses. He built machine shops and roundhouses. He was especially proud of the combination ice, cold-storage, bakery, and laundry facilities he built that kept meat shipped in from the United States cold, produced twenty-five thousand loaves of bread a day, and did the laundry for more than three thousand "white people." He bragged that his employees would order fresh meat from the packinghouses of Chicago and keep it refrigerated every minute until it reached the hands of consumers along the isthmus.

While building towns and roads, however, Stevens still needed to secure workers to dig the canal, and this presented his greatest challenge. He proclaimed, "The greatest problem in building a canal of any type on the Isthmus . . . is the one of labor. The engineering and constructional difficulties melt into insignificance compared with labor."[20] Stevens strongly believed in certain key principles, undoubtedly derived from his work constructing railroads across the United States. First, he believed, the government must find workers of several different ethnicities and nationalities, so as to divide them from one another and let competition between groups spur them to work harder. Theodore P. Shonts, the chairman of the ICC, noted the importance of this at an early stage. Depending on one source of labor, he argued, would lead workers to see themselves as indispensable. More important, "a labor force composed of different races and nationalities would minimize, if it did not positively prevent, any possible combination of the entire labor force which would be disastrous to the work."[21] Second, as an engineer explained to congressmen in 1907, "there must be on the Isthmus a surplusage of labor. Otherwise we will have interminable strikes and everything in the nature of a strike."[22]

But where should this vast surplus come from? Stevens and his staff debated at length the virtues of various kinds of workers, ranking their efficiency by race and nationality. West Indians had supplied most of the labor during the French effort, so they remained a natural choice. Yet many ICC officials believed their labor to be inferior. Stevens considered West Indians the most "harmless and law-abiding" workers he had ever managed, yet he also believed them to be indolent, childlike, and unintelligent. He complained, "I have about made up my mind that it is useless to think of building the Panama Canal with native West Indian labor. It is possible that by flooding the Isthmus with about 40,000 laborers, we could keep our gangs full; but there is no doubt in my mind that, owing to their inferiority as laborers, we are paying a price in gold for labor which we cannot continue."[23]

Displeased by West Indians, Stevens searched for alternatives. He wanted white labor to dig the canal, and he believed whites from the United States could withstand the tropical conditions. Yet he knew this would not be feasible—white Americans would cost too much and would not tolerate the rough labor of canal building. Stevens therefore decided to fight for government approval to import Chinese workers. He had relied on them to build railroads in the U.S. West, and although he conceded that Chinese laborers could be "obstinate," he declared, "I am a little disposed in favor not only of the Chinaman as a laborer, but as a man, from my contact with them on the west coast. In fact, I have a very high respect and regard for Chinese of all classes whom I have ever met."[24]

Winning the right to import Chinese workers proved an uphill battle. In 1905 the Isthmian Canal Commission asked the U.S. attorney general, William Moody, to consider the legal issues involved. Moody analyzed the Thirteenth Amendment, which forbade slavery or involuntary servitude in the United States or "any place subject to their jurisdiction," and found that it did in fact apply to the Panama Canal Zone. Regardless of how well a laborer is treated by the government, Moody argued, and even if he has agreed to the work, he must be free to leave at any time and be able to "choose the work in which he is to engage." The importing of "Oriental aliens" under contracts to perform labor "is not necessarily one of involuntary servitude, but it may be and, in fact, usually is a condition of involuntary servitude." In this way Moody identified a specific ethnic group as particularly vulnerable to involuntary servitude.

Considering the attorney general's report, ICC chairman Theodore Shonts informed Stevens that although it would theoretically be possible to import Chinese laborers, certain steps would need to be taken so as to avoid even the appearance of involuntary servitude. The government would have to provide for repatriation of its laborers. It would have to "minimize the idea of contract labor, to avoid unfavorable public opinion in the United States, and to magnify the fact of direct employment of each laborer by the Government." The government would likewise need to pay wages directly to laborers and not to contractors. Finally, Shonts advised, it would be necessary to protect the Republic of Panama from an "invasion" of such laborers contrary to that nation's immigration laws. Unfortunately, Shonts spelled out, if all these conditions were met and the Chinese workers were truly made "free laborers," there would be no way to guarantee they would remain on the isthmus. The risks and costs would thus be greater—the government would need to pay Chinese workers a much higher wage so they would not desert the project for a higher-paying one, and perhaps pay a higher fee to those who furnished the laborers. This made it impracticable to import Chinese men. As involuntary laborers, Chinese workers were unsavory; as free ones, they were economically impractical.[25]

Stevens tried to make do with West Indians, but a year later, after having observed their work for many months, he despaired that the canal would never be finished if he was forced to rely on them. He began to push aggressively again for access to Chinese workers, ignoring the con-tinued protests from U.S. labor unions. Stevens angrily declared he would not "accept the responsibility, in case the labor question here should be-come acute, of acquiescing in the delay in securing the Chinese labor." He was particularly frustrated to see that "matters of policy rather than those of business have governed the entire proposition." Trying to make the idea of Chinese migrants more palatable, Stevens proposed importing Chinese doctors and allowing some family members to accompany the twenty-five hundred laborers he desired.[26]

In the end, despite Stevens's efforts, a "violent" public reaction against the idea in the United States, Chinese exclusion laws (in the United States and in the Republic of Panama), and opposition from the Chinese government all worked against him. President Roosevelt waffled on the matter, at times putting himself on record as preferring any other source of workers and declaring, "If you could get white labor, . . . I should prefer it. But the prime necessity is to complete the canal as speedily as possible." As late as February 1907, however, Roosevelt agreed "without hesitation" to the hiring of Chinese workers. Soon after he approved the idea, however, the Chinese government issued a proclamation forbidding its citizens to work on the canal. Viceroy Tuan Fang declared that any "coolies" imported to the Canal Zone would be falling into a "dangerous trap." Exploited, unable to make much money, they would be vulnerable to the whims of their employers.[27] This proclamation, combined with Stevens's nearly simultaneous resignation, sealed the matter.

Stevens had cast his eye around the globe for an alternative source of labor, but it seemed every potential worker was either too lazy or too assertive for his tastes. Panamanians and Colombians were believed un-willing to work hard, so the government preferred not to employ them.[28] Shonts strongly favored recruiting Spaniards who were working on rail-roads and sugar plantations in Cuba. "They are white men, tractable, and capable of development and assimilation," he declared. Stevens imported a few hundred of them, but opposition from planters and government officials in Cuba ended the experiment until recruiting stations could open in Spain. Hiring African Americans, it was assumed, would generate protest from employers throughout the South, so the government re-cruited only a few hundred of them.[29]

Lacking any alternative, Stevens regretfully turned back to West In-dians to supply the unskilled labor he needed. Yet when officials began encouraging migration to Panama from across the British and French Caribbean, they found resistance among many Caribbean nations. ICC officials negotiated strenuously when they encountered opposition from the Jamaican government, promising, for example, that they would hire Jamaicans as foremen as well as laborers, so they would not have to work under American foremen.[30] Nonetheless, the Jamaican government se-verely restricted the recruitment of labor by requiring that emigrants pay a steep emigration tax. St. Kitts, Antigua, Montserrat, Grenada, and many others shut ICC recruiters out altogether. Some laborers would migrate to Panama from those islands, but they would have to do so on their own. R. E. Wood, the official in charge of securing labor, complained that American recruiters were being compelled to "wander from island to island, picking up men here and there, like discredited fugitives." Indeed, he declared, many governors in the British Caribbean seemed to lack respect for the U.S. government. They did, however, possess due respect for the British Crown, and so Wood urged Stevens to inform the British government that its Caribbean governors' behavior was inimical not only to American interests but also to the mercantile interests of England itself. This would induce Caribbean governors to cooperate with the United States, he hoped. We cannot tell whether Stevens took this advice, but as the construction project evolved, agents focused on Barbados because its government was agreeable, it had a good supply of English-speaking workers, and they were known to be orderly, peaceful, and obedient. Recruiters opened offices in Barbados, examining potential laborers and offering them contracts that paid their way to Panama and promised them return fare home. More workers came from Barbados than from any other single nation, with Jamaica coming in a close second.[31]

ICC officials remained determined to find further sources of unskilled labor and prevent broad class solidarities from developing. They sent recruiters to Europe, in search of Spaniards, Italians, and Greeks, and finally to India, to sign up "sheiks" or "hindoos," as officials referred to them.[32] Stevens hoped that if it should prove impossible to secure Chinese workers, he might ultimately replace all West Indians with southern Europeans. He found the work of Spaniards to be particularly impressive, in part because they goaded others to work harder: his West Indian laborers, he informed Shonts, had been indifferent to work, "but their complacency has been badly disturbed on account of the introduction of Spaniards and Italians, and to a certain extent their usefulness has been correspondingly increased." Stevens feared, however, that Europe wanted to see the United States fail in Panama and therefore would not allow a sufficient supply of workers. Over time, a greater disadvantage revealed itself when southern Europeans proved more likely to rebel against the Americans' authority.[33]

Securing skilled labor was a simpler task for officials. They turned primarily to white workers from the United States. At any given time, between five and six thousand white Americans worked in the Canal Zone performing jobs as steam-shovel men, machinists, foremen, and the like. A few skilled workers from Panama, from northern European countries like Britain and Germany, and from the Caribbean supplemented the Americans, but their role would grow increasingly problematic when U.S. officials tried to limit skilled jobs to white U.S. citizens. It was not easy to lure white Americans to the Canal Zone, due to the strong economy at home and fears of disease and tropical miasma on the isthmus. The adventurous sorts of men who were most willing to come (many of them with experience in the Philippines or Cuba) often vexed government officials. They didn't work as hard as officials had hoped, yet seemed always to demand higher wages and better benefits. They also tended to engage in heavy drinking and carousing. Stevens observed, "The worst class we have had [in the Canal Zone], to our shame, has been some of our men that have gone down there from here."[34]

During his tenure Stevens pushed the work ahead far more energetically than his predecessor had done, finding sources of labor that would remain largely the same throughout the construction era and influencing the engineering design of the project. Yet by April 1907 he had resigned.

In a letter to Roosevelt he complained bitterly about his discomfort on the isthmus, the attacks on his judgment, and the disruption to his home and family life. He did not think, he confessed, that he could tolerate the strain of the job for the eight years or so required to do it. Roosevelt accepted his resignation and days later summoned the Army major George Goethals, an engineer, to the White House and invited him to accept the job as chief engineer. Frustrated by the resignations of Wallace and Stevens, Roosevelt reportedly declared, "I've tried two civilians in the Canal and they've both quit. We can't build the canal with a new chief engineer every year. Now I'm going to give it to the Army and to somebody who can't quit." Goethals accepted the job, and a new and final era in the construction of the canal began.[35]

"THAT HE IS OMNIPOTENT—ON THE ZONE—NOT MANY WILL DENY"

The man who would shape the character of life in the Canal Zone more than any other was tall, straight backed, and white haired. The same age as Roosevelt, Goethals was quite a different personality. People knew him as an introverted and sometimes stern and judgmental figure. Born in 1858 in Brooklyn to a woodworker and his wife who had emigrated from Ghent, Belgium, some years before, Goethals graduated from the U.S. Military Academy at West Point in 1880 and was then appointed to the Army Corps of Engineers. He met Effie Rodman, the daughter of a New Bedford, Massachusetts, whaling captain, in 1883, and they married the next year. Goethals's Army career for the next decades included teaching at West Point, working on improvements in the Ohio River valley and the Cumberland and Tennessee rivers, building canals in Tennessee and Alabama, and serving with the volunteer army in Puerto Rico during the War of 1898. When tapped by Roosevelt for the job as chief engineer, he was working as an assistant to the Army's chief of staff.[36]

Goethals served as the chief engineer for the remaining, critical years of the canal construction, and particularly for the matters that most concern us—the government's role in shaping the lives and work of Canal

Zone residents—his influence would prove profound. This was due partly to his nature but also to the way Roosevelt reorganized the job when he hired Goethals. After losing two chief engineers as well as receiving great criticism for the amount of second-guessing and endless bureaucracy involved in the project, Roosevelt decided to centralize the job. He appointed Goethals not only chief engineer but also chairman of the Isthmian Canal Commission—previously, these jobs had been held by different individuals. Roosevelt also brought new members onto the ICC, so that five of the eight members (including Goethals) came from the U.S. Army or Navy. Army officers who had a taste for military-style discipline, including D. D. Gaillard, William Sibert, and H. H. Rousseau, would dominate the project. Roosevelt knew that as Army men they would feel honor-bound to remain on the job until its completion, and a sense of military hierarchy and efficiency now pervaded the project. Simultaneously, however, he stripped the ICC of any executive authority. Goethals's government would be a one-man operation. Richard Harding Davis, the journalist who had famously covered the war in Cuba against Spain, wrote in 1912: "As a spectator the writer has been in the field with armies of several nations, but never has he known such an army as this one commanded by Colonel Goethals. For seven years it has been on foreign service, and always in action, always on the firing line. . . . It is an army that knows no rest, no armistices, no flags of truce."[37]

Goethals became known and celebrated mostly as a statesman, yet it's important to remember that he was also an engineer. Stevens had made huge contributions to the basic design of the canal, but much remained to be determined and strategized when Goethals's work began in April 1907. Surveys remained incomplete, little excavation had been done by Wallace or Stevens, and although the decision had been made to build a lock canal, those locks and Gatun Dam had not yet been designed. The railroad would also need to be relocated before the canal could open, as much of its current path would be underwater or on the wrong side of the canal, farthest from Panama City and Colón. Almost all the construction project lay ahead of Goethals, and an army of labor awaited his command.

With much of the infrastructure ready to house and feed the working population, more aggressive excavation work began as Goethals assumed his position in the spring of 1907. The steam shovels and train cars filled with spoil were soon more busily at work. Under Goethals's leadership three million cubic yards of spoil were being excavated along the line each month, whereas the excavation during Wallace's and Stevens's entire combined tenure amounted to less than six million cubic yards.[38] Goethals oversaw a major widening of the floor of the canal (in order to cope with landslides), a reconceptualization of the size and location of the planned locks, and the building of Gatun Dam.[39]

Begun in 1908, the dam would become the largest in the world, at a mile and a half long and half a mile wide at its base. Its base was constructed mostly from the spoils of excavation. To one side of the dam were the Gatun Locks, three pairs that would lower ships from Gatun Lake down to sea level and out into Limon Bay, or raise those approaching from the other direction. In 1910, even before construction of the dam was complete, engineers closed down the diversion they had built for the Chagres River and allowed the waters to begin rising slowly in front of the dam. Gatun Lake would cover more than 160 square miles. Numerous towns that had existed since the earliest days of navigation and commerce across the isthmus were located on land that would be submerged by Gatun Lake. Other towns, including Empire and Culebra, were abandoned as unnecessary once construction was finished; many of the houses and public buildings in those towns were transferred to the new American headquarters at Balboa.[40]

The most spectacular aspect of the project from an engineering standpoint was the design and construction of the locks. All the lock chambers were identical in dimensions (110 by 1,000 feet) and were constructed in pairs so that traffic could flow in either direction. Construction of the lock gates began in August 1909 and lasted four years. They were the only major aspect of the project built by a contractor—the Pittsburgh company McClintic-Marshall, known for efficiently constructing steel bridges—rather than by the U.S. government. The mammoth side walls were constructed by creating a molding of steel and then pouring concrete from overhead to fill them up. The lock gates of steel were built to be hollow in their bottom halves so they would be buoyant in the water and easier to swing back and forth without placing too much pressure on their hinges. Water would flood into the lock chambers through tunnels and culverts using gravity alone. The lock gates then opened and shut using electricity to operate a gigantic cogwheel placed within each gate, which in turn operated a huge steel arm to push the gate out or pull it back. The entire canal used electricity generated by a hydroelectric plant built next to Gatun Dam as the motor for its operation. The complex operation was as one might imagine a child playing in a bathtub. A ship would enter a first lock chamber with water at a low level, and the lock gates would swing shut behind it. The chamber would then flood with water, and the ship would rise naturally with the water. Once the ship rose sufficiently, the lock gates in front of it would swing open, and it would enter the next chamber, where the same process would be repeated. After passing through three lock chambers, a ship would have been raised and then lowered eighty-five feet, from sea level up to the level of Gatun Lake, and back down again.[41]

The locks and Culebra Cut involved the greatest hardship for workers and became terrific sources of fascination for the Americans and tourists from around the world who traveled to the isthmus to see them. They remain celebrated today as a great engineering wonder of the world; less commonly noted is the indispensable role played by U.S. corporate capitalism. Besides the vast machine shops of the Canal Zone, like those in Gorgona and Empire, and in addition to the central role played by McClintic-Marshall, more than fifty factories in Pittsburgh worked making supplies like rivets, bolts, and steel plates for the canal. The locomotives that helped pull ships into and through the locks were built in Schenectady, New York. The Bucyrus Company in Milwaukee built most of the steam shovels. A Wheeling, West Virginia, manufacturer supplied the cogwheels and lifting mechanisms and a great deal of other machinery for the lock gates. Nearly all the electrical equipment was manufactured by General Electric. The canal thus represented a tremendous achievement of American industrialization.[42]

Such a monstrous endeavor required efficient strategies for governing and disciplining the working population and others living in the Canal Zone—more than sixty thousand residents, according to the U.S. government's census of 1912.[43] Despite his obvious contributions to the engineering challenges of the canal, Goethals saw the difficulties of "ruling and preserving order" as the most novel and challenging aspect of his job: "While some experience had been gained in the insular possessions, a new situation existed which had to be solved, and after various changes there was evolved a form of government which was unique, differing from any established methods of administration." Others agreed with him. Joseph Bucklin Bishop, the longtime ICC secretary who worked under Goethals, wrote, "The problems in administration were new and there were no precedents in American experience from which to obtain light for guidance."[44]

How did Goethals see this challenge when he arrived in the Zone in 1907? Years later, in 1915, when the canal had just recently opened and affairs were rapidly shifting away from the demands of construction and into a new era of operating and maintaining the canal, Goethals was appointed by President Woodrow Wilson to be the first governor of the Canal Zone. In a series of public lectures he gave that year, Goethals described his approach to governing. He explained the choices faced by those seeking to create a stable government in the Canal Zone during the post-construction era, and he based his opinions on what he had learned and experienced as chief engineer. There were four main options, he declared: military government, civil government (democracy), commission government, or government via the executive orders of the president of the United States. For the Canal Zone, Goethals believed, a military government was inappropriate. The canal must be a civil rather than a military accomplishment: "As in the United States in time of peace, the military should be subordinated to the civil, and everything on the Isthmus should be considered an adjunct to the canal." A civil, democratic government had been tried during the early days of construction but was found to be lacking as well. Many had argued for democracy in the Canal Zone on the grounds that the United States should create a

model government to educate Central and South Americans on the virtues and benefits of American civilization. Goethals contended that this
had been unwise during the construction era, and it would be unwise
now. The canal was "an administrative problem and political problems
shouldn't be allowed to encumber it." To introduce political institutions
would be "a step backward" and would incur unwarranted costs. Commission government he despised as inefficient, unwieldy, and generating
unnecessary tensions. This left only one feasible form of government: a
one-man operation, headed by the president of the United States.[45]

In fact, Goethals saw himself as the one man who should be in charge.
Soon after arriving in the Zone, he found working with other members
of the ICC difficult and inefficient. He pressed Roosevelt for more authority. When Congress refused to restructure the ICC, Goethals drafted
an executive order that would centralize all powers under his command.
In January 1908, Roosevelt signed the executive order, putting Goethals
in complete charge of the ICC and the Panama Railroad. Goethals would
make all decisions, and he in turn answered only to the president. The
ICC was stripped of all authority. As Goethals described it, the 1908
executive order "resulted in the establishment of an autocratic form of
government for the Canal Zone."[46]

Henceforth the requirements of the construction job would dominate
every aspect of life. To Goethals, efficiency was a necessary prerequisite,
and efficiency in turn required a vast expansion of the powers of the state
and a complete elimination of democracy. He noted that members of
Congress attempted to limit his power in the Canal Zone and create a
more democratic structure, but without success. Democracy, according
to Goethals, would be a frivolous distraction: "Conditions were peculiar,
for there was but one object in view—the construction of the canal; had
the franchise been introduced, the whole structure would have fallen."
He conceded that he may have acted autocratically at times; however,
"the end not only justified the means but could have been accomplished
in no other way."[47]

Over the years many referred to Goethals's government in the Canal
Zone as a "benevolent despotism," a notion that had a long and vigorous

history in Western political philosophy. In 360 B.C., Plato had described an ideal republic in which society would be divided into castes (identified by Plato as the gold, silver, and bronze groups) and everyone would be ruled by a single benevolent philosopher-king. In the nineteenth century the Scottish philosopher and historian Thomas Carlyle, amid the pressures of a rapidly industrializing world, revolted against the materialism and excess democracy around him and imagined an ideal government, which he called benevolent despotism. He modeled this government on his image of heaven, but conceded that it would be impossible to achieve. Carlyle's ideas have long been seen as inspiring both socialism and fascism. Carlyle's peer and sometimes friend John Stuart Mill, the great philosopher of liberalism and representative government, believed despotism to be inappropriate for a mature society like England. Yet Mill, a supporter of British imperialism who worked for many years for the East India Company, strongly defended despotism in an imperial context. In his essay "On Liberty," he declared, "Despotism is a legitimate mode of government in dealing with barbarians, providing the end be their improvement." Thus extensive precedents and justifications existed for Goethals to draw on in dispensing with representative forms of government. Two aspects made his approach particularly significant. First, he was employing benevolent despotism not only among people he identified as inferior but also with a large population of white Americans. Second, it worked—and very effectively indeed. As Willis Abbot, a prominent chronicler of the canal construction, observed, "That crabbed old philosopher Thomas Carlyle would be vastly interested could he but see how the benevolent despotism which he described as ideal but impossible is working successfully down in the semi-civilized tropics."[48]

Goethals not only centralized the state but also extended it deeply into the lives of the residents of the Canal Zone and the Republic of Panama. Whereas Stevens had envisioned constructing much of the canal by contracting work out to individual corporations, Goethals preferred to keep the government in control of almost every feature of the job. The commissaries, cafeterias, hotels, railroad, and hospitals, as well as the actual work of construction (everything except for the locks), were controlled by the government. The government decided how and where people lived, ate, worked, played—or tried to, anyway—and how they should be disciplined. Thus to observers like the journalist John Foster Carr, the Canal Zone government seemed different from that in the United States proper and more akin to an interventionist European government. When Carr described it as a state "with all the machinery and equipment of our home civilization adapted to strange needs," he likely meant something similar to what John Stuart Mill had advised in the case of Britain. A distant population including large numbers of West Indians, southern Europeans, and Panamanians—all of them perceived by ICC officials as lacking the maturity and capability for self-government that white Americans had—required creative adaptations to establish order and efficient government.

Goethals's approach to governing was therefore rather stern and focused on discipline. Marie Gorgas, who was admittedly never fond of Goethals, described him as obsessed with power: "His passion for dominating everything and everybody he carried to extreme lengths. The most desirable gift of the executive is the ability to delegate authority, but this quality Colonel Goethals did not possess. He was impatient of any associate or subordinate whom he could not control." At its gentlest, Goethals's style involved a heavy dose of paternalism. Goethals liked to present himself as a fatherly figure, proudly opening his office every Sunday morning to hear anyone's grievance. The rather saintly portrait of him in the biography by Joseph Bucklin Bishop and Farnham Bishop describes the chief's open-door policy as an exercise in egalitarianism, a $5,000-a-year engineer sitting contentedly next to a Jamaican laundress or Spanish tracklayer as petitioners waited for their moment with the colonel. Marie Gorgas saw it differently, comparing Goethals's behavior during his office hours to that of a "Venetian doge" or a "patriarchal despot."[49]

Goethals did take seriously the complaints made during his open hours. With a full-time inspector working to investigate problems and recommend solutions, including any discipline or punishment deemed necessary, his administration constituted a full-fledged grievance office combined with an independent tribunal. Records maintained by T. B. Miskimon, Goethals's inspector, provide a world of insight into the Zone's daily affairs. ICC employees and their wives complained about everything from drunken or adulterous neighbors to fraudulent commissary managers, insulting foremen, cruel policemen, blackmailing supervisors, women of ill repute, gamblers, abusive spouses, salesmen bearing indecent photographs, and a judge who engaged in sexual harassment. Miskimon dutifully investigated each case and recommended a solution to his boss. In one case where Miskimon found fraud involving commissary books, Goethals suspended the men responsible without pay for fifteen days. When a yardmaster of the Panama Railroad was accused by a colleague of working while intoxicated, Miskimon's detailed investigation resulted in a six-page report for Goethals, in which the inspector concluded that while the yardmaster certainly imbibed, the charge of intoxication on the job may well have been the creation of his jealous and hostile colleague. Thousands of similar examples suggest the challenge of maintaining order in the Canal Zone, with its complicated and diverse cultures.[50]

Even Goethals's admiring biographers noted that he could be strict and unyielding, and the workingmen and -women of the Zone more often saw that side of him. Goethals quickly acquired a reputation (which he relished) for toughness with workers, particularly if they attempted to negotiate with him as part of an organization rather than as individuals. For years he refused to recognize unions or meet with any committee representing the workforce. He proudly declared that in his earlier jobs, "We did not deal with unions; we did not employ unions; we employed individuals and dealt with them individually." When railroad workers in the Canal Zone attempted to organize in 1908, Goethals refused to meet with them. Conferring with one leader of their committee, he explained his refusal: "I will not take another man's word for another man's grievance. If you have a grievance you are the man who can talk to me intelligently about it." This policy continued for years, until President William Howard Taft declared Goethals's position unacceptable, since "organized labor was recognized everywhere." Taft required that Goethals either meet with labor representatives or allow the appointment of a special

labor commissioner to handle workers' grievances. Amid much grumbling, and desiring to avoid the appointment of a labor commissioner at
any cost, Goethals agreed to meet with committees of workers. Even
then, he insisted that most grievances be presented to him not through
unions but through individuals making use of his open door on Sunday
mornings.[51]

In 1910 a locomotive engineer was convicted of involuntary manslaughter and sentenced to a year in the penitentiary because of a train
accident that killed a man. At a mass meeting, transportation workers
demanded that the engineer be released from prison and threatened to
strike if their demand was not met. Goethals refused and declared, "I will
take no action in response to the demand of a mob." Any man who failed
to show up for work the next day would be transported immediately
back to the United States. The threatened strike did not materialize.[52]
Although government officials commented often and publicly on the
affection Zonians felt for Goethals, the latter's reliance on deportation,
police spies, and vagrancy laws for controlling his workers suggested a
different side to his rule. The observation of the Zone policeman Harry
Franck, who conceded Goethals's popularity, is worth keeping in mind:
"That he is omnipotent—on the Zone—not many will deny; a few have
questioned—and landed in the States a week later much less joyous but
far wiser."[53]

THE SILVER AND GOLD SYSTEM

The most important tool the U.S. government relied on for controlling
and managing the Canal Zone's workers and residents was a system of
segregation, and this system reveals how Americans struggled to adapt
domestic policies to the "strange needs" of the isthmus. Although the
origins of the segregation system are somewhat unclear, its roots apparently lay in long-standing practice on the U.S.-built Panamanian railroad
to pay unskilled workers with Panamanian silver and skilled workers with
U.S. gold currency. When the United States began construction, the
story goes, a disbursing officer slapped up signs designating "gold" and

"silver" on the pay cars, and gradually the differential pay scale evolved into segregation. Initially, bosses would reward productive employees by shifting them, regardless of their race, ethnicity, or nationality, from the silver to the gold payroll. Gradually, it hardened into a system of segregation comparable in some ways to the U.S. practice of Jim Crow. Segregation came to shape every aspect of life in the Zone, from work to housing, leisure activities, sexual relationships, and shopping. One would see, for example, large signs at the commissaries denoting the silver and gold entrances. The government paid silver employees far less, fed them unappetizing food, and housed them in substandard shacks. Gold workers earned very high wages and terrific benefits, including six weeks of paid vacation leave every year, one month of paid sick leave every year, and a free pass for travel within the Zone once each month. The government also developed an attractive social life and provided it at no or low cost to white American employees, hiring bands and vaudeville acts to perform regularly throughout the Zone and building grounds for baseball and other sports. Clubhouses provided white Americans with reading rooms, bowling alleys, and gymnasiums. The government allowed only white U.S. citizens to enjoy these leisure activities.[54]

Although the silver and gold system became central to the industrial environment of the Canal Zone, officials apparently felt conflicted and confused about its precise purpose and the principles that should govern it. Amid the confusion, however, racial justifications repeatedly came up. Some people, like the influential C. A. McIlvaine, Goethals's executive secretary, believed it was meant to show quickly how many blacks or whites the government employed at any time, or to avoid conflicts between workers of different races. Others argued segregation would enhance efforts at sanitation and disease eradication by separating outsiders from those native to tropical areas. A more common explanation attributed the system to long-standing worries that white men could not withstand the tropical climate (giving them, for example, extended paid vacations so they could return home). When an engineer inquired whether it was acceptable to have foreigners on the gold roll (by which he meant non-U.S. citizens), the assistant chief engineer J. G. Sullivan responded, "The great distinction between gold and silver basis is that employes on a gold basis are given vacations every year, in which to go to the States to recuperate. The point that I have always maintained is that in deciding whether or not a white foreigner, or semi-white foreigner (Dago) should be put on a gold basis is the fact as to whether or not they would take or whether or not they need, a trip to the States every year." In other words, Sullivan argued, the system should remain as fluid as possible, leaving decisions about where workers belonged up to the officials in charge. There were several Canadians among the nurses, Sullivan noted, and an English foreman came to mind, and he did not think it feasible to move all of them off the gold roll.[55]

Over time, however, the system became more rigid and more emphatically—but never exclusively—a racial hierarchy. This was a murky evolution, difficult to delineate, but upon closer examination some key steps in the process emerge. As early as September 1905, E. S. Benson, the general auditor of the Canal Zone, wrote to Governor Charles Magoon that officials in some departments were giving "silver employes a promotion by putting them on the gold roll. . . . [This] is being done as a mark of favor to certain employes, who may be negroes, the idea being that if a man is on the gold roll he has a certain amount of prestige which he would not otherwise secure." Benson argued that promoting men in this manner was unsatisfactory from "an accounting standpoint when we undertake to distribute certain classes of expenditures between the Departments and Divisions based on the relative number of gold and silver employes." He asked that it be discontinued. John Stevens, then the chief engineer, agreed and issued an order forbidding the practice.[56]

A year later Stevens issued another order. He now required that all "colored employes" be shifted from the gold to the silver roll. He wanted them to see no decrease in their pay; he merely wanted them to serve on the silver rather than the gold payroll. He also excluded "colored" employees who were U.S. citizens from this order but, remarkably, *only* if they had received labor contracts in the United States that stipulated they were being hired on the gold roll. Any other African Americans would, like West Indians, be transferred unceremoniously to the silver roll.[57]

Some officials found this drawing of the racial line to be inconvenient, rude, or threatening to productivity. Most controversial was the issue of skilled workers from the West Indies—did they belong on the gold roll or the silver roll? Henry Burnett, for example, the manager of the Canal Zone commissaries, protested: "It would, I think, be very impolitic to separate all of the Commissary employees, by color putting all the colored men on the silver roll. They would naturally feel it to be in a measure, a humiliation." He added that he had several valuable "colored clerks" who drew higher salaries than some white clerks. Likewise, George Brooke, superintendent of motive power and machinery, responded to Stevens's order by saying he had earlier moved many "colored men" from the gold to the silver roll, and "by doing so I lost a number of excellent men on account of their seriously objecting to begin put on an equality with the ordinary colored laborer." Those still on the gold roll, he argued, "are our best colored men remaining, and I have hesitated about arbitrarily placing them on the silver basis for the reason that I should probably lose more or less of them." Brooke had twelve West Indians working for him on the gold roll in such occupations as machinist, blacksmith, boilermaker, and coppersmith. Most hailed from Martinique, but some came from St. Lucia, Guadeloupe, Antigua, and Jamaica. These were most likely men who had gained experience in the French era of canal construction, which had enabled them to move into skilled positions. John Stevens remained firm, conceding only that a few Afro-Caribbean clerks and "colored policemen, school teachers, and postmasters" could remain on the gold roll. As officials saw it, these latter groups performed key functions and therefore needed some authority and prestige to do their jobs effectively.[58]

As leadership passed from Stevens to Goethals in the spring of 1907, officials continued working to clarify the system, stymied, often, by the complicated ethnic and racial character of the Zone's population. Soon after arriving, Goethals took steps to ensure that white employees would not have to stand in line at the same window as black West Indians to receive their pay. Meanwhile, officials sought guidance for ways to identify individuals' race and thus best fit them into the segregation system.

Hiram Slifer, the manager of the Panama Railroad, wrote in consternation that some of his employees greatly resented their transfer to the silver roll. He seemed especially troubled by a man born in Demerara who claimed to be white. Slifer noted, "There are a number of definitions in the States as to what shall constitute a negro, but I do not believe that we want to go into this subject too deep." Yet he wondered how the commission was handling the matter. The racial issue was creating awkward relations, he declared, particularly in places like the commissary, where they had now divided the gold and silver employees into different areas: "We have already had one or two cases where people who were a little off color have had some difficulty with our employees as to which side of the house they should deal on." Jackson Smith, head of the Department of Labor, Quarters, and Subsistence, commented: "We endeavor to keep those of undoubted black or mixture on the silver rolls." However, if someone from the West Indies claims to be white, then "we place him on the silver roll as a foreigner who has no claim upon us for more than temporary employment, or employment only until we can fill his place with a citizen of the United States."[59]

Officials thus faced two distinct but related issues as they struggled to articulate the meaning and function of segregation. One involved race (the effort to move all "colored" employees to the silver roll) and the other citizenship (the problem of "white" foreigners on the gold roll). In 1908, President Roosevelt issued an executive order that elevated the latter as the key principle, stipulating that gold roll employment would be limited to U.S. citizens except in cases where none were available. Roosevelt later added that Panamanian citizens would also be eligible for gold jobs (in deference to Panamanian leaders who complained that, as the canal was being built across their nation, their citizens should have access to jobs on the gold roll). In 1909 Goethals got the last word, reinterpreting Roosevelt's executive order in ways that defined the system by citizenship and by race. The gold system would consist of all American citizens and "a few Panamanians." Other "white employees" (i.e., not native to the tropics) could be employed when white U.S. citizens were not available. Goethals specifically addressed the matter of African Americans and declared that they should all ideally be carried on the silver roll (although some, he conceded, could remain on the gold roll).[60]

These rather tortured attempts to make segregation more consistent and principled were complicated by a few fascinating exceptions. The first involved the legacies of U.S. imperialism. After Roosevelt's declaration that only U.S. citizens should be hired on the gold roll, some alert officials raised the problem of Puerto Ricans. George Weitzel, for example, the U.S. chargé d'affaires in Panama, noted that several Puerto Ricans were seeking reemployment on the Panama Railroad. He argued that although Puerto Ricans were not citizens, they were "wards of the nation" and "entitled to the protection of the United States." He recommended Puerto Ricans be given preference for jobs over any other foreigners. Goethals agreed, thus ensuring that colonial subjects would benefit from their status.[61]

A more puzzling, albeit rare, quandary emerged for officials when a few white U.S. citizens desired jobs as common laborers in the Atlantic division of the Canal Zone. The clerk in charge asked if hiring them would be acceptable to Goethals and, if so, how they should be classified. Goethals's executive secretary, C. A. McIlvaine, thought through the issues for his boss: "I suppose that, viewed from a strictly impersonal, cold-blooded standpoint, no distinction should be made between white Americans employed as laborers, and aliens. At the same time it does seem rather hard to herd an American citizen with the class of men engaged on this work as laborers." Thus he advised giving the men status as gold roll workers and housing them in gold apartments: "I think that American citizens should be in a preferred class and doubtless these cases will be very few." Goethals agreed and ordered that white American laborers be paid on the gold roll and that housing be found for them so that "they need not come in contact with the alien laborers." Gradually, the problem disappeared as white Americans grasped that laborers' jobs were not meant for them. The policeman Harry Franck confessed he had arrived in the Zone "with the hope of shouldering a shovel and descending into the canal with other workmen, that I might some day solemnly raise my right hand and boast, 'I helped dig IT.' But that was in the callow days before I . . . learned the awful gulf that separates the sacred white American from the rest of the Canal Zone world."[62]

Meanwhile, when Roosevelt in 1908 articulated citizenship as the central principle in the workings of the silver and gold system, Goethals and his subordinates began purging aliens from the gold roll. Goethals ordered department heads to submit lists of foreigners employed on the gold roll and, when possible, shift them to the silver roll. Large-scale purges occurred when reductions of force became necessary—for example, when officials reorganized a division or department. Throughout this process not only did many West Indians lose their jobs or face demotion to the silver roll; Germans, Frenchmen, Britons, and other northern Europeans did so as well. Britain's diplomatic representative in Panama reported that excellent employees faced dismissal because of this "selfish policy." Englishmen had complained to him, he said, that after their dismissal they had "walked from one end to the other of the canal works and the first question that is put to them is 'what nationality are you? . . .' When they answer that they are English they receive the answer that 'only Americans need apply.'" U.S. officials began requiring that any worker on the gold roll who "appeared to be an alien" submit naturalization papers to prove his or her U.S. citizenship. Numerous debates occurred among government officials regarding the degree to which efficiency should be sacrificed in order to comply with the executive order, and many department heads pushed hard—but usually unsuccessfully—to keep aliens on the gold roll.[63]

The government officials' growing emphasis on citizenship had clear racial implications. Goethals indicated this when he responded to a protest from white workers about the government's employing "colored" engineers on the Panama Railroad: "We cannot very well draw a color line, but we can limit the employment of engineers to American citizens." Goethals's treatment of African Americans demonstrates that the system was never purely about citizenship—officials' protests notwithstanding. After 1907 government officials would no longer hire African Americans on the gold roll, although in most cases they allowed the few existing ones to remain in their positions. Officials created a special status for African Americans, which categorized them as silver workers but gave them privileges like paid vacations as a meager acknowledgment of their citizenship. At the same time officials enforced racial segregation off the job, excluding African Americans from YMCA clubhouses and from cafeterias intended for whites. D. D. Gaillard, a division engineer, summed it up in 1909: "It is not the policy of this Division to employ negroes or aliens."[64]

"LIFE IS NOT SUCH A HARDSHIP IN THE ZONE!"

Between 1904 and 1908 the three chief engineers established the basic design of the canal, made considerable progress on the construction, and built the infrastructure needed to house and feed tens of thousands of workers. Particularly under the leadership of Stevens and Goethals, the Canal Zone became a more comfortable place to live, especially for white Americans, and its look would remain much the same until the flooding of Gatun Lake began in 1912 and the surrounding towns were abandoned. Entire settlements emerged where none had existed before, and others were expanded. The Canal Zone became dotted with towns, most of which had American sections as well as labor camps for various ethnic groups. At each end of the isthmus, the Americans had built themselves a town—Cristobal alongside Colón, and Ancon alongside Panama City.

Following the tour that visitors took across the isthmus may help us to visualize the complex world of the Canal Zone. The British traveler Winifred James described in her 1913 book *The Mulberry Tree* how it felt to arrive by ship at the Atlantic side of Panama. She was caught off guard both by "dank and dripping" Colón and by the small encampment she passed known as Monte Lirio, in which West Indian employees were housed in railroad boxcars fitted with wire doors. By contrast, American settlements like Cristobal became known for their scenic wide avenues and, most of all, for "the famous screened houses that safeguard the white man in Panama, the only form of architecture to be found in the whole of the Canal Zone." The wood houses with corrugated iron roofs, a wide veranda running along three sides, and wrapped entirely around with a fine copper wire screen, she said, reminded her of giant meat safes or aviaries. James was struck by the contrast between Colón and Cristobal. The former, home primarily to West Indians, felt like a "ramshackle" place to her, but it was also loud and lively. Late into the night people strolled about, listening to a band in the park, buying lottery tickets, or pausing for a drink at a bar. Cristobal, just down the road, was quiet and lovely. As her rented carriage toured that town's streets, she admired the lights with red or green lamp shades glowing softly inside the copper mesh of the "aviaries," and she could hear rhythmic ocean waves hitting the shore.[65]

The next day James awoke and, like most tourists, caught a train across the isthmus from Colón to Panama City. The trip took two and a half hours, with stops in most towns of the Zone along the way. "Every station," she noted, "is alive with people of every colour." As her train departed Colón and entered the Zone, it passed through a West Indian labor camp with large two-story dwellings complete with balconies (but no copper screening) alongside the railroad tracks: "In these houses scores of families live together, and on the verandahs and balconies everything happens." Her train headed southwest through the isthmus, passing through the old town of Gatun and the twenty-three-mile stretch that would one day be submerged under Gatun Lake. She watched as the train wove in and out of dense jungle, stopping at labor camps like Bohio and Frijoles; passing by Camp Elliott, the headquarters of the Marines ("where the Stars and Stripes were first flown in the Zone"); and moving onward to the major towns of Gorgona, Culebra, and Empire. These last three were at the heart of the Zone, each of them nestled around the gaping Culebra Cut. Gorgona was said to have more and bigger machine shops than anywhere else in the world, while Culebra served as headquarters of the administrators and engineers. At the town of Empire, the largest in the Zone, James observed how "the words 'Welcome to Empire,' done in letters man-size . . . greet you hospitably, while on the hill, and all around, flock the gigantic meat-safes of dark gauze in white painted wood frames."[66]

Soon after her train passed Gorgona, James could see the Chagres

River and then the beginning of Culebra Cut. She found the cut to be "like something seen through the wrong end of a telescope." She observed the trains and steam shovels rushing back and forth: "And over the face of everything crawls a swarm of little ants that might be men or men that might be little ants. One feels like Gulliver in Lilliput." She felt "dazed and stupefied" by the huge scope of the excavation job in the cut and noted especially "the curious manner in which the men and the machines seemed to have changed places; the men had become machines, the machines were uncannily like men."[67]

Onward her train went, passing more labor towns, boxcar settlements, tenements housing Spaniards and Greeks, screened "aviaries," and Pedro Miguel and Miraflores, the towns that would someday provide a home to enormous locks. She finally arrived in Panama City and grabbed a coach that took her back into the Zone, up the hill to Ancon, to deposit her at the Hotel Tivoli, the fine residence built by the United States to house visitors: "In the great cool hall crowds of people are sitting and standing and lining up three deep at the booking-office. Negro bell-boys, dressed in the height of certain American fashions, with low-cut, bulldog-toed shoes, tied with sash ribbons, and enormously full trousers turned up at the hem, go ceaselessly up and down the double staircase, carrying bags and showing people to their rooms in the galleries above."[68]

James was impressed by the Americans' determination to civilize the Canal Zone: "The American 'roughs it' superbly. His desert is made to blossom immediately with all the products of the most modern civilization. . . . The first things with which he plants his jungle are telephones, ice-boxes, and porcelain baths." Of all these, she argued, the icebox was the most important: "Who ever heard of an American without an icebox? It is his country's emblem. It asserts his nationality as conclusively as the Stars and Stripes afloat from his roof-tree, besides being much more useful in keeping his butter cool." James concluded: "The ordinary tourist has every reason to be very grateful to the American for . . . his magnificent way of bringing the tropics to heel." Another British traveler, Charlotte Cameron, put the matter less sardonically: "The U.S. have done more than make a new route for commerce. They have put in training a race of overseas Americans who will one day rival our own Indian administration."[69]

Gradually, American journalists joined travelers like Winifred James in describing the Canal Zone's civilization as impressive. In Cristobal, according to a writer in the trade union magazine *Steam Shovel and Dredge,* living conditions "are not only bearable but so attractive that one thinks he would like to live there." On the train "one finds himself in thoroughly up-to-date coaches, seated among his own race, and altogether it is as if one were taking a summer ride through suburbs of Chicago on trains of the Northwestern or Illinois Central. Only when one looks out of the windows and sees the tropical, luxuriant foliage and thatched cabins of natives perched on the hills is he made to realize that he is in the tropics 2000 miles from home." This writer described how the wives and daughters of canal employees waited at each train station for their menfolk, dressed in lovely summer dresses and hats and waving at the passing trains, thus suggesting to him how "Americanized" the towns throughout the Zone had become. Best of all, he noted, "the fact that work trains carry the Jamaican and Barbadian negroes to and from their work along the canal makes it unnecessary for the casual tourist to mingle with these types en route. Life is not such a hardship in the Zone!" Likewise, a British traveler noticed as she crossed the isthmus by train, "It seems as though we must be dreaming, so curious is the contrast between the highly-civilized train in which we are travelling and the wild luxuriance of the country through which it is carrying us."[70]

As these quotations suggest, the Isthmus of Panama was pervaded by the appearance and the reality of boundaries, themselves generated by notions of difference based on class, gender, race, and nationality. There existed many different "zones" on the isthmus. There was the zone of women versus that of men, the zone of American citizens versus that of foreigners, and the zone of white people versus that of people of color. The isthmus during the construction era was a hierarchical world, and even among white women or white men there were different levels of status and social or cultural acceptance. Such boundaries shaped relations between groups, and between them and the U.S.

government. Furthermore, accepting these boundaries of difference or deciding when or where to contest or transgress them would become central to life in the Zone.

One of the most important and yet most frequently crossed boundaries was that between the Canal Zone and the Republic of Panama. Panama never became a colony of the United States, and American troops did not invade the nation as they did Cuba, Puerto Rico, and the Philippines. Instead, the republic became a protectorate of the United States and a model for the sort of neocolonialism that would dominate U.S. efforts to control the Caribbean and Central America in the twentieth century. ICC officials, U.S. diplomats, and military personnel all became deeply involved in Panama's affairs, and the relationship between Panama and the United States, involving as it did a tense and constant negotiation over sovereignty, sometimes grew explosive. Over the years, while the Canal Zone gradually became an "Americanized" and rigorously civilized world, Panama continued to seem to Americans different, exotic, and uncivilized. The Zone policeman Harry Franck described leaving the ICC administration building one day in Ancon, the American town just outside Panama City. He took a shortcut down the mountainside and suddenly entered "a foreign land." He had unknowingly crossed an international boundary and entered the Republic of Panama. He knew he had left the Zone because of "the instant change from the trim, screened Zone buildings, each in its green lawn, to the featureless architecture of a city where grass is all but unknown; for the formalities of crossing the frontier are the same as those of crossing any village street." Travelers would gain their bearings, Franck advised, by checking to see whether a Zone policeman wearing khaki patrolled the sidewalk, or a black policeman (that is, a Panamanian) in a dark blue uniform and a heavy, wintry helmet. Alcohol was highly regulated in the Zone, while gambling and prostitution were forbidden and rigorously suppressed. Leaving the Zone and crossing into Panama, Americans delighted in finding "everything 'wide open' and raging," particularly in the red-light district of Panama City known as Cocoa Grove. The journey to Cocoa Grove, where the streets were filled with saloons, brothels, Chinese shops, and lottery ticket sellers, provided Americans with an easy escape from the regimented Zone. (Panamanians crossing into the Zone, on the other hand, found themselves suddenly subject to the discipline and sometimes punishment enforced by a vastly superior power.) This particular boundary crossing, with its rich meanings and opportunities for exotic diversions, excitement, and, often, contests over power, emerged as a central motif of life on the isthmus.[71]

AMERICAN OFFICIALS felt compelled on the Isthmus of Panama to adapt the machinery of their home civilization to "strange needs." They wanted to create an industrialized, efficient, and autocratic world, and they used police, spies, and segregation in hopes of maintaining order and keeping workers focused on the job. Officials sought, in short, to create a form of government they deemed suited to the isthmus, a benevolent despotism that would allow them to assert control and subordinate everything to the demands of construction. Yet, sensible as it must have seemed to officials, this was an impossible goal. Shifting the focus away from them and onto the world of those who actually built the canal makes clear how difficult it would be for the officials to achieve their goal. The people of the Isthmus of Panama, both within and beyond the Canal Zone, saw different ways of doing things. They came to the construction project for their own reasons and with different goals in mind. In unexpected ways, they challenged, shook, and transformed the vision of Goethals and his peers. The white American workingmen and workingwomen of the Zone, the people presumed by officials to be their most steady allies, provide our first step into understanding this world.

CHAPTER TWO

"AS I AM A TRUE AMERICAN"

I N 1905, R. B. Elliott, a white American working on the gold payroll as railroad yardmaster in the Panama Canal Zone, was fired from his job. Soon thereafter the U.S. government deported him from the Zone and back to the United States. Like many other skilled U.S. workers in the Zone during the difficult early days of 1904 and 1905, Elliott was unhappy about his working and living conditions. Homesick, scared of disease, and angry about long hours, dangerous conditions, foul food, and lousy quarters, skilled workers had expected better when they got to Panama. It was "not a white man's country," they declared, and while the dampness and tropical heat sapped their strength, precious few diversions existed to help them enjoy their leisure time.[1] Government officials faced "open expressions of discontent and grumbling on the part of the employees in the Canal Zone and frequent resignations."[2] With dissatisfaction widespread, some workers began organizing for change. Elliott was one among this group of men, most of them skilled railroad workers, steam-shovel men, miners, or carpenters, and he gradually emerged as the movement's leader.

By all accounts, Elliott was an intelligent and thoughtful man, well liked and respected. An undercover policeman chatted with him one day and reported that he was "a quiet, sensible, straightforward man. I would not class him as an agitator, as during the time I kept track of him he carried himself as a man should." He drank only a little and didn't engage in unruly behavior. "Regarding this movement of which he is the head, he is acting straightforwardly and refuses to countenance any talk of strike or disorder."[3]

Yet however likable Elliott may have been, his activities raised the ire of government officials. The fact that some of the men involved seemed to lack Elliott's quiet touch didn't help matters. In early March at the Hotel Vienna in Culebra, a town positioned near the most dangerous part of the construction project, some workers convened and demanded a strike. One worker argued that their status as government employees should not prevent them from striking. As evidence he noted the workers' recent militancy at the Brooklyn Navy Yard: "Remember the strike against the U.S. when the Battleship Connecticut was being built." As the discussion grew more heated, one disgruntled worker began shouting out "Dynamite!" Others demurred, saying "before they would strike against the U.S., they would just quit and hit the trail back to civilization." Yet all seemed to agree on their main demands: they wanted an eight-hour day, a six-day week, time and a half for overtime, better housing, and equal pay for a job regardless of a man's color or where he had received his appointment. The latter demands reflected not an effort to include the interests of West Indian workers in their movement, but rather a determination by skilled white men to protect their privileged position: if government officials agreed to pay all workers the same rate regardless of race, they would desire even more vigorously to hire only whites since they would consider the West Indians unworthy of such high pay. Aware that police spies were surely present in the room, most workers conceded that they would obey all laws as well as the U.S. Constitution, yet they stressed that their rights as American citizens entitled them to better treatment.[4]

The movement gradually attracted more recruits as representatives from each of the trades began meeting secretly, away from the prying eyes of policemen. They hoped to create a federation of all the skilled trades and present their demands to the chief engineer, John Wallace. Elliott remained the most active, hustling through the different towns and camps, talking to the men, encouraging them to join his movement. He was aided by a locomotive engineer and a miner, both of whom had served with Roosevelt's Rough Riders in Cuba. Meanwhile, police spies were furiously shadowing each of the leaders, as foremen and supervisors searched for reasons to fire them.

By March 17, officials had found—or concocted—their reasons. Elliott's boss fired him for irregularities in his employees' time cards. Another activist, the miner J. C. Virden, lost his job a couple of days later, supposedly for detonating too powerful a charge of dynamite.[5] Two other leaders resigned their jobs under mysterious circumstances. One, a conductor named Chubb, reportedly drank constantly the next few days until finally leaving the Zone for Panama. Even without their jobs, however, Elliott and the others continued to organize. On March 19, Elliott declared to workers meeting at the Hotel Vienna, "Congress asks for eight hours and we should have it. The 'big men' in Panama are no fools and they will work you ten hours until we demand eight." Police spies reported to ICC officials that dissatisfaction over long hours and low wages was widespread. Police chief George Shanton ordered Elliott shadowed constantly—any threat he might make against the commission was to be reported immediately, so that he could be arrested. One spy reported that "the discharge of Elliott has put a damper on the feelings of the more timid ones, and without his leadership the organization would not hold together."[6] Elliott tried one more tactic, visiting the office of the U.S. minister in Panama, John Barrett, to complain about conditions. Unbeknownst to him, however, John Wallace was visiting Barrett's office when Elliott arrived. Staying hidden, Wallace advised the minister to tell Elliott he could do nothing, and suggest instead that Elliott simply talk with his supervisor.[7]

With the main leaders neutralized, the movement disintegrated. Yet officials were still not finished with Elliott. Several weeks later they intercepted letters he had written that demonstrated, they claimed, that he intended to engage in a counterfeiting scheme. The government soon deported Elliott and he returned to the United States. In 1906 he surfaced one last time. Working now as a switchman for the Illinois Central Railroad in New Orleans, Elliott met with the misfortune of an inquisitive boss. Word somehow had gotten out about his activities in the

Canal Zone. His employer wrote the Canal Zone government for information about his record. Police chief Shanton quickly, and no doubt happily, responded: "He was a labor agitator, and caused the Isthmian Canal Commission, and the Police Department in particular, a great deal of trouble by his repeated attempts to organise labor unions, cause strikes, etc." Shanton concluded that Elliott was an "all-round dangerous man."[8] Presumably, Elliott was soon forced to seek another job.

Although he succeeded in killing Elliott's organizing effort, chief engineer John Wallace apparently did consider the workers' grievances. He felt compelled to ask the ICC back in Washington, D.C., for guidance. He had believed, he said, that skilled men could be worked longer than eight hours a day, and he felt this to be necessary for the construction work to proceed efficiently. In fact, however, Wallace learned to his shock not only that he must observe the eight-hour day for all American citizens but also that he could be fined by the government if he failed to do so.[9] On the matter of hours, at least, Wallace gave in to the workers' demands.

THE ROUGHNECKS' WORLD

The skilled American workers proved a constant irritation for officials like Wallace. Their labor and skills were desperately needed, and they seemed always to be in short supply, particularly during the early years, when yellow fever caused many to board a ship back to the United States soon after arriving. Because of this, and because of the danger of their jobs, Wallace had to pay them higher wages than he felt they deserved. As he saw it, skilled workers were terribly coddled by the government, and despite this they constantly complained. In a letter to the chairman of the ICC, Wallace explained how he perceived his skilled workers: "A great many of the young men who come to the Isthmus have been moved by a spirit of adventure. They have heard of this wonderful country, and are anxious to enlarge their knowledge of it, . . . but arriving here, and surrounded as they are by the conditions that exist, without diversions, without home influences, and especially without the influence of wives, mothers, and sisters, they become discontented and homesick." Worst of all, they seemed to think the United States would pay to send them back home again if unhappiness drove them to quit. To the workers' displeasure, this was most definitely not the case.[10]

Soon after ordering the deportation of Elliott, Wallace left the isthmus as well. His resignation had many causes—by all accounts he was overwhelmed by the job and not performing well or making much progress. But the skilled workers and their demands were certainly a source of frustration to him. Two years later Wallace testified to Congress about conditions on the isthmus and dismissed the skilled workers' grievances: those who complained, he argued, "expected to swing in a hamock and sip mint julips and smoke cigarettes and be fanned, and all that sort of thing. There was no man down there that came . . . to do real work . . . that made any complaint of the way they were fed or the way they were housed."[11]

Wallace's disdain was shared by many other elites in the Canal Zone, who had innumerable nicknames for skilled workers, most of them unflattering. "Roughnecks" was the most popular, though they also called them "huskies," "tropical tramps," "mechanics," "vagabonds," or "soldiers of fortune."[12] Perhaps no one disliked the roughnecks more than the engineers and other white-collar employees did. These college-educated professionals dressed in clean white shirts and worked mostly in spacious, brightly lit offices, yet circumstances often forced them to live alongside the steam-shovel and railroad men. One such professional was Roland Singer, a young electrical engineer who left his home in Lewisburg, Ohio, for the Zone. He found he had nothing in common with the "roughnecks," as he habitually referred to them, and yet he had no choice but to share a life with them and pretend to be friendly. Writing to his mother, Roland described the situation: "Every Sunday night about 10:30 p.m. there are about 8 or 16 fellows come home from spending the day in Panama City. Then they congregate out on the porch in front of the room and adjoining me and cuss and swear and talk about the price fight and hoar houses until 12 p.m. o'clock at night. I sure am getting sick of it." He singled out the steam-shovel men as especially disagreeable. They lacked education and common sense, he declared, yet "they are making from $125 to $200 per month so you may know just how overbearing and repulsive they seem to me." Spending much of his time applying and hoping for a good job back in the States so he could escape the Canal Zone, his letters home sprinkled with references to church and Sunday school, Roland expressed particular shock at having to share quarters with so many "heathens": "I don't mean the natives either. . . . Don't know which I hate worse a Jew or a Catholic." The "Catholic boys"—most likely Irish American workers— seemed the ones most likely to waste their money on gambling, alcohol, and whorehouses in Cocoa Grove.[13]

The policeman and census taker Harry Franck was more generous spirited, but he shared Roland Singer's impression of the roughnecks. Franck referred to the skilled worker as "a bull-necked, whole-hearted, hard-headed, cast-iron fellow . . . a fine fellow in his way, but you some-times wish his way branched off from yours for a few hours, when bed-time or a mood for quiet musing comes. He is a man you are glad to meet in a saloon—if you are in a mood to be there—or tearing away at the cliffs of Culebra; but there are other places where he does not seem exactly to fit into the landscape." Franck uncomfortably shared a bach-elor dormitory with many roughnecks. After supper at a hotel, he ex-plained, he would come home, where "seven phonographs were striking up their seven kinds of ragtime on seven sides of us; and it was the small hours before the poker games, carried on in much the same spirit as Comanche warfare, broke up through all the house." The house wouldn't grow quiet until 4:30 a.m., and soon thereafter "a jarring chorus of alarm clocks wrought new upheaval."[14]

As these stories suggest, the world of male U.S. citizens working on the canal was a complex and hierarchical one. In 1912, according to the U.S. Census, the ICC and the Panama Railroad together employed just over forty-eight hundred male U.S. citizens. Another thousand were em-ployed by independent contractors in the Zone, especially McClintic-Marshall, the company building the lock gates. They came from all over the United States, but most came from northeastern and midwestern industrialized states like New York, Pennsylvania, and Ohio. Almost half of these men, about twenty-five hundred, were married, and of these nearly eighteen hundred had wives living with them in the Zone and keeping house for them. Initially officials discouraged families from coming, but by 1906 they had realized the presence of women and children would comfort these men and civilize and stabilize conditions in the Zone. Increasingly, they encouraged American families to make the trip by doubling the amount of free housing and furnishings allotted to male workers if joined by their wives.[15]

Atop the hierarchy of U.S. employees were men who performed the supervisory tasks and made the major design and labor management decisions: the commissioners and their surveyors, doctors, civil engineers, superintendents, draftsmen, timekeepers, mechanical and electrical engineers, foremen and sub-foremen, supervisors, clerks, accountants, store managers, stenographers, and disbursers. Almost all of these jobs were restricted to white American men. Timekeepers and foremen played a crucial role, and there was a multitude of them. Already by 1907, as excavation got aggressively under way, for example, the Culebra division of the Department of Dredging and Excavation alone had forty-two timekeepers and more than two hundred gold roll foremen (plus dozens more silver roll foremen).[16]

One important step below these white-collar employees in the hierarchy of labor were the men referred to as roughnecks. This in itself was a vast and diverse world, including steam-shovel and railroad engineers, crane operators, conductors, firemen, brakemen, yardmasters, train masters, electricians, teamsters, machinists, blacksmiths, miners (to oversee the drilling and placement of dynamite), boilermakers, pattern makers, carpenters, iron molders, bricklayers, painters, plumbers, pipe fitters, wiremen, and telegraphers. More highly skilled workers like steam-shovel and railroad engineers were paid a monthly salary, while most construction and machine shop workers were paid an hourly rate ranging from forty-four to seventy-five cents. A gulf separated those paid on a monthly versus an hourly basis, to the great consternation of the hourly men. Workers on a monthly salary received significant perks, including the highly desirable six weeks of paid vacation. Hourly workers were eligible for a six-week vacation, but they received pay for only two of the six weeks. On the other hand, monthly workers were expected to work longer than eight hours per day without receiving overtime, while hourly workers received overtime for working longer than eight hours and for working on holidays and Sundays. The hourly employees, especially machinists, blacksmiths, pattern makers, boilermakers, and molders, greatly resented the lack of six weeks of paid vacation and the lower status it suggested. They agitated repeatedly, finally forming a trades council in 1910, and petitioned ICC officials and President Taft for both paid vacation and higher wages. In 1911 officials at last granted them a four-week paid vacation.[17]

The skilled workingmen of the Zone generally had considerable experience and were comfortable in a disciplined, large-scale industrial environment. The construction project was dominated by the most innovative machinery available. The Bucyrus steam shovel used a small team of skilled and unskilled workers to do work that hundreds of West Indians, under French supervision, had once done with hand tools. U.S. officials mechanized every possible aspect of the job, inventing track shifters, uploaders, and dirt spreaders to do the work more efficiently. The foundries, repair shops, and roundhouses all relied on highly advanced technology. As James Bryce, the British ambassador to the United States, observed during a visit to the Zone in 1910: "The work is being prosecuted with the utmost energy, and shows the two features most characteristic of American undertakings—the employment of every kind of device for saving manual labour by means of machinery and a superb disregard of expense."[18] As a result, skilled employees spent much of their time operating and repairing machines, working in the cabs of steam shovels, in the engines of locomotives, or next to lathes in machine shops.

The steam-shovel engineers dominated the skilled workforce from 1905, when construction slowly got under way, until the final years, 1912 to 1914, when dredging machines grew more useful than steam shovels (as water gradually entered the site) and building the enormous locks became the project's focus. They were the most highly paid, most indispensable, and therefore most powerful of all the skilled workers. Their union, the International Brotherhood of Steam Shovel and Dredge Men, was the most vocal and energetic in fighting in Washington, D.C., to extend or maintain their rights. In 1907 the ICC began publishing a Zone newspaper, the *Canal Record,* and editors began publishing the excavation and dredging records achieved by different sections of the construction site, comparing them with one another and with records attained during the French era. In December 1909, for example, the *Canal Record* noted that the most productive excavation had occurred in the Culebra section, with more than one million cubic yards excavated in the previous month alone. Publishing these statistics generated competition and many attempts by engineers and crane operators to outdo other teams of steam-shovel operators. In May 1913 two steam shovels heading from different directions finally met each other on the bottom of Culebra Cut, and within several weeks all dry excavation was finished. There would still be frequent landslides to confront, but dredges would henceforward be used to repair the damage.[19]

The steam-shovel men were nearly matched in power and prestige by the various employees of the Panama Railroad—the engineers, conductors, brakemen, switchmen, track masters, and yardmasters. The constant train traffic (hundreds of trains went by all day long and into the night), and especially the many layers of train traffic in Culebra Cut, made the work challenging for everyone. Train accidents were among the most common causes of injury and death in the Canal Zone, and they presented a special hazard to the employees who worked with trains for eight or ten hours a day. Workers hanging off a train sometimes collided with trees or other obstacles; train collisions injured or killed many; trains running off schedule surprised unwary employees inspecting or repairing the tracks.

Yet despite the dangers—or perhaps because of them—the railroad men had a certain swagger and bravado that other workingmen envied, and they helped set the tone for skilled workers in general. They and the steam-shovel operators were the "labor aristocrats" of the Canal Zone, the men who possessed the most respectability, union and lodge member-ships, more financial resources (often including some savings), nice clothes, and other items indicating success in the world of the working class.

In 1908 the rare misfortune of murder created a snapshot of the be-longings and resources in the life of a locomotive engineer who helped build the canal. Philip Kramer of Tacoma, Washington, worked in the Zone as a locomotive engineer. While asleep in his bachelor's room in the construction town of Paraiso, Kramer had his skull crushed by an unknown assailant. Robbery most likely was the goal. Kramer left as his heirs two young daughters living with his divorced wife in Portland, Oregon. In his possession when he died were shares in a Los Angeles oil company, about $1,000 in gold held in a bank in Panama City, and a funeral benefit fund taken out with the Red Men's Lodge, to which he belonged in Tacoma. His membership in the Red Men also entitled his children to receive money from the lodge's Orphan's Fund. In his room Kramer left behind a small world of objects. Compared with that of the engineers and officials in charge of the construction project, Kramer's wealth was modest indeed. Yet this was a respectable man with many possessions and nice clothes. Along with his marriage certificate, souvenir coins, and lodge ribbons, authorities found oxford shirts, a dress coat, a smoking jacket, a hunting coat, oxford shoes, white pants and cuffs, a leather cigar case, and many books and photographs among the items in his room.[20]

Some of the Canal Zone's American male workers, whether engineers, machinists, or carpenters, came to the isthmus with a taste for adventure after serving in the Philippines or Cuba. George Shanton, for example, who had fought as a member of Theodore Roosevelt's Rough Riders in Cuba during the War of 1898, went to the Canal Zone to create a police force at Roosevelt's request soon after the United States acquired the Zone. J. C. Virden, the miner who worked alongside R. B. Elliott to cre-ate a labor federation, was one who had fought under Shanton's com-mand. When John Foster Carr spent time in the Canal Zone, mingling among the skilled workingmen, he was struck by how many had served in the War of 1898 or, subsequently, in the imperial sites the war created.

Carr painted a vivid picture of skilled workers on their days off: "They generally spent the day . . . on the hotel verandas, smoking, lazily watching the vultures floating high up in the air, 'talking shop,' and telling tales of Cuba and the Philippines, where scores of them have been." The Zone policeman and census taker Harry Franck likewise observed the global origins of these workingmen in his 1913 book on the canal's construction: "We world-wanderers, as are a large percentage of 'Zoners,' with virtually no fixed roots in any soil, floating wherever the job suggests or the spirit moves, have the facts of our past in our own heads only."[21]

Many others hailed from stalwart working-class communities across the United States, from Portland or Los Angeles, Memphis or Little Rock, Detroit or Pittsburgh, Boston or Newark. They were among the most highly paid and skilled members of the working class and were the most likely to have the power and benefits that came with union representation. They could afford relatively pleasant homes in nice neighborhoods. Yet in many cases they were eager for opportunity and higher pay. Some related how recruiters had made the Panama Canal Zone sound enticing, and although during the early years of 1904 and 1905 workers commonly believed they'd been misled, from 1906 onward they typically believed the promises had been kept—although this did not mean they relented in their efforts to maintain or improve their working conditions. Skilled American male workers received pay 25 to 35 percent higher than anything at home plus free quarters, electricity, medical care, and sick leave. Besides such perks, the job in the Zone undoubtedly provided some men with a means of escape—from hard economic times, from blacklisting, or from personal troubles.[22]

"WE ARE ALL PATRIOTIC AMERICAN CITIZENS"

Skilled white male workers from the United States came to Panama already accustomed to certain privileges resulting from their race, gender, skills, and relatively high wages. In the Canal Zone such privileges became heightened: these men knew that the government desperately needed them and that the success of the canal project hinged on their skill, experience, and energetic labor. The government therefore needed to keep them content and avoid desertions. Indeed, although Secretary of War William Howard Taft believed that skilled workers received excessively high wages compared with the payment for similar jobs back home, he resisted efforts by Congress to reduce wages on the grounds that recruiting high-quality skilled workers was one of the great difficulties involved in the construction project. Quality men were simply not willing to go to the isthmus—if they did go, they didn't remain long enough. As late as 1908, when conditions had improved radically compared with the beginning stages of construction, Taft declared that the problem of securing sufficient skilled labor remained, and he blamed it on the tropics: "There is something in the absence of rational amusement, something in the continued high temperature, that puts a man under a nervous strain—something in the remoteness from home . . . that makes labor there dissatisfied; and the men just give up and go home without any reason." Few skilled workers had been on the job for a full year, he noted.[23]

Government officials kept a careful eye on public relations as well, needing to maintain support for the canal project among the taxpaying public back home. They believed that if private contractors had been put in charge of the work, they could risk strikes in order to make the work more efficient. However, the canal construction was a government job, and as Taft explained to congressmen, "There is a good deal more responsibility on the Government officer. . . . The whole public are engaged as critics of the issue; and if it should lead to a disastrous strike, the results would be so burdensome." The silver and gold payrolls irrefutably reinforced white skilled workers' status as aristocrats, differentiating them from other workers by granting highly visible privileges. Skilled workers also enjoyed membership in strong and politically effective unions (like the Steam Shovel and Dredge Men or the International Association of Machinists), and they benefited from lobbying activities carried out by the American Federation of Labor and its high-profile president, Samuel Gompers. The U.S. Senate and House of Representatives conducted innumerable investigations into every aspect of life and work in the Zone, from engineering issues to labor conditions, quarters, housing, and so on, giving skilled workers and their unions an almost constant vehicle for making demands or at least building the case for why they should maintain their excellent pay and benefits. This put great pressure on ICC officials to find ways of controlling, managing, and amusing their skilled workers.[24]

The U.S. government's methods for disciplining labor rivaled those in place anywhere at the time in terms of rigidity and efficacy. Although strikes rarely broke out among skilled workers during the construction years, this was not only because of the lavish pay. Employees might find themselves fired and blacklisted, like Elliott, if they engaged in labor activism, and officials relied heavily on their police force to maintain order and discipline workers.[25] After President Roosevelt sent George Shanton to Panama to create a police force and clear the "criminal element" out of the Canal Zone, Shanton designed a uniform that virtually replicated the one worn by the Rough Riders. Most of the white policemen he recruited had experience in the War of 1898 or the Philippine-American War that followed it. Many of the West Indians he recruited had military or police experience as well. The journalist John Foster Carr observed the police force in action and considered it "possibly the most soldierly and efficient to be found on American territory, and its success was immediate."[26]

The force consisted of roughly 250 officers, half of whom were white Americans and the other half West Indians. The latter policed only the West Indian community. Policemen had to handle many different tasks, keeping the peace in communities often torn by violence, rounding up sailors who fled their ships, suppressing rowdy revelers on a Saturday night. Many towns in the Zone were known for their partying.[27] Often policemen worked undercover, sometimes assisted by marines and soldiers working in civilian clothes, spying on the labor force and targeting any efforts among workingmen to organize themselves. The reformer W. J. Ghent visited the Canal Zone and observed that there existed "in spite of the denials of the Commission, an exasperating system of 'gum-shoeing' or spying on the men." The chief of police chose his undercover policemen from different ethnic groups so as to infiltrate the labor force most effectively. At one time a Swede, a Colombian, a Chinese man from Martinique, and a Greek all worked undercover alongside the more common white U.S. citizens. The young Secret Service of the United States hired an untold number of men, including Chinese assigned to work undercover and help them control gambling and unauthorized liquor sales. The government used information gathered by spies to control the workforce, engaging, for example, in dismissals, blacklisting, or deportation of "troublemakers."[28]

An executive order issued by President Roosevelt had given officials sweeping powers of deportation. Anyone seeking to "incite insurrection, . . . create public disorder, endanger the public health, or in any manner impede the prosecution of the work of opening the canal" could be deported. According to General George Davis, who had served in 1904 as the Zone's first governor, the Canal Zone was the only place under the control of the United States where such broad powers of deportation existed. Testifying during one of many congressional investigations into conditions on the isthmus, the general—as well as the senators questioning him—seemed uneasy because these deportation powers contradicted the Bill of Rights. They resolved the tension by deciding that the U.S. presence in the Canal Zone was a military as well as a civil occupation, and under those conditions the nullification of the Bill of Rights was acceptable. His worries allayed, Davis argued that deportation could and should be used even against U.S. citizens—in particular he cited its usefulness in eliminating workers who threatened to strike.[29]

Officials frequently availed themselves of this right—a peculiar situation, when U.S. citizens could be deported from U.S. territory and sent back home to the United States. It gave government officials absolute power when it came to enforcing productivity on everyone residing in the Canal Zone, and organizing a strike was a principal offense that could result in deportation. The government matched its deportation powers with vagrancy laws, and it enforced the latter, as the executive secretary H. D. Reed put it, "vigorously": "These enable us to compel every man to work, if he is able to work, if he remains in the Zone." The police arrested men for loitering, vagrancy, intoxication, or disorderly conduct, and the number of arrests grew particularly high just after payday.[30]

The three chief engineers, Wallace, Stevens, and Goethals, all prided themselves on their tough responses to skilled workers, and usually officials in Washington, D.C., supported their decisions. The most important effort at labor organizing among gold workers began in February 1907, when steam-shovel operators demanded more pay. Engineers wanted to see their pay rise from $210 to $300 per month, while crane operators sought an increase from $185 to $250 per month and firemen requested a raise from $83 to $110 per month. The workers made this demand of chief engineer Stevens, and their union representative in Washington, D.C., forwarded it to President Roosevelt. While Roosevelt and Stevens considered the grievances, the locomotive engineers and conductors working on the Panama Railroad began organizing too. Stevens offered hints of compromise, but most negotiations waited until Secretary of War Taft visited the isthmus at the end of March 1907. Taft received the various committees and heard their complaints. He understood that a great deal was at stake, because the wages of steam-shovel engineers set the standard for all other American employees. He believed it would be highly embarrassing if they stopped working, yet it would also be embarrassing to pay them much more than they already made.[31]

The men rested their demand for more pay mostly on the discomfort imposed by working on the isthmus: the distance from loved ones, the absence of amusements, the difficulties caused by the humidity and heat, the risk of illness and injury as a result of careless supervisors, and the absence of compensation from the government for injuries. They also expressed concern about frequent dismissals without a hearing or a chance to plead their case, arguing that the result was often unfair and unjust. Taft took more than a month to make a public decision on the steam-shovel operators' grievances. In the meantime, the protest threatened to blossom into a general strike: by now, in mid-April, railroad employees and skilled workers employed on an hourly basis (mostly building trades and machine shop workers) began arguing for higher pay as well. George Brooke, the superintendent of motive power and machinery, reported that "many threats were made by the union men on the Isthmus to make a showing of force at our Gorgona Shops" or send in their resignations. "If we are to have any trouble of this kind," Brooke concluded, "it is much better to have it now than later on." He took a strong stand against the hourly men's demands and refused even to send their petitions on to Secretary of War Taft, stating, "These men were notified that no shop rules or regulations would be recognized or received . . . that our shops must be 'open' shops; and an organization would not be recognized by committee."[32]

When Taft at last responded, the steam-shovel operators considered his offer of a 5 percent pay raise unacceptable. They called a strike in early May 1907. Within two days only thirteen steam shovels were at work, instead of the full force of forty-eight. One member of the ICC ordered the Marines to patrol Culebra Cut and remove all agitators to their base, but Goethals learned of the order and countered it in the belief that it would generate more trouble. For several weeks excavation output remained very low. Gradually, however, Goethals replaced the striking steam-shovel operators through promotions, transfers, or hiring of new workers, and the strikers departed for the United States. In the end, Goethals argued, "the action taken had a wholesome effect on all classes of employees, for the steam-shovel crews had appeared to be indispensable, yet the outcome showed conclusively that defection by them or any other one class of men could not tie up the whole work." In the aftermath of this strike, the conductors and locomotive engineers working for the Panama Railroad again asked for higher pay. Goethals reminded the men that the canal was an "open shop" and that it was "ill-advised to make *demands* for increases in pay or other concessions, and thereafter none such would be given any consideration." He also repeated his policy that he would not meet with committees, but only with individual men.[33]

In 1908, however, government officials in the United States suggested that a labor commissioner be appointed to work with Goethals and represent the interests of workers. Goethals vehemently rejected this idea

("I felt certain that the men themselves did not want such an official," he remembered). The following year Taft, now president of the United States, agreed that a labor commissioner was unnecessary but ordered Goethals to accept meeting with committees representing the skilled workers. Taft, Goethals reported, "thought my position was untenable, for organized labor was recognized everywhere." From then onward, Goethals accepted the "less of two evils" and met periodically with union committees regarding issues of salary, working conditions, and so forth, yet he required that individual grievances be presented to him during his Sunday open-office hours. He continued to brag, years later, that he never relented on his refusal to consider or discuss demands from workers. He would respond to their grievances, he declared, but never their "demands."[34]

Months later an attempt at workplace organizing by boilermakers and machinists in the machine repair shop towns of Gorgona and Empire again demonstrated the difficulties involved. Since officials responded to strikes with such hostility, the workers began a movement to quit en masse instead. When they learned of rumors that police were going to surround the shops in response, the men grumbled that they were being treated like convicts even though they were obeying all the regulations regarding quitting. Their boss defused the situation by confirming that they had the right to quit and that he would not call the police. In the eyes of Goethals's investigator this prevented an inevitable clash between police and "quitters." The boilermakers wanted an increase in pay, saying they made little more than they did back home. Goethals refused their demands, and when push came to shove, the machinists refused to back them up. In the end, thirteen boilermakers quit and found their way to other jobs on the isthmus or headed back to the United States. Before it was over, T. B. Miskimon, Goethals's investigator, reported on the men behind the organizing effort, indicating which one was "the worst agitator of the lot in this trouble" or "one of the first talkers but not strenous as it appears." Miskimon concluded that they were all "like spoiled babies."[35]

The government's arsenal—police spies, vagrancy laws, powers of deportation, and, not least of all, the system of segregation—made it extremely difficult for skilled white male workers to organize on the basis of their workplace power. Gradually they shifted their focus and depended increasingly on their unions in the United States for efficient lobbying of Congress. They also relied more heavily on enunciating and defending their rights as American citizens, as white men, and as representatives of America's empire. Indeed, these rights became inextricable from one another in the eyes of many workers and government officials.[36]

Because the government played such a dominant role in the construction project and intervened so thoroughly in workers' lives, citizenship was perhaps destined to emerge as an important medium through which workers negotiated over the substance of their daily lives on and off the job. Their status as U.S. citizens gave skilled American workers an important source of strength, while noncitizens, by contrast, lacked such bargaining power. Congress oversaw affairs on the isthmus, conducting investigations into labor and housing conditions, sanitation, and health. This gave skilled workers a regular forum for expressing their views, and often they relied on patriotism and citizenship to make their case. As one worker declared, "We are American citizens and . . . proud to have a share in this great work."[37] Arguing on behalf of gold roll employees for a lengthier vacation with pay, the unionist Crawford Moore declared, "We are putting forth our best efforts. We are all patriotic American citizens. We will throw our hats up just as high in the air as anyone when this work is done."[38] Such arguments in the end proved more successful than workplace organizing efforts. Skilled workers maintained or sometimes improved upon the high wages and generous benefits they had won, much to the regret of officials, and in 1908 Congress granted them compensation for injuries on the job.[39]

"OUR CRAFT IS NEARLY TAKEN FROM US"

In early 1908 an executive order issued by President Roosevelt limited employment on the gold roll to U.S. citizens and began to transform life and work in the Canal Zone. It made citizenship vastly more important and began to reshape relations between workers and officials, and between skilled U.S. workers and noncitizens. The ICC immediately began a major transition in its employment policies. It purged the remaining noncitizens (most of them northern and western Europeans or West Indians) from the gold roll, either transferring them to the silver roll or, if that was not possible, eliminating their employment altogether. U.S. gold roll employees strongly supported the policy. Notably, they now began to oppose the presence on the gold roll of Europeans as well as West Indians. A Mrs. Flanagan (the documents suggest nothing else about her identity, but presumably she was married to a skilled American worker) wrote Goethals a few months after the executive order, for example, to report on aliens she had observed still working on the gold roll: "Mr. Hart, an Englishman in the commissary; Mr. Simmons, a Jamaican in the hardware department who served in the English army . . ." One man, she noted, "has got Negro Blood in his veins." Mrs. Flanagan concluded, "As I am a true American I am going to see that all aliens are run out according to your official circular." The records of the ICC contain numerous complaints by U.S. workers and their union representatives regarding aliens holding jobs that, they believed, should belong to Americans.[40]

Yet if Roosevelt's order to purge aliens from the gold roll held the potential to strengthen the hand of skilled American workers, it coincided with a new ICC strategy that profoundly threatened their job security and hence the very basis of their power. In 1907 officials began systematically introducing West Indians and other noncitizens into jobs previously held only by white Americans. Such workers remained on the silver roll, but they began doing jobs once considered the territory of skilled workers. Usually it involved replacing a white man with a West Indian, and this profoundly intertwined the issues of race and citizenship. Supervisors found West Indians to be competent workers and easier to supervise—in part because they lacked union representation and in part because Congress and the American public cared little about their welfare. In many cases, officials argued, West Indians could perform the job more effectively than could white or black U.S. citizens. Officials believed that white men annoyingly pushed for promotion out of the lesser-skilled "helper" jobs, while African Americans, though performing better as workers, irritated supervisors by demanding the same perks and living conditions as their white counterparts. And West Indians always worked much more cheaply, a critical concern in the Zone when Congress was demanding maximal cost efficiency.[41]

So government officials carefully identified those occupations that could be carried out by West Indians and then systematically began replacing white U.S. citizens. In machine shops across the Canal Zone by 1908, West Indians had begun working as machinists, boilermakers, ironworkers, shipwrights, shipfitters, blacksmiths, and blacksmith helpers; on dredges they worked as captains, mates, and engineers. The most widespread substitution occurred among firemen, who assisted the steam-shovel engineers, and among car builders and repairmen. The process of replacing white firemen began shortly after the 1907 strike by steam-shovel engineers, crane operators, and firemen, the most significant strike by skilled workers during the construction period. By the autumn of 1909 no more than a dozen white firemen were working in the central division of the Zone. Previously, a direct line of promotion had connected white firemen to crane operators and upward to steam-shovel engineers (this had been a right steam-shovel workers struggled to protect), so the strategy of substitution sent a strong signal: the boundaries around skill that white workers had jealously guarded were no longer impermeable. Black firemen reminded white workers on a daily basis that whites were dispensable. This was a triple blow, demonstrating the fragility of privileges based on race, citizenship, and skill.[42]

The process of substitution thus made citizenship a more important arena of conflict between skilled workers and the ICC. Union representatives pleaded with ICC officials in the Canal Zone, begged Congress to issue legislation against such substitutions, and petitioned successive presidents to issue executive orders. Skilled workers fought, sometimes successfully, for rules that would determine whether a gold or a silver man should do a certain job. In one case of West Indians working as railroad crew members in 1912, for example, Goethals gave in to the complaints of skilled workers, declaring, "The use of colored men has given rise to such contention among the men that I do not want them used."[43]

In a very different case in 1910, U.S. machinists in the Zone organized a protest against a German named Frank Ertl who was employed as a machinist on the silver roll. He was doing work the gold workers believed belonged to them. The union official Harry Ragsdale argued on behalf of U.S. workers and against Ertl: "He is practically filling the place of an American citizen. The condition of times in the States now is something awful for machinists and we are satisfied that there can be plenty of first-class machinists gotten to do this work." Asked how they felt about West Indians working as machinists, Ragsdale replied: "We do not think that is right, Colonel, that these negroes should be used in there, and especially one case there of a man, he . . . blows it around that he is a machinist and would not work under any other conditions. That gives more or less excitement to the men, for a negroe, and especially a West Indian, for a man to go around and blow that way." Asked if any American Negroes were working in the shops, Ragsdale admitted there were, but not as machinists. He added: "We do not kick against American negroes, if they are citizens; we are complaining against this foreign element." As a result of this exchange, Goethals ordered that Frank Ertl be transferred to unskilled labor.[44]

Even while stressing their rights as citizens, U.S. workers clearly perceived those rights as partially a matter of race. Most often their efforts to establish boundaries around skills they perceived as their property targeted West Indians, and typically their arguments identified race with citizenship. In 1909 skilled workers angrily declared their opposition to the U.S. government's employing "negro 'so-called' mechanics . . . in direct competition with white mechanics and citizens of the U.S.A. (the negroes being subjects of Great Britain and therefore aliens)." Such a policy, they proclaimed, was "Un-American" and "directly against the principles of the U.S. Government as it places the white man in competition with a class, who by their mode of living and habits are on an equal with the Chinese and Japanese, and in general intelligence and mechanical ability are far beneath the Chinese and Japanese." In this way, white workers linked their protest against the hiring of West Indians to a long history of anti-Chinese movements in the United States—movements in which working-class agency helped deny citizenship to Chinese immigrants on the grounds of racial inferiority and simultaneously barred those immigrants from access to certain skills. Workers signing this statement included blacksmiths, boilermakers, machinists, molders, pattern makers, and railway car men. They sent copies of their protest statement to President Taft; the ICC; and the American Federation of Labor president, Samuel Gompers.[45]

Skilled workers' understandings of citizenship were also closely linked to skill and control over certain jobs. Often the links were made in highly complex ways. Skilled workers might argue, for example, that they were better *because* they were white, and therefore they should be given the monopoly over a job that their citizenship afforded them. One union official wrote to Goethals in 1908 and complained about the ICC's employment of "negro engineers." He and the other skilled white workers could understand, he conceded, the need to keep wages low. However, "should these negro engineers be displaced by competent white men . . . the difference in wages paid would be more than compensated for by the better service rendered." The white man would ultimately save the government money by using his cool judgment to avert accidents, for example. Furthermore, and here he explicitly linked citizenship to skill, "as the Commission has shown the disposition to employ none but white American citizens as skilled laborers as far as possible, and as the negro engineers are all aliens with no interest whatever in the great task which brings us all here other than the payment we ask that white engineers be given this preference of the negro alien." Using the same sort of reasoning, William Yates, president of the marine engineers' union, wrote Goethals a year later: "Since American energy, progressiveness, and money have created decent living conditions on the isthmus, there is no question but what the government can secure in the States a number of regularly licensed and reliable masters [and] mates."[46]

By 1913, as the construction project moved toward completion, the building trades had grown more important. Homes had to be moved out of towns that were about to be submerged. They were mostly rebuilt in the new American town of Balboa near Ancon, just outside Panama City, joining a great many new houses and public buildings. More plasterers, carpenters, plumbers, tile setters, copper- and tinsmiths, and electricians now headed from the United States to the Zone. The same dynamic of West Indians taking over jobs that had been worked previously by whites reshaped their trades as well. A U.S. plasterer who had traveled to the Zone for work along with dozens of others in 1914 wrote to the official magazine of his union, the Operative Plasterers' International Association, to say that "English negroes" had infiltrated his trade. They were working alongside him on the new administration building in Balboa. He urged his union to make a fight against West Indian infiltration and declared, "Other trades have let the negro get such a hold that it seems useless for them to try and do anything." He noted, "The plumber is the only trade here which is not hampered by the negro. They had men come here who were good union men and they refused to show the negro anything at all about their craft." This man, who remained anonymous, argued that there seemed to be nothing the men could do while in the Zone. Only union men in the United States could solve the problem. He ended by stressing what he saw as a crucial point: "In order to come down here you MUST be a citizen of the United States, either born or naturalized; no others need apply. Now if that is so, why are they allowed to bring these negroes here, who are subjects of foreign powers, and who knows nothing of the trade at which he is working, while there are thousands of men in the States who are good mechanics, but not citizens, will not be allowed to come here? What is the difference between the two of them? Can you Brothers see any difference? I can't—only in color."[47]

Soon an African American union member criticized the above writer's viewpoint, providing a window into how conditions on the canal were generating debates among both black and white U.S. workers. The African American declared that his white brother had forgotten his "union principles." If the white brother's real concern was foreigners infiltrating the trade, he should focus on conditions in the United States, because the same problem existed. One had only to look around in cities like New York and Newark to see how employers were using foreigners to control their U.S. workforce. Thus he revealed the true point of the white unionist's complaint. Despite his effort to cloak his concerns with issues of citizenship, in fact "the brother's fight is based entirely on the negro question." He concluded, "It would seem to me a more reasonable fight were it aimed at incompetence, in whatever creed, color or nationality it be found."[48]

Ignoring such counterarguments, white trade unionists continued to mobilize against "negro infiltration" and took their complaints to Congress. In 1914 a union man representing the car builders in the Zone testified before Congress and unintentionally shed light on the connections white unionists perceived between race and citizenship. Mr. L. T. Sanders protested, as he put it, against "the way our craft is imposed on here by British subjects; negro laborers, to be plain about it. Our craft is nearly taken from us." A congressman asked: You are protesting on behalf of your union? "No, on an American citizen's rights. . . . We do not feel inclined to work on a level basis with a negro; that is the way it is. As an American citizen, I do not. And what would one of you gentlemen feel like sitting up in Congress even with one of our American negroes?" The chairman demurred, saying that he had sat with Negroes, and that in any case it was up to the American people to elect whomever they wished. Sanders retorted: "It would be different if American negroes were here. The taxpayers are not getting the benefit of it." He concluded, "We are willing to use the negro as a helper, but as far as 'Mr. Negro' being on a job with me, as my equal—" Sanders saw the substitution of blacks for whites as integral to the government's effort to control and cheapen labor on the canal, and he believed this violated his rights as a citizen: "Because they can get the negro at 10 cents an hour, and they lay 'Mr. White Man' off and send him back to the states."[49] Sanders's view of his rights as a citizen thus involved assumptions of his own worth as a producer, his skill and competence, and his racial superiority.

Goethals and his staff saw things very differently. They denied that skilled workers' race, citizenship, or skills afforded them a monopoly over certain jobs. They found placing silver men, mostly West Indians, in jobs formerly held by skilled white U.S. citizens to be an indispensable tactic. Silver men not only worked competently, but they saved money and provided a goad that made skilled white workers perform better and more quickly. In 1912 the socialist Victor Berger wrote Goethals to complain that "negroes" were being hired as blacksmith helpers, and Goethals's response was revealing. He disagreed, he declared, that whites should be hired for this job: "American citizenship entitles a man to preference in employment on the Panama Canal, but not color." In Goethals's view, "white men cannot long withstand heavy muscular exertion in the tropics; that black men can and do withstand the effects of a climate of this kind is a fact which needs no argument. White men do not want these jobs after they get here, as we know from experience, the black men are reasonably contented."[50]

Skilled workers' appeals to their rights as citizens could not prevent them from being replaced by noncitizens on the silver payroll. Substitutions continued throughout the Zone, helping to lower costs and create a more tractable workforce. Furthermore, as the construction project began to wind down in 1912 and 1913, government officials undertook a deliberate policy of systematically phasing out gold workers in favor of silver employees. As early as 1910 in some areas, officials stopped recruiting skilled men from the United States, preferring to replace them with silver workers as their numbers declined. The government had successfully brought its most powerful workers under control. After the canal was completed, in 1915, Goethals celebrated the efforts of his skilled workers, declaring them "an earnest, zealous, and enthusiastic co-operating body of employees." His calm sentiment hid the intense struggles that had been required to create such cooperation.[51]

"WE LOOK TO NO OTHER GOVERNMENT FOR PROTECTION"

Although most U.S. citizens on the ICC's gold roll were white, several dozen African American men also worked on the canal, and for them issues of race, citizenship, and skill interacted in very different ways. The

1912 census recorded only 127 African American employees. During the early years of construction there may have been more, but their numbers likely did not climb higher than 200. However, because of their awkward position in the segregation system, and because of their activism, African American workers powerfully tested the U.S. government. Henry Williams, the young Texas longshoreman, was likely typical: these men felt good fortune knocking at their doors when labor recruiters offered them a prestigious government job working to build the Panama Canal. The jobs were high-paying and, at least initially, on the gold roll. Most of the African Americans who accepted the ICC's offer of work had been born in the rural South. Their very first job had most often involved working the land for a relative or a white employer. Work in the Canal Zone allowed these men to escape the Jim Crow South, with its widespread segregation, racial violence, and economic discrimination. Like African Americans before them who fled for the West after the end of Reconstruction, calling themselves Exodusters, and like participants in the great migrations yet to come, these few African Americans were able to vote with their feet and depart the South for a better life—in this case, jobs in the service of America's empire. Compared with those struggling amid the indignities of the Jim Crow South, then, these were lucky men.[52]

Unlike most other African Americans, these men had already acquired a skill or a knowledge of business that made them contenders for a job in the Canal Zone. Some had found work with a railroad or a foundry in the South and had learned their way around a blacksmith's shop. Others had picked up the essential skills of a riveter or a fireman. And many, like their white counterparts in the Canal Zone, had led lives of unusual adventure before arriving on the isthmus. Henry Hart, a middle-aged man born in Randon, Mississippi, in 1871, provides an example. He had worked on his father's farm for nine years, he informed the ICC personnel officer, beginning when he was no more than two years old. At the age of twelve, Hart got a job in a blacksmith's shop in the town of Hansboro, Mississippi, and then worked fitting iron bridges in Louisiana for nine years. Along the way, he married and had two children. A job milling ore then took Hart to Central America for three years, by the end of which he was fluent in Spanish. He developed rheumatism in Central America, which left him too ill to work for the next two years. While ill and back in the United States, Hart and his wife had a third child, named Icelina. Hart's wife died around that time, perhaps in childbirth. The children went to live with family back in Hansboro, and when Hart recovered his health, his Spanish-language skills must have caught the eye of labor recruiters. He took a job as a blacksmith's helper in 1907 in the gigantic Cristobal shops near Colón, in the Canal Zone. Hart would work in the Zone for eleven years, and gradually he received pay raises and a promotion to blacksmith, before resigning his position and returning to the United States in May 1918.[53]

Charles Arnold took a similar path to the Canal Zone. Born in 1867, Arnold gained experience while still young as a businessman in his home town of Cincinnati. In 1897 he joined the Army, fought in Cuba during the War of 1898, and then remained in Cuba to support the U.S. government's work. After leaving the Army, he lived in Cuba for nine more years, running a business there. In 1909 he became one of many migrants traveling from Cuba to the Canal Zone for work. There Arnold won a position as a fireman on the Panama Railroad, earning $62.50 in gold each month. Unlike Henry Hart, though, Arnold was not well regarded by his employer. Considering his workmanship poor, officials discharged him after only six months of employment.[54]

Black men like Hart and Arnold did not fit easily into the biracial gold and silver system, and this caused discomfort both for them and for government officials struggling to make the system work. In 1907 and 1908 the government had moved most African Americans off the gold roll and created for them a "special" position on the silver roll that granted them certain privileges, like paid vacations, but classified them as colored and refused them many perks. Visible reminders of segregation were pervasive throughout the Zone.[55]

These were matters of great concern to African Americans, and they came to a head in 1912 at a time when the Republican Party, Abraham Lincoln's party, was in power in Washington and in charge of building the canal. This was not meant to be a southern—Jim Crow—operation.

And yet in the name of empire and efficiency a thorough segregation system had been established, a system that trapped African Americans unjustly. That year Dr. R. H. Boyd of Tennessee, a leader in the Colored Baptist Church (the largest denomination among African Americans in the United States), made a journey to the Canal Zone. He wanted to observe the construction effort and examine the work being done by members of his church. He traveled across the isthmus, meeting with ministers and church officials as well as the governor of the Canal Zone. While he described his visit as pleasant in many ways, he was startled by the segregation. He declared that "he never saw in the States as much of a 'Jim Crow' situation as he found here." Most unsettling of all, Boyd later wrote in the *National Baptist Union-Review,* his church's official newspaper, was the treatment he received at the Ancon post office. As he arrived, he "saw the United States flag floating over the post office and felt very much at home." Yet when Boyd walked in and asked for his mail, the clerk told him he must go to the other window: "Sir, you are a Negro, and must get your mail where other Negroes get theirs. Negroes and white men do not get their mail at the same window." Hardly able to conceal his dismay, Boyd remembered, "We looked at him and knew that he was blacker than we were, but wanting our mail so badly, we obeyed orders and went around to the window where Negroes called for their mail." Boyd's article describing his experiences ran in many other African American newspapers, causing consternation in black communities.[56]

Officials were concerned about the construction project's reception in African American as well as white communities back home. Throughout this period Republican Party officials carefully highlighted their work supporting equal rights for Negro citizens of the United States and the records of Presidents Roosevelt and Taft as employers of Negroes in federal jobs.[57] Boyd's revelations hit African American newspapers in the early spring of 1912, just as President Taft prepared for a difficult reelection campaign. Taft would face opposition not only from the Democrat Woodrow Wilson but also from ex-president Theodore Roosevelt, who was running as the candidate of the Progressive Party. In this context the

Republican Party emphasized its concern for equal rights even more forcefully. The *Republican Campaign Text-Book* for 1912 highlighted Taft's "tender solicitude for the brown man of the Philippines" and the fact that "there were more Afro-Americans in the service of the United States government under the Taft administration than ever before in the history of the country." Republicans stressed Taft's fight against peonage and disenfranchisement of African Americans in the South, his opposition to racial segregation, and his denunciation of lynching. Taft's managers worked to fill newspapers like the *Chicago Defender* with such material proving the party's positive impact on black Americans.[58]

Now the reverend's description of racism in the Canal Zone threatened to turn that community against the canal project—and against the Republican Party. In April 1912, Ralph Tyler, an African American serving as auditor of the Navy, alerted President Taft to Boyd's article, and the president ordered an investigation. Goethals immediately complied, asking that both the clerk who assisted Dr. Boyd and the postmaster in charge be identified and interviewed.[59]

Goethals located the clerk in question, a "colored Jamaican" named John Davis who had worked seven years for the Zone post office and was about to take exams to become a lawyer. Davis was also a leader in the Zone's Colored Baptist Church and had met with the Reverend Boyd socially in addition to waiting on him at the post office. Davis declared that nothing had taken place as Boyd described it. He had known who the reverend was as he approached the window: "I saluted him and advised him in answer to his inquiry that there was no mail there for him at the time, told him . . . that I was a member of his church and that if mail arrived, I would see that it reached him by placing it in Rev. Thorbourne's box." Later, Davis testified, when he met with Boyd socially, they discussed the Jim Crow conditions in the Zone and particularly the fact that the post office lobbies were divided into separate areas for whites and blacks: "I explained to him . . . that the West India population was far in excess of any other population and that the division of lobbies facilitated the delivery of the mail." The postmaster at Ancon backed up every detail of John Davis's testimony.[60]

Summarizing the results of his investigation in May 1912, the director of Canal Zone posts, Tom Cooke, carefully defended the racial system in use in the post offices. Separating the races in the post office lobbies is "chiefly beneficial to the West Indians employed on the work here." Only six thousand to nine thousand Americans received their mail at Canal Zone post offices, as compared with forty-six thousand West Indians. Both groups should have an equal opportunity to receive their mail quickly and efficiently, Cooke opined: "There has never been any complaint here on the Isthmus of this service." Ultimately "there is no division which could be construed in any possible manner as race discrimination in the post office work between the American and the West Indian, or between the white and the black, if that expression is better, except that the colored West Indian is provided a lobby and a delivery window of his own . . . and he is given just the same opportunity of receiving his mail . . . as the white American is." Cooke concluded that Boyd's report had been incorrect; he had not experienced any discrimination on the basis of his race or for any other reason. And for good measure, Cooke noted that the same "division of space" existed throughout the Zone, in the commissaries, pay offices, labor trains, and messes, and "for practically the same reason, i.e., to facilitate the work." He added, "This division is made not for race discrimination, but for facilitating the construction of the Canal."[61]

African Americans working in the Zone believed they knew better. They complained about such discrimination, and when this had no apparent effect, they launched protests against their treatment. When government officials treated them differently from white Americans—for example, when they were refused free ice, first-class seats on the train, or payment in gold—African Americans lodged complaints on the grounds of their rights as American citizens. Government officials responded to their protests ambivalently. Anxious to appease them for reasons of public relations, yet determined to uphold the color line, officials never developed a consistent policy.

Consider the case of Walter Eagleson, an African American gold employee working as a watchman for $75 a month in the Commissary

Department. Two years after the Reverend Boyd's accusations of discrimination, Eagleson complained when a clerk at the Balboa post office ordered him to use the silver workers' window: "Will you please inform me, if the Postal clerks have the right to discriminate and draw a color line in the post office on a native born American Citizen?" John Baxter, the head of civil administration, forwarded Eagleson's note to Goethals's executive secretary, asking "whether these people are to be allowed to transact their business in the white lobby of the post office." The latter quickly responded and rejected Eagleson's claim that his citizenship was relevant in this matter: "As you are employed on the gold roll, of course you have a technical right to transact business on the gold roll side of the post office, although, as you are of the negro race, it would seem that you would avoid disputes of this character and save yourself and others annoyance if you would transact your business on the side where others of your race transact their business." Goethals's secretary ended with a quick lecture to Eagleson on race: "It has been found desirable to separate the races to some extent in order to save constant friction of the kind instanced in your letter, and it seems that no man should be ashamed of his race or color, as these are matters which we cannot control." Eagleson must have bridled upon receiving such patronizing advice.[62]

In another case in 1909, six African American blacksmiths working in Empire organized to protest government racism. Since at this time government officials refused to hire African Americans on the gold roll, all six men worked as silver employees. They objected to the fact that Panamanian "negroes" could be hired on the gold roll while they could not, as well as to the government's refusal to issue them free passes on the trains: "Why should not we American Negroes who assisted in fighting so bravely for the independence of our country not parcipitate in all the rights and privilidges, which is by far more than what the Panamanian negroes can say."[63] Goethals investigated the personnel records of all the men who had signed the protest, then responded with some accommodation to their demands. He agreed to issue pass books for the trains to African Americans and to pay them in gold rather than in silver. However, he refused to change the policy of hiring Panamanians since it resulted from a presidential executive order, and he bluntly told them their employment contracts placed them on the silver roll and could not be changed.[64]

The blacksmiths continued their protest, however. They wrote President Taft to say they were dissatisfied with the chief engineer's response and were now looking to him for justice. Calling themselves "Colored American Citizens," they presented the president with a specific request: "Please have us placed *on* the Gold Roll so that we will no longer be deprived of any rights that the other American gets." When they had arrived on the isthmus, they declared, they were ignorant of the ICC's rules and allowed officials to take advantage and employ them on the silver roll. They noted they were "American raised American born know nothing about any other Government only the American Government." Indeed, they said, "We look to no other Government for protection only our own USA and if in case that the USA should see . . . fit to call on us for any use we would not hesitate one moment but gladly and willingly give our aid as we have all ways did."[65] If President Taft ever responded to these workers, no record remains of his reply.

Other African American workers protested government policies as individuals. Henry Williams, the Texan who found work in the Canal Zone as a blacksmith, provides one example. Williams's name does not appear on any petition sent to Goethals or President Taft. Yet ICC personnel records reveal that he believed he faced racial discrimination on the isthmus and he became determined to do something about it. Like many white workers, Williams felt particularly exercised by the role of foreigners in the Canal Zone, but his reactions focused on the disadvantages they posed to black U.S. citizens. He believed the government treated foreigners better than African Americans, allowing them sometimes to work on the gold roll even as officials attempted to "keep all colored men on the silver roll." Williams complained to Goethals, and when ignored, he took his protest to Washington, D.C. While on paid leave in the United States, Williams visited the capital and hired a lawyer to represent him. He met with ICC officials, who then asked Goethals for his view. Goethals responded: "The truth of this whole matter is that Mr. Williams is what the men down here call an 'agitator.' . . . I have been informed that the other colored Americans on the Isthmus are not in sympathy with him or his actions." Williams returned to work in the Canal Zone without seeing his criticisms answered. He worked the next few years without apparent incident and got a small pay raise and a promotion, yet his anger must not have abated. In 1911 he was fired for "insubordination" on the job.[66]

In 1910, Goethals revoked an order that required the few remaining African American gold employees to take off their hats in the commissary since white U.S. citizens faced no such requirement. Goethals conceded that this practice had resulted in "discrimination between American citizens" and thus was inappropriate. When the African American gold employee Charles Arnold complained that same year that he was not being allowed to shop on the gold side of the commissary, the acting chief engineer ruled: "We cannot afford to subject the few American negroes who are employed on the gold roll to any marked discrimination on account of their color. If they claim the privilege, of making their purchases in the commissaries on the gold side, it will have to be conceded to them." Yet African Americans never won inclusion in YMCA clubhouses or in Canal Zone hotels and restaurants. Their housing never measured up to that accorded white workers, and while the government allowed their wives and children to come, they received not married housing but more space in the bachelor dormitories. In short, while officials sometimes responded favorably to African American workers' demands for equality, overall they saw enforcing the color line as a more important priority.[67]

"IT IS NOT THE POLICY OF THE COMMISSION TO HIRE WOMEN"

Like white and African American male employees, the few white women workers in the Zone found that negotiating with the government would be central to their lives, particularly if they hoped to improve their working and living conditions. The 1912 census of the Canal Zone listed 321 women in the employment of the ICC and the Panama Railroad. Most of these women, 251 of them, came from the United States. They hailed from almost every state, but most had made their homes in the upper Midwest and the Northeast, from Illinois and Michigan to Massachusetts and Pennsylvania. These women traveled to the Canal Zone most often to work as stenographers, clerks, teachers, and nurses. A smaller number worked as telegraphers, timekeepers, dietitians, storekeepers, and laundresses. White women who were U.S. citizens were always categorized as gold workers. However, ICC officials preferred not to bring female workers to the Zone unless necessary. When possible, for example they hired female teachers from among the population of wives and daughters of canal employees already living on the isthmus. Likewise, they typically declined to hire female clerical workers on the grounds that affordable housing was not available for them.[68]

Still, a number of women made the trip on their own and managed to secure work. Carrie Townsley of St. Louis, a single woman when she arrived in the Zone at the age of thirty-five, had previously worked for the Mississippi River Commission in various clerical capacities. A division engineer in Cristobal had worked with Carrie in St. Louis, liked her, and hired her to work in the Zone as a file clerk for $150 gold per month. She soon married a foreman working in the Atlantic division of the Zone and suffered through a "reorganization" of the clerical staff that resulted in a demotion and pay cut, but nonetheless she continued working at her job until 1911.[69]

Citizenship could matter as much to American women as it did to their male counterparts. Mary Chatfield, for example, left New England for Panama with many years' experience as a stenographer under her belt, including more than two years working in the engineering department of Columbia University. She had found life as a workingwoman in New York City difficult and thought the Canal Zone's higher salaries would allow her to improve her standard of living. She worried about the risks involved, especially for a single woman in the wild tropical land of Panama, but decided the higher pay made it a worthwhile adventure. She arrived on the isthmus in November 1905 with only her return ticket to New York, her clothes, and $35. Chatfield immediately went to visit John

Stevens and asked for a job, showing him letters of recommendation from Columbia University. When Stevens offered her only $75 per month, she felt insulted and considered walking out on him. But remembering her limited means, she responded, "Having had $3.00 a day in New York City for more than three years, I am not willing to accept less than that on the Isthmus of Panama." Ultimately, they settled on $100 per month, with the agreement that Stevens would raise her pay when he saw that she deserved it.[70]

Chatfield's sixteen months on the isthmus proved difficult. Reorganizations and the search for better pay and working conditions forced her to change jobs several times. All the jobs shared certain qualities: long hours, bosses who (she believed) knew less than she did, and insufficient pay. Like her male counterparts, she found living conditions intolerable and the government food "execrable." She felt miserable and isolated when work took her to towns in the heart of the Zone, but when transferred to a job at Colón Hospital, she found the work even more difficult and the conditions in Panama more unpleasant. Two aspects of life and work in the Zone stood out to her as particularly unjust. First, she observed a widespread bias against women workers. Second, and closely related, she believed that American citizens failed to get the respect due them. She complained vociferously about the unwillingness of canal officials to hire women who were U.S. citizens. In offices known to be understaffed, Chatfield had offered to recruit a friend of hers from the United States, but she always received the same reply: "It is not the policy of the Commission to hire women." The same happened to male friends of hers who sought jobs for their sisters. "Aliens, sots, sharpers, any old thing, will be given a position in an office by the Isthmian Canal Commission, anything but an American woman. . . . Our desire and hope is to get the larger salaries we should receive in this climate to keep us out of the poorhouse when we get too old to work and we should be encouraged, not refused."[71]

All around her, Chatfield believed, she saw talentless or ignorant people, mostly men and many of them foreigners, who had received good and high-paying jobs because they knew someone influential. She resolved to try the same tactic. She secured a better job by visiting a judge she had met and asking him to put in a good word for her with top officials. But the new job was not a sufficient improvement, and she kept hearing that the only way to improve her situation was to visit her congressman or senator. She determined, when she finally earned a vacation to go home, to visit her representatives. There she hoped to find out if it meant anything to be an experienced stenographer and "to have made every effort to comply with the *advertised* Civil Service requirements (barring the impossible one of changing your sex), to be a citizen of the U.S., a native of the U.S. and a descendant of men who fought and women who suffered to make this country a nation." If it meant nothing, she declared, she wanted to know so that she might "not labor longer under delusions."[72]

In August 1906, Chatfield, having earned that paid vacation, boarded a ship and headed to Connecticut, where she met with her aged congressman. She yelled at the top of her voice, she reported, because he was nearly deaf. She told him she had fourteen years of experience as a stenographer and that her family had been in Connecticut for 267 years. She had taken and passed the Civil Service Exam and now asked that her appointment be recognized by the Civil Service Commission so she would receive longer vacations and have her transportation covered. She also requested a raise in pay. Afterward she traveled to Philadelphia to meet with ICC officials, confident that they would grant her request. The officials disappointed her. They declared that women were not allowed to receive civil service appointments and that she was lucky even to have been hired. Her citizenship did not entitle her to special treatment, they informed her. Chatfield was aghast: "Until now I would not have believed that any official of any government in the universe, even the meanest in existence, would have made an official statement that a citizen of his country was the same as 'people from all parts of the globe.'" Sorely disillusioned, Chatfield returned to the isthmus and finished out her time, then packed her suitcases for good and returned happily to the United States. In letters home to her literary club, she offered final advice for American sisters who might follow in her footsteps: "Do not feel proud because you are a citizen of and a daughter of the United States. These facts do not command respect here."[73]

The largest concentration of female employees could be found in the modern hospitals of the Canal Zone. A small group of nurses had been among the very first Americans to arrive on the isthmus after the United States finished negotiating the Hay–Bunau-Varilla Treaty in 1903. Many came to the isthmus with experience in the Philippines, Cuba, or Puerto Rico or on Indian reservations in the United States.[74] At a time when American women were strenuously discouraged from coming to the isthmus, these early nurses entered a land feared for the pervasive death and disease that had handicapped the French construction effort. They nursed American officials and employees through malaria and pneumonia and suffered through the terror in 1905 when yellow fever struck.

By 1908 several dozen nurses were working at each of the two main hospitals in the Zone, at Colón and Ancon. The latter, the larger of the two, could accommodate fifteen hundred patients at once. The lives of female nurses differed from those of male workers in many ways. They lived in female-only housing, and they faced special curfews and received greater scrutiny regarding their behavior (alcohol consumption seemed a particular concern). They also found their work environment extremely challenging. With hospitals divided into wards on the basis of gender, race, and sometimes nationality (there were special wards for women, Spaniards, and "coloreds"), nurses competed for assignments to the best wards. They protested particularly when assigned to the women's ward, as all agreed it lacked basic medical resources. It was difficult for them to assert authority around male patients, and sometimes they felt uncomfortable in the mostly male environment of the Canal Zone.[75]

A young nurse named Alice Gilbert recorded her impressions of the isthmus upon her arrival. Shown to her room in the nurses' quarters near the hospital, she was taken aback by the awful, damp odor emanating from within: "But when one is weary they will sleep and so it was only too soon morning and I was awakened by a great bell being rung on the porch by a colored man, that was the rising bell." She let the exotic sounds of tropical birds outside her room bring her more fully awake, then hurried down the hill to the mess. Gilbert quickly realized she would need to learn a few words of Spanish since the waiters spoke nothing else. At work, she found the hospital a busy place. Each ward had about twenty-two beds, yet "frequently we had cots down the center of the wards and on the porches and all filled." The nurses dreaded mosquitoes and doses of quinine as much as patients did, and Gilbert described her many sleepless nights trying to catch mosquitoes that had somehow slipped inside her netting.[76]

Yet the life of a nurse in the Canal Zone involved some unusual rewards. These included a sense of empowerment that came from working with a group of highly skilled and well-paid women. Nurses were sorely needed, and yet turnover among them was high, as unmarried nurses frequently met and married canal employees. All this could make nurses a difficult group to manage, yet because they were highly visible symbols of the government's authority, officials repeatedly felt compelled to control their work habits and appearance. In 1911 an effort by the government to introduce more stringent rules regarding uniforms demonstrated not only officials' determination to manage every aspect of women's work lives but also how tenaciously nurses stood up for their rights as they perceived them. Unlike many other American workers, these women appealed not primarily to their equal rights as citizens but rather to their right, *as women,* to gender equality.

Previously, nurses had been required only to wear a white skirt and blouse; the rest of their attire was left to their discretion. Now Goethals decided, with input from William Gorgas and the superintendent of hospitals, Charles Mason, to prohibit French heels, require caps and rubber heels, and specify in detail the design of the skirt and blouse. Nurses had to hire a seamstress to make the uniform, and officials allowed a month before the new requirements would take effect. To the officials' surprise, opposition emerged—particularly among nurses at Ancon Hospital.[77]

The historical record does not reveal how nurses initially responded to the new rules, but they must have found a way to express their opposition, because as the deadline approached, their superintendent felt nervous about enforcing the rules. He seemed to panic and wrote his superiors, he said, to "ascertain the extent of my authority in enforcing obedience." Would he be supported if forced to "resort to measures of compulsion"? He anticipated that at least a few nurses would refuse to wear the new uniforms. Therefore, he planned to mark any such nurses as absent without permission. If his superiors felt unwilling to support such discipline, he cautioned, and unless there existed another plan for dealing with "determined insubordination," then "it would seem better to rescind the order than to expose existing authority to an undermining influence."[78]

When sanitary officers decided weeks later to discipline any insubordinate nurses and suspend them without pay, the nurses raised a vocal and effective protest. The nurse Lucy Busbey wrote Goethals a personal note of protest, asking "why, among the many thousand employees of the I.C.C. a special discrimination should be made requiring us to buy and wear a special uniform?" Officials argued that because nurses wore a special uniform while in school, they should wear one now. To this Busbey retorted that undoubtedly many male employees likewise wore uniforms at school. "Therefore why should a few women who happened also to be educated in institutions requiring a school uniform be especially discriminated against in this matter and on their small salaries be required to incur this extra expense?" Other nurses complained to Goethals that the current uniform had been acceptable for seven years and wondered why a change was now suddenly necessary. Bowing to their protests, Goethals delayed the starting date for the new uniforms and ordered an investigation into the entire matter.[79]

To the hospital superintendent the issues involved were relatively simple. A cap would highlight the dignity of nurses, providing them with a "symbol of office" while also enhancing discipline in the wards. The nurse Genevieve Russell agreed, writing Goethals, "As a nurse in the United States and in several foreign countries I have found the wearing of my cap and uniform my surest protection. It is only as men instantly recognize in us women set apart, and in a way consecrated, . . . that they and we can be saved embarrassment and misunderstanding." The cap, Russell argued, was the key, the symbol that established the "relation of patient and nurse—without it we appear simply women in white dresses, working around among the men." But most nurses at Ancon Hospital disagreed with Russell. A letter signed by fifty-three of them, which included the vast majority of nurses there, protested to Goethals against wearing the new uniforms and caps. The latter they particularly despised, saying, "The cap is very impractical and entirely conspicuous in a hospital constructed on the plan of Ancon."[80]

Three months after the issue had first been raised, after a thorough investigation, Goethals ordered the new requirements put into effect. He accommodated the nurses as best he could, saying they could continue wearing their old uniforms as long as possible. Only when normal wear and tear forced replacing their uniforms with new ones would the new regulations be enforced with regard to the style of the skirt and blouse. Nurses must begin wearing the cap and rubber heels immediately, he declared. Perhaps content with this compromise, the nurses apparently ended their protest and complied with Goethals's order.[81]

Another sign that officials thought it important, if difficult, to improve efficiency among nurses can be seen in their reliance on some of the most innovative tools of labor management that had been devised by early-twentieth-century corporate capitalism. The officials made use of scientific management, a system of thought developed in the United States. Taylorism, as it was also known, after its creator Frederick Winslow Taylor, became popular among employers seeking effective labor management strategies. Taylorism combined detailed studies of employees' efficiency with an extensive division of labor in order to better control them and maximize their productivity. Although originally intended for industrial environments, it became influential even in white-collar settings where female workers were predominant (among department store clerks, for example, and clerical workers). Therefore, it is not surprising that officials in the Canal Zone would turn to Taylorism.[82]

In 1908 and 1909 officials decided they should reduce the number of nurses working at Colón Hospital. Forty-two nurses worked there; officials determined seven would be dismissed and three others would be transferred to Ancon Hospital. The nurses were evaluated by the chief nurse and by three doctors. Each evaluator was asked to rank all forty-two nurses in order of their efficiency. Supervisors then compared the four ranked lists to determine which nurses would be retained. Evaluators assessed the medical knowledge of each nurse and her "purely professional ability," as well as her health, temperament, executive ability, and "subordination to discipline." Seniority was not to be included in the evaluation. W. H. May, an assistant of Goethals's, oversaw the process. He confessed that the procedure itself was rather inefficient, particularly since one of the doctors involved had no firsthand knowledge of the nurses.[83]

Virginia Mooney and Margaret Judge, two nurses discharged as a result of this exercise, refused to go without a battle. They protested to Goethals and claimed that personal prejudice had played a role. Virginia Mooney had worked on the isthmus since 1905 and nursed men through the yellow fever epidemic. Margaret Judge, a more recent hire, questioned why her service would suddenly be considered inefficient when previously her superiors considered her more than satisfactory. She also specifically raised the issue of seniority, protesting that more recent arrivals had been ranked more highly than she had.[84]

The evaluators, despite officials' instructions, focused more on behavior, personality, and temperament than on the nurses' skills or lack thereof. Most who testified regarding Margaret Judge's efficiency agreed she possessed fine executive ability. However, some found her unable to maintain order on the wards, especially when a patient proved troublesome. Others declared that she irritated patients more than other nurses did. The chief nurse particularly evaluated nurses with an emphasis on their personal style: "Miss Ledden has a suave, easy manner; takes things easy, and while patients say things that would irritate . . . Miss Judge, they would not her." Another nurse she described as "quiet and not excitable." In the end, government officials decided Margaret Judge should be fired, and the grounds they gave concerned her temperament: "I believe her to be thoroughly competent professionally. I confess, however, that her youth and slight frame, together with her extreme nervous excitement impresses me that she was not among the best suited to the hard conditions of nursing on the Isthmus."[85]

Judge complained and tried to refocus the investigation on her superior's work record. She declared that the chief nurse was herself inefficient and was prejudiced against her. But the chief of hospitals, H. R. Carter, found Judge's claim of prejudice unconvincing. Whenever he had witnessed a disagreement between a nurse and a chief nurse, he declared, the former had always charged the latter with bias. He attributed this to the fact that "a sense of absolute justice does not seem to be a feminine characteristic." While he had qualms about the way the medical staff determined the efficiency rankings, and felt sure they were not entirely correct, he also believed that no "intentional injustice has been done," and he could not think of any way to make the efficiency rankings perfectly accurate. He recommended that the government let the rankings stand. Margaret Judge caught the next ship home for the United States.[86]

"KEEP THE EMPLOYEES CONTENTED AND SATISFIED"

In their struggle to keep productivity high in the Canal Zone, ICC officials sought ways to control employees' leisure as well as work hours. The first chief engineer, John Wallace, had declared in 1905 that amusements and diversions could not feasibly be provided in the Zone. Others thought differently. In 1904, as the U.S. occupation of the Canal Zone began, Secretary of War William Howard Taft worried that he would be sending thousands of men to the isthmus to suffer moral degradation: "As we know from our experience in the Philippines, the one great thing that leads to dissipation and dissolute habits, is the absence of reasonable amusements and recreation and occupation during the hours when the men are not at work." Initially, ICC officials had their hands full combating yellow fever, making decisions about the design of the canal, and building housing, hotels, and cafeterias to provide for the thousands of workingmen. These responsibilities consumed officials through 1904 and 1905. By 1906 and 1907, however, their attention had turned more to engaging employees in pleasant and controlled amusements during their hours away from work. Officials decided that creating a regimented and disciplined workforce required extensive intervention into employees' leisure time.[87]

From the beginning, the tropical environment provided some natural recreational opportunities. The nurse Louise Bidwell recalled that most nurses owned a horse and would go riding on their days off. Visiting the ruins of old Panama was a favorite excursion. Another nurse and one of the first women in the Zone, Alice Gilbert, described her horseback excursions: "The trails were good but the ticks and the red bugs were fierce. There was a trail that led to a tree on a hill in Gorgona in which you could stand and see the Atlantic and Pacific Oceans." She also recalled alligator hunts that lasted two days and involved camping in the jungle. On one trip she traveled with a group that killed fifty large alligators and reflected, "Don't you think that makes up for some of the things we miss by staying down here?"[88]

While they encouraged workers to take advantage of the beaches and other scenic attractions of Panama by giving them a free train pass each month, ICC officials also wanted to provide more organized forms of leisure. They saw this as particularly important for their male employees. Religious organizations eager to play a role in the Canal Zone submitted proposals outlining different possible approaches. The most comprehensive plan came from Clarence Hicks, the general secretary of the YMCA. He assessed conditions in the Zone in 1905 and concluded that his organization could play a beneficial role. Hicks itemized the many evil influences available to men in the Zone or nearby in Panama: gambling, bullfighting, cockfighting, and a great many saloons. On the other hand, influences for good behavior were notoriously missing: no libraries, no places of amusement, no meeting places for clubs or social interaction. Hicks concluded: "It is the deep conviction of the International Committee . . . that the establishing of Young Men's Christian Associations on the Isthmus would do more to make and keep the employees contented and satisfied than any one thing the Canal Commission might do." Because of the YMCA's reputation for instilling a moral sensibility among workers in the United States—and for simultaneously preventing labor unrest—officials chose it to maintain and supervise government club-houses in the Zone.

President Roosevelt personally intervened, writing chief engineer John Stevens in 1906 to urge him to work with the YMCA. The ICC should build "an attractive, wholesome, decent club, to which men won't have to be urged to go, but to which they will actually go of their on ac-cord, probably with the purpose of getting amusement, but with the result also of their own moral and physical betterment." It was important, Roo-sevelt stressed, that the clubhouses offer real diversion, and not just a single little room for prayer meetings. The YMCA had done admirable work among railroad men in the United States, and he knew the same moral improvement could be achieved among canal employees.[89]

By late 1907, ICC officials had built clubhouses in the four major towns of the Canal Zone—Empire, Gorgona, Culebra, and Cristobal—and turned them over to the International Committee of the YMCA to run. The clubhouse bylaws specifically limited membership to "white gold employees of the Canal Commission and Panama Railroad" and "other white residents of the Isthmus" who might be accepted as mem-bers by special action of the executive committee. The YMCA enforced the color line by ordering an investigation of personnel records when its officials suspected a person of color had attempted to pass as white in order to gain admission. White women could make use of the clubhouses for two afternoons—a total of five hours—each week. More than that, argued the YMCA's advisory committee, "would endanger the work for which the organization was intended."[90]

That real work involved encouraging better behavior among the white male American employees. For a fee of $12 per year the clubhouses provided white gold workers ("regardless of belief or creed") with librar-ies and reading rooms, pleasant spaces for writing letters, pool and bil-liards tables, bowling alleys, soda fountains, and gymnasiums equipped with mats, boxing gloves, fencing equipment, and more. Organizations formed by white American employees now had a place to meet, and clubs that focused on photography, Bible study, singing, Spanish, mechanical drawing, chess, checkers, and production of minstrel shows all took advantage of the opportunity. Police chief George Shanton noted the beneficial influence of the YMCA that same year, writing to its manager: "There is less rowdyism, less loafing in and around saloons, and less drinking among the Americans since the organization of the Y.M.C.A. than ever before."[91]

Yet the clubhouses seemed not to achieve their promise. Workingmen again demonstrated that they had a different vision from that of ICC officials. The ICC had planned to build four more clubhouses in 1909 as money became available, but for several reasons officials decided to build only one more. In a revealing report written in 1910, chief engineer Goethals assessed what had happened to the ambitious hopes for the clubhouses. Although there had been significant enthusiasm at first among employees, membership had fallen significantly in the years since they opened. Particularly in Gorgona, the machine shop town with the greatest number of skilled workers, membership had declined from 72 percent of all employees in 1907 to only 44 percent by 1910. Membership currently stood at little more than a thousand men, out of a working population of some five thousand. Goethals explained why: "The clubhouses do not draw the men who work in the ditch." At Empire and Culebra membership remained higher, but both towns had a larger number of white-collar employees. The men who worked in offices found the clubhouses fit more easily into their lives, "as they can always be suitably dressed, [and] present a better personal appearance than men who work in the Cut from eight to ten hours per day."[92]

There was more involved than clothing, however, Goethals admitted. He noted that officials had learned workmen did not care to see the YMCA program expand, "unless the clubhouses were placed under their own management, or they could have more voice in the manner of their operation." Workers most pointedly expressed unhappiness with the fact that on Sundays, the one day of the week most of them had free, many activities were not available at the clubhouses. The reading rooms and correspondence tables were open on Sunday, and club meetings and talks were allowed. The clubhouse rules stipulated that on Sundays "good music and good fellowship will be prominent features" while "games are set aside in keeping with the custom of the American people." Goethals noted that "discontent had started in the Culebra Clubhouse, resulting in a largely-signed petition for Sunday opening of the billiard room and bowling alley." Thus while the YMCA clubhouses continued to operate, overall they proved an expensive and limited experiment. In the United States, YMCA facilities were popular and effective as a medium for instilling middle-class notions of respectability in workingmen. In the Canal Zone, they proved instead another vehicle for negotiations between workers and government officials.[93]

ICC efforts to regulate leisure time extended well beyond the YMCA clubhouses. Officials outlawed gambling and worked strenuously to enforce the law, raiding bachelor dormitories in search of illegal poker games or craps. Dances were held every other Saturday night at the Hotel Tivoli, attended by women and men in their nicest attire and ready to dance until midnight. Officials built baseball fields, and teams sprang up in each major town, their games popular with players and spectators alike. Singing and theatrical groups from the United States toured the Zone frequently. Social clubs like the Masons and the Red Men opened lodges in most towns and quickly signed up many skilled workers. Independent clubs also sprang up. Louise Bidwell remembered being invited by a group called Tropical Tramps to take a boat trip to Taboga Island. A rowdier singing group called the Society of the Chagres Hymnal declared as one of its rules: "Members who have taken less than six drinks will not be allowed to join in the song service. Whiskey tenors will please stick to the key."[94]

As the latter suggests, alcohol was a serious matter in the Zone. It formed an important part of the day for most workers, and so for officials it became a matter of deliberate and careful regulation. They knew workers would acquire alcohol one way or another, and so they reluctantly allowed it but managed consumption as best they could. There were as many as sixty-three saloons in the Zone at any time. The writer Willis Abbot described them as "rough, frontier whisky shops." In order to prevent the saloons from becoming social centers, officials allowed no chairs or tables. No alcohol was sold in ICC hotels, although customers could sometimes bring a libation with them to their table. In July 1913, as the construction project moved toward completion and the challenge of managing workers seemed less worrisome, all liquor licenses were suspended, and the Zone became dry in order to be in agreement with federal law that prohibited alcohol on government property. Even before then, however, the Canal Zone became known for regimentation of leisure hours as well as work, another sign of the extensive state intervention. In the rough and hardworking environment of the Canal Zone, it seemed that every effort by the government to control U.S. workers' lives led those workers to seek outlets beyond the legal boundaries of the Zone even more energetically.[95]

A MERICAN CITIZENS working to build the canal, male and female, white and black, lived and worked in the Zone in ways very different from one another. They were separated by boundaries that granted or denied privileges according to current understandings of race, gender, citizenship, and skill. Because of the nature of government in the Zone, the so-called benevolent despotism, the state intervened thoroughly in their lives. Improving their working and living conditions necessarily involved the government, but it also required choosing whether to enforce or transgress the boundaries that separated them from others. Along the way U.S. employees proved more difficult to manage than officials expected or cared to admit. African Americans challenged the racialized segregation system, while female clerical workers and nurses argued for equal treatment. Citizenship rights emerged most often as the basis of employees' protests.

The most privileged of all employees demonstrated the system's harsh character. By 1907 white male gold workers had bargained, complained, lobbied, quit, or organized strikes in order to achieve comfortable lives in the Canal Zone. The power and perks of skilled workers combined with the demands for full productivity and cost efficiency to prod officials toward a rethinking of the nature and purposes of the silver and gold system. Goethals and his staff fine-tuned existing policies and invented new ones to manage and discipline workers—such as replacing white American workers with lower-paid West Indians. The ICC's strategies placed white skilled workers in a contradictory situation. They became more fully embedded in the system and more actively agents of their expansionist nation—seeking ways to enforce their privileges, emerging as spokesmen for the silver and gold system, pushing for firing of aliens, and complaining when nonwhite workers attempted to break through the color line. Yet simultaneously their positions in the Zone became vulnerable and threatened as officials replaced them with West Indians. This generated unhappiness among skilled workers and unacceptable rates of turnover. Officials had tamed their most powerful employees, but maximum productivity required more. It demanded that workers be satisfied enough with life in the Canal Zone to keep the protracted, ten-year project going. So ICC officials sought other mechanisms for managing and calming their workforce, turning increasingly to leisure activities as a diversion and encouraging workers' wives to come and provide the comforts of home. Yet these, too, emerged as arenas of conflict and mediation.

Meanwhile, a vaster challenge awaited the ICC officials. The tens of thousands of West Indians and southern Europeans who carried out the heaviest and dirtiest labor involved in building the canal, and who lived much less comfortable lives, were explicitly excluded by gold workers' emphasis on their rights as citizens. They labored for a nation that refused to see itself as an empire yet treated them like colonial subjects, a nation that saw them as outsiders yet did not hesitate to use them as a tool to curb the power of their white American employees. Officials never counted on their West Indian workers as allies, but they expected to find them a tractable and pliant source of labor. Those ideas would be dashed at nearly every turn.

CHAPTER THREE

SILVER LIVES

A GRENADIAN man named Isaac McKinzie came to the Canal Zone at age twenty-four and got work as a helper building the canal's lock gates. The year was 1912, and the U.S. government had contracted out to McClintic-Marshall the building and installing of the gigantic lock gates. For unskilled silver employees this was extremely dangerous work, frequently resulting in injuries or even death. McKinzie's job involved climbing down into the gate and guiding or extracting bolts that more skilled workers hammered through from outside. Just the day before, another silver employee had quit when ordered to do this task, but McKinzie accepted the job. He had worked for two weeks at the assignment when one of the bolts went in crooked and he was instructed to direct it as workingmen tried from the outside to straighten it. There was no light inside the gate, and so McKinzie had to get down very close to the bolt to see it. As he was bending down to examine the bolt, a skilled worker on the outside of the lock gate shouted, "Watch out then!" as he hit the bolt hard with his hammer. The bolt shot straight into McKinzie's head and shattered his eyeball. A surgeon removed his eye, and he spent a month in the hospital recuperating without pay.[1]

After he left the hospital, McKinzie sued the company for damages and asked for $10,000. The company's lawyer argued that McKinzie was to blame, that he had failed to take proper precautions, and that many other men were performing the same job and never complained about it. The circuit court of the Canal Zone found in McKinzie's favor but ordered him an award of only $500. The judge argued that he had lost only one eye, thus he was not disfigured, and so would still be able to work. McKinzie wasn't satisfied. He appealed the case to the Supreme Court of the Canal Zone, which found that given the pain and suffering he endured, and because his livelihood would be threatened for the rest of his life, the amount awarded to him should be $1,200.

West Indians inhabited a difficult world and confronted racist hostility and condescension from their U.S. employers. Only after 1908 did the U.S. government provide compensation for disabilities or death, and then only for artisans and laborers engaged in work considered "hazardous," and only if evidence was provided that they were not responsible for causing the injury. Before that time, the U.S. government gave injured silver workers only free medical attention and time off without pay.[2] Like McKinzie, many disabled West Indians fought aggressively for financial support they believed was due to them. McKinzie's case was unusual both because he pursued it all the way to the Supreme Court and because he won a large financial reward. Often West Indians lost their court cases, with judges ruling in favor of the defendants or dismissing the cases altogether. Yet West Indians' energetic use of the legal system to try to achieve justice suggests their creative ability to adapt in the face of an unfamiliar and bureaucratic foreign government.

McKinzie's case not only reflects the pathos of occupational injuries that so often afflicted West Indian workers but also demonstrates a degree of persistence and assertiveness that disproves common assumptions held at the time about West Indians. Officials like John Stevens saw West Indians as exotic creatures, lazy and unintelligent albeit gentlemanly. In fact, West Indians developed a wide range of strategies to shape their personal and working lives, improve their circumstances, and resist attempts by government officials to control them. Some, like McKinzie, used the judicial system to push for recognition and enforcement of their rights. Others devised more subterranean strategies involving careful choices to work and live where or how they wished. For West Indians, geographical and occupational mobility provided one of the most effective tools for creating independence for themselves in the regimented and industrialized Canal Zone. Viewing life and work from their perspective makes the world of the construction project look different. Officials could not conceive that silver workers developed such complex strategies and calculations. Nonetheless, the commissioners, engineers, and foremen of the ICC had to find ways to respond to West Indian laborers' actions, choices, and life strategies.

THE WORLD OF SILVER WORK

When U.S. occupation of the Canal Zone began in 1904, nearly two thousand Jamaicans already lived there, many of them men who had migrated to the isthmus to work for the French canal project during the 1880s.[3] These West Indians witnessed a spectacular transformation of the isthmus as the Americans began to arrive. The story of one young Jamaican, Constantine Parkinson, suggests how dramatic the reconstruction of Isthmian geography must have seemed. Parkinson was born on the isthmus in 1894 and lived in the little town of Playa de Flor on the Atlantic coast near Toro Point, just across the bay from Colón, where the sound and smell of the sea were a part of daily life. The town was made up mainly of Jamaicans. Parkinson's father, originally from Jamaica, probably worked on the French canal effort. When Parkinson was nearly nine, Panama achieved independence, and the United States acquired control over the Zone. Then, like a hurricane hitting the isthmus, the Americans built roads and bridges, housing, cafeterias, hotels, and commissaries. Whole towns sprang up to provide homes for the thousands of canal workers, with sections casually referenced as "Jamaicatown" or "Greektown." Other towns disappeared altogether. Parkinson's home village of Playa de Flor vanished as the United States undertook fortifications of the coastline and built a vast Army outpost named Fort Sherman in its place. Parkinson played a small supporting role in these transformations. As a teenager, in 1909, he felt himself pulled into the eye of the Americans' storm, taking a job as flagman in a surveyor's gang near his home. The survey gang was clearing a path to build a railroad through the area as a preliminary to the fortification work. In that first year alone, Parkinson changed jobs two more times, working as a water boy for a clearing gang and as a chain man with a different survey gang. In the next years he kept switching jobs, finally ending up in 1913 with work as a railroad brakeman back at Toro Point, where construction of Fort Sherman had begun.[4]

Most West Indians working on the canal during the American period were not born on the isthmus, like Parkinson, but came from islands across the Caribbean. From the beginning of the project, West Indians dominated the workforce: according to the ICC's 1912 census, out of a total population in the Zone of sixty-two thousand, more than thirty thousand originated on islands across the Caribbean. Their world included a complex set of cultures, a diversity that is hidden by the generic label of "West Indian" that observers applied to them. West Indians were most often from the British Caribbean, but many came from French islands as well. The major recruiting offices were in Barbados, St. Kitts, and, until 1907, Martinique and Guadeloupe, and thus many West Indians who boarded ships for Panama had come from these islands. Hundreds of others, however, came on their own from islands that had restricted emigration. Most commonly they had left jobs as plantation workers on islands like Barbados, Jamaica, St. Lucia, St. Kitts, Antigua, Grenada, and Trinidad, kissing loved ones good-bye and heading for the Americans' jobs in Panama. They ranged in age from their early teens to their midthirties. They were leaving islands where unemployment, labor surplus, and low wages made it difficult to earn a decent living.[5]

There was a broad range in skill level among West Indians, and they inhabited a wide spectrum of social and economic status and respectability. The ICC classified them according to one of three categories that overlapped rather murkily: laborers, artisans, and those on a monthly salary. Laborers were West Indians who performed unskilled labor; artisans were those engaged in a craft; and the monthly salaried category included both skilled and unskilled West Indians whose hours of work were irregular. During the peak period of construction in 1909, the ICC recorded more than five thousand silver roll employees on monthly salary, at least half of whom would have been West Indians (other silver employees paid on a monthly salary included Europeans, Panamanians, and Colombians). Several hundred of the salaried West Indians were white-collar employees such as policemen, teachers, storekeepers, and clerical workers, who composed the elite of their society in the Canal Zone. Policemen and teachers played especially important roles as figures of authority in the West Indian community, even though their numbers were relatively small. Close behind them were West Indians on monthly payroll whose work was seen as involving some skill and responsibility: bakers, cooks, waiters, barbers, foremen, watchmen, ship captains, steam-shovel and dredge engineers, firemen, and blacksmiths, followed by less skilled workers such as grave diggers, coal passers, janitors, and launderers.[6]

The ICC's use of the term "artisan" to describe West Indian craftsmen was particularly interesting. The label was intended only for West Indians. Although many Europeans worked on the silver roll, they were virtually never referred to as artisans. During congressional hearings into labor conditions in the Canal Zone conducted late in 1909, the chief quartermaster, Carrol A. Devol, characterized the artisans: "Altogether negroes. . . . Very few of the Spaniards are artisans." Although thousands of white U.S. citizens worked at a craft much as these West Indians did, they were referred to as skilled mechanics, not as artisans. Devol explained: "The skilled mechanics are on the gold roll, and what are called artisans are on the silver roll." One gold carpenter (typically a white U.S. citizen) might oversee eight to twelve silver carpenters (West Indians); one gold plumber might manage an area with a few silver plumbers under him. Organizing the work around a small number of mechanics versus a larger group of artisans was useful and efficient, Devol declared, for "there is economy in it." The congressman interviewing Devol in this case finally grasped the situation: "The difference between an artisan and a mechanic is a matter of color?" Devol responded affirmatively.[7]

From 1907 onward, as concerns about cost efficiency led ICC officials to replace white firemen, electricians, painters, masons, and other skilled craftsmen with West Indians, the number of artisans increased. As excavation work moved toward completion after 1910, the number of West Indian laborers diminished. As a result of these trends, artisans became a more important part of the West Indian community. Their group included plumbers, blacksmiths, masons, painters, electricians, carpenters, coppersmiths, car repairers, machinists, boilermakers, drill runners, drill helpers, molders, and pipe fitters. In 1909 the ICC reported having more than thirty-seven hundred artisans on its payroll; by the summer of 1914 that number had risen to more than nine thousand. The ICC paid most artisans the equivalent of sixteen to twenty cents in U.S. currency per hour throughout the construction decade. Several hundred more artisans, those with the greatest skills, were paid as much as twenty-five cents in U.S. currency per hour.[8]

Although the artisanal and white-collar elite might come from any of the Caribbean islands, two main groups were represented: Jamaicans and Martinicans. Most policemen and teachers and many skilled workers were Jamaicans. Their higher status in part derived from the experience many had gained during the French construction era. In addition, the steep emigration tax imposed on Jamaicans by their government meant that those who traveled to the Zone were more likely to have some resources, skills, and education. Because they formed one of the largest groups in the Zone and held elite positions in the community, Jamaicans were at times resented by other West Indians. During the early years of construction, especially from 1905 to 1907, Martinicans also held many of the skilled jobs, although they often spoke little or no English. By 1907, when the Martinican government changed emigration laws, approximately fifty-five hundred Martinicans had entered the employment of the ICC.[9]

Most West Indians, however, filled the much-needed category of unskilled laborers, and this, too, was a complex, regimented, and carefully categorized group. Nearly ten thousand West Indians worked as unskilled laborers as construction hit full intensity in 1909. Unskilled laborers included, at the lowest wage category (five U.S. cents per hour), young water boys and messengers and adult men who had been injured on the job and thus could not perform taxing labor. Most West Indians (more than six thousand in 1909, for example) worked as the classic "pick and shovel" men, earning ten U.S. cents per hour and doing the heaviest, hardest work in Culebra Cut, on building construction sites, or at Gatun Dam. They were typically separated into gangs and supervised at tasks like digging out a steam shovel buried in a landslide, pulling a car along railroad tracks when there was no engine to do the labor, or building roads. A final category of West Indian laborers included some two thousand men who worked as helpers to artisans or skilled mechanics and received thirteen cents per hour.[10]

These differences in pay, skill, and status made for significant disparities among West Indians in terms of their economic resources, their ability to send money home, and their ability to afford comfortable housing in Panama City or in Colón. Those who made a bit more money found it easier to escape the regimentation of the Zone and afford a nicer place in Panama. There were also differences between people who came from the various islands, and these contrasts typically escaped the notice of white observers. French and British West Indians might see life and work in very different ways, and even among the British West Indians tensions emerged. Besides the common resentment toward skilled Martinicans and Jamaicans, and the anger many West Indians reserved for Jamaican policemen they considered particularly cruel, cultural differences separated islanders from one another. Divisions based on language, religion, or the colonial policies of Britain and France meant that the diverse groups often had little in common. The ICC tended to put men from each island in separate gangs, but because they were housed and ate in cafeterias close to one another, disagreements among them often arose. A Jamaican carpenter working for the ICC explained that crowded housing contributed to such disagreements: "There is no sense in putting so many different races together—Jamaicans and Bims [Barbadians] and Martiniques in the same room. It is not right. What use are the Martiniques, anyway? They don't understand English, and when the boss tells one to pick up a stick he will pick up a stone. They ought to get all Jamaicans and pay them better." Over time, their presence in a foreign land and exposure to similar treatment by their U.S. employers would create a common bond among West Indians and consequently some basis for broader solidarities, but during the construction era the divisions between groups remained deep.[11]

"SOMEBODY DYING EVERY DAY"

In the 1960s the Isthmian Historical Society held a competition for the "best true stories" of work and life during the construction era, and this resulted in submissions from several dozen West Indians. The entries came from islands across the Caribbean and from Panama. Most of those who wrote up their memories had worked not as laborers but at a craft or white-collar job, so for the most part they had faced less danger than did the unskilled laborers working in places like Culebra Cut. Nonetheless, the memoirists repeatedly stressed the danger of their work. Dynamite explosions, landslides, steam shovels toppling over, cranes swinging quickly by and crushing heads as they went, railroad accidents, falls from scaffolding while building the enormous locks and gates, and all the various diseases generated significant anxiety. A man named Albert Banister worked in the boiler room at Cristobal and related how casually death appeared in conversations: "Man die get blow up get kill or get drown during the time someone would asked where is Brown he died last night and burry where is Jerry he dead a little before dinner and buried so on and so on all the time." Reginald Beckford, who worked as a messenger, a mail clerk, and then a salesman at a commissary, recalled: "It was nothing unusual to be walking on Front Street and sudenly you sees a yard engine with one I.C.C. flat car attached with dead men streched out, whose faces cannot be seen, because a piece of clean white canvas, the length of the car covers their faces, moving slowly towards the Old Colon Freight House. . . . The people in the vicinity gathers, including myself, trying to get a glimpse of their faces. You can't. The canvas covers their faces. A policeman is on duty to prevent the people from going too near."

Constantine Parkinson remembered various terrors that cast a shadow during the years he worked on the canal. He watched one time as a landslide swallowed a large number of workers, most of them Europeans. Workers toiled day and night to dig the bodies out of the dirt and rocks, finding money tied around the waists of many of the dead men—the safest place, in the eyes of Spaniards and Greeks, to keep the money they were saving. "In construction days," Parkinson concluded, "people get kill and injure almost every day and all the bosses want is to get the canal build." One day Parkinson unfortunately joined the ranks of West Indians injured on the job. In 1913, eighteen years old and working as a railroad brakeman in the Zone, Parkinson fell victim to a train accident. Rushed to the hospital in Colón, he underwent surgery to amputate one leg and part of his other foot. Doctors feared he would die, but Parkinson survived, and years later still remembered what he saw upon awakening: "I notice all kinds of cripples around my bed without arms foot one eye telling me to cheer up not to fret we all good soldiers." The accident ended Parkinson's service on the construction project. After waiting a year, he returned to the hospital, where doctors fitted him with an artificial leg. "It was a big day for me returning home as many said that I would not live."[12]

Yes, one veteran remembered, "the flesh of men flew in the air like birds many days johncrows feed on the bowels of men around the jungles." Illness could be avoided only with great luck. If you missed seeing a friend for a few days or a week, it was said, "don't wonder, he's ether in the hospital or at Monkey Hill [later renamed Mount Hope Cemetery] resting in peace." Nehemiah Douglas recalled working as a rigger on a crane when the cable broke, killing several men instantly: "The amount of blood that flowed gave the appearance of a little gully, and when I saw what appeared an island of blood, I got nervous, I think, because how I got down, I do not know; but I got down and ran like never run a man before, straight home in Paraiso. So fast did I run that when I arrived home I heard the whistle giving the knock off signal." Death became one more matter for the ICC to handle: officials extended railroad tracks all the way to Mount Hope Cemetery so that they might dispose of the dead more efficiently.[13]

Such dangers and threats were reflected in West Indians' songs as well.

Among a vast repertoire of work songs, they frequently chose to sing one plaintively titled "Somebody Dying Every Day." In the geographer Bonham Richardson's interviews with canal workers and their children in Barbados conducted during the 1980s, the death of loved ones remained a vivid memory. When someone died in the Canal Zone, a friend or relative would send a mourning letter, its envelope bordered in black, to break the news to family back home. Claudine Cadogan of St. James, Barbados, remembered the fear of receiving that black symbol of death: "Once when I was a small girl, I heard people moaning and crying out. I went to the house and saw the mother holding a black-bordered envelope and crying. That meant her son had died in Panama."[14]

Government officials' reactions to issues of health and safety provide an indication of how differently they and other white Americans experienced the construction project. According to officials, the death rate in the Canal Zone was remarkably low: by the end of the construction era they specified it was less than 0.08 percent, a lower rate than in even the healthiest states of the United States. This statistic led to boasts that the U.S. government had finally "conquered the tropics for the white race." Certainly conditions were vastly better than during the French era, and they compared favorably to those in many industrial and company towns in the United States and in sites of capitalist development around the world. However, accidents, illness, and death, like everything else in the Zone, followed a color line. Officials conceded that the vast majority of deaths occurred among West Indians. According to government figures, approximately 5,600 people died during the U.S. construction of the canal. Of those, 4,500 were black (predominantly West Indians), and only 350 were white U.S. citizens. However, this figure is inaccurately low, particularly regarding West Indian mortalities. The historian Michael Conniff has shown that poor record keeping, a common tendency among West Indians to change both their jobs and their names, and the fact that they often lived in the towns and cities of Panama rather than in the Canal Zone resulted in many unrecorded deaths. Conniff estimates the mortality figure to be close to 15,000 among West Indians over the course of the U.S. construction decade—or about 10 percent of all immigrants.[15]

Conditions were roughest in the early years. Claude Mallet, the British consul who represented the interests of British West Indians in the Canal Zone, reported on the hardship workers faced in 1905: "I was frequently appealed to by large bodies of labourers who alleged they had not been paid their wages, in some instances for six weeks, and were bordering on a state of destitution." They also complained bitterly about the harshness of Zone policemen and foremen in 1905. And disease was at its worst during this early period. By 1906 sanitation officials had gotten yellow fever under control, and by 1908 sanitation and medical improvements had at last resulted in declining rates of pneumonia and malaria. Yet those diseases remained a threat throughout the construction era, as did accidents on and off the job. Few West Indians managed to avoid harm even if they did avoid death. In fiscal year 1912, for example, the Sanitation Department reported that 23,800 "colored persons" had received treatment in the hospital or at the "sick camps" in each town of the Zone, or had been reported as sick in their quarters. According to the census completed in February of that year, 31,525 West Indians lived in the Zone; even if we add the several thousand more who worked for the United States but lived in the Republic of Panama, this means that as many as two-thirds of all West Indians reported sick or required medical attention during that year. West Indian workers and their families learned their way around the hospitals of the Canal Zone, most of them catching malaria several times and confronting injury more than once. Like Constantine Parkinson, more than a few went home missing a limb or an eye.[16]

With the mortality rate vastly higher among West Indians than among white Americans, it becomes clear that death, like everything else in the Zone, was highly racialized. Poor sanitary conditions in West Indian communities—windows that lacked screens to bar mosquitoes, stagnant water near homes—would never have been tolerated in the white towns of the Zone. West Indians also were typically the ones victimized by landslides, dynamite explosions, or other industrial accidents. They worked through torrential rains, sometimes toiling for hours at digging or drilling in water up to their waists even after the rain subsided. Often they returned home from work with their clothes completely soaked. Most had only one set of clothes, particularly in the early years, and so they would get up the next day, put on wet clothes, and go back to work. "I came wet to my home and leave for work in rain," wrote a West Indian man.[17]

Aaron Clarke arrived in the Canal Zone in December 1906 and poignantly described his life and work. He and the others left the ship and boarded a train for the Jamaicatown near Gatun. Aaron was lucky, he recalled, because he was among the first to be assigned rooms in houses built by the ICC. Their predecessors had all lived in tents. They traveled to a mess kitchen where each received a plate, cup, and spoon (the cost of which would be taken out of their first paychecks). Then they formed a line and received rice and red beans, beef with gravy, bread, and tea. However, "the meals was of very low standard as far cooking was concerned." After eating, Aaron was put to work in the lumberyard. Over the years he held many different jobs. After six months in the lumberyard he cleaned railroad cars, then switched to the Sanitation Department. With the latter he performed several different jobs: "I dug ditches dropped mosquito oil made drains, dug graves acted as pallbearer and sometimes when we could afford the time I performed a short religious ceremony." He found conditions very rough. As late as 1908, he recalled, during the rainy season often all his clothes would be wet, even though by this time he had saved up and managed to purchase two or three sets of clothes. "But the majority of us used a scheme to put on those wet clothes, that is we took the clothes to the bath room with us and immediately leaving the shower without drying our skin we put the wet clothes on, took our breakfast and was off to work for another day of hard toil."

Life in the camps was difficult in other ways. At 7:00 a.m., a watchman would come around and fine those he found, unless they were sick, for their failure to work. At 9:00 p.m., officials would knock loudly on a metal bar to signal that lights must be turned out. The latrine or outhouse was a couple hundred feet away from the camp for sanitary reasons, and men were not allowed to use a basin in the camp to relieve themselves. And so, as Aaron Clarke put it, "you can imagine the hardship and difficulties that we encountered in those days especially on nights when the rain was falling." Even this seemed like paradise compared with the conditions that confronted the earliest workers, who bedded down their first nights on chain-link bunks covered with a piece of canvas, with no sheets, blankets, or pillows, "just the cold chain bunk."[18]

By 1907 conditions had greatly improved. However, visiting that year to investigate life and work in the Canal Zone, the reformer Gertrude Beeks still found a host of problems facing West Indian laborers. She complained about the small amount of space provided them in the dormitories, the metal bunks upon which many men slept, the lack of screens or mosquito netting, and the fact that some camps were built in low areas where the lack of drainage caused poor sanitary conditions. West Indians desperately needed warm showers, more blankets, better food, and sheds built near the heaviest construction areas for resting out of the rain and for keeping their clothes dry. But government officials countered that workers did not need sheds, and even if they did, the government lacked the money to build them. The rooms were large enough, the bunks comfortable enough, the food good enough, and protection from mosquitoes not necessary. Tellingly, Goethals responded to the request for netting by declaring it unnecessary because malaria was not a problem for West Indians: "It is generally admitted . . . that the colored people are immune." Actually, he declared, the greatest death rate among Negroes was due to pneumonia, and so mosquito netting would not make a significant improvement.[19] The government finally did take steps to control the rate of pneumonia, building some sheds where laborers might dry their clothes, selling flannel cloth (which West Indians bought for making undergarments), and making sure the men had blankets. Yet these measures never brought either malaria or pneumonia under control.

In 1912, Gorgas testified regarding two of the biggest health threats among West Indians. The first was nephritis (liver disease), which he declared was due to West Indians' consumption of large quantities of rum. The second was pneumonia, and he testified that it greatly concerned him and his medical staff. In 1906 the medical staff had faced an excessive problem with deaths from pneumonia. More workers died from it than from all other causes combined, and the vast majority of these were West Indians. Doctors carefully studied the situation and found the main cause was that laborers from Barbados and Jamaica generally had only one set of clothes: "They worked in the rain all day; a man would buy a few cents' worth of food in the morning, cook it himself, eat it, and go to work. . . . At night he would go to bed in his wet clothes." When Gorgas was asked what he had done about the high rates of pneumonia, he responded, "We have taken no particular measure," and explained that his board of experts studied the situation and found that the highest rates of pneumonia existed among workers who had recently arrived and caught the influenza that pervaded the isthmus. He therefore recommended that the government's sanitary measures focus not on preventing pneumonia or the spread of influenza but on treating those already ill. Meanwhile, he noted reassuringly, the government should expect that when the numbers of new workers declined, the rates of pneumonia would likewise decrease.[20]

Gorgas's determination to aggressively study pneumonia while doing little to treat it reflects the concerns of an ambitious young medical establishment eager to analyze and tame the tropics in order to make them safe and comfortable—for whites. Gorgas and his staff studied every possible disease, writing up their findings for medical journals. Their overly zealous research is evident in the number of unfortunate West Indians diagnosed as insane. Hundreds of people were committed to the insane wards of Ancon and Colón hospitals. Virtually all of them, to judge from the judicial records of the Panama Canal Zone, were West Indian. The records indicate some of the symptoms laborers manifested. For example, Arthur Andersen from Jamaica, aged eighteen, was admitted to the hospital in June 1911. He developed delusions, believing he had lost some relatives and fearing that someone "desired to have his foot cut off, to which he strenuously objected." He also had a tendency to engage in religious rants, "being obsessed with the idea that the end of the world is near," which caused him to begin preaching to imaginary people. As a result, this young man was permanently committed to the insane ward of the hospital. Likewise, Mary Gowdy, from Bridgetown, Barbados, had lived in the Canal Zone for five years. Her husband, a laborer for Swift and Company in Colón, contacted the insane asylum, as she was acting odd, believing herself persecuted. She refused to let nurses care for her and prayed in a loud voice.[21]

According to official records, these delusions, hallucinations, paranoia, and religious rants were rarely manifested among other groups. The legal records of the Canal Zone include innumerable cases of West Indians committed to the asylum for weeks or sometimes years as a result of such symptoms, and often West Indians complained to the British consul about having been wrongly institutionalized. In 1907 the ICC's annual report mentioned that an insanity ward and an asylum had been built at Ancon Hospital, but little detailed mention of the disease was made. By 1912 more than 550 people were being treated by the ICC for insanity; 9 were U.S. citizens, 43 were Europeans, and more than 500 were black West Indians. One might interpret the incidence of hospitalization for insanity as an unusual exercise in labor discipline, but this seems unlikely. The U.S. government had unlimited powers of deportation; if a laborer or family member proved troublesome, it would be far easier and cheaper to deport him or her. Committing laborers to the hospital, especially for an extended period, cost the U.S. government a significant sum of money. It seems more likely that the burgeoning curiosity of a young medical establishment, combined with a tendency to medicalize certain social and economic problems among West Indians (which in turn reflected their treatment by the ICC), provides the best explanation for this remarkable outbreak of insanity among one specific group of workers.[22]

To the constant presence of death, disease, and crippling accidents was added the strikingly callous response of some Americans to the distressing conditions West Indians faced. Reginald Beckford worked as a salesman in the commissary at Colón, one of the better jobs available to a West Indian. Every day he would watch as the 4:30 train pulled out for Panama City with an engineer named Billy at the throttle. Beckford remembered that Billy had a policy, "whether he is talking truth or not," "that he will stop his train on the tracks for a horse, or a cow but not for a human." One day while Beckford was waiting for the train, he discovered that

Billy had not been joking. After Billy's train roared by, Beckford saw people running toward the tracks. He followed and saw the "half body of a man laying on the tracks. The man had been cut clean across the abdomen. His hands untouched, his eyes opened. Where are his legs? His legs had been carried almost a city block." The train had continued on its journey after killing the unfortunate West Indian, not stopping until reaching its destination at Mount Hope Cemetery.[23]

The testimonies of West Indians about construction days include many references to the indignities to which American officials exposed them. Alfred Dottin declared, "I shall never forget the train loads of dead men being carted away daily, as if they were just so much lumber." Many spoke of feeling they were treated like animals. Jules Lecurrieux arrived on the isthmus and found "to our surprize we were unloaded off the train as animals and not men, and almost under strict guard to camps."[24] Marrigan Austin reached Colón after many days on a crowded ship with very little food. He and the other men were very hungry as they climbed off the ship, he said, after receiving scarce rations for days on end: "We saw . . . a pile of bags of brown sugar. And the whole crowd of us like ants fed ourselves on that sugar without questioning any one, and no one said any thing to us either." Later Austin took a job drilling dynamite holes, and he found conditions harrowing. He concluded: "Life was some sort of semi slavery, and there was none to appeal to, for we were strangers and actually compelled to accept what we got, for in any case of an argument we would have to shut up, right or wrong. And the bosses or policemen or other officials right or wrong could be always winning the game."[25]

Marrigan Austin was not the only one to compare conditions in the Canal Zone to slavery, and it's true that West Indians had few sources of leverage against their new employer. They had neither unions lobbying for them nor representatives who might appear before congressional committees to speak their case. Their main governmental resource, diplomatic representatives from their mother countries of Britain or France, was only inconsistently helpful, and the American public felt indifferent about the conditions they confronted. The U.S. government deliberately kept a huge surplus of unskilled Caribbean laborers on the isthmus in order to forestall any ambitious strategies of collective organizing. The government had many tactics for maintaining discipline among West Indians, including deportation, vagrancy laws, policing, and prison sentences.[26]

The Zone police force, consisting of white Americans (first-class policemen) and West Indians (second-class policemen), played a central role in disciplining residents of labor camps. M. H. Thatcher, the head of civil administration in the Zone, noted that West Indians on the police force were "very useful in dealing with the black population. . . . We do not give them the same police powers that we give white policemen, but we give them sufficient powers to be very useful in their work."[27]

The justice meted out by Zone policemen could be harsh. Harry Franck recalled being instructed as he left to patrol the town of Gatun one night: "New Gatun is pretty bad on Saturday nights. . . . The first time a nigger starts anything run him in, and take all the witnesses in sight along." Likewise, the writer Poultney Bigelow described at length policemen's reputation for petty extortion and harsh treatment of laborers: "I found on all sides among the poor, whether Jamaican negroes or Panamans, this dread of the big policeman who swaggered about as though it was his duty to club people in order to show his zeal for the canal." Police constantly monitored the labor camps, arresting men for vagrancy, loitering, drunkenness, or disorderly conduct. West Indians feared harassment at the hands of policemen and learned to act in a way that would not draw attention. A St. Lucian laborer recalled, "Many get beat up get kill by Canal Zone Police it never happen to me when you are respectible law abiding person Uncle Sam stand by you remember the Laws must be at all cost respected."[28]

Loiterers were either fined anywhere from $5 to $25 or sentenced to time in jail, and since the vast majority of West Indians could not afford such a fine, they typically faced prison. The Jamaican Charles Hamilton, for example, was standing on the porch of his room in Pedro Miguel when policemen came through asking men why they were not working. Hamilton said he had worked twenty-two days already that month and was taking the day off. The police arrested him and, upon checking his record, found he had worked only eight hours that month. Hamilton was tried, convicted of vagrancy, and, because he had also lied to police, given an unusually harsh sentence: thirty days in prison, a $25 fine, and all court costs. Occasionally, men sentenced to the penitentiary would try to escape to Cuba before being transferred to prison, and sometimes they succeeded. Cuba was seen as their refuge, as one man put it.[29]

In one two-week period during the summer of 1911, police sweeping through the labor camps and towns of the Canal Zone arrested thirty people for vagrancy, drunkenness, and such. The number of workers questioned for possible offenses was much higher. In one town alone, police detained and questioned some sixty men. All but five managed to provide a satisfactory explanation for their idleness. They typically declared they worked night jobs or were recovering from an accident or illness. Of the thirty arrested in towns across the Zone and taken to court, more than half were West Indians; the others were mainly Spaniards, Britons, Colombians, and Panamanians. The courts dismissed seven cases of the thirty, including the only two pressed against white Americans (a foreman and a sailor). All others received sentences ranging from five to thirty days in prison and fines from $5 to $20. The ICC records are filled with grievances by West Indians about police mistreatment. They complained of being arrested and imprisoned unjustly, of brutal beatings during the arrest, and sometimes of insulting comments made by policemen. If such an intimidating police presence combined with arrests and possible time in jail proved insufficient to eliminate idleness among canal workers, there was always the threat that serious offenders would be sent to the Zone penitentiary at Culebra, which housed 150 convicts as of 1912, the vast majority of them West Indians. Prisoners at the penitentiary were required to work at hard labor, which consisted most often of road construction. The acting head of civil administration, H. H. Rousseau, also instructed the chief of police to get the word out: "I think that if it becomes generally known that all prisoners in the Canal Zone are required to perform hard labor, it will have a very beneficial influence."[30]

"IF THEY DO NOT WORK THEY WILL STARVE"

Government officials' focus on vagrancy laws, deportation, and hard labor for convicts reflects the central fact that the vast army of West Indians was difficult to manage. The ICC couldn't construct the canal without these workers, yet disciplining them proved a major preoccupation. ICC officials looked to the British and French diplomatic representatives for help in managing West Indians and ensuring efficient labor; yet simultaneously, West Indians looked to the British and French governments for help in protecting their rights. This put the consuls from Britain and France in a complex position. Consider the case of the British consul in Panama, Claude Mallet. Mallet had begun his tenure on the isthmus when the French attempted to build the canal. During the U.S. construction decade he received regular complaints from West Indians regarding problems that ranged from harsh treatment by the Canal Zone or Panamanian police to unjust incarceration in insanity wards or jails, cruel foremen, or destitution when pay from the U.S. government came late. Mallet attended to some complaints, but he generally empathized with U.S. officials and shared their negative opinion of West Indians. Mallet reflected once upon the many strikes he had handled during the French and U.S. construction projects: "What I have always done has been to get the employer to do what is just towards the men and then tell them in unmistakable language to work, and if they do not work they will starve, and that if they disturb public order the government counts upon enough force to keep the peace, and their acts be upon their own heads if they suffer in consequence of defying armed forces."[31]

Throughout his years of service Mallet repeatedly proclaimed himself terribly impressed with American policies. President Roosevelt met with Mallet during his visit to the isthmus and asked him how he thought they were faring. Mallet began by noting that West Indians now lived far better than they had during the French era. Questioned more closely, the consul admitted that he had never personally inspected either the housing or the food supplied to them. Yet he confidently concluded that the complaints coming from them "were so few and trivial I generally found upon investigation that they had no foundation and therefore was convinced the labourers must be well treated and well cared for by the Commission."[32]

The evidence suggests a different reality: West Indians had solid ground for complaining about many aspects of their lives on and off the job. Mallet was certainly correct that conditions had improved since the days of French construction, particularly in terms of disease, but he shared with American officials many notions of West Indian inferiority that precluded him from seeing the necessity for humane treatment. West Indians' grievances were numerous, and one of the major problems they perceived was Mallet's neglectful behavior and reluctance to do more to improve their working and living conditions. Demanding that he be more helpful, West Indians appealed to the rights owed them by the British Commonwealth. When a laborer named Jacob Marsh lost his leg in 1911 and failed to receive a wooden replacement from the U.S. government, he pleaded with the British for assistance: "I know that my Mother Court will not for sake these few lines." Another West Indian wrote more angrily in 1914 about what he perceived as Mallet's dereliction of duty, and his unhappiness over the large numbers of laborers being imprisoned by the Panamanian government as construction neared completion and massive unemployment set in. He declared to Mallet that he knew the laws of England, and he knew West Indians legally deserved more help from their diplomatic representatives.[33]

Even back in Britain some worried that Mallet needed to do more. The socialist member of Parliament J. Keir Hardie declared his concern in 1908 at the high rate of disease (particularly tuberculosis) among West Indians, the fact that some were simply deported home to be cared for by impoverished family members, and the fact that the situation would now only worsen due to a recent order that the men continue working through the rain. He noted, "Surprise is expressed among American officials at the non-interference of the British government." His superiors in London instructed Mallet to investigate and provide a report on the matters Hardie had raised.[34]

Sometimes West Indians appealed directly to ICC officials for improvements. One option was to pursue a grievance through their immediate supervisors. The silver brakemen of Pedro Miguel and Las Cascadas, for example, wrote officials a polite note in 1913 and pointed out that they regularly worked late into the evening, plus Sundays and holidays, and should receive overtime pay for that, as did gold roll employees. They signed themselves "your faithful Servants and workers."[35] Other West Indians showed up at Colonel Goethals's office on Sunday morning to request help, and they tended to express very different concerns from white residents of the Zone. White workers and their families went to Goethals about a wide variety of problems, from troublesome coworkers to abusive or loud neighbors, while the majority of West Indian complaints focused on mistreatment by white police, foremen, or others in positions of authority. Haviland Nevers, for example, a West Indian fireman, complained to Goethals about a conflict with a conductor on the labor train as he headed from Empire to his job in Tabernilla. It began with a small act of rebellion on his part when he was either slow or unwilling to show his pass and pay the ten cents required for the trip. It ended with him getting hit in the head with a lantern, thrown off the train, and finally beaten by ten white workers seeking to assist the conductor and enforce his orders. Goethals's investigator interviewed several witnesses and concluded the beating had been unnecessary, but suggested that the conductor be given only a mild punishment, since Nevers had helped cause the problem through his "bullheaded" behavior.[36]

West Indians not only possessed fewer resources than white workers; they also found themselves scrambling to adjust to different circumstances from those they were accustomed to back home. The work routine in the Canal Zone was highly mechanized and regimented; the U.S. government's style was bureaucratic and more openly racist. A Jamaican carpenter who worked during both the French and the U.S. construction projects compared the two approaches. The United States, he said, was much more orderly. Zone policemen and harsher laws had nearly put a stop to quarrels, cockfighting, drinking, and dancing in the streets, and he approved of this: if a man shoots off a gun now that the United States is in control, "the police catch him and jerk him up to the prison so fast that his feet don't have a chance to touch the ground." Yet he said also that the workers toiled much harder under the Americans, even though they worked fewer hours, and that they were more afraid of the Americans than they had been of the French. The Americans remained quiet until they got really vexed, he observed, and then there was trouble. Finally, he noted, "The Americans are too much of schemers to waste time or money. There are no loafing jobs now, such as there used to be. It is like running a race all the time. You don't mind it for a day, but you can't keep it up."[37]

West Indians who had traveled to the isthmus found these new conditions and expectations challenging. Most of them had labored before coming to Panama on sugar or banana plantations, had cultivated small farms, or had worked in cities in small shops as craftsmen. British elites had encouraged workers' ties to the British Empire as sources of control. The labor system of the Caribbean was profoundly paternalistic and based on thorough legal, economic, and political domination, yet planters nurtured laborers' feelings of independence through piecework and sharecropping arrangements. Plantation laborers struggled, sometimes successfully, to save a bit of money so they could buy their own land. Despite the low pay and harsh conditions at home, many Caribbean workers looked back sentimentally at the way they had been treated there and found it distinctly superior to their treatment in the Zone.[38]

"YOU CAN NOT COERCE THEM VERY MUCH"

To more than a few West Indians, life and work in the Canal Zone seemed a step back from independence, and, perhaps fueled in part by nostalgia for the life left behind, they battled energetically with the U.S. government—especially over the conditions at work, and living and eating arrangements. They brought with them to Panama different work rhythms and attitudes from what the government officials and engineers desired. These latter groups hoped to see Caribbeans adopt industrial-style discipline, efficient work habits, and respect for authority. The contrasting expectations created profound tensions between the two groups, of the same sort that had played out so many times before around the world, for example, when Irish immigrants entered U.S. factories in the 1840s or when African American female sharecroppers moved to a nearby city and began working in domestic service. In such cases, just as in the Canal Zone, workers confronting a more regimented work environment resisted and found a way to assert their own priorities, while employers denounced them for their undisciplined approach.[39]

Government officials constantly compared Caribbeans with other groups and proclaimed that they provided inferior labor. Spaniards, Chinese, Panamanians—all, officials believed, would work harder and more efficiently than Barbadians or Jamaicans. Leading officials like John Stevens did comment on certain virtues of West Indians, describing them as surprisingly literate, gentlemanly, law-abiding, and unlikely to cause trouble. In the Canal Zone those workers arrested for rowdiness or excessive drinking were almost always U.S. citizens, not West Indians. Officials saw them as generally physically fit and strong, yet with some weaknesses. Theodore Shonts, the chairman of the ICC, declared them "strong on the jaw," that is, excessively talkative. Like exaggerated versions of Negroes from the U.S. South, Shonts assessed, Jamaicans in particular "use very good English, and seem to be very proud of it, and they are rolling their words like a sweet morsel under the tongue most of the time." According to Shonts, West Indians' greatest weakness lay in their propensity to "work long enough during the week, for instance, to get enough to live upon and enjoy themselves in their own way, and then, instead of going on and attempting to add to their earnings, they will stop work and go to frolicking and resting."[40]

Usually, officials portrayed the inefficiency of West Indians as proof of their inferiority, their lower development as a culture and as a race. West Indians' laziness, they argued, derived from their vast ignorance and lack of ambition. John Stevens declared, "The West Indian negro is childlike in his disposition, and the ordinary white man, if he treated one of those negroes harshly, would feel . . . if he had any manly feelings, as he would feel toward a child." Yet at times officials conceded that something else was involved. Stevens believed that West Indians willfully sought to control their work environment and resist the exhortations of foremen and supervisors: "Instead of obtaining a fairly continuous amount of labor, as we do from gangs here at home, one-half of the efficiency of this colored labor is lost owing to their deliberate, unceasing, and continuous effort to do as little work as possible."[41]

Though they were powerless in many ways, West Indians forced the ICC to adapt to their needs and desires in certain key respects. They quit and changed their jobs regularly, often changing their names to facilitate the move. Mobility allowed them to seek better conditions, higher pay, a kinder foreman, or more opportunity or simply to resist the pace of the Americans' job. Officials found controlling West Indians a huge challenge because of their constant mobility and the ways it enabled them to demand better working conditions. In late 1909, Goethals issued uniform rates of pay for silver workers that were henceforth to be applied across the entire Zone. His reason was that silver employees had, by changing their jobs, found it possible to force different divisions to pay more for their labor, which was gradually pushing up wages and depriving certain divisions of the requisite number of workers. It was a rare public admission that West Indians sometimes forced bosses at the ICC to adjust their policies in order to tighten management. Officials similarly found it hard to keep track of individual West Indian workers amid the changing of jobs, residences, and names. They pleaded with men not to change their names and asked the British consul to intervene on the issue, but to no avail.[42]

West Indians vexed ICC officials not only by changing jobs but also, frequently, by refusing to show up for work. In 1906 officials admitted they needed to maintain an active workforce of twenty-three thousand to twenty-five thousand West Indians, even though they needed only fourteen thousand to fifteen thousand workers on any given day. This allowed some nine thousand to eleven thousand workers to miss work each day and still left sufficient laborers to accomplish the required tasks. As Shonts put it, "They work two or three days and drop out, and another gang comes in and works. . . . [A]bout a third of them do not show up regularly." Similarly, D. D. Gaillard, the engineer in charge of the central division (which included Culebra Cut), noted that he oversaw roughly fourteen thousand men, although only ten thousand showed up on a typical day. The absences proved especially common during the rainy season. Therefore, while officials found it useful to maintain a surplus in order to discipline workers and prevent strikes, West Indians had also forced them to recruit a much larger workforce simply so foremen would have enough laborers to get the required jobs done.[43]

Chief engineer John Stevens portrayed the situation graphically:

> On Monday the labor ranks are fairly full, on Tuesday they are less so, and on Wednesday a decided shrinkage in the daily force account is shown, and tapering down until Saturday. The force has diminished to such an extent that many of the lines of work are paralyzed, which shows that the mental capacity of the average West Indian negro is limited to the extent that he can in most cases realize his necessities for earning a wage sufficient to cover his animal wants for seven days, and that owing to the high wage which the commission is paying, as soon as two or three days of the week have gone by and he can see five days ahead, his desire to work entirely leaves him.

In fact, West Indians calculated how best to manage life and work in the Canal Zone to their advantage, and with a sophistication Stevens could not imagine. They were eager to find respite from work—unsurprisingly, considering the way foremen drove them at a hard and rapid pace. They would go to great lengths to achieve a break, either staying away from the job for a day or two or, whenever possible, returning to their island homes for a visit. They also found it expensive to live in the Canal Zone because of the high cost of food. They planned carefully and sometimes sacrificed their own comfort in order to save money to send home. One West Indian declared that only by starving themselves could they save money to send home. Often they attempted to supplement their income and their food supply by living and growing sugarcane or bananas, or raising hens, outside the confines of ICC labor camps—and their absences from work sometimes resulted from such responsibilities.[44]

And so tensions between West Indians and government officials easily spilled over from work to food and housing. Food quality differed radically for gold and silver employees. The government spent little on food for the latter, and officials widely acknowledged the result was of poor quality. This proved especially problematic during the early years, when officials contracted the feeding of laborers out to men who organized food for different gangs. The temptation to make as much profit as possible led to shortchanging the laborers, and anger spread among West Indians. It also led to extreme labor mobility, as workers would seek a different gang in hopes of securing better food. As Jacob Markel, a food supplier from Omaha, described the food preparation in 1905 and 1906, cooks would pile whatever food they had for West Indians (yams or beans or bits of bone or meat) into huge kettles and cook it into one big slop: "Just the same as we do for our hogs out on the farm. The only difference I could see between the way they fed those negroes and the way I feed my hogs is that the food was put on a tin plate instead of in a trough."[45]

Discontentment with such conditions during the early years increased, and protests mounted. Chief engineer John Wallace reported trouble with the workers handling freight on the wharves, "just one constant jangle right along between the negroes and their boarding-house keepers, and they were continually expressing dissatisfaction."[46] Undoubtedly, officials heard similar complaints all along the construction line. Matters reached a head in April 1905, when two hundred Jamaicans toiling in Panama City for the ICC's Department of Waterworks and Sewers refused to return to work because they said they had not been properly or sufficiently fed. Their foreman ordered them back to work, but they refused. Unable to manage the situation, he called upon the Panamanian police for assistance.

Canal Zone chief of police George Shanton happened to be near the work site and described seeing sixty to seventy Jamaican laborers running up the street, greatly agitated. The Panamanian police had ordered them back to work, they said, and then used bayonets and beatings to coerce them. Six men had received bad injuries. Shanton declared he would escort the injured to the hospital and asked the others to return to work, but just then twenty-five Panamanian policemen arrived with rifles and fixed bayonets. Shanton informed the police that he had the situation under control, but as one of the wounded began to pass by the police and approach Shanton, the "commander of the detachment drew his saber and struck him over the head with it, knocking him down. I called out to them to 'Hold! Hold!'" Yet the commander's violence seemed a signal to the rest of the policemen, and, "some with drawn bayonets, others clubbing their guns, they charged into the Jamaicans, hitting right and left." The laborers fled, with policemen in pursuit and swinging their clubs. Shanton commented that the Jamaicans had been peaceful and did not provoke the attack. Most ended up with a range of cuts and bruises, and many required treatment at the hospital.[47]

The whole affair, Canal Zone governor Charles Magoon noted, "could cause a serious complication—an injury to a British subject by Panamanian officers at a time when the men were working for the U.S."[48] The British consul was said to be "indignant" about the incident. John Barrett, the American minister to Panama, quickly maneuvered to placate British and Jamaican officials and demanded the Panamanian government investigate the actions of its police force and take steps so such a situation would not recur. He placed the blame on the Panamanian police, not the U.S. foreman or other officials. Barrett did meet with ICC officials to stress that "they must use the utmost care in the future in dealing with the Jamaican laborers and see that they were not treated harshly, that they received proper food," and he asked that the ICC find a way to settle problems without calling in the Panamanian police. But he also cautioned British and Jamaican officials that the Jamaican laborers as a rule were "somewhat difficult to deal with and that they complain, no matter how good provision is made for them. . . . [C]onsequently there must be a certain amount of charity in judging stories about the treatment of laborers by their American employers." He urged the British consul to remind authorities in Jamaica and Britain that "in the inauguration of a great work of this kind there must be a certain amount of difficulties and troubles. . . . [T]he future treatment of the laborers must not be judged by some unforeseen incident. . . . The desire of the Canal Commission is to make the Isthmus attractive for laborers."[49]

During 1905 and early 1906, U.S. officials were especially desperate to keep West Indians on the job. However, the workers' unhappiness with the chaotic conditions in the Canal Zone led to mass desertions. Increasingly, West Indians wanted their wives or sweethearts to join them, but initially officials refused. One account relates that a group of West Indians staged a sit-down strike, declaring, "No women, no work," and government officials conceded their demand and allowed women to come to the Zone. It's not possible to confirm this tale, but certainly ICC officials felt anxious during 1905 and early 1906 to acquire more Martinican laborers and to keep them working once they arrived. Toward this end officials imported several hundred Martinican women to the isthmus in the summer of 1905. By convincing officials to allow women, West Indians may have exerted a powerful influence on their own lives and on conditions across the isthmus.[50]

After confronting strikes over food, officials resolved to improve food preparation and delivery. It took more than a year, but the ICC created government kitchens where West Indians could get better food. Officials also built a silver section of the commissary where West Indians could buy supplies and cook them on their own. The ICC began importing large quantities of sweet potatoes, yams, and codfish from Barbados for cooking in the kitchens, and importing items like jam—of which West Indians were said to be very fond—from England for the commissaries. Still, food supply remained problematic. In 1907 the reformer Gertrude Beeks charged that men were getting dysentery from bad food in government cafeterias. Officials denied her charge but admitted that complaints about the lack of variety and the poor cooking were widespread.[51] A representative from the Bible Society of Barbados visited the isthmus and tried to help officials understand why the laborers shunned government food: "He said the men live on two and frequently only one meal a day in their native country, and that they considered it a sinful waste for a man to pay 30 cents a day for meals when he did not want them and when they could live upon a little sugar cane costing from 1 to 2 cents." But officials would have profited more from listening to their West Indian laborers. John Butcher, who worked for years in the Canal Zone as a plumber's helper, eloquently suggested why so many avoided government food: "a meal of cooked rice which was hard enough to shoot deers, sauce spread all over the rice, and a slab of meat which many men either spent an hour trying to chew or eventually threw away because it was too hard. Along with our rice and meat each one was handed a loaf of bread which seemed so tasty with our metal cup of coffee." The men also objected to the fact that there were no chairs or tables as there were for white workers—West Indians either had to sit on the ground or remain standing to eat their meal. When rainstorms hit at mealtime, men scrambled to find shelter, seeking a spot under buildings when possible.[52]

Chief engineer Wallace concluded: "My experience with . . . [West Indians] has been that, as a rule, you can not coerce them very much. They know what food they want, and what they can get the most benefit out of."[53] The government's inability to coerce West Indians was evidenced in reactions to housing conditions as well. Indeed, housing and food were closely linked, just as both were inextricably bound with dissatisfaction over working conditions. Like their gold counterparts, silver employees received free housing from the government. For some, however, home was a boxcar. Those more fortunate lived in cramped, damp, and dark rooms that lacked privacy or toilet facilities, filled with iron cots covered with canvas. Many spent time outdoors when weather allowed. Others might lounge on their cots during off hours, or sit about on boxes playing cards.[54] West Indians living in the labor camps spent considerable time finding ways to navigate around the ICC's infamous vagrancy laws. They despised the Zone policemen who trolled through the camps, interrogating men who lacked a doctor's note or other excuse. Those who wanted to miss a day of work had to leave and hide out in a Chinese shop, head into the jungle, or face arrest and possible imprisonment.[55]

In 1907 officials added another complication by deciding that only laborers who purchased meal tickets could live in government housing. Theodore Shonts, the chairman of the ICC, denounced West Indians for their "desire to indulge in eatables less suited to their physical needs, and to gratify other desires." His and other officials' reasoning was that men who ate a solid, nutritious meal would work better. Economic efficiency was also on their minds; West Indian cafeterias were losing money because so few workers were buying meal tickets. The officials installed watchmen in the labor camps, placing them on duty night and day to require that men show their meal tickets, which would prove they had a right to be in the camp. The numbers of those living in the free housing quickly plunged. In November 1907 nearly half of all West Indian employees (just under twelve thousand men) lived in government housing. One year later the number had dipped to seventy-five hundred as West Indians voted with their feet. The most precipitous decline occurred after chief engineer Goethals ordered on September 1, 1908, that the requirement that West Indians show a meal ticket in order to sleep in quarters be strictly enforced. Officials hoped this would result in many more men eating government meals, but, they lamented, "the results show it had the opposite effect. As soon as it was enforced, about 1600 of the laborers went into the 'bush' altogether, neither eating nor sleeping in Commission houses." Meal tickets cost twenty-seven to thirty cents a day—a huge sum when most laborers made only ten cents an hour. Even for palatable food this would seem a lot, but West Indians found it insulting to pay such money for intolerable food. Thus they rejected the free housing and instead built themselves shacks or rented apartments in Colón or Panama City. Those residing in the port cities of Panama faced extremely poor living conditions and high rents. Despite the pitiable circumstances, most West Indians preferred life away from the towns of the Canal Zone.[56]

When officials realized the meal-ticket requirement caused a mass exodus from the government's labor camps, they soon removed it. As far as they could tell, chief quartermaster Carrol A. Devol concluded, the laborers' efficiency was not impaired by cooking for themselves. Even after officials relented and let laborers cook their own food, however, West Indians continued to reject the free government housing. One reason was undoubtedly the lack of married housing or any facilities for women at a time when the latter were increasingly traveling to the Zone to join their men, to earn money, or both. Another was the fact that residents of government housing could be evicted if they got into trouble, entered into a disagreement with their employer, or sought work outside the Canal Zone. And they disliked the constant regimentation of the ICC's rule; they could not entirely avoid being driven and disciplined while on the job, but they did at least have the ability to escape the bureaucratic feel of life in the labor camps with the ever-present Zone policemen, watchmen, and sanitation force patrols. For these reasons, as well as for access to agreeable food, most West Indians continued living in the port cities of Panama or in the jungle. The number of those in government housing had declined to little more than six thousand by the end of 1911 and hovered around that level for the remaining construction years—a small group indeed, when one considers that more than thirty thousand West Indians were working for the ICC. Evaluating the problem in early 1909, the chief quartermaster declared, "The time to prevent the West Indians living in the 'bush' has passed. . . . It is not believed that some 16,000 laborers could be driven from their homes into Commission quarters without labor trouble serious enough to interfere with the construction of the Canal."[57] The majority of West Indians had found a way to arrange their lives—despite the overwhelming power of the U.S. government—to gain more control and independence.

Besides moving horizontally from one section of work to another in the Canal Zone, or taking what had been a white mechanic's job as a step to economic mobility, West Indians found they could make more money and enjoy greatly improved conditions working for merchants in Panama City or Colón. Others moved on to banana plantations in Bocas del Toro, Panama, or in Costa Rica, or returned home to their island communities. Canal workers kept in close touch with their families in the Caribbean, sending money home when they could and cherishing a great dream of returning as soon as possible. Bonham Richardson eloquently demonstrated the importance of "Panama money" to Barbadian communities. When the mailman came, it was said, people in Barbados would run out to meet him to see if news—and hopefully money—from Panama awaited them. An "empty letter" was one without money. The Barbadian Cleveland Murrell remembered years later how his father had gone to Panama and worked as a janitor, carefully saving his money. When he had saved about $100, he decided more free-spending men in the barracks would not understand his possession of such wealth, and so he returned to Barbados. He managed to buy some land and cattle, and even opened a small shop. For this family, as for many others, canal work brought an important measure of economic success and independence. Those who returned to Barbados from Panama were easily spotted, flashing money around and wearing the long coats, reaching down below the knee, that were fashionable in Panama at the time. The vast migrations encouraged by the Americans' canal construction pushed many West Indians even farther, to jobs in Cuba or the United States.[58]

Such forms of mobility within and beyond the Canal Zone provided West Indian laborers with their best opportunity to shape living and working conditions and articulate grievances. Organized strikes, like the one in 1905 among Jamaicans protesting insufficient food, were uncommon. Instead, West Indian protests were fleeting and highly subterranean. Sometimes individuals engaged in acts of sabotage, for example, placing large rocks on the railroad tracks to wreck or demobilize a train. In a very different case, West Indians' collective agency could be observed when officials anxiously tried to get laborers to ingest quinine several times a day to prevent malaria. The laborers fiercely protested against drinking the quinine because of its bitter taste. Finally officials resorted to mixing the medication with a gill of rum as the only way to persuade their workers to take it. The St. Lucian Albert Banister, who worked in a Cristobal boiler shop for many years, recalled: "The first gentleman that learn me to drink was Uncle Sammy. . . . When you drink that quinine you feel for 15 minutes you are the sweetest man in the land." Ironically, officials came to see alcohol consumption as one of the West Indians' chief weaknesses.[59]

West Indian laborers' general deference and accommodation to the power of government officials, like slaves or sharecroppers across the United States and the Caribbean before and during this time, masked an ability to rebel—sometimes in very hidden ways—against the world of those in power. One example may suggest the possible form of such expressions. In 1909 a white man working as a steward at one of the government hotels was living with a woman. This was hardly unusual, but a Panamanian newspaper that routinely took the side of West Indians published the fact, printed the steward's picture, and pointed out that West Indians often faced harassment from the authorities for such actions. And so, declared the newspaper, the authorities should investigate this steward, a Mr. Grosse, as well. The paper's publisher was sued for libel for this and other statements. In an affidavit, Grosse complained that "he has a large number of coons under him and they took great delight for many days thereafter leaving copies of the paper on his desk." One can imagine the pleasure West Indians working under Grosse felt as they opened the newspaper to this story and then laid it out on his desk. Without the libel case, such mocking of a white man's power would not be known to us. Undoubtedly similar examples existed that never made it into court affidavits.[60]

Amid the dangers and discomforts and occasional humiliation of life as a canal worker, there remained for most an upside. The tales and memoirs of canal workers suggest that many viewed life on the isthmus as a great adventure. While the Americans sometimes angered or disgusted West Indians, the latter also felt proud of their role in digging the great ditch. A common metaphor in the West Indian canal workers' testimonies is war: "You see most of us came here with the Same spirit as a Soldier going to war, don't dodge from work or we will never finish it," as Prince George Green, who began working as a janitor on the canal in 1909, described it. Among male workers there was often a swagger that came from pride in holding one of the Yankees' jobs and living to tell about it, and many beautiful rocks from the depths of Culebra Cut were taken home as mementos. The ultimate souvenir, however, was a shark tooth. Occasionally canal workers would find one in the dirt dislodged by dynamite, a souvenir from millions of years past when the two oceans were still connected. Such a lucky canal worker would then mount the tooth and wear it proudly on a black watch fob. Reginald Beckford, who worked for a time in a jeweler's shop, remembered mounting many shark teeth for West Indian clients.[61]

In the 1940s the ethnographer Louise Cramer studied the West Indian communities in the Canal Zone and found that at social gatherings and at work, a "love of singing remains an integral part of the West Indian nature in the Zone." Indeed, she observed, "You owe me a song" was commonly declared after friends greeted each other. Many of the songs Cramer analyzed dated from the days of construction. They cover a wide spectrum, from teasing and amusing songs, to tales of courtship, the dangers of work, hard economic times in Jamaica, nostalgia for an island home, death, and the allure of the Americans' construction project. One song devoted to the latter topic called to friends to come work on the "Merican Cut" (in this song, "a" preceding "Merican" means "to," and the first syllable of the word "American" is dropped). The singer acknowledges that the American cut offers a better opportunity than working for one bit (about four and a half pence) a day back home in the Caribbean:

COME OUT A MERICAN CUT
Before me work fe [for] bit a day
Before me work fe bit a day
Before me work fe bit a day
Me wid come out a Merican Cut
Dem a bawl [they cry], oh, come out a Merican Cut
Dem a bawl, oh, come out a Merican Cut,
Come out a Merican Cut, come out a Merican Cut.

Laborers were likely to sing songs like this one as they dug through the long hours in Culebra Cut until the whistle blew at the end of the day. Other songs were clearly meant to be shared during a wake, a celebration that would occur on the ninth night after someone had died, when, supposedly, the spirit of the dead would be laid to rest. As Cramer described, "The entire neighborhood turns out, and tables are loaded with all sorts of choice food, besides plenty of rum, for those keeping the watch. Songs are sung, stories told, and spirits mount during the evening as more rum is consumed."[62]

Churches and other organizations created by West Indians in the

Canal Zone and Panama also sustained them. The U.S. government did little to support social activities among West Indians despite the urging of foreign consuls, but officials allowed laborers to make use of ICC buildings for dances, sports, and other events. Otherwise, West Indians were left to their own devices. Cricket was extremely popular; on Sunday afternoons crowds would gather to watch a competitive game. Dominoes was also a popular evening activity in the labor camps. Friendly and mutual aid societies existed, organized on the basis of each ethnic group and often linked to organizations on their home islands, and they provided assistance for families of injured or killed workers. Like the Americans, West Indians ventured into Panama City and Colón for recreation, visiting rum shops and saloons, nightclubs, and brothels or, if their financial resources did not allow such pleasures, just promenading along the streets to enjoy the diversions of city life.[63]

Religion was a powerful force in West Indians' lives. George Westerman, an important chronicler of West Indian life in Panama, found that there existed in the construction era thirteen Anglican congregations in the Canal Zone—on the isthmus as in Barbados, the Church of England was the most prevalent church. There were as well many congregations of Roman Catholics, Baptists, Methodists, Episcopalians, the Salvation Army, and some nondenominational churches. West Indians prided themselves on their regular church attendance and active engagement in church affairs. Westerman notes that the church tended to see its mission as "providing escape and consolation to those tropical 'ditch diggers.'" The church rose in importance, he argued, simply because there was little else to sustain common laborers. It served as "the only institution which provided an effective organization of the group, an approved place for social activities, a forum for expression on many issues, an outlet for emotional repressions, and a plan for social living." Amos Parks, who worked laying tracks at Frijoles in the Zone, expressed the motivation for regular church attendance more pungently, remembering, "That's the reason we all use to go to Church more regular than today, because in those days you see today and tomorrow you are a dead man. You had to pray everyday for God to Carry you safe, and bring you back."[64]

. . .

ICC OFFICIALS could not build the canal without tens of thousands of laborers, and they had searched the globe for a source of tractable workers. They had settled on West Indians as the most obedient workers they could feasibly bring to the Canal Zone and then sent recruiters through the Caribbean to offer labor contracts. Once on the isthmus, West Indians set out to shape the world around them. Some, like Amos Parks, remembered how workers would rely on God to "Carry you safe, and bring you back." The most powerful weapon West Indians possessed, however, was more mundane. They could vote with their feet, and their mobility carried them safely into better homes or jobs or got them more-satisfying food. Movement of various kinds allowed them to shape their lives and generated the greatest adjustment on the part of their employers. Along the way, as they fought for a bit more independence, they forced officials to develop new approaches to managing and disciplining their supposedly quiescent workers.

Those officials never grasped that West Indians were capable of creating such change and adaptation. They had been dissatisfied with the West Indian workforce from the beginning, but not because they expected wide-scale collective challenges to government policy. Rather, officials believed West Indians would prove insufficient to the grand task of building the canal. So they looked elsewhere, thinking that somewhere there must be white men who could do hard labor in the tropical Canal Zone. Their eyes turned to Cuba, where Spaniards sweated on sugar plantations and on railroads. They expected more energy from Spaniards, and they got it—but with results they never anticipated.

CHAPTER FOUR

LAY DOWN YOUR SHOVELS

I N MARCH 1907 a major riot broke out at a mess hall for Spaniards in the Canal Zone town of Bas Obispo. The hall had just been built to accommodate several hundred Spaniards who came from Cuba to work on the canal, and new government rules had been posted to regulate where people could sit. When one Spanish worker sat in a seat other than the one assigned to him, a West Indian steward instructed him to go to the appropriate spot. Instead of moving, the Spanish laborer punched the waiter, prompting another Spaniard named Angel Negrati to jump onto a table shouting, "Kill the negroes!" Other diners followed Negrati by climbing on tables and throwing plates and glasses while their compatriots attacked and beat the mess hall steward. Police arrived to find the mess hall empty, window screens torn out, lamps destroyed, and "the floor almost entirely covered with stones, cups, saucers, plates, and etc., which had been thrown at the mess steward and his assistants." On a hillside near the mess hall sat about two hundred Spaniards, a Zone policeman reported, "evidently contented with what they had accomplished." Police sent the bruised steward over to the hillside to identify the riot leaders. When he pointed out the first man, "the whole bunch of Spaniards arose as one man and said that we could not take him, but we did, after drawing our revolvers and warning them that we would shoot the first man who attempted to rescue the prisoner." The police then arrested twelve men believed to be the riot's leaders. That night, more Spaniards congregated at the mess hall and stoned the building until again the police came and subdued them.[1]

This riot was one of many acts of protest by Spaniards who joined the workforce as silver employees during 1907 and 1908, and it reveals how tightly intertwined issues of race, ethnicity, and nationality were in the Canal Zone. Spaniards owed their very presence on the isthmus to government officials' beliefs that "whites" would work more productively and energetically than West Indians and thereby solve the nagging labor problems of the construction project. These ideas led officials to go to great lengths to recruit Spaniards, Italians, Greeks, and other southern Europeans. Yet the workers—particularly Spaniards—proved "turbulent," as one official described them. They rioted, protested working conditions, and went on strike far more often than any other group. Moreover, their resistance flowered into an anarchist movement that spread through the labor camps and towns of the Canal Zone in 1911 at the height of the construction project.[2]

Yet as the attack on a West Indian steward suggests, the Spaniards' protests targeted not only the U.S. government but also West Indians. Spaniards inhabited a complex position on the isthmus as "white" men employed on the silver roll alongside black West Indians. In some respects, they received better treatment than other silver workers. At the same time, when they compared themselves with other white workers, most notably the American workers on the gold roll, they felt slighted and victimized by the government's system of hierarchy and segregation. Ordered around by foremen, excluded from restaurants and clubhouses, Spaniards felt themselves marked as inferior on the basis of race, ethnicity, and nationality. They directed their resulting anger at those below and above them: they railed against West Indians and the competition they presented for jobs, even as they fiercely complained about the ICC policies that had put them there.

"THEY ARE WHITE MEN, TRACTABLE, AND CAPABLE OF DEVELOPMENT"

Although most silver employees came from the Caribbean, many traveled to the Canal Zone from southern Europe, from India, and from other parts of Latin America. The 1912 census included as employees of the

ICC or the Panama Railroad one thousand Panamanians, eight hundred Italians, thirteen hundred Greeks, thirty-five hundred Spaniards, and smaller numbers of East Indians, Portuguese, Ecuadorians, Peruvians, Venezuelans, Colombians, Mexicans, Hondurans, Costa Ricans, and Nicaraguans. The vast majority of these individuals worked as common laborers on the silver roll. They shoveled coal, shifted and laid tracks, cut through the jungle bush with machetes, and worked as pick and shovel men in Culebra Cut.[3]

The decision to recruit European laborers grew out of government officials' dissatisfaction with West Indians and their belief that "white" men would do a better job. ICC chairman Theodore Shonts was a strong proponent for the recruitment of Spaniards because, he declared, "they are white men, tractable, and capable of development and assimilation." John Stevens agreed, since he felt that West Indians' laziness and lack of ambition would prevent them from working effectively on the canal. If nothing else, these officials believed, Europeans would at least spur West Indians to work harder and more productively. As it turned out, an easy labor source immediately manifested itself amid transformations generated in Spain by the War of 1898. After the war, Spanish immigration to Cuba soared. *Peninsulares,* as the Spanish immigrants were called, enjoyed many privileges in Cuba, often getting the best-paying jobs and other opportunities unavailable to Creoles or people of color. They could be found working in every sector of the economy, as businessmen and merchants or as skilled workers in urban industries like cigar making. The majority of them, however, flooded into rural areas to take jobs in railroad construction or, more commonly, in the burgeoning sugar industry. Those Spaniards who ended up in rural occupations found the working conditions harsh and the pay lower than they'd hoped and were therefore most susceptible to the pitches of U.S. recruiting agents.[4]

In 1907, ICC labor recruiters learned of a road construction project in Cuba that was relying on laborers from northern Spain. Ten thousand Spaniards had built 347 miles of road in Cuba in only sixteen months, and the foreman declared he "had great success in handling them—that they were intelligent to a degree, docile, tractable, good workers, and had enough ambition." Recruiting agents visiting Cuba sought one thousand men, but U.S. employers in Cuba fought bitterly not to lose their workers. In the end, canal officials succeeded in bringing only about five hundred men to the Canal Zone. Officials confessed to high hopes that these men would solve the labor problem.[5]

The first Spaniards who came to the Zone from Cuba in 1907 so impressed officials with their energy and efficiency that recruiting agents headed directly to Spain and to centers of migrant labor such as Marseilles and Bordeaux, France, to round up several thousand more. They also sought out Italians, Greeks, Frenchmen, Portuguese, and Armenians, but Spain emerged as by far the most common source of European laborers. ICC recruiters found, for example, that one syndicate in Italy controlled the emigration of all laborers from that country and placed a tax on each person so high as to seem like debt peonage. Most of the Italians in the Zone therefore came on their own, either from the United States or from South America.[6]

In Spain, agents focused their efforts in large cities and the economically troubled regions of the northwest. Most came from Galicia, a depressed area in northwestern Spain where subsistence agriculture could not support the growing population. Many others came from nearby Asturias, the Basque Country, or Andalusia, an impoverished southern region of large estates and landless peasants.[7]

The migrants traveling to Panama formed one part of a mass exodus from Spain to the Americas between 1870 and 1914. Spanish immigrants rarely journeyed to the United States, preferring to land in Cuba, Panama, Argentina, or Brazil. Galicia contributed more immigrants to the Americas than any other region of Spain at the turn of the twentieth century, losing roughly half its population between 1850 and 1930. The rise of commercial agriculture and industrialization and the tumultuous changes associated with it explain this mass migration. Those who migrated were typically not the most indigent, but rather working people with some resources and ambition who saw in the vast changes around them an opportunity to make a better life. The historian Jose Moya found, for example, that those who left were often more literate than those who remained behind and that a fierce desire to save money and return home to purchase the land they rented influenced many immigrants.[8]

Once they arrived in the Canal Zone, Spanish workers were surprised by the harsh conditions and poor treatment they received. Recruiting agents had blanketed their towns with leaflets promising spacious houses, pleasant hotels, special housing for married workers and their families, healthful food, and a variety of recreational activities. In reality, as an investigation carried out by the National Civic Federation elaborated, much of this was patently false. Canal officials rarely provided them with married housing, but gave them ragged or torn window screens (allowing insects and disease into their homes), foul water, stale food, and no recreational opportunities. Spaniards learned that the pleasant hotel pictured in the leaflet excluded all but white US citizens. On the job, they found foremen who typically spoke no Spanish and who insulted and mistreated them, long hours (days of twelve hours or more were common), an expectation that they would work even in the heaviest downpours and accept dangerous working conditions without protest, no provision made for families of injured or killed workers, and, of course, grave inequalities in terms of the benefits afforded to gold and silver employees.[9]

A further indignity was the fact that Spaniards' racial identity in the Zone was ambiguous. Whether they would be considered white or non-white shifted according to diverse circumstances. Sometimes U.S. government officials referred to them, along with Italians or Greeks, as "semi-white." At other times, especially when compared with black Caribbeans, they were seen as "white."[10] These notions of race were closely linked to the legacy of empire. The U.S. government consistently perceived Spaniards as common, low, and only questionably civilized, a prejudice in large part derived from the War of 1898, when U.S. journalists had vividly reimagined Spaniards as "monstrous brutes," as uncivilized, or as weak and effeminate, any of which made it easier to perceive them as less than white.[11]

Spaniards chafed at their status as "white" men working on the low-status silver roll, an employment category often defined as being for nonwhites. And it must have been difficult for them to be excluded from hotels, restaurants, and clubhouses reserved for white U.S. citizens, or forced to stand in the line for "coloreds" at the post office. Overall, Spaniards had more in common with West Indians than with white Americans. Like West Indians, they lacked union representation, they could not appeal to the U.S. Congress, and they could not threaten canal officials by saying they would quit, since there was such a surplus of unskilled workers. Spaniards, like many West Indians, did very hard manual labor, most commonly as tracklayers and shifters. Occupational opportunities were actually much more limited for them and other southern Europeans than for West Indians. Thousands of the latter acquired skills and worked as artisans. Spaniards, on the other hand, were rarely allowed to work at jobs other than those demanding simple manual labor. The contrast most likely derived from the French construction period, when many West Indians held positions as craftsmen or their helpers. Spaniards had been recruited to serve specifically as unskilled laborers, and they remained limited to that occupation.

Despite such limitations, Spaniards made as much in wages as most West Indians working as artisans, and sometimes even more. The ICC used a complex pay scale for its silver workers that differentiated them not on the basis of the job they did but according to their race, ethnicity, and nationality. Unskilled West Indians were categorized as "Laborer A" and paid the equivalent of ten cents U.S. currency per hour; Colombians, Panamanians, and other Latin Americans were classified as "Laborer B" and paid thirteen cents per hour (West Indian laborers were explicitly excluded from this category); "Laborer C" received sixteen cents, and the category was reserved for a "European or other white laborer or black American laborer" who came to the Canal Zone on his own, that is, without an official ICC labor contract; Europeans with a contract were classified as "Laborer D" and received twenty cents per hour. Further complicating this hierarchy, the ICC also created classifications of "Artisan C" and "Artisan D" to cover West Indians performing skilled labor; these groups were paid the same amount as Laborers C and D. In other words, a typical unskilled Spanish laborer was paid twice as much as an unskilled West Indian, and as much as or more than a skilled West Indian artisan. These were literally, to adapt W. E. B. DuBois's famous phrase, "the wages of whiteness." Yet in the Canal Zone there were also different shades of whiteness, due mostly to nationality, and, with them, different levels of privilege.[12]

THE "EXCITABLE NATURE OF THE EUROPEAN"

Caught uneasily between West Indians and white U.S. citizens, sensing that their whiteness was somehow a help and yet not helpful enough, Spanish laborers sought support from the one governmental resource they did have: the Spanish consul. His name was Juan Potous, and he responded to workers' complaints much more energetically than did his British and French counterparts. Potous regularly petitioned the U.S. officials with concerns about accidents, demanded investigation into various problems, and asked for compensation to the families of Spaniards killed on the job. In October 1907, for example, a gang of Spaniards at Miraflores loaded a railroad car with large timber while several workers stood atop the pile of logs. To unload the car, the foreman attached a rope to a log near the bottom and pulled it out, bringing down all the logs, along with the workers standing on top of them. Several Spaniards were hurt. One of them was dragged by the logs and broke his neck and one arm. Consul Potous demanded an investigation. U.S. government officials complained privately about the "continual interference of the Spanish Consul with the laborers." They worried he was hurting discipline and encouraging Spanish workers to believe they would win better treatment by going to an outside authority. Publicly, officials responded that the workers' carelessness caused such accidents.[13]

The British consul, Claude Mallet, observed that "Mr. Potous is zealous in taking up with the canal authorities the complaints, however trivial they may be, of his countrymen employed on the canal works. They consist mainly of disputes about wages, infractions of the sanitary regulations, camp quarrels, and etc., and as the American bosses cannot speak Spanish, and are brusque in manner and impatient when demanding obedience to their orders, it is only natural that there have been frequent misunderstandings." Potous often attempted to mediate when such conflicts arose, and Mallet believed his Spanish counterpart often acted rashly. In Mallet's eyes, the fact that the Spaniards remained at work and new ones arrived all the time to join them meant the complaints were unimportant.[14]

Juan Potous did not agree. He and his government angrily complained about deaths and injuries among Spaniards. Responding to such grievances, the ICC in 1907 hired Giuseppe Garibaldi to represent the interests of Spanish and Italian laborers and, revealingly, to mediate quarrels between the two nationalities. Twenty-eight years old at the time, Garibaldi was the grandson of the famous Italian revolutionary of the same name. U.S. officials hoped that he would mediate between them and the foreign consuls, particularly Potous. Once Garibaldi arrived on the job, officials required that Potous and the Spanish laborers first visit him with any complaints before proceeding to anyone more highly ranked. Garibaldi quickly developed into a disciplinarian, criticizing Potous in particular. He objected to the tone in Potous's letters as well as to the influence he exerted on labor relations: "The men should not be guided to think that, by appealing to the Consul, they may obtain redress and privileges that they could not get by going direct to the proper Commission authorities." In general, Garibaldi found it difficult to manage the "rather excitable nature of the European," and he wished labor recruiters would take more care to contract a calmer group of men.[15]

If they believed this young Italian with a famous name would help them resolve their troubles with Spaniards, U.S. officials were sadly mistaken. Garibaldi's presence did not improve matters. In 1908, Potous delivered a fiery report to his government, documenting the miserable living and working conditions Spaniards confronted and the common accidents and frequency of malaria. With particular bitterness he complained that the U.S. government refused to offer compensation to those maimed and left without a way to make a living after working on the canal. Nearly two hundred Spaniards in the Canal Zone or the Republic of Panama had died during 1908, he declared, about half of them canal workers. More than two dozen had been killed by malaria. The isthmus was unacceptably dangerous to the health of Spanish citizens. After receiving Potous's report in November 1908, the Spanish government issued a royal decree forbidding any more emigration to the Canal Zone. Although the number of Spaniards declined, as late as 1912 more than four thousand were still working in the Zone.[16]

Spaniards were happy to ask their consul for assistance, but they relied more wholeheartedly on their own resources, tirelessly resisting the discipline and regimentation of U.S. officials. Immediately upon the arrival of the first group of Spaniards, the chief of police noted that he had been forced to increase the number of Zone policemen by 25 percent because of the "turbulent" Europeans. The records of the ICC are filled with discussions among officials about how to handle such troublesome laborers. In the autumn of 1907, just weeks after some of them had entered the Canal Zone, Spanish workers initiated their first major strike. More than one hundred men laid down their tools, complaining about an abusive foreman and unacceptable food. They described their foreman as somebody they "bear with great patience in spite of his vile language, unfit for an educated man," and claimed that they "complied with his orders notwithstanding the *insults flung at the Spaniards merely because they are Spaniards.*" This same foreman discharged one worker, although the latter had "worked with ardor," simply because "he complained of the food furnished by the ICC. This food can hardly be compared with that furnished in the penitenciary." The foreman soon suspended another man for a minor offense, and after such a pattern of "outrage" the strike began. Two days later U.S. officials sent Italian workers to take the place of the striking Spaniards, assigned a cadre of police to prevent any trouble between the two European groups, and threatened to evict the Spaniards from their housing if they were not back on the job by noon of that same day.[17]

Heavy-handed foremen were the cause of many strikes. Spaniards frequently complained of foremen who spoke no Spanish or abused them verbally or physically. In early 1907 an Italian foreman took charge of a Spanish gang near the construction town of Culebra. The Spaniards resented the Italian's authority over them, and ultimately they attacked the man and beat him. When police arrested a dozen of them and took them off to jail in the nearby town of Empire, about two hundred fellow workers stopped work and headed toward town to liberate them. As the Spaniards marched toward Empire, they attempted to convince other workers to join them, but their effort failed. Instead, police and several foremen met them as they approached town and convinced them to turn back. Of the Spaniards arrested, all but one were convicted and required either to pay a fine or to serve time in jail.[18]

Italians and Spaniards occasionally collaborated in striking, rioting, or mutinying, and some Italians attended Spanish anarchist meetings, but the two groups often fought bitterly. When officials heard rumors of a large strike planned by Spaniards and Italians, their investigator urged them to relax, declaring that no such strike would take place: "There is no union or cohesion between these two nationalities and they mistrust one another." There was hostility also between Spaniards and Greeks. *El Único*, the Spanish anarchist newspaper, complained that Greek foremen in the Zone were treating Spanish workers badly, sometimes causing bloody fights: "Why do these Athenians act so despotically? Are they becoming Americanized?" Such divisions meant that Spaniards usually worked on their own to organize protests and strikes.[19]

Two other grievances generated bitterness among Spaniards: the poor quality of food and job competition with West Indians. Spaniards repeatedly rioted over food and conditions in the mess halls. They assaulted cooks who failed to prepare meals to their liking, they rioted to protest the absence of Spaniards among the cooking staff in their mess halls, and occasionally they quit work to press their protest about the food. Officials made an effort to hire Spanish cooks for the Spanish mess halls, and they imported special foods for them as well—garbanzos, tomato puree, chorizos. When asked by congressmen if he pandered to the tastes of different races, the official in charge of food supply responded, "Oh, yes, indeed. The Spaniard requires the things he is accustomed to in his own country and will have them as he wants them. The negro we feed according to the way he eats back in his own country." Yet there remained limits to what officials would do. Major William Sibert, who headed the

Atlantic division of the ICC, declared, "The food is better than is ordinarily consumed by people of the class in question."[20]

Over time, Spaniards' racial hostility toward West Indians seemed to grow more intense. Joseph Blackburn, who headed civil administration in the Canal Zone, noted (perhaps disingenuously) that "the southern Europeans, white men—the Greeks and the Spaniards and the Italians—are more insistent upon the observation of color lines than you find among the people of the States here at home." In particular, Blackburn observed, his police force had experienced major problems when West Indian policemen attempted to arrest an Italian or a Spaniard. Serious riots had broken out, and "therefore, the scope of service of the colored policemen has been by order restricted to practically the colored camps."[21] When grievances over food became enmeshed with racial hostilities—particularly when black West Indians asserted authority over Spaniards, for example, if they dared to correct a Spaniard's seating choice—the resulting conflicts typically proved even more explosive and difficult for police to handle.[22]

Trouble likewise resulted when Spaniards worked, lived, or commuted to work too close to West Indians. In 1907 Spanish workers at Pedro Miguel threatened a strike, demanding better food and that "all the negroes [be] taken away from their camp."[23] In 1909 crowded labor trains caused a riot between Spaniards and Barbadians in which both sides used clubs and rocks as weapons. Although normally "white" and "colored" workers were given different cars to ride, Barbadians had begun encroaching on cars normally reserved for whites because their own had become intolerably crowded. Policemen who tried to stop the riot were attacked by the Spaniards, leading to several arrests. In response, several hundred Spaniards refused to work, insisting they would wait for the Spanish consul to arrive. In angry speeches, workers declared the consul must achieve justice or they would call upon "all the Spaniards on the Canal Zone to lay down their shovels and organize for the protection of their common rights." These workers demanded both that their compatriots be released from jail and that blacks be prohibited from riding on their train cars. The chief of police responded to their complaints, ordering the officer in charge to "see that the white laborers, who I understand are much in the minority, are not imposed upon in any way by the colored laborers."[24]

The U.S. government generally tried to keep workers segregated by race and citizenship both in transportation and in housing. While West Indians and Europeans often shared the same labor camp, for example, U.S. officials segregated each group to different parts of the camp. Likewise, the government built completely separate mess halls for West Indians and Europeans, but when circumstances prevented complete segregation, conflicts flared. In early 1911 the government assigned a large group of Barbadians to quarters at Cirio camp that had, until that moment, been totally inhabited by Spanish workers and families. Thirty-nine Spanish workers petitioned the U.S. government to remove the Barbadians, saying the latter were thieves and nuisances in terms of "sanitary and moral conditions." The government conceded that when the Barbadians had first entered the camp, the bathhouses were not clearly labeled according to gender, and in some cases male Barbadians had entered a bathhouse and startled a Spanish female. But the government declined to move the Barbadians out of the camp. By August of that same year, racial animosities had grown more bitter. This time, when Barbadians arrived in the town of Paraiso in need of quarters, police visited Spaniards to inform them that the Barbadians would be housed in their dormitory. Spaniards threatened trouble if the government brought Barbadians into the building. Fearing a major conflict, the police quartered the Barbadians instead in an empty building that lacked beds or bedding, then moved them the next day to quarters in a building filled with East Indians. The East Indians protested fiercely against this arrangement, but with less immediate success. Government officials housed the two groups together for nearly two weeks and then found new quarters for the East Indians.[25]

"WE SHOULD ARISE WHEN THEY REPLACE US BY NEGROES"

The arrival of Spaniards and other Europeans increased racial tensions in the Canal Zone; as a policeman described the atmosphere, "Race feeling . . . here is at fever heat and is liable to develop seriously at any moment."[26] What explains this animosity? To some extent, workers brought a sense of racial identity and hostility with them from their country of origin. Racism was hardly unknown in Spain. Reflecting how fluid racial identities can be, Galicians—or, as they are known in Spanish, *gallegos*—were historically thought to be inferior by other Spaniards. In the mines of Asturias in Spain, which began to receive large numbers of Galician immigrants after 1911, tensions also quickly flared, and Galicians became the lowest group in the racial hierarchy that emerged. The special animosity toward Galicians has been observed in other parts of Spain as well. As the anarcho-syndicalist leader Angel Pestaña, who grew up in Basque and León mining towns, commented, "Where this 'race hatred' was most notable was between the *gallegos* and the rest. . . . The *gallegos* were the butt of all the jokes."[27] In the Canal Zone, U.S. officials regularly referred to Spaniards as *gallegos,* even though migrants often came from other parts of Spain. Thus *gallego* seems to have become a pejorative term used for any Spaniard.[28]

Once Spaniards were in Panama, their racial identity became more complex. One can only imagine how differently they must have felt when enjoying their leisure time away from the Canal Zone, footloose in the entertainment districts of Panama City. There they not only spoke the language but also were living representatives of the empire that had colonized Panama, Colombia, and much of Latin America. As Europeans, they stood high on Panama's racial hierarchy, seen not only as white men but as members of a race of conquerors and, as such, as members of a racial aristocracy. In the Zone, however, they were no longer conquerors. They now faced a new imperial power, one that owed its hegemony to victory in a war that had destroyed the Spanish Empire, one that classed them as racial inferiors nearly comparable to people of African descent and yet, contradictorily, left their exact position within the structured racial hierarchy of the Canal Zone distinctly unclear.[29]

Spaniards' position in the Canal Zone was also powerfully shaped by the ICC's labor management strategies. By elevating race and citizenship into key tools of labor management, the silver and gold system encouraged diverse groups to compete with one another for higher status. The system pitted workers against one another as a means of control, bringing them from many different nations for this very reason. As Jackson Smith, who headed the Department of Labor, Quarters, and Subsistence, noted, "It is also imperative to have several nationalities on the work, as these laborers are clannish, and they reason at once that if they are the only people brought here they are the only people that can be secured; and it does not matter whether they are West Indian blacks, Italian, Spanish, or any other, the result would be the same." For the same reason officials replaced certain skilled white workers (such as firemen) with black West Indians, to the fury of whites. When possible, officials used "our higher grade silver men as pacemakers to shame our high grade mechanics in to doing a fair day's work." Foremen likewise would commonly request both a Spanish gang and a West Indian one, so that, as one put it, "I could keep them both on their metal by rivalry between the two."[30]

The government placed Spaniards in a complicated position relative to West Indians. Officials had originally justified paying Spaniards more than West Indians on the grounds that they worked more efficiently. As time went on, however, officials ruefully noted that West Indians' productivity had gradually increased while the Spaniards were doing less work and causing more trouble. This led officials to start replacing Europeans with West Indians during the final years of construction. Over time, Spaniards began to suspect a plot underfoot to replace them altogether with West Indians.[31]

All these factors came together in 1911 as a wave of labor militancy exploded among Spanish workers. The strikes and riots of that year demonstrated the links between labor protest, anarchist politics, and racial hostility. In July, Spanish laborers working in Culebra Cut refused to do certain kinds of work and demanded the right to eat on the job. Culebra Cut had been the site of many previous struggles. As one subforeman put it, Culebra Cut was "the hardest place in the Canal to work on. Nine times out of ten you got to work noon hours, or got to work night time. You got to work hard, because the Canal is sliding in there. . . . [W]e got to work the men hard—sometimes in mud and water up to their waist—and it is pretty hard."[32]

Insubordination quickly spread among Spanish workers in the following days. More than three dozen gangs refused to follow orders, sat down on the job when prohibited from eating, or otherwise showed their determination to improve working conditions. Although striking workers had complaints to varying degrees against all the foremen, they increasingly focused on one American named Pike, the head foreman for about two hundred workers. They accused him of arriving at work drunk, drinking rum on the job, throwing stones at them, verbally abusing them, making them work in heavy rain, and punishing West Indians by kicking or pushing them. The Spanish workers also reasserted their right to eat on the job, a practice that had previously been allowed them.[33]

After some two hundred workers from Miraflores joined the strike in sympathy, bringing the total number of strikers close to eight hundred, workers began holding mass meetings to decide their demands and strategy. At these meetings Spaniards from construction towns like Las Cascadas, Empire, Pedro Miguel, and Gorgona joined those from Culebra and Miraflores, spoke, and contributed to a petition demanding that the government take action. In response, Goethals decided to temporarily remove Pike as foreman and to allow workers to resume eating on the job. He also instructed foremen to stop using abusive language and ordered officials to interview workers and hear their charges against Pike. After much discussion, the strikers returned to work the morning of August 3, 1911. Soon thereafter the committee appointed by Goethals interviewed a few dozen workers and heard their charges. The committee decided the charges were not sufficiently corroborated, and, perhaps more to the point, they decided that keeping Pike on the job would not result in a significant number of desertions. With Goethals's approval, they reappointed Pike to his original position. This represented a major defeat for the workers, for by this time the strike had ended and many of the activists had been urged by the government to leave the Canal Zone. Yet other strikes continued to break out across the Zone, almost all of them among Spanish workers.[34]

Amid this wave of labor militancy, with many strikes defeated but some important demands won, Spanish workers grew increasingly politicized and politically active. Anarchism began spreading as an organized movement across the Zone, winning hundreds of followers among the Spaniards. The politics of Spaniards in the Zone was informed by a rich tradition of rebellion and political protest in Spain, where strategies ranged from violence against property and other spontaneous acts to organized efforts to create associations and build schools. In Galicia, for example, peasants had begun withholding rent payments as early as the eighteenth century in order to fight efforts by landowners to renew their leases. In the early nineteenth century this strategy in Galicia blossomed into a more organized rent strike. Peasants and urban residents similarly rioted against those who charged overly high prices for food. A wave of food riots spread in 1904 and 1905, for example, just before Spaniards began heading to the Canal Zone.[35]

Anarchism in particular had flourished in Spain after the mid-nineteenth century, especially in Andalusia, and wherever Spanish immigrants traveled in the Americas, it tended to follow them—to Brazil, Argentina, Mexico, Uruguay, Ecuador, Cuba, Florida, and the Panama Canal Zone, among other places. Spanish immigrants moved amid an international world of radical politics, their ideology, strategy, and tactics shaped not only by their experiences constructing the canal or time spent in Spain, Cuba, and similar sites of international migration but also by the ideas of a vibrant social and political movement.

In both Spain and Cuba, anarchism became the dominant ideology among workers during the late nineteenth and early twentieth centuries. There were close ties between the anarchist movements in each country, and Spanish anarchist periodicals were distributed widely in Cuban cities. Anarchists in Cuba built effective unions, led strike movements, created schools and workers' associations, and published newspapers. They strove to build unity between workers in different industries and of different skill levels, and they were unusually supportive of women's struggles. They also made antiracism into an important part of their movement, taking an unprecedented stand for solidarity among *peninsulares,* Creoles, and people of color. In the Canal Zone, anarchism evolved differently in one important respect. As the example of Cuba suggests, the ideology

In a photograph that telegraphed to the world the importance of the Panama Canal project, President Theodore Roosevelt poses in the cab of a Bucyrus steam shovel. Roosevelt's visit to the Panama Canal Zone marked the first time an American president left the country while in office. *Library of Congress*

George Washington Goethals, chief engineer of the Panama Canal from 1907 until its completion in 1914, inspecting the construction site. Goethals considered managing and disciplining labor to be an even greater challenge than the medical and engineering difficulties associated with the canal. *National Archives*

The astonishing Culebra Cut, photographed in 1913, after one of many landslides had wrecked a steam shovel and some flatcars. More than eight miles long, Culebra Cut brought together thousands of workers to slice through the Continental Divide. Landslides, premature dynamite explosions, and flooding made it the most dangerous place in the Zone.

National Archives

LEFT: Laborers, like these in Culebra Cut, would sometimes be required to work in the water for hours on end. This, combined with daily torrential rains, caused West Indian and Spanish workers to complain that their clothes never had a chance to dry. Here, workers excavate a ditch at the Cucaracha slide near Gold Hill in Culebra Cut, 1913. *National Archives*

BELOW: U.S. government officials were proud of the fine commissaries they provided for employees, like this one in Balboa in 1915. The dual payroll arrangement— in which white American employees were paid in gold and almost everyone else in silver—became a massive system of segregation that shaped every aspect of life and work in the Zone. Note in this photograph the separate entrances for gold and silver employees, reminiscent of racial segregation in the Jim Crow South. *National Archives*

The railroad played a crucial role in the construction project, carrying workers, machinery, and supplies to and from construction sites, and eliminating excavated dirt and rocks. *Above*, a train prepares to carry laborers to work in Culebra Cut. *Right*, workers line up for payday at Bas Obispo. *National Archives*

ABOVE: In the large, modern blacksmith shop at Gorgona, a few white Americans, *foreground*, are backed up by a small army of West Indians. White U.S workers struggled to uphold their privileges and enforce the racial hierarchy of the Canal Zone, but the possibility that they could be replaced by cheaper West Indian laborers was a constant threat. *National Archives*

LEFT: Dinner on the veranda at the Isthmian Canal Commission's hotel in Gorgona, where gold employees are being served by West Indian waiters.

National Archives

Nurses and medical staff in front of Ancon Hospital. The modern hospitals of the Zone became a challenging and sometimes empowering work site for the dozens of nurses employed there. Nurses clashed with government officials over their uniforms, calling as they did so for equal rights for women. *National Archives*

The reading room at the ICC Clubhouse, run by the YMCA, for gold employees only. YMCA clubhouses were part of an important—but not entirely successful—effort by the U.S. government to make the lives of white American employees more pleasant and thereby reduce turnover. *National Archives*

A ship bringing fifteen hundred Barbadians to work on the canal arrives at Cristobal in 1909. Many of the migrants carried deck chairs, since no sleeping accommodations—or food— were provided during the six-day voyage to Panama. *National Archives*

ABOVE AND RIGHT:
Typical housing
provided by the ICC for
West Indian employees
and their families.
Sharp differences
separated the homes
built for West Indians
from those supplied
to white Americans.
The former usually
confronted congested
spaces and sanitary
problems resulting from
insufficient drainage.
West Indians often
slept on metal cots, and,
despite the prevalence
of malaria, their homes
lacked window screens
and mosquito netting.

National Archives

West Indian employees at a kitchen provided for them by the ICC. These kitchens did not have any seats, and the food was widely considered so intolerable that many West Indians abandoned ICC housing in order to avoid it. *National Archives*

Employees unable to make the trip back to their labor camp for lunch would have to prepare food at their work site. Many workers came to prefer this alternative.

National Archives

ABOVE, RIGHT, AND BELOW: Thousands of
Spaniards traveled to Panama to build the
canal. ICC officials originally thought they
would be preferable to West Indian workers, an
impression that changed once they realized that
Spaniards were more prone to strike. Angry
at their exclusion from the gold roll and from
"white" hotels and cafeterias, Spanish workers
formed a lively anarchist movement in protest
of ICC policies. Here, the so-called *gallegos*
stand next to the railroad cars in which some
of them lived, pose on steps in Las Cascadas,
and work on railroad tracks. *National Archives*

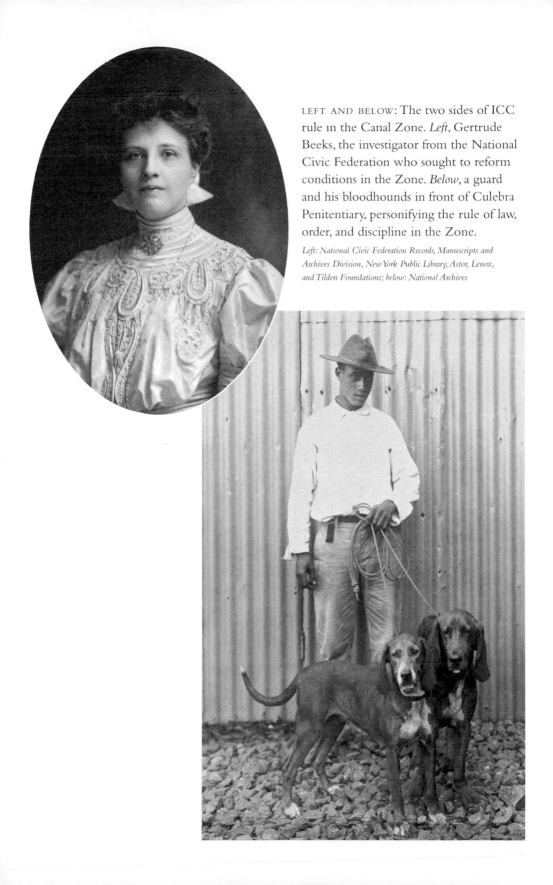

LEFT AND BELOW: The two sides of ICC rule in the Canal Zone. *Left*, Gertrude Beeks, the investigator from the National Civic Federation who sought to reform conditions in the Zone. *Below*, a guard and his bloodhounds in front of Culebra Penitentiary, personifying the rule of law, order, and discipline in the Zone.

Left: National Civic Federation Records, Manuscripts and Archives Division, New York Public Library, Astor, Lenox, and Tilden Foundations; below: National Archives

ABOVE: A West Indian wedding party in Culebra, 1913. Couples from Barbados, Jamaica, and other Caribbean islands often lived together without marrying, much to the chagrin of ICC officials, but few West Indians could afford the elaborate ceremony of the bride and groom pictured here. *National Archives*

RIGHT: Central division engineer D. D. Gaillard and his wife at home. Culebra Cut was later renamed Gaillard Cut in his honor. Like Gaillard and his wife, many Americans living in the Zone placed great emphasis on creating a respectable and civilized domestic sphere. *National Archives*

Carnival celebrations in Cathedral Plaza, Panama City, in February 1912. Cities in the Republic of Panama were less restrictive and regimented than the Zone, and visiting them became a popular leisure activity for canal workers. *National Archives*

U.S. marines scaling a wall during patriotic exercises organized across the Zone and in Panama City and Colón to celebrate America's Independence Day. Riots pitting U.S. military personnel against the Panamanian police broke out in Panama City's Cocoa Grove neighborhood soon after these exercises took place on July 4, 1912. *National Archives*

After many years of work, steam shovels heading from both directions finally met on the floor of the canal in May 1913. Across the Canal Zone, workers and their families celebrated this grand achievement. A year later, in the summer of 1914, the first ship sailed through the canal soon after the outbreak of World War I. *National Archives*

Surveying America's new empire: men and women enjoy a view of Balboa, the town built by the United States to serve as the headquarters of its canal operations, 1919. *National Archives*

CLOCKWISE FROM TOP LEFT: Three views of the Panama–Pacific International Exposition, held in San Francisco in 1915 to celebrate the completion of the canal: the magnificent lights at night; spectators gazing in wonder at the model Panama Canal; and the model canal, which covered nearly five acres and cost $250,000 to build. *San Francisco History Center, San Francisco Public Library*

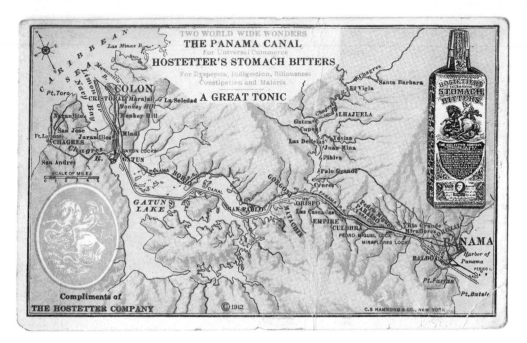

CLOCKWISE FROM TOP: Three postcards capture the popularity of the canal and its meaning in contemporary culture: an advertisement for Hostetter's Stomach Bitters compares the assistance that the elixir provides the human alimentary canal to the wonders in Panama; Santa Claus gazes proudly at the canal; in a pervasive image, "The Kiss of the Oceans" displays two women kissing at the very spot where the canal joined the Atlantic and Pacific oceans. *Author's Collection*

typically emphasized building solidarity across boundaries of skill, status, race, ethnicity, and nationality. In the Panama Canal Zone during the construction era, anarchism became a movement limited to one group—unskilled European immigrants, almost all of them Spaniards—and it never developed antiracism as a part of its ideology.[36]

According to U.S. officials, a belief in the principles of anarchism arrived in the Canal Zone along with the very first Spanish workers in 1907. It became a widespread organized movement only in 1911 as the wave of labor protests climaxed. By the autumn of that year, anarchist clubs existed in Rio Grande, Pedro Miguel, Las Cascadas, Corozal, Culebra, Empire, Gatun, Libertador, and Gorgona—in short, in almost every town where a significant number of Spaniards resided. One close observer of the movement believed it had some eight hundred members in the town of Rio Grande alone, and, he noted, "But for requiring members to pay dues their organization would undoubtedly be much larger than it is." This group in Rio Grande called itself "The Invincibles." Even the chief medical officer, William Gorgas, commented on the ubiquitous movement, observing that hospitalized Spaniards always had anarchist pamphlets among their reading materials.[37]

Bernardo Perez, a Spaniard who had previously spent time in Cuba, stood at the center of this anarchist movement. Perez published an anarchist newspaper, El Único, in Colón and was, according to a police spy, "an excellent orator, a well educated man, and one who appears to have a great deal of experience along this line." He possessed a vast knowledge of labor conditions and anarchist organization around the world and used this to educate and motivate crowds of listeners at protest meetings. Aquilino Lopez, a younger man, assisted Perez. Lopez had been in the Zone for only three months, and "while he is very enthusiastic in the propaganda, very earnest in his efforts to convince, it can be seen that he is young in experience, and lacks the training of his comrade, Bernardo Perez." Lopez demonstrated his enthusiasm when he tried to convince a government official that anarchists were not the bomb throwers suggested by their enemies. He described anarchists as deeply opposed to the Catholic Church and to drunkenness, gambling, war, and prostitution; they advocated reading and education, international peace, and vegetarianism.[38]

In mass meetings and in the pages of *El Único,* Perez sounded fiercer than Lopez. Seeking to recruit more readers, he promised that by supporting his newspaper, "you will have contributed to burying the clericalism that poisons your conscience, capitalism which sucks your blood, and the State which chokes your life." In another article he declared, "We are the junior brothers of those who were hung in Chicago, Vergara, Paris, . . . and of those who were shot in Warsaw, Barcelona, Buenos Ayres and in Japan," thereby placing the Canal Zone's anarchist movement within an international context. He also attended to the specific concerns of canal workers. He demanded public meeting rooms for their organizations, decried deportations of strikers, and attacked the U.S. government for allowing its foremen to abuse workers, for overcrowding them, and for treating them like slaves. Contradicting his own internationalism, he echoed the concerns of most Spanish workers by focusing attention on the threat black Caribbeans seemed to represent. Declaring that "we should arise when they replace us by negroes," Perez argued that the government had already begun moving on such a plan. If Spanish workers failed to unite, West Indians would gradually overtake them, and they would "have to go about the Isthmus begging." Other speakers developed similar themes. One, in a pointed attack on the government overseeing the canal construction, declared, "We are scorned. The American Government despises us. It spits on us."[39]

The anarchists continued meeting throughout the autumn of 1911 and at least through the spring of 1912, and Perez continued to publish *El Único.* One leaflet distributed by the anarchists reflected a sense of grisly humor, noting that a coming meeting would include refreshments such as "Monks' heads, Friars' Juice, Fried Priests' Heart, Tenderloin of Colonel, and Iced Jesuits' blood." These dark images were matched by occasional threats of violence as the anarchist movement grew. In letters and postcards a few anarchists and disgruntled employees threatened to "blow up the works," meaning dynamite the locks. And a rumor spread through the Canal Zone that someone had threatened to assassinate chief engineer Goethals.[40]

The threats of violence increased pressure on the government to respond aggressively. Catholic priests demanded that the government repress the anarchist movement ruthlessly. Some within the government, most notably M. H. Thatcher, who headed the Department of Civil Administration, agreed. Arguing that Perez was an outlaw and encouraging violence, Thatcher urged strong action against him. Gradually, however, most in the government argued for a tolerant policy. The Spanish consul agreed, claiming that there was nothing threatening about the movement. The most influential voice, ultimately, appears to have been that of Goethals's chief clerk, who read over the spy reports and then assessed the anarchist threat for his boss. He declared that the anarchists were not inciting their followers to violence. "They believe that the present organization of society is unjust, and that their class suffers most from the injustice. What intelligent human being would deny this?" Although he believed their activities could lead to a strike or encourage an assassination attack, he noted the government's powerful police and military presence in the Zone and doubted officials would have any trouble repressing either of those. Most emphatically, he warned that suppression would only keep the movement alive. Heeding such advice, the ICC took no steps to prohibit mass meetings and did not deport Perez or any other anarchists—even though they had deported strike leaders in the past. Officials continued to watch the Spanish workers carefully, keeping them and their leaders under tight police surveillance. In March 1912 the final piece of evidence regarding anarchism available to us notes simply that the government refrained from interfering with any further anarchist meetings. Interestingly, the government took a stronger stance against strikers than against anarchists.[41]

After early 1912, Spanish workers in the Canal Zone seem to have suspended their strikes, riots, and anarchist meetings. One can only guess at the nature of the denouement that followed the conflicts of 1911, because little more evidence regarding Spanish workers exists in the voluminous records kept by the ICC. Perhaps the government's strategy worked, and leniency killed the movement. Yet the basic conditions remained the same, and it seems improbable that all tensions and grievances would abruptly disappear. A more likely possibility is that the Spaniards' fears came true, and the U.S. government moved ahead rapidly with its plan to replace Europeans with West Indians. The government had already begun this process by 1911, and Spanish protests had focused precisely on that phenomenon. Furthermore, all the strikes and anarchist agitation must have encouraged the U.S. government to proceed as fast as it could with this strategy, in order to eliminate the troublesome Spaniards. In addition, from 1909 onward few Spaniards entered the Canal Zone because their government prohibited further recruiting. Immigration into the Zone had declined more generally by 1912 as the project's completion neared, and hundreds of men began leaving the Zone for work on United Fruit Company plantations in Guatemala. These changing demographics likely complicated efforts to organize and weakened ties to anarchist movements in Europe.[42]

B EFORE THEIR movement came to an end, Spanish workers launched an articulate protest against the U.S. government's policies in the Canal Zone, one that was expressed through political agitation, food riots, and workplace action. Theirs would stand as the most effective resistance movement during the construction decade. Ironically, however, while the internationalist ideals of anarchism might have encouraged cooperation with men of different races and nationalities, harsh realities in the Zone pushed the Spaniards' protest in a different direction. They became increasingly focused on differentiating themselves from black West Indians to prove their superiority and to clarify their racial identity.

Officials had expected Spaniards would work more productively than West Indians and, by spurring the latter to be more efficient, would serve as a tool in their quest to manage such a large and unwieldy workforce. They found the Spaniards less effective as workers and far more troublesome than they expected. In the end, officials believed the presence of Spaniards helped push West Indians to work harder, but—to their surprise—West Indians helped them manage the Spaniards as well. The system of segregation placed Spaniards in a position uneasily adjacent to that of West Indians and allowed government officials to hold over their heads the threat that they could be replaced by a more lowly paid laborer of African descent. This generated explosive protests among Spaniards that caused headaches for government officials, but it also created a barrier to more widespread solidarities that might have empowered canal workers, given rise to a more potent labor movement, and made possible more significant improvements in workers' living and working conditions.

Even as government officials struggled to discipline and manage the gold and silver workers, another group grew interested in the construction project. The canal was too monumental to be left to the ICC officials alone. Journalists and reformers in the United States— socialists, progressives, and corporate welfare advocates—observed the government's policies in the Zone, often traveling there to see the big ditch for themselves. Increasingly, they used the construction project as a template for evaluating the proper role of the state and its relationship to society during a time of tumultuous change in the United States. They provided suggestions regarding how the United States should treat its workforce and sometimes demanded that government officials heed their advice. For many in the U.S. government, including President Theodore Roosevelt, managing the influence of journalists and reformers back home would prove as important and difficult as any other aspect of building the canal.

CHAPTER FIVE

PROGRESSIVISM FOR THE WORLD

W HERE MIGHT one travel in the early twentieth century to find a society in which profit was not the goal? Where competition did not loom tyrannically over workers and employers? Where the government owned the railroads, the hotels, the stores, and the restaurants and even provided free housing to every resident? Where the ideas of Henry George, the nineteenth-century bestselling author who advocated government ownership of land, had at last become a reality? And where government officials honestly and efficiently intervened to ensure citizens received the best care possible? In 1911 the prominent American socialist Arthur Bullard published a book arguing that such a place already existed—in the Panama Canal Zone.

Bullard had traveled to Panama to observe conditions and interview workers and officials. He declared, "The more one stays here, the more one realizes that the Isthmian Canal Commission has gone further towards Socialism than any other branch of our government—further probably than any government has ever gone."[1]

Bullard was one of many progressive and socialist reformers who observed the government's work on the isthmus and took from it inspiring lessons to apply at home. Born in Missouri in 1879, Bullard quit Hamilton College after two years, so eager was he to get to the world of reform in New York City. There he began working as a probation officer, publishing essays on criminology when he could. Soon he was writing on a variety of topics for the major magazines of the day. He worked as editor of the *Outlook,* as associate editor of the *Masses,* and as a staff member of the socialist newspaper the *Call.* One of the "gentlemen socialists" linked closely to the University Settlement House in New York City, Bullard moved in an invigorating circle of reformers and social workers that included William English Walling, James G. Phelps Stokes, Walter Weyl, Robert Hunter, and Leroy Scott. In 1905, Ekaterina "Babushka" Breshkovskaia, the "Little Grandmother of the Russian Revolution," toured the United States, and Bullard became her constant companion, escorting her as she met with the stars of American reform ranging from Jane Addams to Emma Goldman. Inspired by Babushka, Bullard and Walling visited Russia to cover the 1905 revolution for American periodicals. Soon both men had emerged as experts on Russian affairs.[2]

Bullard's socialist beliefs led him to seek more knowledge about Panama as well as Russia. When the canal construction project was about half completed, he took a ship through the Caribbean, watched U.S. labor recruiters at work in Barbados, and then, when an outbreak of yellow fever on the island meant his journey to Panama would be delayed several weeks due to a quarantine, seized the only opportunity he could find to continue his trip. The American labor recruiter offered him a spot on a British ship carrying West Indians from Barbados to the Canal Zone. He jumped aboard, telling readers that he had been the only white man on board other than the British crew. During the trip, he explained dramatically, he helped the British officers suppress efforts at mutiny by hot and desperately hungry West Indians. Then he breathed a sigh of relief after six long days when land was finally sighted.

Like so many other Americans, Bullard found that a tour of the Canal Zone strengthened his faith in the government. A friend met Bullard and escorted him by train across the isthmus, pointing out the wonders of the construction project. As the train passed the Cristobal machine shops and his friend identified them as the largest of their kind in the world, Bullard initially found himself feeling tired of "this 'largest in the world' talk. . . . The largest dam, the highest locks, the greatest artificial lake, the deepest cut, the biggest machine shops, the heaviest consumption of dynamite, the most wonderful sanitary system." None-theless, he was gradually won over: "It is only as you accustom yourself to the idea that each integral part of the work is of unequaled propor-tions that you begin to sense the grandeur of the whole undertaking." Ultimately, Bullard concluded, "I gained a new respect for Uncle Sam—a new respect for his children who have conceived and are executing this gigantic thing."[3]

Bullard's socialist beliefs gave him a special interest in the extensive government intervention and ownership making the construction proj-ect possible. Everywhere at home, he noted, one hears that the profit incentive must rule and government should remain as limited as possible. And yet the canal, the greatest undertaking of the age, is a government job, the work is done by government employees, and the government controls every aspect of life and work in the Canal Zone. Bullard met and talked at length with a white American worker who belonged to the Socialist Party, an educated and eloquent man who had been work-ing in the Zone for several years. "'Yes,' the worker said, 'this is a fine place to get an idea of what some things will be like when we get the world educated up to Socialism. . . . [T]his Canal Zone is as near Social-ism as you can get to-day—a lot nearer.'" With the nationalization of land, the mechanic noted, Henry George's plan had been realized. The machine shops ran efficiently with no profit incentive, and the commis-saries handled retail distribution cheaply, again because there was none of the waste known as profit. Indeed, he noted, the Canal Zone pro-vided an answer to most of the obvious criticisms of socialism: "I never made a Socialist speech in the States yet without some wise guy getting up and saying that the politicians are all grafters. . . . Well, say, this is a government job. . . . Have you seen any graft running around loose here? I guess not." Likewise, the mechanic declared, the canal project shattered the myth that men would only work well for profit. Everyone there was working for wages, from Goethals on down to the humblest working-man. To this socialist workingman, Goethals treated the workers well precisely because "he won't make any more money if he gouges us. He don't increase his income by neglecting to put a guard on my machine."

In short, this man concluded, Goethals "can afford to be decent. And I guess that is Socialism in a nutshell. We want to revolutionize things so every one can afford to be decent—so nobody will have to cheat, nor underpay, nor overcharge to make a living."

In one important way, the mechanic and Bullard agreed, the Canal Zone was not a socialist society. As the former declared, "First of all, there ain't any democracy down here." Although Goethals was a good boss, the man said, he possessed total control. And while he treated workingmen and their unions with respect, workers nonetheless lacked any say in the policies of the Zone: "Government ownership don't mean anything to us working men unless we own the Government. We don't here—this is the sort of thing Bismarck dreamed of." As Bullard himself noted, "One is used to thinking that if we were deprived of jury trials and the right to vote, we would begin to shoot. But down here the only right which has not been alienated is the right to get out. There are two or three steamers home a week."[4]

Despite these limitations of government, Bullard found a great deal to admire, and so did, he argued, the thousands of Americans in the Canal Zone. Soon the construction would be completed, and most of those Americans would return home. It would be hard, then, to convince them that "government enterprise is necessarily inefficient, extravagant and dishonest." The women of the Canal Zone, likewise, would find it difficult to believe there is "sufficient sanctity in the right of the middleman to his profit to justify the high cost of living." Bullard concluded, "This is the lesson of Panama. . . . 'Collective activity'—this new force which we are developing with such amazing success in the tropics, which we, Americans, have carried further than any other nation—is worth considering as a means of solving our problems at home."[5]

Bullard seems to have taken these lessons to heart. In the years to come he became a strong proponent of state intervention. He supported the United States entering World War I—one of a group of socialists to do so—became a powerful adviser to President Woodrow Wilson, and took a job heading the Russian Division of the reformer George Creel's propaganda machine, the Committee on Public Information. His experiences suggest the ways in which reformers looked to the Canal Zone for insights and lessons about the state's role during the Progressive Era. Books and articles on the construction of the canal pervaded American culture during this period, and writers would routinely assess the meaning of the canal not only in terms of its impact on economics and foreign policy but also in terms of contemporary understandings of the state. This is unsurprising, since state power was the topic of the day. Reformers, politicians, workers, employers, and everyday citizens all debated the proper form and extent of government intervention, and how to reconcile a more powerful state with America's democratic traditions. That tension between authoritarianism and democracy was played out in the Canal Zone as well, but with a much greater emphasis on extensive state intervention and less concern for democratic impulses.

A great many Americans accepted that the government should play a greater role to help cure social ills caused by industrialization, mass immigration, and rapid urbanization, but others worried that state expansion threatened laissez-faire economics as well as popular and democratic government. Under the leadership of presidents like Theodore Roosevelt and Woodrow Wilson, the power and size of the government rapidly expanded. Many agreed with Bullard that the Canal Zone was a place— perhaps *the* place—to watch for insights into the government's proper role. Beyond that, however, there existed a great deal of disagreement. How should the government run the construction effort? What role might progressive ideals play in shaping the project? Did democracy matter? The Canal Zone quickly became a site for contesting diverse approaches to these issues, and ICC policies reflected contemporary views on the state's role and the future of reform.

"THE AMERICAN REVOLUTION AT PANAMA"

One point on which many observers agreed was that the canal project signaled a new and more collectivist approach to government. Individualism and the free market seemed clearly on the decline. Scientific approaches to social responsibility meant more government, more fair treatment of employees, and less interference by private capital. Writing in the *Chicago Daily Tribune* about what he called "the American revolution at Panama," Samuel Merwin praised how "the Canal is being built, and the Canal Zone administered, entirely by wage-earners." Moreover, the employees received decent treatment: "Instead of driving a laborer or other employee to exhaustion, and then turning him over to the nearest saloon or dive for the night, the Commission uses him intelligently and efficiently; removes the usual commercialized temptations from its neighborhood; pays him adequately; and places at his hand an astonishing variety of well-organized and wholesome recreations." Merwin stressed "the efficiency of this extremely modern method of treating employees." Like Bullard, he noted that this was not socialism, because it lacked democracy, and indeed he seemed to desire not socialism, but rather a more powerful collectivism inspired by notions of civic engagement and social responsibility: "The good old individualistic theory that by keeping men down to a state of desperation you give the occasional strong man an 'incentive' to fight his way up" was rejected by Europeans a while ago. Now, at last, the Canal Zone was proving to Americans the futility of expecting laborers to live and work "under the usual conditions of commercialism." Merwin suspected, as others did, that the thousands of enthusiastic young men experiencing the "scientific paternalism" of the Canal Zone, who had learned what it felt like to live amid a sound and modern government, relieved of having to worry about whether they made sufficient wages or how they would pay a bill, would likely "become germ-centers of a thoughtful and healthy sort of discontent when they return and find themselves turned loose at the mercy of a new set of purely commercial forces."[6]

The canal project inspired for some people utopian visions of a future society. William James and H. G. Wells had advocated the adoption of universal conscription so that an army of citizens could undertake public service projects. While some rejected their ideas as unfeasible, the columnist Robert Herrick hailed the canal construction as evidence of the soundness of their idea. He recommended that the army of laborers building the canal not be dispersed upon its completion but be transferred to a site like Alaska, where future railroads and highways required vast human labor. Such a citizens' army would solve many problems at once: it would shift energies away from militarism and toward the public good, it would provide "valuable democratic training," and it would make unnecessary the employment of aliens (which the government unfortunately relied on in the Canal Zone), because universal conscription would make every young citizen of the United States available to the government.[7]

Likewise, some thinkers inspired by the Canal Zone linked it to Edward Bellamy's bestselling utopian novel, *Looking Backward,* published in 1888, which had generated much debate and enthusiasm and helped popularize collectivist approaches to government. *Looking Backward* takes place in the year 2000, when collectivism has finally been achieved. Some have seen Bellamy's vision as a particularly authoritarian sort of socialism, while other historians have argued his collectivism was intended to unleash a new, more fulfilled individuality. Willis Abbot's popular book *Panama and the Canal in Picture and Prose,* which included on its title page "Approved by Leading Officials Connected with the Great Enterprise," saw the canal as a realization of Bellamy's vision, particularly by putting collectivism and state power in the service of consumerism and by exerting a degree of control over vast global markets. Abbot argued, "The dream of the late Edward Bellamy is given actuality on the Zone where we find a great central authority, buying everything imaginable in all the markets of the world at the moment when prices are lowest—an authority big enough to snap its fingers at any trust—and selling again without profit to the ultimate consumers."[8]

More commonly, observers noted a parallel between the Canal Zone's government and the single-tax ideas of the nineteenth-century economist Henry George, whose bestselling book, *Progress and Poverty,* had argued that landowners who received income from rent on land impoverished other Americans, thereby preventing progress and increasing inequality. He proposed a "single tax" on land that would make it economically unfeasible for owners to charge rent for land or do anything other than cultivate it. This would make land more available to poorer Americans, which would result in higher wages for everyone (in part by reducing labor surplus in the cities) and thus generate greater social and economic equality. George became one of the most influential social thinkers of the late nineteenth century, exciting working-class followers across the country—most famously in 1886 in New York City, where he was drafted to run for mayor only to lose to the Democrat Abram Hewitt but handily defeating young Theodore Roosevelt, his Republican opponent. By the first decade of the twentieth century George's single-tax ideas had declined in popularity. Yet they seemed to find new life amid the challenges of America's expansionism abroad. In the Canal Zone, it was said, government ownership of all land was realizing George's dream because speculation and exploitation caused by high rents had become impossible.

The most noteworthy advocate for the idea was William Gorgas, the chief medical officer of the Canal Zone who had defeated yellow fever. Gorgas declared in a speech to the American Public Health Association in 1915 that his experience in the Canal Zone suggested the United States should apply a special tax on uncultivated land in its domestic territory. He conceded that the battle against yellow fever and other diseases had been crucial in improving the quality of life in the Zone, but he added, "The decrease in the general death rate in the canal zone I attribute to the good wages paid." Thus, he argued, in the United States the best thing to lower the death rate and improve living conditions would be to tax idle land. We should make "available the millions of acres of idle lands now held vacant, unproductive and unused. This a special land tax will do. It will increase wages without increasing the burden on labor. Thus it will lower death rates and increase health and efficiency rates."[9]

Throughout the construction decade increasing numbers of middle-class white reformers and journalists evaluated the Canal Zone's government and used it as a site for considering the virtues of state intervention. Often they ducked the question of democracy or contrived a way to argue that the government, despite its apparent authoritarianism, was in fact highly democratic. In 1906, when John Foster Carr traveled to Panama from New York to observe the construction, his reaction was typical: "We are new at the imperial business of creating republics and dependencies, but our success here has been so great . . . the most striking and significant work we are doing on the isthmus is not the completion of a vast and comprehensive scheme for canal digging, but the creation of a state." When the United States arrived on the isthmus, he noted, "we found the old civilization in decay, and throughout a large part of the Zone reverting slowly to savagery." But then the U.S. government began to exert itself, and soon things were made right. Although the approach might seem absolutist, at the municipal level Carr found a workshop of democracy. In the end, he concluded, we are building with idealism, because our labor "has its origins in the very life and traditions of the Republic." Similarly, Willis Abbot characterized the government as a "benevolent despotism" and declared it to be what the czar of Russia might implement if he shared Goethals's dislike of bureaucracies, grafters, and delay. Yet he proclaimed the government "very democratic . . . for it won't issue to Mrs. High-flyer more than three wicker arm-chairs, even if she does entertain every day, while her neighbor Mrs. Domus who gets just exactly as many never entertains at all."[10]

Workers likewise saw the government's policies in the Canal Zone as a testing ground. The Zone's steam-shovel men and machinists struggled to prove that the state was—or should be—a model employer. Labor activists struggling in the United States to build a case for state intervention similarly looked to the Canal Zone. Miners and electrical workers striking in Butte, Montana, in 1917, for example, demanded government ownership of the mines and commented in their strike bulletin: "In no place in the world are better conditions to be found than in the Panama Canal Zone, which is entirely under Government control." The editors of the *Machinists' Monthly Journal* noted in 1908, "When Uncle Sam took hold of the job that was to unite the two oceans, all those who are opposed to the Government taking anything in hand that could be used for the purpose of fattening private interests croaked all kinds of dire prophecies, each one of which declared that the whole thing would end in a miserable failure." They recounted the government's achievements in the Canal Zone:

Uncle Sam took over a festering swamp and made it one of the healthiest spots on earth. He has rebuilt two cities on a modern plan and has constructed a new one on his own account. He has made ports and quays, has driven away contagious diseases and mosquitoes, has reconstructed a railway and enlarged the old canal until it is for much of the way fully completed. All this is very creditable and shows that work prosecuted by the Government is far superior to work done under private contract. And the beauty of it is, the work is done for the nation at large, though the whole world will be benefited. It will stimulate trade and bring the nations of the earth closer together, and thus hasten the day of universal brotherhood.[11]

Life was so pleasant in the Zone, one canal employee wrote in the *International Socialist Review,* that "we are really one of the happiest bunches of workingmen in the world." Most workers would like to stay forever, he declared. "We feel as though we had temporarily escaped the driving lash of Capitalism and the Profit-System and are enjoying a fore-taste of what life will be for all the workers in the Wonderful Days A-Coming."[12]

Middle-class reformers in the United States who, like Bullard, would later become prominent state builders expressed their admiration for the construction project. In the 1920s the technocrat Stuart Chase described his more radical youth during the Progressive Era in the third person: "He made a laborious summary of state-controlled enterprises the world around, and took much comfort in the Panama Canal Zone as the one rocky ledge in a sea of American laissez-faire." The prominent welfare editor and progressive Edward T. Devine visited the Canal Zone and cast a careful eye upon the living conditions, the penitentiary, and the judicial system. Overall he deemed it a perfect representation of his faith in progress, efficiency, and triumphant social science. Although he expressed dismay that prisoners were forced to wear a ball and chain and that there existed no juvenile court or probation system, much about the Zone impressed him. Devine praised the officials' solution to the race problem: "Among the ingenious inventions to which social conditions on the isthmus have given rise, first place must be given to the broad distinction between 'gold employes' . . . and 'silver employes.' " This was not explicitly a racial system, but it rather neatly solved the race problem, according to Devine: "There is no 'Jim Crow car' on the Panama Railway; but there is a first and second class with separate coaches, and on work trains there are separate cars for 'gold' employes. The patent subterfuge might make 'trouble' in some parts of the country; but on the zone, with Negroes who are mainly British subjects, and 'Europeans' who are accustomed to the idea of social classes, the plan seems to work satisfactorily." Devine admired the efficient administration that allowed construction to hum along, and he seemed thrilled to meet "the superb lot of men and boys" doing the actual work. Like most who visited the Zone, he could hardly find sufficient superlatives to describe the project's grandeur: "All honor to them; for this that they are doing . . . is a real wonder of the world."[13]

The Canal Zone thus seemed a living laboratory for the sorts of activist state policies, closely tied to science and the latest technology and managed by experts, that advanced progressives like Herbert Croly advocated. As historian William Leuchtenburg pointed out decades ago, Croly became not only the best-known advocate of expanded state power (coining the term "New Nationalism," which would be adopted, famously, by Theodore Roosevelt) but also one who married the ideals of progressivism to America's new empire. Croly advocated an assertive foreign policy and the creation of an American international system, and he repeatedly noted the interconnections between domestic and foreign policies. He credited the War of 1898 with generating progressivism itself: "That war and its resulting policy of extra-territorial expansion . . . availed, from the sheer force of the national aspirations it aroused, to give a tremendous impulse to the work of national reform." Now the United States had begun the mighty job of creating an international system, both by "pacifying" Cuba and by introducing "a little order into the affairs of the turbulent Central American republics." Furthermore, he noted, "the construction of the Panama Canal has given this country an exceptional interest in the prevalence of order and good government in the territory between Panama and Mexico; and in the near future our best opportunity for improving international political conditions in the Western hemisphere will be found in this comparatively limited but, from a selfish point of view, peculiarly important field." Nor in the long run should these expansionist activities be considered separate from domestic reform: "The irresponsible attitude of Americans in respect to their national domestic problems may in part be traced to freedom from equally grave international responsibilities. . . . [I]t is entirely possible that hereafter the United States will be forced into the adoption of a really national domestic policy because of the dangers and duties incurred through her relations with foreign countries."[14]

POULTNEY BIGELOW AND THE PRESIDENT'S TRIP

How did progressive reformers come to perceive the canal project in such a rosy way? The reactions were not always so positive, and closer examination reveals how the canal came to be seen as a wondrous application of scientific and efficient government policies. In the years after its victory in the War of 1898, as the United States replaced Spain in the Philippines, Cuba, and Puerto Rico, it found the exercise of power difficult and contested by its new subjects. The brutal repression of rebels in the Philippines after 1898 particularly challenged America's positive image of its role in the world. An energetic insurrection had broken out as Filipinos resisted the new occupying power. Under the leadership of Emilio Aguinaldo, thousands of Filipinos took up arms to achieve national independence. The U.S. government was determined to assert its control over the archipelago. For Americans who had sought to portray themselves as using their new power only for civilizing purposes, the Filipino insurrection proved a great embarrassment. Whether measured in duration, resources expended, or the number of mortalities, it ultimately dwarfed the War of 1898. More than 125,000 Americans served in the Philippine-American War; it cost the lives of at least 16,000 Filipino insurgents, perhaps as many as 700,000 Filipino civilians, and 4,200 U.S. soldiers.[15]

The situation in the Philippines generated widespread concern among Americans about the supposed benevolence of their government overseas. In the war's early stages government censorship limited the spread of information. Gradually, as soldiers returned home and particularly as anti-imperialists dug for information, revelations came out in the press about the U.S. military's use of torture. Most infamous was the widespread "water cure" (in which gallons of water would be poured down the victim's throat, then pressure applied to the stomach to force the water back out), but the American press and public also grew concerned about concentration camps, the indiscriminate burning of Filipino villages, and the killing of Filipinos who had surrendered. Brigadier General James Bell reported to the *New York Times* that in the province of Luzon alone, more than 600,000 Filipinos had died, either in battle or from dengue fever, itself at least partially a consequence of famine brought about by the war. Critics of the war effort pressed successfully for an investigation into alleged atrocities committed by the United States. The investigation lasted from January through June of 1902. Although Republicans carefully managed the hearings (refusing to allow the public or the press to attend, and preventing critics of the government from testifying), damning evidence nonetheless horrified the public and led to demands that the United States reform its policy.[16]

The Senate investigating committee learned, for example, that the highest-ranking officer in the Army had protested against the severe methods being employed on the Filipinos. The American governor of the province of Tayabas likewise reported that Army methods included "the extensive burning of barrios in trying to lay waste the country so that the insurgents cannot occupy it," as well as various forms of torture. An Army major accused of killing unarmed Filipinos testified at his trial that he was following orders given him by General Jacob Smith: "Gen. Smith instructed him to kill and burn, and said that the more he killed and burned the better pleased he would be; that it was no time to take prisoners, and that he was to make Samar a howling wilderness."[17] Public outrage grew as the tales of a military seemingly out of control flowed freely. Some newspapers questioned the leadership of President Roosevelt and his secretary of war, Elihu Root. U.S. military officials found themselves compared to their corrupt predecessors in Spain. Anti-imperialists in the United States gained in the Philippines debacle much ammunition for arguing that empire was sapping the manhood of American youth, not energizing it. The arguments put forward by defenders of the military seemed to threaten American respectability even more. Some argued that savage tactics must be used by Americans when they confronted savages, or that the atrocities were committed by Filipinos collaborating with the United States. Still others declared that atrocities carried out by U.S. soldiers derived from a sort of "degeneration" caused by the surrounding environment, culture, and society that lacked civilizing virtues. An article by the writer Poultney Bigelow, titled "How to Convert a White Man into a Savage," described the horrors of warfare in the Philippines he had learned about by interviewing a U.S. soldier who served there. Bigelow concluded that we should be teaching schoolchildren "not merely the gaudy and glorious side of warfare, but at the same time the dark and monotonous murder which is sometimes an ally in imperial progress." An adventure that had seemed an opportunity to bring civilization to the Philippines now was believed to be undermining the very ideals upon which the American Republic had been built.[18]

In this atmosphere of increasing disillusionment with the war, President Theodore Roosevelt launched one of his many brilliant offensives to shape and control public opinion. After meeting with his cabinet, Roosevelt ordered the court-martial of General Smith. This was immediately followed by a series of speeches by cabinet members, by Henry Cabot Lodge, chairman of the pro-war Senate Committee on Insular Affairs, by Army officers, and by Roosevelt himself. Together they articulated a forceful defense of the government's policies in the Philippines. Roosevelt's own intervention occurred during an acclaimed speech on Memorial Day at Arlington National Cemetery. Roosevelt reiterated the reasons for fighting while attacking both Filipino insurgents and American critics of the war. The war in the Philippines, he emphasized, turned on "not only the honor of the flag but the triumph of civilization over forces which stand for the black chaos of savagery and barbarism."

He admitted that U.S. troops had committed atrocities but argued that they had "received terrible provocation from a very cruel and very treacherous enemy," and that enemy had committed more—and more savage—atrocities. He attacked domestic critics as men who "walk delicately and live in the soft places of the earth" and accused them of inconsistency for failing to condemn cruel lynchings at home even as they dishonored men nobly bringing freedom and "the light of civilization" to the Philippines.[19] Soon thereafter, on July 4, 1902, Roosevelt famously declared the war in the Philippines won. Clearly he had won the battle for favorable public opinion. Americans' attention to the war faded even as guerrilla resistance in the Philippines continued for several more years.

The controversy over military atrocities did not shake Roosevelt's belief in the righteousness of American power. He continued to believe, as he had declared in 1899, that the Filipinos "must be made to realize that justice does not proceed from a sense of weakness on our part, that we are the masters. . . . We have put an end to a corrupt medieval tyranny, and by that very fact we have bound ourselves to see that no savage anarchy takes its place. What the Spaniard has been taught the Malay must learn—that the American flag is to float unchallenged where it floats now."[20] Yet at the same time, Roosevelt seemed to grow less interested during these years in formal imperialism and colonialism. He may have been influenced by the public's distaste for aggressive military tactics, the harsh criticism from anti-imperialists over the course of many years, or some instinctive sense that formal rule over distant territories would indeed cause a degeneration of Americans' character. Whatever the explanation, although Roosevelt did not seek to limit the assertion of American power after 1902, he focused on expressing it more effectively through economic and commercial forms of domination, political influence, an aggressive diplomacy, and, when needed, military intervention. He also focused attention on generating favorable publicity regarding the assertion of American power overseas.

Roosevelt's skills in these arenas would prove invaluable as the construction of the Panama Canal got under way, for in the early years the project was firmly associated in the minds of Americans with scandal, corruption, and bureaucratic inefficiency. Poultney Bigelow, a lawyer, a professor of colonial expansion at Boston University, and the author of the article that argued service in the Philippines was turning white men into savages, played a large role in giving Americans this poor impression. His father, John Bigelow, had served in President Lincoln's administration as consul to France and had toured the isthmus with Ferdinand de Lesseps in the 1880s, at which time he began a lifelong friendship with Philippe Bunau-Varilla. And so John's son Poultney naturally developed an interest in Panama and its promised canal. Poultney Bigelow attended Yale and Columbia Law School—he was, in fact, a classmate of Theodore Roosevelt's at the latter. As a grown-up, he even visited Roosevelt's home at Oyster Bay more than once, but the two never became close friends.[21]

A strong, rugged-looking man with an aristocratic air, Poultney Bigelow spent much of his life traveling and writing. He published widely, particularly on topics of German politics and the history and future of colonialism more generally. He excelled as a writer and as a public speaker.[22] In 1905 his career hit the rocky terrain of Panama and never fully recovered. Returning from a journey to South America, Bigelow stopped in Colón and toured the Canal Zone for two days.

He was visiting the Zone at a time when many were still fleeing it due to poor conditions and rapidly spreading disease. Although the worst of the yellow fever epidemic had passed by the time Bigelow visited in November of that year, nerves were undoubtedly still raw, and the government had not yet managed to provide many creature comforts for its workers. Perhaps all this influenced Bigelow's experiences on the isthmus, since clearly he was unimpressed by what he saw. He wrote up his observations and sent them to the *Independent*. His brief essay shook up public opinion and officialdom both in the United States and in the Canal Zone, for it attacked every aspect of the government's work on the isthmus. He described cities so filthy as to be uninhabitable, particularly Colón, the gateway to the canal, a city built on a swamp with no clear drainage system. He noted the absence of clean water and rents preposterously high. Negro laborers, he declared, received far less pay than promised and confronted disdain and disrespect from U.S. officials. He described a Panamanian woman doing laundry for white officials and having nothing but rainwater dripping off her roof as water for the washing. And she dared not complain, lest sanitary officials come and make her dump out even this small bit of water. He noted bureaucratic inefficiency and red tape that prevented work from being done. He found the U.S. officials arrogant and unable to speak Spanish; he saw courts presided over by Spanish-speaking Panamanians, their decisions unintelligible to employees from the United States or West Indies who spoke only English.[23]

Two final charges made by Bigelow struck especially hard and caused an immediate uproar. First, he claimed that the canal was being built through graft and bribes. Ineffective Americans with political connections were traveling to the Zone to play at being doctors or engineers. When he sought to understand the cause of problems in the Zone, Bigelow reported, he "soon learned that So-and-So was the protégé of Senator this or Senator that—there was nothing to do but keep it out of the papers and lay the blame on the climate or the rain." Roosevelt and Taft assure us that "political jobbery is foreign to their natures," he wrote, yet it "flourishes under their noses and they appear to be incapable of stopping it." Finally, Bigelow charged that the U.S. government had imported several hundred Martinican women to work as prostitutes: "Prostitutes are not needed on the Isthmus—and if they were there is no call to send for them at the expense of the taxpayer."

Many others had criticized U.S. policies before Bigelow did. The infamous failure of the French combined with staggering difficulties during the early years of U.S. occupation generated many negative perspectives. ICC secretary Joseph Bucklin Bishop wrote later that the negative newspaper and magazine articles were so common it seemed "to suggest that powerful influences were behind it."[24] Yet Bigelow's were particularly damning charges. The essay concluded that changes were needed in this system, "which already gives ominous signs of rottenness." He wanted someone put in charge who would hold the position for life and who would have the powers of a dictator. Until such reforms took place, "it would be a reckless father who would advise a son to take employment on the Canal Zone."[25]

Roosevelt and his administration aggressively responded to Bigelow's charges. Within a few days Roosevelt issued a special message to Congress attacking the "sensation-mongers" and including reports by Secretary of War William Howard Taft and by chief engineer John Stevens that provided point-by-point rebuttals of everything Bigelow charged. They took special care to disprove his accusations regarding prostitution and graft. The Martinican women, they admitted, were brought to the Canal Zone by the U.S. government, but officials imported them to unite Martinican men with their family members, so that the men would work more efficiently. They argued strenuously that political connections were not influencing appointments and hires on the isthmus and denied that red tape was hindering government bureaucracy. They discredited Bigelow himself for having spent only two days on the isthmus, and they attacked his two main sources as discontented residents who had been refused political appointments by the U.S. government. Theodore Shonts, the chairman of the ICC, assassinated Bigelow's character in a public speech, stooping even to name-calling: "Poultry—I mean Poultney—Bigelow is a completely annihilated man. All his charges of jobbery and immorality were investigated immediately and found to be without foundation." He is "an irresponsible scandal-monger of surprising mendacity."[26]

The U.S. Senate launched an investigation and demanded that Bigelow identify his sources. He refused. He continued to defy the Senate committee even after hours of questioning and after senators threatened to arrest him for contempt. Bigelow melodramatically declared, "You can put me on bread and water and confine me to Colón, but you can't make me disclose the names of persons who have told me these things in confidence." Years later he explained that since residents of the Canal Zone lived "under a reign of political terror," he dared not reveal his informants. The senators adjourned so they could debate their options privately, but in the end, when reminded of a recent Supreme Court decision that protected journalists' right not to reveal their sources, the senators reluctantly backed down. Bigelow remained bitter about his treatment to the end of his life, and continued lecturing and writing about the government's problems in Panama for many years. In his memoirs he accused U.S. government officials of naïveté in running their colonies. They believe, he argued, that all it takes to keep people in the colonies contented is to supply them with Bibles, a book on Lincoln, and the Declaration of Independence. If someone declares that people are not satisfied with their lot, "Congress denounces him as unpatriotic, hales him before an inquisitorial Committee of Investigation, confronts him with a dozen witnesses who prove him to be a liar, and sends him away grateful at having escaped the penalty of high treason."[27]

Meanwhile, negative press continued to appear, which was surely frustrating to Roosevelt and the ICC officials. Editors of the *Independent,* feeling embarrassed at having printed Bigelow's infamous report, sent Edwin Slosson and Gardner Richardson to the Canal Zone to assess the veracity of his charges. Their report ran in four parts during March 1906 and noted that Taft and Stevens had identified many inaccuracies in Bigelow's essay. They attempted to strike a neutral tone, reporting on the many improvements being made in the Zone and the gradual progress in the work. But they also observed that chronic gamblers as well as "human derelicts and habitual adventurers" were numerous throughout the isthmus, and Colón was indeed a filthy and smelly city. On the crucial question of Martinican women, Slosson and Richardson refused to confirm or deny Bigelow's charge that the United States had imported prostitutes. Yet they declared that most people with whom they spoke "stated freely, frankly and emphatically their belief that the women were imported by the Canal Commission to satisfy the demands of the negro laborers" and that they had been deposited arbitrarily along the Zone without regard for the location of family members. Many were leading immoral lives, Slosson and Richardson declared, although others were working at good jobs with the government or private families. In a follow-up article, Slosson and Richardson returned to the topic of women, concluding: "The three things lacking to make life enjoyable on the Isthmus are all feminine—women, cows, and hens." They compared the balls sponsored by the ICC at the Hotel Tivoli to official life in India, where the few married women reigned supreme and feared no competition from debutantes.[28] Later that year, *Cosmopolitan Magazine* sent Bigelow to Panama to reassess conditions. His report repeated many of the original charges, and in particular he taunted Roosevelt, urging him to discover for himself the true conditions in the Zone by visiting "disguised as a plain man."[29]

This scuffle between Bigelow and Roosevelt certainly involved a battle of egos, but its impact was larger than the two men. Bigelow's charges damaged the canal's public image as well as America's sense of its role in the world. Perhaps Roosevelt also saw it as weakening his presidency. Resolving the problem required unusual and dramatic action, a public relations campaign of unprecedented force, drama, and sophistication. Roosevelt needed to refocus public opinion on the virtues of the canal project rather than on the scandals; to do so, he employed his talents for mythmaking and public relations as well as the prestige of the presidency. It is certainly no coincidence that Roosevelt chose, soon after Bigelow published his findings, to become the first president to leave the nation while in office.

On November 8, 1906, Roosevelt and his wife stepped into a carriage at the White House to head for the ship awaiting them in the bay. As he departed, Roosevelt declared, "I want to see how they are going to dig that ditch; how they are going to build that lock; how they are going to get through that cut. It's a business trip. I want to be able to tell people through this congress as much as I can about that canal." A special suite on the USS *Louisiana* accommodated the president and First Lady, with numerous staterooms, bedrooms, a living room, and a smoking room. The *Chicago Daily Tribune* called it a "floating palace," especially outfitted to receive and impress representatives of South and Central American governments. Roosevelt's ship as well as the warships accompanying him received the most advanced wireless technology, and they were in contact with wireless stations at Guantánamo as they crossed the Caribbean Sea. Newspapers noted that Roosevelt would be in immediate contact if needed and that he would be safe. "It is doubtful that even the ghost of the redoubtable Capt. Kidd will care to attempt to board the president's flagship."[30]

Only hours before leaving for Panama, Roosevelt had ordered three companies of African American soldiers who refused to reveal the identity of men who rioted in Brownsville, Texas, in August 1906 dishonorably discharged. Now, during his trip to Panama, he worked to manage the political repercussions resulting from his decision. Many of those discharged had served for years and been decorated for heroism in the War of 1898. There exploded such public outcry across the United States that the secretary of war suspended Roosevelt's discharge order. The protests were most forceful in the black community: African Americans in Washington, D.C., refused, for example, to join in singing the song "America" as a protest and demanded that the president rethink his decision. From Puerto Rico, Roosevelt telegraphed his answer: the order stood, and all 157 African American soldiers must be discharged. Roosevelt thereby became the first president to learn that controversial situations can sometimes be most effectively handled while out of the country.[31]

As Roosevelt's warships steamed their way toward the isthmus, the Canal Zone and port cities of Panama received a scouring. Everything was cleaned, painted, or whitewashed. Extreme precautions were taken to ensure safety and public order. All steamers approaching Panama were inspected, "a number of known Anarchists" and other "suspicious characters" were arrested and imprisoned until Roosevelt completed his visit, and Canal Zone police chief George Shanton, along with a Secret Service officer sent from the United States for this purpose, took virtual command over the police of Panama City and Colón.[32]

The *Louisiana* docked eight hours earlier than expected, so there was a rush as ICC officials boarded trains in Panama City and headed across the isthmus to greet Roosevelt. The president set foot on a pier covered with palms and bunting and then received greetings from Shanton and seventy-two of his best police officers. Next he boarded a "handsomely decorated" train and made the first of many stops where crowds of people greeted him as schoolchildren paraded and sang patriotic songs. When Roosevelt boarded a ship to tour Panama Bay, he saw every steamer, dredge, and tugboat adorned with flags, and as his ship passed each one, "they saluted, blowing their whistles, while the crews . . . cheered the President frantically." In Culebra Cut, Roosevelt received a "21-gun salute" of dynamite explosions as a welcome from the canal employees. In Cristobal he examined the fire brigade and watched as members let loose twenty-one powerful streams of water that washed up over buildings and down the main street of town. Then Roosevelt and chief engineer John Stevens mounted horses and galloped through the town, greeted by cheering crowds at each turn. When Roosevelt entered Panama City, he was escorted by hundreds of mounted police and watched more schoolchildren parade before listening to welcoming addresses by President Amador and other Panamanian officials. Amador declared Roosevelt the "commander in chief of the Panaman-American forces, allied to perform the greatest engineering feat in the world." Roosevelt responded by saying that this "was the first time in the history of the United States that an American President had placed his foot upon territory over which the flag of his country did not fly. He said he was glad this foreign territory was the Panama Republic and spoke of his affection for the young country." Newspapers stressed the warmth and enthusiasm with which the Panamanian people greeted Roosevelt.[33]

Followed about on the isthmus by an army of journalists, and declaring to them early on that he "felt like the commander of a great and successful army," Roosevelt enjoyed endless photo opportunities. He worked hard, demonstrating as he had so many times in the past his rugged approach to the challenges of life. He toured housing for workers, cafeterias, hospitals, foundries, and machine shops, spoke with U.S. and West Indian workers, walked the streets of Colón and Panama City, and examined the ground where dams and locks would be built. He visited the hospitals and found everything, as one journalist put it, in "apple-pie order." Perhaps remembering Bigelow's challenge that he visit "disguised as a plain man," he dramatically slipped away from the scheduled investigations several times, supposedly to see how things really looked. One day, as the *Chicago Tribune* reported it, when Roosevelt and his wife "dropped into the 30 cent lunchroom of the canal employés at La Boca and lunched with a grimy, motley crew of shovelers, his conquest of

Panama was complete."[34] Roosevelt declared the food to be "as good as any one could wish," but the stenographer Mary Chatfield wrote wryly to her women's group back home: "I wonder if he labors under the delusion that they would dare serve him with the same sort of food that they serve to the employees?"[35]

Roosevelt focused his investigation on the more technical aspects of the project and sites like Culebra Cut, where undoubtedly he hoped the American public would focus its attention. He described Culebra Cut to his son: "There the huge steam shovels are hard at it; scooping huge masses of rock and gravel and dirt previously loosened by the drillers and dynamite blasters, loading it on trains which take it away to some dump, either in the jungle or where the dams are to be built. They are eating steadily into the mountain, cutting it down and down."[36] Newspapers lavishly covered this aspect of his trip, describing how Roosevelt ignored warnings of landslides at one spot and insisted on leaving the observation platform, plodding through dirt and over rocks to climb into a steam shovel. Astonished at the machine's power, Roosevelt sat for a few minutes silently watching the "intelligent monster" plunge again and again into the mountainside. Newspaper photographers were clicking shots of Roosevelt at this moment, creating the famous image of his presidency that brilliantly telegraphed to Americans the main values he wished associated with the canal.

As he sat in the steam shovel, he peppered the engineer in charge, a Mr. Gray, with questions and got one surprising request back in response. Gray seized the opportunity to ask the president why steam-shovel engineers didn't receive overtime pay, as the railroad engineers in the Canal Zone did. "Not paid enough?" Roosevelt said with a laugh. "Do you know, some intelligent persons have even said that the President is not paid enough for his work?" Nonetheless, he agreed he would consider the matter. Later, stopped at Culebra, Roosevelt saw a steam shovel at work and decorated with a banner that read, WE WILL HELP YOU TO CUT IT! Another workingman cried out as Roosevelt passed, "WE'RE GOING TO PUT IT THROUGH!" Roosevelt declared that such sentiments pleased him tremendously.[37]

In speeches delivered to American workers and ICC officials, Roosevelt praised the work being done and associated the canal with the great virtues of the United States. He confessed he was going home a "prouder American." "Stevens and his men are changing the face of the continent, are doing the greatest engineering feat of the ages, and the effect of their work will be felt while our civilization lasts." Repeatedly striking a military tone, Roosevelt declared, "Whether you are here as superintendent, foreman, chief clerk, machinist, conductor, engineer, steam-shovel man (and he is the American who is setting the mark for the rest of you to live up to, by the way), whoever you are, if you are doing your duty, you are putting your country under an obligation to you just as a soldier who does his work well in a great war puts the country under an obligation to him." Work on the canal, he declared, should "confer the patent of nobility" upon a man, just as if he had fought valiantly in the Civil War. When someone in a crowd (who Chatfield believed was planted there by Roosevelt's public relations people) shouted out, "What about Poultney Bigelow?" Roosevelt responded that people "should on no account pay attention to such criticisms, as the critics would sink out of sight, while the work the men were doing and had done would remain long after all criticism had been forgotten." In a pointed rebuke to Bigelow's statement that one would not want his son to work on the canal, the president declared he "was so impressed with the magnitude and greatness of this work" that "I wish that any one of my boys was old enough to take part in the work."[38]

Upon his return to the United States, Roosevelt culminated his public relations campaign by issuing a lengthy special message to Congress in which he assessed every aspect of the project and included, for the first time in U.S. history, a photographic supplement. In this message Roosevelt gave an emphatically cheerful appraisal of the work being done. Here and there one might find "some minor rascality" at work on the isthmus, he informed Congress. Yet, "after the most painstaking inquiry, I have been unable to find a single reputable person who had so much as heard of any serious accusations affecting the honesty of the Commission or of any responsible officer under it. . . . [T]he whole atmosphere of the Commission breathes honesty as it breathes efficiency and energy." Furthermore, "the work has been kept absolutely clear of politics." Roosevelt condemned the "immense amount of reckless slander," especially that expressed by U.S. citizens: "I feel for them the heartiest contempt and indignation; because in a spirit of wanton dishonesty and malice, they are trying to interfere with . . . the greatest work of the kind ever attempted." Roosevelt concluded his message powerfully with a final military metaphor: "Our fellow countrymen on the Isthmus are working for our interest and for the national renown in the same spirit and with the same efficiency that the men of the Army and Navy work in time of war. It behooves us in our turn to do all we can to hold up their hands and to aid them every way to bring their great work to a triumphant conclusion."[39]

The journalist William Inglis observed that Americans had greeted news about the canal with "a strange lack of conviction" before Roosevelt visited the isthmus. However, "now that the President has gone to Panama, has seen that the work is progressing, . . . the people are slowly awakening to the fact that our engineers and mechanics and laborers are making a success of the greatest and most difficult engineering feat in the world." Examining articles and books published on the canal, the historian Michael Hogan found that before Roosevelt's visit negative publicity dominated. Afterward, innumerable publications followed Roosevelt's lead, stressing the grandeur of the project, its significance as a gift to world civilization, and especially the engineering and medical achievements that made it possible. One book appearing soon after Roosevelt visited, by Michael Delevante, acknowledged the power the president exerted. Roosevelt, Delevante declared, "has immortalized Panama and the Panama Canal." Gradually the main narrative of the canal shifted from one of disease, inefficiency, and graft to one of national grandeur. Indeed, the ferocity of Roosevelt's public relations campaign was so celebrated at the time that it became, to some people, a joking matter. In a satire published in the New York *Sunday World,* a Mr. Blythe wrote about William Howard Taft's visit to the Zone, which had preceded Roosevelt's by several months: "What did he [Taft] discover there?" "He discovered that steam shovels make fine backgrounds for photographs, and told the President about it." "Is there nothing permanent about the canal?" "Yes." "What?" "The press agent."[40]

Roosevelt's visit certainly triggered the public's favorable new attitude toward the canal, but many others helped transform the project into a proud symbol for Americans. A veritable parade of congressmen, high-ranking government officials, labor representatives, social reformers, and businessmen visited the Zone in these years, using the isthmus as a staging ground to present their vision of American expansionism and the proper form of American government. Each visit provided journalists with another opportunity to broadcast the virtues of construction to the American public back home. The *Chicago Daily Tribune* wrote of this collective project that was "popularizing the canal" in early 1907, soon after a group of Chicago businessmen returned from the isthmus. The *Tribune* editors wrote approvingly, "Such testimony as has been given the country during the last few months is bound to make the average citizen much more sanguine of the early completion of the canal. That means an increasing enthusiasm and pride in American achievement as the day of realization of the world's long dream approaches."[41]

Speaker of the House Joseph Cannon likewise led a group of congressmen to the Zone soon after Roosevelt and declared himself well pleased with the construction effort. Cannon noted, "I don't know whether it's sanitation or civilization. But I know we've introduced here the white man's civilization. We're just as comfortable here as in Illinois." Several times congressmen and senators who served on committees charged with overseeing the construction work visited. Likewise William Howard Taft, who, as secretary of war and, after 1908, as president of the United States, bore responsibility for seeing the construction through to successful completion, traveled to the Canal Zone seven times between 1904 and 1913. His wife, who had frequently visited the Philippines when her husband served as governor-general of that new American colony, wrote when she traveled to Panama that it "seemed more like 'getting home' than like getting to a strange place. The whole atmosphere and surroundings, the people, the language they spoke, the houses and streets, the rank earth odours and the very feel of the air reminded me so strongly of the Philippines as to give me immediately a delightful sense of friendly familiarity with everything and everybody."[42]

Negative publicity declined but did not end after Roosevelt's visit. Poultney Bigelow repeatedly attempted to revive his original charges, and over the years he was joined by others who decried the existence in the Zone variously of white slavery, government corruption, ineptitude, favoritism, mismanagement, bad food, and unfair treatment of U.S. citizens. Congressman Henry T. Rainey of Illinois raised serious accusations in 1907, arguing that the commissary system in the Zone was corrupt and that rotten meat was being served. He declared it a scandal in management "second only to the bum beef scandal of the Spanish-American war." In 1908, Rainey made more serious charges of graft and corruption, alleging that prominent Americans (including William Nelson Cromwell and Charles P. Taft), in their roles as managers of the U.S. government–owned Panama Railroad, were robbing the treasuries of both Panama and the United States. Further, Rainey claimed that both Roosevelt and the incumbent president, William Howard Taft, were aiding their corrupt scheme. The accusation soon faded away, but not before generating bitter arguments in the House of Representatives and significant negative publicity in the newspapers.[43]

BRINGING PROGRESSIVISM TO THE ZONE

Roosevelt's personal charisma and the prestige of the presidency made the canal into headline news and improved public relations, yet even he failed to banish critics, and the government's policies in the Canal Zone remained controversial. As Roosevelt and his administration sought to silence criticisms and ensure that the Canal Zone's government was effective, they increasingly turned to a final weapon: progressivism. By linking U.S. expansionism to progressive ideals—in particular by showing that the government could operate in the Zone in an efficient, orderly, and just fashion—Roosevelt's administration would generate positive publicity about the canal construction project and demonstrate its legitimacy. Yet the goal of bringing progressivism to the Canal Zone took on a life of its own and raised questions about who exactly should benefit from the progressivism of the United States.

The reformer Gertrude Beeks of the National Civic Federation, or NCF, personified the connections between progressivism and the canal project and the complications that resulted. The story of this pioneer in corporate welfare activities also demonstrates how intertwined the worlds of labor activism, settlement houses, corporate welfare, government intervention, and American empire became during this period. Born in Tennessee soon after the Civil War, in 1867, Beeks grew up in Fort Wayne, Indiana, and in Chicago. By the end of the 1890s she had become an active participant in the Chicago Civic Federation, an ally of Jane Addams's at Hull House, and president of the National Association of Women Stenographers. In 1901, International Harvester hired her as its first welfare secretary, with a special request that she develop policies to enhance the comfort of female employees. Beeks quickly made a name for herself by creating a lunchroom so women would have healthy meals, buying a piano so they could dance a bit after lunch each day, and installing additional mirrors in the washroom. Those in charge made a startling discovery, it was said: *"Efficiency was being increased."* Beeks went on to develop policies to improve health and sanitation for male as well as female employees and organized weekend boat trips and baseball games for the "labor element," plus more elaborate trips to resorts for foremen and white-collar workers.[44]

In 1903, Beeks became director of the NCF's Welfare Department. The NCF sought to improve relations between workers and employers by rejecting both socialism and the anti-unionism of employers organizations like the National Association of Manufacturers. At a time of tremendous change in the powers of the federal government, the NCF advocated limited state intervention and preferred to remedy the ills of modern industrial society through a combination of responsible corporate policies and a moderate union movement. Composed of representatives from the worlds of labor, business, and the public, the NCF became a powerful player in progressive America, persuasively presenting its case against socialism and in favor of limited state intervention, moderate unionism, and paternalistic corporate welfare. The NCF's antisocialist philosophy and its warm relationship with corporations also generated biting criticism from left-wing labor activists.[45]

As director of the NCF's Welfare Department, Beeks became a nationally visible leader in the corporate welfare movement. She traveled across the country, working with employers in a range of settings, from factories to mines to department stores, helping them overhaul their welfare policies and seeking ways to make workers more contented and loyal. She organized conferences and symposiums on welfare, published books, and gave lectures. Beeks was a dignified sort of woman, a handsome, gray-eyed figure dressed in the fine businesswoman's fashions of the day. She worked closely with her boss, Ralph Easley, in the day-to-day affairs of the NCF and joined enthusiastically in his antisocialist and antisuffrage activities. Sincerely devoted to improving conditions for workingmen and workingwomen, and striving to nudge employers toward that end, Beeks also disdained the idea of workers contributing to the design of welfare policies. She believed welfare policies should not involve condescension to employees, but neither should they be based on "the so-called democratic idea." Although committees of employees might be useful in implementing policies, their role should go no further: "The chief purpose of committees of employees is advisory and to enlist interest rather than to initiate or execute welfare plans." Beeks seemed to enjoy the power and authority her work afforded in a business world composed mostly of men. Writing Easley about her work for International Harvester in 1903, she exulted: "They say here I should have been a man!"[46]

After Roosevelt visited the Canal Zone in 1906, the NCF announced that Beeks had created a new department devoted to welfare policies for government employees. This signaled the state's rising importance as a force in American political life and as an employer. Despite the NCF's emphasis on voluntary reform by individual corporations, its officers could not ignore the increasing centrality of the state. If only to serve as a model employer, the government itself had to be reformed. According to the *National Civic Federation Review,* many government departments had recently doubled in size, and employees desperately needed improvements in their working conditions. New buildings, like the Library of Congress, were equipped with modern washrooms, good lighting, and ventilated workrooms, but others lacked such conveniences. Patent office employees worked in a building where dust had been gathering "since the time of Lincoln," causing eye irritations and pulmonary problems. The Bureau of Engraving and Printing was said to be a "first-class sweatshop." Why should government employees be forced to tolerate conditions that would not be allowed in private companies? The NCF's new department vowed to survey conditions throughout the government and military and announce its findings at a conference to be held later that year.[47]

There was no better symbol of the government's new power and the importance of its role as employer than the canal project. "Nowhere," declared the *National Civic Federation Review,* "does the Federal Government employ so large a number of persons under circumstances which impose upon it so great a responsibility for providing proper conditions of life as in the Canal Zone." Thus it was hardly surprising that the NCF's new department would be led by Secretary of War William Howard Taft, the man overseeing work on the canal, or that President Roosevelt and Secretary Taft asked Beeks to investigate conditions in the Canal Zone in her capacity as welfare director for the NCF. Taft sent with her a letter of introduction for Goethals: "She has the confidence of the President and of the friends of the President who know her work, and what she reports will be much relied on by the authorities here." Goethals, Taft stressed, should give Beeks every opportunity to explore conditions in the Zone. "She does not come as a spy, or for the purpose of making sensational reports to the newspapers," but rather seeks only to remedy any problems she may find. Taft also noted that because Beeks was tied closely to the trade unions, her suggestions for improving employees' lives would be useful.[48]

And so on a cool, damp day in June 1907, Gertrude Beeks boarded a ship for the long journey to Panama. She spent twenty-three days on the isthmus and examined virtually every inch of the construction project. She toured dormitories, cafeterias, married housing, YMCA clubhouses, and hospitals, and spent time questioning everyone from Colonel Goethals and his top officials to the engineers and foremen, and onward to the skilled and unskilled workers and their wives. She assessed labor conditions, wages, hours, holidays and vacations, housing, sanitary arrangements, water supply, food, commodities for purchase, medical policies, conditions for women and children, and rest and recreation. Beeks was known, a journalist related, for the constant questions she asked: "How could the laborers be happy . . . in dormitories of 60 to 84 cots and less air space than tenement laws require? Why shouldn't they have pneumonia when they were without blankets? Why should families like to live in a camp where there were no schools for the children? Why not organize clubs to make the women content?"[49]

The report Beeks produced after her long stay on the isthmus showed her to be a tough-minded critic with an eye for detail. A reporter for the *New York Times* observed, "Miss Beeks does not mince her words, and she seems to see clearly and sanely."[50] Her critique became an influential but controversial document in the political tug-of-war over government policy in the Canal Zone, one widely distributed among government officials and heatedly debated by many reformers. Beeks found much to praise in the government's work on the isthmus. She reported that Colonel Goethals had won people's confidence because "there is a general feeling that he intends to do 'the square thing,' due to the fact that now the men can get a hearing and to the prompt action taken when fully convinced that some wrong condition has obtained." She found the new dormitories and mess halls quite attractive, making the towns of the Zone more beautiful than almost any factory town in the United States. Beeks exulted over the streets and grounds free from garbage: "Would that our streets and back yards in the U.S. were as clean!" So pleasant did the labor camps appear upon first sight that a temporary visitor might exclaim, as Beeks had heard, "These men are getting all that there is coming to them." She also found that there was, relatively speaking, little vice and drunkenness in the Zone. She did find the "curse of alcohol," especially after payday, but felt that "there is no more orderly a community in the world" than that of the Canal Zone, and the misrepresentation of these fine men was much to be regretted. "Therefore, anxious mothers with well trained sons need not influence their boys to refuse employment on the Canal Zone, for they will be quite as safe as in any other district away from home influence." Borrowing from President Roosevelt's rhetoric, Beeks offered her highest praise: if her two brothers were to choose between jobs in New York City or any other large metropolis in the United States and a job in the Canal Zone, she would not hesitate to recommend the latter.[51]

Nonetheless, the hardheaded social investigator found many problems in the Zone, and no detail proved too small to mention. Beeks criticized the government for housing as many as a thousand men in boxcars and for providing insufficient married housing. She found American bachelors living in poorly ventilated dormitory rooms with as many as three other men. Given the nervousness caused by the tropical climate, she argued, this congestion was particularly harmful. Both nurses and Negro hotel waiters were forced to live in very small quarters. All employees suffered from sharing their quarters with bedbugs, cockroaches, and fleas, so Beeks urged the government to undertake a scientific study to seek improved methods of extermination. Since employees and families alike had access only to cold showers, Beeks strongly recommended that hot-water showers be made available.

The importance of encouraging more families to settle in the Zone proved a major concern for Beeks. The Canal Zone "has become a community and no longer simply affords construction camp life," she stressed, and as such it was crucial to bring more families and to make their lives comfortable. Indeed, the Canal Zone "is a good place for young people to begin housekeeping, not only because of the attractive quarters, but because so much is furnished free . . . there is opportunity of saving and thus getting a good start in life." Furthermore, lovesick men would not remain for long: "A man is much more contented in his own home not only because of the sentiment attached to it, but because there is someone to look after his personal needs, to provide wholesome food suited to his taste and the wife's companionship prevents him from growing discouraged or taking impulsive action when things all seem to go wrong. There is no doubt but that the further development of home life will aid in securing a more permanent force of workers. Men with families there say they 'would not stay ten minutes without them!' "[52]

Because she perceived families as critical for creating a stable and happy workforce, Beeks lavished attention on the problems that discouraged them from coming. It took far too long for workers to receive married quarters—some waited longer than a year—because of a severe shortage. The quarters were often buildings that housed four different families, and Beeks found this to be unsatisfactory—and potentially demeaning, she implied—for white Americans. Workers also complained to her, bitterly, of widespread favoritism in the awarding of married quarters. A man with connections might quickly be able to bring his wife and children to the Zone, while another man of equal rank would wait seemingly forever. And then there was the servant problem. The Jamaicans commonly used as servants by employees' wives were notoriously inefficient and difficult to manage. Beeks observed: "If one will wash she will not iron, one who will iron will not cook, etc." This required housewives to engage in very difficult labor. Officials should remedy the problem, she argued, by importing Chinese laborers to serve as servants, janitors, and cooks. Although they might require higher wages than Jamaicans, they would be well worth the price. Finally, Beeks highlighted insufficient schools as a problem that kept families from coming. She believed the number of schools for black children to be sufficient, but not so for whites. At a town like Empire, where some fifty white children lived, no school had yet been built. Such circumstances required that children either attend one of the schools for blacks or travel by train to another area, something that led many families to return to the United States.[53]

From memoirs they wrote, it is clear that housewives felt extremely isolated on the isthmus, challenged by the weather, illness, and insects of the tropics, and culturally and socially adrift. Beeks observed this and suggested that housewives be included in activities at YMCA clubhouses and that women's clubs be established at every labor camp and affiliated with the General Federation of Women's Clubs. Such clubs might engage in musicals, card parties, bowling contests, afternoon teas, and small groups to entertain bachelors at dinner now and then and "thus give them a little taste of home life." These clubs would help women "become acquainted and less self-centred, for there would be something interesting to talk about." Beeks concerned herself also with the lives of white wage-earning women—nurses in particular. But there her concern for women seemed to end. She included virtually no reference in her report to West Indian, Panamanian, Spanish, or Italian women.[54]

Beeks did assess the conditions facing male laborers from the Caribbean and Europe, although she certainly judged their circumstances according to a different standard from the one she used for white Americans. The closest equivalent she could find were the laws and policies established for poor immigrants in the United States. Tenement laws there required that airspace should not be less than four hundred cubic feet per adult. Virtually all unskilled workers in the Canal Zone lived in dormitories that allowed less airspace than that. This required special attention, Beeks argued, due to the high rate of pneumonia among silver workers. For the same reason she argued strenuously that drying rooms be provided so that workers would not have to sleep and work in wet clothes. The government provided silver workers with neither blankets nor furniture other than metal cots. Officials gave European laborers paper and ink and allowed them to write letters in the mess halls during the evenings, and Beeks believed the same provisions should be made for West Indians. The government provided no furniture for West Indians in the mess halls, and so they would sit under their barracks, "like animals," or inside on the floor. European laborers confronted their own set of problems, and Beeks criticized officials for falsely representing conditions on the isthmus to them. Recruitment literature had pictured a lovely hotel, for example, implying that European common laborers would be allowed to stay there, although it in fact excluded any but white Americans.[55]

While Beeks argued eloquently for improvements in the working and living conditions of West Indians and Europeans, she remained almost entirely silent about race and racism on the isthmus. She noted the existence of "two sets of employes," but she did not clarify the racial nature of this division or mention even once the silver and gold system. In a section devoted to inequalities confronted by workers, she noted that common laborers (that is, West Indians and southern Europeans) worked longer hours than skilled American workers, and she characterized this as a hardship—not for the laborers, but for the American foremen who had to work as long as the common laborers they supervised. The remainder of her discussion of "inequalities" concerned differences between the hours, vacation, and sick leave accorded to different classes of white American employees. She quoted favorably the advice of one Zone resident who implored the U.S. government to "treat all civilized white employes equally and do away with favoritism." In a rare comment about race relations, Beeks praised the ICC officials for replacing black commissary managers with whites on the grounds that black managers treated white workers' wives "rudely." She also emphatically urged the government to extend racial segregation by establishing separate counters for Negroes and whites in commissaries: "Blacks and whites should not be required to mix in making purchases at any of the branch commissaries."[56]

Beeks had little to say about the quality of the food provided for silver workers or their treatment in the mess halls. She devoted incessant attention to the complaints U.S. citizens made about the food provided to them, however. Though she granted that great improvements had been made and that the mess halls were structurally attractive, she found the food monotonous and poorly prepared and the service horrible. One worker complained to her: "Daily egg breakfasts, eggs—eggs—eggs every morning!" Another said, "I do not eat any breakfast at all simply because I can't. The pancakes are so tough I cannot eat them and the coffee is not fit to drink." Others complained of odd sauces poured over the meat or the absence of ice on the table: "You go all the forenoon without water, and then you come in at noon and can't get it cold." Diners received no service at all unless they tipped the waiters generously. It was a wonder the men remained healthy with such poor provisions, Beeks's report commented. Nurses at Ancon Hospital in particular received such poor food they felt compelled to supplement it with commissary purchases. One nurse commented, "Tell the President I not only want a 'square deal,' but very particularly a 'square meal.'"[57]

Beeks devoted considerable space to analyzing why the American workforce changed so rapidly, with employees often returning to the United States after a year or less, and noted the threat this posed to successful construction. Besides general discontent over housing and food, Beeks cataloged complaints of favoritism over the assignment of married quarters, the need for more furniture, and inequalities in wages, hours, and vacation time. Small grievances piled up, like the circular that declared that any man who failed to cover his bed with a sheet would have his mattress removed. This was no way, Beeks argued, to treat Americans. She objected as well to the fact that "there is a strong anti-union sentiment among officials and an unwillingness to deal with union committees." The sense that discrimination existed against union members and resulted sometimes in dismissals had caused great dissatisfaction among workers, she argued.[58]

Beeks pointedly criticized John Stevens's administration for refusing even to allow workers to voice complaints. Goethals's policy of hearing grievances every Sunday and making investigations had generated more hope and confidence in the administration. Still, she observed the oddness of Goethals's policy—he would meet with a committee of boilermakers but not as members of their union, even though every boilermaker belonged to the union. To resolve such problems, Beeks strongly recommended that a conciliation board be established that could hear union complaints. She drew this lesson from labor relations at home in the United States. The importance of a conciliation board "was established by the Anthracite Coal Commission appointed by President Roosevelt and the same rule has been adopted by many employers' organizations making contracts with unions." Nearly every railroad had such a contract with its employees. The conciliation board should be headed up by a labor commissioner who could investigate grievances and help resolve disagreements. Such steps would ensure justice, and this in turn would "serve to attract a good class of laborers, for friends bring friends from the States if conditions are such that they write favorably to them." Beeks also urged that a system of suggestion boxes be created throughout the Zone to allow for anonymous complaints and grievances. She found in her discussions with people a pervasive fear that they would lose their positions if they complained to her about conditions, and furthermore the fear seemed justified. People throughout the government hierarchy, from officials to doctors, from machinists to nurses, asked her to keep their names confidential.[59]

Throughout her visit on the isthmus, Beeks received a warm welcome from everyone. But when it came time to circulate her report among politicians and ICC officials, she and Easley were anxious. As he sent the report to Taft, Easley prepared him to receive it in a good spirit: "In making her criticisms Miss Beeks recognized the fact that never before have there been as good conditions in construction work, but in view of the climatic conditions, the length of time to be consumed in the building of the Canal, and the fact that the Government should be a model employer, she has proceeded on the theory that the surroundings of the employes should be as comfortable as possible. Naturally more can be expected from the Government than from a private employer with limited capital and restricted by competitive conditions." Easley reminded Taft of Beeks's wide-ranging experience developing welfare policies for private corporations, even attaching a list of all the companies she had advised during the previous decade. And in case she might seem to be reacting weakly to tough conditions in the Zone, he carefully noted, "Miss Beeks has endured hardships and knows what it is to subsist on 'corn bread and side meat.' Therefore any reference that she makes to bad food comes not from one who expects conditions to be too ideal."[60]

A copy of the report went immediately to President Roosevelt, and he digested it rapidly. He praised it overall, but one section horrified him. Beeks's report repeated Poultney Bigelow's accusation that graft and bribery existed in the Canal Zone. Roosevelt responded fiercely: "No charge is more easily made nor leaves a more unpleasant taste in the mouth. It is just as if Miss Beeks should say that 'it was alleged' that the wives of various officials were unchaste. Such an accusation must never be publicly repeated unless there is an intention to back such a statement." The yellow press would jump instantly upon the issue, he noted, resulting in no end of trouble. Roosevelt asked Beeks to provide him with any evidence she had, and he would then conduct a separate investigation, but under no circumstances should the discussion of graft be left in the report or otherwise made public. Easley responded that Beeks could only issue vague charges regarding graft because her informants did not want their names revealed. He conceded nonetheless that Beeks would report all her information to Taft and Roosevelt and that he would eliminate any references to graft from the report.[61]

This was nothing compared with the storm of criticism Beeks and the NCF faced from officials on the ground in the Canal Zone. Goethals immediately asked his staff to respond to Beeks's report, and then he compiled a point-by-point rebuttal of every major criticism she made. Although he agreed to adopt several of her suggestions, the overall tone of his response was a weary dismissal: things were not so bad as they seemed, her reforms would cost too much, and she didn't fully understand life and work in the Canal Zone. He appreciated her hard labors and her good intentions, Goethals said, but ultimately her suggestions were simply off the mark. In particular he rejected requests for improvements in the lives of southern Europeans and West Indians. Goethals's labor recruiter in Spain, LeRoy Park, agreed, saying that "the Commission has done all that it promised, and all that can be expected, to take care of these people, and it can scarcely be within the wish of the citizens of this country, who furnish the wealth that goes into the Panama Canal, that such wealth shall be expended for luxuries for foreigners who are receiving a wage adequate to their service, when so many native American laborers know so well the pangs of hunger."[62]

Their polite response masked a great bitterness felt by many officials toward Beeks and her report. No one reveals the depths of anger more clearly than Jackson Smith, the manager of the Department of Labor, Quarters, and Subsistence, who more than any other individual was the target of Beeks's criticisms. Smith was a young man with five years of experience building railroads in Mexico and Ecuador when chief engineer John Stevens catapulted him—above more experienced men—to head the Department of Labor, Quarters, and Subsistence. An efficient but abrasive and often rude man, Smith was charged with providing housing and food to tens of thousands of working people and overseeing their labor. Thus he bore more responsibility than most individuals for the success or failure of the construction project. Like Goethals, Smith favored ruling in the Zone with an iron fist. He became known for his hierarchical approach to housing allowances, giving gold men one square foot of housing for every dollar they earned per month on the job. Disgruntled workers called him "Square-Foot Smith." And if Smith matched Goethals in his tough way of ruling, he lacked the latter's charm and became, in his short tenure, one of the most unpopular officials on the isthmus. By 1908, Goethals had decided, as he wrote Taft, that Smith's "unpopularity is so pronounced as to interfere seriously with the efficiency of his department."[63]

Over the years workers and their unions had raised a crescendo of complaints against Smith. In 1907, Beeks added her voice to the chorus. Most of the problems she observed in the Zone fell into Smith's territory. Although she did not single him out by name, her remarks clearly called Smith's leadership into question: "Tactful, considerate attention on the part of the representatives of the Department of Labor, Quarters and Subsistence would do much toward maintaining content[ment] under adverse circumstances." Beeks knew, she declared, that the department's officials were sincerely interested in employees' welfare; nonetheless, "it is apparent that obnoxious and arbitrary methods too frequently have been pursued." Common sentiment in the Zone was that Smith and his men refused to explain the reasons for poor conditions and refused to hear complaints. Instead, they "suggest that the next boat be taken to the States if not satisfied." Although Beeks knew the department faced an extremely difficult challenge, she concluded, "Its policy of dealing with the human family has been erroneous and is the cause of general dissatisfaction."[64]

Smith could barely control his anger when asked to respond to Beeks's report. His counterattack was twenty-three pages long, his words dripping with bitterness and condescension. He defended his hierarchical approach by saying, "It is the practice the whole world over to provide a little better for men occupying the higher positions than for those in the subordinate ones. The same custom prevails in the Army, with the railroads of the United States, and among other corporations this being part of the reward for which an ambitious man or woman works." Point by point, Smith responded to Beeks's claims, often pungently: "The man who wants to be clean will be so with cold water, while the one who seeks an excuse for his dirt will remain dirty if hot water is provided." The "colored laborers," he claimed, prefer to live in boxcars. Comparing families living in four-family housing to tenements reflects badly "upon the good name of representative American workmen and their wives and daughters," he wrote, and Beeks must bear the responsibility for the damage her comments caused.[65]

Likewise, Beeks's reference to laws regarding airspace in the tenements of the United States was "absurd, if not idiotic," for conditions in the Zone and lack of access to supplies made the work far more difficult. Beeks's critique of the Hotel Tivoli, he argued, "displays a total lack of knowledge of Isthmian conditions and canal affairs in general." The idea that officials should supply mosquito bars to common laborers was an absurdity, for "they are an absolutely ignorant class who do not understand the use of such an article." He denied that favoritism ever influenced the assignment of quarters. He found Beeks's idea of supplying more recreation for employees unacceptable because "too much paternalism is not conducive to the best results." Overall, Smith found Beeks's criticisms to be baseless, and his disdain extended from her to all social welfare types: "The trouble with most investigators who have thus far visited the Isthmus seems to be that they permit the ideal to interfere with the practical, and if all the suggestions offered were adopted, and putting aside the enormous waste of money they involved, the Commission would soon be conducting a gigantic nursery."[66]

In a conversation with Beeks while visiting the United States (a conversation in which Taft also participated, apparently to keep Smith from behaving rudely), Smith began by noting bluntly, "According to your report everything on the Isthmus is wrong except the climate." Relations went downhill from that point. After proclaiming that officials could not supply blankets to laborers since they would only get dirty, Smith was firmly corrected by Beeks: "I told him that blankets are used with the lowest class of employes—the criminal type, drunkards, etc., in New York City's institutions. I shall add now that they are used at Ellis Island for the immigrants and they have no trouble about keeping them clean."[67]

Smith was not the only official who found Beeks's presence in the Zone galling, although others responded more temperately. The vice president of the Panama Railroad, for example, believed Beeks's "various charges are so sweeping and so discouraging where zealous and continuous effort is made . . . to accomplish satisfactory results, that an adequate answer is difficult to prepare."[68] The ICC officials had carefully limited democracy and heightened their own power in the Canal Zone as they sought to maintain order and enhance productivity. Now, because of President Roosevelt's concern for creating a positive public relations campaign, they were forced to tolerate a social investigator poking around in their affairs—and a female one at that.

When the *Providence Journal* published a thinly veiled satire about an investigator named Susie Peeks visiting Providence and basing her examination of the city on the work Beeks had done in Panama, the ICC officials loved it. Susie Peeks found, just as Beeks had, that men were losing the girls who loved them due to unavailability of family housing, that residents of boardinghouses complained of having to eat eggs every day (while residents at other boardinghouses, declared Miss Peeks, requested eggs and failed to get them!), that prices were high, and that drinking was a curse. The ICC distributed the satire throughout the Zone to the great enjoyment of officials and managers and wrote the *Providence Journal* to congratulate its writer for the excellent work. Meanwhile, an associate of Beeks's visited the Zone to follow up on some of her investigation and reported confidentially to Beeks that the isthmus was sprinkled with individuals who had only "spicy" things to say about her. One reaction, probably common, came from an official who found Beeks's report too shaped by her "feminine sentiment—that what would strike you as a hardship for the men, they themselves would not regard as such at all—they actually prefer to rough it in many instances." As one might expect in the early twentieth century, Beeks's gender was mentioned often and by supporters as well as by detractors. The *New York*

Times, reporting on her Panama investigation, commented that workers there had a "warm and powerful friend" visiting them, one who "noticed many little but essential things that would have escaped the eyes of a dozen investigating committees of men."[69]

ICC officials grumbled mightily over Beeks's suggestions, and they rejected many of them. Most important, they refused to appoint a labor commissioner even though Roosevelt favored the idea and John Mitchell, the prominent leader of the United Mine Workers, expressed interest in taking the job.[70] Nor would they change in any significant way their policies regarding unions, and so the pervasive anti-union atmosphere of the Zone continued.

Still, Beeks could take credit for many important reforms. Officials supplied beds, rather than cots, to all white American bachelors, and they built more dormitories to ease congestion. They built drying sheds throughout the isthmus, which Beeks personally considered her greatest achievement because of the improvement in health it afforded workers. Prices at the commissaries were lowered, and their sanitation improved. Officials immediately took steps to extend segregation in the commissaries by creating separate counters for white and black workers (although some officials confessed surprise that Beeks encouraged such a policy, one remarking, "If we had any such arrangement as this in existence, Miss Beeks would doubtless be the first to complain"). A newspaper, the *Canal Record,* was created upon Beeks's recommendation and became a highly effective part of life on the isthmus, credited with generating a stronger sense of community and solidarity. At Taft's request, an organizer visited the Zone to create a network of women's clubs that ultimately affiliated with the General Federation of Women's Clubs. But perhaps the most important reform of all concerned Jackson Smith.[71]

In the summer of 1908, just days after writing his very bitter response to Beeks, Smith was forced to resign. Technically, it was said to be a conflict with Goethals over purchasing orders that led to his departure. But there can be little doubt that the years of protests by employees of all ranks and by unions, especially when reinforced by Beeks's documentation of the failings of Smith and his office, finally convinced Goethals that he needed to install a new manager.[72]

Many of Beeks's criticisms of government in the Zone, though contested by ICC officials, were backed up by workingmen and workingwomen who suffered as a result and kept a record of their experiences. Mary Chatfield, who left the Zone just before Beeks's investigation began, found conditions virtually intolerable there and believed Poultney Bigelow's biting descriptions were closer to the truth by far than the rosy pictures painted by either Arthur Bullard or President Roosevelt. On no point was Chatfield more emphatic than her disgust—which, she declared, was universally shared—with Smith's handling of housing and food and with his personal style. In letters home to her literary club, Chatfield documented endless evidence of Smith's corrupt and inappropriate style: inexperienced people promoted because Smith favored them over others, honest men dismissed because they complained to Washington, D.C., about conditions and the complaint got back to Smith, Smith lying to Chatfield herself about a transfer she desired. And above everything else, his management of hotels, dormitories, and mess halls was abominable. When President Roosevelt visited the isthmus in November 1906, Chatfield hoped Smith would be relieved of his post. She was disappointed: "This man, whose gross mismanagement of the government eating houses has made misery almost incalculable, has been *advanced* by Pres. Roosevelt; he has been made a member of the ICC and retains what he had." Months later Chatfield packed her bags to return home, relieved to escape the poor food and bad working conditions in the Zone. Even then, her one thought was of the despised Smith: "Hurrah for the United States! I will soon be there and Jackson Smith does not run the restaurants."[73]

But to Chatfield the problems in the Zone were systemic, not individual. Not only were favoritism and influence peddling widespread, but it seemed that in every office the least experienced person was in charge. Profiteering and graft were pervasive, for there was no other way to explain why everything in the commissaries cost so much or why the food in the mess halls was so bad. Chatfield recited a poem titled "The Grafter's Version":

My country, 'tis of thee,
Sweet land of jobbery,
Thou best of jokes!
I love thy every cove,
I love each verdant grove,
But most of all I love
Thy verdant folks!

She urged a friend about to visit not to be disappointed as she had been, but to please remember important rules about life in the Zone: "Clear your mind entirely of the idea that the majority of men in high positions here are people to respect and to admire—such are the exception, not the rule." She had found prejudice toward women to be widespread and believed ICC officials had little respect for the rights of U.S. citizens. If Roosevelt hoped everyone would forget Bigelow's scandalous charges, Chatfield mentioned his name repeatedly, asserting that what he described was known to everyone on the isthmus. Reading an exposé of the government's policies in the Philippines, Chatfield observed, "I am glad someone is man enough to talk straight beside Poultney Bigelow."[74] Her perspective on life in the Zone reminds us of the complex challenges faced by advocates like President Roosevelt and by reformers like Beeks. The latter desired to be of help in effecting better and safer conditions in the Zone, but the president's boosterism would remain an obstacle.

DESPITE HER battles with Jackson Smith and other ICC officials, Beeks in the end generated improvements in living and working conditions in the Canal Zone, thus helping officials enhance workers' productivity and discipline. Simultaneously, she tied domestic ideas of progressive social reform more tightly to experiments in state intervention being conducted in the Zone. Her activities and final report were touted in the United States and provided evidence that the science of social reform was alive on the Isthmus of Panama. In this way she helped legitimate the construction project in the eyes of other reformers, journalists, and socialists.

In 1913, while visiting the Canal Zone, the writer Willis Abbot spoke with a financier from New York City, a man he described as "a banker of the modern type with fingers in a host of industrial enterprises." The banker was impressed by the "education in collectivism" which the U.S. government was giving to thousands of people in the Canal Zone through its extensive intervention. As the banker described it, "The big thing is the spirit of paternalism, of modern socialism, of governmental parenthood, if you will, which is being engendered and nursed to full strength by Federal control of the Canal. This is no idle dream, and . . . within three years, it will begin to be felt in the United States." The thousands of workingmen, he anticipated, would return to the United States ready to demand more extensive state intervention on behalf of working people. This would not be a battle of capital versus labor. It would involve no bombs, but rather a peaceful and irresistible momentum that would force the federal government to take over the public utilities—or perhaps all corporations—and adopt the fine standards of "work, wages and cost of living" as existed in the Canal Zone.[75]

Contrary to the imaginings of this banker, no straight line would emerge between the government's policies in the Zone and socialist utopia in the United States. But his reflections suggest how governmental experiments being carried out to further U.S. empire-building fueled notions that a more powerful state, domestically and internationally, could be a force for scientific efficiency and social justice. As Americans built the canal and sought to create a model civilization in the Canal Zone, their efforts were shaped by values and reform traditions they brought from home. Yet they also confronted a world undergoing tremendous change amid U.S. expansionism. This challenge—the project of creating a "progressivism for the world"—emerged as a new and important theme in America's self-definition.

Yet progressivism in the world of the isthmus had significant limitations. As reformers from Bullard to Beeks looked to the Canal Zone to imagine, observe, and apply lessons of social reform, they drew close boundaries around the proper arena in which they and the U.S. government should work. Their concerns focused mainly on the white U.S. citizens in the Zone, and when they did consider southern Europeans and West Indians, they saw them as separate peoples who required lesser standards than those of the more civilized Americans. Beeks focused some attention on the European and West Indian laborers—or at least the men among them—and sought to improve their living conditions, but like other reformers she embraced racial segregation as a natural and desirable approach to maintaining order. Meanwhile, her laboratory for social reform was itself made possible by the support that people just across the boundary line, in the Republic of Panama, provided. The American utopia in the Canal Zone could not exist without the seeming dystopia of Panama. The failure of progressives to acknowledge, much less breach, this boundary line would disrupt life on the Isthmus of Panama in the short run and compromise the reformers' progressive ideals. In the years to come, such neglect of the wider world would shape the character of the American empire.

CHAPTER SIX

THE WOMEN'S EMPIRE

WHEN HER husband went to take a job building the Panama Canal in 1905, Rose Van Hardeveld and her two young daughters left the Wyoming mining town where they had lived for three years and returned to her family's homestead in western Nebraska. There they would "wait as women have waited since the beginning of time, for the call to join my husband." After many months she received word that her husband, Jan, had been assigned married quarters in the Canal Zone. She packed up the family's belongings and dressed Janey and Sister in their best clothes. Heartsick and uneasy, they headed to New York City to catch a ship to Panama. As the ship slowly made its way through the Caribbean, Van Hardeveld read and reread the letters her husband had sent. Then, she remembered, "for the first time I began to picture Panama as 'home.' "[1]

Making the Isthmus of Panama feel like home would prove a challenge to Rose Van Hardeveld and many other American women who journeyed there during the construction decade. Like her, most white American women moved to the Canal Zone not for a job but to work as housewives and support the efforts of husbands building the canal. By re-creating the private, domestic realm of the home in the towns of the Zone, American women became central to the U.S. construction project. Their efforts enhanced canal workers' productivity by making the isthmus more comfortable and soothing—making it feel like "home," as so many observers noted—helping to keep men away from dissipating evils like saloons and red-light districts, and along the way making the Zone a model of civilization. In the United States at this time women were energetically entering the public sphere, but they still lacked full citizenship, as signified in their continued exclusion from the franchise. Supporting the canal construction project through their homemaking labor allowed these women, even while focused on traditional feminine duties and obligations, to participate in a very public episode of American civilization building.[2]

This message was forcefully broadcast by President Roosevelt during his 1906 visit to the isthmus, when he addressed canal employees and their wives: "You are doing the biggest thing of the kind that has ever been done. . . . [I]t is not an easy work. . . . [I]t is rough on the men and just a little rougher on the women. It has pleased me, particularly, to see, as I have, the wives who have come down here with their husbands, the way in which they have turned in to make the best of everything and to help the men do their work well." The General Federation of Women's Clubs similarly highlighted the contributions of white American housewives after the canal had been completed:

> The wives of the civilian employees in their brave efforts to make a semblance of a home in a malarial, insect-infested country, have made it possible for their Government to boast at all times of an efficient force of workers. Without the support and encouragement of their wives these employees would not have remained in the tropics to carry on. . . . Some day there will be a story written of how these women braved the terrors of the sea, challenged the evil reputation of a tropical country, faced the yellow fever mosquito, the perils of a jungle country, nursed the sick and buried their dead with an unfaltering spirit whose armour could only have been that of inspired fortitude.[3]

In other words, contemporaries not only recognized but celebrated the value of American women's domestic labor to the larger goals of the construction project.[4]

Like British and American women who made their homes in other sites of empire—in India, Indonesia, Puerto Rico, or the Philippines, for example—the housewives of the Canal Zone became willing participants in their nation's civilizing mission. Their role differed profoundly from that of their husbands, however. Unlike male employees who left each day to work in the machine shops or construction sites of the canal, housewives were compelled to negotiate the tensions of empire in a supposedly private and intimate realm. Their main interactions with West Indians and Panamanians occurred in their own houses. The labor of West Indian and Panamanian women was indispensable to the canal project, and it often fell to white American housewives to manage them. Their own domesticating mission and their self-image as participants in the canal project were entirely dependent on the labor of these women who cleaned and cooked for them and cared for their children. To succeed at their jobs, however, housewives needed to try to make that labor unnoticed by others. The home therefore served not only as a place to build an "American civilization" in the tropics but also as the fulcrum in which white American housewives defined their identity through the distinctions they discerned between themselves and those who served them. Their reactions to those people—mostly women—were diverse and ranged over time from fear, anxiety, frustration, and dependency to occasional feelings of friendship, admiration, and romanticism.[5]

In important ways the Canal Zone differed from other U.S. expansionist sites around the world. Unlike the Philippines, Cuba, or Puerto Rico, where the United States also established a firm presence, the Canal Zone under U.S. occupation was purposely cut off and distinguished from the Republic of Panama in every possible way. Although the U.S. government was deeply involved in Panamanian affairs and American canal employees and military personnel regularly visited the entertainment districts of Panama City and Colón, the residents of the Canal Zone in their everyday lives remained isolated and insulated from the realities of the Republic of Panama. This was especially true for American women, who less frequently visited the port cities and the beaches of Panama. They mostly inhabited a women's zone, one focused on their homes and neighborhoods and the ICC commissaries where they bought food and other necessities. The public world of work on the canal was unfamiliar to these housewives except when they visited as tourists or took their children to see Culebra Cut.

If the U.S. housewives inhabited in some senses a constrained world, however, it was nonetheless a large one, filled with many other women from the United States and their families, and this provided another contrast with sites like Cuba and the Philippines. Although some U.S. women traveled to the latter countries (most often as wives of government officials, or as teachers or nurses), their numbers were small relative to that of their counterparts in the Canal Zone. The prevalence and importance of skilled white U.S. workers in the Zone and the decision of officials to encourage their wives to accompany them made the demographics and the gender economy of the isthmus distinctive. By 1912 thousands of white American housewives had taken passage to the Canal Zone, accompanied by thousands more of their sons and daughters. The Canal Zone census of that year found nearly eighteen hundred married white women who had been born in the United States. The vast majority had moved to the Zone to provide a home for their husbands. Some were wives of senior officials (Mrs. George Goethals, Mrs. William Gorgas, and so on), engineers, and white-collar employees, but most were the wives of machinists, railroad engineers, carpenters, steam-shovel men, and other skilled workers.[6]

The white American women in the Canal Zone negotiated their lives and work amid an axis of demands. The racial and social hierarchies of the Zone pervaded the world of women as well as of men, and the rough environment of the Canal Zone clashed against many women's desires for respectability. Amid the conflicts, tensions, and sometimes latent violence that resulted, Goethals's staff members found themselves having to serve as social workers and peacekeepers, intervening to resolve white women's quarrels when they had many other—seemingly more urgent—demands pressing on their time. Little did they know, when they encouraged wives to settle in the Zone, that the contributions made by the community of women to enhancing labor productivity would be offset by new sources of disorder and disharmony.

"HERE IN THE ZONE A WOMAN'S A PLEASURE, AND RICH UNCLE SAM FOOTS THE BIG BILL"

Rose Van Hardeveld found her entrance into the world of the Canal Zone in early 1906 a harrowing one. Her husband, Jan, greeted her and her daughters at the dock, and through the heat and humidity they made their way to the train station. After hours of waiting, they boarded a train headed for their new home in Las Cascadas, a construction town near the mouth of Culebra Cut. As the train steamed across the isthmus, she remembered, it would stop every few miles to allow a family to find their home "somewhere in the darkness."[7]

Finally it was their turn. Disgorged by the train, they began walking along the tracks in "the blackest, darkest place I had ever been in." When they reached the house, Jan had no matches, so he let his family rest on the porch while he went to find a light. Van Hardeveld sat clutching her children, with "fleeting mental pictures of the creeping horrors that might pounce on us out of the dark night." Jan returned, and upon entering their new home, they saw bats and lizards scurrying for cover, and then, as they gained their bearings, a vile smell hit them. Jan explained the source of the stench: the house had been built and abandoned by the French. Left unoccupied for years and with double walls, the dwelling had provided a home for hundreds of bats, their nests and droppings now filling the house.[8]

Van Hardeveld believed it was her wifely duty to support and provide companionship to her husband. But like many women she saw her journey to the Canal Zone in larger terms. She and her husband were both Dutch Americans; they passionately supported Theodore Roosevelt and felt a patriotic pride in his canal project. "With Teddy Roosevelt," Jan Van Hardeveld had proclaimed to his wife, "*anything* is possible!" Guided by Roosevelt's vision, and supported by his wife's housekeeping talents, Jan believed they would contribute to the canal construction and help civilization advance. Rose Van Hardeveld was confident that her government appreciated her labor: "The opinion had been expressed by our own Government that the wives and children were as necessary to the success of the job as the men were."[9]

This statement reflected a change in officials' thinking. Initially, in 1904 and 1905, they believed conditions too rough for women. As Rose Van Hardeveld described it, "There seemed to be a general air of Canal Digging first, and women and children are too much trouble."[10] Only rarely did women make the trip except for some nurses and wives of officials. Few comforts were available for wives, and more than one found herself living in a boxcar. In 1905, when hundreds of skilled workers fled the Zone to return to the United States, when disease, accidents, and discomfort made the isthmus seem as much a dreaded land of death as during the French era, it began to seem to officials that women might indeed be the key to success. U.S. officials needed to make the Canal Zone seem not a diseased construction camp but a civilized world—or, as Americans in the Zone described it, "a small bit of the United States, transplanted to alien soil." By early 1906, as they got disease under control, officials began to urge women to come to the isthmus, and simultaneously they began working to make the Zone a more comfortable and hospitable place. They built housing for married couples and their families and provided workers whose wives joined them with double the amount of housing space. They paid wives' way to the isthmus. They built ice plants, cold-storage warehouses, and commissaries, all things men would enjoy but women in particular would find necessary. And, very important, they added a female ward to ICC hospitals.[11]

The argument that women's presence was not only feasible but desirable was forcefully articulated in 1907 by Gertrude Beeks. When she visited the Zone in June of that year, nine hundred families were already living there. Beeks declared the government must treat the Zone like a settled community rather than a construction camp, and toward that end it should build more family houses. ICC officials admitted they were facing hundreds more requests for houses that could accommodate families, but they demurred at spending the extra money, especially for single-family homes. Beeks rebutted, arguing that "the rapid construction of the Canal depends much upon a stable force of employs." Any investment by the government, she noted, would be repaid by keeping workers from returning to the United States and by making those who remained happier: "Men with homes upon the Isthmus are able to have nutritious food tastefully prepared, now impossible at the Government messes. . . . [F]amily life is conducive to contentment, health and, therefore, stability." By the end of 1907 the *New York Times* was publicizing Beeks's opinion that "Panama offers good chances to women." The government proceeded to build more family housing, and by July 1912 a brief note in the ICC annual report curtly showed Beeks's predictions to have been correct. Of the current employees, it declared, 48 percent of married men had been on the job prior to 1908, while only 20 percent of bachelors had been working for the ICC that long.[12]

For the workingmen and engineers in the Zone there were more prosaic reasons to encourage wives and sweethearts to join them. Single American men lived in dormitories, sharing their rooms with one or more others and eating in government cafeterias. Though their quarters were relatively palatial and the food much better than that provided for non-Americans, white workingmen considered conditions rough. The food served in government cafeterias was widely perceived as atrocious. Consequently, men tried whenever possible to marry or bring a wife from the States. This would allow them to apply for married housing, which would provide them with space all to themselves and their family. Their wives would not only provide companionship but also run the household, in turn hiring Caribbean or Panamanian women to cook and clean. As a poem written during the construction era declared:

> *Happy the lot of the man who is married,*
> *With nice little house and furniture free;*
> *Awful the lot of the chump who has tarried,*
> *And turned from the road to fee-lici-tee.*
>
> *Single men think to be free is a pleasure,*
> *And go and come as they will;*
> *But here in the Zone a woman's a pleasure,*
> *And rich Uncle Sam foots the big bill.*

Because of these circumstances, a gendered economy emerged in which women's labor made the Zone feel like home to American men working on the canal, enhanced their comfort, and in this way helped solve the problem of rapid labor turnover that had nagged officials during the early years of construction.[13]

Plaintive letters traveled back and forth as machinists and steam-shovel men entreated their wives or sweethearts to come to Panama. When they failed to convince their sweethearts to make the trip, many men looked for women already living in the Zone, courting daughters of other workers or finding romance in Panama City. One housewife noted that many a bachelor, "after a dinner at a married friend's home, would think longingly of Lucy or Jane, whom he had left behind in the States. The list for assignment to married quarters grew longer and longer and it was eagerly checked as names crept slowly to the top." In one case a man had anxiously waited for married quarters and, when he received them, cabled his fiancée to come at once. Unfortunately, she had grown tired of waiting and married someone else. He went off to another American's house and proposed to the man's daughter. They married the following week and took up residence in his new married quarters.[14]

Housekeeping in the tropical conditions of the Isthmus of Panama was tremendously challenging, and for many housewives this provided a source of pride. As Van Hardeveld put it, "Among some of us first few families to arrive, it often seemed that the job of making a home was more difficult than the job of digging the big ditch." The task facing a white American housewife, surrounded by damp jungle, seemed daunting. On her first morning on the isthmus, Van Hardeveld awoke to a kiss from her husband and the quick advice that she go find food for herself and the children at the "Chink shop" nearby. Then he was gone. At the Chinese shop Van Hardeveld found nothing edible except a few eggs of dubious quality and a handful of beans. She returned home and struggled to build a fire with damp wood so she might feed her hungry girls. Several days later the new commissary at Empire opened, but even then shopping required a hot two-mile walk each way, with Van Hardeveld carrying a basket and her two small daughters trailing behind. The family would walk along the tracks to get there, jumping off onto the slippery footpath whenever a train approached. A trip to the commissary and then lugging the groceries home again demanded an entire day. After a while she simply sent a boy with a note to shop for her, but there remained the tiresome lack of variety: "Day after day I found myself preparing the same meal, from necessity, not from choice: beans, soggy crackers, Danish butter, and fruit."[15]

While her husband had the challenge of overseeing West Indians at work shifting tracks, Rose Van Hardeveld faced the challenge of housekeeping amid numerous pests. Screens and netting barred most mosquitoes, but little could be done to protect the family from roaches and ants. Van Hardeveld arrived home one day from a shopping trip in Empire to see her kitchen taken over by two monstrous streams of ants—each stream more than two inches wide—and hear her daughter calling out, "Look, Mama! They're carrying away our dried apples!" One group of ants marched across the floor, up the wall, and into a can of dried apples. The other group headed back down the wall, each ant bearing a piece of apple and trudging quickly outside with its treasure. Van Hardeveld found oil to swab at the ants and clear her kitchen, tended to her horrified children, and then climbed down the hill again to Empire to inform the quartermaster's office of her problem. Soon two men came to explode chemicals and destroy the ants' nest.[16]

Perhaps an even greater challenge to Van Hardeveld's domesticating efforts, however, resulted from encounters with the West Indians and Panamanians among whom she lived. Van Hardeveld and her family lived atop a hill. Directly below them was a labor camp filled with Jamaicans, Barbadians, and Martinicans. Every day Van Hardeveld listened to their sounds and smelled the scent of their cooking, worrying more than once when she saw people from the camp advancing up the hill toward her home. The nighttime bothered her the most: "With the darkness came noises so weird and uncanny as to make the flesh creep with the strangeness of it all." She grew accustomed to the sounds of alligators, lizards, insects, and birds, but the sounds of humans at night never ceased to rattle her. Just as Van Hardeveld and her husband settled into bedtime rituals, they would hear the "chattering" of the West Indian gang arriving to empty their septic pails: "They seemed like ghouls." Van Hardeveld rarely saw them unless a bright moon showed them "weaving like ponderous shadows . . . down the tracks."[17]

The sounds made by these supposed ghouls, however, were nothing compared to the wailing that rose up out of the labor camp below them when friends and family of West Indians killed by disease or industrial accidents gathered to mourn them: "All night long they would drink rum and wail, and sing Old English Gospel hymns in the flattest, most unmusical way imaginable. No matter how fast asleep I might be, when the first sound of that eerie screeching slapped the air, I was wide awake and out of bed." It was unearthly, she declared, the sound swaying in the air "like the dance of witches." The sound would grow wilder over the course of the night, and then, at the first crack of dawn, the labor camp would suddenly grow quiet. "A night like that interspersed with the squealing of young bats and the distant howling of dogs would leave me utterly unnerved and filled with a vague, mounting dread."[18]

The young housewife had little more friendly regard for West Indians she observed in the daylight. That first day in the Chinese shop, two West Indian women in "ragged dirty dresses" came to her assistance. Speaking Spanish as well as English, they helped her communicate with the Chinese merchant. To make sense of these women, Van Hardeveld drew upon her readings of the great poet of imperialism Rudyard Kipling. With their hair in a "stiff fuzzy brush," the West Indians reminded her of Kipling's poem about the Fuzzy-Wuzzy tribe, and throughout her stay she would refer to West Indians by that title. Van Hardeveld unaccountably found herself despising a Panamanian woman who ran a cantina near her home: "She reminded me of a fat spider waiting for someone to devour. She often smiled and nodded at me in a friendly way, but I hated her."[19]

The Van Hardevelds could not build themselves a comfortable home without assistance from West Indians, no matter how odd, uncivilized, or unreliable they perceived them to be. The family was able to move out of their bat-infested home and into a more agreeable one, but not until a group of West Indians finished fixing the roof on the latter dwelling. The job took forever, according to the Van Hardevelds, because West Indians lacked the work ethic of ambitious Americans. When Rose Van Hardeveld got a West Indian to help her in the house, she perceived the girl, named Miriam, as another burden to shoulder. A St. Lucian who had lived for some years on the isthmus, Miriam seemed to require constant supervision, which drained Van Hardeveld. She and her servant had very different ways of doing basic household tasks, and Miriam would not easily adopt her mistress's approach. Although the historical record provides no hints as to how Miriam perceived the situation, one can imagine that she not only had her own perspective on the white Americans rapidly moving into the new family houses of the Zone but found ways of asserting her ideas and preferred practices. Van Hardeveld's dependence on Miriam's labor and her vulnerability amid the difficulties of tropical housekeeping limited her ability to assert authority over her servant. As in the United States, in the Canal Zone private households as places of work and supervision generated conflicts that were not easily resolved.[20]

Van Hardeveld brightened at the sight of a beautiful sunset or a viewing of Culebra Cut, both of which served as reminders of the grand patriotic adventure in which she and her husband were engaged. Yet in the early days conditions were so difficult, her life so lonely and isolated, respite and recreation so rare, that often her discomfort gave way to bouts of what she called hysteria. Her worst moment came when Sister caught malaria and the doctor feared they would need to move her to the hospital in Ancon. Van Hardeveld tried to give her daughter quinine, but the girl could not keep it down. In desperation one night she left the house with her other daughter and walked to the nearby creek, where she "gave way to old-fashioned screaming hysterics. . . . Poor little Janey clung to me, her frightened eyes searching mine for the cause of such carryings on." Giving vent to her feelings seemed to help, and she returned home stronger and calmer. She realized to her surprise that relief could come from wailing and, when she recalled this moment later, for once did not refer to West Indians as "Fuzzy-Wuzzies": "Though for me, such yielding to hysteria was a matter for private shame, never to be regarded as an accepted social custom, I could concede to the black people whatever gratification they might find in that way."[21]

During these early days on the isthmus, Van Hardeveld confronted her fears that life in the tropics would require a decline into disorder and chaos, a forgetting of civilized ways. She passed the home of a woman who was obviously American and yet had taut yellow skin; the woman's children ran about with distended abdomens and knobby knees. "Oh, dear! I thought, as I looked at my round-cheeked rosy babies. I wonder how long it will be until we look like that?" Attending a party filled with West Indians and Panamanians, at which she was the only white woman, Van Hardeveld worried that "living among this hodge-podge of humanity whose ideas and customs were so different and unfamiliar" would be harmful, especially to her children.[22] She felt particularly concerned on this occasion about the "vulgar and suggestive" dancing of the women. She thought to herself: "Here is where influence makes history, and as far as in me lies my influence shall be for home and decency."[23]

Nonetheless, slowly, painstakingly, Van Hardeveld seemed to relax amid the exotic culture of the isthmus as she realized that she and other Americans were succeeding in domesticating their environment. The dry season arrived and made all of life easier. As Gorgas curbed the incidence of yellow fever and malaria, Van Hardeveld heard less wailing in the labor camp. She found servants she felt were more suitable, Jamaicans who had been trained by the British and who therefore, she believed, understood civilized ways. And as life improved, Van Hardeveld found her reactions to unusual customs on the isthmus changing: "Where before I had been concerned with the need to re-establish our American way of life here in this foreign land, I now found delight in its very foreignness." She began to learn lessons and even find inspiration from the women of color on the isthmus, although she still saw them as exotic beings and identified them with the natural world around her. Van Hardeveld began to enjoy exploring the jungle, finding her "spirits soaring skyward" one day as she followed the trail more deeply into the wilderness. She crossed a stream, and the trail began heading uphill. "Suddenly as though she had dropped from the treetops, a woman was in the path just ahead." They smiled at each other. Van Hardeveld described the native woman as lovely and slender with brown skin. The woman gestured to Van Hardeveld to follow and led her to a small hut. "'A good chance to see how my brown sister keeps house,' thought I." The woman showed her around and offered her water and cacao seeds. Van Hardeveld returned home feeling her "communion with nature" had refreshed and enriched her.[24]

The holidays provided her with a chance to show off her homemaking skills and to share her family's domestic life with bachelor Zone workers. She invited all the "unattached white men" to join them for Christmas dinner. The commissary at Empire stocked obvious Christmas fixings like cranberries and canned mincemeat. Since her dinner would include several doctors from the hospital, Van Hardeveld arranged for the giant stuffed turkey to be cooked in the huge ovens of the hospital. She had worried that her daughters wouldn't experience a true Christmas, for she had managed to buy little for them as gifts. But each of the men brought a gift for her girls, and soon the house was filled with ivory napkin rings and an array of dolls. The Van Hardevelds used boards and boxes to create a table large enough for all, and while they had little silver or linen and not nearly enough dishes, yet "there was American food, and how these fellows did eat!"

As Van Hardeveld and her servants ran up and down the hill to the hospital to get extra dishes and supplies, the male guests played with her children. "Some of them got down on the floor and helped with naming and putting to bed of all the new babies. Home-hungry and heart-hungry men they were." Then they sat down to a delicious dinner, and the table was "uproarious with talk and laughter. Nobody talked of the work. They just talked and laughed and ate. The day was glorious, bright and sunny and not too hot because of a delightful breeze that blew onto the veranda. The white blossoms from our lime tree sent waves of sweet perfume through the house."[25]

Yet even in this moment of domestic triumph, the anxieties of empire did not disappear. Van Hardeveld had hoped to decorate the table with bananas from their own trees, for that "would be something to write about to the folks in western Nebraska." But they found the tree bare of bananas and assumed their servants had come and stolen them during the night. As the family and a few guests sat on the porch after dinner, watching as nighttime fell, they heard a commotion and saw a group of "dusky" figures headed up the hill toward their home. They wondered what the group had come to steal. Seeing the men carrying sticks and pipes, they began to suspect impending violence. As Van Hardeveld considered what she should do, suddenly the group of men clustered together and began singing Christmas carols to her family. Using the sticks and pipes as instruments, the West Indians burst into "Silent Night" and "God Rest Ye, Merry Gentlemen." Van Hardeveld was touched and relieved. Yet she could hardly bear the flat tones of their singing. Her husband bounced down the stairs, thanked the carolers, and handed out coins before ushering them away. While the fine Christmas dinner allowed Van Hardeveld to feel they had transplanted America to the isthmus and created a home for bachelor friends, the carolers helped her remember that "we were still in the tropics after all."[26]

Rose Van Hardeveld was one of the first white American women to arrive in the Canal Zone, so the conditions she faced were undoubtedly rougher than for many who followed. Yet those who came later shared important aspects of her experiences. Elizabeth Parker, the young woman who came to the Canal Zone to marry her fiancé, Charlie, was even more dependent on her servants—perhaps because she was a newlywed. A West Indian boy appeared early that first full day on the isthmus to take Elizabeth's grocery orders. Her husband had also hired a girl named Sarah who arrived with her hair neatly braided into many tiny pigtails, wearing a starched dress and fresh white apron. Sarah showed her mistress how to work the iron stove in the kitchen and explained how to manage shopping and housekeeping chores in the Canal Zone.

Yet like Van Hardeveld, Elizabeth Parker found that managing servants proved one of her greatest trials. Sarah couldn't cook, she used Parker's best Irish linen napkins as cleaning cloths, and she ruined a silver coffeepot Parker had received as a wedding gift. When Parker struggled to throw an elegant dinner party for her husband's boss, Jackson Smith, she hired Sarah's five-year-old brother as a butler, and the boy spilled a tray of martinis over her guests. That same evening Sarah, who could not read, served fish that had been cooked in cleaning rather than vegetable oil. Sarah never returned to work after that incident, and when Parker sought to replace her, she found it difficult. Next came a series of servants who lasted only a few days.[27]

Parker commiserated with a neighbor about what she called her "Battle of the Maids and Houseboys." The neighbor declared, regarding her own struggles with West Indian maids, "They seem so stupid, but when I tried to do without one, I decided they weren't so dumb after all. We have to realize they've never seen the inside of a civilized home before. They've always cooked on charcoal braziers, washed their clothes in the river, and used gourds for dishes." Parker struggled along, and when she found a servant she deemed competent, the isthmus at last became a home for her and her husband. Julius had migrated from British Guiana, where he had been trained by a British family. He was an excellent cook, and he worked energetically and eagerly. Julius became a regular part of their household until finally, years later, he achieved his dream and moved to the United States.[28]

Parker worked hard to conquer the challenges of tropical housekeeping. One day, after indulging in self-pity as she struggled to start a fire without help from a servant, she began scolding herself: "What did I think I was—a Dresden figurine to be put up on a shelf? No, I was a housewife! A housewife with a college degree and, while the degree wasn't in domestic science, I was supposed to have a trained mind." While many a wife grew disgusted with conditions and fled home to the United States, Parker remained entertained by the challenges, she told her friends, even if she complained privately to her husband. She also relied heavily on other white American housewives for companionship and advice, just as Van Hardeveld had. Her friends showed her how to develop a standing order for the commissary so she'd receive a different meat each day, how to keep tinned food and butter in the house at all times in case her commissary order didn't come through or her husband unexpectedly brought company home for dinner, and how to make meat go far if she didn't have enough—or if necessary buy some fish from the Martinican vendor who came regularly by her home.[29] Parker learned to keep sugar in the icebox and put table legs in oil, and if ants were on the cake when company came, she would calmly tap the dish and allow the ants to run away before serving a slice.[30]

Gradually, more American women moved to the Zone. By 1909 they had created a larger social network and encouraged the government to find ways of making their lives more comfortable. Commissaries began by selling a greater diversity of goods, catering more successfully to women with hand-embroidered petticoats, fine linens, fancy dishes, fabric, and hats. It was said that buying such items became a preoccupation for some women, who would set them aside to take home to the United States, thereby accumulating fine goods that might have taken a lifetime to afford back home.[31] As the commissaries became more pleasant, they became a central rendezvous point for housewives eager to see their friends. A traveler visiting the commissary watched "the numerous young matrons with delightful babies and small children, all in pretty summer afternoon array, who made their purchases and then remained to chat with friends, or strolled around the neighborhood, waiting probably for the train which would bring the husbands and fathers home from their work."[32] Those babies and small children provided perhaps the surest evidence that "civilization" had arrived in the Zone. By 1912, as the population of the Zone grew, the maternity wards at Ancon and Colón hospitals filled up, and young mothers met to compare notes on formulas and remedies for teething pain. That year the ICC census listed the number of white children under six years of age living in the Canal Zone who had been born in ICC hospitals at more than thirteen hundred.[33]

By the end of the construction period in 1914, an active social life beckoned to American families in the Canal Zone. The government organized dances every Saturday night at the Hotel Tivoli. Residents of the Zone as well as visitors, whether ordinary tourists or congressional delegations, typically donned their finest garments to attend. The dances quickly became a central part of the Zone's social scene. Churches, including

Catholic, Episcopal, and Protestant ones, were active and well attended. The YMCA clubhouses, though they offered membership only to men, established weekly open hours when women might attend. Women and men created literary clubs and musical societies. The ICC arranged for musical groups, theater companies, lecturers, and minstrel shows to visit the Zone. As each town organized baseball teams, games became common events, and women were encouraged to attend. Invariably, a group of women in white summery dresses could be seen at games, cheering on their team. Families took occasional excursions to tourist spots like Taboga Island and visited the canal construction sites regularly—in part to inculcate in children the patriotic virtues of the project.[34]

Recreation had been one of Gertrude Beeks's top concerns when she visited the Canal Zone in 1907. She believed that the scarcity of recreation, particularly on Sundays, was harmful to the men, women, and children of the Zone. Many of her suggestions, such as her idea that the government might build an amusement park modeled on Coney Island, were ignored. But government officials seem to have taken to heart her critique that American housewives in the Zone were suffering from isolation, monotony, and boredom. To address this, Beeks urged the government to send an organizer from the General Federation of Women's Clubs to create a system of clubs throughout the Zone, and Secretary of War Taft readily acted upon her suggestion.[35]

Beeks chose her good friend Helen Varick Boswell to organize the women's clubs. Born in 1869 in Baltimore, Boswell received a law degree in 1902, a rare achievement for a woman in those days. By 1907 she had gained extensive experience as an organizer for the Republican Party, especially in the state of New York. She was also an active member of the Welfare Department of the National Civic Federation, the Daughters of the American Revolution, and the General Federation of Women's Clubs.[36] She would spend nearly a month in the Canal Zone, arriving in September 1907, her expenses and salary paid by the ICC. Rheta Childe Dorr, writing in *What Eight Million Women Want* in 1910, described Boswell's mission in the following way: "The United States Government asked the co-operation of the women's clubs to save the precarious Panama situation. At a moment when social discontent threatened literally to stop the building of the canal, the Department of Commerce and Labor employed Miss Helen Varick Boswell, of New York, to go to the Isthmus and organize the wives and daughters of Government employees into clubs. The Department knew that the clubs, once organized, would do the rest. Nor was it disappointed."[37] As Dorr's comments suggest, the creation of women's clubs became another opportunity to celebrate American housewives' contributions to improving the Zone's social environment and thereby assist in the canal's construction.

Once she arrived in the Zone, Boswell outlined to interested women how a network of clubs might benefit them. It would bring women together, promote social feeling among them, make it possible for them to play a role in municipal government, and provide classes in subjects like Spanish and home economics. She noted that women were already proving a major positive influence in the Zone. And so she began organizing. Largely retracing Beeks's steps across the isthmus, she found some women anxious for the clubs to succeed. Yet she also encountered obstacles, including a significant elitism among officials' wives. The club movement sought, among other things, to bring women of different class backgrounds together, to unite in one organization wives of steam-shovel men and wives of leading officials. But Boswell found that the more respectable wives had no desire to unite with their working-class counterparts. She observed to Beeks, "There is rather more snobbishness here than elsewhere," and she worked overtime to convince prestigious women like Mrs. Gorgas and Mrs. Goethals to become involved. When finally the latter signed on as president of the federation, other officials' wives decided to participate. By early October 1907, when she departed for the United States, Boswell reported that she had established clubs in Culebra, Empire, Gorgona, Cristobal, Gatun, Ancon, and Pedro Miguel, and in a few smaller towns. Nonetheless, like its counterpart in the United States, the club movement of the Canal Zone remained predominantly a world of middle- and upper-middle-class white women. In the years to come, club leaders would continue to exhort members not to exclude working-class wives.[38]

The clubs organized a diverse array of entertainments, lectures, and philanthropic activities intended to re-create in the Canal Zone the culture and holiday rituals of the United States. In 1907 the Empire club organized a "barn party" for Halloween, supplying apples, corn, doughnuts, Chinese lanterns, a fortune-teller, and a Blarney Stone. The event ended with square dancing and a confetti frolic and was popular and well attended. That same year clubs across the Zone organized the "merriest" Christmas celebrations since the American occupation had begun. In Cristobal on Christmas Eve, for example, five hundred American canal employees and their families came to see fancy decorations, including a tree brought all the way from the United States. Santa Claus showed up with presents for every child. Afterward the guests enjoyed popcorn, candy, nuts, and orangeade while they listened to tunes played by the Canal Zone band. The clubs seemed to search even for small holidays to celebrate, as when the Culebra club held a "colonial tea" to celebrate the Battle of Lexington. The highlight occurred when Miss Eleanor Coolidge recited "The Midnight Ride of Paul Revere."[39] The various celebrations helped Americans feel connected to an "imagined community," one generated by their notions of culture "back home" but simultaneously re-created to meet the new conditions of life thousands of miles away on the Isthmus of Panama.[40]

Clubs presented regular lectures for the enlightenment of members, on topics ranging from horticulture and homemaking challenges (such as the elimination of insects) to the sociology of community development and the culture of Japan. Members visited hospitals to cheer up recovering male patients and attended classes to study Spanish or literary topics (one club tackled the plays of Shakespeare, for example). Back home, charitable work among the poor and efforts to achieve reform became a focus for many clubs, but in the Canal Zone white women focused virtually no attention on improving the lives of West Indians or southern Europeans because they felt their actions might be seen as a critique of the U.S. government.[41] Unsurprisingly, given that government officials had initiated it, the women's club movement focused much energy on serving as a cultural ambassador and all-around booster of the U.S. government's work on the isthmus. Its goals included projecting a positive image for the benefit of Americans at home as well as foreigners abroad. The clubs throughout the isthmus agreed, according to one report, that "women should unite in fostering favorable instead of adverse criticism of conditions in the Zone."[42] The Canal Zone's women's club movement lasted only six years; in 1913 it was disbanded as the canal neared completion. During that time club members contributed to publicizing the role of U.S. women as a visible and honored part of the canal construction project and meanwhile helped the isthmus feel more like "home."

RESPECTABILITY, DIVORCE, AND DESERTION

While white American women struggled to civilize the Zone, there remained domestic and community problems they could neither contain nor resolve. Tensions emerged within and among the American communities in the Zone, along the pleasant tree-lined streets that provided a home to white gold workers and their wives. Notions of respectability and civilized behavior often clashed against a rougher, more raucous approach to life, resulting in frequent conflicts and disagreements among white American married couples.

To save money, the government constructed many of its married quarters in buildings that held four apartments. Single-dwelling quarters existed, but they were difficult to come by. Gertrude Beeks had criticized the four-unit buildings, noting how desperately families preferred the privacy of a home all to themselves. As Beeks put it, "There are so many different types and nationalities concerned. It is difficult to find four congenial families in that heterogeneous population."[43] Beeks's critique is borne out by complaints that residents made to Goethals regarding their neighbors and that open a window for us into the lives of ordinary residents of the Canal Zone. Although the conflicts were sometimes dismissed by Goethals or his investigator as mere "women's disagreements," typically they were in fact infused with distinctions of class or race and issues of respectability. One ongoing battle involved a

Mrs. Tucker and a Mrs. Sessions, who lived across the street from each other and disliked one another so intensely that neighbors felt compelled to side with one or the other. Mrs. Sessions complained to Goethals that whenever she went out on her porch, Mrs. Tucker would imitate her actions. One day, as Mrs. Sessions returned from the town of Empire, Mrs. Tucker could be heard remarking, "The swells have arrived. . . . Yes, I'm an old rubber neck, I came near missing seeing the swells come home this time, but I will be sure to be on the look out for them next time."

The complaints seemed to Goethals to require investigation, so he sent his diligent assistant T. B. Miskimon to interview the women involved. Mrs. Tucker responded that the cutting remarks had begun with Mrs. Sessions, who had commented, "The very next time that old cat looks at me, I am going to ask her how I look." In the end, Miskimon summed up the conflict as one involving class differences. Mrs. Sessions had recently moved into the neighborhood and treated Mrs. Tucker haughtily and arrogantly. She had begun with cutting comments and had a "more refined way" of getting under Mrs. Tucker's skin. "Mrs. Tucker seeing she cannot meet her at that game goes after her on more personal and direct ways." Miskimon recommended that Goethals either move Mrs. Sessions to another neighborhood or wait until she left for the United States, a trip she planned to make fairly soon.[44]

Many residents expressed concern that unruly neighbors would undermine the respectable standards of their community. Goethals often received complaints about people who used bad language, walked on their porch dressed in pajamas, failed to keep their homes clean, drank alcohol, or possessed noisy dogs or children. In one four-unit building, three families united to complain about the Atkins family, which included seven children under the age of fourteen. The children "kept up a regular bedlam both day and night," racing a wagon over the upstairs floor at all hours (to the dismay of their downstairs neighbors), stealing kindling and coal from those who lived next door, and tearing clothes off the line. But in this case as in many others, such minor concerns accompanied more serious ones. Although none of the families complained to Goethals about domestic violence in the Atkins household, the investigator learned that the father regularly punished his children by locking them in a closet or beating them, and neighbors heard their moans and cries. Miskimon proposed that Goethals move the family to a different neighborhood and, hopefully, to a single-dwelling home so that neighbors would not be forced to listen to the verbal and physical battles.[45]

Neighbors who observed or overheard fighting between husband and wife, or between parents and children, routinely asked Goethals to intervene. Neighbors complained when a Mr. Baker cursed at his wife and allegedly choked her. Miskimon interviewed the husband and wife together, and the wife admitted that her husband had a bad temper and that he regularly cursed at her: "I do wish he would quit swearing; I don't like for him to call me a 'MUTT'; a mutt is a dog, and I don't like to be called that." Her husband interrupted her and demanded, "Well, for God's sake, tell them I didn't choke you." Miskimon then asked Baker about neighbors' complaints that his dog barked too much. His notes of the interview concluded: "Mrs. Baker interrupted at this point, and commenced telling the story of her life." Mr. Baker grew impatient, jumped up, and left the room, shouting as he went, "My God! Shut up! I want a drink." This brought an end to the interview. After Miskimon left, fighting commenced at the Baker household, and neighbors called the police. Miskimon suggested to Goethals that he inform Baker he would lose his job unless the "disorder" in his home ceased immediately.[46]

When a woman in the Zone experienced conflict with or violence from a husband or boyfriend, she—or, more commonly, a neighbor who overheard worrisome noises—might seek help from the police or Goethals. Goethals devoted some energy to assessing complaints of domestic violence, but the ICC included no trained social workers, and Goethals's solutions were limited—most often a reprimand or moving the offending party to a different location. In one case an electrician named Louland allegedly acted violently toward his wife, and the police visited his house. Later that day the electrician contemplated who might have called the police on him, and someone overheard him concluding that it must have been a neighbor: "It was Mrs. Dawson or Mrs. Tew, the bitches." Goethals ordered Louland investigated for his bad language, not for abusing his wife. In an interview Louland admitted having said, "If some of these old women bitches would keep out of what doesn't concern them, the place would be worth living in." Miskimon concluded that Louland was a good man, not quarrelsome, not a steady drinker, and thus he should not be reprimanded for his bad language or asked to leave: "He, no doubt, uses talk at times which is more or less rough, but this is due to the bossing of men to a certain degree, and is indulged in by the majority of the people on this street."[47]

Some residents were perceived by officials and other members of the community as disorderly in part because of their race. Miskimon classified one family in Culebra as white Jamaicans, by which he meant, he said, people known to be white but having "negro blood in their veins." They disturbed the peace, several neighbors testified, by staggering about drunk and cursing each other. Miskimon recommended they be evicted from ICC housing. In another case two women took it upon themselves to police the racial boundaries of their neighborhood. They complained to Goethals that a locomotive engineer living near them should not have access to married housing because his wife was not a "pure Caucasian." Miskimon explained to Goethals that she was from Ecuador. The complainants admitted they had seen no immoral or inappropriate behavior by anyone in the house. They felt worried, however, because the husband was leaving for the United States and his wife's sister was going to visit her in the meantime. The complaining women, Miskimon noted, "seem to fear that wrongful practices may be indulged in during his absence, although they admit they have not seen anything in the conduct of the wife to warrant such a presumption." Miskimon informed the women they were encouraged to report any inappropriate behavior but that he could do nothing about the fact that an Ecuadorian lived in married quarters.[48]

As white American housewives struggled to improve their own and their families' living conditions, they often saw the Isthmian Canal Commission's policies as a barrier to building a respectable and civilized environment, and they pushed government officials to make improvements.

Women quarreled with officials over the size and location of quarters given to them, the amount and condition of furniture, the goods available to them at the commissaries, and the quality of meat and produce. Even after managers listened to early complaints and began carrying a wider array of consumer items, commissaries continued to be a source of discontent. Terribly long lines and insufficient help meant a trip there lasted forever. The time spent waiting was especially long after the workday had ended, when ICC employees rushed in. Then a large crowd of people, from West Indian laborers to white American officials, would stand in line with only two or three clerks to assist them. Women complained of receiving bad food and not bothering to return it because such a trip would require too much time. They also complained about exorbitant prices, and some sought to purchase food from other sources as a result, perhaps traveling into Panama or visiting Chinese shops.[49]

Then there was the sensitive issue of fair treatment. An incident at the commissary in the town of Empire reveals that a manager considered unfair by female customers might face an avalanche of criticism. One August morning in 1910 a housewife named Mrs. Bowers visited the Empire commissary and ordered, among other items, some celery and plums. The clerk told her they had no more of either. Later, however, standing on her porch and watching as other housewives returned from the commissary, Mrs. Bowers noticed women who had been behind her in line carrying the coveted celery and plums. She returned to the commissary and complained to Mr. Jensen, the manager. He informed her (rather loudly and sarcastically, she believed) that there had been no celery and plums available. She asked, "Do you mean to call me a liar?" The manager responded, "I don't care what I call you." Mrs. Bowers retorted, "Do you know what I think of you—you are a dirty cur!" Mr. Jensen replied, "I'd hate to tell you what I think you are—send a man down here and I'll tell him."

Jensen's comment was unforgivable in the eyes of Mrs. Bowers. Even Goethals's investigator seemed shocked by the exchange, and he confided to his boss that all of Empire was agitated over the incident. He interviewed many women and found that Mrs. Bowers's story was essentially correct. Women made other charges as well, including allegations of receiving spoiled food or of being treated rudely by Jensen. One woman, Mrs. Rose of Empire, related how she bought a chicken from Jensen's commissary that, she discovered later, was small and rotten on one side. She returned the chicken and asked for a bigger one. Jensen said it wasn't his fault the chicken hadn't been fattened properly, and he refused to take it back. Mrs. Rose angrily told him to keep the chicken: "He threw it under the counter and said he would have it fattened for me." Several times since, she had been to the commissary, and Jensen would simply say that he was still fattening the chicken. She wondered aloud to her interviewer: "Now who could fatten a dead chicken?" Mrs. Rose believed that Jensen showed favoritism: "You can't get nothing unless he loves you—those he loves gets what they want and those he don't don't get anything—WELL I don't want him to love me." Miskimon concluded that although Jensen's commissary was one of the cleanest and most efficiently run, due to his unpopularity with housewives he should be transferred to another town. In this case housewives generated a change for the better in their basic work of consumption. Since shopping for the family was at the center of their labor, eliminating an unfair commissary manager was an important victory.[50]

Some wives of American canal workers struggled with a different sort of hardship. Men working in the Zone tried to convince their wives or sweethearts to come along, as we have seen, and often they succeeded. But many women insisted on remaining at their homes in the United States. Daunted by the idea of homemaking in the wild tropics, worried about stories they'd heard of disease, insects, and snakes, or perhaps simply unwilling to leave their familiar home, many women refused to join their husbands in the Canal Zone. Yet canal workers continued to pressure reluctant wives to come. When wives refused, their husbands often sued for divorce—usually on grounds of desertion—so they would be free to find a wife in the Canal Zone, perhaps marrying a single female working as a stenographer or nurse, or the daughter of another canal worker, or venturing into Panama City in search of a partner. Divorce cases in the judicial records of the Canal Zone shed light on the ways

America's new expansionist role in the world shaped even the most intimate aspects of a married couple's relationship.

Madeline and Brady Owen, for example, had been married in Fort
Smith, Arkansas, where Brady worked as a railroad conductor, and the
couple faced a difficult choice years later when he decided to take a job
working on the canal. He moved to the town of Pedro Miguel and began
working as a conductor foreman. Madeline meanwhile moved with their
two teenage children, Genevieve and Gilbert, to Kansas City. In 1907,
Brady requested married quarters, and after a few months the government notified him that a house would soon be ready for him and his
family. Already by this point Brady had once been assigned married quarters but was forced to forfeit them when his wife did not arrive on the
isthmus. This time he informed her sternly that she was to come, with
their children, two weeks after his letter to her arrived.

Brady's letter sent Madeline into a panic. She had struggled while he
was away, working overtime to raise their children and find a source of
income to supplement the money Brady sent. She worked temporarily
as a stenographer in Kansas City but found it too difficult to continue.
Instead, her seventeen-year-old daughter, who had attended a vocational
school, took a job with the *Kansas City Journal*. With that income and
some money from Brady, Madeline struggled to equip their small apartment with nice things and provide a pleasant home for the children. Yet
the stresses began to show. Fifteen-year-old Gilbert began skipping school.
Finally, he missed so often he had to appear before the juvenile court for
truancy, which greatly concerned his mother.

Letters she wrote suggest that Madeline loved and missed her husband dearly, and yet she found it impossible to contemplate leaving
Kansas City for Panama. She reminded him of promises he had made to
her when they talked one night in their front room: "You said, emphatically, that you *would do nothing more* until you had a positive assertion from me that I was ready and willing to go . . . and *what have you
done* with your usual impulsiveness." She worried about whether the
schools would be good enough, and she felt nervous about dragging
the children all around the globe. She could not forgive her husband

for acting recklessly and refusing her time to arrange their affairs. But most of all she simply couldn't imagine herself in Panama. Her husband's note had left her feeling "an utter wreck." She wanted the family to be together, building a home, and, she wrote, "I would like the trip to Panama above all things—but I am horribly afraid of myself—you know my temperament and how places affect me and I am afraid after the novelty wore off that I would want to leave so badly that nothing could hold me there—these are my misgivings—perhaps you had them before you went down there."

Thus, while Madeline declared that she hated to inflict the humiliation on Brady of having to turn down the government married quarters a second time, she felt she had no choice. She simply couldn't arrange her affairs in order to go, and certainly not in a mere two weeks: "If I were a man—and alone—I might manage it that way." But she was not, and she could not. Angry at this turn of events, Brady sued Madeline for divorce on the grounds that by refusing to travel to the Canal Zone, she had effectively deserted him. He charged that she was duty-bound to come and live with him and that she refused to do so for no reasonable cause whatsoever. When Brady produced Madeline's letters documenting her unwillingness to travel to Panama, the court decided in his favor: divorce was granted to him on grounds of desertion.[51]

Women confronting divorce suits often testified to the financial and emotional difficulties their husbands' absence had bestowed upon them. One can imagine the heartache faced by a married couple when the husband chose to take a job on the isthmus. Separation meant the wife became a single mother, sometimes for years at a time, raising children on her own and struggling to make some income to supplement the wages her husband sent home. Despite the relatively high wages canal workers earned, women often complained that men sent money home only irregularly, or that too little was in the envelope when it did arrive. Minnie Lyons of Elmira, New York, for example, testified she had received only $30 from her husband during the four years he'd been working on the canal. Her husband, Willis, undoubtedly expressed the views of many canal workers when he insisted she come and declared, "I have always contended that it is the husband's place to select the home site, build the house, and say when, and where, his family should live. It is very natural for a man to select a home in a place where it will be pleasant, and where his family will have good advantages, and where he will be able to do the best, and where he can secure his best choice of work."[52]

The case of Cora Gray of Toledo suggested the personal as well as financial toll a husband's absence might take. Living as a single mother with two children and receiving little income from her husband, Jack, pushed her to the limits. To make a living, she went into the rooming-house business, scrubbing and cooking for boarders. She managed to rent a house with seven rooms and rented out four of them. Still she felt herself living on the very edge, unable to save any money. Her children, aged nine and fourteen, needed so many things: "The children are so big now it takes so much for clothes and they eat like pigs Clifton is so fat and so is Nellie they are both of them well." Her letters to her husband were interspersed with comments about her exhaustion, her need to stop writing and go wash clothes or scrub floors. Like many working-class women in the United States, she had taken in boarders to supplement her small income, but this caused her more work and physical strain. A bad fall two years earlier seems to have sapped her strength for good.

Meanwhile, for comfort on the most personal level, Cora had found other male friends. She told Jack about all of it, noting that he himself had said he doubted they would live together again and so she needed to find friends. "Now Jack," she wrote, "I am not trying to lie to you or keep anything from you. I have all ways went and had a good time but in a respectible way. And just as soon as you say you forgive me and are com-ing home to live with me then I will cut all out my friend and live as a wife should." The children never saw anything, she insisted. Her friends visited only in the afternoon. One of her male friends began to scare her, never leaving her alone. She continued seeing her other male friend, but she claimed Jack was the only man she loved and that her only true comfort remained her children: "Clifton is so much comfort to me now realy he seems like a man and when I feel blue or sick why I could never ask for better care and he says only a few more years Mamma and you won't have to work I will take care of you . . . he will come and put his arms around my neck and kiss me and say cheer up Mamma." Cora paid for her frank confessions to Jack. With her letters as evidence, Jack sued Cora for divorce on grounds of adultery. The court decided in Jack's favor and did not require that he pay alimony or child support.[53]

The case of Cora and Jack Gray, in which adultery emerged as the reason for granting divorce to the husband, was unusual. Typically, when a canal worker sued his wife in the United States for divorce, the case was decided in his favor on grounds that the wife had deserted him by refusing to move to the Canal Zone. A white woman in the Canal Zone might sue her husband for divorce on grounds of abandonment, cruelty, or violence, but such cases were quite rare. In citing desertion as the grounds, the men of the Canal Zone were in well-established legal territory, odd as it might seem to us that a woman unwilling to move thousands of miles to a construction camp would be construed as having deserted her husband. In much of the United States, a woman's refusal to reside with her husband had historically constituted desertion. During the early twentieth century, divorce rates were unusually high in the U.S. West, where migrating settlers often confronted wives who refused to go with them. Divorce on grounds of desertion therefore seems to have gone hand in hand with American expansionism both domestically and abroad.[54]

"HER SKIN WAS HERS TO DO WITH AS SHE PLEASED"

While white women's role as homemakers on the isthmus during the construction era has been mythologized, the experiences of their West Indian counterparts have largely been forgotten. The scarcity of written records makes it difficult to uncover the thoughts and lives of West Indians in the Canal Zone, but it's even more challenging to retrace the particular experiences of West Indian women. They emerge from the past as the most invisible, the most forgotten. When they appear in the historical record, most often it's as the objects of other people's fears and anxieties, the wailing women who frightened Rose Van Hardeveld, the seemingly careless or thieving servant girls who annoyed Elizabeth Parker.[55]

Like men from the islands of the Caribbean, West Indian women boarded ships for Panama in large numbers during the early twentieth century. And as in the case of West Indian men, mobility was central to their lives. They might head first to Panama in search of jobs, to join menfolk, or both, but often they headed onward from Panama to plantations in Costa Rica or Colombia, in search of better living conditions. Changing their names, their jobs, or the location of their homes provided them with some control over their lives. Similarly to West Indian men and white housewives from the United States, West Indian women often fell beyond the gaze of ICC officials. Unless their actions seemed potentially threatening to labor productivity, they could often move in a less controlled space. The private households in which most worked as domestic servants offered wide latitude for negotiations and for working in the way they wanted, in part because the housewife supervising them typically knew less than they did about the Isthmus of Panama and effective ways of keeping house there. White American housewives' vulnerability and lack of knowledge surely empowered many West Indian domestic servants. Likewise, their relative independence from ICC regulations does not mean they failed to seek ways of shaping government policies for their own benefit.[56]

At the beginning of the U.S. construction period, in 1904 and 1905, as men began to take leave of their families across islands like Barbados, Jamaica, St. Lucia, and Antigua, some women asked their men not to go. Others set themselves to making do without their men around, just as many of their counterparts in the United States did. After the first year or two, however, many women began making the trip to the Canal Zone. Most went to join husbands, lovers, and fathers, wanting to reunite their families and provide support to their men working at extremely dangerous jobs amid potentially fatal diseases. And more than a few women traveled on their own, some even binding their breasts, according to the oral traditions of West Indians, so they might pass as men to win an ICC contract and board a steamer for Panama. Such women setting off on their own probably thought much like West Indian men had, wanting to make money, see the world beyond Barbados or St. Lucia, and find adventure. Others were simply single mothers desperate to feed their children.[57]

Adina Richards of Holder's Hill in the parish of St. James, Barbados, remembered years later how her mother departed for Panama when Adina was only three years old. Adina's father, a skilled mason, had died just weeks before she was born. With money difficult to come by in Barbados, and Adina's mother undoubtedly hearing stories about the riches to be made in Panama, the steamers heading for the isthmus must have beckoned as the right solution. So off she went, leaving her children in the care of their godmother. Three years later, Adina and her brother journeyed with their godmother to Panama to join their mother, who was now making a good living ironing clothes at an ICC laundry. She was able to support her young family and send a bit of money home to a sister, but most of her savings she kept in a bank in Panama. When she and the children returned home twelve years later, she used her Panama savings to buy an acre of land and thus gain a bit of independence. In 1982, when the geographer Bonham Richardson interviewed Adina about her and her mother's experiences in Panama, she recalled how significantly the Panama money had shaped her life.[58]

Adina's mother traveled on her own, but more commonly West Indian women journeyed to the Zone to meet up with male partners or husbands. According to the Zone census of 1912, West Indian women in the Canal Zone outnumbered North American women by nearly two to one. More than 6,000 women of African descent aged fifteen or older lived in the Canal Zone: this number includes 861 Panamanians and a few Colombians and Venezuelans, but the vast majority were West Indians. They were joined by more than 2,000 family members under the age of fifteen. Several thousand other West Indians lived in rural areas bordering the labor camps of the ICC, building dwellings on their own in order to win more privacy and independence from government rules, thus allowing them to grow a few vegetables and raise chickens. Finally, these numbers include only those who lived within the Canal Zone;

thousands more West Indian men, women, and children made their homes in the congested ghettos of Colón and Panama City.[59]

Like their American counterparts, these women helped their menfolk survive the travails of the construction job, providing them with food and, as much as possible, clean and dry clothes. Unlike American house-wives, West Indian women did all the household labor themselves, calling upon only their children or extended family for help with cooking, cleaning, and child rearing. By 1912 the official census listed nearly two thousand West Indian children six years old and under who had been born in the Canal Zone, further occupying their mothers. Many children labored, like their mothers did, in the households of white Americans. Children as young as five or six worked as servants, showing white American housewives how to light their stoves or get rid of cockroaches. Their small wages helped West Indian families who felt desperate not only to make ends meet but to create a pool of savings that would make their journey to the isthmus seem worthwhile. Photographs tell us as much about the lives of these families as any printed sources. The stagnant water near their dwellings and the absence of screens on the windows meant that disease, especially malaria, was a threat to women and children as much as to men. Women nursed husbands and lovers through illnesses and torrential rains, in wet seasons and dry, and comforted them when they or their co-workers were injured by one of the frequent workplace accidents.[60]

Like Adina's mother, most West Indian women—between two-thirds and four-fifths of them—worked for a wage in the Canal Zone or in the bordering cities of Colón and Panama to bring money into the family economy. The ICC employed only seventy West Indian or South American women in 1912, according to the government census. The census listed four thousand women who were not U.S. citizens working in the Canal Zone for independent employers, and most of these would have been West Indians. Of these, the vast majority, more than three thousand, worked as domestic servants. The remainder were listed as manufacturers, tradespeople, merchants, or agriculturalists. This accords with the memoirs and oral histories of West Indians. Barbadian women remembered their mothers working as laundresses, seamstresses, and domestic servants. They also earned money by selling fruits or other goods, running inns or restaurants, or helping clean up after patients in hospitals.

The most prestigious job for a West Indian woman was teaching in the ICC schools for "colored" children. Only a handful of West Indian women were awarded such jobs, but they were paid very high wages and were admired figures in their communities across the isthmus. Work as a domestic servant in a white American family's home was more readily available, and this was also a popular job since it was accompanied by suitable hours, safe and clean working conditions, and a sense of respectability. Work as a washerwoman could be fairly lucrative, with women able to make nearly $7 each week (a female silver worker with the ICC would make less than $5 per week), but it also proved fairly dangerous, as women typically used rivers as their washbasins.[61]

While white American women were hailed as civilizers, West Indian women were either ignored or considered suspect for poor morals and sanitation. Some of the first West Indian women to travel to the Canal Zone found themselves in the unwelcome gaze of U.S. government officials. Bowing to the demands of Martinican canal workers in 1905, the U.S. government arranged for several hundred women to be brought to Panama from Martinique. Soon after they arrived, Poultney Bigelow made his famous accusation that the women had been brought to Panama by the U.S. government specifically to serve as prostitutes. An uproar resulted. President Roosevelt ordered an investigation, and the U.S. Senate interviewed everyone involved, including the Martinican women themselves.[62]

Chief engineer John Stevens conceded that he not only had ordered the women brought to Panama but also had taken the unusual (and never to be repeated) step of paying for their passage. He also admitted that brothels existed on the isthmus but denied that the Martinican women were brought for the purpose of prostitution. His labor recruiter, who had personally interviewed the women in Martinique before approving them for the trip, defended bringing them as necessary both because the Martinican men wanted their women on the isthmus with them ("The men were clamoring for their wives to come," as he put it) and because of a desperate need for more domestic servants and washerwomen. Facing high rates of return from the isthmus to various Caribbean islands during the early months of construction, officials had accepted that creating a more comfortable family life for all employees, white and black, would be beneficial. As Charles Magoon, the governor of the Canal Zone, noted, "It is no doubt true that private contractors find it advisable, if not necessary, to supply their common laborers with women, and quite possible, if the practice is not permitted in the Zone, that it may affect the question of labor supply from the West Indies or elsewhere." J. W. Settoon, the ICC's labor agent, summarized the situation: "The agents reported that we could get a better class of blacks if they could bring their wives."[63]

Thus, although it is possible that Bigelow's charges were accurate, it is much more likely the government officials were telling the truth. ICC officials certainly accepted the need for prostitution, but the industry was already thriving by 1905 and 1906. Far more pressing for the U.S. government was to create a comforting family life for as many workers as possible. Further complicating matters, and probably inclining Americans to suspect that the Martinican women were immoral, was the fact that many West Indian couples lived together as common-law husband and wife. In the eyes of many U.S. citizens such cohabitation was itself sinful. Upon investigation, Stevens and his staff demonstrated that of the nearly three hundred Martinican women shipped to the Zone, approximately two hundred were married and living with husbands on the isthmus, fifty were living with men but unmarried, and the remainder were single women working for white families as domestics. "As a class these women are neat, clean, and industrious." Only three or four of them had been determined to be prostitutes. The labor recruiter also noted that he had tried to make a point of bringing only "elderly" women of thirty to fifty years of age, believing they would make the best domestic servants.[64]

Members of the U.S. Senate remained concerned despite such assurances. They took the extra step of ordering the Martinican women to testify regarding their marital status, employment, and moral behavior while on the isthmus. More than 150 affidavits provided the women's testimony. Undoubtedly bewildered at being called up in front of a government committee and fearful that they might be deported, many of the women cried as they were questioned. They spoke of wanting to be with their husbands, and they mentioned how labor recruiters promised good jobs with good wages. One woman, Rose Montrose, testified that she made money by washing clothes and sweeping camp quarters. She had been informed, she said, that she must either work or be married, or both. No single woman would be allowed to stay in government quarters unless she worked. Other women testified to working at jobs in the homes of white Americans or in hotels or running cantinas. To the chagrin of investigators, many of the women confessed they were living with men who were not legally their husbands. "I am not married," one reported, "but do not lead an immoral life." The senators clearly were in a quandary, believing it sinful for a woman and a man to live together without a marriage contract. They debated the matter and decided that the key lay in one's intention. If a couple's intention was to live together as a moral, married couple, then it might be permissible that they lacked the benefit of legal sanction. Great care was taken also to clarify the nature of single women's lives. Senators heard testimony that single West Indian females lived in residences with watchmen and policemen keeping an eye on them. Their quarters were closed and locked at 9:30 each night. Alfred Erimus, the watchman responsible for their quarters, testified, "None of them leave and no one is permitted to enter after this hour."[65]

The furor eventually quieted down. In the years to come, thousands more West Indian women made their way to the Canal Zone. Whether they worked as full-time housewives or as wage laborers, their days were difficult, and most leisure activities accessible to American women—the baseball games, open hours at the YMCA clubhouses, and women's club meetings—were not available to them. They did find ways of relaxing together, however, taking walks, visiting Colón or Panama City, or simply socializing with neighbors and singing songs together, perhaps sharing a meal and some rum. They brought with them rich musical traditions from the islands. The folklorist Louise Cramer found that West Indians had songs for virtually any situation—work, spirituality, healing, death, bantering, dancing, social occasions, and so on. Her sources were men and women who had either migrated to the Canal Zone from Barbados or Jamaica at a young age or been born in the Canal Zone and came of age working on the canal. Together the songs provided a fascinating and often humorous commentary on the lives of West Indians and the dangers they faced. One popular song spoke to men's desire to have a woman care for them:

WANT ONE WOMAN

Wan one woman like my cousin Sarah Brown

Wan one woman like my cousin Sarah Brown

Wan one woman like my cousin Sarah Brown

Bayma grass wouldn' kill mi nigga nyams

Woi, woi, woi, woi, woi, Manuel.

Bayma grass wouldn' kill mi nigga nyams.

. . .

Man go da groung da bwoil bun pan,

Man go da groung da bwoil bun pan,

Man go da groung da bwoil bun pan.

Bayma grass wouldn' kill mi nigga nyams.[66]

The song suggests the importance of women in producing good food for their husbands and families. A woman would help weed the crops so that bad grasses ("bayma," or Bahama grass) couldn't kill the yams ("nyams"). "Man go da groung da bwoil bun pan" refers to the fact that men would cook themselves some lunch in the field near where they were working. As they couldn't carry a proper pan all that distance, they would have to use an old, burned one for the job. Having a woman in one's life would ease this burden as well, because she would prepare and pack a lunch for her man.

Another song recognizes women's potential power in their relationships with West Indian men, and the role played by negotiations over money and income:

WOMAN A HEAVY LOAD

Woman a heavy load, hi

Woman a heavy load, hi

Woman a heavy load.

O wen Satidey mornin' com, hi

Wen de money no nuff, hi

Wen de money no nuff, hi

Wen de money no nuff, hi

Wah dem neva go out com back.

Wen de money nuff, hi

Wen de money nuff, hi

Wen de money nuff, hi

Den dey call you honey comb, hi

Wen de money nuff, hi

Why dey call yo sugar stick, hi.

The lyrics declare that if the male singer doesn't bring enough money home on Saturday morning, his woman or wife will leave and not return.[67]

This song reflects sources of disagreement between West Indian men and women; sometimes such conflicts prompted men or women to seek justice from the Canal Zone courts. Contrary to American officials' belief that West Indians eschewed legal marriage ceremonies, there is evidence not only that they married but that they sometimes petitioned the courts for divorce. The dusty judicial records also provide evidence of some women's determination to behave as they wished. In 1912 a Jamaican canal laborer named Courtney Black sued his wife, Mary, for divorce. They had been married a couple of years earlier in the Zone town of Gatun by a Catholic priest. Now Courtney accused his wife of adultery. He claimed she had lain with a man named Charlie Scott; when he confronted her, she was unrepentant and instead left him for Charlie. Courtney's brother testified and corroborated the basic story, saying that when he talked to Mary about her behavior, she retorted unapologetically that "her skin was hers to do with as she pleased." Meanwhile, Mary Black produced a witness who testified she had seen Courtney with another woman. This woman had told Mary about Courtney's adultery, and in the resulting fight Courtney had beaten his wife, and his paramour had abused her as well. Mary also complained to the court that her husband had ordered her to return home to Jamaica, saying he could not save money with her on the isthmus. Despite Mary's complaints and the evidence she offered of her husband's adultery, the Canal Zone courts decided in her husband's favor, although they ordered that he pay her court costs and $10 per month in alimony. The court also ordered that Courtney and Mary Black not marry again so long as the other was alive.[68]

Relatively few divorce suits involving West Indians exist in the Canal Zone court records, at least as compared with the number involving white Americans. There must have been significant financial, political, and psychological barriers to seeking divorce in the white man's court. So those West Indians who went to the courts to sue for divorce undoubtedly possessed some resources and education and had perhaps gained experience navigating through the ICC officials' world. West Indian wives were as likely to sue for divorce as their husbands were. Unlike the suits among white U.S. citizens, West Indian divorce cases never involved charges of desertion. Adultery was a common complaint among West Indian men and women, but equally common were cases in which women sued their husbands for divorce on the grounds of physical violence. A typical case of the latter involved a Martinican woman, Eugenia Peters, who sued her husband, a Trinidadian who worked as a Canal Zone policeman, for divorce on the grounds that he struck and kicked her. Interestingly, as seen above, white American women only very rarely sought a divorce on grounds of violence. The best hope of a white American woman was that a neighbor would complain to Goethals and he would send his investigator over to talk to the man. Fragmentary as the evidence is, existing judicial records suggest that West Indian women were more likely than white American women to seek divorce as a legal solution for domestic violence.[69]

West Indian women also frequently interacted with the British diplomatic representatives serving on the isthmus. It was the responsibility of such officials to send the dreaded letters to wives or other family members of canal workers killed by workplace accidents or disease. Mrs. Benjamin Knight of Bridgetown, Barbados, for example, received such a letter in September 1906: "I have now to inform you of the very sad death of your husband. . . . He was crushed by a freight train while crossing a bridge here." Thomas Knox, the letter's author, offered to send Mrs. Knight the few belongings and final paycheck due her husband. Knox concluded, "I know how you will feel over this sad news, as you were expecting himself shortly, but you must not despair. Trust in him who is our Creator." After hearing such news, the wife or sister of a canal worker would need to arrange for the delivery of any possessions of the deceased. Often this took place with no problems or unreasonable delay, but in many other cases West Indian women had to engage in lengthy negotiations with the British consul in order to receive what they believed was due them.[70]

West Indian women also appealed most often to the British consul—rather than to Goethals—for assistance if they were accused of a crime, facing imprisonment, or mistreated by police. A seamstress named Melvina Ricketts, for example, requested help from the British government when serious misfortune befell her. The troubles began when Ricketts became unable to keep up the payments on her sewing machine. When she refused to pay a debt collector, he called a Panamanian policeman who subsequently robbed and beat her severely. Despite treatment at the hospital, her injuries prevented her from working. By the time she wrote the British consul, the policeman had been arrested for the crime, but Ricketts held little hope of recovering her property. Declaring, "I am a British subject, and as such apply to you for your assistance in this matter," Ricketts asked for the return of her property and for compensation from the Panamanian government for her inability to work, the expenses she had paid to doctors, and her unjust arrest by the policeman. She concluded, "I am a poor woman, and unable to afford the amount of money which would be requisite for a lawsuit." It was left to the consul to do what he could or would to help her, although unfortunately no record remains to tell us what became of the petitioner.[71] Nonetheless, Ricketts's insistence on her rights as a British subject reflects West Indian women's awareness of the British government's responsibilities to help them in times of need.

W HITE AMERICAN housewives became valued citizens and con-tributors during the construction of the Panama Canal. By creating homes for their husbands, they proved essential to U.S. government efforts to civilize the isthmus and maintain a stable and relatively content workforce of skilled white North American workers. Yet beneath the celebratory rhetoric regarding women's civilizing and domesticating mission on the isthmus, there was a more complex reality. Although these women's lives undoubtedly included moments of great pleasure as they cared for husbands and children and watched the blossoming of social networks across the Canal Zone, they also struggled with disagreeable neighbors and numerous threats to the respectability they craved. For wives who refused to travel to the Canal Zone, life alone in the United States became economically difficult, and they faced demands from their husbands—supported by the Canal Zone courts—that they rethink their decision. Those working-class housewives who uprooted their lives and moved to the Zone found themselves confronting boundaries that separated them from the worlds inhabited by men, more elite women, and especially the women of color who made their very mission as civilizers and homemakers possible.

Indeed, a great part of the challenge of tropical housekeeping involved complicated negotiations with the West Indian and Panamanian women whom white housewives depended on and yet disliked and disdained. While West Indian women seemed unknowable to white American housewives, they proved strategic at crafting a life to their liking, either through skilled negotiations with their employers or by exercising their ability to move on to better conditions.

Different as their lives were in many respects, American and West Indian women both found themselves interacting at times with government representatives. West Indians called upon the British consul or, less often, the Canal Zone courts. U.S. housewives complained to Goethals, who then sent his peripatetic inspector, T. B. Miskimon, to investigate and determine a solution. Although the ICC provided them with many comforts, at other times it seemed unfair, lacking in crucial supplies and unwilling to take action in cases of domestic violence. Government officials often considered women's problems small and unimportant. When issues normally deemed domestic and private began to loom as barriers to full labor productivity, however, officials' perspective abruptly changed. An exploration of law, order, and punishment in the Canal Zone reveals how and when "women's issues" could become urgent matters requiring aggressive and efficient state intervention.

CHAPTER SEVEN

LAW AND ORDER

A WEST INDIAN man named Adolphus Coulson had been living and working in the Canal Zone for nearly two years when a personal problem led him to commit murder. He had been sharing a home and bed with another woman when his wife unexpectedly arrived from Barbados one December day in 1906. Coulson immediately acquired a new place for himself and his wife, but he continued to see his mistress. His wife, Mariana, complained vociferously about these visits, even soliciting the help of a policeman to make her husband leave the woman and return to their home. After a few weeks of this, Mariana suddenly became violently ill. She told a doctor that her husband had recently given her medicine in the form of a powder, and the next day she died. An autopsy showed that she had ingested more than twelve grains of arsenic. Adolphus Coulson confessed to having murdered her, and the Second Judicial Court of the Canal Zone sentenced him to death by hanging. But his case wasn't finished yet, and it would end up as one of the most important in the history of the Canal Zone.

Coulson appealed the decision on the grounds that his trial violated the U.S. Constitution, since he had requested a jury trial and was refused. His lawyers argued that Coulson's trial violated the Fifth and Sixth Amendments to the U.S. Constitution, which guaranteed due process of law and the right to an impartial jury. The case went to the Supreme Court of the Canal Zone, where judges upheld the earlier decision. They denied that Coulson had a right to a jury trial by referencing the

Canal Zone's status as a part of the American empire. The judges cited the *Insular Cases* of 1901 to 1904, recently handed down by the U.S. Supreme Court, which had established a legal foundation for America's empire by declaring, in essence, that the Constitution does not follow the flag. In the 1904 case *Dorr v. the United States,* for example, the Supreme Court held that residents of the Philippines did not possess a right to a jury trial. Citing these precedents, the Supreme Court judges of the Canal Zone declared that the power of the United States to acquire territory included the ability "to prescribe upon what terms the United States will receive its inhabitants, and what their status shall be in . . . [the] 'American Empire.' "[1]

Coulson's case therefore raised complex questions regarding the relevance of the U.S. Constitution in the Canal Zone and the legal status of its residents. ICC officials adamantly wanted to avoid jury trials because they felt putting canal workers on juries would compromise the productivity of the construction project. They also claimed that racial divisions on the isthmus would make it impossible to find an impartial jury—whites would not accept blacks on their juries, and blacks would similarly distrust the judgment of whites. Yet to some, it was not a simple matter to abrogate the rights of Canal Zone residents, particularly since they included several thousand U.S. citizens. A delegation of U.S. congressmen happened to be visiting when the Canal Zone Supreme Court decided Coulson's case. Two of the congressmen, known as "sticklers for the rights of the Constitution," hired a Boston lawyer to take Coulson's case to the U.S. Supreme Court.

The day before his scheduled execution in late 1907, Coulson won a temporary reprieve when the U.S. Supreme Court agreed to consider his case. In November 1908, however, the Court refused to overturn the *Insular Cases* and held that the Canal Zone lay outside its jurisdiction. The U.S. Constitution would not apply in the Zone. During the months of waiting for the Supreme Court justices to issue their decision in this case, however, some people had urged President Roosevelt to take matters into his own hands. Joseph Blackburn, the head of civil administration in the Canal Zone, reportedly argued to Roosevelt that refusing

U.S. citizens their constitutional right to a jury trial was "repugnant to American ideas of justice." Ultimately, Roosevelt agreed, and in an executive order issued in February 1908 he extended the right to a jury trial in capital cases to the Canal Zone. This allowed him, in a sense, to have his cake and eat it, too—he preserved the rights of Zone residents to a jury trial while protecting the legal ruling that the Constitution did not apply in the American empire. The executive order was too late to help Adolphus Coulson, however, and he was hanged in the Canal Zone penitentiary at Culebra on March 12, 1909.[2]

Coulson's case reflects the Canal Zone's ambiguous position within the U.S. empire. It also reveals that as a last resort the ICC had numerous judicial strategies for maintaining order in the Zone. Over the years a social and political machine had been built in the Zone, one designed to subordinate everything to the canal construction project. Tools like the silver and gold system, labor spies, Goethals's paternalism, and the importation of white and West Indian women and children were used to try to subdue, comfort, and discipline the population. Yet each of these strategies generated new sources of discontent and rebellion. When disorder grew serious enough that it threatened the construction project itself, ICC officials intervened more extensively by creating laws, courts, and prisons that could punish unacceptable behavior. Officials believed this was important not only for maintaining labor discipline but for generating the boundaries of proper moral and social behavior in a civilized territory like the U.S.-occupied Canal Zone. The judicial and prison systems in the Zone were constructed to play this dual but critical role—to discipline and maximize the productivity of Canal Zone residents and to maintain social and moral order.

The Canal Zone's legal system was shaped by a remarkable amalgam of diverse legal and national cultures. Its courts borrowed as heavily from Colombian and Panamanian law as from U.S. legal traditions, somewhat ironically, given that ICC officials struggled painstakingly to make the Canal Zone seem an outpost of American civilization and to distinguish it in every possible way from the Republic of Panama. In fact, however, the Zone's judicial system reflects how expansionist activity pushed the

United States into a realm where diverse nation-states exercised influence. The colonial experiments undertaken in the Philippines, Puerto Rico, and Cuba in the aftermath of the War of 1898 powerfully carved the contours of law and order in the Zone as well. The new possessions of the United States generated ideological and legal tensions between the rights guaranteed by the U.S. Constitution and the need to rule effectively over foreign populations.

The Canal Zone fit into this larger debate over empire and the Constitution because it was seen as one of the finest examples of the new world leadership being promulgated by the United States. Expansionists believed that the Zone, as part of the American empire, should be treated differently from the United States proper. Yet the more officials worked to make the Zone feel like home, like a bit of American civilization in the tropics, the less effective this argument proved to be. As more and more U.S. citizens made the move to the Zone, first to work on the canal and then to join husbands and fathers already there, the more troubling it seemed to ignore their constitutional rights. Unlike Filipinos or Puerto Ricans, U.S. citizens in the Zone and their supporters at home could clamor for protection of their rights. They might not always see those rights protected—indeed, their rights were often limited in ways that would have been unconstitutional in the United States—but they assertively raised the issue and shaped the debate. Sometimes, as when President Roosevelt responded to the Adolphus Coulson case by guaranteeing the right of Canal Zone residents to a jury trial in capital cases, they saw those rights protected.

"THE CONSTITUTION FOLLOWS THE FLAG, BUT IT DOES NOT CATCH UP WITH IT"

The legal basis of U.S. power in the Canal Zone derived from the Hay–Bunau–Varilla Treaty of 1903, particularly Article 3 of the treaty, which declared that Panama "grants to the United States all the rights, power and authority within the zone . . . which the United States would possess and exercise if it were the sovereign of the territory," rights and powers that were granted in perpetuity. In 1907 the U.S. Supreme Court affirmed that the territory of the Canal Zone belonged to the United States and that the U.S. government did have the right to exercise its power there and build the canal.[3] To ensure discipline and social order, the ICC created a judicial system that ranged from municipal and circuit courts up to the Zone's Supreme Court. The courts were not independent, like their counterparts in the United States, but formed one part of the executive branch of government in the Zone. The principle of separation of powers, the bedrock of constitutional government in the United States, did not apply in the Canal Zone. In legal terms this meant the Zone courts were not constitutional but merely legislative. They lacked important powers such as the right of judicial review.

The ICC divided the isthmus into three circuit courts, with the judge who presided over each serving also on the Canal Zone Supreme Court. Three judges would hear cases appealed to the Supreme Court, one of whom had already passed judgment on the case. Even this seemed an abundance of courts and judges to some observers during the early months of U.S. occupation. As he contemplated the Zone's legal environment in 1904, William Howard Taft argued the government had gone overboard: "All judges in excess of one will have nothing to do. These people do not seem to be litigious. So far they have shown themselves to be very tractable." He acknowledged that more criminal and civil cases would arise once the population increased as the construction project got under way. Yet Taft believed that even if the population rose as high as 50,000, "probably not more than 2,500 of them will be Americans of the white race." He knew most would be unskilled workers from outside the United States since it would not be possible or acceptable for white American citizens to do heavy labor in the tropics. Taft failed to recognize how important the courts would be for maintaining order not only among white Americans but among all residents of the Zone. Over time he discovered his expectations to have been unrealistic, as the courts proved extremely busy in the years to come.[4]

Legal precedents in the United States and the demands of the construction project had the greatest influence over the new judicial system, but it was also shaped by the Spanish Empire, by Colombian law, by tensions between Colombia and Panama, and by U.S. officials' experience with their new colonial acquisitions in the Philippines and Puerto Rico. The Canal Zone judiciary therefore reveals how judicial traditions, precedents, and personnel flowed across the boundaries of diverse nation-states. When the United States took occupation of the Canal Zone, the laws in force were effectively those of Colombia, since Panama as a nation-state was too young to have established its own legal code. Colombia's legal system derived originally from the civil law of Spain. After they won independence in 1819 from Spain, Colombians revised their nation's legal code and moved it closer to legal traditions prevalent in the Anglo-American world. Nonetheless, when the United States began its occupation of the isthmus in 1904, the laws of Colombia still reflected Spain's judicial system.[5]

Nor did the United States shift quickly or decisively away from the laws of Panama and Colombia once occupation began. Roosevelt declared in a 1904 executive order that laws already operating on the isthmus would remain in force until amended or annulled by the ICC. Throughout the construction era, Colombian and Panamanian law remained central to the Zone's judicial system. In the summer of 1912, Frank Feuille, who headed the Canal Zone's Department of Law, complained that the Zone's government consisted of a combination of Colombian and Panamanian laws plus presidential executive orders and ICC ordinances. The Colombian laws, he noted, are "spread throughout a number of books and many of them are inaccessible except to the very few persons who possess a Colombian law library." He recommended an overhaul of Canal Zone law both to simplify administration and to reduce costs.[6]

Because of the urgent need for absolute labor discipline, from early on American officials shaped law and order in the Canal Zone with efficiency in mind. As part of his 1904 executive order, Roosevelt began to reshape the legal structure of the Zone so that it would reflect American jurisprudence while simultaneously reinforcing the ICC's emphasis on maximizing every resident's productivity. Roosevelt declared that "certain great principles of government" would have force in the Zone, by which he meant some of the Bill of Rights. He combined this validation of the Bill of Rights with an ominous proviso giving the ICC sweeping powers of deportation, which in essence negated much of the Bill of Rights. The ICC could deport anyone who might "create public disorder, endanger the public health, or in any manner impede the prosecution of the work of opening the canal." This specifically included "idiots," the insane, epileptics, beggars, felons, anarchists, and those seeking to incite insurrection.[7]

In the years to come, the ICC annulled or amended dozens of acts, gradually bringing the law of the Zone closer to U.S. common law. In particular the ICC issued in 1904 a penal code and a code of criminal procedure that departed significantly from those of Panama (officials used the codes of the state of California as their model), although the Zone's civil law would remain essentially Panamanian until a major revision occurred in the 1930s. Thus lawyers and judges in the Canal Zone had to sort through many judicial traditions as they did their work during the construction era and well into the mid-twentieth century.[8]

The judges who presided over the Zone embodied the hybrid character of its legal culture. The first circuit judge appointed in the Zone was Osceola Kyle, a white Alabaman. Kyle had lobbied hard to win the job, writing Taft with endorsements from prominent Alabama residents, including Booker T. Washington. As the only judge in the Zone during those early months, Kyle was responsible for opening court in all three circuit districts while serving also as the sole Supreme Court judge. He lasted less than five months, however. Kyle neglected important cases for months, and when he was asked to explain, his only defense was that he lacked knowledge of both the Spanish language and Panamanian law. Taft demanded his resignation, declaring that Kyle was "not disposed to fit in with the Spanish law, which . . . ought to prevail in the Zone so far as possible, because it is no purpose of our Government to take from the people of the Zone the laws to which they have been accustomed."[9]

The men appointed to take Kyle's place would all be fluent in Spanish, and two of them, Hezekiah Gudger and Facundo Mutis Durán, had

extensive experience with the laws of Panama. Gudger, a North Caro-
linian, had served as consul general in Panama since 1897 and had extensive experience with the laws, culture, and language of the country.
Mutis had a more glittering vitae. A Panamanian citizen, he had served
twice as governor of Panama before it achieved independence from
Colombia, although one of his terms ended prematurely when a conflict
with the military led to Mutis's fleeing from his home in women's clothes
and hiding out at the American consulate. In between Mutis worked for
many years as an attorney for the Panama Railroad and was later appointed to the Supreme Court of Panama. He was considered one of
the top authorities on Spanish, Colombian, and Panamanian law, and in
1905 Taft appointed him to serve as chief justice of the Canal Zone
Supreme Court.[10]

Similarly, the lawyers arguing cases before courts might be Panamanian or American. Any attorney allowed to practice law on the isthmus
when U.S. occupation began preserved that right in the new Canal Zone.
American lawyers who had been admitted to the bar in any state or territory of the United States could also practice in the Zone, although they
might be asked to sit for an examination on the Zone's legal codes. According to scholar Wayne Bray's analysis of lawyers who argued before
the Canal Zone Supreme Court, approximately two-thirds of them were
American and one-third Panamanian. Some lawyers who often argued
before the Supreme Court were Panamanian, such as Oscar Terán. Only
three lawyers argued more cases before the court than he did. Another
active lawyer was Harmodio Arias, who would later be elected to the
presidency of Panama.[11] In these ways the boundaries between American,
Panamanian, and even Spanish legal cultures were extremely fluid.

Finally, there was the challenge of reconciling the tensions between
constitutional rights and matters of empire. In the aftermath of the War
of 1898, American jurists needed to reassess constitutional law in light of
the colonial expansionism of the United States. Beginning in 1901 in the
Insular Cases, the Supreme Court justices accomplished that, and in doing
so, they provided the framework for legal decisions in the Canal Zone as
well. With rather tortured prose, the same Court that had upheld racial

segregation in *Plessy v. Ferguson* determined that colonial acquisitions by the United States did not contradict the Constitution and that such areas should be considered "unincorporated territories" in which the United States could decide which—if any—constitutional protections would apply to residents. In the most famous case, the 1901 *Downes v. Bidwell,* Justice Edward DouglassWhite justified his decision in this way: "While in an international sense Porto Rico was not a foreign country, since it was subject to the sovereignty of and was owned by the United States, it was foreign to the United States in a domestic sense, because the island has not been incorporated into the United States, but was merely appurtenant thereto as a possession."[12] This decision divided the justices, but in *Dorr v. United States* in 1904 a majority rallied to support the incorporation doctrine. The Supreme Court found in *Dorr* that Filipinos were not fit for jury trials and that Congress need not extend such rights to them until and unless it chose to incorporate the islands.

The *Insular Cases* freed the U.S. government to pursue its expansionist policies with full latitude. They followed closely after the election of 1900, in which William McKinley and William Jennings Bryan had debated imperialism, and the latter, an ardent anti-imperialist, went down soundly to defeat. The relation between the Supreme Court decisions and this election led humorist Finley Peter Dunne to famously quip, "No matther whether th' constitution follows th' flag or not, th' Supreme Coort follows th' iliction returns."[13] The beliefs underlying these decisions closely mirrored the worldview of expansionists like McKinley and Roosevelt. The Supreme Court justices were implicitly agreeing that the empire-building of the United States was a positive development for world civilization; that there existed no conflict between democracy and colonialism; that some racial or ethnic groups were superior to others; and that it was the responsibility of superior groups to help others rise to a higher level of civilization. The *Insular Cases* thus accomplished for empire what *Plessy v. Ferguson* accomplished for domestic race relations. While *Plessy* was famously overturned in 1954, the *Insular Cases* remain decisive even today for questions of "unincorporated territories"— *Downes v. Bidwell* was cited as recently as 1990 as a precedent in a Supreme

Court decision. Furthermore, while *Plessy* argued that segregation could exist amid fundamental equality, the *Insular Cases* forsook even the pretense of equality by asserting that residents of territories could not make claim to equal treatment. Secretary of State Elihu Root summed up the importance of these cases: "The Constitution follows the flag, but it does not catch up with it."[14]

Throughout the construction period, government officials looked closely at the experience of the United States in Puerto Rico and the Philippines as they sought to adjust the laws and legal procedure to U.S. precedents while also retaining, when possible, the flavor of Spanish precedents. By 1904, when the United States established the judicial system of the Canal Zone, officials in the Philippines and Puerto Rico already had several years of experience melding American and Spanish laws. One sign of the close relationship officials saw between the judiciary of the Canal Zone and that of the Philippines and Puerto Rico was the appointment of Charles Magoon as governor of the Canal Zone in 1905. Magoon had previously served as an official with the Bureau of Insular Affairs, where his specialty had been resolving legal problems in the United States' new colonial acquisitions, namely in the Philippines, Puerto Rico, and Cuba.[15] These provided the major models of colonial jurisprudence the ICC relied on when deciding difficult cases.

The case of *Fitzpatrick v. Panama Railroad Company* provides some insight into the ways that judges in the Canal Zone melded these diverse legal cultures in making their decisions. In 1910 the ICC secured permission from the Panama Railroad Company (a corporation owned and run by the U.S. government) to run a special train carrying some of its officials home after they attended an opera in Panama City. That train collided with one run by the Panama Railroad Company as a result of negligence by some of its workers, particularly one brakeman. A man named C. C. Fitzpatrick riding the ICC's special train received injuries during the collision and sued the Panama Railroad Company for damages. The circuit court awarded him $7,000. The Panama Railroad Company appealed this decision, arguing that it should not be liable for an injury caused by its workers. In a lengthy decision the Supreme

Court judges of the Canal Zone considered the issues, casting their net widely for legal advice and precedents. Their decision held that the Panama Railroad was liable for the acts of its servants and employees. It was based on a "careful review" of decisions made by a wide variety of judicial systems: the supreme courts of Panama and of Colombia, the courts of the Philippines and Puerto Rico, and the supreme court of the state of Louisiana.[16] The judiciary of the Canal Zone was thus a complex combination of legal cultures, particularly American and Panamanian courts and sites of U.S. colonialism.

Somehow this hybrid system would have to rule over a society capable of significant conflict, and there were important issues to determine. When was a problem severe enough to require judicial intervention, and then what punishments would be appropriate? Did it matter whether the perceived disorder occurred in public or in private? Were certain forms of conflict tolerated more than others? Most often such questions fell to Goethals's personal investigator as well as to the judges and policemen of the Canal Zone to resolve.

JOLLIFICATION AND LABOR DISCIPLINE

Maintaining discipline among workers required cooperation among various branches of the Canal Zone government. In addition to the municipal, circuit, and supreme courts of the Canal Zone, the police with their labor spies, and the government's powers of deportation and eviction, chief engineer George Goethals held a personal court every Sunday morning. Many of the cases put before him were minor disagreements, but others might have gone to court if the petitioners had chosen that route. Goethals tried when possible to devise a solution that would seem reasonable to all sides, but if no solution presented itself, he was willing to resort to deportation. The socialist Arthur Bullard observed one Sunday morning session, in which a Jamaican couple appealed to Goethals to solve a dispute over who owned the money the wife had earned washing clothes. Goethals ruled that the money belonged to the wife. When the husband demurred that under English law the property should be his,

Goethals responded, "Say the word, and I'll deport you. You can get all the English law you want in Jamaica."[17]

Despite these broad powers of deportation, ICC officials still found it difficult to rule over Zone residents. Deportation meant losing much-needed laborers and was expensive. Although useful in certain situations, deportation alone could not manage the huge population of the Zone. This became apparent as the number of people climbed during 1906 and 1907 and arrests quickly increased. The ICC reported in June 1907 that arrests by Zone policemen had nearly doubled compared with the previous year, from 3,356 to 6,236. Officials attributed this not only to the increase in population but particularly to the importation of many European laborers who were generally "restless, suspicious, and excitable." Intoxication, disorderly conduct, fighting, and violent crimes had all increased, and as a result the ICC began building more jails. Ten police stations and jails were built in 1907, plus three lockups. Four other buildings were adapted to become jails. A penitentiary already existed at Culebra.[18]

In late 1907, ICC officials requested yet more weapons to manage and discipline the Zone's growing population. President Roosevelt complied by issuing an executive order which declared that any vagrant, beggar, or loiterer, or anyone intoxicated or engaging in disorderly conduct or disturbance of the peace, would be guilty of a misdemeanor and punished by a fine of up to $25 and/or one month in prison. With this executive order supporting them, ICC officials began prosecuting men and women even for relatively unthreatening behavior. Police arrested a West Indian woman in 1911, for example, for swearing in public at someone who had angered her: she had cried out, "You damned Antiguan son-of-a-bitch." She was fined $15 plus all court costs.[19] Such trends suggest not only that ICC officials found it difficult to make the Zone as peaceful as they desired but also that the courts and prisons gradually became more important tools of social management.

The executive order was presumably aimed at West Indians and southern Europeans who would find it more difficult than white U.S. citizens to pay a fine as high as $25. Likewise, the courts seemed to reserve relatively stiff penalties for West Indians accused of petty crimes, as if this were a way to ensure law and order among the vast communities of Caribbean workers. One young West Indian man named Abel Scott, for example, forged a pay certificate worth less than $10 during the early days of U.S. occupation and was sentenced to five years' hard labor in the penitentiary. Two years later the judge in the case wrote Joseph Blackburn of the ICC and requested that Scott be pardoned. His reasons reveal the U.S. government's strategy for meting out punishment during the early days of construction. At the time of Scott's original trial, the judge noted, sentences were far more severe since "a great deal of crime was expected in the Canal Zone as it was feared that it would be the refuge for a large criminal class, and it was hoped that by having quick and rather severe sentences this state of affairs would be either remedied or the amount of crime greatly reduced." In fact, perhaps because of such severe sentences, crimes like Scott's were unusual. Now, the judge argued, Scott would have received only a year or two in prison for such a crime, and on those grounds he asked that Scott be pardoned and released from prison. As an added incentive, pardoning Scott would encourage other prisoners to behave well.[20]

A year or two in prison became the norm for such crimes, which still seems rather punitive. Samuel Griffith, a silver employee, changed his pay receipt from $10 to $40 in order to defraud the government of $30 silver (about U.S. $15). The court sentenced him to a year of hard labor. A Barbadian named George Owens, described by the court reporter as a "tall, thin, yellow nigger," forged two U.S. orders, for $10 and $15, and was sentenced to two years of hard labor.[21]

Occasionally men accused of insubordination or mutiny appeared before the courts, as when F. Garcia, a coal passer on a steamship owned by the Panama Railroad, disobeyed his superior captain and then attempted to assault him. Garcia received a sentence of six months of hard labor for his disobedience. Seamen who deserted their ships kept the courts very busy. Some seamen deserted in hopes of securing better jobs in the Canal Zone. This particularly was the case with seamen from Europe. Chinese seamen, on the other hand, more often deserted to escape cruel treatment and poor working conditions. Two men named Ah Mee and Ah Chow, for example, deserted their British ship, claiming their foreman beat them and threatened them with a gun. The court determined that they had been gambling and were indebted to their foreman and that their unwillingness or inability to pay had caused his physical violence. The judge in this case ordered them held in a Zone prison cell until their ship was ready to leave port, partly in order to comply with the Chinese exclusion law of the Republic of Panama.[22]

On a daily basis police spent much of their time inspecting camps, watching for vagrants, and making sure that intoxicated men (or women) did not become so disorderly as to interfere with the construction job the next day. Many tense moments occurred, particularly when West Indians and white policemen confronted each other and their perspectives on a person's rights and the prerogatives of law and order in the Zone clashed. Such conflicts led many laborers to complain to Goethals about police cruelty toward them, providing a vivid picture of how they experienced "labor discipline."

Most of the complaints about police abuse came from silver workers. A man named Walcott, for example, was walking home one day, carrying a package, when a policeman named Arndt began following him. Either Mr. Walcott, a West Indian who delivered ice for a living, declined to state what was in his package, or perhaps his explanation did not satisfy the policeman. The testimony differs on this and many other points. When Walcott reached home, he dropped the package and said to the policeman, "This is what you followed me for." The policeman, "in a rage," one witness observed, stated that he had to take Walcott to jail, but Walcott retorted, "I'm a free man the same as you and I never stole anything." According to a shoemaker who lived next door, the policeman began hitting Walcott over the head with a club. Walcott's wife came out on the porch and grabbed Walcott's hands, as if to show the policeman that he would no longer resist arrest, but the police officer continued beating him over the head until finally his club broke and Walcott fell to the ground.

Walcott quickly rose and ran. When the policeman caught up with him, the two struggled for some time, each holding on to the other. The policeman hollered for someone to help him, but none of the West Indians in the vicinity would come to his assistance. Finally two white men, a foreman and a time inspector from the nearby Empire shops, heard the shouting and ran to help. One of them got the policeman's gun out of his holster and aimed it at Walcott, telling him to stop fighting and go with the policeman to jail or he would be shot. By this time several West Indian women stood about, yelling at Walcott to stop and not risk getting hurt more severely. Walcott was arrested, but before the matter was concluded, the police searched his apartment and arrested three other West Indians, including a shoemaker and a tailor, for failing to assist the officer when he requested it. The police took Walcott to the hospital for treatment only several hours later, by their own testimony. Walcott's wife went to the Empire police station with her five-year-old child, to check on her husband, but police shoved her down the steps and told her to leave. When she would not leave, she testified, they locked her and her child in a cell and refused to give her water or food.

Goethals's inspector on this case, T. B. Miskimon, concluded that the fault lay with Walcott for resisting arrest. Although he did not personally know the policeman Arndt, the inspector noted, "He has never impressed me as having any of what is commonly called the 'bull cop' about him." Miskimon explained that he had looked into the event with unusual care, taking testimony from nearly a dozen people, because there had recently been many complaints about police cruelty in the town of Empire. He succinctly noted that the cause of all the complaints must be one of two things: "Either the police are getting 'strong' or the negroes are."[23] Nine days later Miskimon recommended that the lieutenant in charge of the police force at Empire be discharged, as complaints about police brutality toward West Indians continued to surface. The police were clearly becoming "too strong," but it is also worth noting that in this case, Goethals's investigator recommended that action be taken against a cruel and racist police officer.[24]

Incidents like these spread apprehension among West Indians, and so ICC officials increasingly relied on West Indians to police their own communities. M. H. Thatcher, who headed civil administration in the Zone, noted: "We find [West Indian policemen] very useful in dealing with the black population. . . . We do not give them the same police powers that we give white policemen, but we give them sufficient powers to be very useful in their work."[25] Like other West Indians, however, those wearing the uniform of a Zone policeman had to be cautious in their behavior when they were around white U.S. citizens. The police chief typically did not assign West Indian policemen to patrol in white neighborhoods, but sometimes black policemen found themselves in a situation where their position as policemen conflicted with their racial status in the Zone. When a Jamaican or Barbadian policeman seemed to whites to overstep the boundaries of race, tensions flared. One night in 1908, for example, a West Indian watchman went to a room in an ICC hotel to deliver some shoes he had repaired for a white man. It happened that he was visiting a section of the hotel where many white railroad and construction workers known for their heavy drinking resided. After the West Indian delivered the shoes, an intoxicated white man named A. T. Murphy began shouting epithets at him. Murphy finally came into the hall, grabbed the watchman by the throat, and told him to leave, saying he "did not want a God damned negro spying around there." Murphy began calling to his friends to come and help as he searched for his gun. The watchman blew his whistle for help, and a black policeman named Plummer soon came to his assistance.

The arrival on the scene of a West Indian policeman incensed the crowd. White men began pushing Plummer around and shouting, "Hang him!" and "Kick him out!" while someone placed a rope around his shoulders. After a few minutes of such treatment, Plummer felt himself pushed down the stairs as the Americans yelled at him to go and find a *white* policeman. Plummer hastily retreated as a white policeman appeared and subdued the crowd. Goethals's investigator, Miskimon, took testimony from all sides, including Plummer, who declared he had intended only to calm the crowd. Miskimon, however, was more concerned about whether the American men's carousing in the hotel would disrupt their neighbors—or their own work habits. He noted, "It seems to be a good natured crowd and that while they seem to do considerable drinking they appear to be alright 'on the job' the next day." The inspector concluded that Plummer and the Negro watchman had both been mistreated, but his recommendation to Goethals was simply that "it might be well to keep these people in mind so that their jollifications do not reach such a stage that they will be unfit for work on the days following." If it does reach that point, he noted, it may be necessary to transfer some of the men so as to "break the gang up." In the end, the men faced no consequences for their behavior despite having threatened a black policeman with lynching. Goethals and his investigator knew they needed to allow some "jollification" but prevent it from impeding canal workers' productivity on the job. For reasons like this, West Indians learned to avoid the white workers' dormitories as much as possible.[26]

The most common solution Goethals and Miskimon imagined for social problems ranging from unfair commissary managers to extreme episodes of racial or gender conflict was simply to remove the person causing the problem. When a group of canal employees became too unruly, as the above example suggests, they contemplated separating the men and moving them to different dormitories. At other times Goethals ordered a family moved to a different neighborhood, an employee moved to a different division, or a union-organizing troublemaker deported from the Canal Zone altogether. When none of this worked, he and the ICC had a last weapon in reserve: a prison sentence. The Canal Zone penitentiary provided the final plank in the system of justice and discipline devised by the ICC officials. Like every other aspect of life in the Zone, the prison system was created not only to preserve public order but to maintain labor productivity. The Zone penitentiary at Culebra housed nearly 150 convicts as of 1912, the vast majority of them West Indians, and it was well-known that prisoners worked long days at hard labor. If employees were not contributing to the construction effort, in short, as a last resort the ICC could imprison them and in that way ensure their productivity. One way or another, men and women living in the Canal Zone would be made to assist the construction project.[27]

Prison memoranda from 1908 describe the arduous life of penitentiary prisoners. They woke at 5:30 each morning and spent time cleaning before marching to breakfast. There they received boiled beef, rice and potatoes or yams, coffee, and half a pound of bread. After breakfast, guards shackled each prisoner to a ball weighing between eighteen and thirty pounds and attached to an eight-foot-long chain. The prisoners then marched in their shackles a mile or two to the work site. They labored there for ten hours, while guards carrying double-barreled shotguns watched over them. At noon they received more coffee and another half pound of bread; at night orderlies served them a dinner similar to their breakfast. Afterward, from 6:00 to 9:00, the prisoners' time was their own. During these evening hours prisoners were allowed to talk. On Sundays and holidays, they could receive friends for a couple of hours. At no other time could prisoners speak to anyone. No talking between cells, no talking in the dining hall, no talking on the job. According to the rules, prisoners could not make any sound of any kind unless they required a conversation with a guard or a foreman.[28]

Prisoners performed a variety of jobs, filling in ditches, building roads, and cleaning and maintaining the penitentiary. Officials found that road building in particular provided ideal work for inmates. Any prisoner, regardless of his background, could do this work. Although it required difficult labor in swamps and exposed prisoners to torrential rains, officials argued it was healthy outdoor exercise and better for inmates' health than confinement to cells. Road construction kept prisoners in the public's eye, made it easier to guard them, and as the head of civil administration, Joseph Blackburn, put it, "The deterrent effect of punishment is greater when prisoners are brought frequently before the public."[29] The mild humiliation experienced by prisoners working in public served both as a punishment and as a warning to others. When the Commercial Club of Mobile, Alabama, wrote Canal Zone chief of police and prison warden George Shanton to ask how the use of convict labor on roads was working, Shanton responded with enthusiasm: "This is by all means the most practicable and humane method of handling prison labor." Gradually, officials began relying more heavily on prison labor, assigning not only convicts in the penitentiary to hard labor but also those convicted of lesser crimes by the district judges. They began assigning more work to prisoners such as breaking up rocks and building construction. They also built stockades to house overnight convicts working far from the penitentiary, declaring it a system that had been used effectively with convict labor in the U.S. South and in the Philippines.[30]

Officials praised the prisoners' productivity, estimating that they worked 7 percent to 100 percent more efficiently than other canal workers. This saved the U.S. government a significant amount of money. The assistant engineer overseeing the prisoners' labor conceded that this remarkable efficiency derived partly from the fact that prisoners knew they would receive punishment if they worked poorly (even gazing at visitors was explicitly forbidden); however, he also attributed the fine results to "the perfect discipline and thorough organization possible in working convict labor. . . . [S]plendid results can be obtained if they are properly handled."[31]

Shanton and other officials were keenly aware of how reformers in the United States might react to their prison policies. "It is absolutely necessary," Shanton wrote, "that we establish a reputation on this piece of work that will keep all vagrants and bums, who have once been sent to that place to work, in fear of being arrested and sent back by the judge." We do not want any cruel treatment, but nonetheless a "force of character" should be employed to teach the men that they are to work and work hard. Then "the reputation of the Gatun road will be such that the vagrant class will go most any where in the world to escape going back to that road to work." Shanton also cautioned officials to give prisoners the best and most plentiful food they could, maintain sleeping quarters in fine condition, and provide them with "every care and attention, so that the public in general cannot criticize us along that line."[32]

Yet disciplining prisoners remained a complicated issue. In 1909, after hearing complaints that prisoners were routinely beaten and whipped by guards, Goethals ordered an investigation. Three guards fined for beating prisoners defended themselves by saying they were following instructions from their superiors. One declared his lieutenant had told him how to handle prisoners who misbehaved: "You can get even with them when you get them in the brush." This same guard said he was instructed to whip convicts who required punishment. A policeman argued that they should treat convicts the same way they "handle negroes in Texas." After investigating, Miskimon concluded that the chief of police had approved the use of the whip or strap on prisoners. He noted, "It is a well known fact that in police organizations the rough handling of prisoners is not allowed before the public, and the commanding officer of a precinct will be the first to get after you for it, while if the same happens in the station he will avoid seeing it if possible, if the parties appear to merit such treatment."[33]

Goethals ordered an end to corporal punishment as a result of this investigation. Soon thereafter he received anxious complaints from guards who declared the elimination of corporal punishment was generating widespread insubordination and mutiny, and they feared a large-scale riot would soon result. It was said that prisoners were constantly speaking and joking with one another despite the rule requiring silence. They were engaging in fights, baiting their guards, and, when working in public, begging for tobacco or money from tourists standing nearby. In one case an "American lady" was insulted by a convict who employed language one would not even use in the presence of a "public woman." There were cases of prisoners attempting to assault the policemen guarding them. One policeman was attacked by a prisoner who used his iron ball as a weapon. Police officers strongly requested that Goethals reverse himself and allow the use of the strap on prisoners again.[34]

These problems placed ICC officials in a quandary. They certainly worried about insubordination among prisoners, and they found it difficult to punish them by withdrawing privileges since prisoners enjoyed virtually none. On the other hand, they thought that policemen who complained might be exaggerating the prisoners' offenses, in part due to anger they felt over the government's decision to prohibit corporal punishment. White policemen who worked at the penitentiary had felt especially criticized and insulted by that investigation. Goethals and his officials agreed that policies were urgently needed that could compel good behavior, punish insubordination, and prevent riots. After examining highly regarded penal institutions in the United States and Puerto Rico, they developed a plan that divided prisoners into five grades, each one treated slightly differently in terms of access to privileges and the burden of wearing striped clothing and the ball and chain. By earning points for good behavior, prisoners would gradually attain a higher level. At the highest grade, prisoners would be rewarded with indoor work and full privileges, and be allowed to wear a gray rather than a striped uniform. "In this way an account is kept of each prisoner showing his status as a prisoner," declared M. H. Thatcher, the head of civil administration. Certain prisoners—those sentenced to a life term or still facing more than one third of a five-year term—were prohibited from entering the higher grades because, if not required to wear a ball and chain, they were considered too great an escape risk. Officials also created small cells where troublesome prisoners were ordered to spend up to four hours in dark and solitary confinement on a diet of bread and water.[35] ICC officials believed that with this systematic set of changes, they had brought the Canal Zone's penal system into accordance with the best institutions of the United States. Such reforms helped them make the penitentiary an efficient means of punishing canal workers who lacked discipline or behaved in disorderly ways while simultaneously guaranteeing that prisoners would contribute their labor to the construction project.[36]

MORAL DISORDER, SEX, AND CRIME

In order to build an American civilization in the Canal Zone, officials struggled to curb behaviors they considered unrespectable or immoral. At the same time, they sought to offer certain comforts to workers in order to enhance their ability to perform productively at work and thus to keep them in the Zone. Moral, social, and political order in the Zone, they believed, could not be achieved without a balance between repression and permissiveness. Considering which behaviors they curbed and which they allowed opens a window into the notions of officials—and into a world of Zone residents caught in the unwelcome glare of policemen, courts, and Goethals's personal investigator.

Alcohol, for instance, was one of the most popular vices in the Zone. It formed an important part of the day for most workers, helping them relax and thus endure the challenges of their jobs, yet too much intoxication would hinder labor productivity. So officials carefully regulated alcohol. As Goethals explained to a Senate committee, "Our working men are human; they have got to have their liquor, and if we do not sell it to them they are going to get it elsewhere, and in the towns where liquor is not sold they get it by the bottleful and they stand by that bottle until it is gone; then there is trouble." The government thus allowed not only saloons but also several distilleries throughout the Zone to ensure that workingmen had access to good-quality liquor. Pressed by senators to close them down, Goethals called the distilleries "not a disturbance; they are a source of contentment." The government, he proclaimed, sought not only to provide alcohol to the men but also to ensure they consumed alcohol that was decent in quality. Government officials wanted the business for themselves, however, and so zealously prosecuted anyone caught selling liquor without a license.[37]

Government officials saw gambling, on the other hand, as a vice they should eliminate altogether. They didn't like to talk about it, but gambling was endemic throughout the Zone, particularly in dormitories occupied by single American workingmen. Poker games abounded during workers' leisure hours, and it proved extremely difficult for police to tell whether any of those games involved money bets. Undercover policemen circulated among the workers to try to catch someone wagering in a poker game, craps, or roulette. The police and judges were particularly eager to catch men running games for profit, and prosecutions were common for such behavior. In one of the earliest such cases, in 1905, a man named Charles Christian was found guilty of running a roulette table. The court fined him $100 and sentenced him to thirty days in jail. Christian countered, however, that the Republic of Panama had granted him a concession to run his gambling operation and that, in any case, the Canal Zone had no law against it. The court held that it had the right to punish gamblers, but due to the confusion over jurisdiction it agreed to waive Christian's thirty days in jail. In succeeding cases, gamblers might be sentenced to anything from one day to three months in jail, with the difference in sentence usually depending on the race and ethnicity of those accused.[38]

Regulating sexuality was considered by government officials a far more complicated problem. Officials created multifaceted policies they hoped would ensure clean living and decency, even as they depended on the accessibility of prostitution in the port cities of Panama. Nurses working in Zone hospitals, for example, found their lives carefully monitored and their social activities restricted. Louise Bidwell, who worked as a nurse at Ancon Hospital, recalled that nurses were required to inform the head nurse if they desired even to miss a meal. They had a curfew of 10:30 p.m. and were not allowed to travel beyond Panama City. Women working as stenographers or in other clerical positions seem not to have been subject to such regulations. Nurses, as a symbol of respectability and as representatives of the Zone government, required more careful monitoring.[39]

Men who took or showed pictures of women partially clothed or dressed in bathing suits were investigated for indecency (although the investigator in charge noted that more revealing photographs were readily available for sale in Colón or Panama City).[40] People living in the government's married quarters for white Americans risked being reported to Goethals by neighbors if they engaged in adultery, and then an investigation—and possible dismissals, evictions, or both—would result. Thus a locomotive engineer named O'Neill, for example, left his wife and took up with another married woman. After the husband of O'Neill's mistress complained, Goethals's investigator assessed the situation. O'Neill wound up losing his job and being barred from further employment in the Zone. Judging from the reports of Goethals's investigator, it appears that only white Americans, not Europeans or West Indians, went to Goethals with charges of adultery.[41]

When the courts got involved in cases of adultery, it was usually because West Indians, not white Americans, went to the courts to accuse a husband or wife. Whites were reluctant to rely on the judicial system, but

West Indians perhaps saw it as less damaging because guilty parties would typically not lose their jobs but only be sentenced at most to a day or two of jail or a $10 fine. West Indians did not always get off so easily, however. James Peart, a canal worker from Jamaica, was accused by his brother-in-law of living with a woman in the Zone even though he had a wife back in Jamaica. The court found Peart guilty and sentenced him to three months in prison.[42]

Occasionally the boundaries between adultery and prostitution were difficult to discern. One such case reached the Canal Zone Supreme Court in 1908. A man named James McFarlane, who had once worked as a Zone policeman, rose from his couch one morning and asked his wife to give him their savings of $315. He said he wanted to go into Panama to buy some supplies. He headed to the train station in Culebra and gave the $315 to a Jamaican woman named Mary Cooper. McFarlane testified that he was simply giving Cooper the money to hold for him until he returned. Cooper told a different story. She testified that McFarlane had paid attention to her for some time and had sought to have sex with her, and that because of his attentions she had been beaten by her husband, Dennis Cooper. McFarlane demanded that she rent a house where they could be together, she said, and that if she refused he would "dye her husband with blood." They did have sex, she said, and he had given her money as payment for this act. She in turn had passed the $315 on to her husband, and upon learning this, McFarlane had forced Cooper to return the money to him.

The question facing the court was this: Had the money been taken wrongfully from Dennis Cooper? The court found that McFarlane's story was not believable, declaring, "The story he narrates raises a question of the insane asylum or the penitentiary for him." The judges found Mary's story more probable. They concluded, "The red light of lust illumines this case. A lecherous James and a pulchritudinous Mary, utterly destroy the tissue of falsehoods on which this case is built." Citing the civil code of Panama, the judges held that the husband, Dennis Cooper, was not liable to McFarlane for any money his wife had received from him. And thus the $315 was ordered returned to Dennis Cooper.[43]

If adultery and prostitution were murky areas for officials to navigate, cohabitation outside the boundaries of marriage likewise troubled them. They could agree in theory that it was bad and immoral. But how bad? They could not decide how strenuously to police the problem or how severely to punish offenders. In 1905, Canal Zone governor Charles Magoon ordered punishment of any man and woman living together without being legally married. Anyone sharing a room and bed would be fined a maximum of $25 and thirty days in jail. If the guilty parties married before their case went to trial, they would not be prosecuted. ICC officials devised this law with hopes of nudging West Indian couples, who often lived together without a marriage certificate, to undergo the formal ceremony. Over time, however, officials recognized that expecting all West Indians to marry was unfeasible, and they decided to turn a blind eye to the common practice. To their surprise, meanwhile, cohabitation by white American canal workers proved a more difficult problem, especially since it often involved women of color from the West Indies or Panama.

It is difficult to know how often canal employees engaged in interracial relationships, but popular accounts of the canal construction suggest that it was not uncommon. John Hall, a poet who published a book devoted to the "roughneck" workers of the Zone in 1912, noted the trend. His poem about a steam-shovel engineer, reminiscent in some ways of the African American "John Henry" ballad, added the twist of romance between a skilled white worker and a Panamanian woman. The poem depicted Bill Hicks, a steam-shovel man known for his power:

> The "huskies" swore "Bill" was a wonder;
> A marvel of skill in his line,
> He'd swear by the clock as he loaded the rock
> That he'd "rather pull levers than dine."

Bill, however, hates women and loves only his steam shovel. Until one day, that is, when a Panamanian woman named Juancita comes to watch the steam-shovel engineers:

The little brown "spick" gazed in wonder
Such sights she ne'er had beheld.
Her gaze fell on "Bill," and he felt a great thrill,
but his case-hardened spirit rebelled.

Bill and Juancita soon fall in love. Bill acquires a nickname and is known to all his friends as "Spickety Bill," because of his love for a Panamanian. According to the song, he and his gal remain together until an explosion in Culebra Cut ends his life. Then Juancita can be seen shedding tears at the spot where he died.[44]

ICC officials seem not to have taken strenuous action against interracial relationships until near the end of the construction era. In 1913, however, Goethals ordered investigations into several cases. One involved a locomotive engineer who was living with a light-colored Panamanian woman and their three-year-old daughter in Panama City while working for the ICC. The man, whose name was Frank Day, explained to the inspector that he had a wife at home in the United States in an insane asylum or otherwise would marry the Panamanian woman. Another locomotive engineer living with a Panamanian woman explained he thought it better to live with her than to frequent the houses of ill repute in Cocoa Grove. The response of Oscar Hayes, a white canal worker living with a woman in Panama City, was the most provocative: he declined, the inspector reported, "to state whether he is married to her or not; he says that he pays the house rent, and does not think it is anybody's business. That he gives the commission 9 hours first class service every day, and thinks that is all that is required of him, and he does not want anyone to pry into his private affairs."[45]

Despite Hayes's protests regarding his privacy, government officials saw this as an important public issue. Yet most men living with women of color were doing so on Panamanian soil, not in the Canal Zone, so the U.S. government had little power to change their behavior. Instead, officials sought help from the Panamanian police. If Panama had a law against cohabitation, officials thought, then perhaps they could eliminate or at least discourage such offenses. But this strategy failed as well when the Panamanian chief of police informed the Zone police that "no law is violated and that on account of the quietness observed, and secrecy attempted, it is in no way conducive to disorder or breach of the peace." Since the Republic of Panama would not punish the men, ICC officials decided instead to discharge them the next time the supervisor reduced the working force.[46]

Soon several of the men cohabiting with women of color lost their jobs through force reduction and left the isthmus, including Oscar Hayes and Frank Day. Several others continued living with women in Panama. Commissioner H. H. Rousseau called these remaining men into his office for a conversation in early December 1913. Afterward he felt more empathy for their situation and reported to Goethals: "After taking their side of the matter into consideration . . . it does not appear to me that there are any facts or occurrence remaining unsettled at the present time which would warrant discharge." Rousseau warned the men, however, "that they are expected to conduct themselves outside working hours in a manner that is not detrimental to the Isthmian service as a whole, and that if they do not do so they will have to accept the consequences." The bureaucrats of the Canal Zone agreed with Rousseau's strategy. Another official commented, "While the moral calibre of these men is apparently below par, are they any worse than the men who make a practice of frequenting the dives in Panama and Colón? Without going into any detail it would seem that the single men on the Isthmus are in a somewhat peculiar position as regards sexual intercourse."[47]

Indeed. Officials believed single men required sexual partners, but they wanted no prostitution in the Canal Zone. Yet U.S. government officials found it impossible to create an impermeable border between the Zone and the world of Panama. The perceived immorality of Panama found its way into the Zone, and officials carefully policed the Zone to try to eliminate any houses of prostitution, wandering women "of ill repute," or pimping. Goethals's investigators kept an eye out for prostitutes on the trains and streets, reporting any who appeared and escorting them out of the Zone and back into Panama. Likewise, they investigated charges that white slavery existed in the port cities of Panama. In 1908 an American woman running a boardinghouse in Panama City charged that white American girls under the age of twenty-two were working as prostitutes in Colón. Goethals sent an investigator to canvass every house of prostitution in Colón and Panama City. The investigator reported that he had found only one "white slave," a girl named Rosa Goodwin who claimed to be nineteen. She had come to the Canal Zone from Arkansas via New Orleans along with a Memphis girl, who had since married a dredge captain and no longer worked as a prostitute. The investigator noted that Rosa and her friend had caused more than a little comment because of their drunken behavior and especially their young age: "The rest of them in this town have passed the girlhood stage some time past." But he confirmed that Rosa was not being held against her will.[48]

After the U.S. Congress passed the Mann Act in 1910, also known as the "white-slave act," which outlawed forced prostitution and the interstate transportation of females toward that end, the ICC's Department of Civil Administration became more vigilant. M. H. Thatcher, the department's head, ordered policemen to watch trains and ships entering the isthmus for women being transported through Canal Zone territory to the port cities of Panama or other foreign soil for "immoral purposes." Two men and one woman were arrested and sentenced to one or two years' hard labor in the penitentiary for violating the Mann Act. These became the first successful prosecutions for white-slave trafficking. Thatcher saluted the Zone policemen in his annual report for 1912 for thus clearing the Zone of "dealers, vicious prostitutes, and other undesirables."[49]

Unfortunately the problem was not so easily resolved. Although prostitution rarely received mention in the annual reports of the ICC, concerns were repeatedly voiced over the years not only about prostitutes traveling through the Zone but about canal employees commingling with them. The Zone investigator T. B. Miskimon alerted his superiors in 1909 when a member of the ICC band was seen sitting next to a known prostitute on a train in the Canal Zone: "To my knowledge he sat in the same seat with the woman as far as Culebra, and I suppose entertained her as far as Panama. The fact of this man being in the uniform of the band, and accompanying such a woman, caused considerable comment. The woman, at times, amused herself flirting with the different passengers."[50] Residents persistently complained to Goethals about policemen, including leaders of the force, patronizing prostitutes. One man complained about two Jamaican prostitutes who regularly had policemen, including a sergeant, as clients: "We who are on the Zone and try to support the decent notions of society, who in our best efforts try to protect our wives and families from all knowledge and contact with such characters, are requesting that these women be prosecuted and removed." The police sergeant in particular had been seen caressing a prostitute in public: "This officer is supposed to protect the tenets of the law. He breaks them. He openly encourages these women and parades in the company of one of them before the white women of Bas Obispo." This case went to municipal court, but the judge dismissed it for lack of sufficient evidence.[51]

By 1913 a similar case indicated that officials had grown more determined to rid themselves of prostitutes. The town of Gorgona acquired over the years a special fame as a center of prostitution in the Zone. Residents complained about police and canal employees frequenting prostitutes. Police established surveillance in the area and determined that several women from Jamaica and St. Lucia were seeing white American canal workers. U.S. officials decided they lacked evidence to press charges. Instead, they called the offending men in and informed them they must cease visiting such houses if they wanted to keep working for the ICC. Then they deported the suspected prostitutes, citing their "general reputation and bad conduct."[52]

Male canal employees who sought comfort from other men or from boys were also a problem for government officials, police, and judges. The relatively low number of such cases in the judicial records of the Canal Zone leads one to speculate that homosexual activity usually remained discreet, unobserved, and therefore tolerated. There is no evidence, as there is in the case of prostitution or cohabitation, that the police set up surveillance or otherwise attempted to catch men in the act. Instead, there exist merely a handful of complaints by men or boys alleging they were assaulted, or cases where suspicious sounds led police to come upon men who failed to exercise discretion. Such was the case, for example, of the canal employee John O'Brien and a West Indian boy named Granville Rees.

Rees lived with his mother in Colón and worked as an office boy for a lawyer there. He met John O'Brien one day as they both walked along the main street of Colón. O'Brien invited Rees to his room in the single men's dormitory in Cristobal, took him to his bed, and hugged him, "telling him he was going to use him as he would a girl." Occupants of the room next door heard suspicious noises and beckoned a policeman to investigate. Hearing noise in the room, the policeman broke through the door and found both men partially dressed, O'Brien aroused, while Rees hid under the bed. Rees testified that he had resisted the sexual assault, but the policeman declared he had seen no signs of struggle. The circuit judge found O'Brien guilty of "the infamous crime against nature" and sentenced him to five years in the penitentiary. O'Brien appealed the case to the Canal Zone Supreme Court, arguing that Rees had been an accomplice in the crime and therefore his testimony should not be sufficient to convict the defendant. The court, while finding that Rees had engaged willingly in the sexual act, noted that his testimony was corroborated by others. The judges then abruptly concluded, "We do not think it is productive of any good to enter into a fuller discussion of a question of such revolting character." They upheld the lower court's ruling, and O'Brien was sentenced to the penitentiary.[53]

The case of William Waite, a young Barbadian man, provides insight into how the Zone circuit courts and George Goethals assessed alleged sexual assault on girls. The victim was an eleven-year-old girl named Keturah Lewis. Waite was a twenty-year-old boarder and canal employee in the home of Lewis's parents in the town of Las Cascadas. She was delivering clean clothes to his room one day when, according to her testimony, he took her by force into his bed and "had connection" with her. Waite countered that she had consented to the act and had returned another time, when they again had intercourse. Waite was found guilty of rape in 1905 and sentenced to five years in the penitentiary. Three years later Goethals personally reassessed the crime, noting, "It appears, however, that the girl with whom the offense was committed was of such physical development as to lead Waite to believe that she was more than thirteen years of age." Despite the girl's testimony to the contrary, Goethals declared that she and her parents had all consented to the act and that Waite had offered to marry the child, and therefore Goethals pardoned him.[54]

When it came to problems of sexual assault and domestic violence, particularly if they involved U.S. citizens, the police and courts in the Canal Zone were at a loss for how to respond. This was comparable to treatment of such cases on the U.S. mainland at this time, where family violence was often ignored and few institutional resources existed for its victims. In the Canal Zone, notions of white American women's roles as civilizers and the presence of canal employees' families as a stabilizing and nurturing force made it especially difficult for state authorities to manage effectively—or even publicly acknowledge—the existence of turmoil and violence within a family. Nonetheless, Canal Zone residents complained frequently to Goethals about men who were verbally or physically cruel to their family members. Goethals tended to take little action, but if a man's physical violence toward a woman became threatening to her health and to the public order, then the police and courts typically got involved. In 1905 a woman named Frances Smith was beaten by her partner, Evan Barker. A neighbor got Smith to the hospital, where she received treatment by a doctor. The police were informed of the incident, and Evan Barker was convicted of assault by the circuit court.[55]

Each year thousands of people were arrested in the Canal Zone. The numbers of arrests increased from just over 2,000 during the 1905 fiscal year to more than 7,000 by fiscal year 1912. When one considers that the entire Canal Zone population stood at 62,000 according to the census of 1912, this is a high number of arrests—more than 10 percent of all residents. The West Indian and southern European communities saw a disproportionately high number of arrests: nearly 3,500 West Indians were arrested that year and 538 Spaniards. But U.S. citizens were not far behind, with 517 arrests. Most often those arrested were laborers, but there were nearly 200 each of carpenters and brakemen arrested and more than 100 foremen, firemen, sailors, and teamsters. Nearly 500 domestic servants were also arrested that year. The most common offenses in 1912 were intoxication and/or disorderly conduct (nearly 2,000 people arrested), disturbing the peace (800), assault and battery (547), petit larceny (406), loitering (308), and vagrancy (289). Most of the arrests, in short, were related to the ICC's efforts to keep a lid on the tumultuous labor camps and resulted in a fine or brief jail sentence. Crimes that landed a man or woman in the penitentiary with a sentence of hard labor included assault with a deadly weapon, grand larceny, burglary, manslaughter, murder, rape, trafficking in white slaves, and returning to the Zone after having been deported.[56]

Passions and conflicts in the Canal Zone occasionally erupted into violence, with murder sometimes resulting, and multiple factors help explain why this happened. Tensions in the labor camps and communities of the Zone ran high; men and women worked hard and sometimes drank harder; disagreements within families or between friends or strangers, often of different nationalities or races, could turn violent. A closer look at three murder cases sheds light onto social tensions that ran through life in the Canal Zone. Each case had a different cause and dynamic, but all three involved perceived threats to masculinity and manliness.[57]

One day in 1908 Frank Houston, a skilled American worker, woke up early to prepare for work and went over to the stove in the home he shared with his wife. Taking the lids off the stove to start a fire, he noticed a partially burned letter inside and saw the words "my own wife." He removed the letter, stuck it in his pocket, and read it later that day during a break on the job. The letter was written to his wife by Harry Stern, an assistant manager at the commissary, and it revealed that the two had been carrying on an affair for several months. That evening Houston asked his wife who had visited her the night before, and she said, "No one." He asked her if Stern had visited her, and she said no. He told her about the letter and his discovery of the affair, and showed her the pieces. She tried to eat and swallow the letter, but he forced her to spit it out. She cried out, "If you let me go this time I will never do it again. I will pack up and take the next boat and never bother you again. I will never let another man come in the house." Houston left the house, found Stern in front of the YMCA clubhouse, and asked Stern if he was having an affair with his wife; Stern neither confirmed nor denied it. Pulling out a gun, Houston shot Stern. As Stern fell to the ground, he murmured the words "It is all over." Houston meanwhile walked calmly into the YMCA and said to those gathered, "That is all right. I have got my man." The judge found Houston guilty of murder and sentenced him to ten years in the penitentiary.[58]

Houston appealed on several grounds, including the fact that he had been denied a jury trial. One of the judges wrote regarding this part of his appeal that "there is not a State or Territory in the Union, or any civilized country in the world where he would have been denied a jury on such a charge. . . . The defendant was found guilty by a single judge, and sentenced to 10 years' penal servitude for shooting the destroyer of his home, under circumstances that would probably have resulted in his acquittal by any jury in any State of the Union." But the lower court's sentence was affirmed on the grounds that because he was not charged with murder in the first degree, he did not have the right to a jury trial.[59]

A very different case also involved perceived threats to manliness. Several Spanish workers were playing music, dancing, and drinking together when their party culminated in a fight between two men and, ultimately, manslaughter. Their party must have been a common sort of event in the labor towns of the Zone, particularly among West Indian and southern European workers who lacked other forms of entertainment. In this case the party continued for a while until one of the men decided to escort the women in attendance home since they had to rise especially early the next morning. A Spaniard named Desiderio Rodriguez protested the departure of the women and accused the man escorting them, Andres Oriza, of being a pimp. Their disagreement escalated into a contest over masculinity, with Rodriguez taunting Oriza, "I am a man—come outside here so that you can see." Oriza responded, "You are not a man to fight with me." Their fighting turned physical as Rodriguez pulled out a knife and stabbed Oriza in the neck. "Carajo, you have cut me," Oriza said, groaning. He picked up a club and managed to strike Rodriguez with it before falling to the ground and muttering, "My mother," as his final words. Rodriguez, a twenty-year-old canal worker, told a different story, saying that Oriza attacked him and he used his knife only in self-defense. He had always been afraid of Oriza, he argued. The judge in this case found the witnesses more credible. He convicted Rodriguez of manslaughter but sentenced him to only fifteen months in prison.[60]

A final example began in the red-light district of Panama City known as Cocoa Grove, and it suggests how fine the line between the "civilization" of the Canal Zone and the "disorder" of Panama City actually was. In November 1912, on a moonlit night, two young Panamanian prostitutes named Julia Vega and Petra Garcia were standing outside the cantina where they worked, talking. At about 3:00 a.m., they decided to hire a coach along with a male friend and go for a ride. They waved down a Jamaican driving a horse-pulled carriage and asked him to head out of town. Meanwhile, a man named Francisco Zaldivar was watching them. Zaldivar had arrived earlier that night at the cantina with a bunch of friends and had spent the night joking, singing, and kicking back about twelve beers. He and Vega had lived together for about a year. The day before, the two had quarreled over a man with whom Zaldivar had found Vega, and she had called the police on him. She had also told him that if he continued to threaten her, she would call the police again.

On the fateful night, Zaldivar was still extremely angry with Vega. He observed the two women leave in the coach and decided to hire one himself and follow them. As her coach sped out of town, Vega turned around and saw Zaldivar following her. Scared, she told her driver to speed up but also to turn around and head back to town. The driver urged the horses to go faster, but at some point his hat flew off his head, and he stopped the coach to get out and pick it up. Zaldivar caught up with them, climbed up onto their coach, and demanded to know why Vega had called the police on him. He called her a whore and then shot three bullets into her chest. She gasped, "Aye, Mother," and died. Zaldivar threatened to shoot the coach driver and Petra Garcia as well, but they successfully pleaded with him to spare their lives. A witness who had been with Zaldivar at the bar and had known him for fifteen years said Zaldivar had fought to win independence for the Republic of Panama. Another who knew him said, "Up to now I had always known Zaldivar to be a gentleman."

Because the coaches, in their journey, had crossed the border from Panama into the Canal Zone, the murder case was tried before a jury in the Zone's circuit court. The jury found Zaldivar guilty of murder, and the court sentenced him to death by hanging. The Supreme Court of the Panama Canal Zone affirmed the lower court's decision. One judge dissented, arguing that due to extenuating circumstances (intoxication and the presence of another man in the carriage with Vega), the sentence should be life in prison rather than death. Unfortunately for Francisco Zaldivar, the sentence stood. He was executed at the penitentiary in Culebra the following year.[61]

T HE PROBLEM of law and order in the Zone demonstrates that Goethals's machine of "benevolent despotism" generated more resistance than compliance. Officials had firm notions of acceptable moral and social behavior, but they also needed to allow canal employees and their families some latitude to throw off the regimentation of their workdays in order to relax and prepare for the next one. Officials used the police, the courts, the prisons, and the chief engineer's personal investigator to intervene and set the boundaries of permitted behavior. Their efforts were often futile, however. Disorderly behavior, intoxication, loitering, and vagrancy were epidemic. As the courts grew busier, officials increasingly relied less on deportation and more on imprisonment as the ultimate punishment. And they got the word out: by requiring hard labor of all convicts, even the penal system was structured to serve the need for maximum labor productivity. Despite their best efforts at social engineering, the ICC officials' most efficient machine for creating labor discipline involved a ball and chain and a striped uniform.

Ultimately, their efforts to achieve a balance between repression and permissiveness failed. The world of the Zone was simultaneously too regimented and too wild to serve as the orderly civilization officials hoped to create. The social tensions and pressures generated by the demands of construction and by Goethals's attempt at social control sought an outlet beyond the controlled boundaries of the Canal Zone. The ICC officials tried over the years to insulate the Zone from what they perceived as the disorder and moral disease of Panama City and Colón. The reality was more complex. Even if they had tried, officials could not insulate the port cities of Panama from the social tensions, disorder, and subterranean protests they were generating among canal employees and their families in the Zone. The saloons and dance halls of Panama's port cities tempted canal workers and U.S. troops by the multitude, putting the touted "civilization" of the United States on course to collide with the people of the Republic of Panama.

CHAPTER EIGHT

THE RIOTS
OF COCOA GROVE

URING THE years of the canal's construction, the Fourth of July
emerged as a day for hundreds of American soldiers, marines, canal
employees, and their families to leave the Canal Zone and celebrate their
nation's independence in Panama City. Every year the Army and Marines
hosted several hours of patriotic exercises, band playing, and athletic com-
petitions. Afterward, as the crowds dispersed, many participants and spectators headed to the entertainment district of Panama City, a small area
known as Cocoa Grove, where saloons and brothels lined the streets.
Typically, the Americans' carousing continued throughout the day and well
into the night. Often on such occasions, Cocoa Grove became an explosive site, as long-simmering tensions between the Americans and the Panamanians, West Indians, and other immigrant workers residing there found
an outlet in disagreements small or large. In 1912, however, the celebrations turned deadly and provoked a crisis in U.S.-Panamanian relations.

According to testimony given later to U.S. and Panamanian investigators, U.S. military personnel and canal employees had entered Cocoa
Grove shouting patriotic slogans. Many of them had been drinking
throughout the day. They celebrated late into the night, growing steadily
more unruly and throwing lit firecrackers into saloon windows and carriages passing by. As the Americans' revelry became more boisterous,
residents and business owners of the district began to complain, until at
last the Panamanian police felt compelled to restore order. The police
attempted to subdue the crowd, but when many Americans resisted their

authority, the conflict intensified into a full-blown riot, with Panamanian civilians sometimes stepping in to assist their nation's police. When the violence subsided, Ralph Davis, a U.S. citizen who had been working in Cocoa Grove as a bartender, was dead from a bayonet wound. Many other Americans received serious wounds that required hospitalization, while others were thrown in Panamanian jails, an indignity they considered unacceptable for U.S. citizens.[1]

The United States and the Republic of Panama interpreted the riot in very different ways. Their conflicting perspectives generated a ferocious battle not only over the immediate events but also, ultimately, over each nation's relative power. How did this particular riot, more than any previous conflict, come to both epitomize and exacerbate the hostilities between the two countries? From 1904 to 1914, Colón and Panama City often served as escapes from the regimented world of the Canal Zone, places to engage in activities prohibited in the Zone, and often such behaviors escalated into hostile interactions with Panamanians who resented the presence of the United States and the accommodations their leaders had made to the Americans' power. Rival claims for power by Panamanian police versus Zone police often provoked tensions and violence. The port cities of Panama also served over the years as crucial staging grounds for America's empire, providing not only entertainment districts but also housing and supplies for thousands of canal laborers who chose not to live in the Zone. The Zone itself had been a pressure cooker, creating resentments that had little to do with the Republic of Panama yet could not easily be released or resolved amid the U.S. government's disciplined world. In 1912 hostilities in the Zone and in the Republic of Panama expressed themselves through rival visions of honor, nationalism, and sovereignty. U.S. citizens saw themselves as expressing their patriotism, while residents of Panama City reacted with a sense of injured pride and indignation. It was hardly coincidental, then, that the breakdown of chief engineer Goethals's machine, crafted so carefully to ensure social peace and labor discipline, expressed itself through a deadly conflict between Panamanians and Zone residents.

"THE COUNTRY WAS BEING FOREIGNIZED"

Although the young Republic of Panama faced criticism from many who saw it as a corrupt product of American imperialism, in fact there were striking parallels between the situation of Panama and that of its Latin American neighbors. Panama's leaders had lobbied Colombia for decades for more independence so they could pursue their commercial and economic fortunes. Well-to-do Panamanians felt neglected by Colombia, and so the revolution of 1903 grew out of overlapping ambitions on the part of Panamanian and American elites. When Colombia rejected the treaty that would have granted to the United States the right to build the canal, American leaders *and* their counterparts in Panama felt angry. United both in their portrayal of Colombian politicians as self-interested barbarians denying commercial progress to the isthmus and in their vision of the canal construction as a civilizing force that would benefit the entire world, the Americans and some Panamanian leaders joined together to work toward independence. Once on its own, the new nation-state of Panama moved to fulfill its destiny and bring progress and Western civilizing forces to the isthmus. Its leaders adopted as the nation's motto a phrase that must have pleased President Roosevelt: "For the Benefit of the World."[2] Yet its alliance with the United States brought tumultuous social and economic change to Panama and profound challenges to its sovereignty. In 1910, James Bryce, the British ambassador to the United States, visited the isthmus and observed the control exerted by the United States over Panama. He declared that the Republic of Panama "is so absolutely at its [America's] mercy, created and existing solely by its favour, that the United States can treat the region as its own property, and do just what it likes."[3]

Their partnership with Panamanian leaders was certainly a great boon for U.S. officials, who needed the independent republic to play a variety of roles in support of their empire. Building the canal required efforts to rule over men and women not only in the Canal Zone but also in Panama. Few of Panama's affairs would remain untouched by the United

States in the years that followed. The vast rebuilding of Panama's port cities by the United States—for example, the building of roads, streets, sewers, and water lines—sometimes generated problems that required intervention by both the U.S. and the Panamanian governments. Fumigation work by the ICC Sanitation Department during the early years of construction led to small armies of men sweeping through urban neighborhoods. In February 1905 alone, nearly 350 homes in Panama City were fumigated, with gas bombs of pyrethrum set off to kill any mosquitoes or germs. The fumigation work repeatedly caused fires, and then the United States typically assumed responsibility and agreed to compensate owners. A more difficult challenge lay in deciding the value of the property. In 1906 a major fire in Panama City attributed to U.S. fumigation efforts led to the creation of a joint commission with representatives from both the United States and Panama to decide the property value involved. The two could not agree. Finally, the commission disbanded, and a neutral umpire assessed the damages instead.[4]

The joint commission was indicative of a general trend: the United States became deeply involved in the affairs of Panama, playing an influential role in its government and economy. In 1906, for example, the government of Panama decided a streetcar system should be built throughout Panama City. A man named Henry T. Cook bid successfully to win the job. Part of his contract, however, stipulated that he would be responsible for maintaining the paved streets to either side of the tracks. Since the United States had paved these streets, Cook had to win permission from the United States to lay his streetcar tracks. U.S. officials declared they would give permission only if Cook put up a $25,000 bond contingent on proper repaving of any streets he tore up. Cook declined to put up the bond and began constructing the tracks. The U.S. government then asked the Republic of Panama to enforce an order that forbade anyone from doing excavation work until financial arrangements had been made for the refilling and repaving of the streets—an amount estimated at exactly $25,000. Panama carried out the Americans' request, and construction of Cook's streetcar system was halted until he made the requisite financial arrangements.[5]

U.S. citizens rapidly moved into important government positions in the Republic of Panama. Many Americans became government advisers or inspectors, helping to oversee preparations for elections, overhauling the police, and administering Panama's finances. Americans ran the Instituto Nacional, the country's dominant educational institution. They headed the Santo Tomás Hospital, working with an American woman who supervised nurses at the same institution. "The country was being foreignized," noted one Panamanian observer. ICC officials contracted with Panama's government to build railroads connecting its cities to smaller towns, to care for mentally ill Panamanians in Zone hospitals, and to educate Panamanian children in Zone schools. The United States nudged Panama's leaders to enforce important laws, especially regarding labor recruitment and the maintenance of order.[6] The border separating the Canal Zone from Panama was deliberately kept permeable in many respects. Immigrants traveled freely from one side to the other. Accused criminals could easily be extradited from Panama to the Canal Zone or vice versa. In 1910, when Congress passed the Mann Act, Panama and the ICC worked together to enforce it in the Canal Zone. When ICC officials suspected that white prostitutes were being brought to the isthmus via the ports of Panama and were traveling on the Panama Railroad (which was operated by the U.S. government), they collaborated with Panama to track down and arrest those responsible.[7]

The close ties between U.S. and Panamanian officials were perhaps bound to generate tensions among the citizens of Panama. Sometimes the alliance seemed not only intimate but in visible violation of Panamanian sovereignty. A prime example of this occurred in 1909 when a labor agent attempted to recruit canal workers away to other parts of Latin America. Throughout the construction decade ICC officials went to great lengths to investigate and deport labor agents seeking to "steal" canal workers. Hoping to eliminate the practice in Panama as well as in the Canal Zone, the ICC asked Panama to pass a decree prohibiting the recruiting of laborers within its territory as well, and the Panamanian government complied in 1909. A U.S. citizen named W. P. Spiller violated the decree by recruiting workers in Panama and sending them on to

Colombia, where they awaited his arrival so he could escort them to a plantation in Brazil. The Panamanian government therefore ordered that Spiller be deported, but the Supreme Court of Panama disagreed, arguing that deportation would deprive Spiller of his liberty. The government of Panama then overruled its own Supreme Court in deference to the wishes of the United States and deported Spiller to New York in December 1909. Among Panamanian businessmen and residents generally, the British consul reported, "the action of the Government in deporting Spiller without trial at the request of the Canal Authorities in defiance of the Supreme Court is generally condemned, and expression has been given to much anti-American sentiment."[8]

Meanwhile, foreigners, particularly from the United States and Britain, intervened economically in Panamanian affairs. They dominated much of public finance and commercial agriculture, entering the banking industry as well as the production of coffee, sugar, tropical fruits, cattle ranching, and lumber. The United Fruit Company soared to prominence across the province of Bocas del Toro as Panama granted land concessions. In 1906 the British consul reported that Panama's economy was so vibrant it would soon rival that of the French era. He described the prevalence of U.S. entrepreneurs: "American manufacturers display unusual energy to compete for the new trade; their agents overrun the entire Isthmus, agencies have been opened, and information is gathered which will enable them to understand precisely what kind of purchases of machinery and supplies will have to be made by the Commission during the construction of the Canal." The boundary between Panama and the Zone remained porous economically, much to the disadvantage of the former. Commissaries run by the ICC and private businesses in the Zone paid no import duties on their vast array of commodities, and a thriving unofficial market emerged in Colón and Panama City as entrepreneurs with access to the commissaries purchased excess goods and then sold them to eager consumers. Panamanian merchants, who did have to pay import tariffs, found it impossible to compete with these cheaper goods from Zone commissaries and businesses, and this became a source of great resentment. Soon the republic was awash in Zonian products.[9]

The demographic transformation created by the French and the American canal construction projects caused an explosion in the populations of Panama City and Colón. Tens of thousands of people were drawn to the isthmus, arriving with hopes of jobs in the Zone or the promise of work in the bustling service economy that emerged in Panama City and Colón. Many of these immigrants settled in one of Panama's two cities, preferring not to live in the Canal Zone because of poor conditions and repressive policies, and vast tenement neighborhoods arose to house them. As many as 200,000 West Indians arrived on the isthmus during the construction era and businesses, churches, and social institutions emerged to serve them. The heterogeneous culture that resulted discomfited many Panamanians, who felt uneasy about the African heritage of West Indians as well as the Anglo-Caribbean traditions and language possessed by so many of them.[10]

West Indians constituted only one of many groups arriving on ships day after day. Thousands of others arrived as well, including Americans, Italians, Greeks, Spaniards, Chinese, South Asians, Britons, Germans, Canadians, Colombians, Peruvians, and Costa Ricans. Many of these sojourners were on their way to the Zone, but others were drawn by Panama's expanding economy. The presence of so many diverse groups made Panama City and Colón renowned for their sophisticated, international atmosphere. Added to the polyglot residents were crowds of tourists, especially wealthy Americans and English who put Panama on their world tour so they could witness firsthand the marvels of the canal. One such tourist explored Panama City and described the vision before him: "A Panamanian cart, loaded with English tea biscuit, drawn by an old American army mule, driven by a Hindu wearing a turban, drove up in front of a Chinese shop. The Jamaican clerk, aided by the San Blas errand boy . . . supervise[d] the unloading." This tourist's account continued: "That is Panama every day. Across the street is an Italian lace shop run by a Jew." To some native-born Panamanians, these demographic changes threatened to dilute the Hispanic character of the isthmus. The Jamaican who ran his modest business with a picture of King George on the wall seemed to them entirely out of place and inappropriate. The growing working class of Panama City and Colón had its own needs and appeared ready to make more forceful demands of the nation's small elite. Thus the canal project brought more than diversity: it overhauled social and political relations in a way that compromised the ability of elites to continue their rule.[11]

Cocoa Grove, the major entertainment district of Panama City, stood at the center of these tumultuous changes. The modestly sized neighborhood, about ten square blocks, was packed with saloons, dance halls, and brothels. The latter, with names like the Navaho, La Boheme, and the Tuxedo, crowded up against hotels, Chinese lottery shops, and Chinese and Panamanian restaurants. Panama City was known for its nightlife. The English traveler Winifred James, who explored much of the Caribbean and Central America in the early twentieth century, wrote of Panama City as a busy and cosmopolitan town where the bars played music until late into the night. The streets and sidewalks of Cocoa Grove were typically crowded with carriages and horses, hawkers and peddlers. James toured the city one night by carriage and described a common scene: "As we pass by a cantina at the corner of a square, suddenly there is a pistol shot from upstairs. The men sitting at the tables start and look at one another, and some loiterers upon the pavement gather at the entrance. Only the man who is serving the drinks is undisturbed. He goes on serenely polishing the glass in his hand. This place is known as one where such things as pistol shots have been heard before with rather grim results. It behooves the barman to keep his head lest a panic should attract the law. Our driver is not unduly moved, and shrugs his shoulders when we ask him what it means."[12]

Many Panamanians worked in Cocoa Grove, but so did a great many Americans and Europeans—as bartenders, waitresses, prostitutes, and piano players. One of the most successful madams in Cocoa Grove was a U.S. citizen named Alice Ward, and indeed prostitutes in the district so often hailed from the United States that a slang term for prostitute was "American woman."[13] While visiting the isthmus, Winifred James attended a white-slavery trial held in the Canal Zone courts, and her report gives us firsthand a sense of the international origins of Cocoa Grove prostitutes. A Southampton man had been convicted of white-slave trade and sentenced to a year in prison. Now three women were accused of having arrived on the isthmus with him. All three argued they had come to Panama of their own free will, planning to open a business. They had needed more money, however, and so entered a brothel as prostitutes to earn some cash. Since prostitution was legal in Panama, they would be allowed to practice their trade unhindered if they could prove their story. If not, they would face deportation or prison.

The three women hailed from France, England, and the United States. James described each one. The Frenchwoman had been a milliner off Tottenham Road in London, and James felt no pity for her: "Trim, well-corsetted in a corsetless country, her hair smartly dressed, her face carefully made up, she commanded respect through the respect she showed herself. All through her cross-examination she lied very heartily." Angry and indignant, she rebelled against the proceedings in every way, her foot tapping impatiently through the trial, and James felt she would someday return to respectability in her home country. The second woman, from Hampstead, England, was the mirror opposite: "Untidy, slatternly, she made you feel that she would have been little use either as a servant or a prostitute. Her hair was twisted up anyhow, her dress disordered. She made purpose-less, bewildered movements with her pasty-white, irritating hands, and looked helplessly around her like an animal that is seeking an escape." And finally, there was the American woman, with her "good-natured acceptance of things as they were, whether they turned out dressmaking or the other thing, she apparently had no more sexual morality than the other two, yet she affected one very much as a nice morning does; she seemed clean and nice and fresh." Of the three, James concluded, only the French-woman was likely to see her life turn out right. But James hoped the best for the American, too, as "she was a nice little thing."[14]

Canal employees and U.S. military personnel often turned to Cocoa Grove for adventure and recreation since activities in the Zone were so limited and tame. Gambling and prostitution, effectively banned in the Zone, were omnipresent in Panama City's entertainment district. While the United States had the power to eliminate a red-light neighborhood like Cocoa Grove, ICC officials implicitly depended on it as a place where canal employees could relax before heading back for another period of construction work.[15] The entertainment district offered live music, free-flowing alcohol in comfortable saloons (with chairs!), fascinating crowds of people from all over the world, and partying that lasted most of the night, every night. There was a sense in Colón and Panama City that identities became more fluid and that one might interact with a very different set of people. A poem by John Hall, published in 1912, expressed this mixture of danger and opportunity canal workers enjoyed when they visited Colón. Roughnecks gambling their money away, racial transformations, interracial romances, and the white-slave trade all made entrances into Hall's poem:

AS IT WAS

'Way down in Colon town,
The land of the gambler clan.
'Way down in Colon town,
Where they "trim" the roughneck man.
Where night's turned into day,
And the "live-ones'" coin goes fast:
Where the suckers like to play;
Where the "gringo" hates the past.
Where mateless men soon mate;
Where siren's song sounds sweet;
Where jeering men mock Fate;
Where siren's life is fleet.
Where water man ne'er craves,
And beer the drunkard spurns,
And adds one to the graves
When wine his liver burns.
'Way down in Colon town
Where Mongol mates with Turk;
Where white man's skin is brown;
Where white-slave traders lurk.[16]

In all these ways Panama City and Colón provided an escape from the more regimented, respectable, and segregated world of the Zone. Soldiers and marines on U.S. military bases enjoyed the contrast as much as canal employees did. Their environment was even more segregated than that of canal workers, their only nonleisure contact with Panamanians or West Indians coming when workers brought food into the base or arrived to pick up laundry, or when military duties took them into Panama. And although officials at the time portrayed Panama City and Colón as sources of disorder and worried that the wildness of Panama would cross boundaries and enter the Zone, the truth lay at least equally the other way around. U.S. canal employees and military personnel crossing into Panama after a week or two of hard-driving labor discipline, jockeying for social and economic position, and feeling they had earned a chance to let loose were a source of disorder and disharmony, especially once they entered districts like Cocoa Grove.

The U.S. military already had a long history on the Isthmus of Panama at the time construction began in 1904. In 1856, during construction of the Panamanian railroad by U.S. companies, the United States sent 160 soldiers to put down the Watermelon Riot, an event that eerily echoed the Cocoa Grove riots of the early twentieth century, similarly involving tensions over sovereignty and race. In the decades between that intervention and Panamanian independence in 1903, the U.S. military intervened thirteen more times.[17] Marines began serving in the Zone in 1904, as U.S. possession and preparations for canal construction began. In late 1911, nearly one thousand soldiers representing the U.S. Army's Tenth Infantry Regiment arrived on the isthmus, many of them fresh from their work suppressing the insurrection of Filipinos against the U.S. government. The number of soldiers increased gradually to fifteen hundred. They were new to the Canal Zone and would replace the marines altogether by 1914 (to the dismay of the latter, whose officer had proclaimed his men "as essential for the completion of the Canal as the steam shovel"). The soldiers set to work conducting surveys and maneuvers throughout the Zone and the Republic of Panama. They and the marines served also as an auxiliary police force, and in the decades that followed, Panamanian officials often relied on U.S. troops to help them quell riots, strikes, and popular uprisings, to provide support for endangered presidential administrations, and to oversee elections. The thousands of soldiers and marines in the Panama Canal Zone came most often from rough working-class communities of the United States. Unemployment, a desire for adventure, a migratory life—these were just some of the factors that likely led them to enlist in the military. Not only were their lives more racially segregated than those of canal employees; soldiers and marines also had fewer opportunities for leisure, which led them often to seek entertainment in Panama City.[18]

The chagrin of some white-collar canal employees over blue-collar workers' tendency to go "whoring" and drinking in Cocoa Grove every weekend was noted earlier. U.S. officials had to work to keep not only American canal employees under control but also military personnel and Zone policemen, particularly when they visited Panama City. Goethals's inspector T. B. Miskimon reported on numerous troubles, including marines who begged for money in the streets of Panama City so they could buy drugs. The inspector referred to them as "snifflers," remarking, "They will go in the saloons and beg money, openly stating that they do not want anything to drink but do want the money for Cocaine. I personally saw about eight marines indulging in this practice on the streets of Panama last evening." Even in the relatively tame Zone, policemen engaged in some unprofessional behavior. One afternoon two officers on the Zone police force, for example, rode their horses into a Zone saloon, dismounted at the bar, and ordered drinks. As they drank, one of the horses defecated on the floor. Seemingly unperturbed, the policemen finished their drinks, jumped on their horses, and departed.[19]

Ample evidence suggests that Americans visiting Cocoa Grove sometimes brought with them not only unrestrained behavior but also arrogant and patronizing attitudes. They were tempted by the perceived danger and disorder of Cocoa Grove and wanted to interact with the wilder side of Panama, but they also looked down on the nation and its people. Like more elite Americans, they tended to regard Panamanians as an inferior and less civilized race. Joseph Bucklin Bishop, the secretary of the Isthmian Canal Commission, commented: "The average American has the utmost contempt for a Panaman and never loses an opportunity, especially when drunk, to show it."[20] The combination of their unrespectable behavior and swaggering attitudes led many, not only Panamanians, to question whether the Americans were bringing civilization or barbarism to the isthmus. Innumerable problematic incidents emerged in these years. State Department officials worried over opium and cocaine trafficking and outbreaks of violence that resulted from drunken revelers in Cocoa Grove. Stories spread of canal employees routinely drinking to excess, of men spending all weekend in a drunken state in Cocoa Grove. Tourists received warnings to beware of rowdy Americans in Panama City, and it was said that well-to-do Panamanian women rarely ventured out into the city, fearing the Americans who would crowd them off sidewalks and into the street. Even Americans received warnings to beware their countrymen. When the American traveler Evelyn Saxton arrived in Panama City by train, her husband failed to meet her at the station. A young Panamanian man urged her not to wait at the station as "there are rough Americans about who would not hesitate to insult you." Saxton responded that she had nothing to fear, as she was herself an American. She received the following response: "The Americans I know about Panama are not of your class. They are here in great numbers, and they are very rough and vulgar."[21]

These frictions were indicative of the complex relationship between Panamanians and Americans. Panamanian elites wanted and needed the presence of the United States and its canal construction project, seeing it as a path to modernity and civilization. Yet the American project did not bring the benefits Panamanians had hoped for, and the crowds of Americans flooding into the city streets of Panama often seemed uncivilized and disorderly. In the years after canal construction began, the Panamanian police were often instructed to restore order in Cocoa Grove when violence broke out, using their authority as representatives of the Republic of Panama to calm the behavior of American canal employees, Zone policemen, soldiers, and marines enjoying their off-duty leisure time. Yet when disturbances emerged in Panama City or Colón, when the working masses of Panama made demands, rioted, or went on strike, or when elections caused social disorder, those same American soldiers, marines, or Zone policemen marched in to preserve the power of Panamanian elites. Each side, in short, needed the other, and each side felt disdain for the other.

THE TEMPEST OF PANAMANIAN POLITICS

During the decade of canal construction from 1904 to 1914, Panamanian politics was tempestuous, as conservatives and liberals struggled for control over the government. Conservatives worked to maintain their power as they faced a crescendo of critiques and opposition by liberals and nationalists. Amid the turmoil, however, three themes remained constant: no group reached out effectively to the urban working classes, most of them people of color; the police grew increasingly important for shoring up the regime in power; and Panamanian politics was bound up with the United States in ways that challenged the republic's independence and caused increasing bitterness.

The first president of the Republic of Panama, Manuel Amador Guerrero, recommended to the United States just as his tenure began in 1904 that the Panamanian army be disbanded. A member of the Conservative Party, Amador portrayed the army as beholden to the Liberal forces in his country and requested that the U.S. military and an armed Panamanian police force take the place of the military. Later that year, in the autumn of 1904, an army general demanded resignations of two people in Amador's government, and U.S. officials feared a coup was looming, so they took action. American soldiers entered Panama City, surrounded the presidential palace, and protected Amador as he disbanded the army. This allowed Amador to solidify his tie with the United States and weaken his opposition. Next Amador took steps to strengthen the Panamanian police and turn the force into a loyal band supporting his rule. He created a national guard as the nation's police force, invited the New York City police officer Samuel David to Panama to develop "scientific instruction" for them, and then began using the police to suppress popular unrest and intimidate voters on election day. By 1906 the police had become a "band of armed partisan supporters," enforcing the political wishes of Conservatives. During elections the police were known to vote repeatedly and to protect other Conservatives as they voted repeatedly. Meanwhile, the police served also as the sole defenders of their nation's dignity and security and as the group responsible for maintaining law and order. Their diverse functions sometimes collided with one another, placed them in constant conflict with U.S. citizens and Zone policemen, and made them feared by many canal employees—especially those who lived in Panama. This began the process that, by the 1940s, would make the police a dominant force in the affairs of a fragmented Panamanian nation.[22]

The police became well known for their aggressive and sometimes brutal tactics, and elites regularly relied on them to suppress strikes or riots by working-class Panamanians and to intimidate voters on election day. From the perspective of U.S. officials, the repeated episodes in which the police used heavy-handed tactics against Americans or non-American canal employees were particularly problematic. During the early years of construction the ICC was "embarrassed" by the "daily or hourly" conflicts over territorial jurisdiction that broke out between Panamanian and Zone policemen. Such difficulties decreased but never disappeared, and American and non-American canal employees came to regard Panamanian policemen with suspicion and fear. Over the years Panamanian police were alleged several times to have beaten West Indian canal employees. Of even greater concern to ICC officials was a pattern of violence committed by Panamanian police against U.S. citizens. In June 1906 several U.S. marines and a Navy man were arrested and mistreated by the Panamanian police. On Christmas in 1906 a riot broke out in Colón between Panamanian police and American canal workers. In another incident that same year, Zone policemen, themselves not unwilling to use force when they felt it necessary, seemed shocked when they watched three Panamanian police chase an escaped Panamanian prisoner into the Zone and beat him with clubs and a board. Drunk and exhausted from running, he offered no resistance. The Panamanian police hid their badges before beginning to beat the man, knowing that they were violating their own government's procedures. The three policemen were arrested and put on trial for beating the man and for invading foreign soil. The Canal Zone district court found them guilty and fined each policeman $25.[23]

When Panamanian police manhandled a U.S. citizen, American officials reacted heatedly and, it occurred to many, insultingly. The British consul reported to his Foreign Office that in 1907 several U.S. naval officers had entered a brothel in Colón, gotten drunk, and caused a disturbance. They had been arrested by the Panamanian police, and although they were clearly in the wrong, the Panamanian chief of police "was made the scapegoat and was dismissed to appease the wrath of American citizens in the Canal Zone who considered that officers in uniform should be immune from arrest even if they break the laws in a foreign country." In 1908 a fight in a Colón brothel ended with an American sailor stabbed by a Panamanian. The sailor died, and a U.S. investigation claimed that the Panamanian police had treated him poorly, not providing medical attention or even water in the three hours between the stabbing and his death. U.S. secretary of state Elihu Root sent a note to the president of Panama that, the British consul reported to his superiors, "is rude and insulting, and a warning has been given that the illtreatment of Americans by the Panama police will not be tolerated again." Back in London, a British official watching relations between the United States and Panama deteriorate commented: "Incidents of this kind are not calculated to increase the popularity of the United States in Central America."[24]

In 1908 a broad coalition emerged in Panamanian politics that united landowners and wealthy merchants with foreign investors and middle-class merchants. Hoping to profit from the canal project, this coalition rose to power and elected José Domingo de Obaldía to the presidency. However, although Obaldía invited some Liberals into his government, his policies struck many Panamanians as too conservative and pro-American. Indeed, U.S. officials visibly demonstrated their close alliance with his administration. Goethals's personal investigator noted unhappily after the election that George Shanton, the chief of the Canal Zone police, had ridden his horse in the post-election parade at the lead of the pro-Obaldía forces. Obaldía alienated nationalists and many middle-class citizens, and he angered urban workers by refusing to improve their living conditions and by using the police to suppress strikes.[25]

Obaldía's unpopular presidency ended when he died unexpectedly in 1910. He was succeeded by Carlos Mendoza, a Liberal mulatto, whose politics and race provoked a crisis in Panamanian politics and in U.S.-Panamanian relations. Mendoza was said to have black Panamanians as his base of support, wrote Richard Marsh, a junior diplomatic officer representing the United States, and they are "mostly ignorant and irresponsible, unable to meet the serious obligations of citizenship in a Republic." President Taft, it was said, disliked Mendoza and did not want to see any other Liberal replace him. This was explosive news, suggesting that the United States would not allow Liberals to attain power. The United States pressured Mendoza to resign, and the British consul reported warily: "If that happens, his friends—and he is very popular with the masses—will become very excited, but as four American cruisers are timed to arrive in the Bay when the Assembly meets, and there is a strong military contingent in the Canal Zone, it is unlikely there will be any disturbance of public order."[26]

In the end, Richard Marsh secured Mendoza's resignation by threatening that the U.S. military would occupy and annex his country. Taft and Goethals distanced themselves from Marsh at this point, with Taft declaring, "We have such control in Panama, that no Government elected by them will feel a desire to antagonise the American Government." British diplomats watched the U.S. missteps with stifled amusement. Most of them believed that Marsh had acted on orders from his superiors, and one noted, "This shows how the U.S.G. treat a 'sister Republic.'" Another commented, "The sequence of events constitute a chapter of the most extraordinary acts of diplomatic bungling ever perpetrated in the Latin American Republics by U.S. officials."[27]

After Mendoza resigned, the United States placed Pablo Arosemena in the presidency but also, as a significant compromise, allowed the well-known nationalist Belisario Porras to become Panama's minister to the United States, with the idea that he would be the Liberal candidate for the presidency in 1912. A leader of Panama's Liberal forces in the Guerra de los Mil Días (the Colombian war of 1899 to 1902 in which Liberals rebelled against the Conservative national government), Porras had opposed the Hay–Bunau-Varilla Treaty on the grounds that it compromised Panama's sovereignty. Because of this, President Amador had stripped Porras of his citizenship, forcing him to leave the country, which only reinforced his identity as the nation's leading nationalist. While his leadership over the Liberal and nationalist factions was unrivaled and he possessed strong working-class support, Porras remained the enemy of Conservatives.[28]

The election of 1912 thus emerged as a crucial contest. President Arosemena, originally intended to serve in office only until the next election, decided he enjoyed the position. Although he personally could not run for reelection, he worked to hold on to power by electing his allies. Conservatives nominated a fairly unknown Pedro Díaz and formed a coalition to oppose Porras for the presidency, attempting to discredit the nationalist by accusing him of treason.[29] The United States had been involved in Panamanian politics since the republic's founding—in 1904, for example, it had sent three hundred marines to Panama City and an express shipment of rifles and ammunition to arm the Panamanian police, all in order to help the Conservative candidate Amador win the election. In 1908 the United States had forced President Amador to create the Electoral Inquiry Commission, which was dominated by representatives of the United States and which placed Americans in every election district to observe voting and watch for evidence of fraud.[30]

In the 1910 crisis over Mendoza, the United States had helped create tensions and rising nationalism that would make the election of 1912 extremely bitter and sometimes violent. Ironically, U.S. officials had by the campaign season of 1912 reconciled themselves to the idea of Liberal rule and so worked to ensure a fair election, even though this would mean victory for the Liberal Porras. As a result of these shifting political winds, it was Panamanian Conservatives, especially those organized into the Patriotic Union, who opposed the U.S. role and who became the voice of injured Panamanian nationalism. As in 1908, the United States created an Electoral Inquiry Commission to investigate complaints and observe the voting and counting of ballots. Goethals personally asked the government to postpone its scheduled plan to move half of the marines off the isthmus, and they and members of the Tenth Infantry Regiment fanned out through the country to safeguard the voting.

Meanwhile, Conservative opponents of Porras secretly purchased a supply of rifles from the U.S. War Department, but American election supervisors discovered the rifles. They ordered the disarmament of the Panamanian police and put the entire police force under their own command, sending U.S. Canal Zone police into Panama City to maintain order. Panamanian government officials charged that the United States was sympathizing with Porras and engaging in corrupt activities. Panamanian leaders also took the step of forbidding the right to vote to their police, which caused great resentment. The British consul reported that relations between the parties were "intensely bitter." Recounting innumerable acts of brutality and lawlessness by Conservatives, the consul concluded, "Never, not even in the worst days of the Colombian regime, has such animosity been in evidence as is shown by some of the officials towards their opponents."[31]

With no armed police to enforce a Conservative victory, the Liberal candidate, Belisario Porras, won the municipal elections on July 1, 1912. This meant that Porras would also win the national election to be held two weeks later. Indeed, his Conservative opponent soon withdrew from the election, leaving Porras the unopposed victor, while the Patriotic Union abstained from the election and instead issued a manifesto denouncing the United States for its unfair and corrupt intervention in the election. With Porras as its first nationalist president, Panama seemed poised to assert its authority against American domination. Yet like his predecessors, Porras owed his victory in part to the intervention of the United States. He would soon learn that the U.S. role in his election had inspired a new nationalism among Conservatives and many other

Panamanians as well, and their emotions would soon manifest themselves in explosive ways, complicating his presidency.[32]

An account by the globe-trotter Winifred James captures how charged conditions became during the election of 1912. She arrived in Panama City on election day, July 1, and found the streets barricaded, hardly any cars on the streets, and the few cabs sitting motionless and unwilling to take her up the steep hill to the Hotel Tivoli. James witnessed a mob of people surging down the street while beating a man, his face covered in blood, and "two little Panamanian policemen who had apparently gone in higher up the Avenida to stem the torrent were being swept along in it like sticks in a mill-race." Minutes later she watched as another crowd, this one very orderly, marched along the street. They were disciplined and restrained because "heading the procession and marshaling it on either side walked the puttee-legged, khaki-clad, Stetson-hatted Canal Zone policemen—a blessed and peaceful sight." James's account captures how the U.S. supervision of the election had transformed relations between the police of the two countries, the chaos and violence of the moment, and why so many Conservative supporters felt an indignant and injured pride in its aftermath.[33]

THE RIOTS, HONOR, AND SOVEREIGNTY

As U.S. Independence Day dawned just seventy-two hours later, American soldiers and marines were feeling triumphant about their show of force on election day. Many Panamanians remained embittered, particularly but not exclusively policemen and anyone allied with the Conservative cause. Now, as hundreds of U.S. canal employees, soldiers, and marines headed into Panama City early that morning to enjoy patriotic and athletic exercises in celebration of their nation's independence, conditions had changed. No more Stetson-hatted Canal Zone policemen patrolled the streets—the Panamanian policemen had regained their command. Policemen who had felt humiliation upon being disarmed, disenfranchised, and placed under the supervision of U.S. officials and Zone policemen were eager to reassert their authority as the one armed force of their nation. For many other

Panamanians, the U.S. supervision of the July 1 election had reinforced an already simmering anti-Americanism. In this *Rashomon*-like tale, the two countries constructed vastly different accounts of the events of July 4, and their struggle over the evidence, over how to distribute blame, and over compensation continued for more than three years after the riot. While much remained disputed, certain things are dramatically clear. The riot revealed a deep conflict over notions of honor, respectability, and civilization.

As the thousand or so Americans began arriving in Cocoa Grove in the early afternoon, according to testimony given to U.S. officials who investigated the incident, almost all of them had been drinking, some of them "so much under the influence of drink as not to be able to walk." The crowd amused itself by throwing "lighted fire crackers into passing carriages, saloons, and houses of prostitution," yet the partying was no more boisterous than normal.[34] According to the United States, the crowd consisted about equally of canal employees and military personnel. Many businesses closed their doors for fear of the destructive potential. After several hours, some men demanded entry into saloons and brothels that had closed. When refused, they attempted to break in the doors. If this failed, some climbed up light poles to reach the balcony, but women deterred them by emptying slop buckets over their heads. This so enraged the American soldiers, marines, and canal employees that they forced their way into bars and demanded alcohol. Meanwhile, an argument started between a Panamanian policeman and some soldiers and marines; as the disagreement escalated into a fight, a crowd rushed to the assistance of the soldiers and began beating the policeman. Other policemen came to his aid, but feeling outnumbered, they fled with the Americans in pursuit. At this point, according to the U.S. investigations, the police opened fire on the U.S. soldiers, and quickly several dozen other police arrived, along with many Panamanian civilians. The battle had now become a free-for-all, but while the soldiers and canal workers used stones, bottles, and anything else they could find as missiles, the police had weapons. According to the U.S. Army investigation, the police "lost their heads completely, and got wild and excited in their actions. They used rifles, revolvers, and clubs more than was necessary." They moved through the area, beating in doors, shooting or bayoneting and arresting many Americans, forcing others to "take refuge" in a saloon or a house, until they had cleared the district of all of them.[35] At the end of the day, twenty men had been injured, most of them U.S. citizens, and one U.S. civilian lay dead, bayoneted by a Panamanian policeman.

U.S. officials acknowledged that trouble typically resulted whenever large numbers of military personnel or civilians gathered in the red-light district, but in this case they argued that the police were entirely to blame. In a letter to Panamanian government officials, the U.S. ambassador to Panama, Percival Dodge, summarized his government's view of the incident in 1913, after the U.S. investigation was complete: "The police of Panama virtually ran amuck, shooting and stabbing indiscriminately." Policemen shot at anyone in sight, but they targeted U.S. citizens in particular. A soldier "who knelt and begged for mercy was also ruthlessly beaten."[36] Witnesses interviewed by the ICC, the Marines, and the Army recited a litany of injustices committed that day by the Panamanian police. U.S. military personnel and canal employees shared a common grievance: they felt their clash with the Panamanian police jeopardized their standing as white men, as representatives of the United States, and as military personnel. If this was a world turned upside down, the Americans were left notably discomfited by their new position.

American soldiers and canal workers who testified expressed a common refrain of feeling vulnerable and victimized during the riot. Panama suddenly seemed to belong, powerfully and threateningly, to Panamanians. The Americans observed Panamanian police and civilians in large numbers "walking the streets armed with rifles and revolvers, shooting into cantinas and saloons and at any American that was in sight." Private Thomas Howard reported, "I saw an army man on the ground all covered with blood. I went to help him. There were four policemen around him, kicking him and beating him with clubs." Other soldiers related being cornered by Panamanians and "knowing we would be shot to death for resisting we had to submit to their clubbing." A group of soldiers huddled in front of a building as policemen approached and were heard to say,

"Let's keep together, for God's sake." When they could, canal workers ran back into the Zone for refuge or hid in a saloon or brothel. Amid the violence, soldiers noticed even the smallest indignities: A policeman pushed one off the sidewalk and nearly knocked him over, related a soldier, while a "negress" pushed some marines out of her club. In at least one case, women threw bottles at Americans; in another incident a "negress" shouted names at marines. Another witness saw a crowd of Panamanian boys throwing rocks and using clubs against marines and soldiers. The civilian John McDaid testified that Panamanian police shot a U.S. flag out of his hand.[37]

As the riot escalated, the Marines and Army sent a backup force into Cocoa Grove, and then even officers found their authority challenged by Panamanians. When Marine captain Frank Halford drove into Cocoa Grove, Panamanian police, armed with rifles and bayonets fixed, stopped his car. "I was in a field uniform with Corps devices and rank marks properly placed, and was at first prevented by a policeman from entering the district. He slammed his rifle butt on the ground against my toes and with his hand on the muzzle of his rifle pushed it into my chest." After some tense moments the police allowed Captain Halford to enter the district. He immediately went to a brothel where five marines had barricaded themselves for the last four hours, afraid to come out. Assisted by a Panamanian official, Captain Halford escorted the marines to safety.[38]

U.S. military personnel and canal workers felt particularly targeted because of their nationality. The canal employee Carl DeLeen left the bar where he'd been drinking when the conflict began and headed across the street. He was stopped by a group that included three or four policemen and an equal number of Panamanian civilians. They "asked if I was an American, to which I replied that I was; whereupon I was struck on the arm with a stick by one of the men in civilian clothes, and on the head with a rock by another." Another canal worker, R. L. Swinehart, commented on his experience during the riot: "While the corner was crowded with natives, negroes, and Spaniards, they were unmolested. It was plain to be seen that it was Americans only that they wished to trouble." Some heard the police shouting, "Kill the Americans!" while others heard talk in the days leading up to the riot that police sought to attack Americans. During the riot a crowd of Panamanian police were overheard saying: "Hurry up to Pedro de Obarrio street, . . . we are going to kill gringos."[39]

Dozens of military personnel and canal workers were arrested by Panamanian police and imprisoned, an experience they found humiliating. Private Henry Mitchell of the U.S. Marine Corps described how the police "handcuffed me and marched me through the streets without blouse or leggings to the Central Police Station where I was confined with 9 or 10 negroes." The cell was filthy, he reported, and its floor was wet. Panamanian police arrested the canal employee Thomas Fuentes, a boilermaker in the Gorgona machine shops, and put him in a cell with other Americans, keeping him there until early the next morning. They refused to provide food, "but did state that we might purchase from a negro woman outside the jail some rice and fish, which is not considered a white man's diet." Fuentes asked the police if he and the other prisoners could go out to get some food, accompanied by a guard, and they would pay all expenses. This was also refused.[40]

While the testimony provided by canal employees and soldiers during the U.S. investigations presented a picture of horrifying indignities aimed at them and their countrymen, the evidence provided to investigators in the Republic of Panama, not surprisingly, differed radically. Witnesses testifying to Panamanian officials, most of them Panamanian police and working people from around the world who lived in Cocoa Grove, stressed that the Americans had challenged their dignity. In these accounts, Americans were the aggressors while the Panamanian police had attempted in vain to restore order. Panama's chief of police, Julio Quijano, reported that he had ordered the policemen not to interfere with the boisterous crowd: "The police allowed Americans to hire coaches and not to pay any fare, to knock down and beat natives and foreigners, to storm houses and ransack Canteens and to commit many other disturbances." Americans forced their way into clubs, destroyed furniture, stole money, and attempted to throw prostitutes off balconies.

The riot escalated when U.S. soldiers and civilians began to assault policemen violently and then attacked the police reserves at a substation. This forced policemen to open fire in order to protect the substation and their own lives. Most of the injuries occurred when U.S. citizens fired on Panamanians and the police felt compelled to interfere to defend them.[41]

Police chief Quijano's account undoubtedly reflected his own self-interest. It simplified the nature of the clash and whitewashed his policemen's role in it. Yet many other sources, including people testifying to U.S. investigators, noted that U.S. soldiers and civilians engaged in destructive, violent, and vindictive behavior. As the day started, groups of soldiers stood about on the streets, drinking and shouting, "Viva Porras!" in a way that seemed to bait the Panamanian police (who had generally favored the Conservative presidential candidate). Alice Ward described the escalation of the fight at her brothel: marines and soldiers entered through the balcony and then "started throwing and breaking everything, bags, cups, glasses, doors, a piano . . . some of them then moved towards the bar, where they started hitting the barman who had taken refuge behind it." According to Ward, the soldiers told her they were trashing her place to prove that when they said they wanted to enter a place, they had better be allowed in. Many police testified that they had tried to remain friendly toward the drunken Americans, since there were so many of them. Luis Francisco Ramírez, a Colombian injured in the melee, reported that the riot began when a policeman abandoned his post after a group of marines attacked him. Ordered to return to his post, the policeman complied, only to be attacked again by more marines. One marine fired at him, and soon thereafter six or eight marines began beating any policemen they could find. As the sounds of the fighting reached the brothels, the marines and soldiers inside poured out onto the streets to assist their friends, eighty or a hundred of them at a time.[42]

Violence committed by U.S. military men and canal workers shocked many, including other U.S. citizens. Many marines and soldiers bore arms and fired them at policemen and at district residents. A crowd of people rushed toward one policeman, yelling that the Americans had gone mad: "Los Americanos se habían vuelto locos." A U.S. civilian heard American soldiers saying they would "rip their heads off" in reference to Panamanians. The soldiers brutally beat an older policeman, leaving him for dead on the floor of a saloon. Prostitutes from Nicaragua, Colombia, Panama, Russia, and the United States all reported incidents of destruction committed by the American soldiers and civilians; some reported being kicked or beaten by them. One U.S. soldier, dismayed by the events of the day, confessed to Panamanian investigators that no sober person would have acted as his compatriots had. Another U.S. soldier was so shocked by the behavior of his colleagues and by the Panamanian policemen's inability to control them that he urged the latter, as the riot grew wilder, to call the Canal Zone police and request assistance.[43]

A Panamanian newspaper explained the violent behavior of the U.S. workers and soldiers by reference to race: "Any American, whether from Maine or Alabama, resents being arrested or interfered with in any way by a negro policeman; and the police of Panama are largely negro or mestizo. A large majority of the Americans feel themselves very superior to any Panamanian. This is inherent in their race, in any race of conquerors." Indeed, marines and soldiers often expressed their reactions to Panamanians in racial terms, thereby unintentionally suggesting some of the tensions that existed during the riots. One private, who had participated in the trashing of a brothel, described the moment in this way: "A soldier struck at a coon (negro) when the coon ran out of the door, . . . every chair was thrown out of the door after him (the coon) including the piano stool." The unfortunate man, most likely a West Indian or Panamanian, ended up shot by the soldiers.[44] Yet while race certainly shaped the behavior and attitudes of U.S. marines, soldiers, and canal workers, it alone cannot explain the violence. Americans watched as prostitutes, bartenders, saloon owners, policemen, and children of diverse races and nationalities seemed not to respect their authority. For very different reasons, American military personnel and canal workers as well as the Panamanian police felt themselves victimized and humiliated, and both groups wanted to reassert their authority as representatives of their respective nations. For the working-class residents of Cocoa Grove, caught between two governments, there was no easy path to neutrality.

"THIS ATTITUDE TOWARDS A SOVEREIGN STATE . . . IS INCOMPREHENSIBLE"

After American soldiers and canal workers failed to reassert their nation's authority on July 4, the full machinery of the U.S. government moved swiftly to accomplish the goal. U.S. government and military officials conducted three separate investigations into the rioting, then publicized their findings and portrayed the Panamanian investigation as completely illegitimate. The United States solicited affidavits from prostitutes who said the Panamanians only wrote down certain parts of their testimony. U.S. officials cited unnamed men who said unnamed prostitutes told the Panamanians whatever the latter ordered, "under threat of being sent to jail."[45] In a letter to Ernesto Lefevre, Panama's secretary of state for foreign affairs, U.S. ambassador Percival Dodge declared that "such Panamanian testimony as was not given by interested policemen and other guilty participants in the affair was obtained through force and intimidation." Your evidence, Dodge concluded, is "unworthy of credence." Speaking on behalf of the president of Panama, Minister of Foreign Affairs Eduardo Chiari insisted that his investigation had relied only on the testimony of absolutely impartial witnesses and that the information gathered by the United States must be erroneous. The United States rejected this argument and demanded instead the firing of both the chief of police and his immediate subordinate, the paying of an indemnity to the United States, and a formal expression of regret and apology.[46]

A nineteen-year-old Panamanian policeman was put on trial in Panama City for the murder of Ralph Davis. Found guilty, the young man died in prison before he could be sentenced. The United States demanded that more prosecutions follow. U.S. minister Jennings Price angrily declared: "Every sincere effort, duly made, to fulfill the demands of outraged justice and to comply with the practices of civilization in this matter of moment, would elicit the real gratification of my Government.

Reiteration is made that nothing less than the due and full satisfaction, insistently sought by my Government herein, can bring a termination to a matter of this character."[47]

Month after month the tense negotiations continued, throughout 1913 and well into 1914. A British diplomatic officer noted the difficulty placed on the Panamanian government: "The action of the US Government is certainly harsh, and if the Panama government yield they will sustain a great humiliation in the eyes of the people." But there would be no backing away by the United States. U.S. officials painted a gradually more dramatic and innocent picture of their citizens' role during the riot, declaring that the soldiers and marines, while in "frolicsome holiday spirit," were "viciously wounded and shot down and bayoneted." Finally, in June 1914, U.S. officials threatened that if Panama failed to make amends, the United States would exercise its right under the Hay–Bunau-Varilla Treaty to take over the policing of Colón and Panama City. Belisario Porras responded angrily. He refused to accept responsibility for the riot, noting that similar disturbances occurred throughout the United States near military encampments and describing as particularly far-fetched the idea that the United States would ever dare occupy Panamanian soil.[48] In a private meeting with the Panamanian diplomat Eusebio Morales, Secretary of State William Jennings Bryan sympathized with Panama's circumstances. He noted it was usually difficult to assign blame when such riots occurred, citing a case in Tampa, Florida, that had resulted in the death of an Italian.[49] Yet American diplomats continued to insist on compensation. In the end, Panama and the United States agreed to let a neutral arbitrator set the price. In 1915, Panama paid an indemnity of $12,350 for the death of Ralph Davis and injuries to other American citizens, but explicitly refused to accept responsibility for the violence, declaring American soldiers had provoked it.[50]

Even as these negotiations continued, more conflicts involving the two nations occurred. In 1915 two more riots took the lives of several Americans and Panamanians. Both involved American crowds, mostly soldiers, rioting against Panamanians, most of them police. In the first case, American soldiers had been granted a leave because of a carnival in

Panama City. Once the rioting began, according to newspaper reports, working-class Panamanians joined their police in attacking the soldiers. Before the violence ended, three U.S. soldiers and five Panamanian policemen were dead.[51]

Two months later, in April 1915, another riot broke out. This one resulted in the deaths of an American soldier and a Panamanian citizen and injuries to more than one hundred others. The incident occurred on Good Friday, a national holiday in Panama, after thousands of soldiers came to a baseball game that would determine first place in the Canal League. The game ended in a fight at the baseball field when U.S. soldiers supporting the rival teams fought each other. Canal Zone policemen managed to stop the fight, but then soldiers headed into Colón's red-light district and rioting soon began. Corporal Langdon of the U.S. Army was on patrol duty and attempting to maintain peace when he was shot to death by a Panamanian policeman. Rioting again continued for many hours. Windows throughout the city were smashed and many houses destroyed. Outraged Panamanians stoned the train taking soldiers back to their camps.[52]

The riot of April 1915, and particularly the destruction caused by American soldiers, led Panama's leaders immediately to begin seeking legal action against the United States. They soon abandoned the effort as the United States furiously ordered Panamanian officials to disarm their police force of all rifles. Panama's elected officials insisted that this riot, like the previous ones, had been provoked by U.S. soldiers, and they refused to accept the blame. However, Ambassador Price firmly reminded the Panamanian government that the canal treaty of 1903 gave his government the right to intervene to maintain order in the port cities at any time, and he dictated that all rifles be transported to the U.S. Army, where they would be held "in the event of any occurrence which would make the use of them advisable in the opinion of both Governments." President Porras pleaded in a telegram to President Woodrow Wilson: the weapons were needed to "defend our country and to preserve public order." Porras declared: "This attitude towards a sovereign state which has given to the U.S. evident proofs of friendship and loyalty is incomprehensible to my Government." He described the order as a humiliating violation of Panamanian sovereignty and begged President Wilson to intervene. U.S. secretary of state Robert Lansing quickly responded: "This Government expects immediate compliance with its demand for the complete disarmament of the Police of Panama . . . of high powered rifles." Porras continued to resist, but finally, in May 1916, the police relinquished their weapons. Only a presidential guard of twenty-five men would be allowed to carry rifles. This was to Panamanians a pivotal moment of subjugation to the power of the United States that many still remember today, almost one hundred years later.[53]

THERE WERE numerous causes of the Cocoa Grove riot of 1912. Although many Panamanians initially embraced the canal construction project and hoped to benefit from the Americans' energy, over the years resentment had grown as the promised fruits of the alliance proved sour. U.S. marines, soldiers, and canal workers looked to Cocoa Grove as a place where they could let loose. It helped them forget their position as cogs in Goethals's wheel of labor discipline and productivity. As the months of canal construction turned into years, their sometimes belligerent behavior generated among Panamanians not only fear and suspicion of Americans but also a feeling of injury to their notions of national honor and sovereignty.

U.S. interventions into Panamanian politics further complicated the relationship between the countries and their citizens. The United States had supported and enabled not only the rise of the Conservative Party in Panama after independence was won in 1903 but also its mutually dependent relationship with the Panamanian police force. At first opposed to Liberal rule by someone capable of allying with the working masses, the United States abruptly changed its position and allowed Belisario Porras to run for the presidency. Ironically, these actions by the United States helped ensure that its earlier allies, the Conservatives and policemen who supported them, would feel a powerful resurgence of anti-Americanism and nationalism. Even at the moment when it was helping a Liberal nationalist win power, when it was acting to ensure a fair election, the United States was seen as intervening in a corrupt way and as compromising Panamanian sovereignty. The actions of the United States intensified Panamanians' notions of national honor and sovereignty, which then clashed with U.S. citizens' ideas of their own and their nation's superiority.

To British diplomatic officers observing from the wings, the affair demonstrated the fecklessness and inexperience of the United States. A diplomat commented caustically, "This incident will no doubt enhance the reputation already enjoyed by the USG among the Central American Republics."[54] For a day the Cocoa Grove riots had brought Goethals's efficient machine to a standstill. The affair and its aftermath profoundly challenged the image of the United States as an effective, beneficent, and peaceful power on the Isthmus of Panama. As Americans began looking to the end of the canal construction project in 1913 and 1914, these dynamics made it more imperative than ever to find effective ways of publicizing the canal project. A great world's fair—the Panama-Pacific International Exposition of 1915—would provide the opportunity for seeking positive lessons from the construction project that could be applied back home. At the same time, it would broadcast notions of American power, idealism, and scientific and engineering know-how outward to an increasingly troubled world.

CHAPTER NINE

HERCULES COMES HOME

E VEN AS the Cocoa Grove riot occurred and amid the difficult negotiations that unfolded in the following months, construction of the
canal was moving rapidly toward completion. From 1912 onward the
focus of the work shifted to completing the gigantic lock gates and building docks, mechanical shops, and a coaling station at the Pacific end of
the canal. Culebra Cut—which had held such a grip on the fears and
imaginations of workers and tourists—was nearly conquered. Steam-
shovel operators in the cut had been heading toward each other from
different ends of the isthmus for years in a friendly competition, and now
they began to close in on each other. Rose Van Hardeveld recalled the
rivalry as workers and their families cheered for the steam shovel heading
from her neighborhood in the central division or for the steam shovel
coming from Culebra in the Pacific division. The steam shovels raced to
be the first to break through the final barrier forty feet down at the bottom of the cut. Finally, one day in May 1913, Van Hardeveld recalled, "we
heard the exultant shrieking and blasting of the whistles that told us the
barrier had been penetrated." She and her children ran outside to peer
into Culebra Cut, where they saw men clapping each other on the back
and shouting for joy. "We could see the two shovels with their booms
raised and dippers almost touching. . . . All we could think of was the
victory itself. The last barrier was down." Canal workers and their families celebrated across the isthmus. Within several weeks all dry excavation
was finished.[1]

Several crucial tasks remained for the ICC officials and their employees before the canal could be opened. Plans had to be made for maintaining and managing the completed canal and for governing the people who would remain in the Zone to carry out those duties. In 1912 engineers began allowing the vast stretch in front of Gatun Dam to fill up. As the waters gradually rose into Gatun Lake, the ICC had to conduct a massive relocation of the area's residents. Meanwhile, Goethals and his officers began efforts to reduce the working population of the Zone. At its peak the canal workforce had involved nearly fifty-seven thousand people; by 1921 only fourteen thousand employees would remain. Sending thousands of laborers home or finding them new jobs in Central America or the Caribbean proved as difficult and complex a challenge as anything Goethals had previously encountered.[2]

With the canal nearly completed, Americans' attention shifted to interpreting and comprehending the project's immense significance. Millions traveled to San Francisco in 1915 for a spectacular world's fair held to commemorate the canal's opening. One newspaper declared the fair, known as the Panama-Pacific International Exposition, to be a "monument built to the Panama Canal by San Francisco." One hundred fifty thousand people entered the fair as the gates opened the first day. "Six abreast, singing, cheering, laughing, their hearts lifted and their faces shining with the glory of it all," Americans paraded in to celebrate a great world's fair and the canal that stood at its symbolic heart. "Rich in line with poor," declared the *San Francisco Examiner*. "It was a parade of triumph, a parade of true democracy."[3] It was the first world's fair celebrating, as the exposition's president, Charles Moore, put it, the "vital living, pulsing, present" rather than commemorating a historical triumph, and it would stand as the largest, most successful, most advertised, and most profitable for many years to come. The palaces, arches, murals, sculptures, and gardens honored the same values the canal builders had broadcast: a newly powerful United States, a young nation made into a world power by technology, science, and individuals of genius and able now to contribute more powerfully than ever to human progress, peace, and beauty. The fair signified an important moment in making the canal a symbol of

U.S. power, civilization, and beneficence and provides a window into the myriad connections between the exercise of that power domestically and abroad.[4]

Many observers proclaimed the fair to be most splendid at night, when it was illuminated with a force and beauty unlike anything they had ever seen. General Electric contributed thousands of dollars and assigned its best engineer to design the lighting. Nearly four hundred searchlights flooded monuments like the Fine Arts Palace and the Tower of Jewels, while five hundred open projectors and untold numbers of colored lanterns and underwater lights added a further note of spectacle. Several times a week stunning fireworks shows lit up the dark San Francisco night. A special effect known as the Scintillator combined lighting equal to four billion candles with the city's famous fog to produce an effect considered more beautiful than the aurora borealis. After observing the illuminated city, the poet Edwin Markham declared: "I have seen beauty that will give the world new standards of art, and a joy in loveliness never before reached. This is what I have seen—the courts and buildings of the Panama-Pacific Exposition illuminated at night." The novelist Laura Ingalls Wilder (of *Little House on the Prairie* fame) traveled from her home in the Ozarks to San Francisco for the event and noted, "The lights of the Exposition made it look like fairyland and the lights of the city rising on the hills, row after row behind, linked it all with the stars until one could not tell where the lights stopped and the stars began."[5]

The fair's creators were surely aware that their celebration of the Panama Canal coincided with a dark moment in world history, and that its significance derived in part from that larger context. In the summer of 1914, even as the canal was being flooded with water and preparations had begun for the first ship to cross through from ocean to ocean, World War I broke out. Soon the horrific conflict overtook Europe, seemingly threatening the foundations of civilization. "The lamps are going out all over Europe," British foreign minister Sir Edward Grey famously declared; "we shall not see them lit again in our lifetime."[6] Many who felt trepidation over the events in Europe found in the Panama-Pacific International Exposition a source of optimism about the world's future. As the psychologist G. Stanley Hall reflected after visiting the fair: "The fact that this great Exposition . . . was held in the midst of this awful war, which was the psychological moment for emphasizing the sympathy of nations, will forever give it a unique, pre-eminent character in the history of international expositions."[7]

The war, which began almost precisely as the canal builders completed their work, cast many celebratory plans into disarray. U.S. officials had hoped to mark the opening with a parade of ships through the canal, carefully designing it to be grander than the one that had marked the end of the Suez Canal's construction decades before. President Woodrow Wilson planned to traverse the canal on a battleship en route to the Panama-Pacific International Exposition. World War I made all such ideas unfeasible. After Britain and Germany both refused to participate in the world's fair in San Francisco, some worried about whether it could still be held, but its organizers prevailed, and the fair began as scheduled.[8]

If the war initially dashed many hopes for marking the canal's completion in spectacular ways, in the long run the distant, dark shadow it cast heightened the symbolic importance of the canal and U.S. power in the world more generally. One editor declared in the summer of 1914 that the canal was "the silver lining in the clouds of war," for the serendipitous timing of the canal's opening and the beginning of war in Europe would enhance the ability of the United States to take over a great deal of the world's trade. Others saw in the timing of events a symbol of America's contribution to world civilization. The *Chicago Daily Tribune* noted that the Panama Canal constituted a great constructive project which had united North and South America, while the European war signaled a great work of destruction tearing the Continent apart: "For ten years we have worked with the dredge. For ten years Europe has worked with the cannon. The workers are now in the harvest." More bluntly yet, an article in *Current Opinion* contrasted World War I with the Panama-Pacific International Exposition: "In one case, all the reserves of science and invention are brought into play for the destruction of human life, its comforts and necessities, its works of art, its temples of worship. In the other case, all these reserves are marshaled to enhance human life, augment its comforts, nourish its sense of beauty, and increase its consciousness of human brotherhood. Did the world ever show a more massive and monumental contrast than this—the greatest war of history on one side, on the other the greatest exhibition ever seen of the triumphs of peace and international intercourse?"[9] Like the Panama–Pacific International Exposition itself, World War I gave Americans a signal opportunity to interpret and comprehend the meanings of the canal to their lives and the future of their nation.

KISSING THE ZONE GOOD-BYE

The geography of the Canal Zone was radically transformed as the construction project neared completion. The enormous lock gates rose up as mountains of steel on the landscape. Water began collecting in the spillway of Gatun Dam. Once the canal was filled with water, everything on the farther, northwestern side would become inaccessible. The railroad had already been rebuilt so that it ran from Panama City to Colón along the eastern rim of the canal. Some of the largest settlements in the Zone were abandoned as a result. Empire, the great city of machine shops with a population of more than seven thousand, became a ghost town almost overnight, as did Culebra, where two thousand ICC officials, engineers, and supervisors had lived. The rising waters caused landslides near labor camps presumed to be safe, forcing even more people to flee. Many other towns, including Gorgona (as the industrial heart of the project, it was called the "Pittsburgh of the Canal Zone"), Las Cruces, Frijoles, and Matachin, were obliterated when officials allowed the waters of Gatun Lake to rise in 1912.

In most cases people went willingly, but others were forcibly moved as the floodwaters began licking at their front doors. Zone policemen patrolled the area to prevent people from returning to their homes. Buildings were disassembled by the thousands and moved to towns on the other side of the ditch, most often to the new town of Balboa, built from the spoils of excavation on land reclaimed from the Pacific Ocean. A workforce of approximately five thousand would be required to run and maintain the canal operations, plus their family members, and as many as nine thousand soldiers and marines would be housed on military bases across the Zone. A town of neat landscapes and imperial architecture, Balboa became home for many of the workers and officials who would remain in the Zone after construction ended to maintain the canal.[10]

Elizabeth Parker, who had traveled to the Canal Zone to marry her fiancé in 1907, described Balboa's emergence from muddy swamps along the Pacific. High atop the hills arose spacious homes for Colonel Goethals and other leading officials. Houses salvaged from Empire and other towns were reconstructed for more lowly canal employees. A large administration building, also housing a library and post office, took over a grand hill, with manicured tree-lined avenues leading to it from every direction. Parker warmly welcomed her family's move to Balboa: "There was an air of permanency now. Cement living quarters were being tried out. Roads were built, trees planted, grounds landscaped. Gone were the ugly black stoves, the lone electric bulb dangling from the ceiling on a cord. Electric stoves were being installed in some quarters. We even had telephones!" Parker happily greeted the new social opportunities that came with proximity to Panama City: "We joined the University Club, where we met friendly Panamanians at the weekly dances. There were official receptions and lawn parties. There were teas at the American Embassy, private cocktail parties, and afternoon bridge."[11]

American housewives like Parker may have found that the completion of the canal brought new comforts to their lives, but for many others the transformation sweeping the Zone during the final years brought chaos and displacement. As towns across the Zone were evacuated and jobs eliminated, tens of thousands of West Indians, southern Europeans, and Americans—some of whom had lived on the isthmus for ten years or more—were expected to leave. Officials began to break up Jamaicatowns and other West Indian labor camps throughout the Zone and to develop strategies for removing their army of labor. Even as they worked toward this end in 1912 and 1913, however, workers seeking jobs continued to arrive from across the Caribbean and from India. Goethals complained to the British consul in 1913 that his officials had recruited no new laborers for the last six months and he anticipated no further demand, yet boatloads of West Indians continued to arrive. "In order to avoid the objectionable conditions which would no doubt arise through the presence . . . of a large body of unemployed men," he asked Claude Mallet to inform all Caribbean governments that he desired no more men. Unscrupulous agents in India were likewise continuing to send men, and ICC officials complained because the laborers could find no jobs and were penniless. Even U.S. citizens found themselves searching for work. Some white Americans headed to Costa Rica as the ICC eliminated their jobs, but there they found little work that paid adequate wages. Many American men were ending up, according to the *Canal Record*, in "destitute and desperate situation[s]."[12]

British colonial officials throughout the Caribbean braced themselves for the return of emigrants. As repatriation of thousands of laborers got under way, the Jamaican and Barbadian governments expressed concern about the "disposal" of too many West Indians on their islands, and Barbados passed a law to penalize captains who so overloaded ships as to endanger the health of passengers. On most islands officials anticipated there would be jobs for the returning canal workers, because there had been pervasive labor shortages since the construction project began. The government in Barbados, however, was concerned about the influx of workers, as there were not sufficient jobs and an ongoing drought promised to keep agricultural employment at a minimum for the time being. Colonial officials generally worried about distress among emigrants and potential burdens on their governments if employment was scarce or if the ICC refused to pay the cost of sending men home. The ICC was obligated to pay for contract laborers' repatriation, but the thousands of West Indians who had come on their own had to pay for their return voyage. Thus British officials worked to convince the ICC to pay for repatriating all its laborers.[13]

As the numbers of unemployed laborers grew in Panama City and Colón, officials grew anxious about the potential for disorder. By 1914 large numbers of impoverished West Indians filled the streets of Panama's port cities. The ICC that year lowered the basic wage for silver employees from thirteen to ten cents per hour. Simultaneously, food prices and rents in Panama were rising precipitously. Panamanian police began arresting unemployed men to maintain order and relieve the pressure of congestion. Claude Mallet, the British consul, was inundated with letters of complaint from West Indians who felt they had been imprisoned unjustly. One group of prisoners wrote Mallet complaining that the Panamanian government was routinely imprisoning West Indians and holding them six to eighteen months without trial, then releasing them with no money, no job, and no home. Some West Indians specifically criticized not only the Panamanians and Americans for the social crisis but also the British diplomatic representatives. One man wrote Mallet and demanded: "We Say that this Record country is greatly inhabited by all nation unaccount of the Panama Canal; And there is a counsil of all de damn nation suppose all There counsil was to do there duties; What would happen." This writer concluded by stressing his credentials: "Sir I am not his Counsil But I am an english subject . . . also I has a great knowledge of this Law I know what you can do from what you cant."[14] Congestion, rising prices, and unemployment continued to shape life in the cities of Panama for many years to come.[15]

As American officials sought to reduce the rapidly growing army of unemployed laborers, they found many West Indians reluctant to return to their island homes. Repatriation began on a large scale in the autumn of 1913, but Jamaicans and Barbadians anticipated that wages would be higher and working conditions better if they could remain in the Zone or at least in Central America. In November 1913, Mallet vividly portrayed the ongoing swirl of human migration—and the inability of the ICC to control it—as the canal project began to conclude: in the last three months alone, he reported, nearly thirty-four hundred West Indians had arrived in Colón looking for jobs, some three thousand others had departed the isthmus as the ICC began sending contract laborers home, and another thirteen hundred had departed for jobs throughout Central America. ICC officials and British diplomatic representatives began negotiating with potential employers throughout Latin America, since Chile, Bolivia, Peru, Brazil, Argentina, Venezuela, and Mexico were planning to construct railroads, harbors, and ports to exploit the new commercial opportunities made possible by the canal's opening.[16]

The officials' best hope, however, for finding a place for unemployed West Indians was Central America. The governors of British Guiana and British Honduras expressed interest in receiving laborers from the Canal Zone, and they declared they had land available that could be leased or purchased by canal workers so that they could grow some crops. Unemployed canal workers could also attain work on plantations. The governor of British Guiana declared that West Indians in the Canal Zone "have been receiving high wages: wages much higher than any planter can afford. On the other hand they have been accustomed to work much harder than any agricultural labourer ever works here for his employer; and the comparatively low rate of wages given to agricultural labourers is due to the smallness of the tasks performed by them."[17] The United Fruit Company, or UFCO, sought laborers for its expanding plantations in Panama, Guatemala, Nicaragua, and Colombia. Mallet noted that "the higher wages earned in Central America attract them to remain abroad in preference to going back to the Islands in the West Indies." Hasty arrangements were made for UFCO to hire ten thousand men.

This solution was also problematic. Mallet warned that "the labourers in the Canal Zone are accustomed to work and live under superior conditions such as they will not find on new Banana plantations in the midst of virgin forests which will make them dissatisfied and troublesome." As a result, UFCO's managers preferred to hire laborers directly from Bridgetown. This, however, would leave thousands of laborers on the isthmus, "and the West Indian Governments will be brought face to face with the problem of providing for thousands of their people who are destitute and unable to obtain work in the Republic of Panama or the Central American States."[18]

By 1915 the ICC had reduced the number of its employees by more than twenty thousand. Days were filled with the packing of suitcases and farewell parties. In the final year of construction alone, nearly sixteen thousand people left the Zone for good, mostly canal employees moving back to homes in Europe, the Caribbean, and the United States or, in the case of many West Indians, taking up residence in Colón or Panama City and seeking employment there. The population of Panama's two port cities increased by 50 percent between 1913 and 1921 (from 66,500 to 99,800), as many canal employees sought work there. At the same time, prices and rents both increased significantly in Panama, while the economy entered a depression and jobs became difficult to find.[19] Despite the early worries of British colonial officers, West Indians who returned home to Barbados or Jamaica often had an easier time than those who remained in Panama. The geographer Bonham Richardson, in interviews he conducted with Barbadians decades after the construction effort, found that work on the canal often made possible significant economic mobility once employees returned home. Savings from their jobs in the Zone led to opportunities to buy a bit of land and achieve, in many cases, an important degree of economic independence. The Barbadian Cleveland Murrell, for example, remembered how his father had worked as a janitor in the Canal Zone, all the while carefully saving his money. He returned home with about $100 and used it to rent a bit of land. Rising prices during World War I earned him a solid profit on the sugarcane he grew, which he then used to buy six acres and open a shop. Murrell recalled how proud he felt of his father's economic achievements: "When my father finished working the land, he would peel the mud off of his feet and throw it back on to the land. He would save and save. I don't know how he did it. He was very thrifty—different from those who would sit around and drink rum."[20]

Amid the evacuations and emigration, the canal moved steadily toward completion. In September 1913 officials tested the locks for the first time. A few weeks later President Wilson, in a great publicity stunt and a milestone in the history of telegraphy, pushed a button at the White House to send an electric signal to Panama and blow up Gamboa Dike, the last major earthworks preventing water from flowing through the canal. The telegraphic signal traveled by land from Washington, D.C., to Galveston, Texas, and from there underwater through the Gulf of Mexico to the isthmus, where it detonated forty tons of dynamite in the dike. More than three thousand spectators, including Colonel Goethals, many leading Panamanian officials, and the Frenchman Philippe Bunau-Varilla, came to see the explosion and watch as the vast Culebra Cut quickly filled with water.[21]

Across the United States, people expressed delight at the news of Gamboa Dike's explosion, but nowhere more enthusiastically than in San Francisco, where workers were already busy building the palaces and towers of the coming world's fair. On the day President Wilson sent the electric signal hurtling toward Panama, a large crowd gathered at Union Square in the city's heart. Upon hearing that the dike had exploded, they sang the national anthem while officials hoisted the American flag, bombs were set off, and factory whistles across the city blew. At the fairgrounds Don Lefevre, the official representative of the Republic of Panama, took possession of the site for Panama's building, supervised the hoisting of the Panamanian flag, and received an artillery salute from U.S. battleships stationed off the Presidio.[22]

Officials meanwhile prepared for the end of construction by overhauling the government of the Canal Zone, appointing George Goethals the first governor of the Zone, and restructuring the Zone judiciary to fold it into the district court system of the United States. All the while, the waters gradually rose higher in the canal, and the creatures of the Zone—monkeys, snakes, insects, and sloths—fled to higher ground. Finally, as Elizabeth Parker remembered, "only the mighty hardwood trees remained, their bare branches stretching over the blue water—ghostly reminders of a once-teeming jungle." The day they sent the first tugboat through the locks, Parker and her husband were among the first to watch it pass: "On the prow proudly stood Col. Sibert; on the lock wall stood Col. Goethals, chain smoking, his steel-blue eyes fixed on the tiny craft."[23]

During the summer of 1914, as Europe mobilized for war, Americans along the isthmus prepared for the formal opening of the canal. On August 15 the steamship *Ancon* left Cristobal at 7:00 a.m. and traveled through the canal with Goethals and other American and Panamanian officials, including President Porras of the Republic of Panama, on board. All canal employees had a holiday for the occasion, and they and their families lined the banks of the canal. The *Ancon* smoothly made its way as a band of musicians from the U.S. Army and from Panama on board the ship played "The Star-Spangled Banner." On the ship's foremast flew the flag of the American Peace Society, while the U.S. flag flew on the jackstaff. The ship crossed the isthmus in nine hours, not docking at Balboa but going onward to the deeper waters off the Pacific, then returning to Balboa to deliver its passengers. During the long day's trip the officials and their wives enjoyed a splendid buffet lunch that lacked only wine, the *New York Times* carefully pointed out, as the Zone was now dry territory.[24]

This formal opening drew little attention from the vast majority of Americans, however, distracted as they were by the outbreak of war in Europe. For those leaving the Zone for good, it must have seemed a bittersweet moment. Maybe they felt happy to head back home, to leave a place of toil and struggle. Maybe they expressed a measure of sadness to leave a place that for so long had provided a sense of adventure. Harry Franck, the globe-trotter who worked as a policeman and census taker in the Zone, wrote eloquently of his last visit to Empire, where he had lived for years, when it was about to be abandoned: "It seemed like a different place. Almost all the old crowd had gone, one by one they had 'kissed the Zone good-by.' . . . It was like wandering over the old campus when those who were freshmen in our day had hawked their gowns and mortarboards. . . . I felt like a man in his dotage with only the new, unknown, and indifferent generation about him." Franck visited the old suspension bridge, where he saw some of the last men scurrying about and a few steam shovels digging out final loads of dirt. "Soon the water will be turned in and nine-tenths of all this labor will be submerged and forever hidden from view . . . and palm trees will wave the steamer on its way through what will seem almost a natural channel." Mostly, Franck regretted leaving behind his friends in the Zone police force, but he ended his memoir on a cheery note, declaring he'd see them all again in San Francisco in 1915.[25]

"AMERICA'S GIFT TO THE WORLD"

As people continued to leave the Canal Zone, as machinists and steam-shovel engineers made their way home to Kansas City, Detroit, or Newark, their suitcases filled with souvenirs from Chinese shops, Americans took time to reflect on the larger meanings of the canal project. Over the years businesses had increasingly adopted the canal as an effective way to adver-tise their goods. One pervasive ad from the period declared, "The Two Greatest in History: the Panama Canal and Budweiser Beer!" Another company poignantly compared its contribution to the human alimentary canal to the great effort on the isthmus. "Two World Wide Wonders," proclaimed the ad: "The Panama Canal for Universal Commerce, Hostet-ter's Stomach Bitters for Dyspepsia, Indigestion, Biliousness, Constipation, and Malaria." Keepsake postcards also circulated freely through the United States in these years. A Christmas postcard depicted Santa Claus in his sleigh high above the earth, flaunting a large U.S. flag and looking down content-edly as ships approached the new Panama Canal. Another, titled "The Kiss of the Oceans," introduced a homoerotic note by showing the seas trans-figured into two beautiful women kissing at the very spot where the canal married the Pacific and Atlantic oceans.[26]

Across the United States there was discussion of the canal's signifi-cance for the future of the nation and, indeed, for all of humanity. Amer-icans were proud to see commentators around the world hailing the canal's completion as the most important event of the century. Previous chapters suggested the ways Americans debated the meaning of the canal over the years, particularly in terms of progressivism, the benefits of state intervention, concerns about the government's use of racial segregation in the Zone, and labor's role in the body politic. Now, as completion neared, Americans' feelings about the canal were overwhelmingly posi-tive; they proclaimed it as a beacon of American industrial and techno-logical triumph, a wonder of the world, and a terrific gift to civilization. In 1913, just weeks after helping to dynamite Gamboa Dike, President Wilson issued a proclamation designating the upcoming day of Thanksgiving, and he singled out the canal project as especially deserving of the nation's gratitude: "We have seen the practical completion of a great work at the Isthmus of Panama, which not only exemplifies the nation's abundant resources to accomplish what it will and the distinguished skill and capacity of the public servants but also promises the beginning of a new age, of new contacts, new neighborhoods, new sympathies, new bonds, and new achievements of cooperation and peace." Many described the canal's impact in tones of benevolence, referring to it as *Ladies' Home Journal* did: "America's Gift to the World." A writer in *Manufacturer's Record* considered the canal the "mightiest change in the world's material affairs since the discovery of America." Everyone, from "the far Himalayan Mountains to the wilds of the Andes, from Siberia to the utmost limit of South America," the people of all classes throughout the entire world, would feel the benefits of the canal.[27]

These reflections hint at another common theme. The canal had transformed the earth, profoundly and permanently, including the spatial and commercial relations of all nations. Maps were drawn up to show the new relations of nation-states. A book by Ralph Emmett Avery, titled *The Greatest Engineering Feat in the World at Panama,* included the new miraculous cartography of the world. San Francisco and Honolulu were now five or six thousand miles from New York rather than thirteen thousand; much of Asia could be reached more quickly, and the Suez Canal had suddenly been rendered redundant, at least to the United States, because Melbourne, Manila, Hong Kong, and Yokohama could all be reached more easily via the Panama Canal. The markets of Asia (China, Japan, and the Philippines, as well as Australia and New Zealand) had become as accessible to the United States as to the nations of Europe.[28]

In fact, the most profound spatial consequence of the canal lay in reorienting the nation toward Asia and the Pacific. The American Historical Association convened a special congress in San Francisco during the Panama–Pacific International Exposition to examine the historical significance of the Pacific. It announced that the Panama Canal would transform relations between the Americas, Asia, and Australia: "One era of Pacific Ocean history comes to an end; another begins." Besides papers on the history of China, the Philippines, Australasia, and California, the conference included a powerful essay by Theodore Roosevelt on the history of the canal. He defended at length his actions in acquiring the Canal Zone and the right to build the canal and ended by concluding, "There is not one action of the American government, in connection with foreign affairs, from the day when the Constitution was adopted down to the present time, so important as the action taken by this government in connection with the acquisition and building of the Panama Canal."[29]

The canal's impact on the Americas was likewise seen as transformative. Its opening, particularly since it coincided with World War I, would lead not only to more trade with South America but also to much greater and more permanent settlement of Americans throughout Latin America. The obvious result would be, one author noted, the "Americanization of Latin America," because now U.S. residents would settle there in greater numbers and begin demanding more of the conveniences and comforts of home.[30] One could observe this process of Americanization by considering the case of Panama. The United States had truly made the tropics safe for white men, just as Colonel Gorgas promised, and the inevitable consequence would be a vast diaspora of white North Americans settling permanently throughout the tropics.[31] The editor of the *Independent* reminded readers of Benjamin Kidd's warning years before that whites could not make it in the tropics. Kidd had been proven wrong, the editor averred: "All around the equator there are now experiment stations, where attempts are being made to grow northern races, and among these none is more successful than the one we have established in the region that has the worst reputation for disease and death." This editor concluded: "Our occupation of the Zone is not temporary." More Americans would be living there twenty years from now, and Americanization would gradually produce unimaginable benefits. Consider agriculture alone. As the white man tamed tropical agriculture through scientific methods, what innovations might result? "We can only guess at it by trying to solve the proportion; as the corn of the Indians is to the corn of the white farmer, so is the banana of the Panamanian to the banana of the future."[32]

Thinking further ahead, William Boyce of Chicago proposed that the United States build on its work in Panama by establishing the entire Zone as a vast "duty-free" region. A new era of global connections had begun. Boyce proposed in a speech to the Southern Commercial Congress that the United States should build in the Canal Zone a vast city of 500,000 Americans, where manufacturers and distributors would flock to enjoy freedom from import and export duties. The Canal Zone, he imagined, "would become an immense world's department store, where everything for the use of all people of all nations could be found. It would become the greatest transshipping port in the world." Less visionary commentators agreed that Panama presented remarkable opportunities for "American enterprise," as C. H. Forbes-Lindsay described it. He declared: "One of the most marked characteristics of the Anglo-Saxon is land-hunger— the desire for elbow-room, and the longing to be lord of broad acres." Accordingly, Forbes-Lindsay urged Americans to emigrate to Panama for the cheap land and vast opportunities in agriculture.[33]

As for the commercial impact of the canal, an American diplomat predicted that its results would "far surpass the dreams of the most enthusiastic," and most commentators agreed. U.S. railroad entrepreneurs did worry that the canal would hurt their business, and they lobbied the government to allow a decrease in transcontinental rates without a reduction in rates for the towns and cities along the way. The ICC supported their request, noting, "We are witnessing the beginning of a new era of transportation between the Atlantic and the Pacific coasts. . . . The shrinkage of rates via the Canal from New York to San Francisco has put the transcontinental carriers in serious straits." But most analysts expected the general economic stimulus provided by the canal and cheaper transportation would compensate for any disadvantage to the railroads. The canal, according to George Blakeslee, a professor of international relations at Clark University, would stimulate exports, particularly from the western United States, and industries like coal and steel would benefit. Accordingly, consumer prices would decrease, further stimulating the economy.

Ultimately, shipbuilding would be affected favorably as well, and ports like San Francisco and New York would see a great increase in trade. A study conducted by the French government concluded that American industry would be "incalculably benefitted," while European industry would likely be damaged.

Most American observers addressed the coincidence of the canal's opening with the impact of war and concluded that, economically, things could not be better. Edward Marshall noted in the *New York Times* that together World War I and the canal would open the vast markets of South America to the United States: "That the great European war should have emerged from a nightmare dream of horror into a terrible reality and that the Panama Canal, long regarded as a chimerical extravagance of impractical imagining, should have become a concrete, operative fact almost at the same moment, form a coincidence which may be referred to by future historians not only as one of Fate's greatest gifts to this incomparably lucky Republic but as an adjustment tending to alleviate a great world disaster." Across the country chambers of commerce and merchants' associations feverishly conducted investigations and sought information about Latin markets. Any salesman with knowledge of the Spanish language suddenly became a hot property.[34]

Indeed, over the years many commercial clubs traveled to the isthmus so their members might examine conditions and report back to the community. As early as 1907, for example, more than eighty men, representatives from the Commercial Clubs of Boston, Chicago, Cincinnati, and St. Louis, traveled together to Panama to see "America's Mediterranean" for themselves.[35]

A more muted theme suggested by various writers involved the canal's effect on American military and foreign relations. Many portrayed the canal as a crucial contribution to world peace, but their arguments faltered in the face of Europe's war. Far more compelling were arguments proposing that the canal would play a central role in America's emergence as a major military power. By strengthening the Navy, the canal would have a tremendous impact. Alfred Mahan, whose arguments in favor of greater sea power for the United States had helped move Theodore

Roosevelt to launch the canal construction project, wrote in 1911 that within two decades the canal would be seen to have changed the U.S. role in the world more powerfully than any other historical event except for the War of 1898. Not only would America's interests in the world and its need for defense both expand as a result of these events, but the American Navy would soon be second only to Great Britain's Royal Navy. Perhaps most important, Mahan argued, the world would see a great expansion and strengthening of Anglo-Saxon influence and institutions all along the Pacific, particularly from Alaska to Mexico. By bringing more Americans to the Pacific Coast, the canal would reorient the United States and its commercial and military power toward the Pacific: "More people, more wants; more people, more production. Both wants and production mean more transportation."[36] The editors of *World's Work* put the matter more succinctly: The canal's completion "emphasizes the evolution of a new America. Our splendid isolation is gone. . . . We have become a colonial power with possessions in both oceans. And now we open under our own control one of the great trade routes of the world." They quoted Admiral Mahan as saying it used to be common wisdom that congressmen should avoid serving on a committee like Foreign Affairs, as it meant nothing to one's constituents. The editors concluded: that was a fair observation in the days before the canal, but it certainly did not apply anymore.[37]

Among the dreams indulged in about the canal, perhaps none speaks more powerfully to Americans' quest for a strong sense of national identity than the common notion that the "kiss of the oceans" would unite and homogenize the people of the United States. In a world where pressures and anxieties generated by a host of social changes associated with industrialization seemed to fragment the nation, the great triumph of the canal, and the social and economic benefits it promised, seemed capable of reuniting the American people. Every region of the country appeared poised to benefit and rediscover its connection to the broader nation, but perhaps most emphatically the South. As the historian Alfred Richard noted, the canal seemed to enhance the sense among Southerners that their interests were closely tied to those of the nation as a whole. The former Confederate colonel T. P. Thompson pointed out in *Leslie's Weekly* that the canal's completion would be celebrated in the jubilee year of peace between North and South. He listed the many benefits the canal would bring to the South: "Before the fiftieth anniversary of . . . Appomattox we of the Southland expect a generous stream of immigration in this direction, and when we invite the remnant of the G.A.R. [the Grand Army of the Republic] to celebrate here, as we intended to do, fraternizing with the U.C.V. [the United Confederate Veterans] in the jubilee year of peace between the States, we also expect to have many of the sons of those who wore the Blue here residing in our midst at that time."[38]

A short story by the writer O. Henry popularized this notion that the canal might reunite North and South. In "Two Renegades," O. Henry created a Yankee named Barnard O'Keefe who falls ill on the isthmus while helping Panamanians mobilize for independence from Colombia. He is healed by a grizzly old American doctor who still swears loyalty to the Confederacy. Soon thereafter, O'Keefe is captured by Colombia for his revolutionary activities. The Confederate doctor intervenes and says he can save O'Keefe, but only if he foresakes his Union sympathies and pledges allegiance to the Confederacy. Facing no other option but a firing squad, O'Keefe finally agrees and pledges to serve the Confederacy faithfully. The Confederate doctor then pays a ransom to free O'Keefe, using money he still has from the Confederate States of America. He urges O'Keefe to hightail it back to the United States, before Colombia discovers the ransom has been paid with useless Confederate cash. O'Keefe catches the next ship back, but for years afterward he can still be found in the South, marching and waving the Confederate flag on days of commemoration. In this way O. Henry, a native of North Carolina, portrayed the Isthmus of Panama as the handmaiden of unification and redemption for North and South.[39]

"THE COMING OF A CONQUEROR"

Americans approached the Panama-Pacific International Exposition in 1915 ready to celebrate the "eighth wonder of the world" in grand fashion despite—or perhaps because of—the horrors associated with World War I in Europe. During a trip to the East, Charles Moore, the president of the exposition, had announced the fair's raison d'être: it would be a celebration of America's "greatest achievement, the dream of the ancient navigators fulfilled." He declared bluntly: "Theme: Energy of man, progress of the race, has offered unusual inspiration to the artists, architects, et al., of the world." Future president Herbert Hoover noted the particular utility of the planners' vision: "In these days of stifling struggle our people need something to bring back to them the heritage, not only of the combat of immediate fathers in the upbuilding of the West, but also to bring to the people that they have a heritage of race."[40]

The fair, as the historian Robert Rydell has argued, was suffused with images of racial progress, conquest, and social Darwinism. Explicit references to empire were, for the most part, noticeably absent. Its surrogates, however, were everywhere: the Panama–Pacific International Exposition (PPIE) celebrated civilization, progress, humanity, triumph over nature, and brotherhood. More prosaically, it highlighted the technological, industrial, scientific, and artistic brilliance of the United States. The PPIE celebrated the great city of San Francisco, reborn from the ashes of the 1906 earthquake (another epic triumph over nature). And most of all, the PPIE ecstatically celebrated itself. No fair had ever been more important, more financially successful, more visited, more beautiful, more encouraging of world peace—or, depending on one's point of view regarding international affairs, more effective at preparing the nation for war. Indeed, it was quite an occasion. The fair cost approximately $50 million to build, and its organizers boasted that, thanks to the many millions who visited, they had set a new world's record by making back every bit of the money spent.[41]

The building of the exposition involved a huge effort stretched over four years, and it emerged as a microcosm of struggles that existed in American society and in the construction of the Panama Canal. Many of the workers who toiled to build the fair buildings and landscape the grounds were unionized. Their unions, however, were devoted to the grand cause represented by the fair, and they were eager to display that devotion. In 1912 the San Francisco Labor Council and the Building Trades Council wrote jointly to Charles Moore: "Labor realizes that the PPIE is an institution dedicated to Progress, in the name of humanity, peace, and civilization, held for the purpose of commemorating the greatest engineering feat in the world's history." Furthermore, "all the achievements of modern civilization that are to be placed upon exhibition in the PPIE have been produced by labor." Therefore, unionists declared they would not limit output, would not push for higher wages or shorter hours, would not engage in jurisdictional disputes, and would cooperate with any workers brought to the fair by foreign countries. Organized labor even disavowed its long-term devotion to exclusion of Asians. The Asiatic Exclusion League declared that "organized workers of the U.S. should use the opportunity afforded by the PPIE for furthering the cause of unity and brotherhood among the nations." Toward that end, the league declared, it would welcome all visitors and discontinue all anti-Asian activities.[42]

Motivating the unions' cooperative spirit was also the National Association of Manufacturers, or NAM, which mobilized to limit union power and lobbied Moore and the other fair directors to build the grounds with thoroughly open shop policies. Moore stood against the pressure. He allowed unions and cooperated with them. Yet he may well have used the NAM's visible lobbying and its multiple ways of applying pressure (from Pinkerton spies to threats that employers would not participate in the fair) to encourage concessions from labor.[43]

The question of Asian—particularly Japanese—exclusion was more difficult for the PPIE organizers. In 1913 a fight erupted in California over the Alien Land Bill, which proposed to bar aliens ineligible for citizenship (that is, Asians) from owning land. Charles Moore became outspoken in opposition to the bill, and some white farmers who favored it wrote bitterly about the subject. A farmer named Schmidt complained to Moore, "I see you rich men are fighting it [the anti-alien land bill] and you are trodding upon us in favor of the Japanese." He added, "Must we white farmers be driven away to make room for the Japanese? How would you like to be a poor farmer and have for neighbors a lot of grinning Japs. They have already driven white people away in some part of this state." He concluded that it was unpatriotic to sell land to Japanese farmers and that America must not "kneel down" to Japan.[44]

Japan had threatened to pull out of the exposition if the land bill passed. Its leaders also issued formal complaints about the mistreatment of Japanese citizens by exposition employees and officials. Moore and other organizers believed their fair would fail if Japan did not participate, and they also worried about the consequences for America's trade relations. As American consul general Thomas Sammons stressed, the PPIE was important to the United States in part because of its potential ability to strengthen commercial ties with Japan. Racist incidents would eliminate any such potential. Sammons worked to prevent conflict, negotiating a plan with the consul of Japan whereby the builders of Japan's site at the fair would keep Japanese and American workers segregated from each other. If Americans were needed for a specific task, Japanese workers would be removed until the former finished their job.[45]

While PPIE officials worked to negotiate polite relations with the governments of China and Japan, racial tensions emerged daily at the fair. A concession called "Underground China" included depictions of female slavery and dens in which Chinese addicts seduced white people into smoking opium. The Republic of China and Chinese Americans protested vociferously about the exhibit.[46] As at other world's fairs, an air of social Darwinism and notions of racial progress and hierarchy pervaded the PPIE, and like others it included exhibits of various "inferior" peoples: Samoans, Hawaiians, Somalians, and Mexicans, in addition to the Chinese and Japanese. Sculptures, paintings, and postcards broadcast the fair's themes, including racial progress. The most popular sculpture at the fair, by James Earle Fraser, graphically depicted racial triumph and defeat. Titled *The End of the Trail,* it shows a Native American on his horse, slumped over so far as to be nearly falling off, an emblem of a vanquished race. Author Juliet James wrote at the time that the sculpture portrayed not just the end of the trail but "the end of the Indian race. . . . His trail is now lost and on the edge of the continent he finds himself almost annihilated."[47]

Many of the exhibits on the PPIE's midway, officially called "The Zone," were unsuccessful, particularly those featuring "native villages." The Samoan Village closed early, even though it "provided a glimpse of the life of a race thousands of years behind civilization." A village of Somalians—"thin, black, and hollow-cheeked wanderers," as the PPIE's official chronicler, Frank Morton Todd, described them—was considered boring and tame by fairgoers, even though the residents performed "a great deal of violent flat-foot dancing and spear shaking on their ballyhoo stand." When the concession closed, the Somalians were slow to vacate the site, so exposition guards forcibly removed them. They were then taken to Angel Island and deported.[48] The Hawaiian Village was particularly uninspired; when the Hawaiian commissioner objected that it did not represent the lives of Hawaiians, fair organizers changed the name to "Hula Dancers." Even then, the secretary of the Hawaiian Promotion Committee protested that the hula dancers were not Hawaiians but "fat" women from Chicago who had painted their skin brown.[49]

If patrons grew tired of observing exotic cultures from around the world, or the beautiful sculptures and palaces meant to instill an awesome appreciation of beauty and civilization, innumerable other exhibits demonstrated the wonders of modern technology, industry, and science. To delight and amaze visitors there were the Palace of Food Products, the Palace of Transportation, the Palace of Mines and Metallurgy, the Palace of Varied Industries, the Palace of Machinery, the Palace of Industrial Arts, and buildings erected by individual corporations like the Southern Pacific Railroad Company. Employers big and small displayed their products and inventions in exhibits throughout the different palaces, from Henry Ford's assembly line in the Palace of Transportation (which turned out a car every ten minutes to the pleasure of large crowds) to Gillette Safety Razor, Westinghouse, and Miss Curtis'

Snowflake Marshmallow Creme. The Heinz exhibit showed fifty-seven varieties of the company's food products and gave out free pickle pins. Harley-Davidson showed off the fastest motorcycles in the world. The Excelsior Auto Cycle company presented dozens of bicycles. At the Western Electric exhibit, electrical appliances were displayed along with a gigantic desk telephone and big lamps accompanying a sign that declared, "Every time the lamps flash a Western Electric telephone is manufactured." Paralleling the spatial transformation symbolized by the completion of the Panama Canal, Alexander Graham Bell made the world's first transcontinental telephone call by ringing the exposition from New York City in early 1915. More transcontinental calls were made every day thereafter.[50]

It was left to the Panama Canal to bring together the many themes floating about at the PPIE: the technological genius, geographical and commercial transformation, promise of ascendant industrial might, and the vast benefits to civilization, brotherhood, and world peace. As a souvenir book reminded readers, the reason for the splendid world's fair was "The colossal achievement of mankind, the building of the Panama Canal."[51] There was Perham Nahl's brilliant poster depicting the canal as the thirteenth labor of Hercules serving as the PPIE's main advertisement. Likewise, the architecture and sculptures of the fair were meant to "tell the story of the unification of the nations of the East and the West through the construction of the Panama Canal," according to the contemporary writer Frederic Haskin.[52] A sensational centerpiece of the fair, just inside the main entrance, was the Fountain of Energy, which depicted America's triumph over the isthmus. Juliet James wrote of the aquatic sculpture, "The theme is Energy, the Conqueror—the Over Lord . . . the indomitable power that achieved the Waterway between the Oceans at Panama." At the center of the fountain, "Energy himself is presented as a nude male, typically American, standing in his stirrups astride a snorting charger—an exultant super-horse needing no rein—commanding with grandly elemental gesture of extended arms, the passage of the Canal." The fountain's sculptor, A. Stirling Calder, described his intentions in depicting the triumphant male figure: "His outstretched arms have severed the lands and let the waters pass. Upon his mighty shoulders stand Fame and Glory, heralding the coming of a conqueror."[53]

The canal seemed to inspire fantastic, romantic visions of history and humanity. One man proposed a pageant to the fair organizers around the theme of peace. He imagined a cast of five hundred people acting out the story of humanity, beginning with cavemen and climaxing with the completion of the Panama Canal. It would demonstrate "that in ancient times war was a necessity but is so no longer and that Man's activities should be constructive, as in building Panama Canal, and not mutually destructive." Another, more spectacular pageant was proposed by the president of the Festivals Association of the Pacific Coast. Titled "The Wedding of the Oceans," this pageant of two thousand people would begin with Columbus and march through the history of the Americas (Cabrilho, Balboa, and so on), before climaxing with the exploding of Gamboa Dike. Then the oceans, symbolized as Neptune and Amphitrite, would be joined in wedlock, attended by sea horses, dolphins, Father Panama, and the deities of Earth, Sea, and Sky. Electricity and fireworks would end the pageant in "a blaze of glory."[54]

A poem by Wendell Phillips Stafford, titled "Panama Hymn," used imagery of marriage to represent the canal. Commissioned for the fair's opening ceremonies, the poem was set to music and performed by a chorus of four hundred people. It graphically presented an image of man's triumph over nature:

> We join today the east and west,
>   The stormy and the tranquil seas.
> O Father, be the bridal blest!
>   The earth is on her knees.
>
> As thou did'st give our hand the might
>   To hew the hemisphere in twain,
> Oh, grant the road we lead to light
>   May Never know a chain!

In freedom shall the great ship go
  On freedom's errand, sea to sea,
The oceans rise, the hills bend low,
  Servants of liberty.

The nations here shall flash from foam
  And paint their pennons with the sun
Till every harbor is a home,
  And all the flags are one.

We join today the east and west,
  The stormy and the tranquil seas.
O Father, be the bridal blest!
  Earth waits it on her knees.

Although the editor of *Sunset* magazine found the poem horrible, believing the image of Earth on her knees to be particularly crude (while the image of oceans rising as the hills bent low, he said, made him feel seasick), Charles Moore disregarded his advice, and the poem became the official anthem of the PPIE.[55]

The fair brought together most of the famous men who had played an important role in acquiring and building the Zone, as well as many who would become famous in decades to come. William Jennings Bryan, who as secretary of state had negotiated with the Republic of Panama in the aftermath of the Cocoa Grove riot of 1912, visited to help celebrate America's Independence Day. Newspapers estimated that 100,000 people gathered around to hear the perennial presidential candidate and former secretary of state address the crowd. The day had seen endless marching and Army bands playing in celebration of the holiday. Bryan was greeted with the booming guns of warships as he mounted the podium. Then, in a surprise stunt to honor Bryan, the aerialist Art Smith circled the sky above the grandstand before releasing four doves from his little plane. As the birds winged their way toward the clouds, Bryan stretched his neck to watch. Then he stood and delivered his address, "The Meaning of the

Flag." The Stars and Stripes was draped over his podium, and Bryan caressed the flag at dramatic moments of his speech. Although "the glint of bayonets [remained] in his eyes," Bryan's address focused on the need for peace and brotherly love. His voice shaking with emotion, Bryan invoked Jesus of Nazareth and old-time gospel to plea for peace: "God has given us an opportunity to-day such as no other nation ever had, that may never come again, to lift the world out of this bondage of brute force. The measure of individual and national greatness should be service." And finally: "May the God of our fathers give us light and keep our feet in the path of truth as we strive to fulfill the high mission to which He has called our country." The United States, he exhorted, was the world's best hope for peace.[56]

Soon thereafter, Bryan's old nemesis Theodore Roosevelt had his day, literally, when PPIE officials declared July 21 to be Theodore Roosevelt Day. The ex-president arrived in an automobile surrounded by cavalry troops. He declared, "You did not have to bring me out here. You could not have kept me away. I feel peculiar pride in this Exposition." Roosevelt toured the various exhibits during a long day and attended a banquet in his honor before presenting an address on "war and peace."

Robustly, amid cheers from the audience, Roosevelt evaluated the nation he had worked to build to greatness. He defended his actions in 1903: "In everything we did in connection with the acquiring of the Panama Zone we acted in a way to do absolute justice to all other nations, to benefit all other nations, including especially the adjacent States, and to render the utmost service, from the standpoint alike of honor and of material interest, to the United States." The project had doubled the efficiency of the U.S. Navy, but if unfortified, it would become a great menace to the security of the nation. "The canal is to be a great agency for peace; it can be such only, and exactly in proportion as it increased our potential efficiency in war." As the canal went, so went the nation. The United States must prepare for war, Roosevelt argued, and quickly and efficiently. He decried the way his nation was continuing "with soft complacency to stand helpless and naked before the world," lacking a strong army or navy and trained officers to lead them. He especially attacked the "professional Pacifists, the peace-at-any-price, non-resistance, universal arbitration people [who] are now seeking to Chinafy this country." Although he did not name Bryan, it was surely clear to listeners whom he meant. And as if in further response to Bryan, Roosevelt ended powerfully by reading verses from the Bible that echoed his concerns: "But if the watchman see the sword come, and blow not the trumpet, and the people be not warned; if the sword come, and take any person from among them, he is taken away in his iniquity." The *San Francisco Examiner* reported that when Roosevelt finished with this last Bible verse, he was met with a moment of stunned silence, and then the crowd of sixty thousand broke into cheers and ovation. The applause continued until he had left the stage and his automobile had passed through the exit gates of the exposition grounds.[57]

President Woodrow Wilson and ex-president William Howard Taft were among the many who toured the fair. George Washington Goethals visited and proclaimed, "This is the first International Exposition to commemorate a contemporaneous event. I came to it with the picture in my mind of other great expositions and I found that this one was worthy of the Canal it commemorates."[58] Future presidents Herbert Hoover and Franklin Delano Roosevelt served on the board that planned the exposition. The fair became a cultural crossroads, bringing together Helen Keller, Charlie Chaplin, Henry Ford, Thomas Edison, Fatty Arbuckle, Harry Houdini, Buffalo Bill Cody, William Randolph Hearst, Al Jolson, Samuel Gompers, and many other famous Americans.[59]

Amid the grandeur, pageantry, and posing that took place during the world's fair in San Francisco, two great themes were notably absent. The first was the role played by the Republic of Panama. As a young nation that had ceded control to the United States over the Panama Canal Zone, making the construction project itself possible, as an ally providing resources and labor, as a site of competition and contestation with the United States, as a refuge for canal employees desiring adventure and amusement, and as home to thousands of West Indian canal diggers, Panama had played a central and distinctive role. Yet no building at the exposition displayed the glories of Panama. The Republic of Panama built a pavilion, but it did so unenthusiastically because participation in the fair required a great infusion of money and the U.S. government refused to reciprocate and support the fair Panama planned to hold on its own territory. At one point Panama's government halted construction of the pavilion at the PPIE to protest the U.S. decision but finally agreed to finish the job. PPIE officials had sought to make peace with the Panamanian government by inviting its representatives to attend opening-day festivities, but the U.S. State Department refused even to allow this small gesture. Instead, a luncheon was held to honor Panama's official representative, Don Lefevre, and afterward he addressed PPIE president Charles Moore and other notable officials on his country's sentiments regarding the canal and the exposition.[60]

Lefevre's speech included the polite praise of the United States one might expect at such an event, and yet his comments betrayed a cool and jaundiced perspective on his country's powerful neighbor. He urged listeners not to see him as a stranger, because "I come from the country that made this Exposition a possibility." My young republic, he declared, "furnished the name of 'Panama' for the Panama-Pacific Exposition." Lefevre praised the "energy, the intelligence and the greatness of the Nation that has built the canal," yet he insisted that "we should not forget the important share that Panama and its people have taken in this unparalleled undertaking. We have had our territory pierced in two through the powerful arm of Uncle Sam, to make way for two oceans that will look friendly into each other." Americans, Lefevre declared, should not forget that the Republic of Panama had "put in your hands the Key to the Commerce of the Coast swept by the Ocean of the future."

Lefevre's brief remarks concluded on a dark note. The selfless civic actions of Panamanians had transformed the isthmus into a peaceful republic, making possible the Panama Canal. The canal in turn had destroyed many old Isthmian villages, including Gorgona, where America's own Ulysses S. Grant had camped as a young quartermaster on his way to California. Lefevre spelled out just a few of the personal and social costs to Panamanians: "Many families of natives which lived for years in the picturesque cabins where they were born, have been compelled to abandon their homes and to see gone forever the beloved spot of ground on which they stood . . . [now] covered by the rising waters of the Gatun Lake." If the United States was a phoenix rising from the ashes, the Republic of Panama might be compared to the "mythical bird which opened its breast to give life to its off-spring." In this metaphor the economic and political power of the United States was Panama's offspring. Panama not only gave birth to the canal and to a newly ascendant America but also "tore its entrails to feed international commerce and to strengthen the ties of brotherhood of the world." He hoped the canal would not only shorten the distances of the globe but also bring men closer together and make prejudice toward others disappear forever. To the officials of the PPIE this must have seemed a shockingly frank perspective on America's grand canal and exposition.[61]

Besides the Republic of Panama, another remarkable absence at the fair was the workingmen and workingwomen who actually built the canal. Whether any of the construction era's unsung heroes managed to tour the fair and celebrate their achievements has been lost to history. Surely there must have been a steam-shovel engineer or two, a nurse, or perhaps a typographer who found a way to wander through the grounds. But in all the imagery and gay celebrations of the fair, one sees no references to them. The star attraction of the entire world's fair—a model version of the Panama Canal—demonstrates this erasure of the human labor that made the canal's construction possible. The company that built the model lavished an astonishing amount of resources as well as the latest technological developments in order to reproduce the canal in exquisite and awe-inspiring detail. The model canal covered nearly five acres of land, cost $250,000, and required 225 men working at construction for seven months. The landscaping work employed an additional 60 women, who spent five months planting trees, bushes, and grass. Workers reproduced the canal, locks, and surrounding cities and geographical landmarks over a vast area that looked roughly like a football field. Above and around this reproduction twelve hundred people at a time could be transported via a moving walkway (the longest one in the world at the time, at 1,440 feet), with joints built in to allow the rounding of corners.

The platform was divided into little traveling opera boxes, with two tiers of seats in each one. Spectators sat in the comfortable chairs, placed telephone receivers at their ears, and listened to lectures from a series of 45 rpm phonographic records that employees placed on or off the record player as the moving walkway passed the different sights of the canal. The record player sent its message to telephone transmitters, which then sent the message on to the receivers at each seat. Combining phonograph records and telephone technology to communicate the information seemed quite new and impressive. It had been developed in the laboratory of Thomas Edison.

The model included ingenious details to communicate precisely the workings and feel of the canal. Little ships steamed through the canal, small trains chugged along the landscape, and electric mules pulled the ships through the lock gates. There were lighthouses and hospitals and the administration buildings of the ICC. Towns like Colón and Cristobal were represented with hundreds of tiny buildings, three to six inches in height, with glass windows. They were placed on top of glass so they could be illuminated from underneath. The major parks of Cristobal and Colón were also represented, with each of three main varieties of palm trees included as well. The model showed landmarks like Gold Hill and Mount Hope Cemetery as well as dry docks and hydroelectric plants. Culebra Cut was of course displayed, including the terracing done along the sides of the cut to discourage further slides. The model's designers included Chiriqui Prison and the ruins of old Panama when depicting the region around Panama City. They even took care to show abandoned towns like Pedro Miguel, half submerged under the waters of Gatun Lake, and they showed where old towns like Empire had once existed.[62]

For all the meticulous detail the model included, the tens of thousands of men and women who built the canal, their labors and toil, the malaria and dynamite explosions, their making do with spoiled meat and ants in their fruit pies, were nowhere to be seen. In this sterile landscape, spectators saw no residents of the current cities of the Zone or the port cities of Colón and Panama City, nor any of the thousands of employees who maintained and ran the canal. The model canal depicted the elements Theodore Roosevelt had stressed about the project: the marvels of engineering and technology and the transformed geography of the isthmus.

A journalist described how it felt to visit the canal in this way: "We seat ourselves in a revolving gallery and as we look into the arena below we lose our sense of distance and feel the sensation of peering over the edge of a balloon. We adjust the automatic telephone and a voice . . . tells us that we are above Miraflores locks. . . . Tiny ships nose into the docks and traverse the canal. Wireless messages snap and crackle." This observer noted the absence of people, but it didn't seem to bother him: "It does not require much imagination to see pygmy toilers sweating under the tropical sun, or to hear the clank of machinery and the 'sput–sput' of laboring engines as the steam shovels bite their way through the stubborn earth." He left the miniature canal with a "feeling of reverence" for this project that joined two oceans.[63]

The Panama Canal concession proved to be one of the fair's great success stories. In the first five days of the fair, fifty thousand people toured the model canal. The *San Francisco Call* wrote, "This big attraction in the joy belt has proved to be one of the magnets to attract the thousands of pleasure seekers." Like the fair itself, the model canal was said to be most beautiful at night, as all the buildings, lighthouses, ships, and buoys were illuminated.[64] Laura Ingalls Wilder described in a letter home to her husband how wonderful the concession was, with the electricity managed somehow so that the sky appeared to be at twilight with stars gradually coming out. In a popular children's book by Elizabeth Gordon, *What We Saw at Madame World's Fair,* twin sisters observe that the model canal is "far and away the most educational and interesting thing at the Fair, and helped us to understand really why Madame World was so anxious to have the Canal cut, and why there is so much rejoicing over it." The feminist writer and reformer Charlotte Perkins Gilman reported on the "marvellous mechanics" of the model and inquired, "Could scientific ingenuity farther go?" The model thus gracefully complemented Perham Nahl's poster: the canal construction involved labor, to be sure, but the labor of technological innovation, the labor of a nation, the labor of an empire. Individual laboring men and women shrank like pygmies in significance compared to the broader themes of the project and the nation that made it possible.[65]

I N DECEMBER 1915 the fair, in all its brilliance, came to an end. On the last day nearly 300,000 people crowded in for a final chance to see the sights. As sunset hit, the thousands of lights shined one last time; near midnight a few thousand people gathered to sing "Auld Lang Syne." When the clock struck midnight, PPIE president Charles Moore pushed a button to turn off all the lights, a bugler atop the Tower of Jewels played taps, the aerialist Art Smith spelled out "Farewell PPIE" in smoky letters above them, and hundreds of bombs were set off along the marina to mark the closing of the exposition.[66] Now it was left to the remaining years of the century to demonstrate history's rich use of the Panama Canal's meaning and symbolism.

EPILOGUE

THE CONSTRUCTION of the Panama Canal played a pivotal role in
forging America's self-definition as a nation and as a world power.
As a symbol of American efficiency, enthusiasm, and contributions to
world civilization, the Panama Canal hovered over the twentieth century
like a phantom. It connected the acknowledged strengths of the United
States in medicine, technology, and industry to expansionist aims and in
this way helped make Americans more comfortable with their country's
new role as a world power. The construction project also became a model
for the most prosaic issues of how to exercise power—how to rule over
men and women in America's new sites of empire—and how a nation-
state might effectively operate in an increasingly global economy.

The canal opened to the ships of the world in 1914 just as World
War I erupted in Europe and threatened to bring civilization down with
it. In less than three years the United States would be embroiled as well,
and its war effort would replicate many of the themes, ideals, and language articulated earlier in the Panama Canal Zone. Large-scale mobilization and segregation of labor, special rewards and recognition of
citizenship rights for certain (skilled, white) workers, and a suppression
of political dissent and forms of collective organizing deemed radical: all
this became central to U.S. strategies at home and abroad during World
War I. These practices were carried out in the name of an interventionist state that idealistically articulated the benefits to world civilization to
be gained by U.S. participation in the war. Many of those who led the

construction project in the Canal Zone sought positions of leadership again in World War I. George Goethals, for example, desperately wanted to participate in the U.S. war effort. He wrote General John Pershing to request an appointment, believing his work directing the canal construction would surely be advantageous in the conduct of war. Appointed quartermaster of the U.S. Army, Goethals worked to centralize and streamline the bureaucratic functions of several branches, from the ordering of food, clothing, and equipment, to the assignment of quarters, to transportation. He collaborated closely with the War Industries Board as he sought to bring prices under control—and later was appointed to that board by President Woodrow Wilson.[1]

The strategies first negotiated during the construction of the Panama Canal stretched across the following decades, shaping and defining the twentieth century. The U.S. approach to empire—rejection of formal colonialism in favor of economic, political, and industrial management combined with military engagement as needed—made itself felt in military occupations and political interventions in Puerto Rico, Cuba, and Haiti, among others. In all these cases, the true Herculean labor involved not moving mountains but managing and ruling over men and women. In the Canal Zone during the construction era this had meant that Goethals and his officials had constantly to adapt their ideas about government to the needs, desires, and demands of a diverse population. While officials sought to present the construction project as an efficient machine, in fact the system was sorely tested by the tens of thousands of working people on the Isthmus of Panama. Sometimes it broke down altogether.

In the decades after the canal opened, these tensions—the symbolism of the canal versus the gritty reality of social relationships on the ground, and the designs of officials versus the demands of those they sought to govern—persisted. Canal officials' relations both with their silver employees and with the government of Panama grew increasingly tense during and after World War I. In 1916, six thousand workers (nearly one-third of all silver employees) went on strike for five days, demanding a wage increase. Canal Zone governor Chester Harding commanded that the

Republic of Panama take action against the strikers, and Panamanian police moved quickly to break up meetings and arrest and deport strike leaders, effectively killing the strike.[2] By 1919 and 1920, West Indians were facing pay cuts and widespread unemployment. Many of them had become more militant as a result of both the war and the popular social movement led by Marcus Garvey that emphasized black equality and nationalism. Garveyism surged through Central America, the Caribbean, and the United States after World War I. Explosive labor protests resulted, as West Indians defied officials' assumptions that they were submissive and easy to manage. After the American Federation of Labor began organizing West Indians in 1919, more than a thousand dockworkers at Cristobal went on strike. Governor Harding banned Garvey and his organizers from the Canal Zone, intensified efforts to house West Indians in the Zone so they could be controlled more easily than if they resided in Panama, increased silver workers' wages, and soon thereafter announced that strikers would be evicted from government housing and lose access to the Zone commissaries.

Despite such strenuous measures, dissatisfaction among West Indians across the isthmus was severe, and militancy was running high—much as in the United States, where labor activists in 1919 crippled the steel, mining, meatpacking, and other industries before facing widespread defeat. The West Indian community in the Canal Zone and in Panama increasingly articulated its discontent in the postwar period, influenced both by Garveyism's emphasis on race pride and by the organizing efforts of a union in the United States, the Brotherhood of Maintenance of Way Employees, that stressed the importance of fighting for their rights as workers. West Indian discontent now had a voice in a newspaper, the *Workman,* founded in 1919, which kept up a drumbeat of protest against "Jim Crowism and racial suppression." Its editors denounced a range of unjust conditions, from low wages and expensive housing to racial discrimination in every area of life, cruel treatment by Panamanian police, and inadequate medical care at hospitals and clinics. Furthermore, one editorial proclaimed, "our children do not get the best in the schools; our women are not yet respected as ladies; our capabilities are still spurned by illiterate crackerism and we are still receiving the mouse's share for doing the lion's part of the work." In 1904, the editors argued, the case for silver and gold segregation had been built on claims that Americans were unaccustomed both to the tropical climate and to interactions with large numbers of West Indians and that as U.S. citizens they deserved higher salaries and other privileges. "During all these days, and until 1914 when the water rushed into the great divide, the silver employees found it discreet to continue their work with as little murmuring and as great determination as they could possibly summon. But the times have changed, and what was tolerated between the years 1904 and 1914 will no longer be taken, lying down."[3]

In this atmosphere of determined protest, between twelve thousand and sixteen thousand West Indian silver workers launched a great strike on February 24, 1920. They demanded a pay increase, an eight-hour day, equal pay for women, and a grievance procedure. During the eight days that it persisted, this massive, disciplined strike arguably posed the most effective protest against racism and labor exploitation ever seen on the Isthmus of Panama. With little external support, however, the silver workers' strike was defeated. Their union, based in Detroit, provided no financial assistance. Workers faced dismissal, deportation, and bans on strike meetings. After the strike failed, Governor Harding punished strikers by deporting or refusing to rehire their leaders. Harding categorized those rehired as "new employees" and paid them the lowest possible amount. The strike had signaled not only a new assertiveness among West Indian workers but also the stern determination among Zone officials, in the words of one observer, to lay the "bridle hand on the negroes." Panamanian government officials observed this and other labor troubles in the Zone during the 1920s and tried to demand more jobs for their citizens, but the United States reacted coldly, refusing to make even the gesture of preferential treatment toward Panamanians that it had offered during the construction era. Panama's politicians responded in 1926 by passing a law banning from their country any people of African descent whose native language was not Spanish.[4]

The silver and gold system remained in place until 1955, when U.S.

officials replaced it with a single-wage rate but continued to reserve almost all high-level jobs for Americans. Likewise, Americans retained related perks like travel and tax privileges, and the schools of the Zone remained segregated.[5] Yet World War II and its aftermath heightened antiracism, civil rights consciousness, and nationalism around the world, and these transformations shaped both the United States and Panama. Tensions around sovereignty became more acute as Panama began to demand more control over its territory. U.S. officials felt themselves swept into a dynamic in which concessions they made to the Republic of Panama only reinforced nationalism and led to yet more demands.

In 1940 the United States occupied additional Panamanian territory to better defend the canal, but nationalist protests forced the United States to retreat for the first time and abandon the land. In a 1955 treaty the United States attempted to give more economic benefits in return for the use of Panamanian lands and as a substitute for concessions regarding sovereignty. The treaty generated controversy in the United States, and Panamanians remained dissatisfied. In 1956, Egypt nationalized the Suez Canal, and this reinforced and validated the rising nationalism in Panama. Protests continued, most significantly a movement called Operation Sovereignty that included a march by students into the Canal Zone to raise Panamanian flags. As demonstrations sometimes escalated into rioting, President Eisenhower in 1959 conceded that "we should have visual evidence that Panama does have titular sovereignty over the region." This meant that, in a major concession, the U.S. government would now allow the Panamanian flag to be flown in the Canal Zone.[6]

Throughout this period the Americans living in the Canal Zone—known as Zonians—grew increasingly influential. Much as the skilled white American workers had done during the construction era, Zonians used the patriotism associated with the canal and the sense of entitlement they gained from their status as U.S. citizens to demand the maintenance of sovereignty over the Canal Zone. One Zonian greeted the 1955 treaty, for example, in language similar to that used by skilled workers during the construction era: "*With each replacement of a United States citizen with an alien employee,* Panama's wedge to obtain sovereignty is enlarged."

Zonians found ready allies, particularly among conservative politicians and activists in the United States who perceived any diminution of American power in the region as a sign of appeasement, a failure of leadership, and an unacceptable admission that U.S. control over the Canal Zone since 1904 had been dishonorable. As cold war tensions increased, anticommunism fit neatly into this paradigm. Congressman Daniel Flood linked Panamanian efforts to regain sovereignty over the canal to "the hidden hand of cunning and malignant Sovietism manipulating their local puppet figures to destroy the just rights of the United States and to jeopardize the peace of the world."[7]

Yet agitation continued at both popular and elite levels in Panama, and resentment between Panamanians and Zonians remained very high. By 1964 the governor of the Canal Zone had ordered that U.S. and Panamanian flags both be flown at specific sites. They were not to be raised at schools, but American students at Balboa High School rebelled against their own government and flew the U.S. flag outside their building. To counter this perceived insult, Panamanian students attempted to add their flag to the school. The Panamanian students' demonstration generated widespread riots throughout Panama City and Colón. U.S. troops and Canal Zone police gradually restored order, but the cost in human life was high: nineteen Panamanians and three Americans killed. Canal Zone governor Robert Fleming blamed his countrymen—and particularly Zonians—for the rioting: it was "the perfect situation for the guy who's 150 percent American—and 50 percent whiskey." Although he believed Zonians had provoked the situation, he argued also that the U.S. government failed to take proactive steps to defuse an increasingly volatile situation. Tens of thousands of Panamanians took to the streets to protest the U.S. occupation of their nation's territory, stoning banks owned by North Americans, attacking the U.S. embassy, and setting fire to the U.S. Information Agency, Goodyear and Firestone tire factories, and offices of Pan Am and Braniff Airways. U.S. soldiers dodged bullets, dug into foxholes in front of the Zone's Hotel Tivoli, and were finally ordered to respond by shooting to kill. Before it ended, the fighting had spread to Colón and other regions of Panama. President Roberto Chiari of Panama cut off diplomatic relations with the United States, while President Lyndon B. Johnson praised the U.S. troops for "behaving admirably under extreme provocation by mobs and snipers."[8]

The riots of 1964 and the deaths that resulted proved a turning point in relations between the United States and Panama. They drew sympathy to Panama's demands for greater control over the canal from people around the world. Although President Johnson showed little interest in major negotiations, his successors gradually moved toward the notion that the United States should transfer titular and substantive sovereignty to the Republic of Panama. A military coup in 1968 led by Colonel Omar Torrijos delayed progress and raised concerns about the political future of Panama. In 1973, however, the United Nations Security Council met in Panama City, and the United States was forced to offer the single veto to a resolution calling for a new treaty to "guarantee Panama's effective sovereignty over all its territory." After this vote, the Nixon and Ford administrations began more serious negotiations with Panama.[9]

The stumbling block, however, proved to be public opinion in the United States—and the highly effective mobilization of that public opinion by conservative politicians. President Gerald Ford ceased working toward a new treaty when it became clear during his campaign for reelection in 1976 that the public strenuously opposed transferring the canal. Ford's opponent for his party's nomination, Ronald Reagan, found to his surprise that few issues stirred the public more than the threat of losing the canal. Reagan later confessed he had no intention of raising the issue but discovered as he campaigned that audiences wanted to discuss it. He confronted "utter disbelief" in one community after another at the notion that the United States would give up the canal, and when he responded by arguing the United States should retain sovereignty permanently, he received "tumultuous applause." Reagan turned the canal into a major issue, declaring repeatedly at campaign stops, "We bought it, we paid for it, it's ours, and we should tell Torrijos and company that we are going to keep it." Henry Kissinger tried to educate Reagan on the facts and later complained to a newspaper columnist that he had never confronted "a more gullible pupil with less knowledge." Yet Reagan was not the only one who played the issue to his advantage. Echoing notions formed during the construction era that framed the canal as a triumph of American idealism and technology, Congressman David Bowen, Democrat from Mississippi, declared, "When I am home . . . there is only one thing I can say that invariably makes them cheer. . . . I say that if we can keep the striped-pants boys out of it and leave the canal to the Corps of Engineers, then the thing will work out fine. Many Americans have been raised to regard the canal as an engineering wonder that only the U.S. could have built and run. . . . [It is] emblematic of an entirely beneficent and successful way to help an inferior people."[10]

Negotiations resumed after Jimmy Carter won the presidency in 1976. Although he had promised during the campaign never to support relinquishing control over the canal, Carter as president shared the consensus among many policy makers that the best course for the United States lay, as his future negotiator Sol Linowitz put it, in "adjusting to nationalist aspirations rather than confronting them." Avoiding a difficult battle over the canal's future would allow the United States to control the process toward the inevitable, it was hoped, and thereby allow it to maintain maximum security for the canal. The Carter administration noted that many nations around the world saw the Canal Zone as a "colonial enclave" and believed the existing relationship between Panama and the United States to be inappropriate and anachronistic. Thus Carter sent Linowitz into negotiations with the Torrijos administration. The Torrijos–Carter Treaties were approved by a special plebiscite in Panama and signed by the United States and Panama in September 1977. The treaties promised an end to U.S. control over the canal, affirmed the permanent right of the United States to intervene to defend the neutrality of the canal, but prohibited it from interference in the internal affairs of Panama. They mandated the elimination of the Canal Zone as of October 1, 1979. The United States would continue running the canal until the year 2000, but the treaties arranged for Panamanians to gradually play a greater role. Finally, as of 2000 the Republic of Panama would assume full responsibility for maintenance of the canal and for its defense.[11]

With the treaties signed, the focus turned to winning ratification by the U.S. Senate. As Ronald Reagan had indicated, the American public was strongly opposed to transferring the canal to Panama. This opposition was intensified by mobilization led by conservative activists, innovative direct-mail efforts by Richard Viguerie, and grassroots organizations created throughout the United States by Zonians. Indeed, the historian Michael Hogan has shown that the Panama Canal became a turning point in the emergence of the New Right, allowing conservative activists to rally Americans who lacked unity over other issues. Congressman Daniel Flood of Pennsylvania warned President Carter that if he returned the canal to Panama it "could well be your 'Bay of Pigs' and prevent your renomination or re-election." Although the White House worked hard to unite liberal, labor, church, and business groups, and although Carter ultimately succeeded in winning enough votes in the Senate to pass the treaties, public opinion remained adamantly opposed. Carter frankly admitted to senators the danger involved: "Rarely is a national leader called upon to act on such an important issue fraught with so much potential political sacrifice. . . . I thank you for your personal demonstration of statesmanship and political courage."[12]

Many Americans felt passionate about and devoted to the canal, seeing in it, as Theodore Roosevelt had intended, a symbol of America's selfless contributions to civilization and its technological and industrial accomplishments. Representing all that seemed good about America and extending those virtues to the world, the Panama Canal became an ideological linchpin, justifying and holding together America's role in the world during the American Century. Journalist William Schneider argued during the debate over ratification that the construction project had generated a "primordial attachment" to the canal: "Americans regard the Panama Canal as a monument to our technological know-how and to our humanitarian instincts, as a symbol of Yankee ingenuity, not Yankee imperialism." Take away the Panama Canal, it must have seemed, and the prevailing ideas regarding America's beneficence in the world would potentially collapse as well. Although Carter and his allies portrayed those opposed to the canal as ill informed and tried to educate the public about technical aspects of the canal's history (the United States had *not* bought the Canal Zone, as Reagan and other conservatives contended, for example), it did not matter, because something much larger was at stake.[13]

A housewife from Nebraska, it turns out, helps to illustrate some of these themes. During the winter of 1978, Helen Greene, a fifty-four-year-old mother living in a small town who had long been active in the Democratic Party, received a summons from Washington, D.C. Her newly elected senator, the Democrat Edward Zorinsky, had emerged as a critical undecided vote in the ratification battle. President Carter, seeking every possible means of convincing Zorinsky to support the treaties, had offered to present his case personally to around two hundred Nebraskans. Carter believed Zorinsky was willing to support the treaties but feared political fallout from his conservative constituents back home. Thus, in a creative effort to win Zorinsky's support, Carter planned to reach out to some of those constituents, educate them about the canal, and thereby convince Zorinsky to vote in favor of the treaties.[14]

If Jimmy Carter had known anything about Helen Greene, he likely would have imagined her as the perfect person to win over. She identified herself as a progressive Democrat. She followed political developments closely and was an intelligent and educated woman. Over the years she had combined her work as a mother and housewife with ardent support for Democratic causes, walking the sidewalks of her small town to distribute campaign literature and sending her children out for the same purpose if she was too busy cooking dinner. She had worn a variety of political hats, serving as public relations chairman of Nebraska Citizens for Kennedy during the 1960 presidential campaign, winning appointment in 1964 to the new Nebraska Commission on the Status of Women, and working for two years as public safety coordinator in the administration of Governor Frank Morrison. As president of the Democratic Women's Second Congressional District Caucus in the mid-1970s, Helen Greene was one of the people Senator Zorinsky suggested should receive an invitation to the White House.

Greene was curious to hear what the president would say, she remembered years later, as she packed a light bag for her trip to Washington, D.C. She had bought a new wool coat in Nebraska City for the occasion, and it came in handy when a howling blizzard hit the state just as she headed to the airport. The weather was so bad Greene's husband had to drive her to the airport in their pickup truck. The plane was filled with Nebraskans heading to meet the president, to the surprise of stewardesses serving them snacks and coffee, and discussion about their journey filled the airplane.

As the two hundred Nebraskans arrived at the White House, First Lady Rosalynn Carter greeted each of them individually. They received a personal briefing by President Carter, National Security Adviser Zbigniew Brzezinski, Secretary of State Cyrus Vance, and General David Jones, the chairman of the Joint Chiefs of Staff. Together these men explained the reasons for transferring the canal to Panama, the history of the Hay–Bunau-Varilla Treaty signed in 1903, the security issues at stake, and the larger consequences of attempting to hold on to the canal indefinitely. They stressed that the United States would retain the right to defend the canal even after Panama assumed complete control in 2000, and that the canal had grown gradually less important economically to the United States. Afterward the men and women from Nebraska enjoyed cake decorated with the president's seal and served on china Jacqueline Kennedy had purchased.

Helen Greene was an experienced and well-informed citizen, and now she had attentively received a fine education on the politics and history of the canal. She returned home and dutifully gave a few talks on what she had learned to local schools and Democratic clubs. None of it, however, changed her mind. She continued to have reservations, she wished the United States would not relinquish control, and she felt nervous about the future of the canal once it fell to the Panamanians to maintain. Senator Edward Zorinsky agreed. Despite constant and aggressive courting by President Carter, Zorinsky voted against ratification of the Torrijos-Carter Treaties. Luckily for Carter and for the people of Panama, enough senators voted in favor to ratify the treaties. Zorinsky's vote had not been needed after all.

Latin Americans warmly welcomed the treaties. Torrijos declared the agreement to be a "triumph" because it "decolonizes and does so rapidly." Bolivia designated a "day of national rejoicing" to celebrate the treaties. Costa Rican president Daniel Oduber noted that the "U.S. is showing the Third World that in this hemisphere the relations between the most powerful nation and the small countries are conducted in an atmosphere of equality and mutual respect." In the United States, however, anger and bitterness greeted the "loss" of the canal. The remarkable pride and sense of ownership Americans had historically placed in the canal made it difficult for them to say good-bye. Twelve thousand U.S. citizens living in the Canal Zone—the so-called Zonians—found the changes particularly painful to accept. On September 30, 1979, Panama acquired jurisdiction over the Canal Zone, even though the United States would continue to manage the canal itself until the end of 1999. The *New York Times* described an "unmistakably funereal mood" in Balboa as Zonians prepared to see their way of life disappear. Some families had lived in the Zone since the construction era. One Zonian commented sadly, "The past is dead. Teddy Roosevelt is in the ground." The journalist Alan Riding seemed as emotional as any Zonian, comparing the United States' loss of the Zone to "a nation going down to defeat."[15]

The Torrijos-Carter Treaties did not mean that the United States would remove itself from Panamanian affairs. They provided for the presence of U.S. troops and military bases until the final transfer of power occurred on December 31, 1999, and fourteen bases across the isthmus provided a home to thousands of U.S. military personnel. Over the decades Panama had become a major staging ground for U.S. military intervention in Latin America, with the establishment of such institutions as the Inter-American Air Forces Academy and the School of the Americas (which between them trained nearly eighty thousand Latin American military personnel and police between World War II and 1989). When Manuel Noriega rose to power in 1983, he made Panama into an efficient supporter of U.S. military goals in Central America, for example, allowing the use of his country for covert training and assisting the CIA in establishing a training camp for the Nicaraguan contras. Noriega even supplied men who were demolition specialists to Oliver North in 1985 to help blow up a munitions dump in Managua, Nicaragua.[16]

Despite the strong alliance between Noriega's government and the United States, disagreements between the two increased during the 1980s. By 1989 protests against Noriega had risen within Panama as well because of his authoritarian military rule. Demonstrators in Panama protesting his dictatorship regularly confronted violence at the hands of the Panamanian national guard. President George H.W. Bush increasingly found himself unable to control Noriega, and this seemed particularly problematic at a time when the Torrijos-Carter Treaties were moving the two nations toward joint administration of the canal. Perhaps looking also to demonstrate the potency of his administration, Bush became convinced that Noriega had to be removed from power and that Panama's national guard (known as the Panama Defense Forces, or PDF) had to be eliminated. The U.S. military determined that its goal would be "the disarming and dismantling of the Panama Defense Force." The United States would not only install a new president of Panama but create a new police force under its control. Under the Torrijos-Carter Treaties the PDF was slated to defend the canal after the transfer on December 31, 1999, and the withdrawal of the United States. In a public message immediately after the invasion, President Bush declared his goals: to safeguard the lives of Americans, defend democracy in Panama, combat drug trafficking, and protect the integrity of the Panama Canal Treaty. Ensuring continued U.S. control over Panama and its military as the date of transferring full sovereignty over the canal approached may well have been a central motivation for the invasion, although few documents have been released by the United States to date. Among Panamanians, however—including the many who suffered under Noriega's rule—there is little doubt that this was a primary goal of the U.S. invasion of their country.[17]

The events that triggered the invasion were evocative of the Cocoa Grove riots seven decades earlier. When a Marine intelligence vehicle ran through a roadblock and headed toward Noriega's office, Panamanian national guardsmen fired upon it, and the gunfire killed one marine. In the aftermath of this incident a U.S. soldier and his wife who had observed the killing were taken into custody by the guardsmen, whereupon the soldier received a beating and the wife was threatened with sexual assault. Arguing that Panamanian guardsmen were placing American families' lives at risk, Bush immediately ordered the invasion, along the way seeking to allay worries that he was a spineless president. The United States launched Operation Just Cause in the middle of the night on December 20, 1989, minutes after having sworn into office a new president on a U.S. military base in Panama. The invasion constituted the largest military operation conducted by the United States since the Vietnam War. The United States used overwhelming force to eliminate Panama's small national guard, only three thousand men strong. Eighteen thousand Panamanians had to move into shelters as a result of the invasion, five thousand were detained in prison camps by U.S. soldiers, and the property damage reached higher than $1 billion. As fires spread through Panama City and plumes of smoke rose high, a Panamanian woman interviewed by the *New York Times* declared, "This is horrible. Never in the history of our country has this been seen." According to the Pentagon, more than five hundred Panamanians lost their lives, most of them residents of El Chorrillo, a working-class neighborhood. Human rights observers, however, have estimated that mortalities reached much higher than the Pentagon's figure. Latin American governments, including Argentina, Mexico, Venezuela, and Peru, vigorously condemned the invasion as a violation of Panamanian sovereignty.[18]

The economic, political, and emotional costs of the invasion to Panamanians were difficult to measure. In the short run the invasion clearly changed the power relationship between the United States and Panama to the benefit of the former. Yet over time nationalism within Panama and concerns over sovereignty—both heightened tremendously by Operation Just Cause—generated enormous opposition across the country to any continued U.S. military presence after the transfer of the canal. In persistent rounds of negotiation the United States, under President Bill Clinton, tried to maintain a presence, but Panamanians refused to accede to its demands. Thus on December 31, 1999, not only did the Panama

Canal become the responsibility of the Republic of Panama, but all U.S. military bases shut down permanently, and most remaining troops were shipped out to Puerto Rico. As the sun set on December 30, U.S. soldiers took down their nation's flag for the last time. The United States had planned to lower the flag during the ceremony transferring the canal the following day, but at the last moment officials decided to change course. They worried, they said, that lowering the flag during the official ceremony would inflame anti-Americanism in Panama; many U.S. and Panamanian citizens believed the real worry involved the passions of conservatives in the United States who opposed the transfer. Former Panamanian foreign minister Jorge Ritter stated, "Somehow, I think it would have been nobler to lower the flag at Friday's ceremony. It would have been better for the two countries to end the relationship with a gesture of nobility and patriotism."[19]

Nonetheless, it was a day of national jubilation in Panama as President Mireya Moscoso joined thousands of Panamanian citizens in front of the old commission headquarters to mark the moment in which the canal became Panama's possession. President Moscoso shouted, "The canal is ours!" as Panamanian citizens cheered. Then Moscoso raised the flag of Panama and announced, "I tell the men, women and children of my country that there will be no more fences, no more signs blocking our entrance. This territory is ours again." One Panamanian in the crowd witnessing the transfer, a seventeen-year-old student, captured the feelings of many as he waved a Panamanian flag and announced, "This is the culmination of a pending account. This is the achievement of complete sovereignty."[20]

On the stage among the dignitaries during the ceremony that day was a man, Cecil Haynes, who had worked on the canal as an "office boy" for seventy-one years and whose father had arrived from Barbados in 1904 to help build the canal. Haynes was born in 1913 as the final touches were being put on the huge construction effort. In 1928 he had begun working for the canal commission. Eighty-six years old now, Haynes explained, "My father and others instilled in me that I should respect their efforts in the construction of the canal. It was built mostly with the blood, sweat, and tears of blacks." Although he would be standing among the VIPs during the transfer ceremony, Haynes declared, he was doing so as a living representative of the true VIPs, what he called the "Very Invisible People," those like his father and thousands of other West Indians who built the canal. "I am representing the forgotten workers. They say I'm famous. Famous for what? Did I go to the moon? No. This is for the men who built the canal, who did something international, with loss of life." Haynes described decades of living and working in the Zone among the Americans: "We had to work for them and keep them in the station they were accustomed to. We lived in the zone, too, but we were there to help them on the job and off the job. We were not equals." Thus Haynes had his own reasons for celebrating as the Panamanian flag was raised and the canal was officially transferred to Panama: "I am glad we Panamanians now have the canal, and we will run it as well or better than the Americans did."[21]

"The American Century ended today," a journalist wrote, and perhaps for that very reason no ambitious U.S. politician cared to be present at the event. President Clinton stayed away, as did every significant member of his administration; the ranking U.S. official attending the ceremony was the secretary of the Army. One U.S. citizen who bothered to attend was Howard Phillips of the Conservative Caucus. He flew in to lobby for the reestablishment of U.S. military bases in Panama, offering that in return the United States might help clean up some of the estimated 110,000 pieces of unexploded munitions it had left littering Panama's landscape. He demanded also that Panama cancel its port management contract with a Hong Kong–based company, arguing that its role would allow China to threaten the canal's security. This had been a common refrain in the United States in the weeks leading up to the official transfer ("Asia Moves In On the Big Ditch," one newspaper headline proclaimed). Another presidential campaign was under way in the United States, and the "loss" of the Panama Canal was very much on the minds of conservative activists. One of the rising Republican stars was the son of the president who had invaded Panama in 1989. Just days after the canal was transferred to Panama, the presidential candidate George W. Bush declared during a debate that he would "liberate the Panama Canal if I have to" in order to protect U.S. interests. If the American Century was over, no one had yet told candidate Bush.[22]

A FEW YEARS after the canal's transfer, when I was in the early stages of researching this book, an alumni association invited me to serve as lecturer on a cruise through the Panama Canal. I jumped at the opportunity to embark upon this "sweet gig," as a friend of mine put it. Along the way I learned some unexpected lessons about the canal and its place in American historical memory. My mother, Helen Greene—yes, the same Nebraska woman who had visited the White House in 1978— agreed to go with me.

Preparing my lecture as the ship made its way through the Pacific Ocean, heading toward the canal, I wondered if the audience would care to hear anything other than stories about Theodore Roosevelt, engineering challenges, conquest over nature, and the battle against the mosquito. Finally, I decided my talk should reflect the most interesting aspects of my research, and so I focused not on Roosevelt but on the international workforce that built the canal, particularly the West Indians. I covered topics like segregation, the silver and gold system, and the disadvantages West Indians faced—the housing without screens, the long hours of work standing in water. Audience members seemed engaged by my lecture— indeed, they appeared hungry to learn about the complexities of the construction project even if it meant disrupting their own Rooseveltian notions of the era. The questions audience members asked confirmed that they were more than ready to embrace the history of the canal in all its tragedy and unromantic difficulty. Two specific reactions from audience members, however, suggested to me the dual legacies of the canal construction.

The first came just after my lecture ended. I had answered many questions from the audience and decided somewhat impulsively to introduce my mother to the group. I told the crowd briefly about her 1978 visit to meet with President Carter, and then she stood up and waved to everyone. The audience seemed enchanted to have someone there who had played a part, however small, in the canal's historic transfer back to Panama. And Mom, flushed with the attention, was enjoying the moment. Someone shouted out a question to her: "What did *you* think about giving the canal back to Panama? Did you approve?" Nearly eighty years old now, Helen Greene still possessed the articulate charm of a young woman. She stood up straight and addressed the crowd: "No, I didn't approve. I didn't think it was right back then, and I still don't now. It was our canal and we should have kept it." The crowd responded to Helen's answer with terrific applause—one could imagine how Ronald Reagan felt when he unexpectedly tapped into a similar current of popular sentiment. I interjected some comments about what it meant to Panamanians to gain possession of the canal, how it symbolized independence, honor, and national identity to them, but my audience by now was energetically discussing all the reasons why returning it had been a betrayal of America's responsibilities in the world. I was an alien in someone else's conversation. Audience members eagerly shared with one another their sense of disappointment and frustration, and as they talked, one could discern palpable anger floating through that cruise ship auditorium. Americans no longer owned the canal, and a period of idealism and innocence in U.S. foreign policy had prematurely and unnecessarily ended.[23]

I ruminated over this turn of events the rest of that day while wandering through the cruise ship, which itself was a glorious spectacle of twenty-first-century decadence. I admired the display of food at the twenty-four-hour buffet, watched gamblers in the casino, and sat by the pool while couples around me chatted and sipped margaritas. Harry Franck, who had worked as a Zone policeman during the construction years, came to my mind. As he was leaving the isthmus, Franck had imagined the future: "Then blasé travelers lolling in their deck chairs will gaze about them and snort: 'Huh! Is that all we got for nine years' work and half a billion dollars?'" As the vegetation grew, he figured, the "scars of the steam-shovel" would be healed, and ships would slip along through "what will seem almost a natural channel."[24]

Franck's description of tourists in deck chairs was spot-on, but he underestimated the value people would place on the canal and the connections they would sense between it and their own identity as a people and as a nation.

The next day we woke up early. It was time to traverse the canal. Passengers, nearly nine hundred of them, hustled to the buffet for eggs, waffles, bacon, and blueberry blintzes. Filipino crew members maneuvered around the throngs of passengers, working to refill the buffet, stacking trays high with more papaya and pineapple. I grabbed a bit of breakfast, then raced up on deck as the ship crossed beneath the Bridge of the Americas and into the canal. It was a long but exhilarating day, watching the canal go by, gasping as the ship squeezed through the locks, entered Culebra Cut, and floated by Gold Hill, chatting with other passengers and answering their questions about the construction history. That evening we were exhausted after nearly eight hours of sightseeing. As the ship passed out of the final lock and into the Atlantic Ocean, and as darkness fell, I joined other passengers in the ship's restaurant, where European waiters served us an impeccable five-course meal.

Then some passengers brought a final legacy of the canal's construction to my attention. On board the *Crystal Harmony* there happened to be a large number of African American college alumni, many of them from Howard University. Several had heard my lecture, and I had gotten to know them. One, a New York businessman named Paul Ramsey, had seemed especially interested in the history of the construction and the role played by West Indians. He now approached my table and said, "Professor Greene, I want to tell you that the silver and gold system is still alive and well—and on this very ship!" I must have given him a curious look, because he continued, gesturing as he did so at the chic European waiter placing a plate of salmon on the table. He leaned over, speaking in a low voice, "Look around you! The dining staff is all European while the workers tending the buffet and cleaning our toilets are all Filipinos."[25]

Ramsey had done his homework. He had learned that the two groups received different contracts, with different working and living conditions, different amounts of leisure time, and different pay rates. He discovered that the *Crystal Harmony,* like most other cruise ships, was registered in small countries (like Panama) so its officers need not observe U.S. labor laws. He had talked with workers and learned how the two groups lived while on board the ship. He chatted with Filipinos who had not seen their children since their two-year job contract began and who worked twelve to sixteen hours a day, seven days a week. They described their lives in the cramped and windowless quarters on the lower decks, where passengers were forbidden. Ramsey met with European waiters and learned how much more tip money they earned than did Filipinos who cleaned staterooms or washed dishes. He also observed, and it turned out that this particularly frustrated Ramsey and many other passengers traveling with the Howard University Alumni Association, that there was not a single person of African descent working on the ship. Ramsey and his friends ultimately demanded a meeting with the cruise ship's hotel director to complain about this. As our ship continued on beyond the Panama Canal to visit several Caribbean islands, with populations predominantly of African origin, they believed it unacceptable that no black men or women were employed by the *Crystal Harmony*'s parent corporation. When they met with the hotel director, he seemed to empathize wholeheartedly with their concern. "We try to hire African people, we really do," he confessed, "but when we recruit our laborers in Europe, we just don't find any Africans able to do the job."

During the remaining days of the cruise, I talked more with Paul Ramsey and other alumni about the labor system on the cruise ship and how workers' lives today compare with those of one hundred years ago. We talked about the vast distances Filipinos had traveled in order to work on the cruise ship, and about the difference their pay would make to the lives of family members waiting at home. We compared them to the workers who had built the Panama Canal and wondered if, like West Indians nearly a century earlier, the Filipino maids and cooks found ways to resist workplace discipline. Over coffee we discussed the nature of the twenty-first-century world, when thousands of workers migrate from India or Indonesia to labor on cruise ships, and Mexicans and Central Americans travel to the United States for work—even as U.S. corporations outsource many jobs to other countries in search of cheaper labor. Across history people have moved around the world to improve their lives and seek better jobs. How and when did segregation prove an important means of control? When did governments' powers of deportation emerge as decisive? As we sought answers to such questions, our talks ranged widely from present-day conditions to hundreds of years ago, from Mexican workers fearing deportation in the twenty-first-century United States, to Japanese and Portuguese laborers working on nineteenth-century Hawaiian plantations.

In 1912, John Hall had praised the international working class on the Isthmus of Panama in his poem "The Canal Builders":

> *They're the brawn of every nation!*
> *Nature's best from every station: . . .*
> *For Empire they toil,*
> *In an alien soil.*
> *Unto the end their work will stand.*[26]

The labor Hall celebrated turned out to be invisible to many people, just as the efforts of workers today—on cruise ships, in private households, in retail stores—so often go unnoticed. Much has changed, of course, when we compare the *Crystal Harmony* with the canal that made its journey possible. While the canal workers toiled for empire, their labor also helped create the infrastructure for a global economy—and in the decades since then, the processes of globalization have transformed the world. Yet when we see today how race, ethnicity, gender, and class shape the international division of labor, we might think back to the construction of the Panama Canal and the ways it contributed to many present conditions. Strategies devised during the canal construction project have reached across the decades to the current day. We can see them in the increasing importance of transnational migrant labor and the rapid flow of capital around the globe, in the persistent notion that citizens deserve certain rights that are denied to aliens, and in the sentimental and idealistic ways Americans sometimes approach the exercise of U.S. power around the world. In a poem Bertolt Brecht had once queried, "Every ten years a great man / Who pays the piper?" Approaching the history and future of America's relationship to the world with Brecht's question in mind provides new perspectives. Who are the people toiling and digging today in the ditches of U.S. power abroad? They surely have stories to tell.

ACKNOWLEDGMENTS

ONE HOT DAY in 2002 at the archives of Panama's Ministry of Foreign Affairs, I sat leafing through correspondence memos that told me nothing and led me nowhere. I had traveled to Panama City to search for primary sources that would help me understand the experiences of working people on the Isthmus of Panama during the construction era. I pinned most of my hopes on the Ministry of Foreign Affairs, where documents might shed light on the relations between the United States and Panama—especially during the infamous riots that broke out in Panama City in 1912 and 1915. The director of the archives, Xiomara de Robletto, talked at length with me about the holdings of her institution. She pointed me to several potential areas to explore, but her news overall was discouraging. Her archives held a great deal of information on the construction era and relations with the United States, but she warned that it was poorly organized and that tracking down what I needed might be impossible. For the next several hours I examined records of correspondence sent out from the ministry. Finding nothing of use, I wondered how I would spend the rest of my weeks in Panama City. Then one of the archives' clerical employees walked up to my table and handed me a large volume filled with meticulously organized documents. Might this be useful to you? she asked. Indeed! The volume was filled with letters and testimony related to the riot of 1912. Moments later another employee brought me several more volumes. Soon the table on which I worked was covered with primary-source materials, and as I read, a completely new picture of the riots arose before my eyes. The volumes documented the riots from the perspective of Panamanian officials, U.S. military personnel, canal employees, and the ordinary workingmen and -women of Panama City. Together they told a remarkably different story from the one I had learned in the archives of the United States, and enabled me to see relations between Panama and the United States from multiple perspectives. It turned out that students from the University of Panama had organized the documents related to the riots years before. The director of the archives hadn't known they existed; only clerical workers knew where they were.

Telling the stories of the workingmen and -women who built the Panama Canal seemed, when I first began considering this project, as if it might be impossible because of the apparent absence of primary sources. Yet as I began digging around, I discovered a world more vast than anything I'd known, and this is due to the often hidden labors of students, staff members, archivists, curators, historians, and friends. Together they enriched this project in countless ways. Thanking them and making their many efforts and collaborations more visible is one of the sweetest labors this book has afforded.

The greatest single repository of information regarding the Panama Canal's construction is the National Archives in College Park, Maryland, where the records of the Isthmian Canal Commission are held. Navigating my way through the thousands of boxes in this collection was made much easier due to help from staff members, particularly the expert assistance of David Pfeiffer and Joseph Schwartz. For excellent detective work tracking down the judicial records of the Canal Zone, my thanks to Donald Ford and Martha Campos of the University of Colorado Law School Library, Marie-Louise Bernal and Luis Acosta at the Library of Congress, and Robert Ellis of the National Archives. I am also grateful to staff members and archivists at the National Archives of the United Kingdom in Kew, England; the archives of Wichita State University in Wichita, Kansas; the New York Public Library; the University of California at Berkeley's Bancroft Library; and the University of Colorado at Boulder. For their help identifying primary sources in Panama City I am indebted to staff members and archivists at the University of Panama; the Archives at the Ministry of Foreign Affairs; and the National Archives of Panama, especially its director, Porfirio De Cruz.

Fellowships granted by the American Council of Learned Societies and by the National Endowment for the Humanities made it possible for me to write this book and afforded me the luxury of focusing full-time on the challenges it posed. The University of Colorado at Boulder supported the writing of this book, while CU's Graduate Council on the Arts and Humanities made possible research trips to Panama City, London, and Washington, D.C., as well as a journey to present my work at a meeting of the Caribbean History Association in Havana, Cuba.

Far-flung audiences listened as I presented parts of this project, and I am very grateful to those who organized such opportunities and who read and provided suggestions on my work: Nelson Lichtenstein at the University of California at Santa Barbara, Richard Greenwald at the United States Merchant Marine Academy, Howard Brick at Washington University, F. Tobias Higbie at the Newberry Library in Chicago, and Glenda Gilmore at Yale University. For their thoughtful commentaries and criticism I thank Laura Briggs, Alice O'Connor, Christopher McAuley, Charles Bright, Nicola Miller, Christopher Abel, Thomas Bender, Christopher Boyer, Rick Halpern, Aihwa Ong, Susan Levine, Susan Hirsch, Eileen Boris, Joseph McCartin, Paul Taillon, Sidney Mintz, Amy Kaplan, Harvey Neptune, Paul Kramer, Martha Hodes, Carl Nightingale, Robert Zieger, Diana Paton, James Sanders, William Jones, Willard Gingerich, Anne McPherson, Robert Ferry, Shelton Stromquist, Lynn Hollen Lees, Alexandra Minna Stern, Shelley Streeby, Lok Siu, Steve Striffler, and Sherene Razak. Many others read sections of this manuscript or discussed key issues with me. My hearty gratitude to Marcel van der Linden, Jana Lipman, Donna Gabaccia, Jaquelyn Hall, David Sicilia, Mary Kay Vaughan, Leslie Rowland, Sonya Michel, Daryle Williams, Patricia Limerick, Robyn Muncy, Dylan Tucker, William Pettit, Erika Doss, Sarah Greene, Alex Greene, Constance Clark, Dennis Greene, Martha Gimenez, Mervat Hatem, Jocelyn Olcott, Amanda Greene, and Michael Kazin. For aiding me with specific problems my hat is off to Paul

Sutter, Abigail Markwyn, Mae Ngai, Nancy Cott, John French, Ronald Harpelle, Melvyn Dubofsky, Lee Chambers, Michael Honey, Shirley Gillespie, James Boylan, and Carol Byerly. My friend Bernard Coakley, a geophysicist at the University of Alaska, contributed geological history from the days when no canal was needed to connect the Atlantic and Pacific oceans. I owe a special debt to Heather Thompson, who suggested innovative ways of thinking about writing this book. Many friends kept their eyes out for references to the canal and then sent me wonderful gems of information. Thanks to Donna Stevens, Grace Palladino, Eric Arnesen, Susan Schulten, Geoffrey Klingsporn, Thomas Krainz, Mark Pittenger, John Enyeart, and Bryan Palmer for deepening my perspective on the work and workers of the canal. And I am very grateful to my fellow passengers on the *Crystal Harmony*'s cruise through the Panama Canal: Julia Mullican, William Strickland, Gale Strickland, Harold Freeman, and especially Paul Ramsey.

Finding sources on an international topic like the Panama Canal required advice from a wide range of scholars. I am grateful to Bieito Alonso for providing me with information on consulate records in Spain. The intellectual camaraderie of Caribbeanists and Latin Americanists has been indispensable and enriching. Michael Conniff, Velma Newton, Bonham Richardson, and Lara Putnam each had written books that provided intellectual foundations for this project, and each one kindly provided me with advice on archival sources. Bonham Richardson particularly shaped my understanding of Barbadian workers' experiences through conversations and by lending me his copy of a migrants' registry from Barbados as well as his original notes from interviews he conducted in the 1980s with canal workers. His generosity and trust in this project was marvelous. Lara Putnam's book on West Indians in Costa Rica inspired me to find the legal records of the Canal Zone and shaped the use I made of them; conversations with her about the riches I might find at the National Archives in Kew, England, convinced me to go there; finally, she provided essential advice about where to look for information. The Foreign Office Records at Kew became one of the crucial sources for this book. The friendship of Andrzej Krauze and

Vitek and Dalia Tracz enlivened my days in London. Thanks for befriending this footloose American.

The key in so many ways, of course, was Panama. Aims McGuinness, the historian whose study of nineteenth-century Panama opens a wide window into the country's history, first exhorted me to go to Panama and influenced me in innumerable other ways—for example, urging me to take a taxicab ride across the isthmus to Colón in order to get a sense of working-class life during the construction era. That trip changed the way I saw the canal. Once I got to Panama, Guillermo Castro discussed his country's history with me at great length and kindly took me on a rousing tour of Panama City, Balboa, and the working-class towns of what had once been the Canal Zone. Historian Alfredo Castillero Calvo shared with me his incomparable knowledge of Panama's history and provided tips and advice that shaped my research and helped me interpret my findings. Angeles Ramos Baquero, executive director and curator of the brilliant Museo del Canal Interoceánico de Panamá, illuminated my perspective on the canal in numerous ways. Alfredo and Angie did much to make my family feel at home in Panama City during our weeks there. Together they also located for me *the* most fabulous research assistant, Juana Campbell Cook, who shaped and expedited my work through Panama City's archives, but also shared with me her keen perspective on Panamanian politics and working-class culture.

At the University of Colorado I was privileged to have assistance from excellent research assistants: Cailyn Plantico, Nicki Gonzales, and Gerald Ronning. They provided me with key insights and suggestions as did graduate students John Enyeart, R. Todd Laugen, Carol Byerly, Renee Johnson, John Grider, and Jon Shelton. Colleagues at the University of Colorado lived with this project for many years and found novel ways of providing encouragement. I am especially grateful to Peter Boag, Lucy Chester, Brian DeLay, Francisco Barbosa, Martha Hanna, Susan Kent, Timothy Weston, Eric Love, Marcia Yonemoto, and Virginia Anderson. I have only begun teaching at the University of Maryland, but I am already dependent on Richard Price and Ira Berlin for their wise counsel.

David Montgomery first sparked my interest in the Panama Canal when he asked me to assess the connections between my dissertation research on the American Federation of Labor and politics, and the history of imperialism. Much as I disliked the question, it sure got me thinking. I thank David for his ability to inspire broad intellectual connections across time and space, for sharing my interest in working-class history and empire, and for providing advice on key sections of this book. Five other people encouraged this project and then read the entire draft for me. They provided astonishingly thoughtful suggestions that showed me how I could restructure the book and reshape and sharpen its major arguments. Fred Anderson, Leon Fink, Dana Frank, Aims McGuinness, and James Maffie: this book was terribly lucky to have you involved in such a central way. Fred, a fine craftsman of historical writing, analyzed my manuscript and showed me where improvements could be made. Leon's scholarship has long influenced me, and he brought a tough wisdom regarding working-class and transnational history to bear that illuminated several important themes. Dana and I originally trained together in U.S. working-class history and have shared a growing interest in transnational methodologies; she has been a font of politically sophisticated criticism for years. She provided advice to the very last moment, helping me think up possible titles as the manuscript went to press. (I *still* like "Manifest Ditch Diggers"!) Aims's contributions I have already noted, but I must add that among his many contributions he sent voluminous comments on each of my chapters and nurtured a fuller understanding of the Panama Canal's place in Latin American and Caribbean history. And James Maffie, whose work on Meso-American philosophy has been for me a model of pioneering interdisciplinary scholarship, read multiple drafts of this manuscript. As this project developed, he has been ready to listen, critique, and help me reenvision. As a philosopher he sees things differently, and his reactions to my writing were invaluable.

My agent, Geri Thoma, is better than anyone I know at making me laugh even as she gives me advice I don't want to hear. Thank you, Geri, for finding a place for this project and for providing serious help and frank reactions when I needed them. Glenda Gilmore commented insightfully on an early book proposal, helped me recast my plans for how it should be structured, and suggested it for Penguin's History of American Life series. At The Penguin Press, Scott Moyers provided his savvy perspective on the proposal and an early draft of the manuscript. I owe an especially big debt to Laura Stickney, my main editor at Penguin, who read several drafts of this book and recommended illuminatingly where I should cut and where I should expand. Her big ideas sometimes clashed with my big ideas, but she was as splendid at listening to my perspective as she was at explaining her own. Consequently we found a way to untangle each problem, and the result was a greatly improved book. Even then she kept reading, going over the draft again to look for phrases that could be clearer or smoother. Thanks for all your labor helping me build this book, Laura. I am grateful also to Ann Godoff, Bruce Giffords, Ingrid Sterner, and Darren Haggar at The Penguin Press for their work on this book.

Some thanks are more intimate, personal ones. I am deeply indebted to my family members for their enthusiasm and support over the years. I wish my father, Hank Greene, could have lived to read this book. I can see him now, walking the land of his Nebraska farm, talking about a hawk he spotted or a good book he read. Some of his ways with the world are my ways too, now. Helen Greene, my mother, has forever modeled for me how to be a strong and compassionate woman of the wider world. As readers of this book will have discovered, she kindled in me an early interest in the Panama Canal and then taught me a final, uneasy lesson about it toward the end. I salute her and thank her for her love, passion, and sustenance. James Maffie has been my big-hearted partner in every life adventure. I love his intellectual energy and enjoy laughing with him at the idiosyncrasies of life. Our daughter, Sophia Florence Meinsen Maffie, was named for a great-aunt I cherished, an audacious homesteader. Sophie never got to meet her ancestor who grew potatoes in the hardscrabble earth of Wyoming, yet she possesses all the bravery, imagination, and determined spark one might expect with such a namesake. Sophie and Jim are the homesteaders of my heart. They need not stake a claim; its landscape has belonged to them for a while now.

APPENDIX

TOTAL POPULATION DISTRIBUTED BY PLACE OF BIRTH, SEX, AND PERIOD OF FIRST RESIDENCE IN CANAL ZONE

Place of Birth	Aggregate	Prior to February 26, 1904			Since February 26, 1904*		
		TOTAL	MALE	FEMALE	TOTAL	MALE	FEMALE
Acklin I.	4	—	—	—	4	4	—
Algeria	4	—	—	—	4	4	—
Andros I.	6	—	—	—	6	6	—
Anguilla	1	—	—	—	1	1	—
Antigua	879	10	10	—	869	696	173
Argentina	11	—	—	—	11	10	1
Australia	11	2	2	—	9	7	2
Austria–Hungary	80	2	2	—	78	71	7
Azores	2	—	—	—	2	2	—
Barbados	9,699	67	62	5	9,632	7,893	1,739
Belgium	7	1	1	—	6	5	1
Bermuda	17	1	1	—	16	16	—
Bolivia	18	9	5	4	9	6	3
Brazil	1	—	—	—	1	—	1
British Guiana	454	5	4	1	449	355	94
British Honduras	18	1	1	—	17	13	4
Caicos	1	—	—	—	1	1	—
Canada & Newfoundland	190	—	—	—	190	114	76
Canal Zone	4,615	—	—	—	4,615	2,315	2,300
Canaries	12	—	—	—	12	12	—
Cat Island	9	—	—	—	9	9	—
Ceylon	2	—	—	—	2	2	—
Chili	30	2	2	—	28	24	4
China	447	164	155	9	283	277	6
Colombia	1,449	669	422	247	780	526	254
Costa Rica	113	17	12	5	96	62	34
Cuba	104	17	9	8	87	56	31
Curacao	14	6	6	—	8	8	—

* Treaty between the United States and the Republic of Panama was ratified on February 26, 1904.

Source: *Census of the Canal Zone,* February 1, 1912 (Mount Hope, CZ: ICC Press, 1912), pp. 29–31.

Place of Birth	Aggregate	Prior to February 26, 1904			Since February 26, 1904*		
		TOTAL	MALE	FEMALE	TOTAL	MALE	FEMALE
Denmark	52	—	—	—	52	44	8
Dominica	106	15	8	7	91	75	16
Dutch Guiana	3	—	—	—	3	3	—
Ecuador	54	6	3	3	48	39	9
Egypt	7	—	—	—	7	7	—
England	277	6	5	1	271	194	77
Exuma	1	—	—	—	1	1	—
Fortune I.	277	3	3	—	274	272	2
France	79	13	12	1	66	56	10
French Guiana	7	1	1	—	6	5	1
Germany	267	5	5	—	262	210	52
Gibraltar	1	—	—	—	1	1	—
Grand Cayman	23	—	—	—	23	19	4
Greece	1,285	7	7	—	1,278	1,273	5
Grenada	1,056	6	6	—	1,050	812	238
Guadeloupe	552	20	10	10	532	455	77
Guatemala	17	1	1	—	16	9	7
Haiti	79	5	5	—	74	70	4
Holland	25	—	—	—	25	17	8
Honduras	8	2	2	—	6	5	1
Inagua	5	—	—	—	5	5	—
India	390	1	1	—	389	388	1
Ireland	155	9	9	—	146	117	29
Italy	826	3	3	—	823	809	14
Jamaica	12,204	1,917	1,338	579	10,287	6,794	3,493
Japan	5	—	—	—	5	4	1
Kongo Free State	3	—	—	—	3	2	1
Liberia	1	—	—	—	1	1	—
Long Island	50	—	—	—	50	50	—
Madagascar	3	—	—	—	3	3	—
Malta	1	—	—	—	1	1	—
Martinique	1,840	107	78	29	1,733	1,437	296
Mexico	82	6	3	3	76	71	5
Montserrat	493	7	7	—	486	371	115
Nevis	136	—	—	—	136	124	12
New Providence	147	8	6	2	139	127	12
New Zealand	2	—	—	—	2	2	—
Nicaragua	74	9	5	4	65	48	17
Norway	73	1	1	—	72	59	13
Oruba	1	—	—	—	1	1	—
Panama	6,850	5,352	2,637	2,715	1,498	793	705
Paraguay	2	—	—	—	2	2	—
Peru	220	7	6	1	213	202	11
Portugal	115	—	—	—	115	112	3
Roumania	10	—	—	—	10	10	—
Russia and Finland	118	2	2	—	116	105	11
St. Andrews I.	6	—	—	—	6	6	—
St. Croix	1	—	—	—	1	1	—
St. Kitts	158	7	4	3	151	135	16

* Treaty between the United States and the Republic of Panama was ratified on February 26, 1904.

Source: *Census of the Canal Zone*, February 1, 1912 (Mount Hope, CZ: ICC Press, 1912), pp. 29–31.

Place of Birth	Aggregate	Prior to February 26, 1904			Since February 26, 1904*		
		TOTAL	MALE	FEMALE	TOTAL	MALE	FEMALE
St. Lucia	1,080	299	194	105	781	441	340
St. Martins (Dutch)	4	1	1	—	3	3	—
St. Martins (French)	5	—	—	—	5	5	—
St. Thomas	54	16	8	8	38	27	11
St. Vincent	469	9	9	—	460	412	48
Saba I.	1	—	—	—	1	1	—
Salvador	12	2	1	1	10	8	2
Santo Domingo	4	1	1	—	3	3	—
Scotland	87	3	3	—	84	68	16
Sierra Leone	7	5	5	—	2	1	1
South Africa	16	2	2	—	14	12	2
Spain	4,030	18	18	—	4,012	3,642	370
Sweden	110	2	2	—	108	86	22
Switzerland	28	1	1	—	27	23	4
Syria	23	6	6	—	17	9	8
Tobago	9	—	—	—	9	9	—
Tortola	5	—	—	—	5	4	1
Trinidad	601	16	11	5	585	438	147
Tunis	3	1	1	—	2	2	—
Turkey	29	1	1	—	28	28	—
Turks Island	34	—	—	—	34	33	1
Uruguay	1	—	—	—	1	1	—
Venezuela	56	10	5	5	46	39	7
Wales	16	2	2	—	14	9	5
Watlings Island	11	—	—	—	11	11	—
United States (including territorial possessions)							
Alabama	163	2	1	1	161	108	53
Arizona	5	—	—	—	5	3	2
Arkansas	46	—	—	—	46	35	11
California	131	6	4	2	125	100	25
Colorado	35	—	—	—	35	21	14
Connecticut	111	1	1	—	110	75	35
Delaware	24	—	—	—	24	18	6
District of Columbia	133	—	—	—	133	87	46
Florida	77	3	3	—	74	52	22
Georgia	181	—	—	—	181	136	45
Idaho	6	—	—	—	6	5	1
Illinois	453	1	1	—	452	324	128
Indiana	382	1	1	—	381	277	104
Iowa	238	2	2	—	236	156	80
Kansas	123	1	1	—	122	83	39
Kentucky	369	1	—	1	368	280	88
Louisiana	173	3	2	1	170	126	44
Maine	118	1	1	—	117	86	31
Maryland	259	1	1	—	258	168	90
Massachusetts	386	4	4	—	382	269	113
Michigan	303	—	—	—	303	218	85
Minnesota	88	1	1	—	87	66	21
Mississippi	159	1	1	—	158	109	49
Missouri	282	1	1	—	281	184	97
Montana	15	—	—	—	15	10	5

* Treaty between the United States and the Republic of Panama was ratified on February 26, 1904.
Source: *Census of the Canal Zone*, February 1, 1912 (Mount Hope, CZ: ICC Press, 1912), pp. 29–31.

Place of Birth	Aggregate	Prior to February 26, 1904			Since February 26, 1904*		
		TOTAL	MALE	FEMALE	TOTAL	MALE	FEMALE
Nebraska	77	1	1	—	76	52	24
Nevada	6	—	—	—	6	3	3
New Hampshire	47	1	1	—	46	33	13
New Jersey	305	3	1	2	302	205	97
New Mexico	9	—	—	—	9	6	3
New York	1,372	12	11	1	1,360	969	391
North Carolina	148	4	4	—	144	110	34
North Dakota	13	—	—	—	13	11	2
Ohio	692	—	—	—	692	460	232
Oklahoma	14	—	—	—	14	9	5
Oregon	19	1	—	1	18	12	6
Pennsylvania	1,375	2	2	—	1,373	958	415
Rhode Island	57	1	1	—	56	36	20
South Carolina	91	2	2	—	89	72	17
South Dakota	16	1	1	—	15	8	7
Tennessee	182	2	2	—	180	138	42
Texas	280	3	3	—	277	182	95
Utah	7	—	—	—	7	4	3
Vermont	56	—	—	—	56	39	17
Virginia	338	2	2	—	336	245	91
Washington	27	—	—	—	27	17	10
West Virginia	100	—	—	—	100	74	26
Wisconsin	118	—	—	—	118	86	32
Wyoming	3	—	—	—	3	1	2
Not specified	103	2	1	1	101	54	47
Alaska	1	—	—	—	1	—	1
Hawaii	5	—	—	—	5	4	1
Philippine Islands	6	—	—	—	6	5	1
Porto Rico	43	2	1	1	41	26	15
Grand Total	62,810	8,963	5,191	3,772	53,847	39,972	13,875

* Treaty between the United States and the Republic of Panama was ratified on February 26, 1904.
Source: *Census of the Canal Zone*, February 1, 1912 (Mount Hope, CZ: ICC Press, 1912), pp. 29–31.

NOTES

INTRODUCTION

1. On the number of people who attended the PPIE, see Robert W. Rydell, *All the World's a Fair: Visions of Empire at American International Expositions, 1876–1916* (Chicago: University of Chicago Press, 1984), p. 209. Over the course of the twentieth century, Nahl's poster was joined by many other depictions of the canal in prose, poetry, and visual imagery. One of the most memorable is at the American Museum of Natural History in New York City. Completed in 1935, William Andrew Mackay's grand mural illustrates the construction project. It highlights leadership provided by a handful of men (Theodore Roosevelt, the chief engineers John Stevens and George Goethals, and the sanitation officer William Gorgas) and provides depictions of the gigantic locks and the steam shovels from the Pacific and Atlantic sides joining together in a final act of excavation. Mackay's mural presented the canal as a victory made possible by American technology and the peerless leadership offered by individual men. See "The Murals in the Theodore Roosevelt Memorial Hall," American Museum of Natural History Library. For published depictions of the canal that mirror these themes see, for example, Donald Barr Chidsey, *Panama Passage* (Garden City, N.Y.: Doubleday, 1946); John Hall, *Panama Roughneck Ballads* (Panama and Canal Zone: Albert Lindo, Panama Railroad News Agency, 1912); Willis John Abbot, *Panama and the Canal in Picture and Prose* (New York: Syndicate, 1914).

2. David McCullough, "Knowing History and Knowing Who We Are," transcript of remarks delivered on Feb. 15, 2005, at Hillsdale College's National Leadership Seminar, published in *Imprimis: The National Speech Digest of Hillsdale College* 34, no. 4 (April 2005). The newsletter states it has a readership of more than 1.6 million people per month. I am grateful to Donna Stevens for sending me this newsletter. See also David McCullough, *The Path Between the Seas: The Creation of the Panama Canal, 1870–1914* (New York: Simon and Schuster, 1977), which received the National Book Award and the Francis Parkman Prize, among others.

3. George W. Goethals, *Government of the Canal Zone* (Princeton, N.J.: Princeton University Press, 1915), pp. 2–3; see also Goethals to his wife, March 22, 1907, George Washington Goethals Papers, container 3, Family Correspondence, Library of Congress.

4. See Bertolt Brecht's poem "A Worker Reads History," on p. xiii before this introduction. The poem can also be found in Bertolt Brecht, *Selected Poems,* trans. H. R. Hays (New York: Harcourt Brace Jovanovich, 1947), p. 109.

5. Hall, *Panama Roughneck Ballads;* see especially "The Canal Builders," pp. 34–38, and "The Price of Empire," pp. 65–66.

6. Kristin Hoganson, *Fighting for American Manhood: How Gender Politics Provoked the Spanish-American and Philippine-American Wars* (New Haven, Conn.: Yale University Press, 1998); David Trask, *The War with Spain in 1898* (New York: Macmillan, 1981); Ivan Musicant, *Empire by Default* (New York: Henry Holt, 1998); Walter LaFeber, *The Cambridge History of American Foreign Relations*, vol. 2: *The American Search for Opportunity, 1865–1913* (New York: Cambridge University Press, 1993); Stuart Creighton Miller, *"Benevolent Assimilation": The American Conquest of the Philippines, 1899–1903* (New

Haven, Conn.: Yale University Press, 1982); Louis Pérez, *The War of 1898: The United States and Cuba in History and Historiography* (Chapel Hill: University of North Carolina Press, 1998).

7. Alfredo Castillero Calvo, ed., *Historia general de Panamá* (Panama City: Comité Nacional del Centenario de la República, 2004); John Major, *Prize Possession: The United States and the Panama Canal, 1903–1979* (New York: Cambridge University Press, 1993).

8. William Appleman Williams, *The Contours of American History* (Cleveland: World, 1961), p. 416; "A National Disgrace," *New York Times*, Nov. 6, 1903, p. 8.

9. Shelton Stromquist, *Reinventing "The People": The Progressive Movement, the Class Problem, and the Origins of Modern Liberalism* (Urbana: University of Illinois Press, 2006); Michael McGerr, *A Fierce Discontent: The Rise and Fall of the Progressive Movement in America, 1870–1920* (New York: Oxford University Press, 2003); Maureen A. Flanagan, *America Reformed: Progressives and Progressivisms, 1890–1920* (New York: Oxford University Press, 2007); David M. Kennedy, *Over Here: The First World War and American Society* (New York: Oxford University Press, 1980).

10. Amy Kaplan, "'Left Alone with America': The Absence of Empire in the Study of American Culture," in *Cultures of United States Imperialism,* ed. Amy Kaplan and Donald E. Pease (Durham, N.C.: Duke University Press, 1993); William Appleman Williams, "The Frontier Thesis and American Foreign Policy," *Pacific Historical Review* 24 (Nov. 1955), pp. 379–95; Paul A. Kramer, "Empires, Exceptions, and Anglo-Saxons: Race and Rule Between the British and U.S. Empires, 1880–1910," in *The American Colonial State in the Philippines: Global Perspectives,* ed. Julian Go and Anne L. Foster (Durham, N.C.: Duke University Press, 2003), pp. 43–91. For important examples of the "new imperial" history, see, among others, Paul A. Kramer, *The Blood of Government: Race, Empire, the United States, and the Philippines* (Chapel Hill: University of North Carolina Press, 2006); Mary Renda, *Taking Haiti: Military Occupation and the Culture of U.S. Imperialism, 1915–1940* (Chapel Hill: University of North Carolina Press, 2001); Eric Love, *Race over Empire: Racism and U.S. Imperialism, 1865–1900* (Chapel Hill: University of North Carolina Press, 2004); Eileen Findlay, *Imposing Decency: The Politics of Sexuality and Race in Puerto Rico, 1870–1920* (Durham, N.C.: Duke University Press, 1999); Gilbert M. Joseph, Catherine C. LeGrand, and Ricardo D. Salvatore, eds., *Close Encounters of Empire: Writing the History of U.S.–Latin American Relations* (Durham, N.C.: Duke University Press, 1998); Go and Foster, *American Colonial State in the Philippines;* Ann Laura Stoler, ed., *Haunted by Empire: Geographies of Intimacy in North American History* (Durham, N.C.: Duke University Press, 2006); Amy Kaplan, *The Anarchy of Empire in the Making of U.S. Culture* (Cambridge, Mass.: Harvard University Press, 2005); Vicente L. Rafael, *White Love and Other Events in Filipino History* (Durham, N.C.: Duke University Press, 2000); Aims McGuinness, *Path of Empire: Panama and the California Gold Rush* (Ithaca, N.Y.: Cornell University Press, 2008); Harvey Neptune, "White Lies: Race and Sexuality in Occupied Trinidad," *Journal of Colonialism and Colonial History* 2 (Spring 2001); Jana Lipman, *Guantánamo: A Working-Class History Between Empire and Revolution* (Berkeley: University of California Press, 2008).

11. Walter LaFeber, *The New Empire: An Interpretation of American Expansion, 1860–1898* (Ithaca, N.Y.: Cornell University Press, 1963), p. 6; see also LaFeber's new preface to the 1998 edition of this book, also published by Cornell University Press. Other works that have shaped my approach to these questions include, in addition to those cited above, William Appleman Williams, *Empire as a Way of Life: An Essay on the Causes and Character of America's Present Predicament, Along with a Few Thoughts About an Alternative* (New York: Oxford University Press, 1980); William Appleman Williams, *The Tragedy of American Diplomacy* (New York: Dell, 1972); Emily Rosenberg, *Spreading the American Dream: American Economic and Cultural Expansion 1890–1945* (New York: Hill and Wang, 1982); Emily Rosenberg, *Financial Missionaries to the World: The Politics and Culture of Dollar Diplomacy, 1900–1930* (Cambridge, Mass.: Harvard University Press, 1999).

12. Isabel Hofmeyr's comment can be found in "*AHR* Conversation: On Transnational History," *American Historical Review* 111, no. 5 (Dec. 2006), p. 1444; other works that discuss or employ transnational methods, besides those cited above in note 10, include Thomas Bender, *A Nation Among Nations: America's Place in World History* (New York: Hill and Wang, 2006); Kristin Hoganson, *Consumers' Imperium: The Global Production of American Domesticity, 1865–1920* (Chapel Hill: University of North Carolina Press, 2007); David Thelen, "The Nation and Beyond: Transnational Perspectives on United States History," *Journal of American History* 86 (Dec. 1999), pp.

965–75; Eric Rauchway, *Blessed Among Nations: How the World Made America* (New York: Hill and Wang, 2007).

13. Key works on Panama and the construction of the canal that have influenced this project include Castillero Calvo, *Historia general de Panamá,* especially the following essays: in vol. 3, bk. 2, Carlos Bolívar Pedreschi, "Negociaciones del Canal con los Estados Unidos: 1904–1967," pp. 25–41; and in vol. 3, bk. 1, Gerardo Maloney, "Significado de la presencia y contribución del afro antillano a la nación panameña," pp. 152–71, and Marco A. Gandásegui, "Los movimientos sociales en Panamá: primera mitad del siglo XX," pp. 185–208; Gerstle Mack, *The Land Divided: A History of the Panama Canal and Other Isthmian Canal Projects* (New York: Knopf, 1944); Marco Gandásegui, Alejandro Saavedra, Andrés Achong, and Iván Quintero, *Las luchas obreras en Panamá, 1850–1978,* 2nd ed. (Panama City: CELA, 1990); Alfredo Castillero Calvo, *Conquista, evangelización, y resistencia: Triunfo o fracaso de la política indigenista* (Panama: Mariano Arosemena: Instituto Nacional de Cultura, 1995); Major, *Prize Possession;* McCullough, *Path Between the Seas;* Michael L. Conniff, *Black Labor on a White Canal: Panama, 1904–1981* (Pittsburgh: University of Pittsburgh Press, 1985); J. Michael Hogan, *The Panama Canal in American Politics: Domestic Advocacy and the Evolution of Policy* (Carbondale: Southern Illinois University Press, 1986); Velma Newton, *The Silver Men: West Indian Labour Migration to Panama, 1850–1914* (Mona, Jamaica: University of the West Indies, 1984); Bonham Richardson, *Panama Money in Barbados, 1900–1920* (Knoxville: University of Tennessee Press, 1985); Walter LaFeber, *The Panama Canal: The Crisis in Historical Perspective* (New York: Oxford University Press, 1989).

14. On these themes see, among others, Bender, *Nation Among Nations,* ch. 4. The so-called Spanish-American War is now often referred to as the Spanish-American-Cuban-Filipino War. As even this cumbersome title does not fully grasp the spatial reach of the conflict (Puerto Rico, Guam, and so on), I refer to it simply as the War of 1898.

15. Useful sources on the Open Door Notes include LaFeber, *Cambridge History of American Foreign Relations,* vol. 2, pp. 169–76; Williams, *Tragedy of American Diplomacy,* p. 45; Bender, *Nation Among Nations,* pp. 182–245; Daniel B. Schirmer, *Republic or Empire: American Resistance to the Philippine War* (Cambridge, Mass.: Schenkman, 1972).

PROLOGUE: PRESIDENT ROOSEVELT'S STEAM SHOVEL

1. Roosevelt declared to William Howard Taft, "I have always felt, that the one thing for which I deserved most credit in my entire Administration was my action in seizing the psychological moment to get complete control of Panama." Quoted in John Major, *Prize Possession: The United States and the Panama Canal, 1903–1979* (New York: Cambridge University Press, 1993), p. 63. In his autobiography Roosevelt declares, "By far the most important action I took in foreign affairs during the time I was President related to the Panama Canal." Theodore Roosevelt, *An Autobiography* (New York: Charles Scribner's Sons, 1924), p. 512. Roosevelt's description of his journey to Panama comes from Joseph Bucklin Bishop, ed., *Theodore Roosevelt's Letters to His Children* (New York: Charles Scribner's Sons, 1919), pp. 174, 176–77. See also Kathleen Dalton, *Theodore Roosevelt: A Strenuous Life* (New York: Knopf, 2002).

2. Bishop, *Theodore Roosevelt's Letters to His Children,* p. 174.

3. Ibid., pp. 180–81.

4. Ibid., p. 183.

5. For a fine description of a Bucyrus steam shovel at work, see Willis John Abbot, *Panama and the Canal in Picture and Prose* (New York: Syndicate, 1914), p. 212; see also David McCullough, *The Path Between the Seas: The Creation of the Panama Canal, 1870–1914* (New York: Simon and Schuster, 1977), pp. 496–97; and J. Michael Hogan, *The Panama Canal in American Politics: Domestic Advocacy and the Evolution of Policy* (Carbondale: Southern Illinois University Press, 1986). My interpretation of Roosevelt's role in making the canal a grand symbol of American power predates my reading of Hogan's book, but his treatment of the matter is similar to mine, and, indeed, it is very eloquent on the subject. See esp. chs. 1 and 2.

6. Gail Bederman, *Manliness and Civilization: A Cultural History of Gender and Race in the United States, 1880–1917* (Chicago: University of Chicago Press, 1995), pp. 170–215; Anthony Rotundo, *American Manhood: Transformations in Masculinity from the Revolution to the Modern Era* (New York: Basic Books, 1993); Dana D. Nelson, *National Manhood: Capitalist Citizenship and the Imagined Fraternity*

of White Men (Durham, N.C.: Duke University Press, 1998); Gary Gerstle, "Theodore Roosevelt and the Divided Character of American Nationalism," *Journal of American History* 86, no. 3 (Dec. 1999), pp. 1280–1307.

7. In the 1890s, Roosevelt served on the U.S. Civil Service Commission and the New York City Police Commission and as assistant secretary of the Navy. Dalton, *Theodore Roosevelt;* Julius W. Pratt, *Expansionists of 1898: The Acquisition of Hawaii and the Spanish Islands* (Chicago: Quadrangle Books, 1936); Eric Love, *Race over Empire: Racism and U.S. Imperialism, 1865–1900* (Chapel Hill: University of North Carolina Press, 2004).

8. On the anti-imperialists, see Robert Beisner, *Twelve Against Empire: The Anti-imperialists, 1898–1900* (New York: McGraw-Hill, 1968); Frank Ninkovich, *The United States and Imperialism* (Oxford: Blackwell, 2001).

9. Theodore Roosevelt, "Washington's Forgotten Maxim," address as assistant secretary of the Navy before the Naval War College, June 1897, in *The Works of Theodore Roosevelt* (New York: P. F. Collier, 1897), vol. 13, p. 284.

10. Speech as governor of New York to the Lincoln Club, Feb. 1899; excerpted in Mario DiNunzio, *Theodore Roosevelt: An American Mind* (New York: St. Martin's, 1994), p. 182.

11. This information and the quotation from John Hay are from Major, *Prize Possession*, pp. 28–31.

12. Roosevelt's quotation is cited in Dalton, *Theodore Roosevelt*, p. 254.

13. Major, *Prize Possession*, pp. 34–42; Dalton, *Theodore Roosevelt*, pp. 254–57.

14. Major, *Prize Possession*, p. 49.

15. Gerstle Mack, *The Land Divided: A History of the Panama Canal and Other Isthmian Canal Projects* (New York: Knopf, 1944), pp. 471–72.

16. The Hay–Bunau-Varilla Treaty of Nov. 18, 1903, at the Avalon Project at Yale Law School, *Convention for the Construction of a Ship Canal*, at http://www.yale.edu/lawweb/avalon/diplomacy/panama/pan001.htm (accessed Nov. 2, 2005). See also Major, *Prize Possession*, pp. 38–63.

17. Rich sources on the history of Panama include Alfredo Castillero Calvo, ed., *Historia general de Panamá* (Panama City: Comité Nacional del Centenario de la República, 2004); Alfredo Castillero Calvo, *La ruta interoceánica y el Canal de Panamá* (Panama City: Colegio Panameño de Historiadores and Instituto del Canal de Panamá y Estudios Internacionales, 1999); Celestino Andrés Araúz, *Panamá y sus relaciones internacionales* (Panama City: Universitaria, 1994); Aims McGuinness, *Path of Empire: Panama and the California Gold Rush* (Ithaca, N.Y.: Cornell University Press, 2008); Michael L. Conniff, *Panama and the United States: The Forced Alliance* (Athens: University of Georgia Press, 2001); Alfredo Figueroa Navarro, *Dominio y sociedad en el Panamá colombiano, 1821–1903* (Panama City: Universitaria, 1982); Marco Gandásegui, Alejandro Saavedra, Andrés Achong, and Iván Quintero, *Las luchas obreras en Panamá, 1850–1978*, 2nd ed. (Panama City: CELA, 1990); Luis Navas, *El movimiento obrero en Panamá, 1880–1914* (San José, Costa Rica: Universitaria Centroamericana, 1979); Steve C. Ropp, *Panamanian Politics: From Guarded Nation to National Guard* (New York: Praeger, 1982); Thomas Pearcy, *We Answer Only to God: Politics and the Military in Panama, 1903–1947* (Albuquerque: University of New Mexico Press, 1998); Jorge Turner, *Raíz, historia, y perspectivas del movimiento obrero panameño* (Mexico City: Signos, 1982); Peter A. Szok, *"La Última Gaviota": Liberalism and Nostalgia in Early Twentieth-Century Panamá* (Westport, Conn.: Greenwood, 2001).

18. Szok, *"La Última Gaviota,"* pp. 5, 8, 22–23.

19. Pearcy, *We Answer Only to God*, pp. 39–42; Major, *Prize Possession*, pp. 117–19.

20. Moorfield Storey, *The Recognition of Panama: Address Delivered at Massachusetts Reform Club, Dec. 5, 1903* (Boston: George H. Ellis, 1904), p. 19. The prominent Knights of Labor organizer George McNeill saw American imperialism as linked to, indeed generated by, the industrial system of the United States. Soon after Roosevelt enabled Panama to win independence from Colombia, McNeill declared at an anti-imperialist meeting, "My duty is, if possible, to stir you with some sense of the fact that we are not a free republican government—that we are monarchical, that we are imperialistic, despotic, and that you need not look upon this phenomenon in the Philippine Islands with astonishment—upon that war with Spain, upon the outrages perpetrated in Panama—but only see in these things the development of an industrial system founded in injustice and despotism." George E. McNeill, "Remarks at the Annual Meeting of the New England Anti-Imperialist League," *Report of the Fifth Annual Meeting of the New England Anti-Imperialist League* (Boston: New England Anti-Imperialist League, 1903).

21. Major, *Prize Possession*, esp. pp. 60, 61, 62. While the criticism continued, some expressed praise for Roosevelt. His supporters included Jacob Riis, who declared, "I am not a jingo. But when some things happen I just have to get up and cheer." Roosevelt also found unwelcome support from the Daughters of the Confederacy, who applauded the U.S. recognition of Panamanian independence as vindicating the cause of the South. Jacob Riis, *Theodore Roosevelt, the Citizen* (New York: Outlook, 1904), p. 385. Writing twenty years later, Roosevelt still felt compelled to defend and justify at great length his actions in seizing control of the isthmus. See Roosevelt, *Autobiography*, pp. 512–27. On Roosevelt's civilizing mission, see also Ninkovich, *United States and Imperialism*, pp. 104–18; Frank Ninkovich, "Theodore Roosevelt: Civilization as Ideology," *Diplomatic History* 10, no. 3 (1986), pp. 221–45; Bederman, *Manliness and Civilization*, pp. 170–215.

22. Paul Taillon, "The American Federation of Labor and Expansionism, 1890–1910" (undergraduate honor's thesis, Northwestern University, 1985), pp. 47–51.

23. Daniel B. Schirmer, *Republic or Empire: American Resistance to the Philippine War* (Cambridge, Mass.: Schenkman, 1972), ch. 17; James's quotation is in a letter to E. W. Ordway, Dec. 6, 1903, E. W. Ordway Papers, New York Public Library.

24. Mack, *Land Divided*, pp. 377–404; McCullough, *Path Between the Seas*, pp. 222–35.

25. John Wallace, "The Republic of Panama and the Canal Zone," in *America Across the Seas: Our Colonial Empire* (New York: C. S. Hammond, 1909), p. 72; William D. Boyce, *United States Colonies and Dependencies: The Travels and Investigations of a Chicago Publisher* (Chicago: Rand McNally, 1914), p. 493.

26. Kidd, *The Control of the Tropics*, quoted in Kristin Hoganson, *Fighting for American Manhood: How Gender Politics Provoked the Spanish-American and Philippine-American Wars* (New Haven, Conn.: Yale University Press, 1998), p. 181; Benjamin Kidd, "The Control of the Tropics by the U.S.," *Atlantic Monthly*, Dec. 1898, pp. 721–22. On concerns about the tropics, see also Paul S. Sutter, "Nature's Agents or Agents of Empire? Entomological Workers and Environmental Change During the Construction of the Panama Canal," *Isis* 98, no. 4 (Dec. 2007), pp. 724–54; Nancy Stepan, *Picturing Tropical Nature* (Ithaca, N.Y.: Cornell University Press, 2001); David Arnold, *The Problem of Nature: Environment, Culture, and European Expansion* (Oxford: Blackwell, 1996); David Arnold, *The Tropics and the Traveling Gaze: India, Landscape, and Science, 1800–1856* (Seattle: University of Washington Press, 2006).

27. James Morton Callahan, *An Introduction to American Expansion Policy* (Morgantown: West Virginia University, 1908), p. 36. The many books published on empire in this period make for fascinating reading. See, for example, H. Addington Bruce, *The Romance of American Expansion* (New York: Moffat, Yard, 1909); Archibald Cary Coolidge, *The United States as a World Power* (New York: Macmillan, 1908); Jerome Bruce Crabtree, *The Passing of Spain and the Ascendancy of America* (Springfield: King Richardson, 1898); Hubert Howe Bancroft, *The New Pacific* (New York: Bancroft, 1900).

28. Author's conversation with Dr. Bernard Coakley, professor of geophysics, University of Alaska at Fairbanks (my thanks to Dr. Coakley); H. G. Cornthwaite, "Panama Rainfall," *Monthly Weather Review*, May 1919, pp. 298–302; Froude is quoted in Joseph Bucklin Bishop, *The Panama Gateway* (New York: Charles Scribner's Sons, 1913), p. 90.

29. Marie D. Gorgas and Burton J. Hendrick, *William Crawford Gorgas: His Life and Work* (Garden City, N.Y.: Doubleday, Page, 1924), pp. 140–41.

30. Bonham Richardson, *Panama Money in Barbados, 1900–1920* (Knoxville: University of Tennessee Press, 1985); Bonham Richardson, notes from interviews conducted with Douglas Gay, Niles Corner, Barbados, June 9, 1982. Interviews conducted by Richardson provided him with a crucial source for his pathbreaking book. I am grateful to Dr. Richardson for generously sending me a copy of his notes. On West Indians and Panama, see also Lancelot S. Lewis, *The West Indian in Panama: Black Labor in Panama, 1850–1914* (Washington, D.C.: University Press of America, 1980); Henry De Lisser's account of his travels, *Jamaicans in Colón and the Canal Zone* (Kingston, 1906), p. 13; Velma Newton, *The Silver Men: West Indian Labour Migration to Panama, 1850–1914* (Mona, Jamaica: University of the West Indies, 1984); Michael L. Conniff, *Black Labor on a White Canal: Panama, 1904–1981* (Pittsburgh: University of Pittsburgh Press, 1985). For a fine discussion of the Panama Canal's role in shaping the West Indian diaspora more generally, see also Lara Putnam, *The Company They Kept: Migrants and the Politics of Gender in Caribbean Costa Rica, 1870–1960* (Chapel Hill: University of North Carolina Press, 2002).

31. Richardson, *Panama Money in Barbados*, p. 105.

32. Dr. Carlos E. Russell, *An Old Woman Remembers: The Recollected History of West Indians in Panama, 1855–1955* (Brooklyn: Caribbean Diaspora Press, 1995), pp. 3–4.

33. Bonham Richardson, interview with Howard Skinner, March 23, 1982.

34. Richardson, *Panama Money in Barbados*, p. 106.

35. Mrs. Christine Alberta "Bea" Waldron, interview with Bonham Richardson, March 24, 1982. This is an unusual reaction. More often West Indians felt distant from, even disdainful of, Panamanians, proud of their English linguistic traditions, and reluctant to learn Spanish. See, for example, George Lamming's novel *In the Castle of My Skin* (New York: McGraw-Hill, 1954). On migration from various Caribbean islands, see Newton, *Silver Men*.

36. Winifred James, *The Mulberry Tree* (London: Chapman and Hall, 1913), pp. 190–91. The diverse geographical origins of the people of the Caribbean in conjunction with the history of imperialism across the region generates a problem of terminology for historians. Although most often Afro-Caribbeans referred to themselves as coming from their specific island, they might also, as Lara Putnam has noted, refer to themselves as from a specific parish, town, estate, or even the British or French empire. I refer to specific islands of origin when appropriate throughout this book, but often it is necessary to refer to all Caribbeans as a single category. When doing so, I use the term West Indian, which peoples from the Caribbean sometimes used to refer to themselves. By this term I mean people of African descent from across the British, French, or Spanish Caribbean. Occasionally I refer to them also as Caribbeans or Afro-Caribbeans. On issues of terminology see Putnam, *The Company They Kept*, pp. 15–17; and Michel-Rolph Trouillot, *Silencing the Past: Power and the Production of History* (Boston: Beacon Press, 1995), esp. pp. 113–16.

37. On Indians and Chinese in the region, see Roger Sanjek, ed., *Caribbean Asians: Chinese, Indian, and Japanese Experiences in Trinidad and the Dominican Republic* (Flushing, N.Y.: Asian/American Center at Queens College, CUNY, 1990); Eustorgio Chong Ruiz, *Los chinos en la sociedad panameña* (Panama: Instituto Nacional de Cultura, 1993); Frank Birbalsingh, ed., *Indenture and Exile: The Indo-Caribbean Experience* (Toronto: TSAR, 1989); Luz Maria Martínez Montiel, *Asiatic Migrations in Latin America* (Mexico City: Colegio de México, 1981); Asiatic Exclusion League of San Francisco, *Against Chinese Slavery on the Panama Canal* (San Francisco, 1906); Lok C. D. Siu, *Memories of a Future Home: Diasporic Citizenship of Chinese in Panama* (Stanford, Calif.: Stanford University Press, 2005); Patricia Alma Lee Chung de Lee, *Los Lee Chong: Cinco generaciones de Panamá* (Panama City: Lee Chung de Lee, 1999).

38. The experiences of Ted Sherrard are related in William D. Pennington, "Life and Labor on the Panama Canal: An Oklahoman's Personal Account," *Chronicles of Oklahoma* 56, no. 3 (Fall 1978), pp. 265–73.

39. Personnel records for Henry Williams, Isthmian Canal Commission Records, box 575, National Archives, College Park, Md.; information on lynchings in Texas can be found in *Thirty Years of Lynching in the United States, 1889–1918* (New York: National Association for the Advancement of Colored People, 1919), pp. 97–98.

40. Elizabeth Kittredge Parker, *Panama Canal Bride: A Story of Construction Days* (New York: Exposition, 1955), pp. 9–10.

41. Ibid., pp. 9–10, 13–14, 18.

42. William D. Donadio, *The Thorns of the Rose: Memoirs of a Tailor of Panama* (Colón, Republic of Panama: Dovesa S.A., 1999), p. 112.

43. John Foster Carr, "The Panama Canal: History—Conditions—Prospects," *Outlook*, April 28, 1906, p. 953.

CHAPTER ONE: A MODERN STATE IN THE TROPICS

1. John Foster Carr, "The Panama Canal: History—Conditions—Prospects," *Outlook*, April 28, 1906, p. 963; and John Foster Carr, "Building a State," *Outlook*, June 23, 1906, p. 440. Carr went on to argue, rather unconvincingly, that government at the municipal level of the Zone was less European and more in the style of American democracy. In the latter article he similarly wrote: "We are new at the imperial business of creating republics and dependencies, but our success here has been so great . . . the most striking and significant work we are doing on the Isthmus is not

the completion of a vast and comprehensive scheme for canal digging, but the creation of a state" (p. 436).

2. Marie D. Gorgas and Burton J. Hendrick, *William Crawford Gorgas: His Life and Work* (Garden City, N.Y.: Doubleday, Page, 1924), p. 144.

3. Ibid., pp. 152–55.

4. Among the other passengers on this early ship to Panama were the chief engineer John Wallace, William J. Karner, and four nurses. See William J. Karner, *More Recollections* (Boston: Thomas Todd, 1921), p. 9.

5. Paul Sutter has noted that much of the disease was in fact caused by human impact on the tropics. See Paul S. Sutter, "Nature's Agents or Agents of Empire? Entomological Workers and Environmental Change During the Construction of the Panama Canal," *Isis* 98, no. 4 (Dec. 2007), pp. 724–54; see also David Arnold, *The Problem of Nature: Environment, Culture, and European Expansion* (Oxford: Blackwell, 1996); David Arnold, *The Tropics and the Traveling Gaze: India, Landscape, and Science, 1800–1856* (Seattle: University of Washington Press, 2006); Nancy Stepan, *Picturing Tropical Nature* (Ithaca, N.Y.: Cornell University Press, 2001); Stephen Frenkel, "Jungle Stories: North American Representations of Panama," *Geographical Review* 86, no. 3 (2002), pp. 317–33; Stephen Frenkel, "Geographical Representations of the 'Other': The Landscape of the Panama Canal Zone," *Journal of Historical Geography* 28, no. 1 (2002), pp. 85–99.

6. William Gorgas, "The Conquest of the Tropics for the White Race: President's Address at the Sixtieth Annual Session of the American Medical Association, June 9, 1909," *Journal of the American Medical Association* 52, no. 25 (1909), pp. 1967–69.

7. "Report of the Head of the Department of Municipal Engineering," in *Annual Report of the Isthmian Canal Commission for the Fiscal Year Ending June 30, 1907* (Washington, D.C.: GPO, 1907), app. C, p. 60. For more information, see the annual reports of the ICC and W. C. Gorgas, *Report of the Dept. of Health of the Isthmian Canal Commission for the Month of January 1905* (Washington, D.C.: GPO, 1905).

8. Willis John Abbot, *Panama and the Canal in Picture and Prose* (New York: Syndicate, 1914), pp. 145–49; Gerstle Mack, *The Land Divided: A History of the Panama Canal and Other Isthmian Canal Projects* (New York: Knopf, 1944), pp. 486–95; Wallace to Sir, Feb. 9, 1905, Isthmian Canal Commission Records, RG 185, 2-P-51, box 49, National Archives, College Park, Md. (hereafter cited as ICC Records).

9. David McCullough, *The Path Between the Seas: The Creation of the Panama Canal, 1870–1914* (New York: Simon and Schuster, 1977), p. 452; John Foster Carr, "The Panama Canal—the Commission's White Workers," *Outlook*, May 5, 1906, p. 24.

10. Carr, "Panama Canal—the Commission's White Workers," p. 24.

11. Stevens to Theodore Shonts (chairman, ICC), Dec. 14, 1905, in ICC Records, 2-E-1, Labor Recruiting.

12. For more on the "Great Scare" of 1904 and 1905, see Edwin E. Slosson and Gardner Richardson, "Life on the Canal Zone," *Independent*, March 22, 1906, p. 653; John Foster Carr, "The Panama Canal: The Work of the Sanitary Force," *Outlook*, May 12, 1906, pp. 69–72; "Men in Action," *World's Work* 21 (Dec. 1910), pp. 13809–10.

13. McCullough, *Path Between the Seas*, pp. 459–67; Mack, *Land Divided*, pp. 493–95; C. H. Forbes-Lindsay, *Panama and the Canal To-Day* (Boston: L. C. Page, 1910), pp. 103–20; Harry A. Franck, *Zone Policeman 88: A Close Range Study of the Panama Canal and Its Workers* (New York: Century, 1913), pp. 98–99.

14. Franck, *Zone Policeman 88*, pp. 112, 117; Charlotte Cameron, *A Woman's Winter in South America* (London: Stanley Paul, 1911), pp. 215–16; Joseph Bucklin Bishop and Farnham Bishop, *Goethals, Genius of the Panama Canal: A Biography* (New York: Harper and Brothers, 1930), pp. 208, 211.

15. Winifred James, *The Mulberry Tree* (London: Chapman and Hall, 1913), pp. 235–36; Michael Delevante, *Panama Pictures: Nature and Life in the Land of the Great Canal* (New York: Alden Brothers, 1907), p. 63; Arthur Bullard, *Panama: The Canal, the Country, and the People* (New York: Macmillan, 1911), pp. 47–48; Franck, *Zone Policeman 88*, pp. 119–20; H. H. Rousseau, *The Isthmian Canal* (Washington, D.C.: GPO, 1910), p. 29. According to the official site of the Panama Canal Authority of the Republic of Panama, Culebra Cut was 8.75 miles long, and the lowest point in the mountains above the cut was 333.5 feet above sea level. See http://www.pancanal.com/eng.history/index.html (accessed July 28, 2007).

16. Franck, *Zone Policeman 88*, pp. 119–20.

17. Ibid., p. 100.

18. See, for example, ibid., pp. 105–6; Bullard, *Panama*, pp. 546–59.

19. The anxieties so many people felt about whether a dam would function safely on the isthmus can be traced to the disastrous flood in Johnstown, Pennsylvania, in 1889, in which the South Fork Dam collapsed and killed approximately twenty-two hundred people. On the flood, see David McCullough, *The Johnstown Flood* (New York: Simon and Schuster, 1987). On sea-level and lock canals, see Edwin E. Slosson and Gardner Richardson, "The Sea-Level Versus the Lock Canal," *Independent*, March 29, 1906, pp. 709–16; McCullough, *Path Between the Seas*, pp. 481–89; William L. Sibert and John F. Stevens, *The Construction of the Panama Canal* (New York: D. Appleton, 1915); for further reflections by John Stevens, especially his taking credit for the decision to build a lock canal, see John Stevens, *An Engineer's Recollections* (reprinted from *Engineering News-Record*, 1935; New York: McGraw-Hill, 1936), pp. 40–42. For Theodore Roosevelt's claim that he deserved the credit, see his *Autobiography* (New York: Charles Scribner's Sons, 1924), pp. 527–28.

20. U.S. Senate, *Investigation of Panama Canal Matters: Hearings Before the Committee on Interoceanic Canals of the United States Senate in the Matter of the Senate Resolution Adopted January 9, 1906, Providing for an Investigation of Matters Relating to the Panama Canal, Etc.*, 59th Cong., 2nd sess., Doc. 401 (Washington, D.C.: GPO, 1907), vol. 1, p. 47. I have seen no clear evidence that Stevens quit because of the labor problem; however, we may speculate that it was a likely cause. Stevens railed constantly about the need to find a decent source of labor and pushed aggressively to be allowed to import Chinese workers. About one month after it was finally settled that he would not have access to Chinese labor, Stevens resigned.

21. Shonts to Sir, May 16, 1906, ICC Records, Alpha files, 2-E-2/China, pt. 2, box 93.

22. *Hearings Before the Committee on Interstate and Foreign Commerce of the House of Representatives, on the Isthmian Canal* (Washington, D.C.: GPO, 1906), pp. 33–35; U.S. Senate, *Investigation of Panama Canal Matters*, vol. 2, p. 1574. The need for ethnic/racial competition was articulated by officials so often that journalists covering the construction effort saw it as a central aspect of the government's strategy. For example, see John Foster Carr, "The Panama Canal: The Silver Men," *Outlook*, May 19, 1906, p. 120: "But no large proportion of men is to be brought from any one place, for 'Labor and Quarters' tries to profit by the rivalry that exists between the different islands." For other examples of ethnic division as central to labor management, see Ronald Takaki, *Pau Hana: Plantation Life and Labor in Hawaii, 1835–1920* (Honolulu: University of Hawaii Press, 1983); and Philippe Bourgois, *Ethnicity at Work: Divided Labor on a Central American Banana Plantation* (Baltimore: Johns Hopkins University Press, 1989).

23. *Hearings Before the Committee on Interstate and Foreign Commerce*, 1906, vol. 1, p. 53; Stevens to Shonts, Dec. 14, 1905, ICC Records, 2-E-1. Stevens also declared, "I have no hesitancy in saying that the West Indian Negro is about the poorest excuse for a laborer I have ever been up against in thirty-five years of experience." For this quotation see Michael L. Conniff, *Black Labor on a White Canal: Panama, 1904–1981* (Pittsburgh: University of Pittsburgh Press, 1985), p. 25.

24. *Hearings Before the Committee on Interstate and Foreign Commerce*, 1906, vol. 1, p. 84. It is worth noting that even before Stevens's tenure as chief engineer, officials had assumed they would not be able to secure whites for the unskilled labor they needed on the canal. See, for example, Governor George W. Davis to Benjamin Lyon Smith, Sept. 9, 1904, ICC Records, 95-A-1: "It is impossible to obtain Caucasian labor for this severe tropical work."

25. Moody to Secretary of War William H. Taft, June 5, 1905; Shonts to Stevens, Nov. 29, 1905: both ICC Records, 2-E-1. Readers may recall James Morton Callahan from the prologue, above, who had worried that American imperialism in the tropics would require some form of forced labor in order to succeed, and that, he argued, would endanger the Republic. On Chinese workers in the Americas, see Adam McKeown, *Chinese Migrant Networks and Cultural Change: Peru, Chicago, and Hawaii, 1900–1936* (Chicago: University of Chicago Press, 2001); Madeline Y. Hsu, *Dreaming of Gold, Dreaming of Home: Transnationalism and Migration Between the United States and South China, 1882–1943* (Stanford, Calif.: Stanford University Press, 2000); Erika Lee, *At America's Gates: Chinese Immigration During the Exclusion Era, 1882–1943* (Chapel Hill: University of North Carolina Press, 2007); Alexander Saxton, *The Indispensable Enemy: Labor and the Anti-Chinese Movement in California* (Berkeley:

University of California Press, 1975); and Lok C. D. Siu, *Memories of a Future Home: Diasporic Citizenship of Chinese in Panama* (Stanford, Calif.: Stanford University Press, 2005).

26. Stevens to Shonts, Jan. 18, 1907, ICC Records, Alpha files, 2-E-2/China, pt. 2, box 93; Claude Mallet to Sir Edward Grey, Sept. 12, 1906, Foreign Office Records, FO 371/101, The National Archives, Kew, U.K. Wives and children, Stevens proposed, were to make up no more than 15 percent of the total number of Chinese immigrants.

27. "Chinese on the Canal Zone," *Independent*, Oct. 25, 1906, p. 1009. See also Eugene S. Watson, "Chinese Labor and the Panama Canal," *Independent*, Nov. 22, 1906, pp. 1201–5; and "Chinese Contract Labor in Panama," *Outlook*, Oct. 13, 1906, pp. 343–44; on opposition by the Chinese government, see "Proclamation Forbidding Chinese Coolies to Go Abroad," issued by order of the viceroy, Tuan Fang, March 7, 1907, ICC Records, Alpha files, 2-E-2/China, pt. 2, box 93; on Roosevelt's position, see Shonts to Stevens, Jan. 30, 1907; Roosevelt to Taft, July 27, 1906, and Feb. 1, 1907: all ICC Records, Alpha files, 2-E-2/China, pt. 2, box 93.

28. On Guatemalan Indians, see U.S. Senate, *Investigation of Panama Canal Matters*, 1907, vol. 1, pp. 84–85. On Stevens's preference for white labor, see his letter to Shonts, Dec. 14, 1905, ICC Records, 2-E-1.

29. Shonts to Stevens, June 5, 1905, ICC Records, 2-E-1; Mallet to Grey, Sept. 12, 1906, Foreign Office Records, FO 371/101.

30. Thomas O'Connell (representing the ICC) to the colonial secretary of Jamaica, Nov. 21, 1905, Foreign Office Records, FO 371/101.

31. Wood to Stevens, Oct. 22, 1906, ICC Records, 2-E-1, "Labor Recruiting." On the emigration tax required by Jamaica, see Lancelot S. Lewis, *The West Indian in Panama: Black Labor in Panama, 1850–1914* (Washington, D.C.: University Press of America, 1980), pp. 30–31. It is difficult to estimate precisely the number of laborers who came to the Zone from any one country. However, Velma Newton estimates that some 60,000 Barbadians and Jamaicans entered the Zone during the construction decade. See Newton, *The Silver Men: West Indian Labour Migration to Panama, 1850–1914* (Mona, Jamaica: University of the West Indies, 1984), pp. 92–93.

32. Reference to hiring "sheiks" from India: U.S. Senate, *Hearings Supplement*, Senate Committee on Interoceanic Canals, 62nd Cong. (Washington, D.C.: GPO, 1908), p. 53. It is very difficult to find precise information about laborers from India and their role in the Canal Zone. According to Claude Mallet, the British government's representative in Panama, the U.S. sanitary officials (presumably including William Gorgas) refused to allow the employment of Indians, considering them unsanitary. Between 1871 and 1917, nearly 300,000 Indians migrated to the Caribbean, most of them landing in Trinidad or British Guiana. Over the years a small number made their way to Panama, coming either from India or from islands such as Trinidad. Most often they were refused employment in the Canal Zone, but a small number won jobs on the silver roll. See Mallet, telegram to Foreign Office, 1907, Foreign Office Records, FO 288/94; J. H. Kerr, secretary to the government of Bengal, to the secretary to the government of India, March 30, 1912; Mallet to Grey, July 17, 1912: both Foreign Office Records, FO 371/1417; and Walton Look Lai, *Indentured Labor, Caribbean Sugar: Chinese and Indian Migrants to the British West Indies, 1838–1918* (Baltimore: Johns Hopkins University Press, 1993), pp. 107–9. For more general information on the recruitment of labor, see U.S. Senate, *Investigation of Panama Canal Matters*, vol. 4, pp. 3228–50; Foreign Office Records, esp. FO 370/101 and 371/1417, are also extremely helpful on this subject.

33. On Italians, see Jackson Smith to Taft, May 17, 1907, ICC Records, Alpha files, 2-E-2; for Stevens's comment that the Spaniards had disturbed the complacency of West Indians and also on Europe's desire to see the United States fail, consult Stevens to Shonts, Jan. 18, 1907, ICC Records, Alpha files, 2-E-2/China, pt. 2, box 93. The Alpha files are filled with comments by Stevens, Shonts, and others on the necessity of having a diverse workforce so the laborers could be placed in competition with one another. Regarding opposition by European governments to emigration, the U.S. secretary of war reported there existed a pervasive sentiment among Spanish government officials: "If America needed common laborers, let her seek it among her own people. The American is too proud to work with his hands! He must work with his head, and Spain must be his hands! Spain refuses to be the hands of an American head." Cited in Lewis, *The West Indian in Panama*, p. 35, taken from *Report of the Secretary of War to the President of the United States* (Washington, D.C.: GPO, 1906), pp. 20–23.

34. *Hearings Concerning Estimates for Construction of the Isthmian Canal for the Fiscal Year 1911*, conducted on the Canal Zone by the Committee on Appropriations, 61st Cong. (Washington, D.C.: GPO,

1910); *Message from the President of the United States, Transmitting the Report of the Special Commission Appointed to Investigate Conditions of Labor and Housing of Government Employees on the Isthmus of Panama*, 60th Cong., 2nd sess., Doc. 539 (Washington, D.C.: GPO, 1908), p. 7; *Census of the Canal Zone, February 1, 1912* (Mount Hope, C.Z.: ICC Press, 1912), esp. pp. 29–31; the quotation from Stevens is in U.S. Senate, *Investigation of Panama Canal Matters* (1907), vol. 1, p. 55.

35. Abbot, *Panama and the Canal in Picture and Prose*, p. 162; McCullough, *Path Between the Seas*, pp. 503–8.

36. Bishop and Bishop, *Goethals, Genius of the Panama Canal;* Howard Fast, *Goethals and the Panama Canal* (New York: Julian Messner, 1942); "Mrs. G. W. Goethals; Husband Built Canal," *New York Times*, Jan. 2, 1942, p. 2; McCullough, *Path Between the Seas*, p. 571.

37. George W. Goethals, *Government of the Canal Zone* (Princeton, N.J.: Princeton University Press, 1915), pp. 49–51; McCullough, *Path Between the Seas*, pp. 508–11; Richard Harding Davis, "The Dirt Diggers," *Collier's* 49 (1912), p. 15.

38. Abbot, *Panama and the Canal in Picture and Prose*, p. 168.

39. McCullough, *Path Between the Seas*, pp. 539–41.

40. Abbot, *Panama and the Canal in Picture and Prose*, pp. 177–80; McCullough, *Path Between the Seas*, pp. 550, 590–91.

41. McCullough, *Path Between the Seas*, pp. 590–91, 598; Abbot, *Panama and the Canal in Picture and Prose*, pp. 180–86; Panama Canal Authority, at http://www.pancanal.com/eng/history/history/index.html.

42. McCullough, *Path Between the Seas*, pp. 598–601.

43. Franck, *Zone Policeman 88*, p. 131.

44. Goethals, *Government of the Canal Zone*, pp. 2–3; Joseph Bucklin Bishop, "Personality of Colonel Goethals," *Scribner's Magazine*, Feb. 1915, p. 129; J. Hampton Moore, *With Speaker Cannon Through the Tropics* (Philadelphia: Book Print, 1907), pp. 280–86. Marie Gorgas recalled in her memoir that Roosevelt's choice of Goethals as chief engineer "was based upon the assumption that the Canal needed a persistent driver; one who was possessed, above all, of administrative ability, a talent for handling large masses of men, and even a certain remorselessness of spirit in accomplishing his ends. All these qualities Col. Goethals had in large degree." She noted also that Goethals's account of his work in the Canal Zone "upset" the engineers because he had so little to say about Gatun Dam and Culebra Cut but focused rather on the challenges of governing. Gorgas and Hendrick, *William Crawford Gorgas*, pp. 215–16, 218–19.

45. Goethals, *Government of the Canal Zone*, pp. 83–86, 92.

46. Bishop and Bishop, *Goethals, Genius of the Panama Canal*, pp. 191–93; Roosevelt, *Autobiography*, p. 528; Goethals, *Government of the Canal Zone*, pp. 50–51.

47. Goethals, *Government of the Canal Zone*, pp. 50–51; Bishop and Bishop, *Goethals, Genius of the Panama Canal*, pp. 191–93; Joseph Bucklin Bishop, "A Benevolent Despotism," *Scribner's Magazine* 53 (1913), pp. 303–19.

48. Bishop and Bishop, *Goethals, Genius of the Panama Canal*, pp. 191–93; Goethals, *Government of the Canal Zone*, pp. 50–51; see also Bishop, "Benevolent Despotism"; Abbot, *Panama and the Canal in Picture and Prose*, p. 162. On despotism in the thinking of political philosophers, see Francis McDonald Cornford, trans., *The Republic of Plato* (London: Oxford University Press, 1945), esp. pp. 175–79; Susan Zlotnik, "Contextualizing David Levy's *How the Dismal Science Got Its Name*," in *Race, Liberalism, and Economics*, ed. David Colander, Robert E. Prasch, and Falguni E. Sheth (Ann Arbor: University of Michigan Press, 2006), pp. 95–96; Mark Tunick, "Tolerant Imperialism: John Stuart Mill's Defense of British Rule in India," *Review of Politics* 68 (2006), pp. 586–611; Robert Michels, *Political Parties: A Sociological Study of the Oligarchical Tendencies of Modern Democracy* (New York: Free Press, 1966), p. 113; Michael Moran, "Thomas Carlyle," in *The Encyclopedia of Philosophy*, ed. Paul Edwards (New York: Macmillan, 1967), vol. 2, pp. 22–25. My thanks to James Maffie for helping me trace the philosophical lineage of "benevolent despotism." The phrase was commonly used to describe Goethals's rule. See, for example, Elizabeth Glendower Evans, "The Parable of Panama," *Socialist Review*, July 1914, p. 232. Likewise, General George W. Davis, who served as a member of the Isthmian Canal Commission during the early construction years, testified to the U.S. Senate about the government of the Canal Zone: "The simpler the government the better, and I suppose a benevolent despotism is the only really perfect government that has been conceived by man." U.S. Senate, *Investigation of Panama Canal Matters* (1907), vol. 3, pp. 2261, 2267.

49. Bishop and Bishop, *Goethals, Genius of the Panama Canal,* pp. 241–49: the quotation is on p. 248; Gorgas and Hendrick, *William Crawford Gorgas,* pp. 218–19. In an essay for *Scribner's Magazine,* Joseph Bucklin Bishop actually referred to Goethals's smile as "beatific." See "Personality of Colonel Goethals," p. 145.

50. Miskimon to the acting chairman, March 9, 1909; Miskimon to the secretary to the commission, Feb. 18, 1909: both T. B. Miskimon Papers, MS 86-5, box 2, Special Collections, Ablah Library, Wichita State University. These and similar challenges will be explored further in chapters to come.

51. For Goethals's policy regarding unions, see his letters to Fred Westcott, Dec. 14, 1908, and to Sibert, March 21, 1910: both ICC Records, 2-P-11; and his interview with C. C. Barnett, Dec. 22, 1908, in George Washington Goethals Papers, General Correspondence, box 6, Manuscript Division, Library of Congress. To Sibert, Goethals remarked: "Whatever may be our views in the matter, we are obliged because of instructions from higher authority to recognize the unions, to receive grievance committees, and to extend to them proper treatment." The quotation explaining why Taft wished Goethals to meet with committees representing the workforce is from George W. Goethals, "The Building of the Panama Canal," part 2: "Labor Problems Connected with the Work," *Scribner's Magazine,* April 1915, p. 415.

52. Bishop, "Personality of Colonel Goethals," pp. 147–49.

53. Franck, *Zone Policeman 88,* p. 205. More information on police and deportation can be found in chapters 2, 3, 7, below.

54. Frederic J. Haskin attributes the emergence of the segregation to a disbursing officer in his *Panama Canal* (Garden City, N.Y.: Doubleday, Page, 1913), p. 159; Velma Newton discusses the origins of the silver and gold system in *The Silver Men: West Indian Labour Migration to Panama, 1850–1914* (Mona, Jamaica: University of the West Indies, 1984), pp. 131–33; David McCullough treats the subject briefly in *Path Between the Seas,* p. 576; see also Raymond Allan Davis, "West Indian Workers on the Panama Canal: A Split Labor Market Interpretation" (Ph.D. diss., Stanford University, 1981). Charles Magoon, governor of the Canal Zone, informed senators in 1905 that the differential pay system emerged because of fears that widespread use of U.S. currency would generate runaway inflation, as had happened in the Philippines, Puerto Rico, and Cuba. For this reason, he said, the U.S. government had decided to pay the more numerous unskilled workers in Panamanian (silver) currency. See Newton, *Silver Men,* pp. 131–32.

55. Goethals explained the origins of the system by saying that Americans wanted to be paid in gold, while West Indians preferred to be paid in silver. He concluded: "This divisional designation was found not only convenient but politic, since it avoided all reference to the color line." Goethals, "Building of the Panama Canal," part 2: "Labor Problems Connected with the Work," pp. 395–96; Sullivan to D. W. Bolich, Aug. 4, 1906, ICC Records, 2-F-14, "Transfers, Gold to Silver"; McIlvaine to Mrs. William Swiget, Jan. 1, 1916, ICC Records, 28-B-233, pt. 1. On arguments that segregation would enhance sanitation, see Sutter, "Nature's Agents or Agents of Empire?" According to *American Heritage Dictionary,* the term "dago" is pejorative slang for a person of Italian or, sometimes, Spanish origin. It originated as a contraction of the name Diego.

56. Benson to Magoon, Sept. 4, 1905; Stevens to all department heads, Sept. 5, 1905: both ICC Records, 2-F-14.

57. For Stevens's order, see E. P. Shannon to W. M. Belding, Nov. 12, 1906; Shannon to J. G. Holcome, division engineer, Nov. 15, 1906: both ICC Records, 2-F-14.

58. Shannon to H. D. Reed, Nov. 13, 1906; Burnett to Stevens, Feb. 15, 1907; Reed to Stevens, Feb. 15, 1907: all ICC Records, 2-C-55. Brooke to Stevens, Nov. 1, 1906, ICC Records, 2-F-14.

59. Goethals to all department heads, May 6, 1907; Slifer to Gaillard, Feb. 12, 1908; Smith to Gaillard, Feb. 15, 1908: all ICC Records, 2-F-14.

60. President Roosevelt's executive orders Feb. 8, 1908, and Dec. 23, 1908: both ICC Records, 2-E-11, "Employment of Aliens." See also Goethals to W. W. Warwick, Nov. 16, 1909, ICC Records, 2-F-14.

61. Weitzel to Goethals, Nov. 17, 1908; Goethals to department heads, Nov. 23, 1908: both ICC Records, 2-E-11.

62. Sands (chief clerk, Department of Construction and Engineering, Atlantic division) to McIlvaine, Nov. 25, 1908; McIlvaine to Goethals, memo, Nov. 27, 1908; Goethals to the chief quartermaster, memo, Nov. 28, 1908: all ICC Records, 2-F-14; Franck, *Zone Policeman 88,* p. 12. On the other hand, when Constantine Stephos, a Greek American working as a mate on a ladder dredge, asked

to be transferred from the silver to the gold roll because he was a U.S. citizen, Goethals refused, arguing that such classification was decided on the basis of the sort of work an individual did, not his nationality. See Stephos to Colonel, April 28, 1911, and Goethals to Stephos, May 8, 1911: both ICC Records, 2-F-14.

63. H. T. Hodges to Goethals, March 7, 1908; Smith to the acting chairman, Feb. 28, 1908; Goethals to all department heads, April 18, 1908; W. G. Brewer (master mechanic) to Lieutenant F. Mears (acting superintendent, Panama Railroad), Sept. 24, 1910; Gorgas to Goethals, Aug. 18, 1908: all ICC Records, 2-E-11. For the comments by the British consul Claude Mallet, see his letters to Grey, April 4 and Aug. 21, 1908, Foreign Office Records, FO 371/101.

64. Goethals to Smith, Sept. 25, 1912, ICC Records, 2-P-49, "Demarcation of Grades of Work to Be Performed by Silver vs. Gold Employees"; Gaillard to Goethals, June 19, 1909, ICC Records, 2-P-49/P, "Protest by Labor Organizations Permitting Silver Employees to Perform Grades of Work That Should Be Done by American Citizens." See also McIlvaine (Goethals's executive secretary and the person who presumably drafted the document cited above) to Goethals, Sept. 25, 1912: ICC Records, 2-P-49: "I thought it advisable to make this a question of citizenship, which will accomplish the same end, as I believe the Government cannot very well draw the color line." On African Americans in the Canal Zone, see Charlie Walker, John Hicks, Charlie Woodard, A. Benson, Thomas Onsley, and Sandy Odom to Goethals, Jan. 13, 1909; memo to Goethals, Oct. 10, 1912; Goethals to Henry Hart and John Thomas, March 18, 1910: all ICC Records, 2-C-55, "Employment of Colored American Citizens, General"; and Patrice C. Brown, "The Panama Canal: The African American Experience," *Prologue* 29, no. 2 (Summer 1997), pp. 122-26. On the "special" silver roll for African American employees, see Wood to Henry A. Smith, July 24, 1907; Gaillard to Jackson Smith, Feb. 11, 1908; Jackson Smith to the acting chairman, Feb. 12, 1908: all ICC Records, 2-C-55. By 1912 only forty-four African Americans were working for the U.S. government in the Canal Zone. Twenty-five more worked for a contractor in the Zone. Goethals to Rudolph Forster, July 10, 1912, ICC Records, 2-C-55.

65. James, *Mulberry Tree*, pp. 259-60, 228-32.

66. Ibid., p. 235. James added to her observation of the houses looking like meat safes: "I always felt when I went inside those doors that I ought to be given a dish to sit down on."

67. Ibid., pp. 239-41, 131. The importance of machines and unimportance of humans in the construction of the canal would become a common theme, preceding and helping to generate, no doubt, the complete erasure of human labor that would occur by the time of the Panama-Pacific International Exposition in 1915. For other examples of this, see Arthur Bullard describing Culebra Cut: "It is as busy a place as an anthill. It seems to be alive with machinery; there are, of course, men in the cut too, but they are insignificant, lost among the mechanical monsters which are jerking work-trains about the maze of tracks, which are boring holes for the blasting, which are tearing at the spine of the continent." Similarly, "those midgets of men are not doing the work. They are only arranging it for the monsters of steel whose food is fire." Bullard, *Panama*, pp. 50, 549. Even a writer in the official journal of the International Brotherhood of Steam Shovel and Dredge Men repeated this theme. Describing Culebra Cut, he declared, "Here the steam shovel is king and the tourist realizes that it isn't men but machinery that solve the problem of digging the ditch." Alexis J. Colman, "How the Work of Digging the Canal Strikes a Layman," *Steam Shovel and Dredge* 15, no. 3 (March 1911), p. 196.

68. James, *Mulberry Tree*, pp. 232-41.

69. Ibid., p. 226; Cameron, *Woman's Winter in South America*, p. 221.

70. Colman, "How the Work of Digging the Canal Strikes a Layman," pp. 193-97; Edith A. Browne, *Panama* (London: Adam and Charles Black, 1913), p. 58.

71. Franck, *Zone Policeman 88*, pp. 10, 82. See esp. chapter 8, "The Riots of Cocoa Grove," below.

CHAPTER TWO: "AS I AM A TRUE AMERICAN"

1. *Supplement to Hearings Concerning Estimates for Construction of the Isthmian Canal for the Fiscal Year 1911, Statements of the Representatives of Skilled Employees* (Washington, D.C.: GPO, 1910), p. 21.

2. U.S. Senate, *Investigation of Panama Canal Matters: Hearings Before the Committee on Interoceanic Canals of the United States Senate*, 59th Cong., 2nd sess., Doc. 401 (Washington, D.C.: GPO, 1907), vol. 3, pp. 2265-66, 617.

3. Sergeant George Johnson to George Shanton, March 20, 1905, Isthmian Canal Commission Records,

RG 185, 2-P-11, "Labor Troubles and Spy Reports," National Archives, College Park, Md. (hereafter cited as ICC Records).

4. S. B. Schuck (police sergeant), report of meeting, March 13, 1905, ICC Records, 2-P-11. The battleship *Connecticut* was built in New York at the Brooklyn Navy Yard in 1904 and 1905. Strikes by government employees in shipbuilding and munitions would have provided an important precedent for the organizing activities of skilled workers in the Canal Zone. My thanks to John Stobo, David Montgomery, Grace Palladino, and Joseph Slater for information about this and related strikes. On the history of public employees and labor organizing, see David Ziskind, *One Thousand Strikes of Government Employees* (New York: Columbia University Press, 1940); Joseph E. Slater, *Public Workers: Government Employee Unions, the Law, and the State, 1900–1962* (Ithaca, N.Y.: Cornell University Press, 2004). According to David Ziskind, the earliest recorded strike by civilian employees of the Navy occurred in 1835. He found several strikes by civilian employees of the U.S. military during the early twentieth century.

5. George Shanton to S. G. Schenck, March 17, 1905; Schenck to Shanton, March 20, 1905; R. Gunner to Shanton, March 19, 1905: all ICC Records, 2-P-11.

6. Shanton to Schenck, March 17, 1905; Laurence Angel to Shanton, Sunday noon (n.d.); no signature to Shanton, March 20, 1905: all ICC Records, 2-P-11.

7. Wallace to Admiral John G. Walker (chairman, ICC), March 21, 1905, ICC Records, 2-P-11.

8. Shanton to Dan S. Lehon (Illinois Central Railroad Co.), Jan. 17, 1906, ICC Records, 2-P-11.

9. John Wallace, testimony in U.S. Senate, *Investigation of Panama Canal Matters* (1907), serial set 5097, vol. 1, pp. 641–42; Wallace to Walker, March 21, 1905, ICC Records, 2-P-11; for a lengthier analysis by Wallace of the skilled workers' reasons for discontent, see Wallace to Walker, Feb. 9, 1905, ICC Records, 2-P-51, "Grievances of Employees."

10. Wallace to Walker, Feb. 9, 1905, ICC Records, 2-P-51.

11. Wallace, testimony in U.S. Senate, *Investigation of Panama Canal Matters*, vol. 1, p. 611.

12. John Hall, *Panama Roughneck Ballads* (Panama and Canal Zone: Albert Lindo, Panama Railroad News Agency, 1912), pp. 9–15.

13. Singer to his family, Sept. 4 and Nov. 23, 1913, letters in author's possession. For more examples of complaints about improper behavior in the bachelor dormitories, see "Letters from the Line," *Canal Record,* March 11, 1908, p. 219.

14. Harry A. Franck, *Zone Policeman 88: A Close Range Study of the Panama Canal and Its Workers* (New York: Century, 1913), pp. 86–87. Skilled workers also believed they were resented by Army officers. A Panama Railroad conductor complained to Goethals in 1908 that Army officials had declared himself and his peers to be "high-priced conductors getting as much as Captains in the Army." See "Interview Between Col. George W. Goethals and C. C. Barnett," Dec. 22, 1906, in George Washington Goethals Papers, General Correspondence, box 6, Manuscript Division, Library of Congress.

15. *Census of the Canal Zone, February 1, 1912* (Mount Hope, C.Z.: ICC Press, 1912), pp. 16, 32–38, 52; *Supplement to Hearings Concerning Estimates,* passim and pp. 347–48; *Supplement to Hearings on the Panama Canal, Senate Committee on Interoceanic Canals* (Washington, D.C.: GPO, 1908), pp. 52, 89; John Foster Carr, "The Panama Canal—The Commission's White Workers," *Outlook,* May 5, 1906, pp. 21–24. On the government at first discouraging women and children from accompanying their menfolk to the Zone, see Mrs. Charles C. J. Wirz, "Some of My Experiences on the Isthmus of Panama," in *The American Woman on the Panama Canal: From 1904 to 1916,* ed. Mrs. Ernest von Muenchow (Balboa Heights, Panama: Star and Herald, 1916), p. 25. For more on women in the Canal Zone, including the wives of U.S. workers, see chapter 6, below.

16. *Annual Report of the Isthmian Canal Commission for the Fiscal Year Ending June 30, 1907* (Washington, D.C.: GPO, 1907), plate 137.

17. *Hearings Concerning Estimates for Construction of the Isthmian Canal for the Fiscal Year 1911,* conducted on the Canal Zone by the Committee on Appropriations, House of Representatives, 61st Cong. (Washington, D.C.: GPO, 1910), pp. 75–78; Canal Zone Trades Council to Goethals, n.d., ICC Records, 2-D-39, pt. 2, box 32. For a summary of the differences between monthly and hourly employees' situations, see George W. Goethals, "The Building of the Panama Canal," part 2: "Labor Problems Connected with the Work," *Scribner's Magazine,* April 1915, pp. 395–418.

18. Bryce to Sir Edward Grey, Nov. 28, 1910, Foreign Office Records, FO 371/943, National Archives, Kew, U.K.

19. "Record of Excavation Since American Occupation," *Canal Record,* Dec. 8, 1909, p. 116; David Mc Cullough, *The Path Between the Seas: The Creation of the Panama Canal, 1870–1914* (New York: Simon and Schuster, 1977), p. 604.

20. Estate of Philip F. Kramer, deceased, Jan. 14, 1908, case 134, Records of District Courts of the United States, RG 21, District of the Canal Zone, 2nd Judicial Circuit, Empire, Gorgona, Ancon, Civil Case Files, 1904–14, box 3, National Archives, Washington, D.C. According to the *Canal Record,* Philip Kramer's gold watch was soon found in the possession of a Spanish workman, who was immediately arrested for the murder. The workman claimed to have found the watch, however, and interrogation of the gang of men with whom he worked generated no more evidence. It's unknown what happened in this case. See *Canal Record,* Jan. 29, 1908, p. 170.

21. On Shanton and the police department, see McCullough, *Path Between the Seas,* pp. 494–95; Carr, "Panama Canal—Commission's White Workers," pp. 21–24; Franck, *Zone Policeman 88,* p. 107.

22. When the construction project began, the International Brotherhood of Steam Shovel and Dredge Men negotiated a salary of $190 per month for steam-shovel engineers and $165 per month for crane operators. These salaries soon rose to $210 and $185, respectively. A study of wages in the United States conducted by the union found the average wage to be $163 per month for steam-shovel engineers and $110 per month for crane operators. See E. Tipping, "The History of the Panama Canal," *Steam Shovel and Dredge* 18, no. 11 (Nov. 1914), pp. 931–34. ICC secretary Joseph Bucklin Bishop estimated that the average pay of workers in the Canal Zone ranged from 25 to 100 percent higher than that of their counterparts in the United States, but the union's more conservative estimate is probably more accurate. See Joseph Bucklin Bishop, "A Benevolent Despotism," *Scribner's Magazine* 53 (1913), p. 303.

There is a vast scholarship on white male skilled workers in the United States at the turn of the twentieth century. Useful portrayals of skilled workers at this time include Michael Kazin, *Barons of Labor: The San Francisco Building Trades and Union Power in the Progressive Era* (Urbana: University of Illinois Press, 1988); David Montgomery, *The Fall of the House of Labor: The Workplace, the State, and American Labor Activism, 1865–1925* (New York: Cambridge University Press, 1987); Walter Licht, *Working for the Railroad: The Organization of Work in the Nineteenth Century* (Princeton, N.J.: Princeton University Press, 1983); Patricia Ann Cooper, *Once a Cigarmaker: Men, Women, and Work Culture in American Cigar Factories, 1900–1919* (Urbana: University of Illinois Press, 1987); Julie Greene, *Pure and Simple Politics: The American Federation of Labor and Political Activism, 1881–1918* (New York: Cambridge University Press, 1998).

23. William Howard Taft, testimony in *U.S. Congressional Hearings Supplement, Senate Committee on Interoceanic Canals* (Washington, D.C.: GPO, 1908), pp. 6–8.

24. Ibid., pp. 6–7.

25. U.S. Senate, *Investigation of Panama Canal Matters,* vol. 3, pp. 2265, 2668; Michael L. Conniff, *Black Labor on a White Canal: Panama, 1904–1981* (Pittsburgh: University of Pittsburgh Press, 1985), p. 37.

26. On Shanton and the Rough Riders, see McCullough, *Path Between the Seas,* pp. 494–95; the best source on the Zone policemen is Franck, *Zone Policeman 88.* See also John Foster Carr, "Building a State," *Outlook,* June 23, 1906, p. 440. Franck reports (p. 150) that almost all of the American policemen came to the job with military training under their belts, as did Carr, who visited the Zone in 1906. The organization of the police force, Carr noted, is "half military." "Most of its officers and petty officers come from the army and have seen active service in Cuba and the Philippines" (p. 440).

27. For a profile of the police department see Franck, *Zone Policeman 88,* esp. pp. 145–47.

28. W. J. Ghent, "Work and Welfare on the Canal," *Independent,* April 29, 1909, p. 909; Franck, *Zone Policeman 88,* 154, pp. 205–6. The use of spies was a time-tested technique in U.S. factories. On this see, for example, Stephen Norwood, *Strikebreaking and Intimidation: Mercenaries and Masculinity in Twentieth-Century America* (Chapel Hill: University of North Carolina Press, 2001); Robert Michael Smith, *From Blackjacks to Briefcases: A History of Commercialized Strikebreaking and Unionbusting in the United States* (Athens: Ohio University Press, 2003); Gary M. Fink, *The Fulton Bag and Cotton Mills Strike of 1914–1915: Espionage, Labor Conflict, and New South Industrial Relations* (Ithaca, N.Y.: Cornell University Press, 1993).

29. General Davis, testimony in U.S. Senate, *Investigation of Panama Canal Matters,* vol. 3, pp. 2262–65. For more on deportation, see chapter 7.

30. Theodore Roosevelt's executive order is discussed in ibid., pp. 2261–65; Reed to Stevens, Oct. 22, 1906, ICC Records, 2-E-1; J. P. Fyffe to M. H. Thatcher (head of Deptartment of Civil Administration), July 29, 1911; D. D. Gaillard to Taft, Dec. 14, 1907; Rousseau to Shanton, Jan. 3, 1908: ICC Records, 94-L-9.

31. Taft gives his views on the matter in *U.S. Congressional Hearings Supplement, Senate Committee on Interoceanic Canals,* pp. 23–24. See also Brooke to Rousseau, April 13, 1907, and Taft to Roosevelt, "Labor Issues in the Canal Zone, Isthmus of Panama," May 9, 1907: both ICC Records, 2-D-39, box 32.

32. Brooke to Rousseau, April 13, 1907, ICC Records, 2-D-39, box 32.

33. According to the official journal of the International Brotherhood of Steam Shovel and Dredge Men, this strike was an independent movement among steam-shovel operators in the Canal Zone and was not supported by the union's national leadership. Secretary of War Taft later testified that the striking steam-shovel engineers had all returned home to the United States; he did not clarify whether they went voluntarily or were deported, but his wording suggests the former. "The Trouble at Panama," *Steam Shovel and Dredge* 11, no. 6 (June 1907), pp. 273–75; Goethals, "Building of the Panama Canal," pt. 2: "Labor Problems Connected with the Work," esp. pp. 413–16; Goethals, testimony in *Panama Canal—Skilled Labor: Extracts from Hearings of the Committees on Appropriations of the Senate and House of Representatives, Fiscal Years 1907 to 1915 Inclusive,* 63rd Cong., 2nd sess. (Washington, D.C.: GPO, 1914), pp. 276–81. Taft's testimony is in *U.S. Congressional Hearings Supplement, Senate Committee on Interoceanic Canals,* pp. 23–24. See also Gerstle Mack, *The Land Divided: A History of the Panama Canal and Other Isthmian Canal Projects* (New York: Knopf, 1944), p. 541.

34. Goethals, "Building of the Panama Canal," pt. 2: "Labor Problems Connected with the Work," esp. pp. 413–16. For an insightful window into Goethals's views on labor and his strategy for dealing with it, see "Interview Between Col. George W. Goethals and C. C. Barnett."

35. T. B. Miskimon to Goethals, memos, n.d., T. B. Miskimon Papers, MS 86-5, box 2, FF 47 and 48, Special Collections, Ablah Library, Wichita State University.

36. Strikes continued to occur, but infrequently. An important strike broke out among plasterers working to complete the new Hotel Washington in 1913, for example. It began in part as a conflict over aliens (West Indians) being hired on the job. See the documentation on this strike at ICC Records, 2-P-21, box 48, in Jan. and Feb. 1913.

37. *Message from the President of the United States, Transmitting the Report of the Special Commission Appointed to Investigate Conditions of Labor and Housing of Government Employees on the Isthmus of Panama,* 60th Cong., 2nd sess., Doc. 539 (Washington, D.C.: GPO, 1908), p. 3. Important works focusing on the relationship between U.S. imperialism, race, and citizenship in the early twentieth century include José Cabranes, *Citizenship and the American Empire* (New Haven, Conn.: Yale University Press, 1979); Hazel M. McFerson, *The Racial Dimension of American Overseas Colonial Policy* (Westport, Conn.: Greenwood, 1997); Andrew Neather, "Labor Republicanism, Race, and Popular Patriotism in the Era of Empire, 1890–1914," in *Bonds of Affection: Americans Define Their Patriotism,* ed. John Bodnar (Princeton, N.J.: Princeton University Press, 1996); Christina Duffy Burnett and Burke Marshall, eds., *Foreign in a Domestic Sense: Puerto Rico, American Expansion, and the Constitution* (Durham, N.C.: Duke University Press, 2001). On citizenship more generally, see Rogers M. Smith, *Civic Ideals: Conflicting Visions of Citizenship in U.S. History* (New Haven, Conn.: Yale University Press, 1997), esp. pp. 429–39; Ian F. Haney-López, *White by Law: The Legal Construction of Race* (New York: New York University Press, 1996); Paul Taillon, "Americanism, Racism, and 'Progressive' Unionism: The Railroad Brotherhoods, 1898–1916," *Australasian Journal of American Studies* 20 (July 2001), pp. 55–65; Paul Taillon, "To Speak for the People? Citizenship, the State, and Railway Labor Politics, 1917–1920," unpublished paper presented at the 2003 American Historical Association Conference; Joseph A. McCartin, *Labor's Great War: The Struggle for Industrial Democracy and the Origins of Modern American Labor Relations, 1912–1921* (Chapel Hill: University of North Carolina Press, 1997); Hendrik Hartog, "The Constitution of Aspiration and 'The Rights That Belong to Us All,'" *Journal of American History* 74 (Dec. 1987), pp. 1013–34; Charles Tilly, "Citizenship, Identity, and Social History," *International Review of Social History* 40, supp. 3 (1995), p. 10; Kathleen Canning and Sonya O. Rose, "Gender, Citizenship, and Subjectivity: Some Historical and Theoretical Considerations," *Gender and History* 13 (Nov. 2001), pp. 430–33.

38. U.S. Senate, *Investigation of Panama Canal Matters*, p. 3231; *Supplement to Hearings Concerning Estimates*, pp. 24, 49.

39. Department of Commerce and Labor, *Bulletin of the Bureau of Labor*, no. 59, July 1905; U.S. Senate, *Investigation of Panama Canal Matters*, pp. 51, 641–45, 808; Goethals, "Building of the Panama Canal," pt. 2: "Labor Problems Connected with the Work," p. 418; Greene, *Pure and Simple Politics*, passim.

40. Mrs. Flanagan to Goethals, Sept. 12, 1908; Goethals to Sibert, Aug. 11, 1908: both ICC Records, 2-E-11, "Employment of Aliens."

41. See Brooke to Goethals, Feb. 1, 1909; S. B. Williams to Goethals, Jan. 26, 1909; and Gaillard to Goethals, Jan. 19, 1909: all ICC Records, 2-P-49/P, box 49.

42. Goethals testifying in *Hearings Concerning Estimates for Construction of the Isthmian Canal*, pp. 46–47, 234; Brooke to Goethals, Feb. 1, 1909, ICC Records, 2-P-49/P; Goethals, "Building of the Panama Canal," pt. 2: "Labor Problems Connected with the Work," pp. 401–2, 411–14.

43. Goethals to J. A. Mears, July 12, 1912, ICC Records, 2-P-49, "Demarcation of Grades of Work to Be Performed by Silver v. Gold Employees."

44. Sibert to Goethals, April 21, 1910; Goethals to Sibert, April 25, 1910: both ICC Records, 2-P-49.

45. "Resolutions Proposed and Adopted by Employes of the ICC Regarding Certain Conditions Prevailing on the Canal Zone, January 1909," ICC Records, 2-P-49/P. On the anti-Chinese movement in the United States, see Erika Lee, *At America's Gates: Chinese Immigration During the Exclusion Era, 1882–1943* (Chapel Hill: University of North Carolina Press, 2007); Alexander Saxton, *The Indispensable Enemy: Labor and the Anti-Chinese Movement in California* (Berkeley: University of California Press, 1975); Andrew Gyory, *Closing the Gate: Race, Politics, and the Chinese Exclusion Act* (Chapel Hill: University of North Carolina Press, 1998); Lucy E. Salyer, *Laws Harsh as Tigers: Chinese Immigrants and the Shaping of Modern Immigration Law* (Chapel Hill: University of North Carolina Press, 1995).

46. Fred Westcott to Goethals, Dec. 21, 1908, ICC Records, 2-E-11, pt. 1; Yates to Goethals, Dec. 4, 1909, ICC Records, 2-P-11.

47. Letter from Corozal, Canal Zone, Panama, to the editor, *Plasterer*, June 1914, pp. 6–7.

48. Member of Local 148, Atlanta, Operative Plasterers' International Association, to the editor, *Plasterer*, Aug. 1914, p. 6. I am grateful to Grace Palladino for these letters from *Plasterer* and for informing me that Local 148 was represented at the 1914 union convention by an African American delegate—and so was presumably a local composed of African Americans.

49. *Panama Canal—Skilled Labor: Extracts from Hearings of the Committees on Appropriations of the Senate and House of Representatives, Fiscal Years 1907 to 1915 Inclusive*, 63rd Cong., 2nd sess. (Washington, D.C.: GPO, 1914), pp. 372–81.

50. Goethals to Berger, Sept. 9, 1912, ICC Records, 2-E-11; Brooke to Goethals, Feb. 1, 1909, ICC Records, 2-P-49/P, "Protest by Labor Organizations Against Permitting Silver Employees to Perform Grades of Work That Should Be Done by American Citizens."

51. T. H. Dickson to Rousseau, Dec. 23, 1910, ICC Records, 2-P-49; Goethals, "Building of the Panama Canal," pt. 2: "Labor Problems Connected with the Work," p. 418.

52. *Census of the Canal Zone, February 1, 1912*, pp. 32, 52. According to the census, African Americans in the Canal Zone came most often from the following states (listed in order): Virginia, Florida, Georgia, Texas, and Louisiana.

53. Personnel records for Henry Hart, ICC Records, box 167.

54. Personnel records for Charles Arnold, ICC Records, box 10.

55. On the "special" silver roll for African American employees, see R. E. Wood to Henry A. Smith, July 24, 1907; Gaillard to Jackson Smith, Feb. 11, 1908; Jackson Smith to Gaillard, Feb. 12, 1908: all ICC Records, 2-C-55.

56. Boyd's comments are in a clipping attached to a letter from Ralph Tyler to Charles D. Hilles, secretary to President William Howard Taft, April 12, 1912, ICC Records, 28-B-233.

57. Rudolph Forster to Major F. C. Boggs (chief of office, ICC), July 5, 1912; Goethals, cable sent July 10, 1912: both ICC Records, 2-C-55. For material stressing the Republican Party's support for Negroes, see "Sustaining the Colored Man's Rights and Protecting the Colored Man's Liberties," in *Republican Campaign Text-Book, 1906* (issued by the Republican Congressional Committee, 1906), pp. 72–73.

58. "The Afro-American Citizen," in *Republican Campaign Text-Book, 1912* (Philadelphia: Dunlap, 1912), pp. 239–46. Note the change in terminology from the *Republican Campaign Text-Book* of 1906 (cited in previous note) and that of 1912, as the "Colored Man" became the "Afro-American Citizen."

59. Tyler to Hilles, April 12, 1912, ICC Records, 28-B-233. Ralph Tyler held one of the highest political offices of any African American in Washington, D.C., in 1912. During World War I, he would be appointed official war correspondent with the American Expeditionary Force, charged with covering all news regarding the "colored" troops in France. See Emmett J. Scott, *Official History of the American Negro in the World War* (1919; New York: Arno, 1969), ch. 20.

60. Tom M. Cooke to head of Department of Civil Administration, Canal Zone, May 9, 1912; Davis to Cooke (director of posts, Ancon, Canal Zone), May 7, 1912; J. W. Tannehill (postmaster) to Cooke, May 8, 1912: all ICC Records, 28-B-233.

61. Cooke to head of Department of Civil Administration, May 9, 1912, ICC Records, 28-B-233. In the United States similar arguments—that it would reduce racial conflicts and tensions—were used to justify racial segregation. This argument was used by President Woodrow Wilson, for example, as he extended Jim Crow segregation through the federal bureaucracy after winning the election in 1912. See Leon Litwack, *Trouble in Mind: Black Southerners in the Age of Jim Crow* (New York: Knopf, 1998), p. 373.

62. Eagleson to Baxter, Aug. 28, 1914; Baxter to C. A. McIlvaine, Aug. 31, 1914; and McIlvaine to Eagleson, Sept. 2, 1914: all ICC Records, 28-B-233, pt. 1.

63. Charlie Walker, John Hicks, Charlie Woodard, A. Benson, Tom Onsley, and Sandy Odom (blacksmiths of the Mechanical Department of Empire) to Goethals, Jan. 13, 1909, ICC Records, 2-C-55.

64. Goethals to Walker, Jan. 20, 1909, ICC Records, 2-C-55. As we saw in chapter 1, President Roosevelt had ordered the hiring of Panamanians on the gold roll in deference to the fact that the canal was being built across their territory.

65. Odom, Onsley, Thomas Motley, Benson, Woodard, James Starks, Grinard T. Elder, Jesse Wenly, and James McKnight to Taft, Feb. 3, 1909, ICC Records, 2-C-55.

66. Williams's case is discussed in the ICC Personnel Records for Gold Employees, box 575.

67. Goethals to Hart and John Thomas, March 18, 1910; H. F. Hodges (acting chairman) to Major E. T. Wilson (subsistence officer), Oct. 19, 1910: both ICC Records, 2-C-55, "Employment of Colored American Citizens, General." On exclusion of African Americans from YMCA clubhouses, see discussion below.

68. *Census of the Canal Zone, February 1, 1912*, pp. 52–54; "Women in the Isthmian Service," *Canal Record*, May 27, 1908, p. 310. Women employed by the ICC and the Panama Railroad who were not U.S. citizens were mostly West Indians who worked at various forms of domestic service.

69. *Census of the Canal Zone, February 1, 1912*, pp. 52–54; personnel records for Carrie Townsley, ICC Records; "Women in the Isthmian Service," p. 310. Based on what we know about the history of female clerical workers, these women were most likely educated daughters of skilled workers in the United States. For the broader context of clerical workers' history, see Ileen A. Devault, *Sons and Daughters of Labor: Class and Clerical Work in Turn-of-the-Century Pittsburgh* (Ithaca, N.Y.: Cornell University Press, 1990); Jerome P. Bjelopera, *City of Clerks: Office and Sales Workers in Philadelphia, 1870–1920* (Urbana: University of Illinois Press, 2005); Jurgen Kocka, *White Collar Workers in America, 1890–1940: A Social-Political History in International Perspective*, trans. Maura Kealey (London: Sage Publications, 1980); Lisa M. Fine, *The Souls of the Skyscraper: Female Clerical Workers in Chicago, 1870–1920* (Philadelphia: Temple University Press, 1990).

70. Mary A. Chatfield, *Light on Dark Places at Panama* (New York: Broadway, 1908), pp. 45–50, 185.

71. Ibid., pp. 102–3.

72. Ibid., pp. 87, 130.

73. Ibid., pp. 144, 177.

74. On the links between nurses in Panama, the Philippines, and other sites of U.S. imperialism, see Catherine Ceniza Choy, *Empire of Care: Nursing and Migration in Filipino American History* (Durham, N.C.: Duke University Press, 2003), pp. 28–29; Marie D. Gorgas and Burton J. Hendrick, *William Crawford Gorgas: His Life and Work* (Garden City, N.Y.: Doubleday, Page, 1924), p. 185. To compare nurses' experiences in the United States, see Susan Reverby, *Ordered to Care: The Dilemma of American Nursing, 1850–1945* (New York: Cambridge University Press, 1987); Barbara Melosh, *"The Physician's Hand": Work Culture and Conflict in American Nursing* (Philadelphia: Temple University

Press, 1982); Darlene Clark Hine, *Black Women in White: Racial Conflict and Cooperation in the Nursing Profession, 1890–1950* (Bloomington: Indiana University Press, 1989).

75. Willis J. Abbot, *Panama and the Canal in Picture and Prose* (New York: Syndicate, 1914), pp. 253–72; W. H. May, memorandum, Dec. 30, 1908; Goethals to May, Dec. 28, 1908; "Investigation Held at Colón Hospital, January 11th, as to the Nature of the Services of Misses Margaret M. Judge and Virginia Mooney, Nurses," p. 21: all ICC Records, 2-P-40.

76. Alice Gilbert described her experiences in "Hospital," ch. 2 in Muenchow, ed., *The American Woman on the Panama Canal*, pp. 3–6.

77. Goethals to Miss E. Jeanette George, Ancon Hospital, Aug. 21, 1911; Mason to Gorgas, Sept. 18, 1911: both ICC Records, 2-P-40.

78. Mason to assistant chief sanitary officer, Nov. 1, 1911, ICC Records, 2-P-40.

79. Busbey to Goethals, Nov. 27, 1911; Goethals to Gorgas, Nov. 27, 1911; Goethals to Colonel J. H. Phillips (acting sanitary officer), telegram, Dec. 1, 1911: all ICC Records, 2-P-40.

80. Mason to Phillips, Dec. 4, 1911; Russell to Goethals, Dec. 3, 1911; Frances P. Sprouse and fifty-two other women to Goethals, Dec. 4, 1911: all ICC Records, 2-P-40.

81. Goethals to Phillips, Dec. 4, 1911, ICC Records, 2-P-40.

82. On Taylorism there exists a vast scholarship; most influential to me have been Susan Porter Benson, *Counter Cultures: Saleswomen, Managers, and Customers in American Department Stores, 1890–1940* (Urbana: University of Illinois Press, 1986); Daniel Nelson, *Frederick W. Taylor and the Rise of Scientific Management* (Madison: University of Wisconsin Press, 1980); Samuel Haber, *Efficiency and Uplift: Scientific Management in the Progressive Era* (Chicago: University of Chicago Press, 1964); Montgomery, *Fall of the House of Labor.*

83. May, memorandum, Dec. 30, 1908; "Investigation Held at Colón Hospital," p. 3: both ICC Records, 2-P-40.

84. Goethals to Captain Robert E. Noble (acting chief sanitary officer), Jan. 9, 1909; Judge to H. R. Carter (director of hospitals, Ancon), Jan. 9, 1909: both ICC Records, 2-P-40.

85. "Investigation Held at Colón Hospital"; Goethals to Judge, Jan. 15, 1909: both ICC Records, 2-P-40.

86. "Investigation Held at Colón Hospital," p. 38; Carter to Goethals, Jan. 12, 1909; Goethals to Judge, Jan. 15, 1909: all ICC Records, 2-P-40.

87. Taft to Davis, Aug. 23, 1904, ICC Records, 28-A-31, "Religious Organizations."

88. Louise C. Bidwell Collection, MS 86-13, folders 2 (copies of invitations) and 4 (memoir written by Bidwell), Special Collections, Ablah Library, Wichita State University; Gilbert, "Hospital," pp. 3–6.

89. Clarence Hicks, "Report of International Committee of Young Men's Christian Association on Panama," Feb. 4, 1905; Roosevelt to Stevens, May 21, 1906: both ICC Records, 95-A-1. For another example of preliminary thinking by ICC officials on the need for leisure activities, see the assessment by Canal Zone governor George Davis to Benjamin Lyon Smith (secretary of Home Missions), Sept. 21, 1904, ICC Records, 95-A-1.

90. Goethals to Secretary of War J. M. Dickinson, March 30, 1910; "By-Laws for the Conduct of Young Men's Christian Association Work on the Canal Zone," n.d.; minutes of Gorgona Council Meeting, Oct. 10, 1910; statistical report for month of September 1907, Young Men's Christian Association; announcement of the YMCA clubhouses, May 1907; minutes of meeting of the advisory committee of the YMCA of the Canal Zone, June 5, 1907: all ICC Records, 95-A-1.

91. Statistical report for month of September 1907, Young Men's Christian Association; Shanton to Bruce Minear (general secretary, YMCA, Culebra), Aug. 21, 1907: both ICC Records, 95-A-1.

92. Goethals to Dickinson, March 30, 1910; statistical report for month of September 1907, Young Men's Christian Association: both ICC Records, 92-A-1.

93. Goethals to Dickinson, March 30, 1910; Announcement of the YMCA Canal Zone, May 1907: both ICC Records, 92-A-1. See also "Commission Club Houses: Activities of the Young Men's Christian Association," *Canal Record*, Feb. 19, 1908, p. 196. On the YMCA in the United States, see Thomas Winter, *Making Men, Making Class: The YMCA and Workingmen, 1877–1920* (Chicago: University of Chicago Press, 2002). Winter argues that YMCA officials worked for moral improvement in part by impressing middle-class standards of manhood upon workingmen.

94. Gorgas and Hendrick, *William Crawford Gorgas*; Bidwell Collection, MS 86-13, folder 2 (copies of invitations).

95. Abbot, *Panama and the Canal in Picture and Prose*, pp. 346–47. For a fascinating comparison of the French and American eras in terms of leisure activities, see Edwin E. Slosson and Gardner Richardson, "Two Panama Life Stories," *Independent* 60 (1906), pp. 918–25. The authors interviewed a Jamaican laborer who worked for both the French and the Americans. There was much he preferred about the French approach to managing workers, but he found the regimented nature of life under the United States to be an improvement: "The best thing the Americans have done is to stop bad language and gambling, which leads to quarrels. There is a big fine and prison for gambling. In the French days there used to be cock fighting, and drinking, and shooting, and dancing all the time. Now it is all stopped."

CHAPTER THREE: SILVER LIVES

1. *Isaac McKinzie v. McClintic-Marshall Construction Company,* Aug. 12, 1912, civil case 119, RG 21, Judicial Records of the Canal Zone, 1st Circuit, National Archives, Washington, D.C. For other examples of suits against this company, see cases 143, 145, 157, 169. The information in the following paragraphs about McKinzie's case comes also from the case cited above. Important studies on West Indian life and work include Velma Newton, *The Silver Men: West Indian Labour Migration to Panama, 1850–1914* (Mona, Jamaica: University of the West Indies, 1984); Bonham Richardson, *Panama Money in Barbados, 1900–1920* (Knoxville: University of Tennessee Press, 1985); Lancelot S. Lewis, *The West Indian in Panama: Black Labor in Panama, 1850–1914* (Washington, D.C.: University Press of America, 1980); Michael L. Conniff, *Black Labor on a White Canal: Panama, 1904–1981* (Pittsburgh: University of Pittsburgh Press, 1985); Gustave Anguizola, "Negroes in the Building of the Panama Canal," *Phylon* 29, no. 4 (Fall 1968), pp. 351–59; Gerardo Maloney, *El Canal de Panamá y los trabajadores antillanos* (Panama City: Universidad de Panamá, 1989); Luis Navas, Hernando Franco Muñoz, and Gerardo Maloney, *El movimiento obrero en Panamá* (Panamá: Autoridad del Canal de Panamá, 1999); George Westerman, *The West Indian Worker on the Canal Zone* (Panama: Liga Civica Nacional, 1950); Elizabeth McLean Petras, *Jamaican Labor Migration: White Capital and Black Labor, 1850–1930* (Boulder, Colo.: Westview, 1988); Rhonda A. Frederick, *"Colón Man a Come": Mythographies of Panama Canal Migration* (Lanham, Md.: Lexington Books, 2005). Fictional accounts that provide insightful reimaginings of West Indian life include Dr. Carlos E. Russell, *An Old Woman Remembers: The Recollected History of West Indians in Panama, 1855–1955* (Brooklyn: Caribbean Diaspora Press, 1995); George Lamming, *In the Castle of My Skin* (New York: McGraw-Hill, 1954); Maryse Condé, *Tree of Life: A Novel of the Caribbean* (New York: Ballantine Books, 1992); Eric Walrond, *Tropic Death* (New York: Collier Books, 1926).

2. *Hearings Concerning Estimates for Construction of the Isthmian Canal for the Fiscal Year 1911*, conducted on the Canal Zone by the Committee on Appropriations, House of Representatives, 61st Cong. (Washington, D.C.: GPO, 1910), pp. 145–47. The Liability Act providing for compensation took effect on Aug. 1, 1908. Between that date and Nov. 1, 1909, the U.S. government received two thousand claims. During that period it disbursed $54,000 for injuries but less than $700 for deaths. See also Newton, *Silver Men*, p. 142; and George W. Goethals, "The Building of the Panama Canal," pt. 2: "Labor Problems Connected with the Work," *Scribner's Magazine*, April 1915, p. 418. In 1912 the Panama Canal Act increased compensation and extended it to more employees.

3. *Census of the Canal Zone, February 1, 1912* (Mount Hope, C.Z.: ICC Press, 1912), pp. 29–31. Only Panamanians were more numerous in the region when the United States took possession of the Zone in 1904, at about five thousand men and women.

4. Constantine Parkinson, "Isthmian Historical Society Competition for the Best True Stories of Life and Work on the Isthmus of Panama During the Construction of the Panama Canal," Panama Collection of the Canal Zone Library-Museum, box 25, folders 3–4, Manuscript Division, Library of Congress, Washington, D.C.

5. *Census of the Canal Zone, February 1, 1912*, pp. 8–12, 29–31; Newton, *Silver Men*, esp. pp. 88–97.

6. *Hearings Concerning Estimates for Construction of the Isthmian Canal for the Fiscal Year 1911*, pp. 67–72; Newton, *Silver Men*, p. 136. There were just over one hundred West Indian policemen, for example, and thirty West Indian teachers.

7. *Hearings Concerning Estimates for Construction of the Isthmian Canal for the Fiscal Year 1911*, pp. 65–76, 135.

8. Ibid., pp. 67–72; Newton, *Silver Men*, pp. 134–38; *Canal Record*, Sept. 2, 1914, p. 15. The gradual rise

in the number of artisans employed by the ICC can be tracked in the *Canal Record* and in the annual reports of the ICC. See, for example, "Report of the Department of Labor, Quarters, and Subsistence,"*Annual Report of the Isthmian Canal Commission, 1908* (Washington, D.C.: GPO, 1908), app. J, p. 249.

9. *Hearings Concerning Estimates for Construction of the Isthmian Canal for the Fiscal Year 1911*, pp. 67–72; Newton, *Silver Men*, p. 41; Lewis, *West Indian in Panama*, p. 30.

10. *Hearings Concerning Estimates for Construction of the Isthmian Canal for the Fiscal Year 1911*, pp. 67–72; Newton, *Silver Men*, p. 136.

11. Carla Burnett, "'Are We Slaves or Free Men?' Labor, Race, Garveyism, and the 1920 Panama Canal Strike" (Ph.D. diss., University of Illinois at Chicago, 2004), pp. 33–37; Edwin E. Slosson and Gardner Richardson, "Two Panama Life Stories," *Independent* 60 (1906), pp. 918–23. Harry Franck, the American policeman and census taker who described life in the Canal Zone, noted how different Barbadians appeared as compared with Jamaicans. Revealing his distrust of West Indians, he declared, "Of the great divisions among [West Indians], Barbadians seemed more well-mannered than Jamaicans—or was it merely more subtle hypocrisy?" Harry A. Franck, *Zone Policeman 88: A Close Range Study of the Panama Canal and Its Workers* (New York: Century, 1913), p. 43.

12. Constantine Parkinson wrote his story and entered it in the "Isthmian Historical Society Competition." The pages detailing Parkinson's story all derive from this source.

13. Albert Peters, John Holligan, Mitchell Berisford, and Nehemiah Douglas, ibid. A letter submitted to this same competition by Clifford Hunt likewise recalled, "Men in my gang tell the Boss I am going out to ease my bowels and they die in the bush and nobody look for you."

14. Leslie Carmichael, ibid.; interview notes taken by Bonham Richardson in Barbados during 1982. These interviews provided Richardson with a crucial source for his pathbreaking book, *Panama Money in Barbados*. I am very grateful to Dr. Richardson for allowing me to see his notes.

15. Conniff, *Black Labor on a White Canal*, pp. 30–31; David McCullough, *The Path Between the Seas: The Creation of the Panama Canal, 1870–1914* (New York: Simon and Schuster, 1977), pp. 581–83, 610; William Gorgas, "The Conquest of the Tropics for the White Race: President's Address at the Sixtieth Annual Session of the American Medical Association, June 9, 1909," *Journal of the American Medical Association* 52, no. 25 (1909), pp. 1967–69.

16. On destitution during the early period, see Mallet to Charles Magoon, Jan. 17, 1906, Foreign Office Records, FO 371/101, The National Archives, Kew, U.K. Statistics on illness and treatment in hospitals are from "Report of Col. W. C. Gorgas, Head of the Department of Sanitation," in *Annual Report of the Isthmian Canal Commission for the Fiscal Year Ending June 30, 1912* (Washington, D.C.: GPO, 1912), app. P, p. 544. For statistics on population, see *Census of the Canal Zone, February 1, 1912*, pp. 8–12.

17. Norton Brownie, "Isthmian Historical Society Competition."

18. Slosson and Richardson, "Two Panama Life Stories"; "Isthmian Historical Society Competition," see letters by Aaron Clarke and Thomas Gittens.

19. Gertrude Beeks's report and the government's response can be found in the Isthmian Canal Commission Records, RG 185, 28-A-5, National Archives, College Park, Md. (hereafter cited as ICC Records). See also Goethals to Beeks, Aug. 23, 1907, in the same collection. As late as Nov. 1907, Gertrude Beeks wrote that laborers still lacked mattresses or blankets, and were lying directly on canvas or metal cots. The floors of their quarters were also wood, which retains moisture, rather than the concrete used by the British government at Cape Town. See "Reply of Miss Gertrude Beeks," Nov. 16, 1907, ICC Records, 28-A-5, p. 47.

20. Gorgas testifying in *The Panama Canal: Hearings Before the Committee on Interstate and Foreign Commerce*, House of Representatives, 62nd Cong., 2nd sess. (Washington, D.C.: GPO, 1912), pp. 275–76. For a similar opinion that West Indians were to blame for their illnesses, see Theodore Shonts, chairman of the ICC, testifying in U.S. Senate, *Investigation of Panama Canal Matters: Hearings Before the Committee on Interoceanic Canals of the United States Senate*, 59th Cong., 2nd sess., Doc. 401 (Washington, D.C.: GPO, 1907), serial set 5097, vol. 1, p. 478: "Our people [white Americans] have greater vitality, and they probably take better care of themselves." For more on medical efforts in the Zone, consult J. Ewing Mears, *The Triumph of American Medicine in the Construction of the Panama Canal* (Philadelphia: Wm. J. Dornan, 1911); Gorgas, "Conquest of the Tropics for the White Race";

William Crawford Gorgas, *Sanitation in Panama* (New York: D. Appleton, 1915); Joseph A. Le Prince and A. J. Orenstein, eds., *Mosquito Control in Panama: The Eradication of Malaria and Yellow Fever in Cuba and Panama* (New York: G. P. Putnam's Sons, 1916).

21. Civil case files from the 3rd Judicial Circuit, Panama Canal Zone, National Archives, Washington, D.C.; see esp. case files 377, 380, and 446.

22. On West Indians complaining to the British consul, consider the case of Nataniel Brown, who complained he had been held against his will for seven months but never received any treatment for insanity. Brown to the Honorable Colonial Secretary of Jamaica, July 24, 1908, Foreign Office Records, FO 288/110; *Annual Report of the Isthmian Canal Commission for the Fiscal Year Ending June 30, 1907* (Washington, D.C.: GPO, 1907), p. 31; *Annual Report of the Isthmian Canal Commission for the Fiscal Year Ending June 30, 1912* (Washington, D.C.: GPO, 1912), p. 550. For more on such themes, see David Arnold, *Colonizing the Body: State Medicine and Epidemic Disease in Nineteenth-Century India* (Berkeley: University of California Press, 1993); Warwick Anderson, *The Cultivation of Whiteness: Science, Health, and Racial Destiny in Australia* (New York: Basic Books, 2003); Julyan Peard, *Race, Place, and Medicine: The Idea of the Tropics in Nineteenth-Century Brazilian Medicine* (Durham, N.C.: Duke University Press, 2000).

23. Reginald Beckford, "Isthmian Historical Society Competition."

24. Alfred Dottin and Jules Lecurrieux, ibid.

25. Marrigan Austin, ibid.

26. For evidence on officials' determination to maintain a labor surplus, see William Burr's testimony in U.S. Senate, *Investigation of Panama Canal Matters: Hearings Before the Committee on Interoceanic Canals of the United States Senate*, serial set 5098, vol. 2, p. 1574.

27. Thatcher's testimony is in *The Panama Canal: Hearings Before the Committee on Interstate and Foreign Commerce*, vol. 1, p. 320.

28. Franck, *Zone Policeman 88*, p. 167; Poultney Bigelow, "Panama—the Human Side," pt. 3, *Cosmopolitan Magazine* 42 (1906), pp. 53–60; Fitz. A. Banister, "Isthmian Historical Society Competition."

29. An ordinance allowed arrest for vagrancy, mendicancy, trespass, intoxication, and disorderly conduct. Any person found idle, begging, drunk, disorderly, or without visible means of support would be punished by a fine of no more than $25 or imprisonment for no more than thirty days, or both. This ordinance took effect on Jan. 1, 1908, and was added to the penal code of the Canal Zone by executive order of President Roosevelt on Jan. 9, 1908. See extracts from the minutes of meeting of the ICC, Dec. 9, 1907, and Roosevelt's executive order: both ICC Records, 94-L-9. For the case of Charles Hamilton, see Inspector Miskimon to Goethals, Aug. 31, 1910, T. B. Miskimon Papers, MS 86-5, box 2, FF 39, Special Collections, Ablah Library, Wichita State University.

30. J. P. Fyffe, "In Re: Labor Conditions," to M. H. Thatcher, July 29, 1911; "Persons Arrested for Loitering and Vagrancy in the Various Towns of the Canal Zone, and the Results of Their Trials, from 6:00 p.m., July 12, 1911, to 6:00 p.m., July 27, 1911"; Rousseau to George Shanton, Jan. 3, 1908: all ICC Records, 94-L-9. See also Thatcher's testimony in *The Panama Canal: Hearings Before the Committee on Interstate and Foreign Commerce*, vol. 1, p. 320. For accounts of West Indians alleging mistreatment by police, see the manuscripts of Miskimon, Goethals's investigator, in Miskimon Papers. For example, see Miskimon's memo to Goethals, Aug. 10, 1910, MS 86-5, box 2, FF 33. For more on prisons and prison labor, see chapter 7, below.

31. Mallet to Consul Cox, Dec. 8, 1910, Foreign Office Records, FO 371/944.

32. Mallet to Sir, marked confidential, Nov. 19, 1906, Foreign Office Records, FO 288/98.

33. Marsh to the foreign secretary of state, United Kingdom, Jan. 7, 1911, FO 371/1176; no author to no one (but presumably to Mallet), Sept. 26, 1914, Foreign Office Records, FO 288/160.

34. Hardie to Colonel Seely (MP, Colonial Office), Nov. 24, 1908, and see also accompanying letters, document #42743, Foreign Office Records, FO 371/494. Available evidence suggests the French consul played a role similar to that of his British counterpart. In one case he took action when, in 1905, a group of Martinican laborers protested their treatment on board a ship and were forcibly ejected from it. The Panamanian police physically punished the Martinicans, and the French government became concerned about charges of cruelty. Consequently, the French consul conducted an investigation into living and working conditions for Martinicans, and requested several changes

from the U.S. government. See G. Bonhenry, Vice Consulate of France in Colón, Panama, "Report," Nov. 13, 1905; Bonhenry to the Department of Foreign Affairs, Nov. 16, 1905: ICC Records, 2-P-69, pt. 1, box 50.

35. Brakemen of Pedro Miguel and Las Cascadas to Goethals, April 13, 1913, ICC Records, 2-P-22, box 48.
36. Miskimon, memorandum for the chairman, n.d., Miskimon Papers, MS 86-5, box 2, FF 47.
37. Slosson and Richardson, "Two Panama Life Stories."
38. See Richardson, *Panama Money in Barbados*, esp. ch. 2 and 3; Conniff, *Black Labor on a White Canal*, pp. 8–11; Lewis, *West Indian in Panama*, pp. 72–73; and George Westerman, "Historical Notes on West Indians on the Isthmus of Panama," *Phylon* 22 (Winter 1961), p. 342.
39. On this common theme in history and anthropology, many examples abound. Among others, consult Herbert Gutman, *Work, Culture, and Society in Industrializing America: Essays in American Working-Class and Social History* (New York: Knopf, 1976); Tera Hunter, *To 'Joy My Freedom: Southern Black Women's Lives and Labor After the Civil War* (Cambridge, Mass.: Harvard University Press, 1997); and James C. Scott, *Weapons of the Weak: Everyday Forms of Peasant Resistance* (New Haven, Conn.: Yale University Press, 1985).
40. U.S. Senate, *Investigation of Panama Canal Matters*, vol. 1, pp. 81, 55, 347, 485–86.
41. Stevens considers West Indians to be childlike in ibid., p. 81. Similarly, William Nelson Cromwell testified that the Caribbean laborers were "plain people" who were "densely ignorant." See ibid., vol. 2, p. 1163; and Stevens notes West Indians' deliberate efforts not to work in "Exhibit A," in *Message from the President of the United States Transmitting Certain Papers to Accompany His Message of January 8, 1906* (Washington, D.C.: GPO, 1906), p. 24.
42. *Hearings Concerning Estimates for Construction of the Isthmian Canal for the Fiscal Year 1911*, p. 66; on the changing of names, see, for example, Basil Blackman (acting governor of Jamaica) to the minister in Panama, Aug. 17, 1908, Foreign Office Records, FO 288/110.
43. *Hearings Before the Subcommittee of the House Committee on Appropriations, in Charge of Sundry Civil Appropriation Bill for 1907* (Washington, D.C.: GPO, 1906), p. 9. See also on this point *Hearings Before the Committee on Interstate and Foreign Commerce of the House of Representatives, on the Isthmian Canal* (Washington, D.C.: GPO, 1906), p. 38; *Panama Canal—Skilled Labor: Extracts from Hearings of the Committees on Appropriations of the Senate and House of Representatives, Fiscal Years 1907 to 1915 Inclusive*, 63rd Cong., 2nd sess. (Washington, D.C.: GPO, 1914), p. 109; U.S. Senate, *Investigation of Panama Canal Matters*, vol. 3, p. 1574; *Hearings Concerning Estimates for Construction of the Isthmian Canal for the Fiscal Year 1911*, p. 327.
44. Stevens, "Exhibit A," in *Message from the President*, p. 21; Slosson and Richardson, "Two Panama Life Stories."
45. U.S. Senate, *Investigation of Panama Canal Matters*, vol. 3, p. 1296, vol. 1, p. 773.
46. Ibid., vol. 1, pp. 620–21.
47. Shanton to the governor of the Canal Zone, April 27, 1905, in *Papers Relating to the Foreign Relations of the United States, with the Annual Message of the President Transmitted to Congress, Dec. 5, 1905*, House of Representatives, 59th Cong., 1st sess. (Washington, D.C.: GPO, 1906), pp. 711–12.
48. Magoon, testimony in U.S. Senate, *Investigation of Panama Canal Matters*, vol. 1, p. 773.
49. Barrett to the minister of government and foreign affairs, May 8, 1905, and Barrett to the British consul, May 8, 1905: both in *Papers Relating to the Foreign Relations of the United States*, pp. 710–11. See also George Davis to Wallace, May 3, 1905, in U.S. Senate, *Investigation of Panama Canal Matters*, vol. 3, pp. 2500–2505, 2665. Lewis discusses this incident in *West Indian in Panama*, pp. 46–49. The Panamanian police would be a recurring source of trouble for West Indian laborers in the Canal Zone. On this subject a useful source is Anguizola, "Negroes in the Building of the Panama Canal."
50. Eyra Marcela Reyes Rivas, *El trabajo de las mujeres en la historia de la construcción del Canal de Panamá, 1881–1914* (Panama: Universidad de Panamá, Instituto de la Mujer, 2000), p. 103; Fannie P. Hernandez, "Men Dug the Canal . . . but Women Played a Vital Role," *Panama Canal Review* (Spring 1976), cited in the richly documented dissertation by Paul W. Morgan Jr., "The Role of North American Women in U.S. Cultural Chauvinism in the Panama Canal Zone, 1904–1945" (Ph.D. diss., Florida State University, 2000), pp. 40, 51–52. Many works cite this tale of a sit-down strike by West Indian workers declaring "No women, no work," but the only direct evidence I've found

for this is the 1976 reminiscence, cited above, by Fannie Hernandez. On the importation of Martinican women, see Poultney Bigelow, "Our Mismanagement at Panama," *Independent*, Jan. 4, 1906, reprinted in *Message from the President*, pp. 79–91; and U.S. Senate, *Investigation of Panama Canal Matters*, vol. 1, pp. 56–57, 931–82. Many West Indians began sending money home so women might join them on the isthmus, but this also complicated the housing situation. The U.S. government provided some married housing to laborers, but required that only legally married couples might make use of it. In 1907 the ICC stopped building married housing for the laborers on the ground that it cost too much money. See Newton, *Silver Men*, pp. 148–49.

51. On Beeks's charge about food and the government's response, see R. E. Wood (acting manager, Department of Labor, Quarters, and Subsistence) to Goethals, Aug. 23, 1907, ICC Records, 28-A-5, p. 10. For sample menus supplied to gold versus silver employees, see U.S. Senate, *Investigation of Panama Canal Matters*, vol. 2, p. 1330. On the importing of food from Barbados, England, and other places, see *Hearings Before the Committee on Interstate and Foreign Commerce of the House of Representatives on Panama Canal* (Washington, D.C.: GPO, 1909), pp. 83–86. Also useful is the discussion in *The Panama Canal: Hearings Before the Committee on Interoceanic Canals*, U.S. Senate, 62nd Cong. (Washington, D.C.: GPO, 1912), pp. 162–63.

52. The comment by the representative of the Bible Society of Barbados is in *Hearings Concerning Estimates for Construction of the Isthmian Canal for the Fiscal Year 1911*, p. 76. For John Butcher's opinion, see "Isthmian Historical Society Competition."

53. Wallace's comment is in U.S. Senate, *Investigation of Panama Canal Matters*, vol. 1, p. 624. Thus gradually the government shifted its strategy to a looser approach. Whereas initially officials believed it essential to make West Indians consume more meat so as to improve their efficiency, they soon discovered they would need to let laborers decide for themselves what and how they would eat.

54. The descriptions of how men spent their time come from Henry De Lisser's account of his travels: *Jamaicans in Colón and the Canal Zone* (Kingston, 1906), p. 13. See Newton, *Silver Men*, for her very useful discussion of food and housing and West Indians' complaints regarding both.

55. See comments by the Jamaican carpenter interviewed in Slosson and Richardson, "Two Panama Life Stories."

56. U.S. Senate, *Investigation of Panama Canal Matters*, pp. 3087, 596; *Hearings Concerning Estimates for Construction of the Isthmian Canal for the Fiscal Year 1911*, pp. 74, 76; "Labor Problems: Laborers Who Prefer 'the Bush' to Commission Quarters," *Canal Record*, Jan. 13, 1909, p. 157; Newton, *Silver Men*, pp. 150–51.

57. By the summer of 1915, fewer than five thousand West Indian men were living in government housing. See U.S. Senate, *Investigation of Panama Canal Matters*, vol. 4, p. 3087, vol. 1, p. 596; *Hearings Concerning Estimates for Construction of the Isthmian Canal for the Fiscal Year 1911*, pp. 74, 76; *Canal Record*, Aug. 11, 1915, p. 445; "Report of the Quartermaster," in *Annual Report of the Isthmian Canal Commission for the Year Ending June 30, 1910* (Washington, D.C.: GPO, 1910), p. 312; *Canal Record*, Sept. 2, 1914, p. 1; "Labor Problems," p. 157. See also Newton, *Silver Men*, pp. 150–51.

58. The Jamaican newspaper the *Daily Gleaner* reported that in 1907 alone, Barbadians had sent home nearly $300,000 through the Canal Zone post office, while Jamaicans had sent home nearly $125,000, and Grenadians had sent $30,000. See "Canal Work," *Daily Gleaner*, March 30, 1908; Richardson, *Panama Money in Barbados;* and interview notes taken by Bonham Richardson in Barbados during 1982, in author's possession. Another excellent discussion of the Panama Canal's impact on international migration by Caribbeans is Lara Putnam, *The Company They Kept: Migrants and the Politics of Gender in Caribbean Costa Rica, 1870–1960* (Chapel Hill: University of North Carolina Press, 2002).

59. John Wallace, testimony in U.S. Senate, *Investigation of Panama Canal Matters*, vol. 1, p. 373. Albert Banister in "Isthmian Historical Society Competition."

60. See *Canal Zone v. Thomas F. B. Davis,* filed Jan. 27, 1909, cases 629–32, Judicial Records of the Canal Zone, Criminal Cases, 2nd District, National Archives, Washington, D.C.

61. Prince George Green and Reginald Beckford, "Isthmian Historical Society Competition."

62. Louise Cramer, "Songs of West Indian Negroes in the Canal Zone," *California Folklore Quarterly* 5, no. 3 (July 1946), pp. 243–72. For a useful approach to folk songs as sources, see Scott Reynolds Nelson, *Steel Drivin' Man: John Henry, The Untold Story of an American Legend* (New York: Oxford University Press, 2006).

63. Newton, *Silver Men*, pp. 156–57; Lewis, *West Indian in Panama*, pp. 76–77.

64. Westerman, "Historical Notes on West Indians on the Isthmus of Panama," pp. 342–43; Amos Parks's recollection is in "Isthmian Historical Society Competition."

CHAPTER FOUR: LAY DOWN YOUR SHOVELS

1. J. P. Cooper (sergeant, Zone policeman) to George Shanton, March 13, 1907; Shanton to H. D. Reed, March 14, 1907: both Isthmian Canal Commission Records, RG 185, 2-P-59, National Archives, College Park, Md. (hereafter cited as ICC Records). For the broader context of southern European immigration to the Americas during the early twentieth century, consult Yolanda Marco Serra, *Los obreros españoles en la construcción del Canal de Panamá: La emigración española hacia Panamá vista a través de la prensa española* (Panamá: Portobelo, 1997); William D. Donadio, *The Thorns of the Rose: Memoirs of a Tailor of Panama* (Colón, Republic of Panama: Dovesa, 1999); James R. Barrett and David Roediger, "Inbetween Peoples: Race, Nationality, and the 'New Immigrant' Working Class," *Journal of American Ethnic History* (Spring 1997), pp. 3–44; Thomas Guglielmo, *White on Arrival: Italians, Race, Color, and Power in Chicago, 1890–1945* (New York: Oxford University Press, 2003); Jose C. Moya, *Cousins and Strangers: Spanish Immigrants in Buenos Aires, 1850–1930* (Berkeley: University of California Press, 1998); Louis A. Pérez, *Cuba: Between Reform and Revolution* (New York: Oxford University Press, 1988); Ada Ferrer, *Insurgent Cuba: Race, Nation, and Revolution, 1868–1898* (Chapel Hill: University of North Carolina Press, 1999).

2. On the "turbulent" character of Spaniards, see *Hearings Before the Committee on Interstate and Foreign Commerce of the House of Representatives, on the Panama Canal* (Washington, D.C.: GPO, 1908), p. 32.

3. *Census of the Canal Zone, February 1, 1912* (Mount Hope, C.Z.: ICC Press, 1912), pp. 54–55. The one important exception involved some Panamanians, who were occasionally allowed to work at clerical or supervisory jobs on the gold payroll. Their privileged status was made possible by President Theodore Roosevelt, who included them on the gold roll in his 1908 executive order in deference to Panama's having given effective control over the Canal Zone to the United States.

4. Shonts to Stevens, June 5, 1905, ICC Records, 2-E-1; see Pérez, *Cuba*; Ferrer, *Insurgent Cuba*; Joan Casanovas, *Bread, or Bullets! Urban Labor and Spanish Colonialism in Cuba, 1850–1898* (Pittsburgh: University of Pittsburgh Press, 1998); Jackson Smith, "European Labor on the Isthmian Canal," March 25, 1907, ICC Records, 2-E-3.

5. Shonts testifying in U.S. Senate, *Investigation of Panama Canal Matters: Hearings Before the Committee on Interoceanic Canals of the United States Senate*, 59th Cong., 2nd sess., Doc. 401 (Washington, D.C.: GPO, 1907), vol. 1, p. 484; Smith, "European Labor on the Isthmian Canal."

6. William J. Karner, *More Recollections* (Boston: Thomas Todd, 1921), pp. 206–7; William R. Scott, *The Americans in Panama* (New York: Statler, 1913), pp. 188–89. On Italian migrants and their role in the Canal Zone, see also Diego dal Boni, *Panamá, Italia, y los italianos en la época de la construcción del Canal, 1880–1915* (Bogotá: Panamerica, 2000). For a comparison with Italian migration to North America, see Gunther Peck, *Reinventing Free Labor: Padrones and Immigrant Workers in the North American West, 1880–1930* (New York: Cambridge University Press, 2000).

7. Smith, "European Labor on the Isthmian Canal."

8. Spain sent more migrants abroad than any other European country during these decades except for Britain and Italy. See Moya, *Cousins and Strangers;* Salvador Palazón, *Los Españoles en América Latina, 1850–1990* (Madrid: CEDEAL, 1995), pp. 130–34; Walter Nugent, *Crossings: The Great Transatlantic Migrations, 1870–1914* (Bloomington: Indiana University Press, 1992), pp. 101–5; Adrian Shubert, *A Social History of Modern Spain* (London: Unwin Hyman, 1990); Marco Serra, *Los obreros españoles en la construcción del Canal de Panamá.* The 1912 census of the Panama Canal Zone includes statistics on literacy. Of the nearly thirty-five hundred Spaniards employed by the U.S. government, thirteen hundred were recorded as being illiterate. *Census of the Canal Zone, February 1, 1912,* pp. 50–54.

9. Gertrude Beeks, "Report for the National Civic Federation," issued to William H. Taft, Jan. 28, 1908, esp. pp. 43–46, ICC Records, 28-A-5; "Statements Made by a Delegation of European Laborers," Aug. 9, 1911, ICC Records, 2-P-59.

10. J. G. Sullivan, the assistant chief engineer, referred to Europeans as "semi-white" in a letter to D. W. Bolich, Aug. 4, 1906, ICC Records, 2-F-14; for an example where Spaniards are unambiguously referred to as white, see acting chief of police to commanding officer, Culebra, Feb. 25, 1909, ICC Records, 2-P-59.

11. Amy Kaplan and Donald E. Pease, eds., *Cultures of United States Imperialism* (Durham, N.C.: Duke University Press, 1993), especially the article by Amy Kaplan, "Black and Blue on San Juan Hill"; Theodore Roosevelt, *The Rough Riders* (New York: Modern Library, 1999).

12. *Hearings Concerning Estimates for Construction of the Isthmian Canal for the Fiscal Year, 1911,* conducted on the Canal Zone by the Committee on Appropriations, House of Representatives, 61st Cong. (Washington, D.C.: GPO, 1910), pp. 67–68. Silver workers were paid in silver, which was worth roughly half the value of gold. When discussing the pay they gave to silver workers, U.S. officials always referred to what the silver pay would be worth in U.S. currency, and I follow the same convention in this book. Thus in the case discussed here, Laborer A is described as earning ten cents U.S. currency per hour, although in reality he would have been paid twenty cents silver per hour. David Roediger employs W. E. B. DuBois's notion in *The Wages of Whiteness: Race and the Making of the American Working Class,* 2nd ed. (New York: Verso, 2007); by "wages of whiteness" both DuBois and Roediger referred to the psychological and cultural wage white workers historically earned as a result of privileges their race afforded them.

13. Potous to Joseph Blackburn, Oct. 5, 1907; G. Garibaldi to Joseph Bucklin Bishop, Oct. 16, 1907; Blackburn to Potous, June 18, 1907: all ICC Records, 2-P-69. I've seen no evidence of involvement by the Italian or Greek consuls, for example, in the records of the ICC, but the archives of those countries—as well as of France—might contain more information.

14. Mallet, annual report for 1908, delivered in May 1909, Foreign Office Records, FO 371/708, The National Archives, Kew, U.K.

15. Garibaldi to Bishop, Oct. 16, 1907; R. E. Wood to Blackburn, July 27, 1907; Potous to D. D. Gaillard, March 4, 1908; Garibaldi to Goethals, June 9, 1908: all ICC Records, 2-P-69.

16. Mallet, annual report for 1908, Foreign Office Records, FO 371/708. For the correspondence between Spanish and U.S. government officials over issues like compensation in the years before Potous issued his report in 1908, see, for example, Potous to Blackburn, June 17, 1907, and Spanish minister R. Piña y Millet to secretary (presumably to William Howard Taft, the secretary of war immediately responsible for Canal Zone policies), June 25, 1907: both ICC Records, 2-P-69. See also *Hearings Concerning Estimates for Construction of the Isthmian Canal for the Fiscal Year 1911,* p. 64; *Census of the Canal Zone, February 1, 1912,* p. 30.

17. Spanish workmen to Potous, Oct. 30, 1907; Potous to Blackburn, Oct. 31, 1907; and governmental memo, Nov. 1, 1907: all ICC Records, 2-P-69.

18. Shanton to Reed, Feb. 26, 1907; S. B. Schenk to Shanton, Feb. 26, 1907; Benjamin Wood to Shanton, Dec. 13, 1906: all ICC Records, 2-P-59.

19. See A. E. Verdereau to Shanton, April 27, 1907; *El Único,* May 18, 1912: both ICC Records, 2-P-59.

20. Sibert to Blackburn, Sept. 6, 1907; Shanton to Blackburn, June 1, 1908; A. K. Evans (Zone policeman) to Shanton, May 2, 1907: all ICC Records, 2-P-59. The comment regarding pandering can be found in *Hearings Before the Committee on Interstate and Foreign Commerce of the House of Representatives on Panama Canal,* Hotel Tivoli, Ancon, Canal Zone (Washington, D.C.: GPO, 1909), pp. 83, 84.

21. *Hearings Before the Committee on Interstate and Foreign Commerce of the House of Representatives, on the Panama Canal* (1908), p. 30.

22. Cooper to Shanton, March 13, 1907; Shanton to Reed, March 14, 1907: both ICC Records, 2-P-59.

23. Clipping from the Panama *Sunday Sun,* March 31, 1907; Stanley Ross (Zone policeman) to Shanton, May 2, 1907: ICC Records, 2-P-59.

24. Sergeant Kennedy to Shanton, Feb. 25, 1909; Captain G. A. Porter (acting chief of police) to commanding officer of Culebra, Feb. 26, 1909; Porter to Potous, Feb. 26, 1909; Charles Palacio (Zone policeman) to Porter, Feb. 26, 1909: ICC Records, 2-P-59. For another example of trouble between Spaniards and West Indians riding together on labor trains, see *Canal Zone v. George Playfair,* March 13, 1905, case 6, Judicial Records of the Canal Zone, 2nd Criminal District, RG21, National Archives, Washington, D.C.

25. Memo, March 7, 1911, to Colonel Carrol A. Devol (chief quartermaster); Devol to Goethals, March 17, 1911; J. B. Cooper to chief of division, Aug. 24, 1911; M. H. Thatcher to Goethals, Sept. 9, 1911; Devol to Goethals, Sept. 12, 1911: all ICC Records, 28-B-233.

26. Shanton to Reed, April 9, 1907, forwarding a letter written by G. H. Skinner (Zone policeman), ICC Records, 2-P-59.

27. Shubert, *Social History of Modern Spain,* pp. 124–25.

28. Jose C. Moya found this to be the case in Argentina as well. See his *Cousins and Strangers,* p. 15.

29. On the decline of the Spanish Empire and its impact on Spanish immigrants, see Sebastian Balfour, *The End of the Spanish Empire, 1898–1923* (Oxford: Oxford University Press, 1997); Jordi Maluquer de Motes Bernet, *España en la crisis de 1898: De la gran depresión a la modernización económica del siglo XX* (Barcelona: Peninsula, 1999). For the experiences of Spaniards in Cuba and Argentina, see Casanovas, *Bread, or Bullets;* Moya, *Cousins and Strangers.*

30. See Julie Greene, "Race and the Tensions of Empire: The United States and the Construction of the Panama Canal, 1904–1914," unpublished paper presented at the Johns Hopkins Conference "Between Two Empires," Nov. 2000; George Brooke to Goethals, Feb. 1, 1909, ICC Records, 2-P-49/P; and Smith, memo, March 25, 1907, ICC Records, 2-E-3.

31. U.S. Senate, *Hearings Supplement, Senate Committee on Interoceanic Canals,* 62nd Cong. (Washington, D.C.: GPO, 1908), p. 90.

32. "Notes of Investigation Held on Sunday, July 30, 1911, in Office of Division Engineer at Empire Regarding Complains of Spanish Laborers in Culebra District," p. 6, ICC Records, 2-P-59.

33. A. S. Brook, memo to C. A. S. Zinn, July 28, 1911; petitions of the strikers, n.d.; José Buigasy de Dalmau (Spanish consul) to Goethals, July 28, 1911; Paul S. Wilson, "Memo re the European Laborers of the Culebra District," July 28, 1911; Goethals, "Notice to the Spanish Laborers on Strike," Aug. 2, 1911: all ICC Records, 2-P-59. Traditionally, Spaniards drank only coffee at breakfast time. Prohibiting eating on the job meant they would eat nothing between 6:20 a.m., when they arrived at work, until lunchtime at 1:00 p.m.

34. J. P. Fyffe to Thatcher, Aug. 3, 1911; Goethals, "Notice to the Spanish Laborers on Strike"; for the workers' petition to the government, see La Asamblea a la ICC, n.d.; Goethals to Gaillard, Aug. 7, 1911; "Notes of Investigation Held on Sunday, July 30, 1911"; Zinn (acting division engineer) to Joseph Little (superintendent of construction), July 31, 1911; A. Cornelison to assistant division engineer, Aug. 10, 1911; Cornelison to division engineer, Sept. 2, 1911: all ICC Records, 2-P-59.

35. Shubert, *Social History of Modern Spain,* pp. 90–103, 193–96.

36. See especially Casanovas, *Bread, or Bullets!;* and Temma Kaplan, "The Social Base of Nineteenth-Century Andalusian Anarchism in Jerez de la Frontera," *Journal of Interdisciplinary History* 6, no. 1, (Summer 1975), pp. 47–70; George Reid Andrews, "Black and White Workers; Sao Paulo, Brazil, 1888–1928," *Hispanic American Historical Review* 68, no. 3 (Aug. 1988), pp. 491–524; Shubert, *Social History of Modern Spain,* pp. 97–99; George R. Esenwein, *Anarchist Ideology and the Working-Class Movement in Spain, 1868–1898* (Berkeley: University of California Press, 1989); Raymond Carr, *Spain, 1808–1975* (Oxford: Oxford University Press, 1982); Edward Malefakis, *Agrarian Reform and Peasant Revolution in Spain: Origins of the Civil War* (New Haven, Conn.: Yale University Press, 1970); Eric Hobsbawm, *Primitive Rebels: Studies in Archaic Forms of Social Movement in the 19th and 20th Centuries,* 2nd ed. (New York: Praeger, 1963); Gary R. Mormino and George E. Pozzetta, *The Immigrant World of Ybor City: Italians and Their Latin Neighbors in Tampa, 1885–1985* (Urbana: University of Illinois Press, 1987); Maxine Molyneux, "No God, No Boss, No Husband: Anarchist Feminism in Nineteenth-Century Argentina," *Latin American Perspectives* 13, no. 1 (Winter 1986), pp. 119–45; Barry Carr, "Marxism and Anarchism in the Formation of the Mexican Communist Party, 1910–1919," *Hispanic American Historical Review* 63, no. 2 (May 1983), pp. 277–305; John M. Hart, *Anarchism and the Mexican Working Class, 1860–1931* (Austin: University of Texas Press, 1978); Vicente Díaz Fuentes, *La clase obrera: Entre el anarquismo y la religión* (Mexico: Universidad Nacional Autónoma de México, 1994); Anton Rosenthal, "The Arrival of the Electric Streetcar and the Conflict over Progress in Early Twentieth-Century Montevideo," *Journal of Latin American Studies* 27, no. 2 (May 1995), pp. 319–41; Jose C. Moya, *Cousins and Strangers.*

37. Paul Wilson to Bishop, Aug. 31, 1911; Gorgas to Goethals, Sept. 9, 1911; F. H. Sheibly to Bishop, Sept. 25, 1911: all ICC Records, 2-P-59.

38. Wilson to Bishop, Aug. 31, 1911; Corporal 5 (Zone police) to Shanton, Sept. 19, 1911; Father Henry Collins to Goethals, Oct. 13, 1911: all ICC Records, 2-P-59.

39. *El Único, Suplemento al número 1,* Sept. 12, 1911; P.V. (police spy) to Shanton, Sept. 25, 1911; Sheibly to Bishop, Sept. 25, 1911: ICC Records, 2-P-59.

40. Collins to Goethals, Oct. 10, 1911; F. B. (alias Punatazot) to Goethals, Nov. 6, 1911; R. J. Cochran to Goethals, Oct. 24, 1911; C. A. McIlvaine to Goethals, Aug. 17, 1911: all ICC Records, 2-P-59.

41. Father D. Quijano to Charles Mason, Sept. 26, 1911; Collins to Goethals, Oct. 13, 1911; Gorgas to Goethals, Sept. 30, 1911; Thatcher to Goethals, Sept. 29, 1911; J.K.B. to Goethals, n.d.; Eugene T. Wilson to acting chairman, March 21, 1912: all ICC Records, 2-P-59.

42. *Hearings Concerning Estimates for Construction of the Isthmian Canal for the Fiscal Year 1911,* p. 64; "Report of Lieut. Col. C. A. Devol, Quartermaster's Department," Appendix J, in *Annual Report of the Isthmian Canal Commission for the Fiscal Year Ending June 30, 1912* (Washington, D.C.: GPO, 1912), pp. 377–78.

CHAPTER FIVE: PROGRESSIVISM FOR THE WORLD

1. Arthur Bullard, *Panama: The Canal, the Country, and the People* (New York: Macmillan, 1911), p. 562. See also Albert Edwards, *Testing Socialism in the Canal Zone* (Girard, Kans.: A. W. Ricker, 1908). Technically, Bullard pointed out, one of the two railroads in the Canal Zone—the Panama Railroad, for passenger travel—was in private hands. But as the government owned virtually all stock in the company, he considered that as well to be government owned. For an interesting exploration of how the construction of the Panama Canal shaped the thinking of British Socialists, see Kevin Morgan, "British Guild Socialists, and the Exemplar of the Panama Canal," *History of Political Thought* 28, no. 1 (Spring 2007), pp. 120–57.

2. Arthur W. Thompson, "The Reception of Russian Revolutionary Leaders in America, 1904–1906," *American Quarterly* 18, no. 3 (Autumn 1966), pp. 452–76; James Boylan, *Revolutionary Lives: Anna Strunsky and William English Walling* (Amherst: University of Massachusetts Press, 1998), p. 68; Mark Pittenger, *American Socialists and Evolutionary Thought, 1870–1920* (Madison: University of Wisconsin Press, 1993); Jane E. Good, "America and the Russian Revolutionary Movement, 1888–1905," *Russian Review* 41, no. 3 (July 1982), pp. 273–87. See also Jane E. Good, "Strangers in a Strange Land: Five Russian Radicals Visit the United States, 1890–1908" (Ph.D. diss., American University, 1979), pp. 20, 161–62.

3. Bullard, *Panama,* pp. 48–49.

4. Ibid., pp. 572–78, 507.

5. Ibid., pp. 577–78.

6. Samuel Merwin, "The American Revolution at Panama: An Impression . . . and a Question," *Chicago Daily Tribune,* July 14, 1912, p. H3. For a similar analysis, see Willis J. Abbot, *Panama and the Canal in Picture and Prose* (New York: Syndicate, 1914), pp. 325–29.

7. Robert Herrick, "Imagination and the State," *Chicago Daily Tribune,* Jan. 10, 1915, p. A5; see also H. G. Wells, *Social Forces in England and America* (New York: Harper and Brothers, 1914); for arguments about employing similar methods in Alaska, see Merwin, "American Revolution at Panama"; and Abbot, *Panama and the Canal in Picture and Prose,* pp. 325–29.

8. Edward Bellamy, *Looking Backward: 2000–1887* (New York: Signet Classics, 2000); Abbot, *Panama and the Canal in Pictures and Prose,* p. 328. For interpretations of Bellamy, see Shelton Stromquist, *Reinventing "The People": The Progressive Movement, the Class Problem, and the Origins of Modern Liberalism* (Urbana: University of Illinois Press, 2006), pp. 39–42; Arthur Lipow, *Authoritarian Socialism in America: Edward Bellamy and the Nationalist Movement* (Berkeley: University of California Press, 1982); James Gilbert, *Designing the Industrial State: The Intellectual Pursuit of Collectivism in America, 1880–1940* (Chicago: Quadrangle Books, 1972).

9. Henry George, *Progress and Poverty: An Inquiry into the Cause of Industrial Depressions and of Increase of Want with Increase of Wealth: The Remedy* (New York: D. Appleton, 1882); on Gorgas and the single tax, see "Tax Idle Land to Aid Health, Plan of Gorgas," *Chicago Daily Tribune,* Sept. 7, 1915, p. 7. See also Stromquist, *Reinventing "The People"*; David M. Scobey, "Boycotting the Politics Factory: Labor Radicalism and the New York Mayoral Election of 1884," *Radical History Review* 28–30 (1984), pp. 280–325; John L. Thomas, *Alternative America: Henry George, Edward Bellamy, Henry Demarest Lloyd, and the Adversary Tradition* (Cambridge, Mass.: Harvard University Press, 1983). For others who mentioned the government ownership of all land in the Canal Zone as a positive feature, see Bullard, *Panama;* and Merwin, "American Revolution at Panama."

10. John Foster Carr, Sixth Paper, "Building a State," *Outlook,* June 23, 1906, pp. 435–45; Abbot, *Panama and the Canal in Picture and Prose,* pp. 328–29.

11. Joint strike bulletin, July 9, 1917, issued by the Metal Miners Union and the Electrical Workers' Union in Butte, Butte–Silver Bow Public Archives, Labor History Collection, Butte, Mont.; *Machinists' Monthly Journal,* Oct. 1908, p. 872. Others besides Bullard believed skilled workers would be converted to socialism as a result of seeing the lovely benefits accruing from government control. See, for example, Abbot, *Panama and the Canal in Picture and Prose,* pp. 326–27; Edith A. Browne, *Panama* (London: Adam and Charles Black, 1913), p. 74. For connections between socialism and imperialism in the British context, see Anna Davin, "Imperialism and Motherhood," in *Tensions of Empire: Colonial Cultures in a Bourgeois World,* ed. Frederick Cooper and Ann Laura Stoler (Berkeley: University of California Press, 1997), pp. 95–97. My thanks to John Enyeart for providing the Butte miners' perspective on the canal.

12. A Comrade, "The Isthmian Canal Today," *International Socialist Review* 11, no. 1 (July 1910), p. 15.

13. Stuart Chase, "Portrait of a Radical," *Century Magazine,* July 1924, p. 296; Edward T. Devine, "The Canal Builders," *Survey,* March 1, 1913, pp. 764–68. For background information on Devine, see Clarke A. Chambers, *Paul A. Kellogg and the "Survey": Voices for Social Welfare and Social Justice* (Minneapolis: University of Minnesota Press, 1971), esp. pp. 6–11, 29–30, 44. Born in 1861, Devine was one of the pioneers of what Chambers calls "social work journalism." He headed the New York Charity Organization Society and created the journal *Charities,* which later became the *Survey.* Often the analyses of government in the Canal Zone ducked the race question. Others besides Devine found the segregation system to be praiseworthy. Willis J. Abbot described it thus:

> The brilliant idea occurred to someone in the early days of the American campaign that as the West Indians, Panamanians and Latin-Americans generally were accustomed to do their monetary thinking in terms of silver all day labor might be put on the silver pay roll; the more highly paid workers on a gold pay roll. Thenceforward the metal line rather than the color line was drawn. The latter indeed would have been difficult as the Latin-American peoples never drew it very definitely in their marital relations, with the result that a sort of twilight zone made any very positive differentiation between whites and blacks practically impossible. . . . [O]n the Zone the man is silver or gold according to the nature of his work and the size of his wages.

See Abbot, *Panama and the Canal in Pictures and Prose,* pp. 324–25. I am grateful to Mark Pittenger and Thomas Krainz for informing me of the articles by Chase and Devine.

14. William E. Leuchtenburg, "Progressivism and Imperialism: The Progressive Movement and American Foreign Policy, 1898–1916," *Mississippi Valley Historical Review* 39, no. 3 (Dec. 1952), pp. 483–504, esp. pp. 501–3; Herbert Croly, *The Promise of American Life* (1909), at http://www.gutenberg.org/catalog/world/readfile?fk_files=117114&:pageno=1 (accessed April 29, 2005), pp. 173, 177.

15. For statistics on mortality see Frank Ninkovich, *The United States and Imperialism* (Oxford: Blackwell, 2001), p. 51; on the number of military personnel, see Richard Welch, *Response to Imperialism: The United States and the Philippine-American War, 1899–1902* (Chapel Hill: University of North Carolina Press, 1979), p. xiii.

16. Daniel B. Schirmer, *Republic or Empire: American Resistance to the Philippine War* (Cambridge, Mass.: Schenkman, 1972); Paul A. Kramer, *The Blood of Government: Race, Empire, the United States, and the Philippines* (Chapel Hill: University of North Carolina Press, 2006), pp. 143–46; Welch, *Response to Imperialism,* pp. 133–49.

17. Schirmer, *Republic or Empire;* see also "Address of Mr. Herbert Welsh" at the "Mass Meeting of Protest Against the Suppression of Truth About the Philippines," at http://www.boondocksnet.com/ai/ailtexts/massmtg11.htm (accessed Feb. 6, 2007).

18. Kristin L. Hoganson, *Fighting for American Manhood: How Gender Politics Provoked the Spanish-American and Philippine-American Wars* (New Haven, Conn.: Yale University Press, 1998); Ninkovich, *United States and Imperialism,* esp. pp. 51–53; on the racial implications of the war and "degeneration," see

Kramer, *Blood of Government*, p. 146; for Poultney Bigelow's article see "How to Convert a White Man into a Savage," *Independent* 54, no. 2789 (1902), pp. 1159–61.

19. Schirmer, *Republic or Empire;* Welch, *Response to Imperialism*, pp. 133–49; for a fine discussion of Roosevelt's speech, see Kramer, *Blood of Government*, pp. 154–57; quotation from the speech may be found in Theodore Roosevelt, *Addresses and Presidential Messages of Theodore Roosevelt, 1902–1904* (New York: G. P. Putnam's Sons, 1904), pp. 56–67.

20. Speech as governor of New York to the Lincoln Club in New York, Feb. 1899; excerpted in Mario DiNunzio, *Theodore Roosevelt: An American Mind* (New York: St. Martin's, 1994), p. 182.

21. On John Bigelow's career, see Margaret Clapp, *Forgotten First Citizen: John Bigelow* (Boston: Little, Brown, 1947); and David McCullough, *The Path Between the Seas: The Creation of the Panama Canal, 1870–1914* (New York: Simon and Schuster, 1977), esp. pp. 187–88. On John and his son Poultney, see Poultney Bigelow's memoir, *Seventy Summers* (New York: Longmans, Green, 1925). When his father served as minister to Prussia, Poultney was a boy of nine and became close friends with the future kaiser Wilhelm II. The two boys wandered about the Hohenzollern family estate playing as Indians in the Wild West. See Poultney Bigelow, *Prussian Memories, 1864–1914* (New York: G. P. Putnam's Sons, 1915); and "American Tells of Kaiser as a Playmate," *New York Times*, Nov. 7, 1915, p. SM7, ProQuest Historical Newspapers.

22. A sampling of Poultney Bigelow's books might include *History of the German Struggle for Liberty* (New York: Harper and Brothers, 1896); *The Children of the Nations: A Study of Colonization and Its Problems* (New York: McClure, Phillips, 1901); *White Man's Africa* (New York: Harper and Brothers, 1900).

23. Poultney Bigelow, "Our Mismanagement at Panama," *Independent*, Jan. 4, 1906, reprinted in *Message from the President of the United States Transmitting Certain Papers to Accompany His Message of January 8, 1906* (Washington, D.C.: GPO, 1906), pp. 79–91. This government publication includes many useful documents related to Bigelow's charges, including lengthy responses from Secretary of War William Howard Taft and chief engineer John Stevens.

24. The *Independent* published follow-up articles on Panama soon thereafter and noted defensively that many other articles had appeared criticizing the canal project before Bigelow's. See Edwin E. Slosson and Gardner Richardson, "The *Independent*'s Report on Panama," *Independent*, March 15, 1906, pp. 589–96. For Bishop's quotation, see J. Michael Hogan's pathbreaking article on Roosevelt's public relations effort: "Theodore Roosevelt and the Heroes of Panama," *Presidential Studies Quarterly* 19 (Winter 1989), p. 81; the essay is also included in Hogan's *Panama Canal in American Politics* (Carbondale: Southern Illinois University Press, 1986).

25. Bigelow, "Our Mismanagement at Panama."

26. Taft to Roosevelt, Jan. 8, 1906; and John Stevens, "Exhibit A": both in *Message from the President;* "Canal in Nine Years Is Shonts's Promise," *New York Times*, Jan. 21, 1906, p. 5, ProQuest Historical Newspapers.

27. "Bigelow Defies Arrest at the Canal Inquiry," *New York Times*, Jan. 19, 1906; "May Not Punish Bigelow," *New York Times*, Jan. 20, 1906, ProQuest Historical Newspapers; Bigelow, *Seventy Summers*, pp. 217–18, 232, 273–86. Around the time this scandal broke, Bigelow resigned his position at Boston University because of objections to his views "on the negro and on Christian missionaries in the Far East." He credited this and especially the Senate investigation with making him "in worldly eyes a ruined man," and he retired at the age of fifty: *Seventy Summers*, p. vii. We will see below, in chapter 6, that Congress followed up its investigation of Bigelow by investigating the unfortunate Martinican women to determine if they were prostitutes or not.

28. Slosson and Richardson, "*Independent*'s Report on Panama"; Edwin E. Slosson and Gardner Richardson, "Life on the Canal Zone," *Independent*, March 22, 1906, pp. 653–60.

29. Bigelow's article is cited in Hogan, "Theodore Roosevelt and the Heroes of Panama," p. 82; for the follow-up articles by Bigelow, see "Panama—The Human Side," pts. 1–3, *Cosmopolitan Magazine* (1906–7), vol. 41, pp. 455–62 and 606–12, and vol. 42, pp. 53–60.

30. "Roosevelt on Way to See the Ditch," *Chicago Daily Tribune*, Nov. 9, 1906, p. 1; "Roosevelt to Say Adieu," *Chicago Daily Tribune*, Nov. 5, 1906, p. 1; "Floating Palace for President: Suite of Rooms on Louisiana Outfitted to Impress South Americans," *Chicago Daily Tribune*, Nov. 6, 1906, p. 4.

31. On the Brownsville incident, see "Negro Troops Disarmed at Roosevelt's Orders," *Chicago Daily*

Tribune, Nov. 13, 1906; "President Expels an Army Battalion," *New York Times*, Nov. 7, 1906; "Roosevelt and Taft Said to Have Clashed," *New York Times*, Nov. 21, 1906; "Roosevelt Is Firm, and Taft Gives Way," *New York Times*, Nov. 22, 1906; Kathleen Dalton, *Theodore Roosevelt: A Strenuous Life* (New York: Knopf, 2002), pp. 321–23.

32. "President at Panama: Makes a Quick Trip; Anarchists Under Arrest," *New York Times*, Nov. 15, 1906; "Canal 'Tidied Up' to See Roosevelt," *Chicago Daily Tribune*, Nov. 14, 1906; on the cleaning up of the isthmus, see also McCullough, *Path Between the Seas*, p. 494.

33. "Roosevelt Delivers Warning to Panama," *New York Times*, Nov. 16, 1906, p. 1; "Cruise in Panama Bay," *New York Times*, Nov. 16, 1906; "President Inspects Canal Workers' Homes," *New York Times*, Nov. 18, 1906; William Inglis, "At Double-Quick Along the Canal with the President," *Harper's Weekly* 50 (1906), pp. 1740–45.

34. "Roosevelt Delivers Warning to Panama"; "Roosevelt Sees the Dirt Flying; Lunches with Diggers," *Chicago Daily Tribune*, Nov. 16, 1906, p. 1.

35. Inglis, "At Double-Quick Along the Canal with the President"; "Roosevelt Sees the Dirt Flying"; Mary A. Chatfield, *Light on Dark Places at Panama* (New York: Broadway, 1908), p. 195.

36. Roosevelt to Kermit, Nov. 20, 1906, in *Theodore Roosevelt's Letters to His Children*, ed. Joseph Bucklin Bishop (New York: Charles Scribner's Sons, 1919), pp. 182–83.

37. "The President Climbs a Steam Shovel," *New York Times*, Nov. 17, 1906; Michael Delevante, *Panama Pictures: Nature and Life in the Land of the Great Canal* (New York: Alden Brothers, 1907); Inglis, "At Double-Quick Along the Canal with the President." See also "The Panama Canal as the President Saw It," *Review of Reviews* 35 (1907), pp. 66–73.

38. "Ignore Criticisms, Says the President," *New York Times*, Nov. 19, 1906, ProQuest Historical Newspapers; Address of Theodore Roosevelt to the Assembled Panama Canal Force, Colón, Nov. 16, 1906: "The Work You Have Done Here Will Remain for the Ages," http://www.czbrats.com/Builders/speechTR.htm (accessed May 5, 2004); "Address to the Employees of the I.C.C., Culebra, CZ," http://www.czbrats.com/Builders/EarlyOnes.htm (accessed April 4, 2007); Roosevelt to Kermit, Nov. 20, 1906, in Bishop, *Theodore Roosevelt's Letters to His Children*, p. 182; Chatfield, *Light on Dark Places at Panama*, pp. 195–96. Chatfield's reaction to the president's visit is quite interesting. She opened the subject in her letters home by stating: "I will now give you my version of the flying visit of the greatest ruler on earth" (p. 194). She concluded: "We were told that he would visit our office in the afternoon and were instructed to rise when he entered. I told the man that sat opposite me that I would not rise for any 'mere man' that afternoon. I felt sure that he [Roosevelt] would not waste his time coming up there and he did not" (p. 196).

39. "Message of the President on the Panama Canal, Communicated to the Two Houses of Congress by President Theodore Roosevelt," Dec. 17, 1906, http://www.czbrats.com/Builders/presmes8.htm (accessed April 4, 2007); J. Hampton Moore, *With Speaker Cannon Through the Tropics: A Descriptive Story of a Voyage to the West Indies, Venezuela, and Panama* (Philadelphia: Book Print, 1907), p. 265. See also Hogan's treatment of this topic: "Theodore Roosevelt and the Heroes of Panama," pp. 82–84.

40. William Inglis, "The Progress and Promise of the Work at Panama," *Harper's Weekly* 50 (1906), pp. 1852–56; Hogan, "Theodore Roosevelt and the Heroes of Panama," pp. 84–86; Delevante, *Panama Pictures*; Moore, *With Speaker Cannon Through the Tropics*, pp. 245–46.

41. "Popularizing the Canal," *Chicago Daily Tribune*, March 16, 1907; "Commercial Men Praise Ditch Job," *Chicago Daily Tribune*, March 13, 1907. For more on the businessmen's trip, see Walter B. Stevens, *A Trip to Panama: The Narrative of a Tour of Observation Through the Canal Zone, with Some Account of Visits to Saint Thomas, Porto Rico, Jamaica, and Cuba, by the Commercial Clubs of Boston, Chicago, Cincinnati, and St. Louis, February 18–March 14th, 1907* (St. Louis, 1907); another example of the interest in the canal shown by businessmen is Cincinnati Chamber of Commerce, *Trade Expansion Tour: Panama Canal, Jamaica, Havana, and Southern Points, February 14 to March 9, 1913* (Cincinnati: printed by Tom Jones, 1913). Taft visited the canal in 1909, albeit with much less fanfare than Roosevelt; see "Canal Progress Praised by Taft," *Chicago Daily Tribune*, Feb. 8, 1909. On labor representatives' visit to the Canal Zone, see "Chief of Steam Shovelers to Investigate at Panama," *Chicago Daily Tribune*, Jan. 4, 1908.

42. Speaker Joseph Cannon is quoted in "The Speaker Home: Life of His Party," *New York Times*,

April 8, 1907, p. 2, ProQuest Historical Newspapers; Helen Herron Taft, *Recollections of Full Years* (New York: Dodd, Mead, 1914), p. 284; on Speaker Cannon's visit, see Moore, *With Speaker Cannon Through the Tropics.*

43. Poultney Bigelow, "An American Panama: Some Personal Notes on Tropical Colonization as Affected by Geographic and Political Conditions," *Bulletin of the American Geographical Society* 38, no. 8 (1906), pp. 489–94; "Panama Meat Is Bad; All Else Is Fine," *Chicago Daily Tribune*, April 3, 1907; "Rainey Sees Canal Graft: Congressman Makes a Bitter Attack on Taft and Others," *Chicago Daily Tribune*, Jan. 27, 1909; "Congress to Act on 'Canal Graft'?" *Chicago Daily Tribune*, Dec. 8, 1908. For other criticism about the construction project, see "Panama a Sodom, Editor Declares: Temperance Worker Holds Roosevelt Responsible for 'White Slaves' on Isthmus," *Chicago Daily Tribune*, June 4, 1907; "Sees War Measure in Canal," *Chicago Daily Tribune*, Jan. 28, 1909; "Canal Zone Called Satrapy," *Chicago Daily Tribune*, Feb. 26, 1911. See also, for a harsh critique of the government, Chatfield, *Light on Dark Places at Panama.*

44. Nikki Mandell, *The Corporation as Family: The Gendering of Corporate Welfare, 1890–1930* (Chapel Hill: University of North Carolina Press, 2002); Bradley Rudin, "Industrial Betterment and Scientific Management as Social Control, 1890–1915," *Berkeley Journal of Sociology* 17 (1972–73), p. 62; Stuart D. Brandes, *American Welfare Capitalism, 1880–1940* (Chicago: University of Chicago Press, 1970); Andrea Tone, *The Business of Benevolence: Industrial Paternalism in Progressive America* (Ithaca, N.Y.: Cornell University Press, 1997); the quotation about efficiency comes from Sarah Comstock, "A Woman of Achievement: Miss Gertrude Beeks," *World's Work*, Aug. 1913, p. 445; Beeks to Ralph Easley, Saturday, 1903, National Civic Federation Papers, reel 417, New York Public Library (hereafter cited as NCF Papers).

45. Marguerite Green, *The National Civic Federation and the American Labor Movement, 1900–1925* (Washington, D.C.: Catholic University of America Press, 1956); Christopher J. Cyphers, *The National Civic Federation and the Making of a New Liberalism, 1900–1915* (Westport, Conn.: Praeger, 2002).

46. In 1917, after Easley's first wife had died, he and Beeks married. See Comstock, "Woman of Achievement," p. 448; Rudin, "Industrial Betterment and Scientific Management as Social Control," p. 62; Gerd Korman, *Industrialization, Immigrants, and Americanizers: The View from Milwaukee, 1866–1921* (Madison: State Historical Society of Wisconsin, 1967), pp. 90–91; Beeks to Easley, Saturday, 1903, NCF Papers, reel 417; see also Green on Beeks's activities in *National Civic Federation and the American Labor Movement,* esp. pp. 276–77; on her antisuffrage and antisocialist activities, see Cyphers, *National Civic Federation and the Making of a New Liberalism,* pp. 78–79.

47. "Welfare Work for Government Employes," *National Civic Federation Review,* Sept. 1907, pp. 10–16. On voluntary welfare activities as a "political ideology" for the NCF and for Beeks particularly, see Tone, *Business of Benevolence,* p. 43.

48. "Conditions in the Canal Zone," *National Civic Federation Review,* Sept. 1907, p. 9; Taft to Goethals, May 16, 1907, NCF Papers, reel 376, Subject Files, Panama Canal.

49. "Panama Labor Inquiry," *New York Times,* June 8, 1907, p. 8, ProQuest Historical Newspapers; details on weather from *New York Times,* June 8, 1907, p. 18; no author or date but presumably by Gertrude Beeks, "Steam Shovel Work and Steam Shovel Men in Panama," NCF Papers, reel 376, Subject Files, Panama Canal; "Conditions in the Canal Zone," p. 9; Comstock, "Woman of Achievement," p. 448. Beeks also published a short summary of her lengthy report in an article titled "The Nation's Housekeeping at Panama," *Outlook,* Nov. 2, 1907, pp. 489–93.

50. "What a Woman Saw in the Canal Zone," *New York Times,* Sept. 30, 1907, p. 3, ProQuest Historical Newspapers.

51. Gertrude Beeks, "Conditions of Employment at Panama," *National Civic Federation Review,* Oct. 1907, pp. 2–19, esp. pp. 2, 3, 14. The complete report is also available in NCF Papers, reel 376, Subject Files.

52. Beeks, "Conditions of Employment at Panama," p. 4.

53. Ibid., pp. 5–6, 13–14. Regarding the servant problem, Beeks noted that janitor service in bachelor dorms was also unsatisfactory. Some men complained that a mop had never been used in their rooms.

54. Ibid., p. 13.

55. Ibid., pp. 6, 16. In a response to this issue of falsely representing conditions to Europeans, the ICC labor recruiter LeRoy Park argued that the hotel picture had clearly stated on it the words "Em-

ployes' Hotel" and that no one ever referred to Europeans as anything but laborers. So it was not, in fact, a misrepresentation, he claimed: Park to Jackson Smith, June 24, 1908, Isthmian Canal Commission Records, RG 185, 28-A-5, National Archives, College Park, Md. (hereafter cited as ICC Records).

56. Beeks, "Conditions of Employment at Panama," p. 10; "Rebuttal of Miss Gertrude Beeks," Nov. 15, 1907, ICC Records, 28-A-5, p. 9.

57. Beeks, "Conditions of Employment at Panama," p. 8.

58. Ibid., pp. 9, 15; the quotation is on p. 16. Beeks's comment about treatment of American citizens is quoted in Jackson Smith's response to her report, Smith to Goethals, June 18, 1908, ICC Records, 28-A-5, "NCF Investigations."

59. Beeks, "Conditions of Employment at Panama," p. 17.

60. Easley to Taft, Aug. 6, 1907, NCF Papers, reel 376, Subject Files, Panama Canal.

61. Roosevelt to Easley, Aug. 10, 1907; Easley to Roosevelt, Aug. 14, 1907: both NCF Papers, reel 376.

62. Park to Smith, June 24, 1908, ICC Records, 28-A-5.

63. If their wives joined them, men received double their monthly pay in square footage. Joseph Bucklin Bishop and Farnham Bishop, *Goethals, Genius of the Panama Canal: A Biography* (New York: Harper and Brothers, 1930), pp. 177–78; see also Gerstle Mack, *The Land Divided: A History of the Panama Canal and Other Isthmian Canal Projects* (New York: Knopf, 1944), pp. 546–47; and McCullough, *Path Between the Seas*, pp. 470, 478–79.

64. Beeks, "Conditions of Employment at Panama," p. 9.

65. Smith to Goethals, June 18, 1908, ICC Records, 28-A-5, pp. 2, 3, 4.

66. Ibid., pp. 8, 11, 16, 23.

67. "Interview with Mr. Jackson Smith," NCF Papers, n.d., but apparently 1907.

68. Vice president, Panama Railroad Company, to Goethals, Sept. 24, 1907, ICC Records, 28-A-5.

69. "Civic Federation's Report on Providence," *Providence Journal,* reprinted in *Star and Herald,* Nov. 19, 1907; see also unsigned letter to the editor of the *Journal,* Nov. 21, 1907: both ICC Records, 28-A-5. Lady Helen Varick Boswell, confidential, to Beeks, Sept. 18, 1907, NCF Papers, reel 376; "What a Woman Saw in the Canal Zone," *New York Times,* Sept. 30, 1907, p. 3, ProQuest Historical Newspapers.

70. See correspondence between Mitchell and Beeks on Aug. 27 and Aug. 30, 1907, NCF Papers, reel 376, Subject Files, Panama Canal.

71. For a complete index of ICC responses to Beeks's report, including action taken or denied, see Col. Goethals to Lieut. H. F. Hodges, Sept. 27, 1907, ICC Records, 28-A-5; also "What a Woman Saw in the Canal Zone." For the quotation regarding Beeks and segregation, see Hiram Slifer (general manager, Panama Railroad Company) to Goethals, April 2, 1908, ICC Records, 28-A-5.

72. On Smith's resignation, see Bishop and Bishop, *Goethals, Genius of the Panama Canal,* pp. 177–80.

73. Chatfield, *Light on Dark Places at Panama,* pp. 213, 244.

74. Ibid., pp. 138–39, 144, 189, 265–67.

75. Abbot, *Panama and the Canal in Picture and Prose,* pp. 326–27.

CHAPTER SIX: THE WOMEN'S EMPIRE

1. Rose Van Hardeveld, *Make the Dirt Fly!* (Hollywood, Calif.: Pan Press, 1956), pp. 8, 17; Rose Van Hardeveld, "From 1906 to 1916," in *The American Woman on the Panama Canal: From 1904 to 1916,* ed. Mrs. Ernest von Muenchow (Balboa Heights, Panama: Star and Herald, 1916), p. 10.

2. References to the Canal Zone being like "home" are common in contemporary articles and books. See, for example, William Inglis, "The Progress and Promise of the Work at Panama," *Harper's Weekly* 50 (1906), p. 1852: "Any American can live and work in the Canal Zone as safely as home." Harriet Verner, a white American housewife in the Zone during the construction era, declared of her counterparts, "And then they made it home. . . . No woman, no home." In Muenchow, *American Woman on the Panama Canal,* p. iv.

Similarly, in chapter 1, above, the *Steam Shovel and Dredge* compared a train ride across the Isthmus of Panama to "taking a summer ride through suburbs of Chicago." The scholarship on women and empire is vast. Particularly influencing my notion of women's role in building a home for their husbands is Rosemary Marangoly George, "Homes in the Empire, Empires in the Home,"

Cultural Critique 27 (Winter 1993–94), pp. 95–127. Other studies that have shaped my approach include Vicente L. Rafael, "Colonial Domesticity: White Women and United States Rule in the Philippines," *American Literature* 67, no. 4 (Dec. 1995), pp. 630–66; Mary Louise Pratt, *Imperial Eyes: Travel Writing and Transculturation* (New York: Routledge, 1992); Ann Laura Stoler, *Carnal Knowledge and Imperial Power: Race and the Intimate in Colonial Rule* (Berkeley: University of California Press, 2002); Mrinalini Sinha, *Colonial Masculinity: The 'Manly Englishman' and the 'Effeminate Bengali' in the Late Nineteenth Century* (Manchester: Manchester University Press, 1995); Lora Wildenthal, "Race, Gender, and Citizenship in the German Colonial Empire," in *Tensions of Empire: Colonial Cultures in a Bourgeois World,* ed. Frederick Cooper and Ann Laura Stoler (Berkeley: University of California Press, 1997), pp. 263–86; Dipesh Chakrabarty, "The Difference—Deferral of a Colonial Modernity: Public Debates on Domesticity in British Bengal," in Cooper and Stoler, *Tensions of Empire,* pp. 373–405; Amy Kaplan, *The Anarchy of Empire in the Making of U.S. Culture* (Cambridge, Mass.: Harvard University Press, 2002); Nupur Chaudhuri and Margaret Strobel, eds., *Western Women and Imperialism: Complicity and Resistance* (Bloomington: University of Indiana Press, 1992); Ruth Roach Pierson and Nupur Chaudhuri, eds., *Nation, Empire, Colony: Historicizing Gender and Race* (Bloomington: University of Indiana Press, 1988).

3. Address of Theodore Roosevelt to the Assembled Panama Canal Force, Colón, Nov. 16, 1906: "The Work You Have Done Here Will Remain for the Ages," http://www.czbrats.com/Builders/speechTR.htm (accessed May 5, 2004); General Federation of Women's Clubs, "Protection for the Wives of Panama Canal Employees," n.d., Louise C. Bidwell Collection, MS 86-13, Special Collections, Ablah Library, Wichita State University.

4. Contemporaries' emphasis on U.S. women's contributions to the canal project stands in stark contrast to their neglect by historians. One historian who focused attention on the white housewives of the Zone is Paul W. Morgan Jr., "The Role of North American Women in U.S. Cultural Chauvinism in the Panama Canal Zone, 1904–1945" (Ph.D. diss., Florida State University, 2000); David McCullough devotes a few pages to women, which is more than most scholars, in *The Path Between the Seas: The Creation of the Panama Canal, 1870–1914* (New York: Simon and Schuster, 1977). The bulk of research on the canal's construction has approached it from the perspective of engineering, politics, and diplomacy, hence missing the significance of women's participation.

5. On women's work as "emotional labor" and the tendency for it to be invisible to others, see Arlie Russell Hochschild, *The Managed Heart: Commercialization of Human Feeling* (Berkeley: University of California Press, 1983); for an application of this idea to twentieth-century flight attendants' work, see Kathleen M. Barry, " 'Too Glamorous to Be Considered Workers': Flight Attendants and Pink-Collar Activism in Mid-Twentieth-Century America," *Labor: Studies in Working-Class History of the Americas* 3, no. 3 (Fall 2006), pp. 119–38. On white women's relationship to colonial subjects on imperial sites, see the excellent collection edited by Tony Ballantyne and Antoinette Burton, *Bodies in Contact: Rethinking Colonial Encounters in World History* (Durham, N.C.: Duke University Press, 2005).

6. *Census of the Canal Zone, February 1, 1912* (Mount Hope, C.Z.: ICC Press, 1912), pp. 16–23. According to the census, of 62,810 total inhabitants in the Zone, 9,770 were whites who had been born in the United States. Of these, roughly 1,300 were children fourteen years of age or younger, 6,700 were males aged fifteen or older, and 2,900 were females aged fifteen or older. Of the women aged fifteen and older, 1,767 were identified as married. There were a few hundred workingwomen in the Zone—for example, nurses, stenographers, and teachers—but they were almost always unmarried. Thus the 1,767 married white female U.S. citizens listed in the census were almost all living in the Zone as housewives. For other cases of white American women's involvement in imperial projects, see Rafael, "Colonial Domesticity"; Ian Tyrrell, *Woman's World/Woman's Empire: The Woman's Christian Temperance Union in International Perspective, 1880–1930* (Chapel Hill: University of North Carolina Press, 1991); and on intimacy, gender, and empire, see the articles in Ann Laura Stoler, ed., *Haunted by Empire: Geographies of Intimacy in North American History* (Durham, N.C.: Duke University Press, 2006).

7. Van Hardeveld, *Make the Dirt Fly!,* pp. 18, 20.

8. Ibid., p. 21.

9. Ibid., pp. 5, 68.

10. Van Hardeveld, "From 1906 to 1916," p. 13. See also in Muenchow's collection the essay by Mrs.

Chas. C. J. Wirz, which notes that the first governor of the Canal Zone, General George Davis, actively opposed the presence of U.S. women in the Zone. "Some of My Experiences on the Isthmus of Panama," p. 25.

11. Van Hardeveld, *Make the Dirt Fly!*, pp. 68, 87.

12. Becks to William H. Taft, Jan. 17, 1908, Isthmian Canal Commission Records, RG 185, 28-A-5, National Archives, College Park, Md. (hereafter cited as ICC Records); "Panama Offers Good Chances to Women," *New York Times,* Oct. 20, 1907, p. SM11; Colonel Carrol A. Devol (Quartermaster's Department) to Goethals, July 1, 1912, in *Annual Report of the Isthmian Canal Commission for the Fiscal Year Ending June 20, 1912* (Washington, D.C.: GPO, 1912), p. 378.

13. John Hall, "Mrs. Mac-Dasher," in *Panama Roughneck Ballads* (Panama and Canal Zone: Albert Lindo, Panama Railroad News Agency, 1912), p. 30.

14. Elizabeth Kittredge Parker, *Panama Canal Bride: A Story of Construction Days* (New York: Exposition, 1955), pp. 44–45.

15. Van Hardeveld, *Make the Dirt Fly!*, pp. 68, 40.

16. Ibid., pp. 112–13.

17. Ibid., p. 49.

18. Ibid., pp. 49–50.

19. Ibid., pp. 26–27, 23, 34. Her husband similarly objectified his West Indian workers, referring to them as "grinning black monkeys."

20. Ibid., pp. 39, 41–44.

21. Ibid., pp. 52–53. On domestic servants and their negotiations with female employers, see, for example, Tera W. Hunter, *To 'Joy My Freedom: Southern Black Women's Lives and Labors After the Civil War* (Cambridge, Mass.: Harvard University Press, 1997).

22. Van Hardeveld, *Make the Dirt Fly!*, pp. 28, 33.

23. Rose Van Hardeveld, "Personal Experiences," in Muenchow, *American Woman on the Panama Canal,* p. 14.

24. Van Hardeveld, *Make the Dirt Fly!*, pp. 91–95.

25. Ibid., pp. 83–85.

26. Ibid., pp. 85–87.

27. Parker, *Panama Canal Bride*, p. 34.

28. Ibid., pp. 27, 40.

29. Ibid., pp. 28, 36–37.

30. Ibid., pp. 37, 28, 30.

31. Van Hardeveld, "Personal Experiences," p. 14.

32. Mary L. McCarty, *Glimpses of Panama and of the Canal* (Kansas City, Mo.: Tiernan-Dart, 1913), pp. 130–31.

33. Parker, *Panama Canal Bride,* 76; *Census of the Canal Zone, February 1, 1912,* pp. 42–43.

34. Muenchow, *American Woman on the Panama Canal.* For an overview of social activities the *Canal Record* provides a fine source of information. On literary clubs, see Mary A. Chatfield, *Light on Dark Places at Panama* (New York: Broadway, 1908), passim. On patriotism and visits to the construction sites, see Morgan, "Role of North American Women in U.S. Cultural Chauvinism in the Panama Canal Zone," p. 65.

35. Gertrude Beeks, "Conditions of Employment at Panama," *National Civic Federation Review,* Oct. 1907, p. 12. See also Mary I. Wood, *The History of the General Federation of Women's Clubs for the First Twenty-Two Years of Its Existence* (New York: History Department, General Federation of Women's Clubs, 1912); Mildred White Wells, *Unity in Diversity: The History of the General Federation of Women's Clubs* (Washington, D.C.: General Federation of Women's Clubs, 1953); Karen J. Blair, *The Clubwoman as Feminist: True Womanhood Defined, 1868–1914* (New York: Holmes and Meier, 1980); Ann Firor Scott, *Natural Allies: Women's Associations in the United States* (Urbana: University of Illinois Press, 1991); Mary Jean Houde, *Reaching Out: A Story of the General Federation of Women's Clubs* (Chicago: Mobium, 1989); Anne Ruggles Gere, *Intimate Practices: Literary and Cultural Work in U.S. Women's Clubs, 1880–1920* (Urbana: University of Illinois Press, 1997).

36. On Boswell, see Melanie Susan Gustafson, *Women and the Republican Party, 1854–1924* (Urbana: University of Illinois Press, 2001), ch. 3.

37. Rheta Childe Dorr, *What Eight Million Women Want* (1910), at http://www.gutenberg.org/files/12226/12226-h/12226-h.htm (accessed July 8, 2005).

38. Boswell to Beeks, Sept. 23, 1907, National Civic Federation Papers, reel 376, Subject Files, New York Public Library; see also "Women's Clubs in Panama," *National Civic Federation Review*, Feb. 1908, p. 24. On continuing reminders against exclusivity, and for more general coverage of the women's club movement in the Canal Zone, see Morgan, "Role of North American Women in U.S. Cultural Chauvinism in the Panama Canal Zone," pp. 87–108. My understanding of the subject here is indebted to Morgan's dissertation.

39. See the weekly column titled "Social Life of the Zone" in the *Canal Record* for a detailed report of club events. For the activities discussed above, see in particular the issues of Oct. 30, 1907, p. 6; Jan. 1, 1908, p. 140; and April 29, 1908, p. 276.

40. The notion of "imagined communities" is from Benedict Anderson, *Imagined Communities: Reflections on the Origin and Spread of Nationalism* (New York: Verso, 1983).

41. Jeanette Ferris Brown, "Socials and Clubs," in Muenchow, *American Woman on the Panama Canal*, pp. 47–51.

42. "Women's Clubs in Panama," p. 24; Morgan, "Role of North American Women in U.S. Cultural Chauvinism in the Panama Canal Zone," pp. 87–108. For information on women's clubs and working-class issues in the United States, see Wells, *Unity in Diversity*; Priscilla Murolo, *The Common Ground of Womanhood: Class, Gender, and Working Girls' Clubs, 1884–1928* (Urbana: University of Illinois Press, 1997).

43. Beeks, "Conditions of Employment at Panama," p. 4.

44. Miskimon to Goethals, memorandum, March 26, 1910, T. B. Miskimon Papers, MS 86-5, box 2, folder 30, Special Collections, Ablah Library, Wichita State University.

45. Miskimon to Goethals, memorandum, March 5, 1910, Miskimon Papers, MS 86-5, box 2, folder 28. The Miskimon Papers at Wichita State University include many other examples of troubles with neighbors as well as child abuse and domestic violence.

46. Miskimon to Goethals, memorandum, Aug. 12, 1910, Miskimon Papers, MS 86-5, box 2, folder 37.

47. Miskimon to Goethals, Oct. 30, 1909, Miskimon Papers, MS 86-5, box 2, folder 16. On the history of domestic violence, see Linda Gordon, *Heroes of Their Own Lives: The Politics and History of Family Violence, Boston, Massachusetts, 1880–1960* (New York: Viking, 1988); Elizabeth Pleck, *Domestic Tyranny: The Making of Social Policy Against Family Violence from Colonial Times to the Present* (New York: Oxford University Press, 1989); David Peterson, "Wife-Beating: An American Tradition," *Journal of Interdisciplinary History* 23, no. 1 (Summer 1992), pp. 97–118.

48. Miskimon to Goethals, July 13, 1908, MS 86-5, box 1, folder 22; Miskimon to Goethals, May 13, 1909, MS 86-5, box 2, folder 9: both Miskimon Papers.

49. Chatfield, *Light on Dark Places at Panama*, pp. 139, 142, 152.

50. Miskimon to Goethals, memorandum, Aug. 26, 1910, and accompanying testimonies, Miskimon Papers, MS 86-5, box 2, folder 39; for other negative discussion of the commissaries, see Chatfield, *Light on Dark Places at Panama*, esp. p. 139.

51. *Brady Owen v. Madeline Owen,* May 1, 1911, case 96, Records of District Courts of the United States, RG21, District of the Canal Zone, 1st Judicial Circuit, Balboa, Civil Case Files, 1904–14, box 1, National Archives, Washington, D.C.

52. *J. Frank McKeever v. Florence McKeever,* July 18, 1910, case 82, and *Willis E. Lyons v. Minnie E. Lyons,* July 24, 1913, case 167, Records of District Courts of the United States, District of the Canal Zone, 1st Judicial Circuit, Civil Case Files, 1904–14, box 1.

53. *John W. Gray v. Cora Gray,* May 17, 1910, case 393, Records of District Courts of the United States, District of the Canal Zone, 2nd Judicial Circuit, Empire, Gorgona, Ancon, Civil Case Files, 1904–14, box 6.

54. Glenda Riley, *Divorce: An American Tradition* (New York: Oxford University Press, 1991), esp. pp. 86–89; Robert L. Griswold, *Family and Divorce in California, 1850–1890: Victorian Illusions and Everyday Realities* (Albany: State University of New York Press, 1982), esp. pp. 78–79; Norma Basch, *Framing American Divorce: From the Revolutionary Generation to the Victorians* (Berkeley: University of California Press, 1999); Nancy F. Cott, "Marriage and Women's Citizenship in the United States, 1830–1934," *American Historical Review* 103, no. 5 (Dec. 1998), pp. 1440–74; Nancy F. Cott, *Public*

Vows: A History of Marriage and the Nation (Cambridge, Mass.: Harvard University Press, 2001); Elaine Tyler May, *Great Expectations: Marriage and Divorce in Post-Victorian America* (Chicago: University of Chicago Press, 1983).

55. Little has been written on the lives of West Indian women in Panama or the Canal Zone. One of the best sources is Eyra Marcela Reyes Rivas, *El trabajo de las mujeres en la historia de la construcción del Canal de Panamá, 1881–1914* (Panama: Universidad de Panamá, Instituto de la Mujer, 2000). See also Lara Putnam, *The Company They Kept: Migrants and the Politics of Gender in Caribbean Costa Rica, 1870–1960* (Chapel Hill: University of North Carolina Press, 2002); Jack L. Alexander, "Love, Race, Slavery, and Sexuality in Jamaican Images of the Family," in *Kinship Ideology and Practice in Latin America*, ed. Raymond T. Smith (Chapel Hill: University of North Carolina Press, 1984), pp. 147–80; Christine Barrow, *Family in the Caribbean: Themes and Perspectives* (Kingston: Ian Randle, 1996); Christine Barrow, ed., *Caribbean Portraits: Essays on Gender Ideologies and Identities* (Kingston: Ian Randle, 1996); Roy Simon Bryce-Laporte, "Crisis, Contraculture, and Religion Among West Indians in the Panama Canal Zone," in *Blackness in Latin America and the Caribbean*, ed. Norman E. Whitten and Arlene Torres (Bloomington: Indiana University Press, 1998), vol. 1, pp. 100–118; Ronald N. Harpelle, *The West Indians of Costa Rica: Race, Class, and the Integration of an Ethnic Minority* (Montreal: McGill-Queen's University Press, 2001); Elizabeth McLean Petras, *Jamaican Labor Migration: White Capital and Black Labor, 1850–1930* (Boulder, Colo.: Westview, 1988); Verene Shepherd, "Gender, Migration, and Settlement: The Indentureship and Post-Indentureship Experience of Indian Females in Jamaica, 1845–1943," in *Engendering History: Caribbean Women in Historical Perspective*, ed. Verene Shepherd, Bridget Brereton, and Barbara Bailey (Kingston: Ian Randle, 1995), pp. 236–42.

56. Reyes Rivas, *El trabajo de las mujeres en la historia de la construcción del Canal de Panamá*, pp. 134–61.

57. Bonham Richardson interview notes, 1982, passim, in author's possession; Dr. Carlos E. Russell, *An Old Woman Remembers: The Recollected History of West Indians in Panama, 1855–1955* (Brooklyn: Caribbean Diaspora Press, 1995), esp. pp. 8–9.

58. Richardson interview notes with Mrs. Adina Richards (née Fordringham), March 15, 1982, in author's possession.

59. *Census of the Canal Zone, February 1, 1912*, pp. 16–55.

60. Ibid., pp. 42–43. Nearly three-fourths of all black children living in the Canal Zone in 1912, or 1,847 of 2,459, had been born in the Zone.

61. Reyes Rivas, *El trabajo de las mujeres en la historia de la construcción del Canal de Panamá*, pp. 151–56; *Census of the Canal Zone, February 1, 1912*, p. 55.

62. For Bigelow's article ("Our Mismanagement at Panama") and the resulting investigations, see *Message from the President of the United States Transmitting Certain Papers to Accompany His Message of January 8, 1906* (Washington, D.C.: GPO, 1906).

63. Examination of John F. Stevens and J. W. Settoon; John Stevens, "Exhibit A, Memorandum of Comments"; and Magoon to Taft, Nov. 16, 1905: all in ibid.; U.S. Senate, *Investigation of Panama Canal Matters: Hearings Before the Committee on Interoceanic Canals of the United States Senate,* 59th Cong., 2nd sess., Doc. 401 (Washington, D.C.: GPO, 1907), pp. 54–57, 20–31, 41.

64. George Shanton to Magoon, Nov. 21, 1905; see also examination of Settoon: both in *Message from the President*.

65. U.S. Senate, *Investigation of Panama Canal Matters*, vol. 1, pp. 930–33, 941–81.

66. Louise Cramer, "Songs of West Indian Negroes in the Canal Zone," *California Folklore Quarterly* 5, no. 3 (July 1946), p. 255. Cramer listened as a woman sang this song for her. The woman reportedly had originally learned it in Jamaica in 1906.

67. Ibid., p. 256.

68. *Courtney Black v. Mary Black,* Oct. 10, 1912, case 124, Records of District Courts of the United States, District of the Canal Zone, 1st Judicial Circuit, Civil Case Files, 1904–14, box 1.

69. *Eugenia Justine Peters v. Arthur Joseph Peters,* June 30, 1913, case 163, Records of District Courts of the United States, District of the Canal Zone, 1st Judicial Circuit, Civil Case Files, 1904–14. For similar cases, see also in the 1st Judicial Circuit: *Samuel Donovan v. Elida V. Donovan,* Nov. 16, 1910, case 90, box 2; and *Beatrice Ford v. Frederick A. Ford,* June 20, 1912, case 115, box 2. Putnam, *Company They Kept,* includes a detailed discussion of marriage and cohabitation among West Indians, but her sources provided little information about divorce.

70. Knox to Knight, Sept. 11, 1906, Foreign Office Records, FO 288/101, The National Archives, Kew, U.K. See also the 1908 petition of Jane Moseley, Port of Spain, Trinidad, regarding the belongings of her deceased brother Samuel Cox, Foreign Office Records, FO 288/109.

71. Ricketts to the British consul, Jan. 21, 1913, Foreign Office Records, FO 288/149. For another example, see Lorline Cargell (imprisoned by the Panamanian government, unjustly, she claimed) to the British consul, Sept. 27, 1914, Foreign Office Records, FO 288/160.

CHAPTER SEVEN: LAW AND ORDER

1. *Canal Zone v. Coulson,* case 28, decided May 8, 1907, in *Canal Zone Supreme Court Reports,* vol. 1: *Cases Adjudged in the Supreme Court of the Canal Zone from July Term, 1905, to October Term, 1908* (Ancon, C.Z.: ICC Press, 1909), pp. 50–55; see also "Trial by Jury on the Zone," *Canal Record,* Sept. 25, 1907, p. 5.

2. On this, see Wayne D. Bray, *The Common Law Zone in Panama: A Case Study in Reception* (San Juan, P.R.: Inter American University Press, 1977), pp. 62, 87–88; Frederic J. Haskin argues in his book *The Panama Canal* (Garden City, N.Y.: Doubleday, Page, 1913), p. 258, that Joseph Blackburn, who headed Civil Administration in the Zone, influenced Roosevelt to issue this executive order. According to Haskin, Blackburn "regarded it as repugnant to American ideas of justice to deny to Americans on the Isthmus the right to be tried for felonious offenses by juries of their peers." The execution of Adolphus Coulson is listed in the index to the Gorgas Hospital Mortuary Registers, 1906–91, available on the National Archives Web site through its Access to Archival Databases.

3. On the Hay–Bunau-Varilla Treaty, see Bray, *Common Law Zone in Panama,* pp. 40–41; *Wilson v. Shaw,* 1907, at http://caselaw.lp.findlaw.com/cgi-bin/getcase.pl?court=us&vol=204&invol=24 (accessed Sept. 15, 2005); see also J. Michael Hogan, *The Panama Canal in American Politics: Domestic Advocacy and the Evolution of Policy* (Carbondale: Southern Illinois University Press, 1986), pp. 13, 34; David McCullough, *The Path Between the Seas: The Creation of the Panama Canal, 1870–1914* (New York: Simon and Schuster, 1977), pp. 388–94.

4. Bray, *Common Law Zone in Panama,* pp. 72–74, 79–80.

5. Ibid., pp. 3–18.

6. Ibid., pp. 94–95, 63–64; "Report of Hon. Frank Feuille, Head of the Department of Law," in *Annual Report of the Isthmian Canal Commission for the Fiscal Year Ending June 30, 1912* (Washington, D.C.: GPO, 1912), app. O, p. 518.

7. Bray, *Common Law Zone in Panama,* pp. 94–95, 63–64. Bray cites President Roosevelt's executive order of May 9, 1904.

8. Ibid., esp. ch. 7 and pp. 100, 116.

9. Ibid., pp. 77–84.

10. Ibid., pp. 84–85.

11. Ibid., pp. 86–87.

12. *Downes v. Bidwell,* accessed at http://caselaw.lp.findlaw.com/cgi-bin/getcase.pl?court=us&vol=182&invol=244 (accessed Sept. 13, 2005). *Dorr v. United States,* at http://caselaw.lp.findlaw.com/cgi-bin/getcase.pl?court=us&vol=195&invol=138 (accessed Sept. 13, 2005). See also Walter F. Pratt Jr., "*Insular Cases,*" in *The Oxford Guide to United States Supreme Court Decisions* (New York: Oxford University Press, 1999), pp. 136–37; James E. Kerr, *The Insular Cases: The Role of the Judiciary in American Expansionism* (Port Washington, N.Y.: Kennikat, 1982); Efrén Rivera Ramos, *The Legal Construction of Identity: The Judicial and Social Legacy of American Colonialism in Puerto Rico* (Washington, D.C.: American Psychological Association, 2001).

13. Sanford Levinson, "Installing the *Insular Cases* into the Canon of Constitutional Law," in *Foreign in a Domestic Sense: Puerto Rico, American Expansion, and the Constitution,* ed. Christina Duffy Burnett and Burke Marshall (Durham, N.C.: Duke University Press, 2001), pp. 134–35.

14. Quoted in Frank Ninkovich, *The United States and Imperialism* (Oxford: Blackwell, 2001), p. 56.

15. Bray, *Common Law Zone in Panama,* p. 4; see also Gustavo Adolfo Mellander, "Magoon in Panama" (master's thesis, George Washington University, 1960); and Gustavo Adolfo Mellander, *The United States in Panamanian Politics* (Danville, Ill.: Interstate Printers and Publishers, 1971), p. 74.

16. *Fitzpatrick v. Panama Railroad Company,* decided Jan. 31, 1913, in *Canal Zone Supreme Court Reports,*

vol. 2: *Cases Adjudged in the Supreme Court of the Canal Zone from October 1908 to June 1914* (Mount Hope, C.Z.: Panama Canal Press, 1915), pp. 111–32. The quotation is from p. 118.

17. Albert Edwards, *Panama: The Canal, the Country, and the People* (New York: Macmillan, 1911), p. 503. Edwards was a pseudonym for Arthur Bullard, the well-known socialist.

18. Joseph Blackburn, "Report of the Head of the Department of Civil Administration," in *Annual Report of the Isthmian Canal Commission for the Fiscal Year Ending June 30, 1907* (Washington, D.C.: GPO, 1907), pp. 162–63. In fiscal year 1907, 56 people were deported from the Canal Zone; in 1912 the number deported was 156, 100 of whom had finished serving terms in the Zone penitentiary. See ibid., p. 152, and *Annual Report of the Isthmian Canal Commission for the Fiscal Year Ending June 30, 1912*, pp. 464–65.

19. The ordinance took effect on Jan. 1, 1908, and was added to the penal code of the Canal Zone by executive order of President Roosevelt on Jan. 9, 1908. See extracts from the minutes of meeting of the ICC, Dec. 9, 1907, and Roosevelt's executive order: both Isthmian Canal Commission Records, RG 185, 94-L-9, National Archives, College Park, Md. (hereafter cited as ICC Records); *Canal Zone v. Rebecca Merchant*, for disorderly conduct, Nov. 11, 1911, case 127611-11-11, Records of District Courts of the United States, RG 21, District of the Canal Zone, 2nd Judicial Circuit, Empire, Gorgona, Ancon, Criminal Case Files, 1904–14, box 7, National Archives, Washington, D.C.

20. *Canal Zone v. Abel Emanuel Scott*, March 14, 1905, case 9, Records of District Courts of the United States, District of the Canal Zone, 2nd Judicial Circuit, Criminal Case Files, 1904–14, box 1.

21. *Canal Zone v. Samuel Griffith*, case 215; *Canal Zone v. George Owens*, Dec. 17, 1908, case 207: both in Records of District Courts of the United States, District of the Canal Zone, 3rd Judicial Circuit, Cristobal, Criminal Case Files, 1904–20, box 1.

22. *Canal Zone v. Garcia*, June 29, 1907, case 115; *Canal Zone v. Ah Mee and Ah Chow*, July 16, 1909, case 247: both in Records of District Courts of the United States, District of the Canal Zone, 3rd Judicial Circuit, Criminal Case Files, 1904–20, box 1.

23. T. B. Miskimon to Goethals, memorandum, Sept. 10, 1910, T. B. Miskimon Papers, MS 86-5, box 2, folder 40, Special Collections, Ablah Library, Wichita State University.

24. Miskimon to Goethals, memorandum, Sept. 19, 1910, Miskimon Papers, MS 86-5, box 2, folder 41.

25. Thatcher's testimony is in *The Panama Canal: Hearings Before the Committee on Interstate and Foreign Commerce*, House of Representatives, 62nd Cong., 2nd sess. (Washington, D.C.: GPO, 1912), vol. 1, p. 320.

26. Miskimon to Goethals, memorandum, Dec. 16, 1908, Miskimon Papers, MS 86-5, box 1, folder 30.

27. On convict labor in the United States, see Karin A. Shapiro, *A New South Rebellion: The Battle Against Convict Labor in the Tennessee Coalfields, 1871–1896* (Chapel Hill: University of North Carolina Press, 1998); Alex Lichtenstein, *Twice the Work of Free Labor: The Political Economy of Convict Labor in the New South* (New York: Verso, 1996).

28. L. G. Thom (assistant engineer) to Major W. L. Sibert (division engineer), Aug. 13, 1908, ICC Records, 62-B-78, pt. 1. Prisoners sentenced to less than one year were not required to wear shackles. See also "Instructions to Prisoners," ICC Records, 55-A-1, pt. 1.

29. Blackburn to Goethals, Aug. 18, 1908, ICC Records, 62-B-78, pt. 1.

30. Shanton to Blackburn, July 23, 1908; Sibert to H. H. Rousseau, Jan. 25, 1908: both ICC Records, 62-B-78, pt. 1.

31. Thom to Sibert, Aug. 13, 1908, ICC Records, 62-B-78, pt. 1; and "Instructions to Prisoners," ICC Records, 55-A-1, pt. 1.

32. Shanton to police officer in command, Cristobal, Feb. 19, 1908, ICC Records, 62-B-78, pt. 1. In 1905, as the government made its plans for recruiting labor to build the canal, one enterprising newspaper journalist wrote a treatise to convince officials they should import convicts from the United States to the Canal Zone and use them as a major source of labor. According to this journalist, Samuel Fox of Kansas City, Missouri, the Department of Labor and Commerce considered his suggestion sufficiently feasible that it asked him to forward his ideas to the Isthmian Canal Commission. Fox declared: "Important Government Work has been accomplished in foreign lands by the use of Convicts or Criminals. The Australian Colonies attest that fact." Fox anticipated officials would have no trouble securing convicts in the United States except in those areas where their labor was already sold to contractors. One is reminded, upon hearing of Fox's scheme, of the

worries in the 1890s that America would not be able to launch large projects in the tropics without recourse to forced or indentured labor. The ICC rejected Fox's proposal. See Fox to the chief clerk, July 19, 1905; and Samuel Fox, "Convict Labor for the Panama Canal," July 19, 1905: both ICC Records, 62-B-78, pt. 1.

33. Miskimon to Goethals, memoranda, May 11, 1909, Oct. 28, 1910, Miskimon Papers, MS 86-5, box 2, folders 9 and 42. It is difficult to know for sure whether beating of prisoners continued after this investigation, but the inspector's critical tone in his report to Goethals suggests that it may hence-forth have been discouraged. One year later a black policeman hit a prisoner and was himself then beaten by a white policeman in the presence of the warden. The black policeman, angry at his treatment, responded that he "was as good as any Damn white officer" and then moved as if to pick up an inkstand on the desk in front of him to use against the police officer, at which point the warden himself got involved. The black policeman made a complaint against the warden and the white policeman for this incident, but Goethals's inspector believed that the white men had done nothing wrong. Miskimon to Goethals, March 30, 1910, Miskimon Papers, MS 86-5, box 2, folder 30.

34. First-Class Policeman George Fisher to Sergeant Joseph Seeger, April 30, 1909; Seeger to Blackburn, May 2, 1909: both ICC Records, 46-D-7.

35. Thatcher to Sir, Dec. 14, 1910; Peter Johnson (second lieutenant, Zone policeman) to Shanton, May 4, 1909; Seeger to Blackburn, May 2, 1909; J. P. Fyffe, "Grading of Prisoners," n.d.; J. P. Fyffe, "Instructions to Prisoners" (approved by Blackburn and Goethals), n.d.; Fyffe to Thatcher, Feb. 10, 1912: all ICC Records, 46-D-7.

36. Edward T. Devine, "The Canal Builders," *Survey,* March 1, 1913, pp. 765, 768.

37. In July 1913, as the construction project moved toward completion and the challenge of managing workers seemed less worrisome, all liquor licenses were suspended, and the Zone became dry in order to comply with federal law that prohibited alcohol on government property. See Willis J. Abbot, *Panama and the Canal in Picture and Prose* (New York: Syndicate, 1914), pp. 346–47; George Goethals in *Panama Canal: Hearings Before the Committee on Interstate and Foreign Commerce,* vol, 1, p. 328.

38. As in the case of R. B. Elliott in chapter 2, above, police sometimes relied on gambling charges to harass workers involved in union organizing. For the court cases discussed in this paragraph, see the following in the Records of District Courts of the United States, District of the Canal Zone, 2nd Judicial Circuit, Criminal Case Files, 1904–14: *Canal Zone v. Charles Christian,* filed Jan. 26, 1905, case 5, box 1; *Canal Zone v. Uriah Lee, George Gordon, and others,* July 18, 1911, case 1166, box 7; *Canal Zone v. Geo Tolluck, Joseph Johnson, and George Wray,* July 21, 1911, case 1175, box. 7. These last three men were charged with playing at a game of dice for money. Two were sentenced to ten days in prison; the other was found not guilty.

39. Louise C. Bidwell Collection, MS 86-13, folder 1, Special Collections, Ablah Library, Wichita State University.

40. Miskimon to D. D. Gaillard, Feb. 27, 1908, Miskimon Papers, MS 86-5, box 1, folder 38; Miskimon to the acting chairman, May 27, 1910, Miskimon Papers, MS 86-5, box 2, folder 35.

41. Miskimon to C. A. McIlvaine, memo, Sept. 15, 1909, Miskimon Papers, MS 86-5, box 2, folder 13. The concluding assessment is based on a reading of the Miskimon Papers, which span several years.

42. See especially *Canal Zone v. James Peart,* filed Dec. 27, 1908, case 606, Records of District Courts of the United States, District of the Canal Zone, 2nd Judicial Circuit, Criminal Case Files, 1904–14, box 4.

43. *Canal Zone v. Cooper,* case 52, in *Canal Zone Supreme Court Reports,* vol. 2: *Cases Adjudged in the Supreme Court of the Canal Zone from October 1908 to June 1914,* pp. 16–19.

44. John Hall, "Spickety Bill," in *Panama Roughneck Ballads* (Panama and Canal Zone: Albert Lindo, Panama Railroad News Agency, 1912), pp. 27–29. On John Henry, see Scott Nelson, *Steel Drivin' Man: John Henry, the Untold Story of an American Legend* (New York: Oxford University Press, 2006).

45. Peter Johnson to Goethals, Sept. 19 and 28, 1913, ICC Records, 62-B-248, pt. 1, box 364, "Co-habitation or Immoral Conduct of White Employees with Native or Colored Women." The title given to this file by the ICC indicates what sort of cohabitation troubled them: white men cohab-iting with women of color.

46. Captain Barber (Zone police) to Goethals, memo, Oct. 21, 1913, ICC Records, 62-B-248.

47. Rousseau to Goethals, Dec. 3, 1913; and WPC, memo, Dec. 4, 1913: both ICC Records, 62-B-248.

Rousseau was the head of the Department of Municipal Engineering, Motive Power and Machinery, and Building Construction.

48. *Canal Zone v. John Lane,* for pimping, Dec. 18, 1908, case 607, Records of District Courts of the United States, District of the Canal Zone, 1st Judicial Circuit, Balboa, 1904–14, box 4; Miskimon to Gaillard, Jan. 30, 1908, Miskimon Papers, MS 86-5, box 1, folder 32; Miskimon to Goethals, Oct. 21, 1907, Miskimon Papers, MS 86-5, box 1, folder 6.

49. "Report of M. H. Thatcher, Head of the Department of Civil Administration," *Annual Report of the Isthmian Canal Commission for the Fiscal Year Ending June 30, 1912,* app. N, pp. 465–66.

50. Miskimon to Goethals, April 5, 1909, Miskimon Papers, MS 86-5, box 2, folder 7.

51. B. W. Caldwell, M.D., to Charles Magoon, June 22, 1906; Magoon to Caldwell, June 23, 1906: both ICC Records, 62-B-248, pt. 1, box 364.

52. H. G. Belknap, memo, June 10, 1913; Belknap to Captain Barber, June 23, 1913; Barber to M. H. Thatcher, June 24, 1913; C. F. Johnson to chief of division, July 2, 1913: all ICC Records, 62-B-248, pt. 1, box 364.

53. *Canal Zone v. John T. O'Brien,* Feb. 12, 1908, case 154, Records of District Courts of the United States, District of the Canal Zone, 3rd Judicial Circuit, Criminal Case Files, 1904–20, box 1; *Canal Zone v. O'Brien,* case 43, in *Canal Zone Supreme Court Reports,* vol. 1: *Cases Adjudged in the Supreme Court of the Canal Zone from July Term, 1905, to October Term, 1908,* pp. 121–22. To contrast arrests for sodomy in the Canal Zone with those in the United States, see George Chauncey, *Gay New York: Gender, Urban Culture, and the Making of the Gay Male World, 1890–1940* (New York: Basic Books, 1995); Peter Boag, *Same-Sex Affairs: Constructing and Controlling Homosexuality in the Pacific Northwest* (Berkeley: University of California Press, 2003).

54. *Canal Zone v. William Waite,* Nov. 7, 1905, case 27; and Goethals, memo, Dec. 21, 1908: both Records of District Courts of the United States, District of the Canal Zone, 2nd Judicial Circuit, Criminal Case Files, 1904–14, box 1. Supporting the pardon, the judge of the Second Circuit Court noted, "The girl was under 13 but gave her consent to the act, and was well grown for her age; I may say almost fully developed." In a similar case a white conductor named Campbell was accused of attempting to rape two girls aged nine and ten. This case was not taken to the courts, because none of the parties wanted the bad publicity that would come from legal action. Instead, the parents complained to Goethals. He ordered an investigation, which in turn recommended that Campbell be discharged and refused any other job in the Zone. See T. B. Miskimon, "Personal: Memorandum for the Chairman," Jan. 16, 1910, Miskimon Papers, MS 86-5, box 2, folder 23.

55. *Canal Zone v. Evan Barker,* Sept. 26, 1905, case 20, Records of District Courts of the United States, District of the Canal Zone, 3rd Judicial Circuit, Criminal Case Files, 1904–20, box 1. On the politics of family violence in U.S. history, see Linda Gordon, *Heroes of Their Own Lives: The Politics and History of Family Violence—Boston, 1880–1960* (Urbana: University of Illinois Press, 2002).

56. "Report of M. H. Thatcher," pp. 482–87; *Census of the Canal Zone, February 1, 1912* (Mount Hope, C.Z.: ICC Press, 1912). To compare views on crime in the United States during this period, see John Goebel Jr., "The Prevalence of Crime in the United States and Its Extent Compared with That in the Leading European States," *Journal of the American Institute of Criminal Law and Criminology* 3, no. 5 (Jan. 1913), pp. 754–69. After 1912 the number of arrests declined slightly, to 6,827 in 1913; 4,911 in 1914; and 5,157 in 1915. See "Report of the Governor," in *Annual Report of the Isthmian Canal Commission for the Fiscal Year Ending June 30, 1914* (Washington, D.C.: GPO, 1914), p. 56; and "Report of the Governor," in *Annual Report of the Isthmian Canal Commission for the Fiscal Year Ending June 30, 1915* (Washington, D.C.: GPO, 1915), p. 51.

57. "Report of M. H. Thatcher," p. 487; on constructions of manliness and masculinity in the United States, see Gail Bederman, *Manliness and Civilization: A Cultural History of Gender and Race in the United States, 1880–1917* (Chicago: University of Chicago Press, 1995); Kristin L. Hoganson, *Fighting for American Manhood: How Gender Politics Provoked the Spanish-American and Philippine-American Wars* (New Haven, Conn.: Yale University Press, 1998).

58. *Canal Zone v. J. Frank Houston,* Feb. 17, 1913, case 615, Records of District Courts of the United States, District of the Canal Zone, 3rd Judicial Circuit, Criminal Case Files, 1904–20, box 3.

59. *Canal Zone v. Houston,* case 119, in *Canal Zone Supreme Court Reports,* vol. 2: *Cases Adjudged in the Supreme Court of the Canal Zone from October 1908 to June 1914,* pp. 238–52.

60. *Canal Zone v. Desiderio Rodriguez,* May 11, 1911, case 375, Records of District Courts of the United States, District of the Canal Zone, 3rd Judicial Circuit, Criminal Case Files, 1904–20, box 3.

61. *Canal Zone v. Francisco Zaldivar,* Nov. 30, 1912, case 700, Records of District Courts of the United States, District of the Canal Zone, 1st Judicial Circuit, Criminal Case Files, 1904–14, box 3; see also *Canal Zone v. Zaldivar,* case 113, in *Canal Zone Supreme Court Reports,* vol. 2: *Cases Adjudged in the Supreme Court of the Canal Zone from October 1908 to June 1914,* pp. 227–37.

CHAPTER EIGHT: THE RIOTS OF COCOA GROVE

1. For one account of the riot see FO 304, "Record of Proceedings of a Board of Investigation Convened at Camp Elliott, Isthmian Canal Zone, by Order of the Commanding Officer, Camp Elliott, to Inquire into a Disturbance Which Occurred in the City of Panama," in Embajada de los Estados Unidos en Panamá: Expediente de los disturbios del 4 de julio de 1912 y 1915 en Cocoa Grove, vol. 1, Archivos de Ministerio de Relaciones Exteriores, Panama City. For specific information on the injuries and fatality, see, for example, "Examination of Past Assistant Surgeon B. H. Dorsey, U.S. Navy," in this same vol. 1.

2. Peter A. Szok, *"La Última Gaviota": Liberalism and Nostalgia in Early Twentieth-Century Panamá* (Westport, Conn.: Greenwood, 2001), p. 32; Fernando Aparicio, "'Alcanzamos por fin la victoria': Tensiones y contradiciones del 3 de noviembre de 1903," in *Historia general de Panamá,* ed. Alfredo Castillero Calvo (Panama City: Comité Nacional del Centenario de República, 2004), pp. 372–92.

3. Bryce to Sir Edward Grey, Nov. 28, 1910, General Correspondence of the Foreign Office, Panama, Foreign Office Records, FO 371/943, The National Archives, Kew, U.K. On Panama during the early twentieth century, see Carlos Bolívar Pedreschi, "Negociaciones del Canal con los Estados Unidos: 1904–1967"; Gerardo Maloney, "Significado de la presencia y contribución del afro antillano a la nación panameña"; and Marco A. Gandásegui, "Los movimientos sociales en Panamá: Primera mitad del siglo XX": all three are included in Calvo, *Historia general de Panamá,* pp. 25–41, 152–71, and 185–208, respectively; and see also the essays in Marco A. Gandásegui, ed., *Las clases sociales en Panamá* (Panama: Del Centro de Estudios Latinoamericanos, 1993).

4. W. C. Gorgas, *Report of the Department of Health of the Isthmian Canal Commission for the Month of January 1905* (Washington, D.C.: GPO, 1905), p. 6. "Report of the Department of Civil Administration," in *Annual Report of the Isthmian Canal Commission for the Fiscal Year Ending June 30, 1907* (Washington, D.C.: GPO, 1907), app. F, pp. 146–57.

5. "Report of the Department of Civil Administration," pp. 149–50.

6. "Report of M. H. Thatcher, Head of the Department of Civil Administration," in *Annual Report of the Isthmian Canal Commission for the Fiscal Year Ending June 30, 1910* (Washington, D.C.: GPO, 1910), app. O, pp. 364–65.

7. Szok, *La Última Gaviota,* p. 60; "Report of M. H. Thatcher, Head of the Department of Civil Administration," in *Annual Report of the Isthmian Canal Commission for the Fiscal Year Ending June 30, 1912* (Washington, D.C.: GPO, 1912), app. N, pp. 465–66.

8. W. Chalkley to Grey, Dec. 20, 1909, General Correspondence of the Foreign Office, Panama, Foreign Office Records, FO 371/943, 1910.

9. Claude Mallet to Sir, Jan. 31, 1906, Foreign Office Records, FO 288/98; Szok, *La Última Gaviota,* p. 48; William D. McCain, *The U.S. and the Republic of Panama* (Durham, N.C.: Duke University Press, 1937).

10. Michael L. Conniff, *Black Labor on a White Canal: Panama, 1904–1981* (Pittsburgh: University of Pittsburgh Press, 1985).

11. Szok, *"La Última Gaviota,"* pp. 45, 47–48; the quotation is from George A. Miller, *Prowling About Panama* (New York: Abingdon, 1919), p. 41.

12. Winifred James, *The Mulberry Tree* (London: Chapman and Hall, 1913), pp. 243–44.

13. David McCullough, *The Path Between the Seas: The Creation of the Panama Canal, 1870–1914* (New York: Simon and Schuster, 1977), p. 561; John Major, *Prize Possession: The United States and the Panama Canal, 1903–1979* (New York: Cambridge University Press, 1993), p. 130.

14. James, *Mulberry Tree,* pp. 253–55.

15. For a fine analysis of prostitution's history that sheds light on the relationship between the sex trade and labor discipline, see Luise White, *The Comforts of Home: Prostitution in Colonial Nairobi* (Chicago: University of Chicago Press, 1990).

16. John Hall, "As It Was," in *Panama Roughneck Ballads* (Panama and Canal Zone: Albert Lindo, Panama Railroad News Agency, 1912), p. 18.

17. On the Watermelon Riot and on U.S.-Panamanian relations more generally in the nineteenth century, see Aims McGuinness, *Path of Empire: Panama and the California Gold Rush* (Ithaca, N.Y.: Cornell University Press, 2008); on U.S. military interventions, see also Michael L. Conniff, *Panama and the United States: The Forced Alliance,* 2nd ed. (Athens: University of Georgia Press, 2001).

18. On the background of U.S. military personnel, see Mary Renda, *Taking Haiti: Military Occupation and the Culture of U.S. Imperialism, 1915–1940* (Chapel Hill: University of North Carolina Press, 2001); for information about the U.S. military in the Canal Zone, see Major, *Prize Possession,* esp. pp. 155–61.

19. T. B. Miskimon to the chairman, Dec. 20, 1909, folder 20; Miskimon to Goethals, June 2, 1908, folder 18: both T. B. Miskimon Papers, MS 86-5, Special Collections, Ablah Library, Wichita State University.

20. Major, *Prize Possession,* pp. 120–28; the quotation is on p. 121.

21. On this point, see Szok *"La Última Gaviota,"* esp. pp. 60–61. Also see Evelyn Saxton, *Droll Stories of Isthmian Life* (New Orleans: L. Graham, 1914), pp. 14–15, 19. Saxton did note, as she learned her way around the city, that the Americans she met, "no matter how drunk they appeared to be," always showed her "some courtesy." See also Mary A. Chatfield, *Light on Dark Places at Panama* (New York: Broadway, 1908), p. 52.

22. For useful commentary on corruption during elections and the role of the police, see the reports by British consul Claude Mallet, for example, Jan. 31, 1906, FO 288/98, and Mallet to Grey, July 2, 1912, FO 371/1417, Political Correspondence, Panama, 1912: both Foreign Office Records. See also Thomas Pearcy, *We Answer Only to God: Politics and the Military in Panama, 1903–1947* (Albuquerque: University of New Mexico Press, 1998), pp. 39–42; Major, *Prize Possession,* pp. 117–19, 126–27; "Porras Wins in Panama," *New York Times,* July 14, 1912, p. 9, ProQuest Historical Newspapers.

23. "Report of the Head of the Department of Civil Administration," pp. 163–64; Major, *Prize Possession,* p. 121; *Canal Zone v. Gregorio Serress, Manuel Jeminez, and Jose Gonzales,* April 8, 1906, case 43, Records of District Courts of the United States, RG 21, District of the Canal Zone, 3rd Judicial Circuit, Cristobal, Criminal Case Files, 1904–20, box 1, National Archives, Washington, D.C.

24. Mallet to Grey, Jan. 1, 1909, Political Correspondence, Panama, Foreign Office Records, FO 371/708.

25. Pearcy, *We Answer Only to God,* pp. 43–44.

26. Mallet to Grey, Aug. 24, 1910, General Correspondence of the Foreign Office, Panama, Foreign Office Records, FO 371/943.

27. Mallet to Grey, Aug. 29 and Sept. 10, 1910: both General Correspondence of the Foreign Office, Panama, Foreign Office Records, FO 371/943. On both letters, see also the additional commentaries signed by "R.S."

28. Major, *Prize Possession,* pp. 121–27; Pearcy, *We Answer Only to God,* pp. 39–40; Patricia Pizzurno Gelós, *Antecedentes, hechos, y consecuencias de la Guerra de los Mil Días en el Istmo de Panamá* (Panama: Fomato 16, 1990).

29. Major, *Prize Possession,* pp. 126–27; "Porras Wins in Panama," *New York Times,* July 14, 1912, p. 9.

30. Major, *Prize Possession,* pp. 119–30; Pearcy, *We Answer Only to God,* pp. 38–46.

31. See Mallet to Grey, July 2, March 18, and May 16, 1912: all Political Correspondence, Panama, Foreign Office Records, FO 371/1417.

32. Mallet to Grey, July 16, 1912, Political Correspondence, Panama, Foreign Office Records, FO 371/1417; Major, *Prize Possession,* pp. 119–30; Pearcy, *We Answer Only to God,* pp. 38–46; "Police in Panama," *Los Hechos: Diario Politico, Organo de la Union Patriotica,* July 8, 1912, p. 1, Isthmian Canal Commission Records, RG 185, 62-B-199, National Archives, College Park, Md. (hereafter cited as ICC Records); "Want Us to Intervene," *New York Times,* May 4, 1912, p. 4, ProQuest Historical Newspapers; "To Guard Panama Election," *New York Times,* May 5, 1912, p. C3; "Guns

for Panama Election," *New York Times,* May 11, 1912, p. 2; "No Guns for Panamanians," *New York Times,* June 13, 1912, p. 1; "Vote in Panama Today," *New York Times,* June 30, 1912, p. 13; "Porras Wins in Panama," *New York Times,* July 1, 1912, p. 6; "Porras Wins in Panama," *New York Times,* July 14, 1912, p. 9; "Las Elecciones en Panama" and "El Derechode Sufragio": both in *La Estrella de Panamá,* June 23, 1912.

33. James, *Mulberry Tree,* p. 262.

34. FO 304, investigation conducted by U.S. Army at Camp Otis, Las Cascadas, July 5, 1912; and "Record of Proceedings of a Board of Investigation Convened at Camp Elliott, Isthmian Canal Zone, July 6, 1912," especially the summation of findings at end of report: both Legación de los Estados Unidos en Panamá, Archivos de Ministerio de Relaciones Exteriores, Panama.

35. "Unanimous Conclusions of the Board of Army Officers," U.S. Army investigation, July 5, 1912; statement of Mr. Otto W. Nichols, FO 304, "Record of Proceedings of a Board of Investigation Convened at Camp Elliott, Isthmian Canal Zone," July 6, 1912, from Embajada de los Estados Unidos en Panamá.

36. Dodge to Ernesto Lefevre (secretary of state for foreign affairs), Feb. 25, 1913, FO 305, Correspondencia relacionada con los desórdenes que tuvieron lugar en el Barrio de Torolancia, Legación de los Estados Unidos en Panamá.

37. See testimony of Private Lucas Joretti (hospital corps), Private Emile Barbonese, R. L. Swinehart, Private George DeWolff, Private Harry G. Gebhart, and John McDaid, all in FO 304, "Record of Proceedings of a Board of Investigation," investigation conducted by U.S. Army at Camp Otis, Las Cascadas, July 5, 1912, Legación de los Estados Unidos en Panamá.

38. Testimony of Captain Frank Halford, USMC, FO 304, "Record of Proceedings of a Board of Investigation Convened at Camp Elliott, Isthmian Canal Zone, by Order of the Commanding Officer, Camp Elliott, to Inquire into a Disturbance Which Occurred in the City of Panama."

39. Carl DeLeen, testimony in ICC investigation, and Rafael Alzamora, testimony in ICC investigation, July 5 and 9, 1912: both ICC Records, 62-B-199, box 363; R. L. Swinehart, testimony in USMC investigation; Whiting Andrews (secretary of the American legation) to Mr. Minister, July 9, 1912, FO 304, Embajada de los Estados Unidos en Panamá.

40. Statement of Thomas Fuentes, July 10, 1912, ICC Records, 62-B-199, box 363.

41. Quijano to the director of *La Estrella de Panamá,* July 8, 1912; "Copy of Report to the Secretary of Government Justice," n.d.: both ICC Records, 62-B-199, box 363. See also the editorial regarding these events in *La Estrella de Panamá,* July 9, 1912.

42. Testimony of Juan Muñoz ("la actitud de mis camaradas y yo durante los acontecimientos fue atenta y amisstosa para con los soldados Americanos, puesto que su estado de beodez y su número nos lo pedían"); of Alice Ward; and of Luis Francisco Ramírez: all from the investigation carried out by the Panamanian government, Legajo 14, Legación de los Estados Unidos en Panamá.

43. Testimony of Davis Gilbert, Cupertino Garrido, Eugenio Mateos, Ricardo Andrade, María Arosemena, Margaret Graham, Alice Ward, Enriqueta Gómez, Petra De León, Robert Davis, Charles Muller, Panamanian investigation, Legajo 14.

44. "Racial Differences," *Los Hechos,* July 8, 1912, ICC Records, 62-B-199; testimony of Private Stephen Crow, U.S. Army investigation. References to race or racial insults are surprisingly rare in the testimony offered to Panamanian investigators.

45. Becky Kaatz (prostitute), testimony to ICC investigation, July 9, 1912, ICC Records, 62-B-199; Andrews to Mr. Minister, July 9, 1912, in Embajada de los Estados Unidos en Panamá, vol. 1.

46. Dodge to Lefevre, Feb. 25, 1913, FO 305; Chiari to Dodge, Aug. 27 and Sept. 27, 1912, letters 2806 and 3079; Dodge to the minister, Sept. 25, 1912, letter 255: all Legación de los Estados Unidos en Panamá, vol. 1.

47. Superior Court sentence, April 28, 1914, signed by Juan Demóstenes Arosemena; letter FO 58, Price to Lefevre, May 14, 1914, Legación de los Estados Unidos en Panamá, vol. 1.

48. Memo accompanying Mallet to Grey, Oct. 3, 1912, Political Correspondence, Panama, Foreign Office Records, FO 371/1417; Price to Lefevre, FO 68, June 9, 1914; Willing Spencer to Lefevre, Dec. 24, 1915; Porras to Lefevre, Feb. 1, 1916: all Legación de los Estados Unidos en Panamá, vol. 1.

49. Morales to Lefevre, letter 22-1915, dated June 3, 1914, Legación de los Estados Unidos en Panamá, vol. 1.

50. Lefevre to Robert Lansing, Dec. 8, 1916; Legation Royale des Pays-Bas, signed by WLFC de Rap-

pard, arbitrator, Oct. 20, 1916: both Legación de los Estados Unidos en Panamá, vol. 1; Lefevre to Price, letter S-6439, dated April 24, 1915, Legación de los Estados Unidos en Panamá, vol. 21.

51. Dodge to Lefevre, March 13, 1913, FO 310, *Legación de Washington en Panamá,* Legajo 14A; "Soldiers and Police Slain in Panama Riot," *New York Times,* Feb. 14, 1915, p. 1.

52. "American Soldier Slain in Colon Riot," *New York Times,* April 3, 1915, p. 1.

53. José B. Calvo to Morales, telegram, S-6252; Lefevre to Price, April 24, 1915, letter S-6439: both Legación de Panamá en Washington, vol. 21; Price to Lefevre, FO 247, Oct. 15, 1915, Legación de Washington en Panamá, vol. 16; Porras to Wilson, telegram, May 11, 1915, and Lansing to American legation in Panama, telegram, May 13, 1915: both Legación de Washington en Panamá, vol. 16; Major, *Prize Possession,* p. 134. My understanding of the meaning of this disarmament in Panamanians' collective memory today is also indebted to a discussion with Guillermo Castro, July 2002, in Panama City.

54. Memo accompanying Mallet to Grey, Oct. 3, 1912, Political Correspondence, Panama, Foreign Office Records, FO 371/1417.

CHAPTER NINE: HERCULES COMES HOME

1. Rose Van Hardeveld, *Make the Dirt Fly!* (Hollywood, Calif.: Pan Press, 1956), p. 139; David McCullough, *The Path Between the Seas: The Creation of the Panama Canal, 1870–1914* (New York: Simon and Schuster, 1977), p. 604.

2. Sharon Phillips Collazos, "The Cities of Panama: Sixty Years of Development," in *Cities of Hope: People, Protests, and Progress in Urbanizing Latin America, 1870–1930,* ed. Ronn Pineo and James A. Baer (Boulder, Colo.: Westview Press, 1998), p. 252; Omar Jaén Suárez, *La población del Istmo de Panamá del siglo XVI al siglo XX* (Panama: Impresora de la Nación, 1978), charts 77, 460 and 78, 460. The figure of fifty-seven thousand employees includes the employees of the ICC and the Panama Railroad, as well as workers contracted privately by corporations building the lock gates.

3. "Exposition Promise Is Victoriously Accomplished, World's Greatest Fair Opens Its Gates to Public, Monument Built to Panama Canal by San Francisco," *San Francisco Examiner,* Feb. 20, 1915; "150,000 People of All Nations in Exposition Parade, Rich in Line with Poor, Babel of Noises Thunders Greeting to All the World," *San Francisco Examiner,* Feb. 21, 1915.

4. Charles Moore's comment was made in a speech at a State Department dinner hosted by William Jennings Bryan on Dec. 15, 1913, Records of the Panama-Pacific International Exposition, box 13, Bancroft Library, University of California at Berkeley (hereafter cited as PPIE Records). For more information on the PPIE, see Frank Morton Todd, *The Story of the Exposition: Being the Official History of the International Celebration Held at San Francisco in 1915 to Commemorate the Discovery of the Pacific Ocean and the Construction of the Panama Canal,* 5 vols. (New York: G. P. Putnam's Sons, 1921); Robert W. Rydell, *All the World's a Fair: Visions of Empire at American International Expositions, 1876–1916* (Chicago: University of Chicago Press, 1984); Donna Ewald and Peter Clute, *San Francisco Invites the World: The Panama-Pacific International Exposition of 1915* (San Francisco: Chronicle Books, 1991); Burton Benedict, *The Anthropology of World's Fairs: San Francisco's Panama Pacific International Exposition of 1915* (London: Scolar, 1983); Eugen Neuhaus, *The Art of the Exposition: Personal Impressions of the Architecture, Sculpture, Mural Decorations, Color Scheme, and Other Aesthetic Aspects of the Panama-Pacific International Exposition* (San Francisco: P. Elder, 1915); Abigail Markwyn, "Inviting the Alien: Images and Reality of China and Japan at the Panama-Pacific International Exposition," unpublished paper in author's possession.

5. Todd, *Story of the Exposition,* pp. 343, 348; the Markham quotation is in Elizabeth Platt Deitrick, *Best Bits of the Panama-Pacific International Exposition and San Francisco* (San Francisco: Galen, 1915), p. 64; Roger Lea MacBride, ed., *West from Home: Letters of Laura Ingalls Wilder, San Francisco, 1915* (New York: Harper and Row, 1974), p. 63.

6. Sir Edward Grey, *Twenty-Five Years* (1925), vol. 2, ch. 18, cited in *The Oxford Dictionary of Quotations* (New York: Oxford University Press, 2004). Grey's comment was made on the eve of World War I.

7. Hall's quotation is in *The Legacy of the Exposition: Interpretation of the Intellectual and Moral Heritage Left to Mankind by the World Celebration at San Francisco in 1915* (San Francisco: Panama-Pacific International Exposition Company, 1916), p. 80.

8. "No Canal Trip for Wilson," *Chicago Daily Tribune,* March 4, 1915, p. 7; "Mammoth Fleet Will Pass Canal with President," *Chicago Daily Tribune,* Jan. 10, 1915; "Panama Parade by War Vessels of Five Nations," *Chicago Daily Tribune,* Jan. 14, 1915, p. 7.

9. "Panama—the Silver Lining in the Clouds of War," *Current Opinion* 57 (1914), p. 210; "Two Openings," *Chicago Daily Tribune,* Aug. 15, 1914, p. 6; "The European War and the Panama-Pacific Exposition—Monumental Contrast," *Current Opinion* 58 (1914), p. 315. For other commentary on the canal and World War I, see "The Mastery of Peace," *New York World,* reprinted in *Chicago Daily Tribune,* Aug. 17, 1914, p. 6; "The Panama Canal and World History," *Outlook* 111 (1915), p. 59.

10. Elizabeth Kittredge Parker, *Panama Canal Bride: A Story of Construction Days* (New York: Exposition, 1955), pp. 80–81; for population figures, see *Census of the Canal Zone, February 1, 1912* (Mount Hope, C.Z.: ICC Press, 1912), p. 16; William R. Scott, *The Americans in Panama* (New York: Statler, 1913), ch. 16; Frederic J. Haskin, *The Panama Canal* (Garden City, N.Y.: Doubleday, Page, 1913), p. 315; "Panama Canal Open in a Month," *Chicago Daily Tribune,* Sept. 20, 1913, p. 15.

11. Parker, *Panama Canal Bride,* p. 85.

12. Goethals to Mallet, July 10, 1913, FO 288/150, Miscellaneous Consular Correspondence, 1913; J. H. Kerr (secretary to the government of Bengal) to the secretary to the government of India, Department of Commerce, March 30, 1912, FO 371/1417; and Mallet to Grey, July 17, 1912, FO 371/1417: all Foreign Office Records, The National Archives, Pew, U.K.; "No Work for Americans in Costa Rica," *Canal Record* 7, Nov. 5, 1913, p. 99.

13. Mallet to Grey, Oct. 28 and 30, 1912; Sydney Olivier (governor, Jamaica) to Lewis Harcourt (secretary of state for the colonies, London), May 9, 1912; Leslie Probyn (governor of Barbados) to Mallet, Sept. 30, 1912: all Political Correspondence, Panama, Foreign Office Records, FO 371/1417.

14. Mallet to Grey, Aug. 21, 1913; Mallet to Grey, received Sept. 30, 1913; Mallet to the governor of Jamaica, Sept. 8, 1913; Mallet to Grey, Nov. 8, 1913: all Political Correspondence, 1913, Foreign Office Records, FO 371/1703. For examples of complaints about unemployed West Indians facing arrest, see, for example, W. B. Letvole to Honorable Sir, Sept. 23, 1914, and especially no author to Mallet, received Sept. 26, 1914: both Miscellaneous Consul Records, 1914, Foreign Office Records, FO 288/160. See also Probyn to Harcourt, Consular Records, Panama, 1913, Foreign Office Records, FO 369/604.

15. Carla Burnett, "'Are We Slaves or Free Men?' Labor, Race, Garveyism, and the 1920 Panama Canal Strike" (Ph.D. diss., University of Illinois at Chicago, 2004), pp. 2–4; John Major, *Prize Possession: The United States and the Panama Canal, 1903–1979* (New York: Cambridge University Press, 1993), pp. 88–89.

16. John Barrett (director general of the Pan American Union), memo for the media about the Panama Canal, Sept. 20, 1912, FO 371/1417; Mallet to Grey, Nov. 8, 1913, FO 371/1703: both Political Correspondence, Panama, Foreign Office Records.

17. Charles T. Cox to Harcourt, April 20, 1912, Political Correspondence, Panama, 1912, Foreign Office Records, FO 371/1417.

18. Cox to Harcourt, April 20, 1912; K. J. E. Swayne (governor of British Honduras) to Harcourt, May 7, 1912; Mallet to Grey, Oct. 28, 1912; Mallet to Olivier, April 15, 1912; Mallet to Probyn, Oct. 30, 1912: all Political Correspondence, Panama, 1912, Foreign Office Records, FO 371/1417; Mallet to Grey, Nov. 8, 1913, Political Correspondence, Panama, Foreign Office Records, FO 371/1703.

19. "Emigration of Laborers Continues," *Canal Record,* Aug. 12, 1914, p. 513; Collazos, "Cities of Panama," p. 252.

20. Interview notes taken by Bonham Richardson in Barbados during 1982, in author's possession; see also Bonham Richardson, *Panama Money in Barbados, 1900–1920* (Knoxville: University of Tennessee Press, 1985).

21. "Panama Canal Open in a Month," p. 15; "Wilson Blows Up Last Big Barrier in Panama Canal," *Chicago Daily Tribune,* Oct. 11, 1913, p. 1; "Will Blow Open Big Canal Today," *Chicago Daily Tribune,* Oct. 10, 1913, p. 1; see also McCullough, *Path Between the Seas,* pp. 605–7.

22. Moore to Ira Bennett, Oct. 10, 1913, PPIE Records, box 59, "Panama Canal" folder.

23. Parker, *Panama Canal Bride,* pp. 81–83.

24. "The Panama Canal Officially Opened," *New York Times,* Aug. 16, 1914; "Canal Opened to Traffic of World Ships," *Chicago Daily Tribune,* Aug. 16, 1914.

25. Harry A. Franck, *Zone Policeman 88: A Close Range Study of the Panama Canal and Its Workers* (New York: Century, 1913), pp. 311–14. For other reminiscences of the Canal Zone, see Winifred Lewellin James, *A Woman in the Wilderness* (New York: George H. Doran, 1916), pp. 94–103.

26. Alfred Charles Richard Jr., *The Panama Canal in American National Consciousness, 1870–1990* (New York: Garland, 1990), p. 235. Hostetter's Stomach Bitters advertisement (n.d.), "X-mas Greetings" from Santa Claus (postmarked 1909), and "The Kiss of the Oceans" (n.d.): all postcards in author's possession.

27. Richard, *Panama Canal in American National Consciousness*, pp. 237, 232; "Designates Thursday, Nov. 27, as Day for Thanksgiving," *Chicago Daily Tribune*, Oct. 24, 1913, p. 11; "What the Panama Canal Will Do for the World," *Current Opinion* 56 (1914), pp. 230–31, quoting from the *Manufacturer's Record*.

28. Ralph Emmett Avery, *The Greatest Engineering Feat in the World at Panama: Authentic and Complete Story of the Building and Operation of the Great Waterway—the Eighth Wonder of the World* (New York: Leslie-Judge, 1915), pp. 253–56. For similar reckonings of the spatial transformation wrought by the canal, see Willis J. Abbot, *Panama and the Canal in Picture and Prose* (New York: Syndicate, 1914), pp. 384–87; Haskin, *Panama Canal*, esp. ch. 30, "A New Commercial Map," pp. 347–57.

29. Theodore Roosevelt, "The Panama Canal," in *The Pacific Ocean in History: Papers and Addresses Presented at the Panama-Pacific Historical Congress Held at San Francisco, Berkeley, and Palo Alto, California, July 19–23, 1915*, ed. H. Morse Stephens and Herbert E. Bolton (New York: Macmillan, 1917), p. 150.

30. Avery, *Greatest Engineering Feat in the World at Panama*, pp. 253–56.

31. William Gorgas, "The Conquest of the Tropics for the White Race: President's Address at the Sixtieth Annual Session of the American Medical Association, June 9, 1909," *Journal of the American Medical Association* 52, no. 25 (1909), pp. 1967–69.

32. "The Americanization of Panama," *Independent*, Feb. 25, 1909, pp. 429–30. In a similar vein, Frederick Palmer exulted in the *Chicago Daily Tribune* about the marvelous impact of American occupation: "American Rule Vivifies Panama: Health, Peace, and Prosperity Are Brought to the Little Republic," *Chicago Daily Tribune*, March 4, 1909. See also "Gorgas's Conquest of Disease: The Marvelous Cleaning Up of the Canal Zone Means Occupation of the Tropics by the White Race," *New York Times*, Sept. 22, 1912.

33. "Wants Free City in Panama Zone," *Chicago Daily Tribune*, Oct. 29, 1913, p. 20; C. H. Forbes-Lindsay, "Panama, a Field for American Enterprise," *Independent* 67 (1909), pp. 910–15; C. H. Forbes-Lindsay, "Opportunities for Americans in Panama," *Lippincott's Magazine*, Oct. 1911, pp. 492–95.

34. The unnamed American diplomat is cited in George H. Blakeslee, "The Results of the Panama Canal on World Trade," *Outlook* 111 (1915), pp. 490–97; for the French government's study, see "Canal Will Make U.S. Trade Power," *Chicago Daily Tribune*, Oct. 28, 1913, p. 7; for an analysis similar to Blakeslee's, see Theodore P. Shonts, "The Value of the Panama Canal," *World's Work*, April 1914, pp. 704–7; Edward Marshall, "European War Opens South America's Big Market to Us," *New York Times*, Aug. 23, 1914.

35. Walter B. Stevens, *A Trip to Panama: The Narrative of a Tour of Observation through the Canal Zone, with Some Account of Visits to Saint Thomas, Porto Rico, Jamaica, and Cuba, by the Commercial Clubs of Boston, Chicago, Cincinnati, and St. Louis, February 18th–March 14th, 1907* (St. Louis, 1907), p. 233; see also Cincinnati Chamber of Commerce, *Trade Expansion Tour: Panama Canal, Jamaica, Havana, and Southern Points. February 14 to March 9, 1913* (Cincinnati: Printed by Tom Jones, 1913). Analyses of the impact the canal would have on the commerce of the United States abounded. See, for example, Agnes C. Laut, "Preparations on the Pacific for Panama," *Review of Reviews* 44 (1911), pp. 705–13; Irving Fisher, "Some Probable Economic Effects of the War," *New York Times*, Aug. 30, 1914, p. SM4; "Effect on Trade Routes Discussed by London Times Man," *Chicago Daily Tribune*, Oct. 19, 1913, p. A2.

36. On the canal and world peace, see, for example, Shonts, "Value of the Panama Canal"; Alfred T. Mahan, "The Panama Canal and Sea Power in the Pacific," *Century Magazine* 82 (May–Oct. 1911), pp. 240–48.

37. "Panama and a New United States," *World's Work*, Dec. 1913, pp. 132–33. For other attempts to analyze the impact the canal would have on the relationship between the United States and the

world, see "The Panama Canal and Its Relation to the World," *Steam Shovel and Dredge,* Sept. 1914, pp. 751–54.

38. Richard, *Panama Canal in American National Consciousness,* pp. 230–31; for Thompson's essay, see "What the Panama Canal Will Do for the South," *Leslie's Weekly* 112 (1911), pp. 384–400; Westerners also saw the canal as crucial to their future. See Zoeth Skinner Eldredge, *The Key to the Pacific* (San Francisco, 1906); and Richard, *Panama Canal in American National Consciousness,* p. 231. The GAR and the UCV were fraternal organizations for veterans who served in the Union and Confederate Armies, respectively, during the Civil War.

39. O. Henry was born William Sydney Porter in Greensboro, North Carolina, in 1862. In 1897 he began serving a sentence in the penitentiary for embezzlement and while there began writing short stories. After his release he changed his name to O. Henry, moved to New York City, and became a prolific and very popular short story author. This information comes from http://www.online-literature.com/o_henry/; O. Henry's story "Two Renegades" may also be accessed online at http://www.literaturecollection.com/a/o_henry/117/.

40. Notes from a speech given by Charles Moore during his Eastern trip, PPIE Records, box 13; the Hoover comment is quoted in Rydell, *All the World's a Fair,* p. 208.

41. Avery, *Greatest Engineering Feat in the World at Panama,* pp. 353, 384.

42. San Francisco Labor Council and Building Trades Council to Moore, Aug. 22, 1912; P. H. McCarthy, resolution passed by Asiatic Exclusion League, n.d.: both PPIE Records, box 36.

43. See particularly the documents in folders 1 and 2, box 36, PPIE Records.

44. Schmidt to Moore, April 28, 1913, PPIE Records, box 9, folder on complaints.

45. Thomas Sammons, Oct. 14, 1912, PPIE Records, box 36, folder 9. See also the two folders on relations with Japan and the Alien Land Law in PPIE Records, box 63.

46. See the "Underground China" folder, PPIE Records, box 23; Shehong Chen, *Being Chinese, Becoming Chinese American* (Urbana: University of Illinois Press, 2002), ch. 3; Rydell, *All the World's a Fair,* p. 229; Todd, *Story of the Exposition,* vol. 2, p. 358.

47. William Lipsky, *San Francisco's Panama-Pacific International Exposition* (Charleston, S.C.: Arcadia, 2005), p. 67; Juliet James, *Sculpture of the Exposition Palaces and Courts: Descriptive Notes on the Art of the Statuary of the Panama-Pacific International Exposition, San Francisco* (San Francisco: H. S. Crocker, 1915); or see online at http://www.books-about-california.com/Pages/Sculpture_of_the_Exposition/The_End_of_the_Trail.html. Another popular sculpture of a Native American was Edward Berge's *Scalp,* which shows an exultant, beast-like man waving a human scalp in the air. See Lipsky, p. 67. See the Web site of the National Cowboy and Western Heritage Museum for pictures of the sculpture: http://www.nationalcowboymuseum.org/g_trai_high.html.

48. Todd, *Story of the Exposition,* vol. 2, p. 375; Rydell, *All the World's a Fair,* p. 228; Lipsky, *San Francisco's Panama-Pacific International Exposition,* p. 83.

49. Secretary of the Hawaiian Promotion Committee, complaint to the PPIE, PPIE Records, carton 9, "Hawaiian Village"; Todd, *Story of the Exposition,* vol. 2, p. 352.

50. Ewald and Clute, *San Francisco Invites the World,* pp. 67–99.

51. Deitrick, *Best Bits of the Panama-Pacific International Exposition and San Francisco,* p. 3.

52. Haskin, *Panama Canal,* p. 375.

53. James, *Sculpture of the Exposition Palaces and Courts,* accessed online at http://www.gutenberg.org/dirs/etext04/scipt10.txt; A. Stirling Calder, *The Sculpture and Mural Decorations of the Exposition* (San Francisco: P. Elder, 1915). James concluded, "The Fountain embodies the mood of joyous, exultant power and exactly expresses the spirit of the Exposition. . . . [It suggests] 'The Power of America rising from the Sea.' " Another example of the canal inspiring the architecture of the fair could be seen in the Court of the Sun and Stars, where two more sculptural fountains, according to Frederic Haskin, depicted the rising and setting of the sun to present the theme of "the world united and the land divided." Juliet James noted that the sculpture *The Rising Sun,* which again presented a nude American man with arms outstretched and taut muscles, represented "the new light occasioned by the opening of the Panama Canal."

54. Robert Goldstein to PPIE Pageant Committee, April 27, 1913; George L. Hutchin to Louis Levy (chief of publicity, PPIE), Oct. 21, 1913: both PPIE Records, box 21, folder 2.

55. Stafford was a supreme court justice for the District of Columbia. His poem "Panama Hymn" is in

PPIE Records, box 19, "Poems and Songs" folder. See also Charles K. Field (editor, *Sunset* magazine) to Joseph M. Cumming (executive secretary, PPIE), Aug. 28, 1913, PPIE Records, box 19.

56. "Bryan Talks at World's Fair on Keeping the Peace," *San Francisco Examiner,* July 6, 1915.

57. "Prepare Against War: Roosevelt; Blood on Our Hands if We Fail," *San Francisco Examiner,* July 22, 1915; "We Must Have Fighting Edge: Roosevelt," *San Francisco Examiner,* July 22, 1915. As if unable to resist continuing his argument with Roosevelt, Bryan addressed three thousand people at a Congregational church in San Francisco just days after Roosevelt had visited to repeat his call for world peace. Bryan referred to Roosevelt's speech as "useless" and cried out, "The big stick was not mentioned by Christ at all." In fact, he declared, "The trouble is you can't find a soft voice with a big stick. If a man . . . gets a big stick he loses his soft voice." See "Bryan Hits at Colonel and Big Stick," *San Francisco Examiner,* July 26, 1915.

58. The quotation by Goethals is from *Legacy of the Exposition,* p. 68.

59. Ewald and Clute, *San Francisco Invites the World,* p. 98.

60. Moore to Bennett, Feb. 1, 1915; Bennett to Moore, Feb. 2, 1915: both PPIE Records, "Foreign Pavilions: Panama" folder.

61. Speech of Don J. E. Lefevre, n.d., PPIE Records, box 31, "Special Events" folder.

62. Todd, *Story of the Exposition,* vol. 2, pp. 150–51; Panama Canal Exhibition Co., "Specification and Discription of Reproduction of Panama Canal," PPIE Records, box 95, "Panama Canal Concession."

63. Jack Burroughs, "Learn While You Laugh," n.d., newspaper clipping, vol. 10 of clippings, PPIE Records.

64. "More Than 50,000 Visit Zone Canal," *San Francisco Call,* Feb. 26, 1915; see also "Miniature Canal Is Exposition Feature," *San Francisco Bulletin,* Feb. 24, 1915: both vol. 10, newspaper clippings, PPIE Records.

65. MacBride, *West from Home,* p. 37; Elizabeth Gordon, *What We Saw at Madame World's Fair* (San Francisco: Samuel Levinson, 1915), pp. 82–83; Charlotte Perkins Gilman, "The Gorgeous Exhibition," *Forerunner,* May 1915, p. 121.

66. "Sing Swan Song at Panama Fair," *San Francisco Examiner,* Dec. 5, 1915.

EPILOGUE

1. Joseph Bucklin Bishop and Farnham Bishop, *Goethals, Genius of the Panama Canal: A Biography* (New York: Harper and Brothers, 1930), pp. 371–401. Other prominent ICC officials who served in the war included William Gorgas (as surgeon general of the Army), S. B. Williamson, and R. E. Wood.

2. Carla Burnett, "'Are We Slaves or Free Men?' Labor, Race, Garveyism, and the 1920 Panama Canal Strike" (Ph.D. diss., University of Illinois at Chicago, 2004), pp. 2–4; John Major, *Prize Possession: The United States and the Panama Canal, 1903–1979* (New York: Cambridge University Press, 1993), pp. 88–89.

3. "United We Stand," *Workman,* April 26, 1919; "Cold Facts, but Warm Thoughts," *Workman,* Oct. 18, 1919. On the postwar mobilization by West Indian workers, see also Burnett, "'Are We Slaves or Free Men?'" pp. 2–4.

4. Burnett, "'Are We Slaves or Free Men?'" pp. 1–27; Major, *Prize Possession,* pp. 92–96.

5. Major, *Prize Possession,* pp. 227–28.

6. On diplomacy with Panama during these decades, see J. Michael Hogan's excellent *The Panama Canal in American Politics: Domestic Advocacy and the Evolution of Policy* (Carbondale: Southern Illinois University Press, 1986), esp. pp. 68–75. Eisenhower's quotation is on p. 74. On the expropriation of the Suez Canal by Egyptian president Gamal Abdel Nasser, consult William Roger Louis and Roger Owen, eds., *Suez 1956: The Crisis and Its Consequences* (Oxford: Oxford University Press, 1989).

7. Hogan, *Panama Canal in American Politics,* p. 73; emphasis added to the quotation by the Zonian representative. See also Major, *Prize Possession,* pp. 331–34; and Walter LaFeber, *The Panama Canal: The Crisis in Historical Perspective* (New York: Oxford University Press, 1978), p. 142.

8. Major, *Prize Possession,* pp. 335–36; Hogan, *Panama Canal in American Politics,* p. 76; LaFeber, *Panama Canal,* pp. 137–40; John Lindsay-Poland, *Emperors in the Jungle: The Hidden History of the U.S. in Panama* (Durham, N.C.: Duke University Press, 2003), p. 86. For an example of the "utopian" lifestyle of Zonians at mid-century, see Philip Harkins, "Panama: This Is America—This Week," *Los Angeles Times,* reprinted in the *New York Times,* June 30, 1946, p. D8.

9. Major, *Prize Possession*, pp. 340–44.
10. Sol M. Linowitz to Secretary of State Cyrus Vance, May 2, 1977, White House Central File, Jimmy Carter Library and Museum, at http://www.jimmycarterlibrary.org/education/panama/document04.pdf (accessed April 24, 2007). For analysis of this and related arguments, see LaFeber, *Panama Canal*. Congressman Bowen's comment about "striped-pants boys" is a reference to career diplomats in the State Department and is quoted in Alfred Charles Richard Jr., *The Panama Canal in American National Consciousness, 1870–1990* (New York: Garland, 1990).
11. Linowitz to Vance, May 2, 1977; Hogan, *Panama Canal in American Politics,* pp. 87–88.
12. Flood to Carter, White House Central Files, Jan. 27, 1977, Jimmy Carter Library and Museum, at http://www.jimmycarterlibrary.org/education/panama/document01.pdf; Hogan, *Panama Canal in American Politics;* President Carter to senator, April 1978, Staff Secretaries File, Jimmy Carter Library and Museum, at http://www.jimmycarterlibrary.org/education/panama/document16.pdf. Adam Clymer, *Drawing the Line at the Big Ditch: The Panama Canal Treaties and the Rise of the Right* (Lawrence: University Press of Kansas, 2008), makes an argument similar to Hogan's about the link between the conservative movement and the Panama treaties. Clymer's book appeared too late for me to consult it fully before sending my book to press.
13. William Schneider is quoted in Hogan, *Panama Canal in American Politics.* Hogan's source for the Schneider comment is "Behind the Passions of the Canal Debate," reprinted from the *Washington Post;* U.S. Congress, Senate Committee on the Judiciary, *Panama Canal Treaties,* U.S. Senate debate, 1977–78, 95th Cong., 2nd sess., pp. 3309–10; see also LaFeber, *Panama Canal,* pp. 217–27. On assumptions that opponents of the canal were uninformed, see George Gallup, "Support for Panama Treaties Increases with Knowledge," Oct. 23, 1977, vertical file, Jimmy Carter Library and Museum, at http://www.jimmycarterlibrary.org/education/panama/document11.pdf.
14. Information in this and the following paragraphs is from the author's interview with Helen Greene, May 18, 2007; and "The Wooing of Senator Zorinsky; or, Love's Labors Lost, a Washington Comedy of Manners," *Time,* May 27, 1978.
15. Robert A. Pastor (Latin American specialist on the National Security Council) to associate press secretary for the National Security Council Jerry Schecter and press secretary Jody Powell, Sept. 7, 1977, Jody Powell Press Files, Jimmy Carter Library and Museum, at http://www.jimmycarter library.org/education/panama/document07.pdf; "Americans in Canal Zone Sadly Witness End of an Era," *New York Times,* Oct. 1, 1979, p. A1.
16. Lindsay-Poland, *Emperors in the Jungle,* pp. 103–11.
17. Ibid., pp. 112–20; Michael R. Gordon, "Ordered by Bush: Alternative Government Sworn," *New York Times,* Dec. 20, 1989, p. A1. "A Transcript of Bush's Address on the Decision to Use Force in Panama," *New York Times,* Dec. 21, 1989, p. A19.
18. Lindsay-Poland, *Emperors in the Jungle,* pp. 116–21; R. W. Apple, "War: Bush's Presidential Rite of Passage," *New York Times,* Dec. 21, 1989, p. A1; "Fires and Helicopters Transforming Panama City," *New York Times,* Dec. 21, 1989, p. A23; Andrew Rosenthal, "16 Americans Dead; General Is in Hiding," *New York Times,* Dec. 21, 1989, p. A1; "Excerpts from Briefings on U.S. Military Action in Panama," *New York Times,* Dec. 21, 1989, p. A20; James Brooke, "U.S. Denounced by Nations Touchy About Intervention," *New York Times,* Dec. 21, 1989.
19. "Panama Canal Sees the Last of the Stars and Stripes," *New York Times,* Dec. 31, 1999, p. A10. The *Times* referred to the Zone in this article as "this former outpost of American military and engineering might." See also Gustavo Gorriti, "Running Away from History," *New York Times,* Dec. 14, 1999, p. A1.
20. "To Cheers, Panama Takes Over the Canal," *New York Times,* Jan. 1, 2000, p. A16; "A Century Ends in Panama," *New York Times,* Dec. 18, 1999, p. A22; "Panama Canal Sees the Last of the Stars and Stripes."
21. "Panama Canal Sees the Last of the Stars and Stripes"; "A Canal Celebrity Honors Unheralded Workers," *New York Times,* Dec. 14, 1999, p. A4.
22. The *New York Times* editorial team called the decision of the Clinton administration not to attend the official ceremony "a shabby way to treat a monumental human achievement created at the dawn of this century." See Adam Clymer, "Mirror on the Past: Canal's Fate Reflects Shift by U.S.," *New York Times,* Dec. 15, 1999, p. A14; "Asia Moves In On the Big Ditch," *New York Times,* Dec. 19, 1999, p. WK3; "Bush Willing to 'Liberate' Panama Canal," *Milwaukee Journal Sentinel,* Jan. 8, 2000, p. 6.

23. Notes from a journal kept by the author during the Panama Canal *Crystal Harmony* cruise in Feb. 2003.

24. Harry A. Franck, *Zone Policeman 88: A Close Range Study of the Panama Canal and Its Workers* (New York: Century, 1913), p. 312.

25. This and the following paragraphs describing conversations that took place during the cruise are from the author's journal kept during Feb. 2002.

26. John Hall, "The Canal Builders," in *Panama Roughneck Ballads* (Panama and Canal Zone: Albert Lindo, Panama Railroad News Agency, 1912), pp. 34–38.

SELECT BIBLIOGRAPHY

MANUSCRIPT COLLECTIONS

Belisario Porras Archives. Sección de Gobierno y Justicia. University of Panama, Panama City.

District Courts of the United States. Records of the Panama Canal Zone, Record Group 21. U.S. National Archives Building, Washington, D.C.

Embajada de los Estados Unidos en Panamá. Expediente de los disturbios del 4 de julio de 1912 y 1915 en Cocoa Grove. Archivos de Ministerio de Relaciones Exteriores, Panama City.

Foreign Office Records. The National Archives, Kew, England, United Kingdom.

George Washington Goethals Papers. Manuscript Division. Library of Congress, Washington, D.C.

Isthmian Canal Commission Records. Record Group 185. U.S. National Archives, College Park, Maryland.

Legación de los Estados Unidos en Panamá. Correspondencia. Archivos de Ministerio de Relaciones Exteriores, Panama City.

Legación de Panamá en Washington. Correspondencia. Archivos de Ministerio de Relaciones Exteriores, Panama City.

National Civic Federation Records. Manuscripts and Archives Division. New York Public Library, New York City.

Panama Collection of the Canal Zone Library-Museum. Manuscript Division. Library of Congress, Washington, D.C.

Panama-Pacific International Exposition Records. Bancroft Library, University of California at Berkeley.

T. B. Miskimon Papers. Special Collections. Ablah Library, Wichita State University.

GOVERNMENT PUBLICATIONS

Annual Report of the Isthmian Canal Commission. Washington, D.C.: Government Printing Office, 1904–1915.

Census of the Canal Zone, February 1, 1912. Mount Hope, C.Z.: ICC Press, Quartermaster's Department, 1912.

Hearings Before the Committee on Interstate and Foreign Commerce of the House of Representatives, on the Isthmian Canal. Washington, D.C.: Government Printing Office, 1906.

Hearings Before the Committee on Interstate and Foreign Commerce of the House of Representatives, on the Panama Canal. Washington, D.C.: Government Printing Office, 1908.

Hearings Before the Committee on Interstate and Foreign Commerce of the House of Representatives, on the Panama Canal. Washington, D.C.: Government Printing Office, 1909.

Hearings Before the Subcommittee of the House Committee on Appropriations, in Charge of Sundry Civil Appropriation Bill for 1907. Washington, D.C.: Government Printing Office, 1906.

Hearings Concerning Estimates for Construction of the Isthmian Canal for the Fiscal Year 1911. Conducted on the Canal Zone by the Committee on Appropriations, House of Representatives. Washington, D.C.: Government Printing Office, 1910.

Investigation of Panama Canal Matters: Hearings Before the Committee on Interoceanic Canals of the United States Senate in the Matter of the Senate Resolution Adopted January 9, 1906, Providing for an Investigation of Matters Relating to the Panama Canal, Etc. Washington, D.C.: Government Printing Office, 1907.

Message from the President of the United States Transmitting Certain Papers to Accompany His Message of January 8, 1906. Washington, D.C.: Government Printing Office, 1906.

Message from the President of the United States Transmitting the Report of the Special Commission Appointed to Investigate Conditions of Labor and Housing of Government Employees on the Isthmus of Panama. Washington, D.C.: Government Printing Office, 1908.

The Panama Canal: Hearings Before the Committee on Interoceanic Canals. Senate. Washington, D.C.: Government Printing Office, 1912.

The Panama Canal: Hearings Before the Committee on Interstate and Foreign Commerce. House of Representatives. Washington, D.C.: Government Printing Office, 1912.

Panama Canal—Skilled Labor: Extracts from Hearings of the Committees on Appropriations of the Senate and House of Representatives, Fiscal Years 1907 to 1915 Inclusive. Washington, D.C.: Government Printing Office, 1914.

Papers Relating to the Foreign Relations of the United States, with the Annual Message of the President Transmitted to Congress, Dec. 5, 1905. House of Representatives. Washington, D.C.: Government Printing Office, 1906.

NEWSPAPERS AND MAGAZINES

The Canal Record
Century Magazine
The Chicago Daily Tribune
Cosmopolitan Magazine
Current Opinion
The Daily Gleaner (Jamaica)
The Independent
International Socialist Review
La Estrella de Panamá
Lippincott's Magazine
Machinists' Monthly Journal
National Civic Federation Review
The New York Times
The Outlook
Review of Reviews
The San Francisco Examiner
Scribner's Magazine
Steam Shovel and Dredge
The Survey
The Workman (Panama)
The World's Work

BOOKS AND DISSERTATIONS

Abbot, Willis John. *Panama and the Canal in Picture and Prose.* New York: Syndicate, 1914.

Araúz, Celestino Andrés. *Panamá y sus relaciones internacionales.* Panama City: Universitaria, 1994.

Arnold, David. *The Problem of Nature: Environment, Culture, and European Expansion.* Oxford: Blackwell, 1996.

———. *The Tropics and the Traveling Gaze: India, Landscape, and Science, 1800–1856.* Seattle: University of Washington Press, 2006.

Avery, Ralph Emmett. *The Greatest Engineering Feat in the World at Panama: Authentic and Complete Story of the Building and Operation of the Great Waterway—the Eighth Wonder of the World.* New York: Leslie-Judge, 1915.

Ballantyne, Tony, and Antoinette Burton, eds. *Bodies in Contact: Rethinking Colonial Encounters in World History.* Durham, N.C.: Duke University Press, 2005.

Bederman, Gail. *Manliness and Civilization: A Cultural History of Gender and Race in the United States, 1880–1917*. Chicago: University of Chicago Press, 1995.

Bellamy, Edward. *Looking Backward: 2000–1887*, reissue. New York: Signet Classics, 2000.

Bender, Thomas. *A Nation Among Nations: America's Place in World History*. New York: Hill and Wang, 2006.

Benedict, Burton. *The Anthropology of World's Fairs: San Francisco's Panama Pacific International Exposition of 1915*. London: Scolar, 1983.

Benson, Susan Porter. *Counter Cultures: Saleswomen, Managers, and Customers in American Department Stores, 1890–1940*. Urbana: University of Illinois Press, 1986.

Bigelow, Poultney. *Seventy Summers*. New York: Longmans, Green, 1925.

Bishop, Joseph Bucklin, ed. *Theodore Roosevelt's Letters to His Children*. New York: Charles Scribner's Sons, 1919.

Bishop, Joseph Bucklin, and Farnham Bishop. *Goethals, Genius of the Panama Canal: A Biography*. New York: Harper and Brothers, 1930.

Boag, Peter. *Same-Sex Affairs: Constructing and Controlling Homosexuality in the Pacific Northwest*. Berkeley: University of California Press, 2003.

Boyce, William D. *United States Colonies and Dependencies: The Travels and Investigations of a Chicago Publisher*. Chicago: Rand McNally, 1914.

Bray, Wayne D. *The Common Law Zone in Panama: A Case Study in Reception*. San Juan, P.R.: Inter American University Press, 1977.

Browne, Edith A. *Panama*. London: Adam and Charles Black, 1913.

Bullard, Arthur. *Panama: The Canal, the Country, and the People*. New York: Macmillan, 1911.

Burnett, Carla. "'Are We Slaves or Free Men?' Labor, Race, Garveyism, and the 1920 Panama Canal Strike." Ph.D. dissertation. University of Illinois at Chicago, 2004.

Burnett, Christina Duffy, and Burke Marshall, eds. *Foreign in a Domestic Sense: Puerto Rico, American Expansion, and the Constitution*. Durham, N.C.: Duke University Press, 2001.

Callahan, James Morton. *An Introduction to American Expansion Policy*. Morgantown: West Virginia University, 1908.

Calvo, Alfredo Castillero. *Conquista, evangelización, y resistencia: Triunfo o fracaso de la política indigenista*. Panama: Mariano Arosemena: Instituto Nacional de Cultura, 1995.

———, ed. *Historia general de Panamá*. Panama City: Comité Nacional del Centenario de la República, 2004.

Cameron, Charlotte. *A Woman's Winter in South America*. London: Stanley Paul, 1911.

Casanovas, Joan. *Bread, or Bullets! Urban Labor and Spanish Colonialism in Cuba, 1850–1898*. Pittsburgh: University of Pittsburgh Press, 1998.

Chatfield, Mary A. *Light on Dark Places at Panama*. New York: Broadway, 1908.

Chaudhuri, Nupur, and Margaret Strobel, eds. *Western Women and Imperialism: Complicity and Resistance*. Bloomington: University of Indiana Press, 1992.

Chauncey, George. *Gay New York: Gender, Urban Culture, and the Making of the Gay Male World, 1890–1940*. New York: Basic Books, 1995.

Choy, Catherine Ceniza. *Empire of Care: Nursing and Migration in Filipino American History*. Durham, N.C.: Duke University Press, 2003.

Conniff, Michael L. *Black Labor on a White Canal: Panama, 1904–1981*. Pittsburgh: University of Pittsburgh Press, 1985.

———. *Panama and the United States: The Forced Alliance*, 2nd ed. Athens: University of Georgia Press, 2001.

Cooper, Frederick, and Ann Laura Stoler, eds. *Tensions of Empire: Colonial Cultures in a Bourgeois World*. Berkeley: University of California Press, 1997.

Croly, Herbert. *The Promise of American Life*, 1909. http://www.gutenberg.org/catalog/world/readfile?fk_files=117114&:pageno=1.

Cyphers, Christopher J. *The National Civic Federation and the Making of a New Liberalism, 1900–1915*. Westport, Conn.: Praeger, 2002.

Dalton, Kathleen. *Theodore Roosevelt: A Strenuous Life*. New York: Knopf, 2002.

Davis, Raymond Allan. "West Indian Workers on the Panama Canal: A Split Labor Market Interpretation." Ph.D. dissertation. Stanford University, 1981.

Delevante, Michael. *Panama Pictures: Nature and Life in the Land of the Great Canal.* New York: Alden Brothers, 1907.

De Lisser, Henry. *Jamaicans in Colón and the Canal Zone.* Kingston, 1906.

Donadio, William D. *The Thorns of the Rose: Memoirs of a Tailor of Panama.* Colón, Republic of Panama: Dovesa, S.A., 1999.

Esenwein, George R. *Anarchist Ideology and the Working-Class Movement in Spain, 1868–1898.* Berkeley: University of California Press, 1989.

Ewald, Donna, and Peter Clute. *San Francisco Invites the World: The Panama-Pacific International Exposition of 1915.* San Francisco: Chronicle Books, 1991.

Ferrer, Ada. *Insurgent Cuba: Race, Nation, and Revolution, 1868–1898.* Chapel Hill: University of North Carolina Press, 1999.

Findlay, Eileen J. Suárez. *Imposing Decency: The Politics of Sexuality and Race in Puerto Rico, 1870–1920.* Durham, N.C.: Duke University Press, 1999.

Forbes-Lindsay, Charles Harcourt. *Panama and the Canal To-Day.* Boston: L. C. Page, 1910.

Franck, Harry A. *Zone Policeman 88: A Close Range Study of the Panama Canal and Its Workers.* New York: Century, 1913.

Frederick, Rhonda A. *"Colón Man a Come": Mythographies of Panama Canal Migration.* Lanham, Md.: Lexington Books, 2005.

Fuentes, Vicente Díaz. *La clase obrera: Entre el anarquismo y la religión.* Mexico: Universidad Nacional Autónoma de México, 1994.

Gandásegui, Marco A., ed. *Las clases sociales en Panamá.* Panama: Del Centro de Estudios Latinoamericanos, 1993.

Gandásegui, Marco, Alejandro Saavedra, Andrés Achong, and Iván Quintero. *Las luchas obreras en Panamá, 1850–1978,* 2nd ed. Panama City: CELA, 1990.

George, Henry. *Progress and Poverty: An Inquiry into the Cause of Industrial Depressions and of Increase of Want with Increase of Wealth: The Remedy.* New York: D. Appleton, 1882.

Gilbert, James. *Designing the Industrial State: The Intellectual Pursuit of Collectivism in America, 1880–1940.* Chicago: Quadrangle Books, 1972.

Go, Julian, and Anne L. Foster, eds. *The American Colonial State in the Philippines: Global Perspectives.* Durham, N.C.: Duke University Press, 2003.

Goethals, George W. *Government of the Canal Zone.* Princeton, N.J.: Princeton University Press, 1915.

Gorgas, Marie D., and Burton J. Hendrick. *William Crawford Gorgas: His Life and Work.* Garden City, N.Y.: Doubleday, Page, 1924.

Gorgas, William Crawford. *Sanitation in Panama.* New York: D. Appleton, 1915.

Green, Marguerite. *The National Civic Federation and the American Labor Movement, 1900–1925.* Washington, D.C.: Catholic University of America Press, 1956.

Greene, Julie. *Pure and Simple Politics: The American Federation of Labor and Political Activism, 1881–1917.* New York: Cambridge University Press, 1998.

Guglielmo, Thomas. *White on Arrival: Italians, Race, Color, and Power in Chicago, 1890–1945.* New York: Oxford University Press, 2003.

Hall, John. *Panama Roughneck Ballads.* Panama and Canal Zone: Albert Lindo, Panama Railroad News Agency, 1912.

Harpelle, Ronald N. *The West Indians of Costa Rica: Race, Class, and the Integration of an Ethnic Minority.* Montreal: McGill-Queen's University Press, 2001.

Hart, John M. *Anarchism and the Mexican Working Class, 1860–1931.* Austin: University of Texas Press, 1978.

Haskin, Frederic J. *The Panama Canal.* Garden City, N.Y.: Doubleday, Page, 1913.

Hogan, J. Michael. *The Panama Canal in American Politics: Domestic Advocacy and the Evolution of Policy.* Carbondale: Southern Illinois University Press, 1986.

Hoganson, Kristin L. *Consumers' Imperium: The Global Production of American Domesticity, 1865–1920.* Chapel Hill: University of North Carolina Press, 2007.

———. *Fighting for American Manhood: How Gender Politics Provoked the Spanish-American and Philippine-American Wars.* New Haven, Conn.: Yale University Press, 1998.

Hunter, Tera W. *To 'Joy My Freedom: Southern Black Women's Lives and Labor After the Civil War.* Cambridge, Mass.: Harvard University Press, 1997.

James, Juliet. *Sculpture of the Exposition Palaces and Courts: Descriptive Notes on the Art of the Statuary of the Panama-Pacific International Exposition, San Francisco*. San Francisco: H. S. Crocker, 1915.

James, Winifred Lewellin. *The Mulberry Tree*. London: Chapman and Hall, 1913.

———. *A Woman in the Wilderness*. New York: George H. Doran, 1916.

Joseph, Gilbert M., Catherine C. LeGrand, and Ricardo D. Salvatore, eds. *Close Encounters of Empire: Writing the History of U.S.–Latin American Relations*. Durham, N.C.: Duke University Press, 1998.

Kaplan, Amy. *The Anarchy of Empire in the Making of U.S. Culture*. Cambridge, Mass.: Harvard University Press, 2002.

Kaplan, Amy, and Donald E. Pease, eds. *Cultures of United States Imperialism*. Durham, N.C.: Duke University Press, 1993.

Kazin, Michael. *Barons of Labor: The San Francisco Building Trades and Union Power in the Progressive Era*. Urbana: University of Illinois Press, 1988.

Kerr, James E. *The Insular Cases: The Role of the Judiciary in American Expansionism*. Port Washington, N.Y.: Kennikat, 1982.

Kramer, Paul A. *The Blood of Government: Race, Empire, the United States, and the Philippines*. Chapel Hill: University of North Carolina Press, 2002.

LaFeber, Walter. *Cambridge History of American Foreign Relations*, vol. 3: *The American Search for Opportunity*. New York: Cambridge University Press, 1993.

———. *The New Empire: An Interpretation of American Expansion, 1860–1898*. Ithaca, N.Y.: Cornell University Press, 1963.

———. *The Panama Canal: The Crisis in Historical Perspective*. New York: Oxford University Press, 1978, 1989.

Lai, Walton Look. *Indentured Labor, Caribbean Sugar: Chinese and Indian Migrants to the British West Indies, 1838–1918*. Baltimore: Johns Hopkins University Press, 1993.

Lee, Erika. *At America's Gates: Chinese Immigration During the Exclusion Era, 1882–1943*. Chapel Hill: University of North Carolina Press, 2007.

Lewis, Lancelot S. *The West Indian in Panama: Black Labor in Panama, 1850–1914*. Washington, D.C.: University Press of America, 1980.

Lindsay-Poland, John. *Emperors in the Jungle: The Hidden History of the U.S. in Panama*. Durham, N.C.: Duke University Press, 2003.

Lipsky, William. *San Francisco's Panama-Pacific International Exposition*. Charleston, S.C.: Arcadia, 2005.

Love, Eric. *Race over Empire: Racism and U.S. Imperialism, 1865–1900*. Chapel Hill: University of North Carolina Press, 2004.

MacBride, Roger Lea, ed. *West from Home: Letters of Laura Ingalls Wilder, San Francisco, 1915*. New York: Harper and Row, 1974.

McCullough, David. *The Path Between the Seas: The Creation of the Panama Canal, 1870–1914*. New York: Simon and Schuster, 1977.

McGerr, Michael. *A Fierce Discontent: The Rise and Fall of the Progressive Movement in America, 1870–1920*. New York: Oxford University Press, 2003.

McGuinness, Aims. *Path of Empire: Panama and the California Gold Rush*. Ithaca, N.Y.: Cornell University Press, 2008.

Mack, Gerstle. *The Land Divided: A History of the Panama Canal and Other Isthmian Canal Projects*. New York: Knopf, 1944.

Major, John. *Prize Possession: The United States and the Panama Canal, 1903–1979*. New York: Cambridge University Press, 1993.

Maloney, Gerardo. *El Canal de Panamá y los trabajadores antillanos*. Panama City: Universidad de Panamá, 1989.

Mandell, Nikki. *The Corporation as Family: The Gendering of Corporate Welfare, 1890–1930*. Chapel Hill: University of North Carolina Press, 2002.

Miller, Stuart Creighton. *"Benevolent Assimilation": The American Conquest of the Philippines, 1899–1903*. New Haven, Conn.: Yale University Press, 1982.

Montgomery, David. *The Fall of the House of Labor: The Workplace, the State, and American Labor Activism, 1865–1925*. New York: Cambridge University Press, 1987.

Moore, J. Hampton. *With Speaker Cannon Through the Tropics: A Descriptive Story of a Voyage to the West Indies, Venezuela, and Panama*. Philadelphia: Book Print, 1907.

Morgan, Paul W., Jr. "The Role of North American Women in U.S. Cultural Chauvinism in the Panama Canal Zone, 1904–1945." Ph.D. dissertation. Florida State University, 2000.

Moya, Jose C. *Cousins and Strangers: Spanish Immigrants in Buenos Aires, 1850–1930*. Berkeley: University of California Press, 1998.

Muenchow, Mrs. Ernest von, ed. *The American Woman on the Panama Canal: From 1904 to 1916*. Balboa Heights, Panama: Star and Herald, 1916.

Musicant, Ivan. *Empire by Default*. New York: Henry Holt, 1998.

Navarro, Alfredo Figueroa. *Dominio y sociedad en el Panamá colombiano, 1821–1903*. Panama City: Universitaria, 1982.

Navas, Luis. *El movimiento obrero en Panamá, 1880–1914*. San José, Costa Rica: Universitaria Centroamericana, 1979.

Navas, Luis, Hernando Franco Muñoz, and Gerardo Maloney. *El movimiento obrero en Panamá*. Panama: Autoridad del Canal de Panamá, 1999.

Newton, Velma. *The Silver Men: West Indian Labour Migration to Panama, 1850–1914*. Mona, Jamaica: University of the West Indies, 1984.

Ninkovich, Frank. *The United States and Imperialism*. Oxford: Blackwell, 2001.

Parker, Elizabeth Kittredge. *Panama Canal Bride: A Story of Construction Days*. New York: Exposition, 1955.

Pearcy, Thomas. *We Answer Only to God: Politics and the Military in Panama, 1903–1947*. Albuquerque: University of New Mexico Press, 1998.

Pérez, Louis A. *Cuba: Between Reform and Revolution*. New York: Oxford University Press, 1988.

———. *The War of 1898: The United States and Cuba in History and Historiography*. Chapel Hill: University of North Carolina Press, 1998.

Petras, Elizabeth McLean. *Jamaican Labor Migration: White Capital and Black Labor, 1850–1930*. Boulder, Colo.: Westview, 1988.

Pierson, Ruth Roach, and Nupur Chaudhuri, eds. *Nation, Empire, Colony: Historicizing Gender and Race*. Bloomington: University of Indiana Press, 1988.

Pratt, Mary Louise. *Imperial Eyes: Travel Writing and Transculturation*. New York: Routledge, 1992.

Putnam, Lara. *The Company They Kept: Migrants and the Politics of Gender in Caribbean Costa Rica, 1870–1960*. Chapel Hill: University of North Carolina Press, 2002.

Rafael, Vicente L. *White Love and Other Events in Filipino History*. Durham, N.C.: Duke University Press, 2000.

Ramos, Efrén Rivera. *The Legal Construction of Identity: The Judicial and Social Legacy of American Colonialism in Puerto Rico*. Washington, D.C.: American Psychological Association, 2001.

Renda, Mary. *Taking Haiti: Military Occupation and the Culture of U.S. Imperialism, 1915–1940*. Chapel Hill: University of North Carolina Press, 2001.

Reyes Rivas, Eyra Marcela. *El trabajo de las mujeres en la historia de la construcción del Canal de Panamá, 1881–1914*. Panama: Universidad de Panamá, Instituto de la Mujer, 2000.

Richard, Alfred Charles, Jr. *The Panama Canal in American National Consciousness, 1870–1990*. New York: Garland, 1990.

Richardson, Bonham. *Panama Money in Barbados, 1900–1920*. Knoxville: University of Tennessee Press, 1985.

Riley, Glenda. *Divorce: An American Tradition*. New York: Oxford University Press, 1991.

Roediger, David. *The Wages of Whiteness: Race and the Making of the American Working Class*, 2nd ed. New York: Verso, 2007.

Roosevelt, Theodore. *An Autobiography*. New York: Charles Scribner's Sons, 1924.

Ropp, Steve C. *Panamanian Politics: From Guarded Nation to National Guard*. New York: Praeger, 1982.

Rosenberg, Emily. *Financial Missionaries to the World: The Politics and Culture of Dollar Diplomacy, 1900–1930*. Cambridge, Mass.: Harvard University Press, 1999.

———. *Spreading the American Dream: American Economic and Cultural Expansion 1890–1945*. New York: Hill and Wang, 1982.

Russell, Dr. Carlos E. *An Old Woman Remembers: The Recollected History of West Indians in Panama, 1855–1955*. Brooklyn: Caribbean Diaspora Press, 1995.

Rydell, Robert W. *All the World's a Fair: Visions of Empire at American International Expositions, 1876–1916*. Chicago: University of Chicago Press, 1984.

Saxton, Alexander. *The Indispensable Enemy: Labor and the Anti-Chinese Movement in California.* Berkeley: University of California Press, 1975.

Saxton, Evelyn. *Droll Stories of Isthmian Life.* New Orleans: L. Graham, 1914.

Schirmer, Daniel B. *Republic or Empire: American Resistance to the Philippine War.* Cambridge, Mass.: Schenkman, 1972.

Scott, James C. *Weapons of the Weak: Everyday Forms of Peasant Resistance.* New Haven, Conn.: Yale University Press, 1985.

Scott, William R. *The Americans in Panama.* New York: Statler, 1913.

Serra, Yolanda Marco. *Los obreros españoles en la construcción del Canal de Panamá: La emigración española hacia Panamá vista a través de la prensa española.* Panama: Portobelo, 1997.

Shepherd, Verene, Bridget Brereton, and Barbara Bailey, eds. *Engendering History: Caribbean Women in Historical Perspective.* Kingston: Ian Randle, 1995.

Sibert, William L., and John F. Stevens. *The Construction of the Panama Canal.* New York: D. Appleton, 1915.

Sinha, Mrinalini. *Colonial Masculinity: The 'Manly Englishman' and the 'Effeminate Bengali' in the Late Nineteenth Century.* Manchester: Manchester University Press, 1995.

Stepan, Nancy. *Picturing Tropical Nature.* Ithaca, N.Y.: Cornell University Press, 2001.

Stevens, John. *An Engineer's Recollections.* New York: McGraw-Hill, 1936.

Stoler, Ann Laura. *Carnal Knowledge and Imperial Power: Race and the Intimate in Colonial Rule.* Berkeley: University of California Press, 2002.

———, ed. *Haunted by Empire: Geographies of Intimacy in North American History.* Durham, N.C.: Duke University Press, 2006.

Stromquist, Shelton. *Reinventing "The People": The Progressive Movement, the Class Problem, and the Origins of Modern Liberalism.* Urbana: University of Illinois Press, 2006.

Szok, Peter A. *"La Última Gaviota": Liberalism and Nostalgia in Early Twentieth-Century Panamá.* Westport, Conn.: Greenwood, 2001.

Todd, Frank Morton. *The Story of the Exposition: Being the Official History of the International Celebration Held at San Francisco in 1915 to Commemorate the Discovery of the Pacific Ocean and the Construction of the Panama Canal.* New York: G. P. Putnam's Sons, 1921.

Trask, David. *The War with Spain in 1898.* New York: Macmillan, 1981.

Turner, Jorge. *Raíz, historia, y perspectivas del movimiento obrero panameño.* Mexico City: Signos, 1982.

Van Hardeveld, Rose. *Make the Dirt Fly!* Hollywood, Calif.: Pan Press, 1956.

Westerman, George. *The West Indian Worker on the Canal Zone.* Panama: Liga Civica Nacional, 1950.

Williams, William Appleman. *The Contours of American History.* Cleveland: World, 1961.

———. *Empire as a Way of Life: An Essay on the Causes and Character of America's Present Predicament, Along with a Few Thoughts About an Alternative.* New York: Oxford University Press, 1980.

———. *The Tragedy of American Diplomacy.* New York: Dell, 1972.

Winter, Thomas. *Making Men, Making Class: The YMCA and Workingmen, 1877–1920.* Chicago: University of Chicago Press, 2002.

INDEX